NOLO® Products & Services

⇨ Books & Software

Get in-depth information. Nolo publishes hundreds of great books and software programs for consumers and business owners. They're all available in print or as downloads at Nolo.com.

⇨ Legal Encyclopedia

Free at Nolo.com. Here are more than 1,400 free articles and answers to common questions about everyday legal issues including wills, bankruptcy, small business formation, divorce, patents, employment and much more.

⇨ Plain-English Legal Dictionary

Free at Nolo.com. Stumped by jargon? Look it up in America's most up-to-date source for definitions of legal terms.

⇨ Online Legal Documents

Create documents at your computer. Go online to make a will or living trust, form an LLC or corporation or obtain a trademark or provisional patent at Nolo.com. For simpler matters, download one of our hundreds of high-quality legal forms, including bills of sale, promissory notes, nondisclosure agreements and many more.

⇨ Lawyer Directory

Find an attorney at Nolo.com. Nolo's unique lawyer directory provides in-depth profiles of lawyers all over America. From fees and experience to legal philosophy, education and special expertise, you'll find all the information you need to pick a lawyer who's a good fit.

⇨ Free Legal Updates

Keep up to date. Check for free updates at Nolo.com. Under "Products," find this book and click "Legal Updates." You can also sign up for our free e-newsletters at Nolo.com/newsletters/index.html.

8th edition

The
Small Business
Start-Up Kit
for California

By Peri H. Pakroo

Edited by Marcia Stewart

Eighth Edition	FEBRUARY 2010
Editor	MARCIA STEWART
Cover Design	SUSAN PUTNEY
Book Design	TERRI HEARSH
Proofreading	SUSAN CARLSON GREENE
Index	ELLEN SHERRON
CD-ROM Preparation	ELLEN BITTER
Printing	DELTA PRINTING SOLUTIONS, INC.

Pakroo, Peri.

  The small business start-up kit for California / by Peri H. Pakroo. -- 8th ed.

    p. cm.

  Includes index.

  ISBN-13: 978-1-4133-1100-6

  ISBN-10: 1-4133-1100-8

  1. Small business--Law and legislation--California--Popular works. 2. New business enterprises--Law and legislation--California--Popular works. I. Title.

  KFC84.B87P35 2010

  346.794'0652--dc22

                                    2009037820

Please note

We believe accurate, plain-English legal information should help you solve many of your own legal problems. But this text is not a substitute for personalized advice from a knowledgeable lawyer. If you want the help of a trained professional—and we'll always point out situations in which we think that's a good idea—consult an attorney licensed to practice in your state.

Acknowledgments for the First Edition

All authors should be so lucky to have such a swell team of people helping them through the process of writing a book. Thanks to Jake Warner for giving me the inspiration and encouragement to start this book, and to finish it when my mind and fingertips were weary. Major thanks to Beth Laurence for tightening up the information and streamlining it into a finished product. And thanks to the whole editorial staff at Nolo for convincing me I would eventually reach the light at the end of the tunnel with my brain intact.

Thanks to Terri Hearsh for her layout and design of the book. And also to Ely Newman for patiently walking me through the technicalities of putting forms on disk. Sincere thanks to David Rothenberg for lending a CFO's eye to my discussion of small business finances.

Thanks to all my family and friends for their patience and sensitivity in not asking too often "Is your book done yet?"

Most of all, love and thanks to Turtle for keeping my soul happy and free when my mind was not.

—PHP 1998

Dedication

I dedicate this book to my mom and dad, Kay and Reza Pakroo, who, for better or worse, somehow convinced me I could do anything—even write a book.

About the Author

Peri Pakroo is a consultant and media developer, specializing in legal and start-up issues for businesses and nonprofits. She owns and runs P-Brain Media (www.pbrainmedia.com), a strategic consulting and communications firm that develops information-rich media for Web, print, video, and other formats. She received her law degree from the University of New Mexico School of Law in 1995 and a year later began editing and writing for Nolo, specializing in small business and intellectual property issues. She is the author of *The Small Business Start-Up Kit* (national and California editions) and *Starting and Building a Nonprofit,* and has edited such titles as Nolo's *Starting & Running a Successful Newsletter or Magazine; Getting Permission: How to License & Clear Copyrighted Materials Online & Off; Music Law;* and *How to Write a Business Plan.* Peri teaches adult education courses at WESST (www.wesst.org) in Albuquerque, a nonprofit whose mission is to fight poverty by facilitating entrepreneurship among women and minorities in the state of New Mexico. She is active in supporting local, independent businesses and is a co-founder of the Albuquerque Independent Business Alliance.

Table of Contents

Appendixes

The following spreadsheets are available only on the CD-ROM.

> Cash Flow Projection Worksheet
>
> Profit/Loss Forecast Worksheet
>
> Break-Even Analysis Worksheet
>
> Billable Rate Worksheet
>
> Warranty Track Worksheet

These forms are also included on the CD-ROM that comes with this book.

Partnership Agreement

California Registered Limited Liability Partnership Registration

California LLC Articles of Organization

California Sample Articles of Incorporation

California Certificate of Limited Partnership

Application for Employer Identification Number (IRS Form SS-4)

Instructions for IRS Form SS-4

California Fictitious Business Name Statement

California Application for Seller's Permit and Instructions (Individuals, Partnerships, Corporations, and Organizations)

California Resale Certificate

California Swap Meets, Flea Markets, or Special Events Certification (BOE-410-D)

California Board of Equalization Publications Order Form

California Limited Liability Company Tax Voucher (FTB Form 3522)

Entity Classification Election (IRS Form 8832)

Election To Have a Tax Year Other Than a Required Tax Year (IRS Form 8716)

Determination of Worker Status for Purposes of Federal Employment Taxes and
Income Tax Withholding (IRS Form SS-8)

Your Small Business Start-Up Companion

You don't have an MBA. Hell, you've never taken a business class. You spent your college years studying literature and art history and periodically dropping out to travel the world. And now you find yourself thinking about going into business for yourself—maybe restoring antiques, illustrating books, running a café, or selling software. "Me, a businessperson?" you skeptically ask. You keep trudging to work each morning, but as the hours tick by, you find yourself fantasizing more and more about kissing your 9-to-5 job goodbye. You jot down some notes, work out some kinks in your plan, and continue to wonder whether it just might fly....

Unfortunately, most people who have toyed with business ideas this way never get to find out whether they would have worked or not. For a variety of practical, financial, and psychological reasons, most folks just don't take the leap from idea to reality. This is really a shame, since there's nothing that complex or difficult about turning a business idea into an actual working business. Most prospective entrepreneurs would be surprised—and encouraged—to know that they can get most of the way across the line between "I'm thinking about starting my own business" and "I own and run my own business" simply by completing a short list of bureaucratic tasks. This book will explain what those tasks are and how to complete them.

Stephen Parr, owner and director of Oddball Film and Video, a stock footage company in San Francisco, California:

I started making video art in the 1970s. After a while, I started collecting all these weird bits of film because it was cheaper than shooting it myself. I gathered all kinds of old, found footage, like military training films, educational films, home movies, and all kinds of other images, and put them together into montages, which I screened in nightclubs as background visuals. I was showing them all over—nightclubs in New York, Chicago, San Francisco—and I made some money by selling the tapes to the clubs.

Then I started getting calls from these companies in Silicon Valley that produce industrial videos, like training films and promotional programs for corporate trade shows. Video game companies were calling, too. Companies like Sega, Sun Microsystems, and Silicon Graphics wanted to pay me for my footage. The guy I lived with at the time thought I should go into business selling the stock footage I had collected, but I didn't know if I could make a living doing it. I didn't know anything about the stock footage business. There were a few companies doing it, but they were in New York or L.A., and they seemed really huge.

But since I liked working with images and since the business had already started to take off on its own, I finally decided to formalize it. I started by picking a company name. I wanted something interesting that conveyed what I did. We came up with Oddball. It's a word that people don't really use anymore, more of a '40s or '50s expression—an oddball is someone kind of weird, unbalanced, or unusual, you know? Well, from there, I just kept compiling more footage, and over the years I started logging it, and buying more.

At the most basic level, my business involves finding, organizing, and preserving historical footage. And then distributing it. Our clients include ad agencies, news organizations, documentary and feature filmmakers, industrial, corporate, and music video producers, educational filmmakers, and anyone who needs offbeat and unusual images. In one way we're like a library. We archive and license historical visual information.

These days, I spend most of my time trying to organize and publicize my business. We just launched our website, and that takes time to maintain. And I spend a lot more time trying to obtain films than actually looking at them. Still, what I do at Oddball is an extension of the work I've been doing since the 1970s. I guess it became a business the day I decided I wasn't going to do anything else.

You undoubtedly already know that getting a business off the ground isn't easy. You've got a million different details to work out—how you'll produce your product or service, how much you'll charge, what marketing strategies to use, how to manage your cash flow—and you need to nail all of this down before you stand to make a dime. You'll likely find that very few, if any, other businesspeople have done exactly what you're setting out to do, so you'll have to answer a lot of questions on your own (or with your partners). It can be scary and lonely—and while exhilarating, it's almost always stressful.

But compared to working out the details of how your business will run and become successful, clearing the bureaucratic hurdles isn't a big deal at all. Dealing with governmental start-up requirements has been done millions of times before by all types of different businesses. Though the bureaucracy governing small business often seems like a convoluted maze, you can take comfort in the fact that the procedures are standard; they apply more or less the same to everybody, and the answers are out there. Unlike your unique business strategy that you'll need your best creative wits to devise, conquering the bureaucracy is essentially a no-brainer. Yes, it requires some patience and fortitude, but by no means do you need any special skill, education, or experience. As long as you do a bit of homework and arm yourself with an overview of the process (as you're doing by reading this book), you'll be able to meet all the small business registration requirements without breaking a sweat.

You can usually start a sole proprietorship (the legal term for a one-owner business) or a partnership (a business with more than owner) by registering with just one government office. And for business owners who want protection from personal liability for business debts—often referred to by the legal jargon "limited liability"—the simplest corporations or limited liability companies (LLCs) require only a couple more registration tasks. In other words, once you've got your business idea developed to a certain degree, all you need to do is visit a few government offices, fill out some forms, and pay some fees—and suddenly your idea will have become an actual, legitimate business.

Keep in mind that there's certainly a lot more to launching a successful small business than dealing with bureaucratic requirements. For starters, you'll need to have a sound business idea, and you'll need to be able to develop good management skills to guide it to success. This book, however, largely leaves these issues for other resources to cover. Unlike many other small business guides, we're not going to spend your precious time quizzing you on whether you have the right personality to be your own boss, evaluating your business idea, or helping you to identify the personal goals that you hope to achieve by starting a business. If you need more help deciding whether or not to start a business or what kind of business you should start, you should probably buy a different book. If, on the other hand, you want a book that cuts to the chase and explains systematically what you need to do to launch a business in California, this book is for you.

This book is also for those of you who are fairly certain you want to give your idea a try, but not quite ready to march down to city hall to register your business. In addition to explaining the start-up requirements in California, this book also outlines the preliminary work you should do before heading out to file all your official forms. Chapters 1 through 4 discuss fundamental tasks such as choosing the right legal structure for your business (sole proprietorship, partnership, LLC, or corporation), coming up with a catchy and legally sound business name, and finding a location that's good for business. We also explain how to draft a business plan that will help you define your business, plan for profitability, and attract lenders and investors. If you've already taken care of some these tasks, you can either skip these chapters or use them as a guide to evaluate what you've already done.

To help you through your start-up days, later chapters introduce you to a number of basic issues that every ongoing business needs to master. These include insurance, taxes, contracts and agreements, marketing (including taking your business online), and bookkeeping, accounting, and financial management (with cash flow projection and other useful worksheets included on the CD-ROM that comes with this book). Though they're not exactly start-up requirements, you should devote some time to them in the dawning days of your business so that you'll be up to speed when business is fast and furious.

Finally, keep in mind that businesses with employees have significant additional responsibilities. Chapter 15 offers a general overview of the laws and regulations that govern businesses with employees. If you're thinking about hiring employees, that chapter will help you figure out if you're ready to tackle the many requirements that come with your first hire. Chapter 15 also explains the difference between employees and independent contractors—an important distinction—because using independent contractors does not subject you to most of the laws that apply when you hire employees. If you decide that you need to hire any employees, you'll probably need to do further reading. An excellent and exhaustive resource is *The Employer's Legal Handbook*, by Fred S. Steingold (Nolo).

One of the main ideas we want you to take away from this book is that there's nothing mysterious or even terribly complex about the process of starting your own business. Whether you've drafted a highly specific business plan with the help of accountants and consultants or you've scratched it out on a cocktail napkin, the process of turning your idea into a legitimate business is the same. That process is covered in this book.

How you build and run your business, on the other hand, is where the real challenge comes in. You'll need confidence to get your business rolling—and you'll need guts, too. You may well find that some of the questions burning in your mind have no defined answer, because no one has asked that question or tried that idea before. You probably wanted to start a business in the first place so that you could make your own decisions—but this can often be quite a heavy burden. You may not believe it now, but some days you'll probably find yourself wishing you had a boss.

You'll need to learn to trust yourself, both when you feel optimistic and when you suspect that one of your ideas is less than brilliant. You'll also have to develop a sense for when you need help and learn to be judicious in taking the advice of people around you. Part of the art of controlling your own destiny is accepting the wisdom of others while maintaining your own focus and direction. It's not always an easy balance to maintain, but you'll undoubtedly get better at it as you gain experience in running your own show. The bottom line: Think hard, keep your mind open—and fight like hell to make your ideas a reality.

Take the leap.

More Small Business Products From Nolo

Nolo's website (www.nolo.com) offers books, software, online legal forms, (including California-specific forms, such as an online application to form an LLC in California), eProducts, and free legal information to help businesses solve specific legal problems. Here are some of the most popular business titles. You'll find more online.

Business Plans

Business Plan Pro 2009

by Palo Alto Software (available through Nolo)

A fast, easy way to generate the plan you need to launch or expand your business.

How to Write a Business Plan

by Mike McKeever

Explains how to write a business plan, whether for your own purposes or to attract money from lenders or investors—including how to evaluate the profitability of your business idea; estimate operating expenses; determine assets, liabilities, and net worth; and find potential sources of financing.

Business Operations

Negotiate the Best Lease for Your Business

by Janet Portman and Fred S. Steingold

A guide to the ins and outs of finding a space for your business, negotiating a lease, and solving problems that arise from it.

Legal Forms for Starting & Running a Small Business

by Fred S. Steingold

Dozens of legal forms and documents crucial for the success of a small business.

Legal Guide for Starting & Running a Small Business

by Fred S. Steingold

All the legal info you need to get your business off the ground and running—including how to raise start-up money, attract the best help, buy or sell a business or franchise, negotiate a favorable lease, insure your business, and resolve legal disputes.

Quicken Legal Business Pro 2010

A software package containing more than 140 legal forms and the complete text of five of Nolo's bestselling business titles—including *Legal Guide for Starting & Running a Small Business, Tax Savvy for Small Business, The Manager's Legal Handbook, How to Write a Business Plan,* and *Marketing Without Advertising.*

Running a Side Business: How to Create a Second Income

by Richard Stim and Lisa Guerin

Have the drive but need the know-how to start and run a side business (while working full time)? Find answers to your business questions in this book.

Save Your Small Business: 10 Crucial Strategies to Survive Hard Times or Close Down and Move On

by Ralph Warner and Bethany K. Laurence

Packed with the ideas, strategies, and lessons that have kept a successful entrepreneur in business for more than 30 years.

Forms of Ownership

Business Buyout Agreements: A Step-by-Step Guide for Co-Owners

by Anthony Mancuso & Bethany K. Laurence

Explains how to protect your business interests by drawing up a "premarital" agreement between you and the other business owners that sets out a plan for what happens if you or a co-owner leaves the company. A must for any new business with more than one owner.

Form Your Own Limited Liability Company

by Anthony Mancuso

Offers instructions and forms to create an LLC in your state, as well as a full explanation of LLCs and how they work.

How to Form a California Professional Corporation

by Anthony Mancuso

Current tax info, forms, instructions, and other information needed to form a professional, rather than a standard, corporation in California.

How to Form Your Own California Corporation

by Anthony Mancuso

The forms, information, and instructions you need to incorporate your business in California.

More Small Business Products From Nolo (cont'd)

How to Form Your Own California Corporation
(with Corporate Records Binder & CD-ROM)
by Anthony Mancuso

Incorporate your business in this all-in-one binder bursting with forms, instructions, certificates, and more.

LLC Maker
by Anthony Mancuso

Windows software that assembles LLC articles of organization according to state legal requirements, plus an operating agreement and other LLC formation paperwork.

Nolo's Quick LLC: All You Need to Know About Limited Liability Companies
by Anthony Mancuso

Explains the basics of limited liability companies and helps you figure out whether structuring your business as an LLC is the right way to go.

Form a Partnership: The Complete Legal Guide
by Denis Clifford and Ralph Warner

Describes the legal and practical issues of creating a partnership—including financial and tax liabilities, contributions and distributions, and changes in ownership.

Intellectual Property

Trademark: Legal Care for Your Business & Product Name
by Stephen R. Elias and Richard Stim

The information and forms you need to choose a distinctive trademark, register it, and fight infringers.

Marketing

Marketing Without Advertising: Easy Ways to Build a Business Your Customers Will Love and Recommend
by Michael Phillips and Salli Rasberry

Explains the secret of attracting customers without pricey ads—including how to build trust with potential customers, encourage customer recommendations, improve customer service, list

products and services widely and inexpensively, and use the Internet to market services and products.

Tax

Deduct It! Lower Your Small Business Taxes
by Stephen Fishman

Take all the business tax deductions you're due! Write off travel expenses, meals, entertainment, and much more.

Home Business Tax Deductions: Keep What You Earn
by Stephen Fishman

The complete guide to the tax deductions your home business can claim—including your home-office costs.

Tax Savvy for Small Business
by Frederick W. Daily

Offers plain-English tax laws and rules on business deductions, plus tax info on LLCs, partnerships, corporations, and more.

Workplace Laws

The Employer's Legal Handbook
by Fred S. Steingold

All the basics of employment law in one place. It covers safe hiring and firing practices, wages, hours, employee benefits, taxes and liability, discrimination, and sexual harassment.

The Manager's Legal Handbook
by Lisa Guerin and Amy DelPo

A quick reference to employment law, combining legal information and practical ideas.

Working With Independent Contractors
by Stephen Fishman

Explains all the tricky IRS rules and provides forms and instructions for hiring independent contractors.

Choosing a Legal Structure

You probably already have a rough idea of the type of legal structure your business will take, whether you know it or not. That's because, in large part, the ownership structure that's right for your business—a sole proprietorship, partnership, LLC, or corporation—depends on how many people will own the business and what type of services or products it will provide, things you've undoubtedly thought about quite a bit.

For instance, if you know that you will be the only owner, then a partnership is obviously not your thing. (A partnership by definition has more than one owner.) And if your business will engage in risky activities (for example, trading stocks or repairing roofs), you'll want not only to buy insurance, but also to consider forming an entity that provides personal liability protection (a corporation or a limited liability company), which can shield your personal assets from business debts and claims. If you plan to raise capital by selling stock to the public or want to give your employees stock options, then you should form a corporation.

If you've considered these issues, then you'll be ahead of the game in choosing a legal structure that's right for your business. Still, you'll need to consider the benefits and drawbacks of each type of business structure before you make your final decision.

In California, the basic types of business structures are:

- sole proprietorships
- partnerships
- limited liability companies (LLCs), and
- corporations.

To help you pick the best structure for your business, this chapter explains the basic attributes of each type.

Stephen Parr, owner and director of Oddball Film and Video, a stock footage company in San Francisco, California:

What a business really is, is you deciding you have a business. It's really nothing more than that.

Making the Decision to Go Official

Some of you may be grappling with a more preliminary question than what legal structure you should choose and wondering whether or not to formalize your business—to go the official route and register your business with the appropriate agencies in your state. For instance, maybe you've been doing freelance graphics work on the side for a number of years, but now you're thinking of quitting your 9-to-5 job to take on graphics work full time.

Generally speaking, anyone with a good-sized or otherwise visible business should bite the bullet and complete all of the necessary registration tasks to become official. Operating under the table can all too easily be exposed, and the government can come after you for fines and penalties, and might even padlock your business simply for operating without the necessary paperwork. And if you're making a profit, ignoring the IRS is definitely a bad idea. Besides fines and back taxes, you could even face criminal charges and jail time.

On the other hand, tiny, home-based, hobby-type businesses can often operate for quite some time without meeting registration requirements. If you're braiding hair or holding an occasional junk sale out of your garage, for instance, you can probably get by without formal business registration—at least for a while. Keep in mind, however, that just because it may be possible doesn't mean it's the best option. Often, formally registering your business can benefit you, the owner, as well, since you can then write off business expenses and reduce your personal taxes. In Chapter 8, we discuss hobby businesses in more depth, including how tax laws deal with businesses that continually lose money.

If you're not sure whether you want to register your business and open it up to the world of government regulations, the information about registration requirements in this book will put you in a better position to make a decision. Chapter 6 walks you through the many governmental requirements that apply to all new businesses, and explains how to go about finding and satisfying any additional requirements that may apply to your specific business.

This chapter will help you answer the most common question new entrepreneurs ask about choosing a business form: Should I choose a business structure that offers protection from personal liability—a corporation or an LLC? Here's a hint as to what the best advice will be: If you focus your energy and money on getting your business off the ground as a sole proprietorship or a partnership, you can always incorporate or form an LLC later.

Limited Liability

One basic distinction that you'll probably hear mentioned lots of times is the difference between businesses that provide their owners with "limited liability" and those that don't. Corporations and LLCs both provide owners with limited personal liability. Sole proprietorships and general partnerships do not.

Limited liability basically means that the creditors of the business cannot normally go after the owners' personal assets to pay for business debts and claims arising from lawsuits. (Liability for business debts is discussed in detail later in this chapter.)

As you read about specific business types in this chapter, you'll see how a decision to form a limited liability entity (a corporation or an LLC, mainly) can dramatically affect how you run your business. On the other hand, sole proprietorships and partnerships (which are somewhat simpler to run than corporations and LLCs) may leave an owner personally vulnerable to business lawsuits and debts.

Sole Proprietorships

 SKIP AHEAD

Sole proprietorships are one-owner businesses. Any business with two or more owners cannot, by definition, be a sole proprietorship. If you know that there will be two or more owners of your business, you can skip ahead to "Partnerships," below.

A sole proprietorship is simply a business that is owned by one person and that hasn't filed papers to become a corporation or an LLC. Sole proprietorships are easy to set up and to maintain—so easy that many people own sole proprietorships and don't even know it. For instance, if you are a freelance photographer or writer, a craftsperson who takes jobs on a contract basis, a salesperson who receives only commissions, or an independent contractor who isn't on an employer's regular payroll, you are automatically a sole proprietor. This is true whether or not you've registered your business with your city or obtained any licenses or permits. And it makes no difference whether you also have a regular day job. As long as you do for-profit work on your own (or sometimes with your spouse—see "Running a Business With Your Spouse," below) and have not filed papers to become a corporation or a limited liability company, you are a sole proprietor.

 CAUTION

Don't ignore local registration requirements. If you've started a business without quite realizing it—for example, you do a little freelance computer programming, which classifies you as a sole proprietor by default—don't let the fact that you're technically already a sole proprietor fool you into thinking that you've satisfied the governmental requirements for starting a business. Most cities and counties require businesses—even tiny home-based sole proprietorships—to register with them and pay at least a minimum tax. And if you do business under a name different from your own, such as Custom Coding, you must register that name—known as a fictitious business name—with your county. In practice, lots of businesses are small enough to get away with ignoring these requirements. But if you are caught, you may be subject to back taxes and other penalties. (See Chapter 6 for an explanation of how to make the necessary filings with the appropriate government offices.)

Running a Business With Your Spouse

If you plan to start a sole proprietorship and expect that your spouse may occasionally help out with business tasks, you should be aware of a fuzzy area in federal tax law that you can use to your advantage. The IRS typically allows a spouse to pitch in without pay without risking being classified as an owner or as an employee of the other spouse's business. This situation is sometimes erroneously called a "husband-wife sole proprietorship."

The normal rule is that someone who does work for a business must be one of three things from a legal standpoint: a co-owner, an employee, or an independent contractor. But when that someone is your spouse, this rule is softened somewhat. Your spouse can volunteer—that is, work without pay—for your sole proprietorship without being classified as an employee, freeing the business from paying payroll tax.

That saves you money—and, if you have no other employees, also allows you to avoid the time-consuming record keeping involved in being an employer. Similarly, a spouse who is not classified as a partner or an independent contractor won't have to pay self-employment taxes and your business won't have to file a partnership tax return.

Also consider that under marital property laws, which vary from state to state, if a business is started or significantly changed when a couple is married, both spouses may have an ownership interest in the business regardless of whose name is on the ownership document.

If you are concerned about the possible consequences of divorce, read Chapter 14, "Planning for Changes in Ownership." It discusses how divorce and other life events, such as retirement and death, can affect ownership of a business and explains how to plan in advance to accommodate the possibilities. You may also want to check with a lawyer who is experienced in handling marital property issues to see how your business could be affected in your particular state in the event of a divorce.

Finally, if you and your spouse both want to be active partners in a co-owned business—each with an official say in management—you should create a partnership or an LLC or a corporation, even though this will mean filing somewhat more complicated tax returns and other business paperwork. If your spouse tries to squeak by as a volunteer in a so-called husband-wife sole proprietorship when you're really working together as a partnership, you run the risk of being audited, having the IRS declare you're a partnership—and socking your spouse with back self-employment taxes.

Pass-Through Taxation

In the eyes of the law, a sole proprietorship is not legally separate from the person who owns it. This is one of the fundamental differences between a sole proprietorship and a corporation or an LLC. And it has two major effects: one related to taxation (explained in this section), and the other to personal liability (explained in the next).

At income tax time, a sole proprietor simply reports all business income or losses on his or her individual income tax return. The business itself is not taxed. The IRS calls this "pass-through" taxation, because business profits pass through the business to be taxed on the business owner's tax return.

You report income from a business just like wages from a job except that, along with Form 1040, you'll also need to include Schedule C, on which you'll provide your business's profit and loss information. One helpful aspect of this arrangement is that if your business loses money—and, of course, many start-ups do in the first year or two—you can use the business losses to offset any taxable income you have earned from other sources.

EXAMPLE: Rob has a day job at a coffee shop, where he earns a modest salary. His hobby is collecting obscure records at thrift stores and rummage sales. Contemplating the sad fact that he has no extra money to spend at the flea market on Saturday morning, he decides to start selling some of the vinyl gems he's found. Still working his day job, he starts a small business that he calls Rob's Revolving Records.

During his first full year in business, he sees that a key to consistently selling his records is developing connections and trust among record collectors. Unfortunately, while he is concentrating on getting to know potential buyers and others in the business, sales are slow. At year-end, he closes out his books and sees that he spent nearly $9,000 on records, his website, marketing items such as business cards, and other incidental supplies, while he made only $3,000 in sales. But there is some good news: Rob's loss of $6,000 can be counted against his income from his day job, reducing his taxes and translating into a nice refund check, which he'll put right back into his record business.

! **CAUTION**

Your business can't lose money forever. See the discussion of tax rules for money-losing businesses in Chapter 8.

RESOURCE

Be ready for the day you'll owe taxes. Once your business is under way and turning a profit, you'll have to start paying taxes. (See Chapter 8 for an overview of the taxes small businesses face.) Taxes can get fairly complicated, however, and you may need more in-depth guidance. For detailed information on taxes for the various types of small businesses, see *Tax Savvy for Small Business*, by Frederick W. Daily (Nolo). This book gives exhaustive information on deductions, record keeping, and audits—all of which will help you reduce your tax bill and stay out of trouble with the IRS.

Personal Liability for Business Debts

Another crucial thing to know about operating your business as a sole proprietor is that you, as the owner of the business, can be held personally liable for business-related obligations. This means that if

your business doesn't pay a supplier, defaults on a debt, loses a lawsuit, or otherwise finds itself in financial hot water, you, personally, can be forced to pay up. This can be a sobering possibility, especially if you own (or soon hope to own) a cool house, car, or other treasures. Personal liability for business obligations stems from the fundamental legal attribute of being a sole proprietor: You and your business are legally one and the same.

As explained in more detail in the sections that discuss corporations and LLCs, below, owners of these businesses enjoy what the law calls "limited personal liability" for business obligations. This means that, unlike sole proprietors and general partners, owners of corporations and LLCs can normally keep their houses, investments, and other personal property, even if the business fails. In short, if you are engaged in a risky business, you may want to consider forming a corporation or an LLC—although a thorough insurance policy can often protect you from lawsuits and claims against the business.

! **CAUTION**

Commercial insurance doesn't cover business debts. Commercial insurance can protect a business and its owners from some types of liability (for instance, slip-and-fall lawsuits), but insurance never covers business debts. The only way to limit your personal liability for business debts is to use a limited liability business structure such as an LLC or a corporation (or a limited partnership or limited liability partnership).

Creating a Sole Proprietorship

Setting up a sole proprietorship is incredibly easy. Unlike starting an LLC or a corporation, you generally don't have to file any special forms or pay any special fees to start working as a sole proprietor. You simply declare your business to be a sole proprietorship when completing the general registration requirements that apply to all new businesses, such as getting a business license from your county or city, or a seller's permit from the California Board of Equalization.

For example, when filing for a business tax registration certificate with your city, you'll often be asked to declare what kind of business you're starting. Some cities require only that you check a "sole proprietorship" box on a form, while others have separate tax registration forms for sole proprietorships. Similarly, other forms you'll file, such as those to register a fictitious business name and to obtain a seller's permit, will also ask for this information. (These and other start-up requirements are discussed in detail in Chapter 6.)

Partnerships

Bring two or more entrepreneurs together into a business venture, stir gently, and—poof!—you've got a partnership. By definition, a partnership is a business that has more than one owner and that has not filed papers with the state to become a corporation or an LLC (or a limited partnership or limited liability partnership).

CAUTION

Beware of local registration requirements. If you're going into business with others, don't let the fact that you're automatically a partnership fool you into thinking that you've satisfied the governmental requirements for starting a business. Most cities and counties in California require all businesses to register with them and pay at least a minimum tax. And if you do business under a name other than the partners' names, you must register that name—known as a fictitious business name—with your county. (See Chapter 6 for an explanation of how to make the necessary filings with the appropriate government offices.)

General Versus Limited Partnerships

Usually, when you hear the term "partnership," it means a general partnership. As we discuss in more detail below, general partners are personally liable for all business debts, including court judgments. In addition, each individual partner can be sued for the full amount of any business debt (though that partner can turn around and sue the other partners for their shares of the debt).

Another very important aspect of general partnerships is that any individual partner can bind the whole business to a contract or business deal—in other words, each partner has "agency authority" for the partnership. And remember, each of the partners is fully personally liable for a business deal gone sour, no matter which partner signed the contract. So choose your partners carefully.

There are also a couple of special kinds of partnerships, called limited partnerships and limited liability partnerships. They operate under very different rules and are relatively uncommon, so they are only briefly described here.

A limited partnership requires at least one general partner and at least one limited partner. The general partner has the same role as in a general partnership: He or she controls the company's day-to-day operations and is personally liable for business debts. The limited partner contributes financially to the business (for example, invests $100,000 in a real estate partnership) but has minimal control over business decisions or operations and normally cannot bind the partnership to business deals. In return for giving up management power, a limited partner gets the benefit of protection from personal liability. This means that a limited partner can't be forced to pay off business debts or claims with personal assets, but can lose the entire investment in the business. But beware: A limited partner who tires of being passive and starts tinkering under the hood of the business should understand that personal liability can quickly become unlimited that way. If a creditor can prove that the limited partner acted in a way that led the creditor to believe that he or she was a general partner, that limited partner can be held fully and personally liable for the creditor's claims.

RESOURCE

More on limited partnerships. See *Form a Partnership: The Complete Legal Guide,* by Denis Clifford and Ralph Warner (Nolo).

Another kind of partnership in California, called a limited liability partnership (LLP), provides all of its owners with limited personal liability. These partnerships are only available to professionals—licensed lawyers, accountants, and architects—and are particularly well suited to them. Most professionals aren't keen on general partnerships because they don't want to be personally liable for another partner's problems—particularly those involving malpractice claims. Forming a corporation to protect personal assets may be too much trouble, and California won't allow these professionals to form an LLC. The solution is often a limited liability partnership. This business structure protects each partner from debts against the partnership arising from professional malpractice lawsuits against another partner. (A partner who loses a malpractice suit for his or her own mistakes, however, doesn't escape liability.)

As attractive as they are, limited partnerships and limited liability partnerships (and limited liability companies, discussed below) are not cheap to create. The filing fee is just $70, but California also charges a minimum annual tax of $800 for both types of limited partnerships. The tax is due in the first quarter of operations, whether or not you're making a profit.

Pass-Through Taxation

Similar to a sole proprietorship, a partnership (general or limited) is not a separate tax entity from its owners; instead it's what the IRS calls a "pass-through entity." This means the partnership itself does not pay any income taxes; rather, income passes through the business to each partner, who pays taxes on an individual share of profit (or deducts a share of losses) on an individual income tax return (Form 1040, with Schedule E attached). However, the partnership must also file what the IRS calls an "informational return"—Form 1065—to let the government know how much the business earned or lost that year. No tax is paid with this return. Just think of it as the feds' way of letting you know they're watching.

Personal Liability for Business Debts

Since a partnership is legally inseparable from its owners, just like a sole proprietorship, general partners are personally liable for business-related obligations. What's more, in a general partnership, the business actions of any one partner bind the other partners, who can be held personally liable for those actions. So, if your business partner takes out an ill-advised high-interest loan on behalf of the partnership, makes a terrible business deal, or gets in some other business mischief without your knowledge, you could be held personally responsible for any debts that result.

EXAMPLE: Jamie and Kent are partners in a profitable landscape gardening company. They've been in business for five years and have earned healthy profits, allowing them each to buy a house, decent wheels, and even a few luxuries—including Jamie's collection of garden sculptures and Kent's roomful of vintage musical instruments. One day Jamie, without telling Kent, orders a shipment of exotic poppy plants that he is sure will be a big hit with customers. But when the shipment arrives, so do agents of the federal drug enforcement agency who confiscate the plants, claiming they could be turned into narcotics. Soon thereafter, criminal charges are filed against Jamie and Kent, resulting in several newspaper stories. Though the partners are ultimately cleared, their attorney fees come to $50,000 and they lose several key accounts, with the result that the business runs up hefty debts. As a general partner, Kent is personally liable for these debts even though he had nothing to do with the ill-fated poppy purchase.

Before you get too worried about personal liability, keep in mind that many small businesses don't face much of a risk of racking up large debts. For instance, if you're engaged in a low-risk enterprise, such as freelance editing, landscaping, or running a small band that plays weddings and other social events, your risk of facing massive debt or a huge lawsuit is pretty small. For these types of small, low-risk businesses, a good business insurance policy that covers most liability risks is almost always enough to protect owners from a catastrophe such as a lawsuit or fire. Insurance won't cover regular business debts, however. If you have significant personal assets, like fat bank accounts or real estate, and plan to rack up some business debt, you may want to limit your personal liability with a different business structure, such as an LLC or a corporation.

Partnership Agreements

By drafting a partnership agreement, you can structure your relationship with your partners pretty much however you want. You and your partners can establish the respective shares of profits (or losses) each will receive, what the responsibilities of each partner will be, what should happen to the partnership if a partner leaves, and how any number of other issues will be handled. It is not legally necessary for a partnership to have a written agreement. The simple act of two or more people doing business together creates a partnership. But only with a clear written agreement will all partners be sure of the important—and sometimes touchy—details of their business arrangement.

In the absence of a partnership agreement, California's version of the Revised Uniform Partnership Act (RUPA) kicks in as a standard, bottom-line guide to the rights and responsibilities of each partner. For example, if you don't have a partnership agreement, then California's RUPA states that each partner has an equal share in the business's profits, losses, and management power. Similarly, unless you provide otherwise in a written agreement, a California partnership won't be able to add a new partner without the unanimous consent of all partners. (Cal. Corp. Code § 16401.) But you can override many of the legal provisions contained in the California RUPA if you and your partners have your own written agreement.

There's nothing terribly complex about drafting partnership agreements. They're usually only a few pages long and cover basic issues that you've probably thought over to some degree already. Partnership agreements typically include at least the following information:

- name of partnership and partnership business
- date of partnership creation
- purpose of partnership
- contributions (cash, property, and work) of each partner to the partnership

- each partner's share of profits and losses
- provisions for taking profits out of the company (often called partners' draws)
- each partner's management power and duties
- how the partnership will handle departure of a partner, including buy-out terms
- provisions for adding or expelling a partner, and
- dispute resolution procedures.

These and any other terms you include in a partnership agreement can be dealt with in more or less detail. Some partnership agreements cover each topic with a sentence or two; others spend up to a few pages on each provision. Of course, you need an agreement that's appropriate for the size and formality of your business, but it's not a good idea to skimp on your partnership agreement.

RESOURCE

More information on partnerships. *Form a Partnership: The Complete Legal Guide,* by Denis Clifford and Ralph Warner, is an excellent step-by-step guide to putting together a solid, comprehensive partnership agreement. Also, *Business Buyout Agreements: A Step-by-Step Guide for Co-Owners,* by Anthony Mancuso and Bethany K. Laurence, explains how to draft terms that will enable you to deal with business ownership transitions. (Both books are published by Nolo.)

If you think you may need more than the simple partnership agreements provided in this book, there are more detailed partnership agreement forms on CD (as well as many other resources for running your business) in *Quicken Legal Business Pro 2010.* You can learn more about all of these resources at www.nolo.com.

Take a look at the short sample partnership agreements on the following pages to see how a very basic partnership agreement can be put together. (You'll also find a blank partnership agreement in Appendix C and on the CD-ROM that comes with this book.) These samples are about as basic as it gets—the bare minimum—and you'll almost surely want to use something more detailed for your business.

Partnership Agreement #1

Alison Shanley and Peder Johnson make the following partnership agreement.

Name and Purpose of Partnership

As of September 22, 20xx, Alison and Peder are the sole owners and partners of the Dunsmuir Fly-Fishing Company. The Dunsmuir Fly-Fishing Company shall be headquartered in Dunsmuir, California, and will sell fly-fishing equipment by mail order.

Contributions to the Partnership

Alison and Peder will make the following contributions to the partnership:

Alison Shanley	cash	$10,000
	desk, miscellaneous office furniture	1,000
	Total contribution:	$11,000
Peder Johnson	cash	$7,000
	computer system	2,000
	Total contribution:	$9,000

Profit and Loss Allocation

Alison and Peder will share business profits and losses in the same proportions as their contributions to the business.

Management of Partnership Business

Alison and Peder will have equal management powers and responsibilities.

Departure of a Partner

If either Alison or Peder leaves the partnership for any reason, including voluntary withdrawal, expulsion, or death, the remaining partner shall become the sole owner of the Dunsmuir Fly-Fishing Company, which shall become a sole proprietorship. The remaining owner shall pay the departing partner, or the deceased departing partner's estate, the fair market value of the departing partner's share of the business as of the date of his or her departure. The partnership's accountant shall determine the fair market value of the departing partner's share of the business according to the partnership's book value.

Mediation of Disputes

Alison and Peder agree to mediate any dispute arising under this agreement with a mutually acceptable mediator.

Amendment of Agreement

This agreement may not be amended without the written consent of both partners.

Alison Shanley	Peder Johnson
Signature _____	Signature _____
Date _____	Date _____
Address _____	Address _____
_____	_____
Social Security # _____	Social Security # _____

Partnership Agreement #2

Christine Wenc, Simon Romero, and Brendan Doherty agree to the terms of the following agreement.

1. **Name of Partnership.** Christine, Simon, and Brendan are partners in the Wenc & Romero Partnership. They created the partnership on July 12, 20xx.

2. **Partnership Purpose.** The Wenc & Romero Partnership will provide newspaper clipping services to clients.

3. **Contributions to the Partnership.** Christine, Simon, and Brendan will contribute the following to the partnership:

    Christine: $1,000 cash; one Macintosh computer (value $1,500); and one monitor (value $500)

    Simon: $1,000 cash; one fax machine (value $400); one laser printer (value $1,200)

    Brendan: $500 cash; various office equipment (value $500)

4. **Profits and Losses.** Christine, Simon, and Brendan shall share profits and losses as follows:
Christine	40%
Simon	40%
Brendan	20%

5. **Partnership Decisions.** Christine, Simon, and Brendan will have the following management authority:
Christine	2 votes
Simon	2 votes
Brendan	1 vote

    No partner may accept a new client without the agreement of the others.

6. **Additional Terms to Be Drafted.** Christine, Simon, and Brendan agree that in six months they will sign a formal partnership agreement which covers the items in this agreement in more detail and the additional following items:
    * each partner's work contributions
    * provisions for adding a partner
    * provisions for the departure of a partner, and
    * provisions for selling the business.

7. **Amendments.** This agreement may not be amended without the written consent of all partners.

Christine Wenc   Social Security # _____

Signature _____   Date _____

Simon Romero   Social Security # _____

Signature _____   Date _____

Brendan Doherty   Social Security # _____

Signature _____   Date _____

What a Partnership Agreement Can't Do

Although a general partnership agreement is an incredibly flexible tool for defining the ownership interests, work responsibilities, and other rights of partners, there are some things it can't do. These include:

- freeing the partners from personal liability for business debts
- restricting any partner's right to inspect the business books and records
- affecting the rights of third parties in relation to the partnership—for example, a partnership agreement that says a partner has no right to sign contracts won't affect the rights of an outsider who signs a contract with that partner, and
- eliminating or weakening the duty of trust (the fiduciary duty) each partner owes to the other partners.

Limited Liability Companies (LLCs)

Like many business owners just starting out, you might find yourself in this common quandary: On the one hand, having to cope with the risk of personal liability for business misfortunes scares you; on the other, you would rather not deal with the red tape of starting and operating a corporation.

Fortunately for you and many other entrepreneurs, you can avoid these problems by taking advantage of a relatively new form of business called the limited liability company, commonly known as an LLC. LLCs combine the pass-through taxation of a sole proprietorship or partnership (business taxes are paid on each owner's individual income tax returns) with the same protection against personal liability that corporations offer. And now that California no longer requires LLCs to have at least two members, solo business owners also have the option of forming an LLC.

However, professional services businesses may not use the LLC structure in California. "Professional services" are "any type of professional services that may be lawfully rendered only pursuant to a license, certification, or registration authorized by the Business and Professions Code, the Chiropractic Act, or the Osteopathic Act" or the Yacht and Ship Brokers Act. (Cal. Corp. Code §§ 13401(a), 13401.3.)

If you're a professional services provider and want a business structure with limited personal liability for the principals, all is not lost. You may recall from the discussion of partnerships, above, that accountants, lawyers, and architects may form limited liability partnerships (LLPs). If you want limited personal liability with another type of professional services business, you'll need to use the corporate business structure, discussed below (see "Corporations").

Limited Personal Liability

Generally speaking, owners of an LLC (called "members") are not personally liable for the LLC's debts. (There are some exceptions to this rule, discussed below.) This protects the members from legal and financial liability in case their business fails or loses a lawsuit and can't pay its debts. In those situations, creditors can take all of the LLC's assets, but they generally can't get at the personal assets of the LLC's members. Losing your business is no picnic, but it's a lot better to lose only what you put into the business than to say goodbye to everything you own.

> **EXAMPLE:** Callie forms her own one-person mail-order business, using most of her $25,000 in savings to establish a cool website and buy mailing lists. Callie realizes that she'll have to buy a significant portion of her sales inventory up front to be able to ship goods to her customers on time, so she plans to buy those items on credit. While she is willing to risk her $25,000 investment to pursue her dream, she is worried that if her mail-order business fails, she will be buried under a pile of debt. Callie decides to form an LLC so that if her business should fail, she'll only lose the $25,000; no one will be able to sue her personally for the business debt that she owes. She feels more secure going into business knowing that even if her business fails, she can walk away without the risk of losing her house or her car.

While some LLCs opt for a structure in which the company is run by specially designated managers, most LLCs are simply managed by the members. This more common setup is called a "member-managed" LLC; one that is run by managers (who are elected by the members) is called a "manager-managed" LLC. A manager-managed LLC might be appropriate if some of the LLCs owners are passive investors (similar to limited partners), while a smaller group intends to actively run the company. If all the LLC owners intend to actively manage the company, you'll generally use the more common member-managed structure.

With this in mind, remember that, like a general partner in a partnership, any member of a member-managed LLC can legally bind the entire LLC to a contract or business transaction. In other words, each member can act as an agent of the LLC. In manager-managed LLCs, any manager can bind the LLC to a business contract or deal.

While LLC owners enjoy limited personal liability for many of their business debts, this protection is not absolute. There are several situations in which an LLC owner may become personally liable for business debts or claims. However, this drawback is not unique to LLCs. The limited liability protection given to LLC members is just as strong as (if not stronger than) that enjoyed by the corporate shareholders of small corporations. Here are the main situations in which LLC owners can still be held personally liable for debts:

- **Personal guarantees.** If you give a personal guarantee on a loan to the LLC, then you are personally liable for repaying that loan. Because personal guarantees are often required by banks and other lenders, this is a good reason to be a conservative borrower. Of course, if no personal guarantee is made, then only the LLC—not the members—are liable for the debt.
- **Taxes.** The IRS or the California Franchise Tax Board may go after the personal assets of LLC owners for overdue federal and state business tax debts, particularly overdue payroll taxes. This is most likely to happen to members of small LLCs who have an active hand in managing the business, rather than to passive members.
- **Negligent or intentional acts.** An LLC owner who intentionally, or even carelessly, hurts someone will usually face personal liability. For example, if an LLC owner takes a client to lunch, has a few martinis and injures the client in a car accident on the way home, the LLC owner can be held personally liable for the client's injuries.
- **Breach of fiduciary duty.** LLC owners have a legal duty to act in the best interest of their company and its members. This legal obligation is known as a "fiduciary duty," or is sometimes simply called a "duty of care." LLC owners who violate this duty can be held personally liable for any damages that result from their actions (or inactions). Fortunately for LLC owners, they normally will not be held personally responsible for any honest mistakes or acts of poor judgment they commit in doing their jobs. Most often, breach of duty is found only for serious indiscretions, such as fraud or other illegal behavior.
- **Blurring the boundaries between the LLC and its owners.** When owners fail to respect the separate legal existence of their LLC, but instead treat it as an extension of their personal affairs, a court may rule that the owners are personally liable for business debts and liabilities. Generally, this is more likely to occur in one-member LLCs; in reality, it only happens in extreme cases. You can easily avoid it by opening a separate LLC checking account, getting a federal employer identification number, keeping separate accounting books for your LLC, and funding your LLC adequately enough to be able to meet foreseeable expenses.

LLC Taxation

Like a sole proprietorship or partnership, an LLC is not a separate tax entity from its owners; instead, it's what the IRS calls a "pass-through entity." This means the LLC itself does not pay any income taxes; instead, income passes through the business to each

LLC owner, who pays taxes on the individual share of profit (or deducts his or her share of losses) on an income tax return (for the feds, Form 1040 with Schedule E attached). But a multiowner LLC, like a partnership, does have to file Form 1065—an "informational return"—to let the government know how much the business earned or lost that year. No tax is paid with this return.

LLCs give members the flexibility to choose to have the company taxed like a corporation rather than as a pass-through entity. In fact, partnerships now have this option as well. (See Form 8832, *Entity Classification Election,* in Appendix C.)

You may wonder why LLC owners would choose to be taxed as a corporation—after all, pass-through taxation is one of the most popular features of an LLC. The answer is that, because of the income-splitting strategy of corporations (discussed in "Corporate Taxation," below), LLC members can sometimes come out ahead by having their business taxed as a separate entity at corporate tax rates.

For example, if the owners of an LLC become successful enough to keep some profits in the business at the end of the year (or regularly need to keep significant profits in the business for upcoming expenses), paying tax at corporate tax rates can save them money. That's because federal income tax rates for corporations start at a lower rate than the rates for individuals. For this reason, many LLCs start out being taxed as partnerships, and when they make enough profit to justify keeping some in the business (rather than doling it out as salaries and bonuses), they opt for corporate-style taxation.

LLCs face significant taxes and fees at the state level. California charges a minimum annual tax of $800, which is due in the first quarter of operations, whether or not you're making a profit. Additional fees may be charged as well. (LLC taxes and fees are discussed in more detail in Chapter 8.)

LLCs Versus S Corporations

Before LLCs came along, the only way all owners of a business could get limited personal liability was to form a corporation. Problem was, many entrepreneurs didn't want the hassle and expense of incorporating, not to mention the headache of dealing with corporate taxation. One easier option was to form a special type of corporation known as an S corporation, which is like a normal corporation in most respects, except that business profits pass through to the owner (as in a sole proprietorship or partnership), rather than being taxed to the corporation at corporate tax rates. In other words, S corporations offered the limited liability of a corporation with the pass-through taxation of a sole proprietorship or partnership. For a long time, this was an okay compromise for small to medium-sized businesses, though they still had to deal with many of the corporate requirements of running an S corporation (discussed in more detail below).

Now, however, LLCs offer a better option. LLCs are indeed similar to S corporations in that they combine limited personal liability with pass-through tax status. But a significant difference between these two types of businesses is that LLCs are not bound by the many regulations that govern S corporations.

Here's a quick rundown of the major areas of difference between S corporations and LLCs. (Keep in mind that corporations, including S corporations, are explained in more detail in the next section.)

- **Ownership restrictions.** An S corporation may not have more than 75 shareholders, all of whom must be U.S. citizens or residents. This means that some of the C corporation's main benefits—namely, the ability to set up stock option and bonus plans and to bring in public capital—are pretty much out of the question for S corporations. And even if an S corporation initially meets the U.S. citizen or resident requirement, its shareholders can't sell shares to another company (like a corporation or an LLC) or a foreign citizen, on pain of losing S corporation tax status. In an LLC, any type of person or entity can become a member—a U.S. citizen, a citizen of a foreign country, or another LLC, corporation, or limited partnership.

- **Allocation of profits and losses.** Shareholders of an S corporation must allocate profits according to the percentage of stock each owner has. For example, a 25% owner has to receive 25% of the profits (or losses), even if the owners want a different division. Owners of an LLC, on the other hand, may distribute profits (and the tax burden that goes with them) however they see fit, without regard to each member's ownership share in the company. For instance, a member of an LLC who owns 25% of the business can receive 50% of the profits if the other members agree (subject to a few IRS rules).

- **Corporate meeting and record-keeping rules.** For S corporation shareholders to keep their limited liability protection, they have to follow the corporate rules—issuing stock, electing officers, holding regular board of directors' and shareholders' meetings, keeping corporate minutes of all meetings, and following the mandatory rules found in the corporation code. By contrast, LLC owners don't need to jump through most of these legal hoops—they just have to make sure their management team is in agreement on major decisions and go about their business.

- **Tax treatment of losses.** S corporation shareholders are at a disadvantage if their company goes into substantial debt—for instance, if it borrows money to open the business or buy real estate. That's because an S corporation's business debt cannot be passed along to its shareholders unless they have personally cosigned and guaranteed the debt. LLC owners, on the other hand, normally can reap the tax benefits of any business debt, cosigned or not. This can translate into a nice tax break for owners of LLCs that carry debt.

Forming an LLC

To form an LLC, you must file Articles of Organization with the California Secretary of State. You should also execute an operating agreement, which governs the internal workings of your LLC. Before you decide the LLC is the best thing since easy cheese, you should be aware that an LLC is generally not as cheap to start as a partnership or sole proprietorship. While the filing fee itself isn't terribly expensive ($70), the California Franchise Tax Board requires that you pay a minimum annual LLC tax of $800 when you start your LLC.

Many brand-new business owners aren't in a position to pay this kind of money right out of the starting gate, so they start out as partnerships until they bring in enough income to cover these costs. Since California lowered its corporate start-up fees in 2000, some entrepreneurs are tempted to start out as corporations, which are now cheaper to start than LLCs. However, keep in mind that the added expenses of running a corporation (legal and accounting fees, for example) can often make a corporation more expensive in the long run than an LLC.

CAUTION

Some LLCs must comply with securities laws. LLCs that have owners who do not actively participate in the business may have to register their membership interests as securities or, more likely, qualify for an exemption to the registration requirements. For information about the federal securities laws, visit the Securities and Exchange Commission's website at www.sec.gov and click on "Information for: Small Businesses."

RESOURCE

For more on LLCs. *Form Your Own Limited Liability Company*, by Anthony Mancuso (Nolo), gives detailed information on LLCs, including step-by-step instructions and forms for creating one in every state. For a briefer treatment, consult *Nolo's Quick LLC: All You Need to Know About Limited Liability Companies*, also by Anthony Mancuso. It offers an overview of LLCs as well as comparisons to other business structures, but does not include any start-up forms. Nolo also offers an online application for California LLCs and LLC software to form your LLC online (see www.nolo.com for details).

Corporations

For many, the term "corporation" conjures up the image of a massive industrial empire more akin to a nation-state than a small business. In fact, a corporation doesn't have to be huge, and most aren't. Stripped to its essentials, a corporation is simply a specific legal structure that imposes certain legal and tax rules on its owners (also called shareholders). A corporation can be as large as IBM or, in many cases, as small as one person.

One fundamental legal characteristic of a corporation is that it's a separate legal entity from its owners. If you've already read this chapter's sections on sole proprietorships and partnerships, you'll recognize that this is a major difference between those unincorporated business types and corporations. Another important corporate feature is that shareholders are normally protected from personal liability for business debts. Finally, the corporation itself—not just the shareholders—is subject to income tax.

 CAUTION

Publicly traded corporations are a different ball game. This section discusses privately held corporations owned by a small group of people who are actively involved in running the business. These corporations are much easier to manage than public corporations, whose shares are sold to the public at large. Any corporation that sells its stock to the general public is heavily regulated by state and federal securities laws, while corporations that sell shares, without advertising, only to a select group of people who meet specific state requirements are often exempt from many of these laws. If you plan to sell shares of a corporation to the general public, you should consult a lawyer.

Limited Personal Liability

Generally, owners of a corporation are not personally liable for the corporation's debts. (There are some exceptions to this rule, discussed below.) Limited personal liability is a major reason why owners have traditionally chosen to incorporate their businesses: to protect themselves from legal and financial liability in case their business flounders or loses an expensive lawsuit and can't pay its debts. In those situations, creditors can take all of the corporation's assets (including the shareholders' investments), but they generally can't get at the personal assets of the shareholders.

EXAMPLE: Tim and Chris publish *Tropics Tripping*, a monthly travel magazine with a focus on Latin America. Because they both have significant personal assets, and because they will have to borrow a lot of capital to start up their magazine, they form their business as a corporation to protect their personal assets in case their magazine fails. They do great for a few years, but suddenly their subscription and advertising revenue starts to suffer when a recession plus political unrest in several Latin American countries reduce interest in travel to that area. Hoping the situation will turn itself around, Tim and Chris forge ahead—and go deeper into debt as it proves impossible to pay printing and other bills on time. Finally, when their printer won't do any more print runs on credit, Tim and Chris are forced to call it quits. *Tropics Tripping*'s debts total $250,000, while business assets are valued at only $90,000—leaving a $160,000 debt to creditors. Thankfully for Tim and Chris, they won't have to use their personal assets to pay the $160,000, because as owners of a corporation, they're shielded from personal liability.

 TIP

Corporations aren't the only option. With the advent of limited liability companies, corporations aren't the only business entities that provide limited liability status for all owners. (See the section on LLCs, above.)

Forming a corporation to shield yourself from personal liability for business obligations provides good, but not complete, protection for your personal assets. Here are the principal areas in which corporation owners still face personal liability.

- **Personal guarantees.** If you give a personal guarantee on a loan to the corporation, then you are personally liable for the repayment of that loan. Because banks and other lenders often require a personal guarantee, this is a good reason to be a conservative borrower. Of course, if no personal guarantee is made, then only the corporation—not the shareholders—is liable for the debt.

- **Taxes.** The IRS or the California Franchise Tax Board may go after the personal assets of corporate owners for overdue corporate federal and state tax debts, particularly overdue payroll taxes. This is most likely to happen to owners of small corporations who have an active hand in managing the business, rather than to passive shareholders.

- **Negligent or intentional acts.** A corporate owner whose negligent (that is, careless), or perhaps even intentional actions end up hurting someone can't hide behind the corporate barrier to escape personal liability. Shareholders are subject to personal liability for wrongs they commit—such as attacking a customer or leaving a floor wet in a store—that result in injury.

- **Breach of fiduciary duty.** Corporate owners have a legal duty to act in the best interest of the company and its shareholders. This legal obligation is known as a "fiduciary duty," sometimes simply called a "duty of care." An owner who violates this duty can be held personally liable for any damages that result from those actions (or inactions). Fortunately for corporate owners, run-of-the-mill mistakes or lapses in judgment aren't usually considered breaches of the duty of care. Most often, breach of duty is found only for serious indiscretions, such as fraud or other illegal behavior. For example, if a corporate officer has falsified some financial data in order to seal a deal with a client, that officer may be held personally liable for any damages that result from that breach of duty to the company.

- **Blurring the boundaries between the corporation and its owners.** When corporate owners ignore corporate formalities and treat the corporation like an unincorporated business, a court may ignore the existence of the corporation (in legal slang, it may "pierce the corporate veil") and rule that the owners are personally liable for business debts and liabilities. To avoid this, it's important that corporate owners not allow the legal boundary between the corporation and its owners to grow fuzzy. Owners need to scrupulously respect corporate formalities by holding shareholders' and directors' meetings, keeping attentive minutes, issuing stock certificates, and maintaining corporate accounts strictly separate from personal funds.

Also, bear in mind that although limited personal liability can prevent you from losing your home, car, bank account, and other assets, it won't protect you from losing your investment in your business. A business can quickly get wiped out if a customer, employee, or supplier wins a big lawsuit against it and the business has to be liquidated to cover the debt. In short, even if you incorporate to protect your personal assets, you should purchase appropriate insurance to protect your business assets. (Insurance is discussed in Chapter 7.) But remember, insurance won't help if you simply can't pay your normal business debts.

Corporate Taxation

The words "corporate taxes" raise a lot of fear and loathing in the business world. Fortunately, the reality of corporate taxation is usually less depressing than the hype. Here are the basics—think of it as Corporate Tax Lite. If you decide to incorporate, you'll likely want to consult an accountant or small business lawyer who can fill you in on the fine print. (See Chapter 16 for information on finding and hiring a lawyer.)

The first thing you need to know is that you'll be treated differently for tax purposes, depending on whether you operate as a regular corporation (also called a C corporation) or you elect S corporation status. An S corporation is the same as a C corporation in most respects, but when it comes to taxes, C and S corporations are very different animals. A regular, or C, corporation must pay taxes, while an S corporation is treated like a partnership for tax purposes and doesn't pay any income taxes itself. Like partnership profits, S corporation profits (and losses) pass through to the shareholders, who report them on their individual returns. (In this respect, S corporations are very similar to LLCs, which also offer limited liability along with partnership-style tax treatment.) These two types of corporations are explained in more detail just below.

C Corporations

As a separate tax entity, a regular corporation must file and pay income taxes on its own tax return, much like an individual does. After deductions for such things as employee compensation, fringe benefits, and all other reasonable and necessary business expenses have been subtracted from its earnings, a corporation pays tax on whatever profit remains. In small corporations in which all of the owners of the business are also employees, all of the corporation's profits are often paid out in tax-deductible salaries and fringe benefits—leaving no corporate profit and thus no corporate taxes due. (The owner/employees must, of course, pay tax on their salaries on their individual returns.)

Fringes and Perks

Like they can for employee salaries, corporations can deduct many fringe benefits as business expenses. If a corporation pays for benefits such as health and disability insurance for its employees and owner/employees, the cost can usually be deducted from the corporate income, reducing a possible tax bill. (There's one main exception: Benefits given to an owner/employee of an S corporation who owns 2% or more of the stock can't be deducted as business expenses.)

As a general rule, owners of sole proprietorships, partnerships, and LLCs can deduct the cost of providing these benefits for employees, but not for themselves. (These owners can, however, deduct a portion of their medical insurance premiums, though it's technically a deduction for the individuals, not a business expense.)

The fact that fringe benefits for owners are deductible for corporations may make incorporating a wise choice. But it's less likely to be a winning strategy for a capital-poor start-up that can't afford to underwrite a benefits package.

Initial rates of corporate taxation are comparatively low (15% to 25%). (See "Marginal Tax Rates for Corporations," below.) Corporations that keep some profits in the business from one year to the next—rather than paying out all profits as salaries and bonuses—can take advantage of these low tax brackets. This practice, sometimes called income splitting, basically involves strategically setting salaries at a level so that money left in the business is taxable only at the 15% or 25% corporate tax rate (which applies to profits up to $50,000 or $75,000). Since any amount of "reasonable" compensation to employees is deductible, corporate owners have lots of leeway in setting salaries to accomplish this.

EXAMPLE: Alexis and Matt run Window to the Past, Inc., a glass manufacturing business that specializes in custom work for architectural renovations. Toward the end of the year, they calculate that year's profit to be approximately $145,000. They decide to give themselves each a $50,000 bonus out of the profit (on top of their $40,000 salaries). Because both salaries and bonuses are tax-deductible business expenses, this reduces Window to the Past's taxable income to $45,000. The resulting corporate profit of $45,000 will be taxed at only 15%, the lowest rate. (If Alexis and Matt had left all the profits in the business, the profits over $75,000 would have been taxed at 34%, and profits over $100,000 would have been taxed at a whopping 39%.) Of course, the bonuses Alexis and Matt give themselves increase their personal incomes, which will be taxed on their individual returns. Still, their personal tax rates are lower than the high corporate rates of 34% and 39%.

Marginal Tax Rates for Corporations

The following chart shows tax rates for corporations. For example, if a corporation's taxable income was $75,100, it would pay 15% of its first $50,000 of income, 25% of the next $25,000, and 34% on its remaining $100 in income. The corporation's marginal tax rate—the tax rate a corporation would pay on the last dollar of its income—would be 34%.

Taxable Income	Tax Rate
0 to $50,000	15%
$50,001 to $75,000	25%
$75,001 to $100,000	34%
$100,001 to $335,000	39%
$335,001 to $10,000,000	34%
$10,000,001 to $15,000,000	35%
$15,000,001 to $18,333,333	38%
Over $18,333,333	35%

Keep in mind that these corporate rates don't apply to professional corporations, which are subject to a flat tax of 35% on all corporate income.

This income-splitting strategy is available only to shareholders who also work for the corporation. If they're not at least part-time employees, then shareholders won't be in a position to earn salaries or bonuses and will be able to take money from the corporation only as dividends.

Double Taxation

This brings us to the vexing problem of double taxation, routinely faced by larger corporations with shareholders who aren't active employees. Unlike salaries and bonuses, dividends paid to shareholders cannot be deducted as business expenses from corporate earnings. Because they're not deducted, any amounts paid as dividends are included in the total corporate profit and taxed. And when the shareholder receives the dividend, it is taxed at the shareholder's individual tax rate as part of personal income. As you can see, any money paid out as a dividend gets taxed twice: once at the corporate level and once at the individual level.

You can avoid double taxation simply by not paying dividends. This is usually easy if all shareholders are employees, but probably more difficult if some shareholders are passive investors anxious for a reasonable return on their investment.

S Corporations

Unlike a regular corporation, an S corporation does not pay taxes itself. Any profits pass through to the owners, who pay taxes on income as if the business were a sole proprietorship, a partnership, or an LLC. Yet the business is still a corporation. This means, of course, that its owners are protected from personal liability for business debts, just as are shareholders of C corporations and owners of LLCs.

Until the relatively recent arrival of the LLC (discussed above), the S corporation was the business form of choice for those who wanted limited liability protection without the two-tiered tax structure of a C corporation. Today, relatively few businesses are organized as S corporations, because S corporations are subject to many regulations that do not apply to LLCs. (See "LLCs Versus S Corporations," above, for more information.)

Forming and Running a Corporation

Unlike sole proprietorships and partnerships, you can't clap your hands twice and conjure up a corporation. In addition to tax complexity, the major drawbacks to forming a corporation—either a C or an S type—are time and expense. Now that California has reduced the up-front fees for incorporating, however, most of the expense involves legal and other professional fees that are almost always incurred in forming a corporation. To incorporate, you must file Articles of Incorporation with California's Secretary of State, along with a filing fee of $100. (Significantly, the minimum annual tax of $800 is no longer due in the first business year for corporations created on or after January 1, 2000.) You will have to file a Statement by Domestic Stock Corporation every year, beginning within 90 days of filing your Articles of Incorporation. (These requirements are covered in detail in Chapter 6.) And if you decide to sell shares of the corporation to the public—as opposed to keeping them in the hands of a relatively small number of owners—you'll have to comply with lots of complex federal and state securities laws.

Finally, to protect your limited personal liability, you need to act like a corporation, which means adopting bylaws, issuing stock to shareholders, maintaining records of various meetings of directors and shareholders, and keeping records and transactions of the business separate from those of the owners.

CAUTION

Corporations must comply with securities laws. Corporations must either register their shares with the Securities and Exchange Commission or qualify for an exemption to securities registration requirements. For information about small business exemptions to the federal securities laws, visit the Securities and Exchange Commission's website at www.sec.gov and click on "Information for: Small Businesses."

RESOURCE

More on running corporations. For more information on the many complexities of running a corporation, read either *How to Form Your Own California Corporation* or *The Corporate Records Handbook: Meetings, Minutes & Resolutions*, both by Anthony Mancuso (Nolo).

Choosing the Best Structure for Your Business

Although there are many differences between the various types of business organizations, most business owners choose an operating structure based on one major legal issue: the personal liability of owners for business debts. It's true that the issue of personal liability can have a huge impact on successful small businesses a few years down the road. But business owners who are just starting out on a shoestring often care most about spending as little money as possible on the legal structure of their business. This is certainly an understandable

approach; far more new businesses die painful deaths because they don't control costs than because they lose costly lawsuits. In short, for many new small businesses, incorporating or organizing as an LLC is as unnecessary an expense as a swank downtown office or a gleaming chrome espresso machine in the lunchroom.

That said, owners of any business that will engage in a high-risk activity, rack up large business debts, or have a significant number of investors should always insist on limited personal liability, either with an LLC or a corporation. This is even more true if the business can't find or afford appropriate insurance.

If you decide that your personal liability is worth the extra cost, you still need to decide whether to form a corporation or an LLC. Many business owners who want limited liability protection realize that incorporation normally makes sense only if a business needs to take advantage of the corporate stock structure to attract key employees and investment capital. No question, corporations may have an easier time attracting capital investment by issuing stock privately or publicly. And some businesses may find it easier to attract and retain key employees by issuing employee stock options. But for businesses that never go public, choosing to operate as an LLC rather than a corporation normally makes the most sense, if limited liability is your main concern. If the corporate stock structure isn't something you want or need for your business, the simplicity and flexibility of LLCs offer a clear advantage over corporations.

Analyzing Your Risks

Starting a business is always risky. In some businesses, however, the risks are particularly extreme. If you're planning to launch an investment firm or start a commercial building construction company, there is little doubt that you'll need all the protection you can get, including limited personal liability as well as adequate insurance. Other businesses are not so obviously risk laden, but still could land you in trouble if fate strikes you a blow. When analyzing your business, note that red flags for riskiness include:

- using hazardous materials, such as dry cleaning solvents or photographic chemicals, or hazardous processes, such as welding or operating heavy machinery
- manufacturing or selling edible goods
- driving as part of the job
- building or repairing structures or vehicles
- caring for children or animals
- providing or allowing access to alcohol
- allowing activities that may result in injury, such as weightlifting or skateboarding, and
- repairing or working on items of value, such as cars or antiques.

If you've identified one or more serious risks your business is likely to face, figure out whether business insurance might give you enough protection. Some risky activities, such as job-related driving, are good candidates for insurance and don't necessarily warrant incorporating. But if insurance can't cover all of the risks involved in your business, it may be time to form an LLC or a corporation.

Keep in mind that insurance will never insulate you from regular business debts. If you foresee your business going into serious debt, an LLC or corporation may be the best business structure for you.

(For more information on risk management and insurance, see Chapter 7.)

Chapter 1 Checklist: Choosing a Legal Structure

☐ Identify the number of owners of your business.

☐ Analyze your business's risks and decide how much protection from personal liability you'll need.

☐ Determine how you'd like the business to be taxed (as a pass-through entity or as a corporation).

☐ Decide if your business would benefit from the stock structure of a corporation (by being able to distribute stock options and sell stock).

☐ Choose a business structure.

☐ If you will structure your business as a partnership, draft and sign a partnership agreement.

☐ If you will structure your business as an LLC or corporation, file articles with the California Secretary of State and draft bylaws (for corporations) or an operating agreement (for LLCs).

Picking a Winning Business Name

There's a lot of room for personal and professional creativity when picking a business name, but there are also legal requirements and pitfalls that you absolutely need to understand. In particular, it's important for all business owners to understand the basics of trademark law, which establishes and protects the legal right to use a particular name for a business, product, or service.

If you choose a business or product name that's too similar to a competitor's name, for instance, you could find yourself accused of violating the competitor's trademark (called "infringement" or "unfair competition") and be forced to change your business name and possibly pay money damages. Having to change a business name can be a serious blow to a business that has worked hard to build name recognition among its customers—not to mention the cost of changing signs, stationery, preprinted invoices, and the like.

But suppose you plan to open a local business so small that you don't even expect to compete with businesses in the next county, much less in another state or country. You probably wonder if the arcane world of trademark law really affects you. Until the 1990s the answer would have clearly been no—you didn't really have to worry too much about national or global name conflicts back then. As long as a quick search of your phone book didn't reveal any obvious local conflicts and you didn't call your business "Ford," "IBM," or some other famous name, you were fine. But in today's world of the Internet, mail order, and rapidly growing national chains, "local" obviously isn't what it used to be. Even if you're opening just a tiny bookstore in a small town, if you inadvertently choose the same name as an Internet store that sells books, you may very well be accused of infringing the online store's trademark— even if the online store's headquarters are on a different continent.

One good way to figure out how concerned you need to be about trademark law is to consider the consequences of having to change your business name. If a name change would be cheap and easy and wouldn't seriously confuse your customers, then don't lie awake nights worrying about picking a name that's absolutely bulletproof. However, if changing your name would be messy or expensive, you'll want to take the time and trouble to be sure the name you plan to use doesn't already belong to someone else.

Are you convinced that paying attention to the law of business names is important? Good. Now you'll learn how to choose a name that won't land you in legal hot water and how to secure the maximum legal protection for it. This chapter will also cover some nonlegal aspects of naming your business, including tips and advice on how to choose the most effective name for your particular business.

> **CAUTION**
>
> **Watch out for other legal issues.** Besides watching out for trademark conflicts, business owners also need to comply with other legal rules. Many businesses must comply with fictitious business name requirements. (See "Step 3: Register Your Fictitious Business Name" in Chapter 7.) Typically, this means you'll need to register a fictitious business name statement (or similar document) with your county clerk and possibly publish it in a local newspaper. And for corporations, LLCs, and limited partnerships, the California Secretary of State must approve your business name before it will accept Articles of Incorporation, Articles of Organization, or a Statement of Limited Partnership.

An Overview of Trademark Law

In a nutshell, trademark law—which is really a catchall term referring to a large body of statutes, regulations, and court decisions—prevents a business from using a name or logo that is likely to be confused with one that a competing business already uses. This general rule applies both to the name of a business and to the names of any of its products or services.

Allowing businesses to have exclusive use of certain names helps consumers to identify and recognize goods in the marketplace. When you buy Racafrax brand of wood glue, for instance, you'll know that it will be similar in quality to the Racafrax glue you bought last time. By contrast, if any company was allowed to call its glue "Racafrax Glue," customers would never know what they were

Getting the Terms Straight

One reason the law of business names often seems confusing is that it is riddled with lots of arcane and often overlapping legal jargon. For example, local, state, and federal agencies often use different terms to describe the same or very similar legal concepts. Here's a brief rundown of the terms you need to know, all of which are discussed in greater detail in the rest of this chapter.

- The term **legal name** means the official name of the entity that owns a business. The legal name of a sole proprietorship is simply the full name of the owner—for example, John Potter. If a general partnership has a written partnership agreement that gives a name to the partnership, then that name is the legal name. Otherwise, the legal name of the general partnership is simply the last names of the owners. (Many sole proprietorships and partnerships present their businesses to the public under names that are different from their legal names—see fictitious business name, below.) And for corporations, LLCs, and limited partnerships, legal names are the names registered with the California Secretary of State.

- A **trade name** is simply the name that a business uses with the public, which may or may not be the same as the name of the business owner or the business's legal name. John O'Toole's Classic Cars, Amoeba Records, and Nolo are examples of trade names. You see trade names on business signs, in the telephone book, and on invoices. In many transactions, such as opening a bank account or applying for a loan, you'll need to provide the owners' names, the legal name of the business (if different), and the trade name of the business (if different).

- The term **fictitious business name** is used when the trade name of a business is different from its legal name. For instance, if John O'Toole named his sole proprietorship Turtle's Classic Cars, the name "Turtle's Classic Cars" would be a fictitious business name because it does not contain the owner's last name, O'Toole. A fictitious

business name is sometimes called a **DBA** name. DBA stands for "doing business as," as in "John O'Toole, doing business as Turtle's Classic Cars." Corporations and LLCs may also have to file fictitious name statements if the name they hold out to the public differs from the legal name they registered with the state. For example, if the owners of Southern Colusa County Auto Mechanics Ltd. Liability Co. decide to operate a repair shop under the fictitious name "Grease Monkeys," they'll have to file a fictitious business name statement.

- When a business incorporates, it must choose and register a **corporate name** with the California Secretary of State. Similarly, a limited liability company (LLC) must register an **LLC name** and a limited partnership (LP) must register an **LP name** with the California Secretary of State. Corporate, LLC, and limited partnership names must have the Secretary of State's approval before they will be registered. If a corporation, an LLC, or a limited partnership operates under the same name that's registered with the Secretary of State, then its name will be both its legal name and its trade name.

- A **trademark** (sometimes called simply a mark) is any word, phrase, design, or symbol used to market a product or service. Technically, a mark used to market a service, rather than a product, is called a service mark, though the term "trademark" is commonly used for both types of marks. Owners of trademarks have legal rights under both federal and California law, which give them the power in some cases to prevent others from using their trademarks to market goods or services.

- **Business name** tends to be a catchall term that can refer to any of the names used by a business—the name of a business itself, a corporate name, a fictitious business name, or the name of a business's product or service.

Business Names and Trademarks Often Overlap

Many trade names double as trademarks and service marks for products and services of the business. For instance, when McDonald's (trade name) advertises McDonald's French fries, the trade name "McDonald's" also becomes a trademark because it is used to identify the maker (or brand) of French fries. And when the company puts up a sign in front of its restaurant, the term "McDonald's" becomes a service mark, identifying who's providing the fast food service of that restaurant. In other words, any time you use your trade name to identify a product, service, or business location, you're using the trade name as a mark—either a trademark or a service mark. As you can see, a name can wear a bunch of different hats: It can be a trade name, a legal name, and a trademark (or service mark) all in one.

Legal Name	Trade Name	Trademarks/Service Marks
McDonald's Corporation	McDonald's	McDonald's French fries Big Mac Mayor McCheese Golden arches symbol
Microsoft Corporation	Microsoft	Microsoft Word Windows 2000 Internet Explorer "Where do you want to go today?" slogan
Nolo Press/Folk Law, Inc.	Nolo	Nolo Scales symbol "Your legal companion" slogan
Trader Joe's Company	Trader Joe's	Trader Joe's Baked Tortilla Chips Trader Giotto's Italian Roast coffee beans Trader Darwin's vitamins
Ronco, Inc.	Ronco	Popeil Pocket Fisherman Dial-O-Matic Food Slicer
Kraft Foods, Inc.	Kraft	JELL-O Gelatin Cheez Whiz Tang Instant Breakfast Drink "It's the cheesiest" slogan for Kraft Macaroni & Cheese "Good to the last drop" slogan for Kraft Maxwell House Coffee

getting. And because customers would never know when they were using the Racafrax company's glue, the Racafrax company wouldn't be able to build customer trust or goodwill, even if its glue was the best available. In this way, consumers and businesses alike benefit from trademark protection.

This section will give you a rundown of what's protected by trademark law and how to determine and protect your rights to the names you use. This will help you understand what steps you should take as part of forming your business to avoid infringing others' rights (and opening yourself up to lawsuits). And it will also give you the legal basics you'll need to protect your business name and to figure out whether your rights are being infringed by others down the road.

Trademark Protects More Than Names

This chapter focuses on how trademark applies to business names. But the rules discussed here apply to a lot more—logos, designs, slogans, and packaging features can also be protected by trademark. For example, Nike's slogan, "Just Do It," and American Express's mantra, "Don't leave home without It," are protected by the law of trademark. For more information on using trademarks in other aspects of your small business, read *Trademark: Legal Care for Your Business & Product Name*, by Stephen Elias and Richard Stim (Nolo).

 CAUTION

Pick a name that won't bring legal trouble. The main reason to learn the basics of trademark law is not so you can successfully defend your name in court against another business that tries to use it. Even if you were to win a complex and expensive court fight, you'd be a huge loser when it comes to time, worry, and legal fees. Far better to avoid disputes in the first place by choosing a safe name that has a very low likelihood of leading to customer confusion and, therefore, an infringement lawsuit.

What Is a Trademark?

The definition of "trademark" is simple: any word, phrase, logo, or other device used to identify products or services in the marketplace. This includes the names of products or services themselves and often the name of the business that's selling them. Using a name in public commerce to identify goods or services for sale is enough to make it a trademark; there is no registration requirement. However, registration with the U.S. Patent and Trademark Office will greatly strengthen your power to enforce your rights to the trademark. For example, if you federally register your trademark, you can stop any subsequent user in your field from using the same or a confusingly similar mark anywhere in the United States. (See "Trademark Registration," below.)

Keep in mind, however, that a key part of the definition of a trademark is that it must be used in public to identify goods or services for sale. So if you don't use the name of your business or product or service in public in conjunction with something you're trying to sell, it isn't considered a trademark. For example, if a software company called ZZP Web Masters markets bookmarking software for the Internet called "WebWorm," then the name WebWorm is a trademark. If the only marketing done for WebWorm is an ad that reads, "Manage your bookmarks with WebWorm," then the business name ZZP Web Masters will not be a trademark because it's not used in public to sell WebWorm. But an ad that reads, "WebWorm: The best bookmarking software on Earth, by ZZP Web Masters," includes two trademarks: the product name WebWorm and the trade name ZZP Web Masters.

By the same token, a name that appears only in nonpublic documents—for example, an internal memo or a product sample that isn't available to the public—isn't a trademark.

For practical purposes, many if not most business names are also considered trademarks, since most businesses do use their names to promote or sell their products or services.

Trademarks Versus Service Marks

You've probably heard the term "trademark," which applies to names, logos, and slogans that identify products (such as Chia Pet), a whole lot more than the term "service mark," which is used when a name identifies a service (such as H&R Block Tax Preparation Services). Because the legal rules for trademarks and service marks are virtually identical, the term "trademark," or sometimes just "mark," is commonly used for both types of marks. But since the two terms do refer to technically different things, you should be aware of the distinction, especially if your businesses will primarily provide services.

Trademark Rights

The power of a trademark comes from the fact that you may be entitled to exclude others from using the same mark. If you were the first to use a trademark, then you own certain rights to it and can take legal action against others who use it illegally. In legal terms, if others "infringe your trademark" by using it in a way that's likely to confuse your customers or that has "diluted" your trademark, you can take them to court and force them to stop using it, and maybe even to pay damages.

For example, if ZZP Web Masters had been selling WebWorm for two years and then another company started selling a similar product called "WebWorm," ZZP Web Masters could sue the other company and force it to stop using the product name "WebWorm." If ZZP Web Masters could prove that its business suffered because of the infringement, it might also be entitled to some financial compensation (damages) from the other company.

So far, so good—you're probably even wondering why everyone says trademark issues are such a bear to deal with. Here's why: Just because you own a trademark doesn't mean you can always prevent someone else from using it (and likewise, another owner of a trademark can't always prevent you from using that mark). Unlike a copyright, which generally gives the same level of protection to all owners, a trademark gives widely varying degrees of protection to the owner, depending on a variety of circumstances. So, as explained below, the key legal point isn't so much whether you own a trademark but whether it qualifies for trademark protection—and if so, how much.

Strong Versus Weak Marks

The general rule is that distinctive business names, such as Google and Mountain Dew, receive the strongest legal trademark protection. What makes a mark "distinctive" is explained in more detail below, but, for the moment, it's important that you understand why distinctive names get more protection. The theory is that distinctive names such as Pepsi or Xerox make strong connections in the minds of consumers and play a big role in their buying choices. The opposite is considered to be true for names that aren't very distinctive, such as Quality Vitamins or Brite Paint.

Because distinctive names are thought to play such a big role in helping consumers choose among brands, it follows that the more distinctive a name is, the more likely it is (in legal theory at least) that customers will be confused by more than one business using the name. To avoid this confusion, the law gives more protection to distinctive names, and less or none to names that are merely ordinary and descriptive.

A truly distinctive trademark (also called a "strong trademark") is one that clearly distinguishes the product or service it represents from others. Memorable, unusual names, such as Xerox or Google, are good examples of distinctive marks. While there's no magic formula for what makes a trademark distinctive, strong marks tend to be surprising or fanciful names that often have nothing to do with the business, product, or service. Still more examples of distinctive marks include Chia Pet, Velcro, and Comet, the cleanser.

On the flip side, a weak trademark consists of ordinary, descriptive words that merely describe aspects of the product or business, such as durability ("Sturdy Knapsacks"), location ("The Edge of Town Tavern"), or other qualities ("Speedy Dry Cleaners" or "Tasty Vegetables"). Also, trademarks that include personal names are usually considered to be ordinary marks and therefore weak. (But, as we explain below, weak trademarks can become stronger with use.)

An additional reason why ordinary, descriptive trademarks aren't strongly protected, at least at first, is to make sure that competitors aren't unfairly prevented from using common words to describe their own products. For example, a food delivery service company called "Galloping Gourmet" wouldn't be able to monopolize the word "gourmet" and stop a deli from using the name "Tom's Gourmet Sandwiches."

How Trademarks Can Grow Stronger

A weak trademark can eventually offer good protection if it becomes distinctive and therefore stronger through use. Called "acquiring a secondary meaning" in legalese, this is particularly likely to occur when a product or service with a weak mark becomes a lasting success, making it likely that the public will associate the mark with the product or service being sold. For example, as the designer clothing brand Tommy Hilfiger has become popular worldwide, its previously weak trademark has grown stronger as customers have come to associate the ordinary name with a particular company. Examples of the weak-to-strong phenomenon include Burger King, Tom's Natural Toothpaste, and Ben & Jerry's Ice Cream.

Unfair Competition Laws

What if your weak trademark never becomes strong? Just because you have a weak trademark doesn't mean that others are free to use your business name. Because of a legal doctrine called unfair competition, you may be able to prevent others from using your descriptive name, as long as you used it first. Although unfair competition law is a separate body of law from trademark law, it can have the same effect. It's based on the same idea—that it's not fair for another business to rip off your business's good reputation.

For example, if you've been selling dry cleaning services in Bakersfield under the name Jean's Quick Cleaners, and someone else in the same city opens Jeanne's Quick Cleaners, you could claim unfair competition and convince a court to prevent the newcomer from using that name. As you can see, unfair competition law can have the same result as trademark law: It can prevent another business from using a name identical or confusingly similar to yours, if you used the name first. Keep in mind, however, that your right to stop trademark infringement is stronger than your right to stop unfair competition, so it will be easier to prevent someone from using your business name if it's trademarked.

When Do Trademarks Conflict?

As you surely know, plenty of businesses share the same names, or at least parts of the same names, without violating each other's trademark rights. Examples include United Airlines and United Van Lines; Ford Motor Company and Ford Modeling Agency; and Scott Paper Products and Scott Sunglasses. This is perfectly legal, because trademark infringement occurs only when the use of a mark by two different businesses is likely to cause customer confusion. (An exception to this rule is explained in "The Dilution Exception," below.) If customers aren't likely to be confused, then both businesses may legally use the same mark. But if customer confusion is likely, then the rightful owner of the mark can prohibit the other businesses from using it and can sue for damages (financial compensation) for any unauthorized use.

Dual uses of the same or similar mark can cause customer confusion if it's unclear which company actually makes a product or service, or if customers will be misled as to the source of the product. Customer confusion can happen in a number of different ways. Sometimes dual uses of a mark lead customers to believe that a certain company made a product when it actually did not. Or a customer may see trademarks being used in two different places and think that the companies are jointly owned or somehow affiliated, which may not be true.

Determining whether two marks legally conflict (in other words, whether customer confusion is likely) is one of the trickiest bits of trademark law. In making this determination, courts deem the following factors to be particularly important:

- how strong (distinctive or well known) the original trademark is
- how much the products or services really compete against one another, and
- how similar the trademarks are in appearance, sound or meaning.

We'll look at each of these in more depth in the next few sections. As you read on, keep in mind that trademark conflict is a legal question—which means that legal rules, as opposed to common sense, will dictate the outcome.

How Strong Is the Mark?

As discussed above, distinctive (strong) marks receive the most protection because, in legal theory, they are more likely to stick in consumers' minds and play a role in their buying choices. Because strong trademarks tend to stick in customers' minds, so the theory goes, customer confusion is likely if more than one company uses a strong trademark. To protect consumers from such confusion, courts will typically prohibit more than one company from using a strong trademark. In addition to protecting consumers, prohibiting multiple uses of a strong trademark prevents businesses from stealing customers or getting a free ride off another business's good reputation by using its established trademark.

For example, the very strong and well-known trademark Microsoft is firmly implanted in millions of people's minds. If a company called itself Microsoft Consulting, plenty of people would be confused about whether Bill Gates had anything to do with that consulting company. If Bill Gates sued Microsoft Consulting for trademark infringement, he would have a very good chance of winning.

Trademark law doesn't give much, if any, protection to weak trademarks because they don't trigger a strong association in customers' minds between the mark and a particular product or service (or so the legal thinking goes). For that reason, courts are less inclined to find that customer confusion is likely when more than one business uses a weak trademark. Note that this is true even if customer confusion does in fact exist. For example, if Smith Jewelry and Smith Hardware exist in the same town, customers may wonder if they're owned

by the same family. Nonetheless, trademark law won't protect the name of either business, since the name Smith is so common. (However, unfair competition law may protect the hardware store Smiths if the jewelry store Smiths started getting into the hardware business, making the businesses direct competitors.)

Do the Products or Services Actually Compete?

If the products or services that share the same trademarks are in completely unrelated fields or industries, or if they're sold in different geographical regions (and not on the Internet), there's obviously far less chance that customers will be confused. In other words, the less products or services actually compete, the less likely it is that there will be a trademark violation. For example, a pizza joint named Rocket Pizza probably won't be confused with a record store named Rocket Records, even if they exist in the same city. And an auto shop named Armadillo Repairs in Portland, Maine, most likely won't run into any trademark conflicts with Armadillo Auto Repairs in San Diego. Because they are so far apart and serve purely local customers, chances are slim that customers would confuse the two companies.

> **EXAMPLE:** You open a coffee shop in Weed, California, and name it Pam's Coffee Stop. A year later, you're driving through Barstow and notice a small café also named Pam's Coffee Stop. After thinking about it, you decide that there's little chance of a trademark violation by either business. The trademark is ordinary and descriptive and therefore weak, plus the shops are so far away from each other that they're not competitors. But this gets you wondering what you'd do if a big national chain started using the name and moved into your area. The answer is, you would retain the right to use the name because you were the first to use it in your area (as long as the national chain hadn't registered the name with the U.S. Patent and Trademark Office before you first used it). But the chain could prevent you from expanding into other areas of the country if this ever became your goal.

⊘ CAUTION

New marketing techniques, new competitors. As mentioned at the beginning of this chapter, with the arrival and widespread use of the Web, the fast expansion of mail-order catalog businesses, and ever more frequent travel, the old rule that small, local businesses don't have to worry about trademarks from other geographical regions has largely gone out the window. Today, even small, local businesses commonly establish websites, hundreds of thousands of businesses send out catalogs, and some local restaurants and hotels seek to reach a national (or even worldwide) pool of tourists. The upshot is that many formerly local businesses that just a few years ago never would have been confused with each other are now competitors, which of course increases the likelihood of customer confusion and trademark infringement if their names are the same. (Be sure to read "Trademark Issues Online," below, on new trademark issues and considerations in today's ever smaller world.)

Of course, there are plenty of gray areas in which two businesses aren't in head-to-head competition but use the same marks for products that are similar enough to make a customer stop and think, for example, "Is a Parker calendar made by the same company as Parker pens?" Even though a company with the same name may not be stealing business from a competitor, it may be unintentionally taking advantage of that company's goodwill and getting a free ride from its advertising.

Whether infringement exists in these gray areas often depends on how strong the original trademark is (as discussed above). If the original trademark is weak, there's probably not much goodwill or reputation to rip off (few customers would be confused by the similar name), so a court wouldn't be likely to find infringement. But if the original trademark is strong, there's a greater likelihood that the newer trademark will rip off the older one's reputation, making it likely for the court to agree that there's been an infringement.

EXAMPLE: Your pet products company begins selling a toy that looks like a cross between a dog and a weasel, which you name the Garden Weasel. Soon after your toy hits the market, the makers of the nationally marketed Garden Weasel 5-in-1 garden tool contact you, claiming that you are infringing their trademark. Because you feel that the products are unrelated enough to minimize the chance of customer confusion (the products don't compete with one another), your first thought is to stick with the Garden Weasel name.

Think again. The Garden Weasel trademark is distinctive (memorable and unusual) and therefore strong. If you are sued—and you may well be—defending the lawsuit is likely to cost you tens or possibly even hundreds of thousands of dollars that you almost surely can't afford. And if the Garden Weasel mark is strong enough, you may lose the suit, even though the products don't compete. A better approach would probably be to tweak your name a bit, to something like the Lawn Weasel or the Garden Ferret, for instance.

Sight, Sound, and Meaning Test

Obviously, dual use of identical trademarks can cause customer confusion, as discussed above. But what about merely similar trademarks? If two marks look alike, sound alike, or have the same meaning, a court could decide that they conflict with each other, just as if they were identical. Small or superficial differences between two trademarks may not be enough to prevent customer confusion. The difference in spelling, for example, does not make the name "Ekzon" sufficiently different from "Exxon" to avoid trademark problems. And even though they're expressed in two different languages, the names "Le Petit Fleur" and "The Little Flower" have the same meaning, which increases the likelihood that some customers could confuse the two.

EXAMPLE: You open an auto lubrication business and name it Jiffy Oil. A few weeks later, you receive a stern letter from the attorneys of Jiffy Lube, a national chain of auto lubrication businesses. The letter informs you that the name "Jiffy Oil" infringes on the rights to the trademark "Jiffy Lube," because customer confusion is likely because the names are very similar, are used to describe an almost identical service, and mean pretty much the same thing. They demand that you change your business's name or be taken to court. You'd be wise to comply. The "Jiffy Lube" trademark, though a descriptive term (for fast lubrication), has become a very strong mark over time—customers have come to recognize it as a specific brand of service. And because your shop is a direct competitor of Jiffy Lube, the chance of customer confusion is high.

The Dilution Exception

As mentioned several times, there is a big exception to the rule that one trademark infringes another only where there is the likelihood of customer confusion. Even when customer confusion is improbable, courts will stop a business from using a trademark that's the same as or similar to someone else's if the use has diminished—or "diluted"—its distinctiveness. This legal protection kicks in only when a mark is so well known that even if you were to use it in a different context than the original trademark, lots of people would think of the original trademark. For example, a court might stop an athletic shoe manufacturer from using the trademark Exxon or a gas station from calling itself Nike. Even though customers would not be likely to confuse an oil company with a shoe maker, this sort of copying is a legal no-no, because allowing others to use the very famous trademark can chip away at its distinctiveness and slowly reduce its legal strength.

Trademark Issues Online

As in many other legal areas, the traditional principles of trademark law are scrambling to keep up with the fast clip of technological change. The Internet has changed many of the rules regarding trademark issues, just as it has created some entirely new ones. This section outlines a number of Internet-related concerns about trademarks and business names.

The Web Has Changed the Rules

As described in the previous section, one of the touchstones of trademark infringement is whether or not the two trademarks in question are likely to cause customer confusion. In the pre-Internet world, a small, local business didn't have to worry too much about name conflict as long as no one in their area had a similar name. But geographical distance is irrelevant in cyberspace.

Particularly if you plan to put your business online, you'll have to consider not only the trademarks of businesses already on the Web, but also those of businesses located anywhere the Web reaches—which, of course, is just about everywhere. If you create a Web page for a small home-based business, your business is no longer local in character. You're essentially launching a national or worldwide business that can compete with businesses everywhere, whether or not those businesses are online.

For example, if you create a website for your antique restoration business, Dalliance Designs, you could be competing with every antique restoration business in the country. If one of these owns the trademark "Dalliance Designs," your effort to share the market with that business opens a potentially ugly can of legal worms.

The Web has changed trademark rules for everybody—even for businesses that don't go digital. As more and more small businesses launch websites introducing themselves in a keystroke to consumers all over the globe, your purely local, offline business might find itself in competition with businesses several time zones—or even continents—away. Although courts are still chewing over many trademark issues raised by online commerce, it is already clear that, in some circumstances at least, a Web business with the same name as yours poses just as great a threat of a trademark lawsuit as does a real-life, bricks-and-steel business across the street.

> **EXAMPLE:** Jarrod is a mechanic who opens a small machine shop in a rural area of California. He's lived in the area for 30 years, and knows every business for miles around. Nevertheless, as part of choosing a name for

his business, Jarrod carefully checks the phone book and the county register for fictitious business names and ultimately settles on his first choice, Checkers Tool and Die.

All goes smoothly for a few months, until a customer compliments Jarrod on his slick-looking website. This leaves Jarrod totally confused since he hates computers and has only a vague notion of what the Web is. But in talking with his customer about this mysterious website, Jarrod realizes that a machine shop in Florida is also using the name "Checkers Tool and Die," and sells a number of specialized parts via an online catalogue. This doesn't particularly worry Jarrod until his customer (a lawyer, naturally) goes on to explain that if the distant business can prove it owns the trademark to "Checkers Tool and Die" and convince a court that it shares the same market as Jarrod, it might be able to force Jarrod to stop using the name.

Although at least one customer has been confused, Jarrod doesn't really expect the Florida outfit to go after him—after all, his business is small and local, provides primarily repair services (with parts as a sideline) and doesn't sell on the Web. Nevertheless, even the possibility of legal trouble worries him— especially because he'd like to open a retail machine parts shop next to his repair shop. After learning that the Florida outfit has been using the name Checkers Tool and Die for years and seems to be putting lots of energy into expanding its website, Jarrod decides to be safe and spend the time and money necessary to change the name of his business to White Mountain Tool & Die before he expands.

Domain Name Conflicts and Cybersquatting

Besides making sure that your business name won't create trademark trouble, if you plan to create a website for your business, you'll also need to choose a domain name that's legally safe. A domain name (such as nolo.com) is part of a website's URL (such as http://www.nolo.com/index.html), which functions as its Internet "address." Later sections of this chapter discuss the process of choosing and registering a domain name; for now, the focus is on the trademark issues that can surround domain names.

The first thing you should understand is that, generally speaking, your domain name will function as a trademark if you conduct business at your site—that is, if you offer products or services for sale. This is true whether or not you register your domain name with the U.S. Patent and Trademark Office (PTO). As discussed in "Trademark Registration," below, registering your domain name with the PTO will strengthen your power to enforce your trademark rights to it, but using it for a commercial purpose is all that's technically necessary to establish your trademark rights. For instance, amazon.com is the domain name for a huge website that sells books, videos, and other products—and the name amazon.com also serves as a trademark. This means that trademark law prohibits anyone else from using the name amazon.com for a business.

Keep in mind, however, that if your domain name is generic such as software.com or books.com, it won't qualify for much trademark protection. This rule applies to generic business or product names, such as lawyer, building supplies, or pet food; the law will generally not allow you to establish any trademark rights to these generic terms. But as we discussed earlier (in talking about weak trademarks), even generic domain names can grow stronger with use. Consider etrade.com, which has become almost synonymous with online stock trading. Originally, the name wouldn't have deserved much trademark protection since it wasn't distinctive at all—anyone can slap an "e" on the beginning of a word. Now, however, the mark has acquired "secondary meaning" and is probably entitled to trademark protection.

For most business owners, the best way to make sure their customers will find them online is simply to tack ".com" onto their regular business names. However, while trademark law will allow two or more companies to use the same name as long as it won't confuse customers, the technical limitations of the Web won't allow for two identical domain names. In other words, Ford Trucks and the Ford Modeling Agency won't both be able to use ford.com as a domain name. Because each website must have its own unique address, you may be out of luck if someone is already using your business name plus .com as a domain name. As you can imagine, this is where things can get sticky.

Dealing With Domain Name Conflicts

If you're starting a brand-new business that you haven't named yet, choose a name that also can be used as a domain name. That way, you can register it as a domain name right away and sidestep the whole issue of what to do if your domain name is already taken. You'll need to decide for yourself how important it is to you to have a domain name that's the same as your business name. If it's really important, then you may have to work hard to come up with a business name that's good for business, available as a domain name, and available as a trademark. If it's not that important, then your naming process will be somewhat easier—but you may regret it down the road when your business name can't be registered as a domain name.

A few possible scenarios may arise when someone is using your business name as a domain name. One is that you may simply have missed your chance to get that domain name yourself—even though you have trademark rights to it—and will either have to choose a different name or buy it from whomever registered it first. These are likely to be your only options if your mark isn't nationally famous and customers aren't likely to be confused by another business using your name.

EXAMPLE: Gene and Beth run a bookstore in San Diego called Lexicon. After about a year of planning, they decide to launch a website—but are disappointed to find out that the domain name lexicon.com has already been taken. By doing a search on the Web and going to the lexicon.com website, Gene and Beth discover that the owner of lexicon.com is a freelance editor in Chicago. Since Gene and Beth's bookstore doesn't have any national exposure,

they probably won't be able to force the editor in Chicago to give up the name—the editor's site probably would not confuse customers into thinking there was some association with their bookstore.

On the other hand, you may be able to assert your trademark rights against someone who is using your trademark as a domain name if:

- his or her use of the trademark is likely to cause customer confusion, or
- your trademark is distinctive and nationally known—even if the other party's use of it is not likely to cause customer confusion. (As discussed above, laws against trademark dilution protect famous marks from use by others, even if customer confusion is not likely.)

EXAMPLE: Assume that Gene and Beth's bookstore, Lexicon, already had a well-established national mail-order catalog business and the name Lexicon was familiar to a national audience. In this situation, they might be able to assert their trademark rights in court and force the Chicago editor to give up the lexicon.com domain name.

You will have to weigh carefully the pros and cons of attempting to force someone to give up a domain name based on a potential trademark infringement. On the one hand, the possibility of prevailing and getting the domain name you want may make this course worth it. On the other hand, remember that lawsuits cost time and money, and can easily exceed $10,000 in legal and court fees (and sometimes ten times that amount). You may be better off simply choosing a different domain name or even buying the name from the other party.

> **CAUTION**
>
> **Come to your own defense.** Your trademark rights can become weakened if you fail to defend your trademark when you know or should know that it's being infringed. For this reason, it's probably a good idea to go after a website or any other business or individual that

infringes your trademark. For more in-depth information on defending your trademark and dealing with infringers, see *Trademark: Legal Care for Your Business & Product Name,* by Stephen Elias and Richard Stim (Nolo).

Dealing With Cybersquatters

You may find that the domain name you want has already been registered by someone who wants to sell it back to you at a profit. For instance, say you own a well-known car racing magazine called *Auto Racing Today.* When you are ready to launch a website, you discover that the domain name autoracingtoday.com is already registered by another business, which offers to sell the name back to you for $250,000 (actually a modest amount compared to similar sales). This practice, known as "cyber-squatting," became a real problem in the late 1990s before businesses realized the importance of reserving domain names as early as possible.

A 1999 federal law known as the Anticybersquatting Consumer Protection Act makes cybersquatting illegal and provides remedies for those who suffer harm from it, including getting the domain name back and possibly receiving money damages. To win a cybersquatting lawsuit, you'll have to sue the cybersquatter in federal court and prove that:

- the cybersquatter acted in bad faith by registering the name solely to make a profit by selling it back to you
- your mark was distinctive at the time the domain name was registered
- the domain name is identical or confusingly similar to your trademark, and
- you were the first to use the trademark in commerce.

An alternative to a lawsuit is to use a procedure set forth by ICANN (short for International Corporation for Assigned Names and Numbers), the international group now in charge of Internet domain name policy. ICANN's process for resolving cybersquatting disputes is known as the Uniform Domain Name Dispute Resolution Policy (UDRP), and typically will cost far less and take less time than a lawsuit. You'll have to prove that:

- the domain name is identical or confusingly similar to your trademark

- the registrant has no legitimate interests in or rights to the domain name, and
- the domain name was registered or is being used in bad faith, or both.

Another advantage of the ICANN procedure is that it can be used in international domain name disputes, while a lawsuit based on the Anticybersquatting Act can only be brought against domain name registrants in the United States. For more information, visit ICANN's website at www.icann.org.

Name Searches

By now you get the picture that a dispute over business names can be thorny. To avoid potential trademark hassles later on, you need to do some early digging before you finally settle on a name for your business. The main way to accomplish this is to conduct a name search to find out whether another business is already using a name that's identical or similar to the one you want to use. The information in this section will help you figure out how to go about researching your chosen name, and what to do once you've found one that you'll be able to use— and protect—as a trademark.

 TIP

Searching domain name availability. It's easier to find out whether a name is available as a domain name than to figure out whether it's being used as a trademark. To find out if a domain name is available, simply go to one of the many domain name registrars online (a good list is available at www.internic.com). Once you enter the name you want, the registrars tell you whether it's available and, if not, who has registered it.

The scope of your search will depend largely on the size and geographical scope of your business and your plans for its future. If you plan from day one to sell a product nationally—whether via catalog, through retailers, or online—you'll obviously need to worry about trademarks across the country. If, on the other hand, you're starting a small home-based service business, don't plan to advertise, and are relatively certain you won't expand geographically, a search of names in your county, and perhaps state, may be all you need—though it is always wise to search widely so that you at least know what's out there.

Keep in mind that the extent of your search encompasses not only how widely you search geographically, but also how deeply you search—in terms of looking not only for identical names, but also for those that are merely similar or have a slight resemblance to yours. Searching for the exact name (also called a "direct hit" search) is quick and cheap, but risks missing look- and sound-alikes. A more in-depth search, such as one that looks for names with slight variations in spelling, is safer, but can get quite complicated and expensive.

Sources of Name Information

Name research can be difficult because there is no one place to look. In large part, this is because a business can—and millions do—establish a trade-mark simply by using it. Since millions of marks aren't registered with the government, in addition to checking federal and state trademark databases you'll want to check many other sources of information, such as business directories and phone books, for unregistered trademarks. You should check some or preferably all of the following resources for name conflicts, depending on how extensive a search you need.

The World Wide Web

It is probably best to start with the Internet because this resource is huge, fast, and free. Just use a search engine such as Google to quickly see whether someone else on the Web is using a specific term and how it is being used.

Another easy way to check trademarks online is to go to a domain name register online and put in variations of the name you want to use. (Go to www.internic.com for a list of registrars.) If another company has reserved a domain name that contains your proposed trademark, chances are you won't be able to use it as a trademark. If the domain name qualifies as a trademark—which essentially means it is being used to sell a product or service online—then, as described earlier in this chapter, you won't be able to use it as a trademark if your use would be likely to confuse customers.

Phone Directories

Don't overlook the phone book as a valuable source of local name information. If you find someone who's using the name you want in your local area and your businesses are similar, there's no reason to waste money searching the federal trademark register or other government databases. However, if your businesses are different enough, you might be able to use the name.

Industry Sources

Trade publications and business directories can be great sources of business name information (and they can also give you good ideas for names). You can also call trade associations and chambers of commerce to ask if they can provide lists or directories of businesses in the area.

Federal Trademark Database

All those starting a business, no matter how tiny and local, should search the federal trademark database to determine whether the name they want to use has already been registered by a similar business in the United States. The most important reason to do this is to avoid being sued for "willful infringement." If you use a trademark already registered at the federal level (even if yours is a tiny, local business), you can be sued for knowingly violating someone else's trademark—even if you didn't actually check the federal database and had no idea it was there. Searching the federal database can be complicated, and there are a few different ways to go about it—including hiring a trademark search firm to do the work for you. (See "Searching the Federal Trademark Database," below.)

California Secretary of State Databases

The California Secretary of State maintains databases of registered names of corporations, limited partnerships, and LLCs. Be aware, however, that these databases do not overlap, even though they're all maintained by the Secretary of State. In other words, you need to check each database separately.

To find out whether a name appears in the corpo-rate, LLC, or limited partnership database, you can contact the Secretary of State by mail, by phone, or in person. Inquiring by phone costs a small fee—$4 in 2009—and requires a prepaid account. Visit the Secretary of State's website at www.sos .ca.gov for the current phone number and additional information about checking name availability.

California's Trademark Unit

The California Secretary of State also maintains a state trademark registry at its Trademark Unit. This database is a good one to check—and you can search by phone for free. You're allowed to have two names checked per phone call. To contact California's Trademark Unit, check the Secretary of State's website for the current phone number.

You may also want to check some or all other states' trademark registries. You can check them by calling the states yourself and finding out their individual rules for searching the state trademark register, or you can hire a trademark search firm to do the work for you.

County Fictitious Business Name Databases

Each county maintains a database of fictitious business names (FBNs) that have been registered in that county. If you register a fictitious business name statement with your county (discussed in Chapter 6), you'll be asked to check the county's FBN database to see if any other business in the county has already registered that name. But even if you won't be using an FBN—because you'll use your own name or your corporate, limited partnership, or LLC name—it's a good idea to check the FBNs used by other businesses. In all counties these databases can be searched in person for free, or you can submit a name by mail and have it checked by a staff person at the county clerk's office for a small fee (from $5 to $30 or so, depending on the county). You can check any and all county databases for a name, even if you don't plan to register an FBN statement there. (A list of websites for California county clerks appears in Appendix A.)

CAUTION

State and county agencies usually check only exact matches. These agencies won't tell you whether a similar name is included in that database. If, for example, the county clerk's office tells you that "The Dog House" does not appear in its fictitious name database, you might be surprised later to find that "The Dawg Haus" has been in business for years. In short, you may have to do a more extensive search than the one provided by the state or county office.

CAUTION

County and state databases have limits. Just because a name doesn't appear in any county or state name databases, that doesn't mean another business doesn't already own that trademark. Use of the name, not registration, is what creates trademark ownership. Plenty of businesses own trademarks that they have never registered, so it's important to check for unregistered trademarks using the resources discussed above. And many businesses won't bother registering at the state level, but will register a federal trademark. If you plan to invest time and money in establishing your trademark, it's essential that you do a federal trademark search, too.

> **EXAMPLE:** Tom and Jen, both veterinarians in California, search their county's fictitious business name database for the name "Critter Care," which they want to use for the animal hospital they're planning to open. They don't find anyone else using the name in their area, so they believe they can use it. But just to be safe, Jen decides to check the California state trademark directory for the name. She finds out that a California corporation has already obtained state trademark protection for the name "Critter Care." Because that corporation was doing business under its own name and not a fictitious one, it didn't have to register with any county fictitious name databases. (Tom and Jen also would have found the name by checking the Secretary of State's corporate name database.)

Searching the Federal Trademark Database

As discussed above, to avoid a charge of willful infringement, it's a very good idea to check the federal trademark registry, maintained by the U.S. Patent and Trademark Office (PTO). Only the tiniest of microbusinesses should even consider skipping this step, and then only after careful thought and consideration. The Internet and other communication technologies have simply created too many potential trademark conflicts, even for small businesses.

If possible, begin your search with the free trademark database on the PTO's website. The PTO's database consists of all federally registered marks and all marks for which registration is pending. To start, go to the PTO's Trademark Electronic Business Center at www.uspto.gov/ebc/index_tm.html and choose "Search." Then follow the instructions you see on the screen.

If using the Internet isn't feasible for you, visit your local Patent and Trademark Depository Library (PTDL) and use its research materials. (The PTO maintains a list of PDTLs nationwide; you'll find the list at the PTO website at www.uspto.gov.) If a PTDL isn't convenient, a large public library or special business and government library near you should carry the federal trademark register, which contains all federal trademarks and service marks arranged by categories of goods and services.

Another option is to hire a professional search firm to do the work for you. You can order a complete search of registered and unregistered marks through Trademark Express, Thompson and Thompson, CCH Trademark Research Corporation, or one of the PTDLs that offer electronic search services for very reasonable fees.

If you decide to hire a search firm, the cheapest and easiest type of national search is a direct-hit search, which will reveal whether another business has registered an identical name with the PTO. You can often hire one of the companies mentioned above to do a direct-hit search for you for less than $50. But while direct-hit searches are quick and cheap, they usually won't turn up trademarks that are similar, but not identical, to the name you're considering. For example, if you want to name your softball training center "The Strike Zone," a direct-hit search may not turn up a trademark for "The S. Zone." And as discussed above, any mark that looks like, sounds like, or means the same as your name could present a trademark conflict.

More extensive national searches take a lot more time and money, but may be necessary if you plan for your business to reach a wide audience and want to eliminate any risk of infringing someone else's existing trademark. For an in-depth search, it may make the most sense to hire a search firm; expect a fee of roughly $200 to $350 for a professional, comprehensive search. If you do decide to hire search services, you're likely to save money if you do some quick, preliminary searches on the Internet yourself—to rule out some of your choices.

 RESOURCE

For more information on national trademark searches. See *Trademark: Legal Care for Your Business & Product Name,* by Stephen Elias and Richard Stim (Nolo).

Analyzing Your Search Results

If, after your search, you determine that the name you've chosen does not already belong to someone else (or that someone else isn't using a similar name), you can go ahead and use it. Assuming you really are the first user of the name, you'll own the trademark, which will give you the right to stop others from using it in certain situations. But since registering a trademark conveys important additional rights and protections, you may want to register your name with the PTO, and maybe with the State of California as well. (See "Trademark Registration," below, to learn more.)

But what if your search (or a search done by a professional firm) turns up an identical or similar name to the one you want to use? If the name is a famous trademark, it's probably time to pick a new name. Remember that if using your business name diminishes a famous trademark's distinctiveness or disparages its reputation for quality, the owner of the famous trademark may stop you from using your name, even if its customers aren't likely to be confused between its products and yours.

TIP

Be sure to check domain names. If your Internet business will be important to you, pick a name that can also be used as a domain name. You can check whether a domain name is available at any domain name registrar—you can find a list of registrars at www.internic.com.

Even if the name isn't famous, if it has been registered for official trademark protection, especially at the federal level, consider that as a huge "No Trespassing" sign that should be taken seriously. Owners of federally registered trademarks have the right to use their trademarks anywhere in the country, and it is easy for them to sue and recover damages. If your search shows that the name is being used, but isn't registered at the federal or state levels, then you might have a bit more leeway—but not much more. Because use, not registration, conveys trademark rights, you still need to be very careful not to infringe that owner's rights.

That said, there are a few instances when taking a name that is already being used by someone else is okay. If the name is being used for a company that provides a very different product or service than the one you plan to sell, then you may have good reason to move forward with your plans to use the name. This is especially true if the two businesses serve only local markets and are hundreds of miles apart.

For example, just because a tiny clothing store in Newport Beach calls itself Nature's Calling doesn't mean that you, in Humboldt County, can't use Nature's Calling for your plumbing business. But if you wanted to start a clothing store in your town called Nature's Calling, and one already exists in Newport Beach, then you should at the very least do more research before using it. If a federal trademark register search indicates that the Newport Beach store has registered the mark "Nature's Calling," your subsequent use is a clear legal no-no. But even if the name is not registered and the Newport Beach store seems like a local outfit, it could have plans to expand its territory—or, as is even more likely, to create a website. Neither of these actions would necessarily prohibit your use of the name on your original store, but they could prevent you from using it more widely. The bottom line is that even if you feel certain that your business is different enough

from that of the trademark owner to allow you to use the name, you should proceed only with lots and lots of caution.

TIP

How would you feel? If you are uncertain as to whether your proposed trademark would infringe an existing trademark, use a variant of the Golden Rule: How would you feel if you owned the existing trademark and someone started to use it? Ask a few friends the same question. If any of the answers is "pissed off," consider choosing a different name or at least invest a few hundred dollars in a consultation with an experienced trademark lawyer.

RESOURCE

Other resources on name and trademark issues. For more help understanding the nuances of different types of trademarks, picking a bulletproof name, and searching and registering trademarks, by far the best source of sophisticated information is *Trademark: Legal Care for Your Business & Product Name*, by Stephen Elias and Richard Stim (Nolo). And you'll find lots of free information on trademarks and business names in the Patents, Copyright & Trademark area of Nolo's website at www.nolo.com.

Choosing a Domain Name

Assuming that your business will create a website—usually recommended—you'll need to choose a domain name and register it. (See Chapter 13 for more on doing business online.)

A great domain name should be memorable, clever, and easily spelled. But names that are straightforward and descriptive won't qualify for much trademark protection. Many good domain names—for instance, coffee.com, drugs.com, and business.com—are not eligible for trademark protection because they are the names of whole categories of products or services. Besides, virtually every such generic domain name is undoubtedly already registered by someone else. Likewise, domain names that use surnames or geographic names are unlikely to get trademark protection.

(Of course, it's possible for a generic name, such as etrade.com, to become famous and develop "secondary meaning."

TIP

You may want to register several domain names. In addition to your business name, you may want to register the names of your products or services, or other related names. For example, if you design and sell gourmet aprons and your primary domain name is kitchenstuff.com, you might also want to register aprons.com so that customers who are looking for aprons and enter "aprons.com" into their browsers will land at your site. Remember, names of your products or services may be as important as your business name from a marketing perspective. It's also a good idea to register common misspellings of your primary domain name and of the names that reflect the nature of your products or services. It will, of course, cost more for multiple registrations, but the increased traffic may be worth it.

One potential problem in picking a domain name is that millions of names are already taken. For example, if your business name is Flaky Cakes, you may find that FlakyCakes.com already belongs to someone else, so you'll have to use a different domain name or change your business name if it's important to you that your business and domain names are the same.

If you do find a domain name that's available, make sure the one you pick doesn't conflict with someone else's trademark. Even if you come up with a domain name that is brilliant from a marketing standpoint, be aware that your domain name is at risk if it legally conflicts with any of the millions of commercial trademarks that already exist. Remember, your domain name will probably function as a trademark just as your regular business name will—assuming you conduct business at your site. (This is true whether or not you register it with the U.S. Patent and Trademark Office. Registering your domain name with the PTO will strengthen your enforcement rights, but using it for a commercial purpose is all that's technically necessary to establish your rights to it.) It follows that you are not allowed to use a domain name that's likely to cause

customer confusion between your company and another, whether that company is online or off. (See Chapter 13 for detailed information on registering domain names.)

TIP

Apply for federal trademark registration. In addition to applying for protection for your business name, you should also try to register your domain name with the PTO. While you don't need to register to establish your rights to your domain name, registering it will strengthen your power to enforce your rights to it against infringers. It will also prevent someone else from registering the same name—which could save a lot of headaches in the future.

RESOURCE

For more information on domain names. Check out Nolo's website at www.nolo.com under the Business tab for more on choosing a domain name for your business. Also see *Trademark: Legal Care for Your Business & Product Name*, by Stephen Elias and Richard Stim (Nolo) and Nolo's Online Trademark Application.

Trademark Registration

By now, you should understand that registering your trademark will strengthen your rights to it and make it easier to protect the name in case of a dispute. Registration is simply the process of notifying the state or, more commonly, the U.S. government that you're using a particular trademark. When registration is complete, the trademark gets placed on an official list of registered names, commonly called a trademark register.

The U.S. Patent and Trademark Office (PTO) maintains two registers, the Principal Register and the Supplemental Register. When people refer to a federally registered trademark, they're generally talking about marks on the Principal Register. Trademarks that appear on the Principal Register get the most protection, and the penalties can be harsh for those who improperly use a name that appears on it. The Supplemental Register, on the other hand, is reserved for weaker, less distinctive trademarks that don't qualify for the Principal Register. The main function of the Supplemental Register is to provide notice of a mark's current use to anyone who does a trademark search. After five years on the Supplemental Register, a mark may qualify to be moved to the Principal Register if it's been in continuous use during that period.

The PTO provides registration forms and instructions. These are available from a number of sources, including the PTO's website at www.uspto.gov. For simple trademarks such as business names (as opposed to trademarks for special packaging or product design—called "trade dress" in the biz), the instructions will probably be easy enough to follow. (You can also fill in and submit the form online at the PTO's Trademark eBusiness Center.)

California (and most other states) maintain just one register for all trademarks. State registration doesn't give as many benefits as federal registration, so it generally makes most sense to register federally for the widest scope of protection. Some trademarks, however, don't qualify for federal registration because they aren't used in national, international, or territorial commerce—in other words, they're only used within the state. These marks can only be registered at the state level. Although use of a trademark on the Internet almost guarantees the right to apply for federal registration, if you are only using the mark within California, state registration may be the only option.

The process of registering a trademark with the state of California is similar to the federal system's procedure. State trademark registration forms are available from the Trademark Unit of California's Secretary of State, or you can download them from the SOS's website at www.sos.ca.gov.

Winning Names for Your Business, Products, and Services

Now that you have a general idea of the legal hurdles you need to clear and the snags and traps to watch out for, let the naming begin! Despite the trademark hassles involved, choosing names for your business and its products or services remains one of the more fun parts of starting your business. It gives you a chance to use your creative juices to come up with a name that is both marketable and infused with your individual personality (or the collective personalities of all the business partners). A business name can help you establish the overall vibe of your business, from strictly professional to downright funky, to a dozen things in between.

Besides legal restrictions and personal preferences, the traditions and realities of your particular industry or business will probably have a lot to do with what kind of business name you choose. Good, memorable business and product names range from the clever (SuperFantastic Bubble Plastic, Garden Weasel, Liquid Paper) to the straightforward (24-Hour Fitness, Fruit Roll-Ups, Jenny Craig Weight Loss Centers) to sometimes even the cryptic (Yahoo!, Chia Pet, Floam). In part because there really are so many different kinds of businesses and so many approaches to choosing a distinctive name, it's impossible to give any kind of specific advice on choosing a great name. There are, however, a few things that are helpful to keep in mind when choosing your business names.

- **Especially for small local businesses that don't plan to expand geographically, straightforward, informative names often work better than evocative ones.** For example, if you plan to open a shop selling aquarium supplies and tropical fish in Oakland, East Bay Aquariums & Fish may be a far more effective name than The Lure of the Ocean. Also, choosing an ordinary name—especially one with a geographic identifier—will make you less likely to infringe on someone else's trademark since humble, descriptive names qualify for less trademark protection (unless they are already famous). Of course, you have to make sure no one else is already using your proposed ordinary name in your immediate area.
- **Think about how your customers will locate your business and your products.** If you don't expect customers to seek out or remember your company as a whole, but only its products, it's silly to focus much attention on the business name (which you may never use as a trademark). For instance, while millions of people know the product The Clapper and

its commercial jingle ("Clap on! Clap off! The Clapper!"), few know or care who its makers are.

- **Before you finally commit to a name, get some feedback from potential customers, suppliers, and others in your support network.** They may come up with a downside to a potential name or suggest an improvement you haven't considered. Doing this type of homework is especially important if you will market your goods or services to customers who are members of several different ethnic groups. You obviously don't want to choose a name or symbol and learn later that it offends or turns off a key group of customers. For example, one organization we know couldn't figure out why it got such a cold shoulder from Mexican-Americans. The answer turned out to be that the shape, size, and type used on its signs were similar to a "No Trespassers—Keep Out" sign widely used in Mexico. And virtually everyone with email has by now seen a widely circulated humor piece on a number of advertising translation blunders—such as Kentucky Fried Chicken's "finger lickin' good" slogan translated in China as "Eat your fingers off."

- **Niche businesses are often identified by their trade names, even when the focus is on the products.** This means that it is wise to pay particular attention to picking a memorable name if you will try to capture a particular, small field. The publisher of this book, Nolo, is a good example. Even though book buyers in other fields usually identify books they want by title or author, Nolo customers have come to recognize its name, often going into a bookstore and asking where the Nolo books are. In other words, Nolo has come to mean "self-help law" to many customers familiar with it, in contrast to the name HarperCollins—a large publisher of books on many topics—which might not evoke anything particular in most book customers' minds.

- **In certain service businesses in which an owner's personal attention and savvy is important (for example, architecture or accounting), it is common to use the owner's name, as in Charles Schwab.** In other service and retail businesses, it is more common to use creative names—Kinko's and Fuddrucker's come to mind—and not only for the business itself, but sometimes for its products, too.

EXAMPLE: Jerri and Orlando operate a car wash named Storm, which develops a good deal of name recognition in the city. Besides relying on the reputation of their trade name, they come up with clever names for various service packages (such as Sunday Shower, Typhoon Tuesday, and the Everyday Squall Special) in hopes that those names will catch on as well.

- **Be sure your trade or business name will still be appropriate if and when your business grows.** If you open Berkeley Aquariums & Fish, will it be a problem (or an advantage) if you want to open a second store in San Rafael? Especially if you plan to sell products on the Internet, you should think twice about giving your business a geographical identifier. Similarly, if you start a business selling and installing canvas awnings using the name Sturdy Canvas Awnings, your name might be a burden if you decide to also start making other products such as canvas signs. On the other hand, the name Sturdy Canvas would let you move into all sorts of canvas products, such as duffel bags, canvas signs, and drop cloths.

TIP

Think nationally even if you act locally. As discussed throughout this chapter, even though you may plan to open just one local office or store, it's a good idea to be sure your name is safe from trademark conflicts on a statewide or even national basis (and, if appropriate, from domain name conflicts). Then, if your business takes off, you won't bump into someone else who already uses the name in another area or online.

Chapter 2 Checklist:
Picking a Winning Business Name

☐ Become familiar with the basics of trademark law, including what types of trademarks qualify for maximum legal protection.

☐ Draft lists of business, product, and domain names that could work.

☐ If you plan to do business online, check to see whether your proposed business names are available as domain names. (Ideally, your domain names will be the same as your business or product names.)

☐ If the online aspect of your business will be important to you, narrow your list of names to those that are available as domain names.

☐ Do a trademark search of the names on your list.

☐ If any names are already being used as trademarks, eliminate the ones that are either already famous trademarks or would lead to customer confusion if you also used the name.

☐ Choose between the names that are still on your list.

☐ Register your business and product names as domain names whenever possible.

☐ Register your business and product names as trademarks.

Choosing a Business Location

For many types of businesses, location can mean the difference between feast or famine. Other enterprises will do more or less the same whether they're located in downtown Manhattan or in a deep crevasse on Mars. Not only does the importance of location vary greatly from business to business, but what makes a location desirable for one business might not work for another. Since there's no universal definition of what makes a location good for business, it's important for every business owner to figure out how location will (or will not) contribute to the success of the business—and to choose a spot accordingly.

That said, there are some basic issues to consider when choosing a business location. For starters, make sure the location makes economic sense. You won't want to spend a fortune for a spot on an exclusive commercial strip unless it's really going to pay off. It's obviously important that the rent for your business space fits into your overall budget. But don't be too frugal in this area—even the best-run business will fail if its customers can't find it or don't want to go to an unsafe neighborhood. And, of course, the location that you choose needs to be legally acceptable for whatever you plan to do there. Especially if you are planning to work from home or in a nonbusiness area, you'll need to check zoning laws to see if they prohibit your type of business. This chapter will help you figure out how to find a suitable place that meets all the needs of your business and complies with your local laws.

SKIP AHEAD

Planning to work from home? If you've already decided that you want to run your business from home, you can skip most—but not all—of this chapter. Read "Complying With Zoning Laws," below, for a good introduction to zoning rules. And see "Zoning Rules for Home Businesses," below, for more detailed information. After you read this material, turn to Chapter 9 for a more in-depth treatment. That chapter is devoted to the special issues facing home business owners—including zoning, the home business tax deduction, and risk management.

Picking the Right Spot

Your first task is to figure out how important location is to your business. For some businesses, the classic "location, location, location" advice definitely applies. But for others, location may be a lot less important than getting affordable rental space. And for plenty of businesses, location is practically irrelevant: wholesalers, service businesses that do all their work at the customer's location (like roofers or plumbers), mail order companies, and Internet-based businesses, for example. Especially if you can pass on your rent savings to your customers, picking a spot in an out-of-the-way area might be to your advantage. In other words, if location isn't that crucial to your business, don't blow all your start-up money on an expensive space in a thriving location.

If, on the other hand, you determine that location will be important to your business success, you'll need to figure out the best place to locate so that lots of customers can find you. It's one thing to know that you need a good location, but it can be harder to figure out what makes a location good. Ask yourself these questions:

- Will customers come on foot?
- Will customers drive, and, if so, where will they park?
- Will more customers come if you locate near other similar businesses?
- Will the reputation of the neighborhood or even of a particular building help draw customers?

As you ponder these and similar questions, here are a few things you'll want to consider.

Planting Yourself in Rich Soil

The key to picking a profitable location is to figure out what factors will increase customer volume for your unique business and then to concentrate on finding a location that achieves as many of them as possible. For example, if you're opening a coffee shop, you may assume your customer volume will be highest if there's lots of pedestrian traffic nearby during the hours you plan to be open. Furthermore, if you envision your cafe to be a mellow place to sit and read, you'd probably prefer a university area or shopping district full of people with time to kill, rather than an area buzzing with busy business-people. If, on the other hand, you plan to open a small coffee shop with no tables—just fast, high-volume service—a busy downtown office district might be the right spot.

> **Audrey Wackerley, owner of RetroFit, a vintage clothing store in San Francisco, California**
> *When we first opened we got a space in the perfect neighborhood, with lots of thrift stores, coffee shops, and other walk-in–type businesses on a strip with lots of foot traffic (plus, it was only a few blocks from my apartment). But we were on a cross street a few doors around the corner from Valencia Street, the main strip. We did okay, but nothing like the shops on Valencia itself. Finally we got a good deal on a storefront on Valencia Street, and we moved. Our business practically tripled! We do pay a bit more for the better space, but our boost in sales more than makes up for it.*

Keep in mind that different types of businesses attract customers in different ways. One key distinction is foot traffic versus automobile traffic. An auto repair shop, for example, will obviously draw customers in radically different ways from the coffee shop. For the auto shop, the choicest locale is a well-traveled street, where it will be seen by many drivers who will be able to pull into the lot easily. For an urban coffee shop, on the other hand, a popular location might be in an area where there are lots of people passing on foot. But of course no rule is absolute—for example, some coffee shops thrive on busy thoroughfares because commuters stop for "to go" coffee and baked goods every morning.

Also think about whether it would benefit your business to be around similar businesses that are already drawing the type of customers that you want. A women's clothing store, for example, would no doubt profit from being near other clothing shops, because many women shopping for clothes tend to spend at least a few hours in a particular area. The point is, the perfect location for any business is a very individual matter. Spend some time figuring out the habits of the customers you want to attract, then choose a location that fits.

Keeping Rent Within Your Budget

One obvious and important factor in finding a business space is how much you can afford. Chances are that you have found or will find a fabulous spot that you can only dream about because the monthly rent is so high. While it's okay to dream, don't be foolish enough to overpay for a space that you can't afford. As part of your business planning (discussed in detail in Chapter 4), determine how much rent you can afford each month, and stick to it.

One good way to find out how much rent is reasonable for an area is to call a commercial broker or agent in your area and have a chat about how much space generally goes for in the areas you're considering. Brokers and agents generally give you an average figure for what commercial space costs per square foot per year in a given area; once you have this figure, you can compare it to the costs of any potential spaces you're considering. But keep in mind that agents and brokers are self-interested professionals who may benefit from higher rents. In other words, don't necessarily accept the figures they give you at face value.

Square footage rates are generally given in cost per year, so once you multiply the rate by the square footage of a space, you'll need to divide it by 12 to determine the monthly rent.

> **EXAMPLE:** Jennifer and Oliver are planning to open a theater in a certain neighborhood of their city. They call a few real estate brokers out of the phone book whose ads indicate they handle commercial space leasing. All the brokers say that commercial space in the area they like generally goes for $10 per square foot. (Jennifer and Oliver know that this is an annual figure, which works out to about $0.83 per square foot per month.) A few weeks later, Jennifer and Oliver notice a building for rent, and call the agent for more information. The agent tells them that the monthly rent is $1,800 and that the space is 2,400 square feet. Jennifer

and Oliver do the math and see that this rent is slightly less than the going rate for the area:

Monthly rent	$ 1,800 per month
x 12 months	= $21,600 per year
÷ 2,400 square feet	= $ 9 per year/sq. ft.

For comparison's sake, they do the math to determine what the rent would be if the space rented out for the going rate, $10 per square foot:

Cost per sq. ft./month	$ 10
x Square footage	= $24,000 per year
÷ 12 months	= $ 2,000 per month

They're not quite ready to enter a lease, but the fact that this space is somewhat of a bargain puts it near the top of their list.

Though being realistic about your rent is important, don't sabotage your business by picking a cheap but bad location. This may seem obvious, but sometimes new business owners become blind to common wisdom when presented with an opportunity to rent a super-cheap space. Even if they've already determined that location will play a key role in their success, they either believe that the savings in rent will make up for slow sales or convince themselves that they'll be the pioneers in a new area that is sure to swell into a hot business district by the middle of next week. While this does occasionally happen (bless those brave pioneers), it's generally a poor idea to move into a dead section of town, since it almost certainly won't bloom fast enough to support your business in its financially vulnerable start-up days.

Unless you have a sound reason to believe that you'll get enough customers in your oddball location, don't let the lure of low rent tempt you into a bad business decision. At least in popular urban areas, rent can be the highest overhead expense for many new businesses.

Getting the Right Physical Features

When picking your space, your biggest consideration might not be where it is but what it is. Ask yourself whether the building facilities are appropriate or adaptable for your business. For example, if you're planning to open a coffeehouse, you might fall in love with a beautiful brick warehouse space in a funky shopping district. But if the place doesn't have at least minimal kitchen facilities, you should probably forget it. Unless you can convince your landlord to put in the needed equipment—plumbing, electrical work, and the rest (discussed below)—it's highly unlikely that laying out the cash to do it yourself will be worth it.

Sure, some improvements might be relatively cheap, such as putting up a wall or two or adding new light fixtures. But if the building lacks something major that is essential to your business operation, take it as a sign that the place isn't right for you—even if it has loads of other great qualities. You'll have to decide for yourself which features your business absolutely can't live with or without.

EXAMPLE: Charlotte and Sandra plan to open an alternative health store that will offer products such as medicinal herbs, aromatherapy products, and yoga supplies. They also plan to offer services such as aromatherapy sessions and consultations with nutritionists and herbalists. Charlotte and Sandra have high hopes for the service side of their business, so their physical space needs to be comfortable and appealing to customers. After looking at a number of storefront spaces in their chosen neighborhood, they find one that seems just perfect—until they notice the lack of windows. Except for the glass front door, the place has almost no natural light. Even though not having windows doesn't absolutely prevent them from doing business, Charlotte and Sandra decide that, given their expected customer base and their own feelings, they need a brighter space.

Another consideration that's important for many businesses these days is having modern phone lines and broadband Internet access, either via cable, DSL, or a T1 line. Anyone who spends much time on the Web knows that a low-bandwidth connection can seriously impact your productivity (and drive you crazy to boot). Outdated phone lines can also slow down your faxes and may even result in dropped telephone connections—not exactly a good thing for business. When you're considering a specific space, ask the agent or the landlord for information on the phone and data lines into the space, such as whether it's connected to a fiber optic network or has broadband Internet access. Also, find out if the landlord has sold the rights to the risers (wire conduits) in the building to a single telecommunications provider, such as Verizon or AT&T; if so, you could be stuck with that provider.

In addition to dealing with concerns about high-tech communications wiring, don't overlook plain old electrical power as an important consideration in choosing a business space. Make sure that any space you're looking at has enough power for your needs, both in terms of the number of outlets and the capacity of the circuits. If you'll mostly be running computer equipment, a copier, a coffee machine, and the like, chances are that any reasonably equipped commercial space will have enough power for you. But if you'll be running machinery or other electricity-hungry equipment, make sure to find out from the landlord how much juice the circuits can handle and whether a generator is available during power outages. Also, if you'll keep sensitive computer equipment at your office, ask the landlord how many hours of air conditioning are included in the terms of your lease, and negotiate longer hours if necessary.

Another common need for many businesses is adequate parking. If a significant percentage of your customers will come by car and there isn't enough parking at your chosen spot, it's probably best to look elsewhere. In fact, the city might not allow you to operate there if parking isn't adequate.

 TIP

Check local planning or health department requirements. If, for example, you're starting a small food manufacturing business to produce energy bars, you may need to rent a space with a certain number of vents, a fire-resistant roof, and walls of proper material and adequate thickness. You may also need a safe place to park refrigerated delivery trucks. And your business may be subject to special waste disposal requirements, so you may need extra space for waste storage or equipment. Contact your city or county departments of planning, health, or fire, or another appropriate agency to find out. You should also check out state and federal laws that apply to your business. (See Chapter 6 for a discussion of licenses and permits.)

Complying With Zoning Laws

A certain spot may be good for your business, but if it's not properly zoned for what you plan to do, forget it. Local zoning laws (often called "ordinances" or "land use regulations") prohibit certain activities from being conducted in particular areas. To use an obvious example, a nightclub wouldn't be allowed to operate in a district zoned for residential use. Sure, only a fool would try to open a disco on a quiet residential street—but there are less obvious zoning restrictions that you must observe.

Zoning ordinances typically allow certain categories of businesses to occupy different districts of a city or county. For example, mixed commercial and residential uses might be allowed in one district while another district allows heavy industry and warehouses. So if you open your small jewelry-making business in a space zoned for commercial use, you could be in for a real headache if zoning officials decide you're a light-industrial business that's not allowed to operate in a commercial district. Similarly, you may not be allowed to run a commercial business—particularly one that's open to the public—in an industrial zone.

In addition to regulating the types of businesses allowed in certain areas, zoning laws also regulate specific activities. Depending on your area, you might be subject to laws regulating parking, signs, water and air quality, waste management, noise, and the visual appearance of the business—especially in historic districts. In addition to these regulations, some cities restrict the number of a particular type of business in a certain area, such as allowing only three bookstores or one pet shop in a certain neighborhood. Finally, some zoning laws specifically regulate home businesses.

RELATED TOPIC

If you have a home business. Zoning rules for home businesses are explained in detail in Chapter 9, "Laws, Taxes, and Other Issues for Home Businesses." Refer to that chapter for a full discussion of several special issues facing home business owners—including zoning, the home business tax deduction, and risk management.

Expect Zoning Laws on Parking Spaces and Business Signs

Local zoning laws commonly require a business to provide parking, and they also may regulate the size and type of business signs. Be prepared for your city or county to look into both these issues. If there's already a parking problem in your proposed area, you may have to come up with a plan for how to deal with the increased traffic your business will attract.

Also, be ready for zoning officials to get really nitpicky about your business sign. Many local laws limit the size of business signs (no signs over five feet by three feet, for instance), their appearance (such as whether they're illuminated, flashing, colorful, or made of neon), and their placement (flat against the building, hanging over the sidewalk, or mounted on a pole). There are even some regulations attempting to limit the use of foreign language on signs. Be sure to find out what your local regulations are before spending money on having signs made.

TIP

Know your neighbors. More often than not, zoning laws are enforced for the sake of the other people and companies in the neighborhood (this is particularly true of home-based businesses). While some areas are strict about their zoning laws, most of the time you won't have a zoning official knocking unannounced on your door unless neighbors have complained or you're in flagrant violation of the laws. Enforcement is often triggered by complaints, so it's a good idea to get to know your neighbors and develop good relationships with them. And, if you plan to run your business from home, be sure to read Chapter 9, which covers special zoning issues for home businesses.

Never sign a lease for a business space without first knowing that you'll legally be able to do business there. However, it's okay to sign a contingent lease, with a clause stating that the lease won't be binding if you don't get zoning approval. Being forced to move your business is a headache enough, but not nearly as catastrophic as having to pay rent on a lease for a space that you can't use.

When determining whether you'll be able to do business at a potential location, never assume that you'll be allowed to do a certain activity simply because the previous tenants of the space did it. For all kinds of reasons, some businesses get away with zoning violations, even for long periods of time. But new occupants are sometimes scrutinized more carefully than already-existing businesses. It may not be fair, but a new business may be told it can't do what an old one had long been doing.

It's also possible that the previous tenants had an official okay to operate outside the zoning restrictions. For example, the previous occupants might have had a zoning variance (an exception to zoning laws) for their particular business—one that won't necessarily be extended to you. And lots of times when zoning laws change, businesses that are already in place are allowed to keep doing what they were doing, even if the activity violates the new zoning law (a system referred to as "grandfathering"). When a tenant with a grandfathered exception leaves and new occupants come in, however, the new business usually has to abide by the new, more restrictive zoning law.

Finding Out What Laws Apply

How do you find out whether a given location is properly zoned for your business and whether you need to get any approvals? The answer varies from area to area. In some cities and counties, zoning approval is part of the tax registration process (discussed in Chapter 6). In San Diego, for instance, when you apply for your business tax certificate, you must also pay a Zoning Use Clearance fee to have your business approved for the location listed on your application. And the city of Oakland won't accept your new business application without prior approval of your business location by the city's zoning division. Other cities don't require proof of zoning approval before issuing a tax registration certificate—but that doesn't mean you should take the zoning laws any less seriously. Whether or not you're required to deal with your local zoning department before starting your business, you'll still be subject to its monitoring and enforcement.

If your city doesn't include zoning approval as part of its start-up requirements for new businesses, you'll need to do some detective work. Generally, this involves talking with your local zoning officials. Most zoning agencies are part of city or county planning departments. Look under "Planning" or "Zoning" in the government section of your phone book. If your business will be located in a city, you probably only need to worry about city zoning ordinances. Businesses in rural areas should contact the county zoning or planning offices.

Getting zoning approval typically begins with filling out a form issued by the city planning department in which you provide information about your proposed location and what you plan to do there. In some cities, you may be required to submit detailed building plans to show exactly how you intend to use the space in question. Your application may be evaluated simply on the information you provide in the form, or the zoning department may send out an inspector to more closely examine the potential business space. Once the zoning department has all the information it requires to make a decision, it will either approve your application without limitations, approve it with certain conditions, or deny it altogether.

How Vigilant Are Zoning Officials?

There's a world of difference from area to area in how strict zoning officials are. Many zoning departments aren't terribly rigid about enforcement, mostly responding to complaints from neighbors or other citizens about businesses that create a nuisance or other trouble. In a few areas, however, zoning agents relish sniffing out minor infractions and enforcing zoning ordinances to the letter.

If you're considering going ahead with your business despite what you consider to be a minor zoning problem, do your best to find out how strict the zoning police are in your area. Start by asking other local businesspeople about their experiences. If they tell you that there's little enforcement other than responding to complaints, you can breathe a little easier about what might be a minor infraction, such as including tennis-racket stringing (which officials might consider a light-industrial activity) at your sports shop in an area zoned only for commercial use. Even so, it never pays to engage in a prohibited activity that is fundamental to your business. While tennis rackets could be strung elsewhere, a health club wouldn't want to have to locate its juice bar two blocks away.

But no matter how mellow your zoning department, at the very least you need to know what the rules are for your proposed location. Ignoring the rules while counting on lax enforcement is just plain dumb.

Dealing With Zoning Snags

If your zoning board has a problem with any of the activities you plan to conduct at your chosen location, you have a few options, usually ranging from making appropriate changes to your business to giving up on that location and finding a new one. Obviously, some zoning conflicts are simply not fixable—for example, you'll never be allowed to open a nightclub on a quiet cul-de-sac. But a creative (and, when necessary, assertive) business owner can often persuade zoning officials or the zoning appeals board to work out an acceptable accommodation that will allow the business to use the desired location.

For borderline situations, one approach is simply to advocate an interpretation of the zoning law that's favorable to you before you get an official "No." Communicate with zoning officials, and try to persuade them to give you their seal of approval.

If the zoning officials have already denied your application, it's often possible to appeal their decision, usually to a higher authority such as a board of appeals within the zoning agency or the city council. If you're successful, the zoning board may grant you a "variance," which is basically a one-time exception to the local zoning laws. Or the board may give you a "conditional use permit," which essentially gives you approval to operate your business as long as certain conditions are met, such as restricting the maximum occupancy to a certain number or providing additional parking spaces.

When lobbying for an exemption from a zoning requirement, be aware that you're asking for special treatment, so make your case as persuasive as possible. If your business will be valuable to the community, present evidence of that fact. Proof can include demographic data about the area, testimony from community leaders, or statements from other local businesspeople. Your goal is to show that the value of allowing your business in the area is greater than the trivial zoning conflicts that may exist. If you can compromise in some other area, offer to do so.

> **EXAMPLE:** Carolyn wants to open a small printing shop, Nelson's Press, on a commercial strip where storefront space is cheap and plentiful. Before signing a lease, she applies for zoning approval. The local zoning board rejects her application because Carolyn's proposed location is zoned commercial, but her print shop would technically be a light-industrial business. Carolyn decides to try to get an exception, because her printing operation will be small (only one small offset printing press) and would be an asset to the neighborhood, which has been struggling economically.
>
> She submits detailed plans of her business to the zoning board, showing the business's small scope and including specific protocols for dealing with toxics such as ink. She also submits letters from other business owners in the neighborhood documenting how commerce in the area has languished for years and arguing that new businesses would help revitalize the strip. Many of the business owners also note that a local printer would be convenient for the existing area businesses, which currently have to go across town for their print jobs. A few weeks later, Carolyn gets a conditional use permit allowing her to proceed with her printing business, as long as she doesn't expand her business with additional presses and follows a number of standard rules governing the chemicals she'll use in printing.

Zoning Rules for Home Businesses

Similar to business owners who operate from commercial office spaces, those who run home businesses need to make sure they don't violate their local zoning rules. As home businesses have exploded in popularity, more local governments have adopted specific provisions in zoning laws controlling them. Mercifully, most of the rules are straightforward and fair—with some exceptions. If you're unlucky and find that you're subject to prohibitive municipal ordinances or private land use restrictions, take a hard look at whether you should set up shop in your home after all. But more often, you'll find that you'll need to jump through a simple hoop or two and pay a modest fee to run your business from home.

Dwellings in residential or mixed-use zones are often allowed to run businesses that have little likelihood of causing noise or pollution, creating traffic, or otherwise disturbing the neighbors. A few examples include freelance writers, artists, attorneys, accountants, architects, insurance brokers, and piano teachers.

To find out local rules, contact your city's planning or zoning department and ask for information on its rules for home businesses. Often, home businesses are allowed with some restrictions—such as limiting employees to residents, curbing the number of customers allowed, and prohibiting business signs posted outside. Also ask the local zoning authority whether any special rules exist for the specific type of business or activities you plan to conduct.

As to whether or not you need a permit to run a home business, local rules vary. If a permit is required, getting one is usually a simple matter of filling out a form provided by the planning department and paying a fee. You may also need to deal with other departments in addition to the zoning office. For example, depending on your business activities, you may need to get approvals from your county health or fire department.

 RELATED TOPIC

For more on home office zoning. For more detail on permits for specific business activities, see Chapter 6 on start-up requirements. And see Chapter 9 for a full discussion of special issues facing home business owners—including zoning, the home business tax deduction, and risk management.

Commercial Leases

Chances are that you'll rent rather than buy a space for your business. After all, most small start-ups don't have the funds to purchase real estate, and it's usually not a good idea to saddle your business with high interest payments, anyway. But just because you've rented plenty of apartments or flats over the years, don't assume that you know the score when it comes to leasing business space.

Practically and legally speaking, there are significant differences between commercial leases and residential leases. Commercial leases are not subject to most consumer protection laws that govern residential leases—for example, there are no caps on deposits or rules protecting a tenant's privacy. Also, commercial leases are generally subject to much more negotiation between the business and the landlord, because businesses often need special features in their spaces, and landlords are often eager for tenants and willing to extend special offers. While a residential tenant will usually just take an apartment or flat more or less as is, a business owner will often need to modify the existing space—for example, by adding cubicles, raising a loading dock, or rewiring for telephones, Internet access, and computer networks.

Because company owners must negotiate modifications suitable for their own operations, commercial leases are relatively flexible creatures. Of course, your bargaining power will vary a great deal from situation to situation. For example, getting a landlord to accept your demands would probably be a lot easier for a long-term lease in a largely vacant office building than for a six-month lease in a hot commercial area. Likewise, local, independent landlords are often more willing to make concessions than huge property management companies or real estate investment trusts.

When negotiating a commercial lease, keep in mind that the success or failure of your business may ride on certain terms of the lease. The amount of the rent is an obvious concern, as is the length of the lease. (You probably don't want to tie yourself to a five- or ten-year lease if you can help it, in case your business grows faster than you expect or the location doesn't work out for you.) But other, less conspicuous items spelled out in the lease may be just as crucial to your business's success. For instance, if you expect your shoe repair business to depend largely on walk-in customers, be sure that your lease establishes your right to put up a sign that's visible from the street. Or, if you are counting on being the only sandwich shop inside a new commercial complex, make sure your lease prevents the landlord from leasing space to a competitor. If you are starting a new service company that you expect to grow quickly, make sure there's room for expansion.

The following checklist includes many items that are often addressed in commercial leases. Pay attention to terms regarding:

- rent, including allowable increases and method of computation

- whether the rent includes insurance, property taxes, and maintenance costs (called a gross lease), or whether you will be charged for these items separately (called a net lease)
- whether the rent includes heat, air conditioning, phone, garbage collection, water, and other utilities
- the security deposit and conditions for its return
- who is responsible for code compliance, security, and fire safety
- the length of the lease (also called the lease term) and when it begins
- whether there's an option to renew the lease or expand the space
- how the lease may be terminated, including notice requirements, and whether there are penalties for early termination
- exactly what space is being rented, including common areas such as hallways, rest rooms, and elevators, and how the space is measured (some measurement practices include the thickness of the walls)
- specifications for signs, including where they may be placed
- whether there will be improvements, modifications (called buildouts when new space is being finished to your specifications), or fixtures added to the space; who will pay for them; and who will own them after the lease ends (generally, the landlord)
- who will maintain the premises and provide janitorial services
- whether the lease may be assigned or subleased to another party, and
- whether disputes must be mediated or arbitrated as an alternative to court.

TIP

Beware the Americans with Disabilities Act. The Americans with Disabilities Act (ADA) requires all businesses that are open to the public or that employ more than 15 people to have premises that are accessible to people with disabilities. Make sure that you and your landlord are in agreement about who will pay for any needed modifications, such as adding a ramp or widening doorways to accommodate wheelchairs.

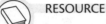 RESOURCE

For more on leasing office space. For detailed information on finding a space and negotiating a lease, see *Negotiate the Best Lease for Your Business,* by Janet Portman and Fred S. Steingold (Nolo).

Chapter 3 Checklist: Choosing a Business Location

☐ Determine how much rent you can afford.

☐ Decide what neighborhood would be best for your business.

☐ Find out what the average rents are in the neighborhoods you're considering.

☐ Identify the features and fixtures your business space will need.

☐ Make sure any spaces you're considering are, or can be, properly zoned for your business.

☐ Examine any commercial lease carefully before signing and negotiate the best deal you can.

☐ If working from home, make sure your business activities won't violate any zoning restrictions on home offices.

☐ Become familiar with the rules on home office deductions before claiming them on your tax return.

☐ Be sure your home office is adequately insured. (Insurance is further discussed in Chapter 7.)

Drafting an Effective Business Plan

I f you think only Type A personalities compose business plans, think again. Talk to a random sample of successful business owners—even the most laidback—and you'll be amazed at how many took the time to put their business plans into writing. If you're truly determined to succeed, you'll follow their example because without a plan, you're leaving far too many things to chance. Just as a blueprint is used to ensure that a building will be structurally sound, a business plan will help you make sure that your business will be able to stay afloat.

The purpose of a business plan is simple: to bring together in one document the key elements of your business. These include the products or services you'll sell, what they'll cost to produce, and how much sales revenue you expect during your first months and years of operation. Most important, your plan will help you see how all the disparate elements of your business relate to one another, which will allow you to make any necessary alterations to increase your business's potential to turn a profit.

Business plans are often written by business owners who want to borrow money or attract investment. This is good as far as it goes—lenders and investors do want to understand as much as possible about how a business will work before deciding whether to back it financially. Unless you're prepared to show them a well-thought-out plan for making your business profitable, you won't have much chance of convincing them to finance your project.

But creating a business plan is a good idea even if you don't need to raise start-up money. The planning process often brings up issues and potential problems that you hadn't thought of before. And the discipline involved in developing financial projections, such as a break-even analysis and a profit and loss forecast, will help you decide whether your business is really worth starting, or whether you need to rethink some of your key assumptions. As any experienced businessperson will tell you, the business you decide not to start (often because its business plan doesn't pencil out) can play a greater role in your long-term success than the one on which you bet your economic future.

This chapter explains how to create a thorough business plan and describes basic types of business

financing and lending sources. The approach to business planning here is simple and straightforward: It outlines a number of descriptive sections and a number of financial reports. When you have completed these sections, you will have the essential elements that will help guide you in running your business—and that will help attract funding if you need it.

SKIP AHEAD

For those who already have a plan. If you've already written a business plan, you may want to skip ahead to the financing discussion (see "Using Your Plan to Raise Start-Up Money")—although you might also want to review the sections on writing a business plan as a way of evaluating the work you've already done.

RESOURCE

For more help on the business of business plans. Nolo offers a couple of resources for those in need of setting up or revising business plans. *How to Write a Business Plan*, by Mike McKeever, is a comprehensive guide explaining how to write a business plan—including how to evaluate the profitability of your business idea; estimate operating expenses; determine assets, liabilities, and net worth; and find potential sources of financing. And *Business Plan Pro 2009* is software that offers a fast, easy way to generate the plan you need to launch or expand your business.

Different Purposes Require Different Plans

All good business plans have two basic goals: to describe the fundamentals of the business idea, and to provide financial calculations to show that it will make good money. But, depending on how you intend to use it, a business plan can take somewhat different forms.

- If you will use your plan to borrow money or interest investors, write it with an eye toward selling your vision to skeptical people. Generally, you should include a persuasive introduction and a request for funds, in-depth market research information, an evaluation of your main competitors, your key marketing strategies, and a management plan. In addition, your plan should contain detailed financial information—including your best estimates of start-up costs, revenues, and expenses. Finally, since your plan will be submitted to people who don't know you well, the writing should be polished and the format clean and professional. (See "Using Your Plan to Raise Start-Up Money," below, for a discussion of business financing basics.)

- If your plan will primarily be for your own use—that is, if you don't need to raise money—don't worry so much about making a sales pitch or slick presentation (although you'll probably want to do a quick market and competitive analysis). But don't skimp when it comes to doing your numbers. You'll need to include estimates of start-up costs, revenues, and expenses. The last thing you want is to experience the very real misery of realizing too late that your business never had a chance to make a solid profit.

TIP

Plan to get the help you need. Not all businesspeople are great writers. But excellent writing skills can be a big help in creating a compelling business plan. Consider paying a freelance writer with small business savvy to help you polish your plan. Similarly, if you are challenged by numbers, find a bookkeeper or accountant to provide some help with the math.

Describing Your Business and Yourself

The first several sections of your plan should describe the beauty of your business idea. If you will show your plan to potential lenders, investors, or colleagues, you'll want to show them right up front that you've hit upon a product or service that customers really want. In addition, you'll want to show that you are exactly the right person to make

this fine idea a roaring success. Your goal is to have them say, "Wow! What a great business idea! And yes, I see exactly why Carlos Burns is the ideal person to make it a big success."

To accomplish these goals, you should include the following in your plan:

- a statement of the purpose of your business
- a detailed description of how the business will work
- an analysis of your market
- an analysis of your competitors
- a description of your marketing strategy, and
- a résumé setting forth your business accomplishments to date.

Again, depending on how you intend to use your business plan, you may be able to skip some of these elements. For example, if you don't need to raise start-up money and are writing a plan mostly for your own use, you may decide to skip the résumé of your own business accomplishments. But think twice before you leave out too much. Any new business will need to be introduced to loads of people—suppliers, contractors, employees, and key customers, to name a few—and showing them part or all of your business plan can be a great way to do it.

State Your Business's Purpose

What will your product or service be? And why does the great big world—or your small town or narrow niche market—need the product or service you want to offer? The first paragraph of your plan should address this question as directly and compellingly as possible. For example, if you're planning to open a pet-grooming salon, you might start with the proposition that in today's increasingly busy world, pet owners need and want to keep their pets clean and groomed, but often don't have time to do it themselves. Similarly, if you want to start a sea kayaking guide service, you might start with the proposition that more and more people are participating in this exciting sport, but need equipment, planning, training, and logistical help to do it in other parts of the world.

A statement of business purpose doesn't need to be complicated or lengthy. In fact, some of the best simply state the obvious. If the need for your business will be clear to lenders or investors (for example, a sandwich shop in a fast-growing office area), one paragraph may be all you need. But if the value of your business idea isn't so readily apparent (for example, an innovative software company), you will want to say more. Show how your business will solve a real problem or fill an actual need. And explain why customers will pay you to accomplish the task.

Describe Your Business

Once you've stated the need that your business will fill, describe exactly how you'll go about filling it. Don't write a bunch of fluffy text about the brilliance of your entrepreneurial idea. Instead, outline in detail exactly how your business will operate. While the degree of detail may vary depending on what kind of business you're starting and who will be reading your business plan, your description should include specifics such as:

- how you will provide the product or service
- where you will buy key supplies
- how customers will pay you
- how many employees you will have and what they will do
- your hours of operation, and
- your business location (if possible, include details about how your customers will find you).

CAUTION

Be sure to include the costs of creating a website and doing business online. You can end up spending a bundle, especially if you're running a full e-commerce operation. When budgeting for online business activities, remember to include not only the costs to develop a website, but also the ongoing costs of maintaining and promoting it. Put careful thought into your online operations early on in your business planning efforts to make sure they don't become an unexpected drain on your business later on. See Chapter 13 for advice on developing an online presence, including selling and marketing online.

Keep in mind that even the smallest, simplest business involves a swarm of pesky details. While you're writing your business description, don't assume there's anything obvious about your business, even if it's a tiny one-person operation. For example, if you plan to start a pet-grooming business, how many different types of services will you offer: Shampooing? Flea bathing? Nail cutting? Hair trimming? Teeth cleaning? Will you charge separately for each individual service, sell them in packages, or both? How will you attract customers and regularly stay in touch with the best ones? How will you accommodate animals with special needs such as allergies or behavioral problems such as aggressiveness? How will people drop off and pick up their pets? Will your business need insurance in case an animal is injured or dies while in your care?

TIP

A little repetition is okay. The description of how your business will operate is likely to be the longest section of your plan and will probably discuss topics that are also covered elsewhere. No problem. For example, in your big-picture business description and in your marketing strategy section, you should discuss the key issue of how you will establish and keep a competitive edge. (See "Describe Your Marketing Strategy," below.)

Use the process of writing your business description as an opportunity to change or refine your business idea. When you write and rewrite this section, you'll probably come up with ideas and questions you haven't yet thought through. If so, great—this gives you an opportunity to fill in the gaps before you actually open for business. And even if you discover a flaw so big that you decide not to start the business after all, your business plan has done its job. While such a decision is undoubtedly disappointing, it's far better for your business to fail on paper than in real life.

Define Your Market

Who will buy your product or service? Even the most innovative business will fail if it doesn't quickly find enough customers to make a profit. In this section, your task is to demonstrate to a potential investor or lender (or convince yourself) that there are indeed customers out there, ready and willing to buy your product or service. Show that there is a demand for your product or service by referring to news reports, trade journal articles, or other reports. Use whatever data you can get your hands on. And don't neglect your imagination—unconventional arguments are fine as long as they are convincing. Here is a brief list of points you may wish to make:

- **Similar businesses have been successful.** For example, if several fitness clubs with business service centers (Wi-Fi access, computers, and fax machines) are all the rage in L.A., you might explain why this is a good indication that your similar business would succeed in Sacramento, where the market is currently dominated by less-cutting-edge gyms.
- **Marketing surveys or demographic reports point to a growing need for your product or service.** For instance, to buttress your contention that there will be a need for your new line of paralegal training materials, point to U.S. government reports listing paralegals as one of the fastest-growing occupations.
- **Media reports confirm the popularity of and demand for your business.** For example, include newspaper clips or transcripts of television news reports on the surge of demand for antibacterial air fresheners as evidence that your germ-killing Sani-Scent™ will sell.
- **Your conversations with potential customers show a need for your business.** It's often a good idea to carry out an informal survey of your most likely customers and include the results. For example, if you will run a business repairing and reconditioning acoustic guitars and similar stringed instruments, you might include results of a survey of guitarists and other musicians on what kind of repair services they need, as well as quotes from them saying that they'd use your services.

In addition to establishing that there is a solid demand for your business, do your best to define and describe exactly who your customer base will be. If you're opening a bar with live entertainment, for instance, you might identify your market as primarily childless, urban 21- to 35-year-olds, who tend to have more disposable income and leisure time than others. Similarly, if you're planning an antique restoration service, you might identify your target market as professionals and others in the 40 to 70 age range with household incomes of $100,000 or more. The better you can show that you know exactly who your target customer is, the more confident lenders and investors will be that you can actually find these people and sell to them.

TIP

Include a profile of your target customer. Explain why and how this fictional person would need your product or service. Do your best to flesh out a believable person. Creating a typical customer gives a face to an otherwise abstract market definition and gives your market analysis more impact. For more information on defining your target customer, see Chapter 12.

Analyze Your Competition

Just because you have a great business idea doesn't mean you'll be successful. Other businesses may have already cornered the market or be poised to do so. For example, lots of small business owners who ran successful movie-rental businesses were wiped out when chains such as Blockbuster rolled out thousands of megastores. It's often all too easy for a bigger, better-capitalized outfit to copy your best features and pull the rug out from under your business. Use this section to explain why your business really will have few direct competitors— or, if competitors will abound (as is far more likely), to show how your business will develop and keep an edge. Don't be shy about detailing competitors' strengths as well as weaknesses as part of showing why your business will better meet customers' needs.

In discussing the competition, it's important to put yourself in the shoes of a customer who is comparing your business to a competitor's. From the customer's perspective, what factors are most important in choosing which business to patronize? Some obvious considerations are quality of products or services, convenience (access), reliability, and price. Your competitors will probably excel in some of these areas and be weaker in others. The same will probably be true of your business. The trick is for you to find a spot, or niche, among the competition, and offer a combination of elements—such as price and convenience—that no one else offers.

CAUTION

Think twice before competing on price. No matter how efficient your business is and how little you charge, someone will always charge less. Given the purchasing power and other efficiencies of big business, few small operators can successfully compete on pricing alone. Far better to look for another edge—quality, uniqueness, or customer convenience, to mention a few.

Businesses With Specialized Knowledge Are Hard to Copy

The business owner who knows the most about how to beat out competitors usually wins. But what is business knowledge, and how can you exploit it? In the broad sense, it's anything a business knows how to do that can give it a meaningful edge over competitors. Common examples include:

- the ability to buy products for resale cheaper than competitors
- a great location
- a unique, hard-to-duplicate product
- excellent customer service, and
- superior customer accessibility—through longer hours or better parking, for example.

Consider the example of Laura and Brad's import business. They were importing clothing from Guatemala, but with competition from hundreds of other small importers, it was hard to make a dime. Leaving Brad to manage the business for a few weeks, Laura spent some time working with a dozen weavers in a small Guatemalan town. They focused on creating specially woven and dyed fabric suitable for luxury window coverings. Realizing that the high end of the import business was an underexploited niche, Laura quickly created a product with a hard-to-copy look and a solid profit margin. In short, she transformed a not particularly savvy, barely profitable import business into a highly intelligent, highly profitable one.

EXAMPLE: John wants to open a business to sell and service classic cars. In developing his business idea, he discovers that there are about a dozen existing companies within a 20-mile radius of his proposed location that already provide some or all of the services he envisions. Before finally committing to opening the business, he needs to identify and create a convincing competitive edge. One day, talking to a friend, he realizes that his edge could be a better system for finding parts. If he could locate new and used classic car parts nationwide rather than just in his region, he would have a huge advantage over other shops. John begins by developing a database of websites that specialize in classic and reproduction car parts, organized by make and model. By using these online dealers—plus other dealers nationwide who aren't online but whom John will get to know as he attends regional trade shows and does more national business—John will be able to get parts faster than any of his competitors. Putting some extra energy into the parts aspect of his business gives John a key marketing hook to convince his knowledgeable (and often finicky) customers that his business really is a step ahead.

Describe Your Marketing Strategy

By now you've shown that there are people out there who will buy your product or service from you instead of from your competitors. Great, but your job isn't done. Investors and others interested in supporting your business will want to know how you'll reach your customers in a cost-effective way. The answer to this question is, in a nutshell, your marketing strategy.

RELATED TOPIC

Learn about marketing in Chapter 12: Small Business Marketing 101. Refer to that chapter for a detailed explanation of crafting a marketing strategy and using cost-effective tools. For the purposes of your business plan, you'll need at least a cursory description of your marketing approach. Some businesses may want to go a step further and draft a separate marketing plan.

Any marketing strategy worthy of the name should be based on the particular characteristics of the market you're trying to reach, with the goal of reaching as many customers as possible for the least expense. For instance, if you're trying to reach a very tiny group of people, such as left-handed ophthalmologists, or even a slightly larger audience, such as digital video editors, it makes no sense to spend the big bucks required for television advertising. On the other hand, if your market consists of all children between the ages of six and ten, TV advertising might be an efficient way to reach them.

In describing your plan for reaching your customers, explain what methods you will use, such as radio or newspaper advertising, Web marketing, or directory listings, such as trade directories or the yellow pages. If you plan to use nontraditional guerrilla marketing tactics, such as putting up posters all around town or staging publicity stunts, explain exactly what you plan to do. And no matter what kind of marketing strategy you outline, be sure to explain why you think it will work.

Small businesses that don't have much of a marketing budget shouldn't be shy about their smaller-scale plans. Even if you don't plan to spend much (if any) money on marketing or advertising, you should have a plan for how you'll reach your first customers. In your business plan, simply explain what this strategy is. The following example shows how a small business with a minimal advertising and marketing budget might explain its strategy.

EXAMPLE: Rather than spending money on traditional advertising, Turtlevision, a video post-production firm, plans to keep its marketing costs very low, at least for the first year or two. The company plans to list its services in local video-related directories and use various online communities to promote the business. In addition, the company will offer services at a discount to various nonprofit organizations to develop a strong portfolio and to generate good word of mouth. (For example, it plans to offer discounted services to a nonprofit film foundation to stream videos on the Web.) Turtlevision hopes that it will receive recommendations from satisfied customers, which will give it a start in the right direction.

CAUTION

Spam is bad. No matter how delectable you find the potted meat product, do not fool yourself into believing that sending out masses of unsolicited emails (a practice known as "spamming") will be good for your business. Most Web-savvy entrepreneurs already know what nutritionists have told us for years—spam is bad for you. At the very least, it's bad for any goodwill that may exist for your business. No one likes getting junk email, no matter what fabulous deal it may offer. Be a good Net citizen and use more savory marketing tactics than spam.

TIP

Marketing without advertising can be successful. Especially in niche or local markets, people often make purchasing decisions based on the recommendations of people they respect, not on ads. If you doubt this, think about how you chose your dentist, plumber, or the company that recently fixed your roof. Chances are good that you got a recommendation from someone you trusted. To be the beneficiary of positive word of mouth, you need to run an excellent business. Assuming you do, there are loads of cost-effective ways to let potential customers know about your great service. For a book full of great ideas, read *Marketing Without Advertising: Easy Ways to Build a Business Your Customers Will Love and Recommend*, by Michael Phillips and Salli Rasberry (Nolo).

Describe Your Business Accomplishments

Above and beyond demonstrating the beauty of your business, you'll want to show that you're the right person to run it. Do this by creating a résumé showing your business accomplishments. Here you have the chance to highlight all of your relevant experience and training, as well as any other personal information likely to inspire confidence in you as a businessperson.

Prospective lenders and investors will want to know a number of things about you.

- **Do you understand the business?** Emphasize that you understand the basic tasks of the business inside and out. Surprisingly, lots of people start small businesses in areas in which they are amateurs. For example, a person who isn't mechanically inclined but who loves German cars may want to open a VW repair shop. Lack of hands-on experience will likely be a red flag to investors, who know a nonexpert boss can't roll up his or her sleeves and help out in emergencies. Do your best to show them otherwise.

- **Can you manage people?** All sorts of organizations, including small businesses, fail because their leaders—no matter how technically competent—can't work well with others. Bad management of people is one of the surest ways to create a poor workplace atmosphere, one with low morale, mediocre productivity, and high turnover. If you have successfully worked with, and preferably led, people, emphasize this experience.

- **Do you understand money?** A surprising number of people who open small businesses don't know how to manage—or make—money. Even though their business idea is a good, competitive one and their employees are energetic, they make such poor financial decisions that their businesses don't prosper. Knowing this, people who will consider funding your business will want to see if you or another key person in your business has money management skills. If you do—even if your experience was in a very different business—emphasize it.

Making Financial Projections

In addition to describing how your business will work, including how it will reach plenty of customers and fend off competitors, you'll also need to do some number crunching to show that it will in fact turn a profit. All the rosy descriptions in the world won't make it a success if the numbers turn up red.

Projecting the finances of your business may seem intimidating or difficult, but in reality it's not terribly complex. Basically, it consists of making educated guesses about how much money you'll need to spend and how much you'll take in, then using these estimates to calculate whether your business will be sufficiently profitable.

Predicting and planning the finances of your business are important not only to attract investors, but also to demonstrate to you and your family that your business idea will fly. If your first projections show your business losing money, you'll have an opportunity while still in the planning stage to make sensible adjustments, such as raising your prices or cutting costs. If you neglect to make financial projections, you won't realize your plan is a money loser until you actually start losing money. At that point, it may be too late to turn things around.

Nonetheless, many new entrepreneurs avoid crunching their numbers, often due to fear that their estimates will be wildly off-base and yield useless results. This is a poor reason to avoid forecasting your finances. If you do your best to make realistic predictions of expenses and revenues and accept that your guesstimates will not be absolutely correct, you can learn a great deal about what the financial side of your business is likely to look like in its early months and even years of operation. Even a somewhat inaccurate picture of your business's likely finances will be much more helpful than no picture at all.

For a basic understanding of your business's projected financial situation, you'll need to make the following estimates and calculations, all of which are discussed in detail in the rest of this chapter.

- **A break-even analysis.** Here you use income and expense estimates for a year or more to see whether, in theory at least, your business will be able to turn a profit. If you have trouble projecting a solid profit, you might need to consider abandoning your idea altogether.

- **A profit/loss forecast.** Here you'll refine the sales and expense estimates that you used for your break-even analysis into a formal, month-by-month projection of your business's net profit for at least the first year of operations.

- **A start-up cost estimate.** As the name suggests, this is simply the total of all the expenses you'll incur before your business opens. These costs should be included in your business plan to give a true picture of how much money you'll need to get your business off the ground.

- **A cash flow projection.** Even if your profit/loss forecast tells you that your business will have higher revenues than expenses, that doesn't mean that you'll always have enough cash available on key dates, such as when rent is due or when you need to buy more inventory. A cash flow projection lays out how much cash you'll have—or how much you'll be short—month by month. This lets you know if you'll need to get a credit line or set up other arrangements to make sure funds are available.

Get to Know Your Numbers

The calculations involved in accounting aren't terribly complex. The main reason people get confused is not that they're bad at math—it's that they don't understand what the numbers mean. It's important that you take a little time early on to learn what your key financial numbers are and how they relate to one another. To help you keep the numbers straight, keep in mind this formula (see "Categorizing Your Expenses," below, for an explanation of "costs of sale" and "fixed costs"):

> Sales revenue
> – Costs of sale (variable costs)
> = Gross profit
> – Overhead (fixed costs)
> = Net profit
> – Taxes
> = After-tax profit

You'll have a much easier time understanding all the various financial calculations involved in accounting—including break-even, profit/loss, and cash flow analysis—once you're familiar and comfortable with this basic formula.

The best way to do your financial projections is to use spreadsheet software such as Microsoft *Excel*. If you have never used spreadsheet software, take heart: It is quite easy to learn. Ask a friend to show you how it works or even tackle it yourself, and in a couple of hours you'll likely be able to start your number crunching in earnest.

It usually makes sense to develop your initial financial projections with spreadsheet software and not the fuller-featured accounting software that you should use to track your actual income and expenses once your business launches. Accounting programs such as *QuickBooks* or *Peachtree Accounting* work great for ongoing bookkeeping and financial management, but are not nearly as flexible for the task of developing estimates and projections. Also, it's generally wise to steer clear of business planning software, which is usually nothing more than a word processing function and some empty spreadsheets to fill in. Most readers of this book probably already have word processing and spreadsheet software, which will offer better and fuller features than whatever is offered with a business plan program.

The rest of this chapter will walk you step-by-step through each of these financial forecasts. When you're done, you should be able to tell whether your business will actually make enough money to pay the bills and turn a profit. Assuming the answer is yes, you'll also see whether you need to obtain start-up money from investors or lenders and if so, how much. Finally, once your business is up and running, you can refer back to your forecasts to see how your performance is measuring up.

Break-Even Analysis

Your break-even point is the point at which the income you'll bring in just covers your expenses. Expenses include the costs of providing your product or service (also known as variable costs, since they change depending on how many products or services you provide), plus your overhead, which includes rent, salaries, and utility bills (commonly called fixed costs).

FORM ON CD-ROM

Break-Even Analysis Worksheet. On the CD-ROM that comes with this book, you'll find an interactive worksheet to help you calculate your break-even point. The file name of the worksheet is BreakEven.xls. For the automatic calculations in the worksheet to be active, you'll need to open the worksheet in a spreadsheet program such as Microsoft *Excel*.

To use the worksheet on the CD-ROM, follow the steps outlined below. Each step is also explained in greater detail later in this section. You should read the detailed information before using the worksheet. Enter figures only into white cells; do not enter anything in blue cells.

Step 1: Enter your estimated total annual revenues. This figure will not be used in the worksheet calculations, but will help you in the next step, in which you will break down your estimated revenues into categories.

Step 2: This step will result in an average gross profit percentage for your business as a whole, based on calculations for up to three categories of products or services your business will provide. First, enter the name for the category, then enter an average sales price, variable cost, and estimated revenues for each category. The total of your estimated revenues for all categories should equal your estimated total annual revenues from Step 1. If they do not, the worksheet will still calculate an average gross profit percentage based on the total of your category revenue estimates. However, you may want to evaluate why your category revenue estimates do not match the estimate for your business as a whole. Once you have entered numbers for all categories you plan to use (you do not need to use all three categories), your average gross profit percentage for your business as a whole will be displayed at the bottom of the section.

Step 3: Enter the type and amount of all fixed costs you anticipate for your business. Enter monthly figures; the worksheet will automatically calculate an annual amount.

Result: The worksheet will show you your break-even point, which is the amount of revenue you'll need to bring in before your business starts making any profits.

Because break-even analysis offers a glimpse of your ultimate profitability, it's a great tool for weeding out losing business ideas. For example, if you see that you'll need to achieve a highly optimistic sales number just to cover your costs, you should rethink your entire business plan. Maybe you'll figure out a way to adjust parts of your business so that you can realize a profit from lower sales. If not, it might be best to ditch your less-than-brilliant business idea.

To find your break-even point, first make a best-guess estimate of your sales revenue for the products or services you plan to sell. Then predict how much profit you'll make on each sale (by subtracting the costs of the sale from the revenue it will generate), and figure out a "gross profit percentage"—how much of each sales dollar exceeds the cost of the product or service itself. Finally, estimate what your fixed costs (such as rent and insurance) will be. After a few calculations, you'll see whether the profit you'll make on each individual sale (also called gross profit) will cover your fixed costs.

Before examining the details of calculating your break-even point, look at a very simple example that illustrates the overall process. All the calculations are explained in more detail below; for now, just focus on the process as a whole.

> **EXAMPLE:** Michele is starting a side business selling her own handmade jewelry. To calculate her break-even point, she makes her very best estimate of how much jewelry she thinks she could sell in a year. She figures she could sell an average of 20 pieces a month at $20 apiece, making her yearly income $4,800. Then she figures out how much she'd make on each sale, above the cost of materials. (For this super-simplified example, let's leave the cost of her time out of the equation.) Since the materials for each piece cost Michele $5, she'd be making $15 on each sale. In other words, her gross profit would be $15 per piece. Next she calculates her gross profit percentage, which is her gross profit ($15) divided by her selling price ($20). This puts her gross profit percentage at 75%, which means that $0.75 of each sales dollar exceeds of the cost

of the piece of jewelry itself. Next, Michele would figure out what her fixed costs would be—the cost of her tools and the monthly fee for her booth at a local arts and crafts mall. She figures that these fixed costs total $50 per month, or $600 per year.

To calculate her break-even point, Michele will divide her annual fixed costs ($600) by her gross profit percentage (.75) to arrive at $800. This means that just to cover the costs of the materials and her tools and booth, Michele must bring in $800 per year; anything above that amount will be her pretax profit. Since she earlier estimated that she could sell $4,800 worth of jewelry per year, Michele figures that she'll easily reach her break-even point—and make a $4,000 profit as well.

Before explaining exactly how to do the calculations, this chapter quickly discusses two items that you need to understand before actually crunching your numbers: making financial estimates and categorizing your expenses.

Making Estimates

When you estimate your income and expenses, your estimates should extend over enough time to catch up with seasonal fluctuations. Depending on your type of business, your revenue and expenses may vary wildly from month to month. For example, if you plan to manufacture custom snowboards, most of your sales will be in the late fall and early winter months, while the opposite will be true if you made surfboards. A good way to account for this is to make estimates for each month of the year, then add them up to get a yearly figure. In making these estimates, it is wise to cover at least a one-year period, which is enough time to account for normal ups and downs, but not so long as to be overly speculative.

Categorizing Your Expenses

Your business expenses break down into two categories: fixed expenses (fixed costs) and variable expenses (variable costs). This division is not only important for your break-even analysis, it's also a standard method of categorizing expenses for accounting and tax reporting. Here's the difference.

- **Fixed costs.** Commonly referred to as "overhead," these include all regular expenses not directly tied to the product or service you provide. Rent, utility bills, phone bills, payments for outside help such as bookkeeping services, postage, and most salaries (except in service businesses) are common fixed costs.
- **Variable costs.** These costs—sometimes also called product costs, costs of goods sold (or COGS), or costs of sale—are directly related to the products or services you provide and include inventory, packaging, supplies, materials, and sometimes labor used in providing your product or service. They're called "variable" precisely because they go up or down depending on the volume of products or services you produce or sell. In the case of services, one of the biggest variable expenses is almost always the wages or salary of the service provider. (See "Salaries and Labor Costs—Fixed or Variable?" below, for a more complete explanation.)

Estimate Your Sales Revenue

Start your break-even analysis by making your best estimate of annual sales revenues. Your estimate will obviously depend on several different variables, such as your type of business, what you plan to charge for each product or service you'll offer, and how successful you'll be at selling products and services.

Though at first it may seem overwhelming to project revenues based upon so many untested variables, it is essential that you take the plunge and try out some numbers. Even though your estimates won't be anywhere near 100% accurate, they'll force you to focus and refine key elements of your business idea and may even help you spot big potholes in your plan. And besides, you need these estimates before you can move ahead with your break-even calculations, so get over it and start estimating.

One good way to estimate how much money you'll be bringing in is to compare your business

Salaries and Labor Costs—Fixed or Variable?

Whether you'll categorize labor expenses as fixed or variable costs often depends on the type of workers you pay and the kinds of products or services you're selling. Salaries or wages of the managers and employees who are necessary to keep your business going (you or your bookkeeper, for example) are usually best seen as fixed costs. But salaries or wages for employees who create the products or provide the services you sell may be more appropriately treated as variable costs. For example, an ad agency that pays six freelance copywriters to service clients' accounts should treat their paychecks as variable costs.

To figure out whether a labor cost should be designated as fixed or variable, ask yourself: If I sell one, ten, or 100 more products or services this week, will my labor costs go up? If not, you're probably looking at a fixed cost. For instance, suppose you're trying to decide whether your receptionist's salary should be categorized as a variable cost or a fixed cost. If you produce and sell 100 more Snuggie blanket-robes, will your reception costs go up? Probably not. So your receptionist's salary should be part of your overhead. But if you have to hire five temporary employees to handle the phones at Christmastime to handle the spiking demand for Snuggies, their wages should be classified as variable costs. (Hint: Money paid to workers who are temps or independent contractors are usually categorized as variable costs because those payments are usually tied to providing a product or service.) Of course, if you sell more products or services regularly, you'll probably decide to expand your business and increase your overhead, because you'll have to hire more support staff, managers, and other necessary employees just to get along. At that point, you might revisit your allocation of fixed and variable costs.

to similar ones. Retail businesses, for example, often measure annual sales revenue per square foot of retail space. Thus, if you plan to open a pet supply store, you'll want to find out the annual sales revenue per square foot of other pet supply shops. Although direct competitors probably won't share this information with you, industry trade publications almost always provide it. Attending industry trade shows where you can meet and talk to people who own similar businesses in other parts of the country is another good way to gather valuable information.

EXAMPLE: Inga is planning to open a used bookstore in San Francisco called Inga's Book Haus. She plans to sell mostly used books, which generally have a high profit margin, but she'll also stock a limited selection of new books at the front of the store to attract more customers. She'll sell some miscellaneous trinkets, such as postcards and magnets, as well.

To figure out how much sales revenue she can realistically expect for Inga's Book Haus, Inga calls up a couple of friends who are in the book business. One who works at a nearby used bookstore confides to Inga that the store sells approximately $450 worth of books per square foot per year. Another friend owns a new and used bookstore in Pasadena; she tells Inga that they bring in about $400 annually per square foot. Neither of these stores is exactly like the one Inga envisions; the one in San Francisco doesn't sell any new books, and the one in Pasadena does a healthy trade in textbooks, which Inga doesn't expect at her store. To round out her information, Inga also looks into some trade publications and does a bit of sleuthing at local new-and-used bookstores, examining their prices and how busy they seem to be. Ultimately she decides that an annual income of $350 per square foot is realistic. She has her eye on a few storefronts, all around 1,200 square feet, so she estimates her annual revenues to be $420,000.

Basing your projected revenue on the numbers of similar companies also works for nonretail businesses, such as wholesaling or manufacturing companies—but, it can be somewhat tricky to find a solid basis for comparison. Unlike retail businesses, sales per square foot doesn't really apply. If you're not already well acquainted with your field, you'll have to do some research. Study similar businesses to find out how many employees they have, how wide their distribution is, and how much annual income they earn. Base your income projections on similarly sized businesses with a comparable range of distribution.

If yours is a service business, your estimate of sales revenue will depend on how many billable sales you'll be able to make each month. A big part of this calculation is how many hours you and any employees will work and how much you'll be paid per hour by your clients. But don't overlook the fact that all of your time won't be billable—you won't be providing services every hour you're at work. For example, if you run a landscaping business, a sizable portion of your time will not be spent performing landscaping work, but managing your accounts, maintaining your equipment, and soliciting new clients. You'll need to make a realistic assessment of how much of your time will be taken up by these nonbillable activities and how much time you'll spend providing actual services to clients to get an accurate picture of how much money will be flowing in.

Calculate Your Average Gross Profit Percentage

Your next task is to figure your average gross profit percentage. That may sound complex, but basically it's just a figure that represents how much of each sales dollar will be left over after paying for the costs of the products or services themselves. There are a number of steps involved in calculating this figure, but none involve anything more than simple math: addition, subtraction, multiplication, and division. Once you know your average gross profit percentage, you'll easily be able to figure out how much money you'll need to bring in to cover all the costs of your business.

In a nutshell, to figure your average gross profit percentage you'll need to:

1. Figure out your gross profit for each major category of your products or services.

2. Determine an average gross profit for your business overall, including all your products and services.

3. Divide your average gross profit by your average selling price.

In case you're wondering what the difference is between "gross profit" and "average gross profit," here's a quick explanation. The details will be covered while going through the calculations below. When you sell an individual product, the money that you earn above the cost of the item itself (called your variable cost, or sometimes cost of goods) is called gross profit. For instance, if your pet store sells a doghouse for $200, and you bought the doghouse for $110, then what's left over for you after the sale is $90—your gross profit. If your business sells more than one kind of product, you'll need to calculate an *average* gross profit for your total product line to get a realistic figure. The average gross profit for your pet store would include all of your products—cat scratching posts, pet food, play toys, and so on—including their sale prices and what they cost you.

The next few subsections take you through the process of calculating your business's average gross profit.

Figure Your Gross Profit by Category

As described above, your gross profit is the amount of money you make on each sale, above what it costs you to provide the product or service—that is, the variable cost, or cost of sale. Gross profit is determined simply by subtracting the variable cost of your product or service from its sales price.

Variable costs are generally fairly easy to estimate. If you're selling products bought from a wholesaler, your variable costs may be as simple as what you pay for the products themselves. If you'll assemble the products, then include your costs for the parts and labor needed to put them together. Also remember to include items such as packaging or freebies in your variable costs.

If you sell only services, variable costs basically include what you pay to whomever provides the services (you or perhaps an employee), not including time spent on administrative tasks and managing accounts, which is generally considered to be a fixed, not variable, cost. It can sometimes be tricky to figure out the variable costs of a service business. Do your best to separate out the costs that are not associated with individual projects—those are your fixed costs.

EXAMPLE: Turtlevision, a digital video editing service, pays its staff editor $50 per hour for 80 hours per month of editing work. In addition, Turtlevision pays an office assistant $15 per hour for 100 hours per month of administrative work. Turtlevision's monthly variable costs would include the editor's salary of $4,000, but not the salary paid to the office assistant, which is not tied to any particular client or project.

One kink in figuring out your business's gross profit is that your selling prices and variable costs may vary a great deal from product to product (or service to service). For instance, say you buy cat collars for an average of $4, and sell them for an average price of $10 (your gross profit per cat collar would be $6). Doghouses, on the other hand, cost you an average of $110, and you sell them for an average price of $200 (your gross profit per doghouse would be $90).

To account for these differences, you should categorize your products or services and figure an average gross profit for each category. There are a few steps to follow, but hang in there—each one is pretty simple.

First, estimate the average selling price and average variable cost for products or services with roughly similar selling prices and variable costs. For instance, you might group all your animal collars together—for cats, dogs, and ferrets—since their selling prices ($9 to $13) and variable costs ($3 to $5) aren't too different. Don't lump together products or services with considerably different selling prices or variable costs. As a general rule, the more tightly you define your categories, the more accurate your estimates will be.

After you've estimated the average selling price and average variable cost for each category, subtract the average variable cost from the average selling

price for each category, and you'll have an average gross profit dollar figure for each category.

	Animal collars	Bird-houses	Dog-houses
Average selling price	$ 11	$ 60	$ 200
− Average variable cost	4	30	110
= Average gross profit	$ 7	$ 30	$ 90

The next step is to figure out a gross profit percentage for each category. A gross profit percentage tells you how much of each dollar of sales income is gross profit. To calculate each category's gross profit percentage, divide the average gross profit figure by the average selling price.

Animal collars category:

	Average gross profit	$ 7
÷	Average selling price	$ 11
=	Gross profit percentage	63.6%

Using the above example, it follows that if you sold $1,500 in cat collars, 63.6% of that—$954—would be gross profit, or the amount left over after paying costs of sale. As you can see, converting your gross profit into a percentage allows you to quickly figure out how much of your income will be left over after variable costs have been covered.

Calculate Your Average Gross Profit

After you've found the gross profit percentage for each category, you'll be able to determine your average gross profit for your business as a whole.

First, estimate your annual sales revenue per category. Earlier, you estimated your total annual sales revenues; now divide that figure as best you can into your estimates for each category. For example, if you estimated total annual revenues of $100,000 for your pet supply business, divide that among your categories, such as collars, birdhouses, and doghouses—say $25,000 in collar sales, $40,000 in birdhouses, and $35,000 in doghouses. Base your division on your best sense of which categories and products will make up a big part of your business, and which will have a smaller share. Then, for each product category, multiply the estimated sales revenue by the category's gross profit percentage (arrived at above) to figure out your total gross profit dollars per category.

> Animal collars category:
>
> | | | |
> |---|---|---|
> | | Estimated sales revenue | $ 25,000 |
> | x | Gross profit percentage | 63.6% |
> | = | Total gross profit | $ 15,900 |

Finally, add together the gross profit dollar amounts for each category to arrive at a total annual gross profit for your business. Divide the total annual gross profit figure by the total annual sales that you estimated for all products or services. The result will be an average gross profit percentage for your business.

Let's look at how this process works with Inga's Book Haus.

> **EXAMPLE:** As you may recall, Inga plans to sell new and used books, plus some peripheral items, such as postcards and refrigerator magnets. Because the profit margins for new books, used books, and trinkets are different, Inga figures a gross profit percentage for each of these categories. (Inga might want to establish separate categories for hardback, paperback, and coffee table books, but we'll keep things simple.)
>
> To accomplish this, first Inga estimates an average variable cost for each category. In addition to the cost of the merchandise, she includes the cost of free bags, bookmarks, and wrapping paper for gifts. For instance, used books cost her an average of $3, and she figures the bookmarks and bags that go with each sale will cost her an average of 10¢. So her total average variable cost in the used book category is $3.10. She doesn't include fixed costs, such as rent or salaries, here.
>
> Next, Inga fills in an average selling price for each product category. Her average selling price for used books, for example, is $7. She then subtracts the average variable cost (arrived at above) from the average selling price to get an average gross profit figure for each product category. Subtracting her average variable cost for used books ($3.10) from her average selling

price for used books ($7) leaves her with an average gross profit for used books of $3.90.

> Used book category:
>
> | | | |
> |---|---|---|
> | | Average sales price | $ 7.10 |
> | − | Average variable cost | 3.10 |
> | = | Average gross profit | $3.90 |

Inga does the same calculations for new books, which also shows an average gross profit at $3.90, and trinkets, which has an average gross profit of $1.40.

To determine the gross profit percentage, she'll simply divide the gross profit by the selling price in each category to get a gross profit percentage for each category. Dividing her average gross profit for used books ($3.90) by her average selling price ($7) gives Inga a gross profit percentage of 56% for used books, a good percentage. That means that for every dollar she'll bring in from used books, 44 cents per dollar will be eaten up on Inga's costs, leaving 56 cents per dollar to cover fixed costs and go towards a net profit. Her gross profit percentage for new books is 33%, and for trinkets it's an impressive 70%, as shown below.

> New book category:
>
> | | | |
> |---|---|---|
> | | Average gross profit | $ 3.90 |
> | ÷ | Average selling price | $12.00 |
> | = | Gross profit percentage | 33% |
>
> Trinkets category:
>
> | | | |
> |---|---|---|
> | | Average gross profit | $ 1.40 |
> | ÷ | Average selling price | 2.00 |
> | = | Gross profit percentage | 70% |

Using the gross profit percentages and estimated sales revenues for each category, Inga can calculate the gross profit dollar figure for each category. For example, her estimated annual sales of used books is $300,000. (Remember that Inga estimated her total annual sales revenue to be $420,000. She thinks used books will account for a little over two-thirds of her sales.) By multiplying $300,000 by the used book category's gross profit percentage

(56%), she estimates an annual gross profit of $168,000. Adding up the gross profit figures for each category, Inga figures that her total gross profit will be $215,000. Finally, by dividing this amount by her annual estimated revenues of $420,000, she easily determines her overall average gross profit percentage, which is 51.2%.

	New books	Used books	Trinkets
Average variable cost per product	$ 8.00	$ 3.00	$ .50
+ Bookmarks, bags	.10	.10	.10
= Average total cost	$ 8.10	$ 3.10	$ .60
Average selling price	$ 12.00	$ 7.00	$ 2.00
− Average total variable cost	8.10	3.10	60
= Average gross profit	$ 3.90	$ 3.90	$ 1.40
Average gross profit	$ 3.90	$ 3.90	$ 1.40
÷ Average selling price	12.00	7.00	2.00
= Gross profit percentage	33%	56%	70%
Average sales	$100,000	$300,000	$20,000
x Gross profit percentage	33%	56%	70%
= Annual gross profit	$ 33,000	$168,000	$ 14,000

Annual gross profit	
New books	$ 33,000
+ Used books	168,000
+ Trinkets	14,000
= Total annual gross profit	$215,000
÷ Total annual sales	$420,000
= Average gross profit percentage	51.2%

Estimate Your Fixed Costs

You're done with the hard part. Compared to calculating your gross profit percentage, fixed costs are a breeze. Simply estimate your monthly fixed expenses, including items such as rent, utility bills, office supplies, uncollectable debts—basically, any anticipated costs that don't depend on the product or service you sell. Since many of these costs recur monthly, it's usually easiest to estimate them per month and total them for one year. It's also a good idea to throw in a little extra—say 10% or so—to cover miscellaneous expenses that you can't predict. Once you've arrived at a total, you'll know that you'll need to make at least this much gross profit (and probably a healthy chunk more) to keep your business afloat.

EXAMPLE: Here is a list of Inga's monthly estimates for fixed costs.

Rent	$ 3,500
Wages for part-time clerks	2,500
Utilities	800
Telephone	700
Office equipment	700
Insurance	500
Advertising	700
Accounting	300
Electronic payment system fees	300
Miscellaneous	1,000
Total fixed expenses per month	$ 11,000

Total fixed expenses per month	$ 11,000
x Number of months in a year	12
Annual total fixed expenses	$132,000

CAUTION

Don't forget you have to eat. Notice that Inga has chosen not to list a salary here as an expense. She, like many sole proprietors, figures that her savings, help from friends and family, and some extra crumbs the business may produce should be enough to live on for the short term. Once she figures out how much profit the business will bring in regularly, she'll decide how much profit she can expect to take out of the business and add that number to her fixed costs. Leaving out payments for your own living expenses in your break-even analysis, however, can be dangerous, at least if you're planning to live off your business's profits from the get-go. If this is your plan, you should add to your fixed costs the minimum amount you'll need to take out of the business to cover your living expenses. Then, if you can't project your income to be higher than your fixed costs when the amount you'll need for living expenses is included, you'll know you can't plan on living off the company. This may be a clue that your business is not a good bet.

> **TIP**
>
> **Keep fixed costs as low as reasonably possible.** If your business is slow to get started—and lots of businesses take months or even years to become solidly profitable—high fixed costs can quickly eat up your savings. Rather than committing yourself to high overhead, it's usually better to keep expenses low, allowing increases only when your income justifies spending more. For example, few businesses really depend on a pricey physical location for their success. If your business won't depend on a big, casual walk-in trade, don't overpay for a trendy zip code. Operating from a low-cost warehouse district, an older office building, or even your garage may work just fine, at least at the beginning.

Calculate Your Break-Even Point

Once you have estimated your average gross profit percentage and your fixed costs, it's easy to figure out how much revenue you'll need to break even. Remember, your gross profit percentage represents how much of each dollar of revenue is actual profit, money left over after paying for the product or service itself. To figure out your break-even point, you'll divide your estimated annual fixed costs by your gross profit percentage. The result will be the amount of sales revenue you'll need to bring in just to cover your costs.

> **EXAMPLE:** The break-even point for Inga's Book Haus will equal her annual fixed expenses divided by her average gross profit percentage.
>
> | | |
> |---|---|
> | Annual fixed expenses | $132,000 |
> | ÷ Average gross profit percentage | 51.2% |
> | = Break-even point | $257,813 |

If you're having trouble understanding how this equation works, you're not alone. Conceptually, it's a little tricky to see how dividing your fixed costs by your gross profit percentage yields your break-even point. Think of it this way: However much money your business brings in, some of it will be eaten up by the cost of the product or service itself (your variable costs), leaving you a reduced amount left over to pay your bills. How much is left over is determined by your gross profit percentage—this number tells you just how much will be left over, on average, from each dollar, after paying for your product or service itself (your variable costs). When you divide your estimated annual fixed costs by your gross profit percentage, the resulting number (the break-even point) is the exact amount that's enough to cover all of your costs.

> **EXAMPLE:** Another extra-simplified example should help illustrate this concept. Michele plans to go into business selling jewelry. Her gross profit percentage was 75%, meaning that for every dollar she brought in, 25¢ would be eaten up by the cost of the jewelry materials, leaving Michele 75¢ to cover her fixed costs. Michele's fixed costs were $600 per year. So, you're wondering, why isn't Michele's break-even point $600? Because if Michele earned exactly $600 in a year, only 75% of that would be available to cover her fixed costs—the other 25% would have already been eaten up by the costs of her jewelry, and she wouldn't be able to pay all of the $600 in fixed costs. To account for this, Michele needs to divide her fixed costs ($600) by her gross profit percentage (75%) to arrive at the higher amount that she'll need to bring in to cover both her fixed costs and her variable costs. Dividing $600 by .75 results in $800, her break-even point; if Michele brings in $800, 25% of it will go toward the cost of the product, and the rest ($600) is just enough to cover her fixed costs.

Analyze Your Result

If your estimated revenue exceeds your break-even point, great—but that's not the same thing as saying you are free to put the excess money in your pocket. Again, remember that every dollar you bring in doesn't come for free; you had to pay something for the products or services that brought in that money. The portion of excess sales revenue that's really yours (ignoring taxes for the moment) is equivalent to your gross profit percentage of that excess revenue. To determine how much of the excess revenue is pretax profit, multiply the excess by your gross profit percentage. The result is your estimated net profit.

EXAMPLE: Earlier, Inga estimated her annual sales revenue to be $420,000—over $160,000 more than she needs to break even.

Estimated revenue	$420,000
– Break-even point	257,813
= Excess revenues	$162,187

To figure out how much of her excess revenue will be actual pretax profit, Inga multiplies it by her gross profit percentage.

Excess revenues	$162,187
x Gross profit percentage	51.2%
= Net profit	$ 83,040

Inga is happy to see her projections show a profit. But she needs to remember that none of her estimates included any payments to herself, meaning she'll probably need to take some of that net profit just to meet her living expenses.

If, on the other hand, your break-even point is higher than your expected revenues, you'll have some decisions to make. For example, you'll have to decide whether certain aspects of your plan can be amended to come up with an achievable break-even point. For instance, perhaps you could find a less expensive source of supplies, do without an employee, or save rent by working out of your home. But don't change your numbers without a very good reason. When confronted by a break-even point that exceeds your estimated revenues, you may be tempted to tweak and squish your numbers into a profitable forecast, even if those numbers aren't realistic. Unless you really do have a good reason to think you can break even at a lower point,

you'd be wise to guard against this temptation. For example, to have your plan pencil out in the black, you might boost your sales estimates in hopes that you'll somehow be able to pull it off. But can you really sell 50,000 Sausage Shooters™, 3,000 books on medieval dentistry, or 2,000 Tori Spelling mini-tees per month?

Generally speaking, when trying to pencil out a more profitable break-even point, it's best to focus on your costs. The most reliable way to tilt a business from the red to the black is to reduce what you will pay out, not to make a more optimistic projection of what you'll take in.

Profit/Loss Forecast

If your break-even analysis shows that, based on realistic estimates of revenue and expenses, your business will turn a profit, your next job is to use these figures to create the profit/loss forecast component of your business plan. Similar to a break-even analysis, a profit/loss forecast (sometimes called a P & L forecast) uses your estimates for sales revenue and variable costs to calculate your gross profit, then subtracts your fixed expenses from gross profit to arrive at net profit. If you use accounting software, it will generate a P & L statement automatically once you enter monthly sales and expense estimates. You can also use the worksheet on the CD-ROM that comes with this book, as described below.

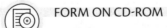 **FORM ON CD-ROM**

Profit/Loss Forecast Worksheet. On the CD-ROM that comes with this book, you'll find an interactive worksheet to help you do a profit/loss forecast. The file name of the worksheet is ProfitLoss.xls. For the automatic calculations in the worksheet to be active, you'll need to open the worksheet in a spreadsheet program such as Microsoft *Excel*.

To use the worksheet, follow the steps outlined below. Each step is explained in greater detail later in this section. You should read the detailed information before using the worksheet. Enter figures only into white cells; do not enter anything in blue cells.

Step 1: Enter your estimated sales revenues for each month. If you will be starting a business in a month other than January, you may change the months to begin with your starting month.

Step 2: Enter the average gross profit percentage for your business as a whole. You need to enter this figure just once, in the first column under "January." The worksheet will automatically enter it for every other month.

Step 3: Enter your anticipated fixed expenses for each month. The worksheet uses common categories, and contains some rows you may customize for expenses specific to your business. If you do not anticipate a certain type of expense, you may leave cells blank.

Result: When you have entered estimated sales revenues, a gross profit percentage, and fixed costs for all months, the worksheet will display your estimated net profit or loss for each month.

The main difference between a P & L and a break-even analysis has to do with timing. A break-even analysis looks at profit and loss on a yearly basis, while your P & L forecast calculates monthly net profit. A P & L forecast also differs from a cash flow projection (discussed below) in the kinds of income and expenses that it includes. A cash flow projection looks at all sources of income and expenses, including loans, transfers of personal money into the business, start-up costs, and all other types of cash inflows and outflows. A P & L forecast, on the other hand, is only concerned with money earned from normal business operations. For this reason, a P & L forecast will tell you whether your business operations are generating enough income to cover your expenses, which is something you can't glean from a cash flow projection.

Here's how to translate your break-even figures into a profit/loss forecast. Start by breaking down your annual sales estimate into monthly amounts. If you expect significant seasonal fluctuations in sales, account for them here.

Next, figure your gross profit for each month. The easiest way to do this is to multiply each month's

sales revenue by the gross profit percentage for your business as a whole, which you calculated earlier. (If you rounded off your gross profit percentage, you'll get a slightly different gross profit figure here than you did in your break-even analysis.)

Enter your monthly fixed expenses by category, and add them together to get monthly totals. Then, for each month, subtract your total fixed expenses from your gross profit and enter the result in the net profit row. If the result is a negative number, it means your expenses are more than your gross profit. Put parentheses around the result; in accounting symbols, a number in parentheses is a negative number.

! CAUTION

Your profit/loss forecast doesn't include the whole picture. Other income and costs, such as loans and start-up expenses, aren't included in your P & L forecast, which reflects only money earned and spent as part of providing your products or services. For the full picture of all money that comes into and goes out from your business—including start-up costs, loans, taxes, and other money that isn't earned or spent as part of your core business operation—you'll need to do a cash flow analysis. (See "Cash Flow Projection," below, for a complete explanation.)

A completed P & L forecast will outline your business's profitability month by month. If your expenses are higher than revenues for a month or two, don't panic—most start-up businesses lose money for at least a few months—but you will need to figure out how to make it through these lean months (for example, by getting a start-up loan). More important in the big picture is whether you can see a trend toward stable profitability. If not, you may need to revisit parts of your plan (or possibly scrap your idea all together). But, as mentioned earlier, resist the temptation to inflate your sales estimates; a more realistic approach is to lower your costs. Once you have a P & L forecast that shows consistent profits each month, based on realistic estimates, you're ready to move forward.

A one-year profit/loss forecast for Inga's bookstore is shown below.

Inga's Book Haus Profit/Loss Forecast: Year One Total

	Jan	Feb	Mar	April	May
Sales Revenues	$ 30,000	$ 35,000	$ 35,000	$ 35,000	$ 35,000
Gross Profit (51.2%)	15,360	17,920	17,920	17,920	17,920
Fixed Expenses					
Rent	3,500	3,500	3,500	3,500	3,500
Salaries	2,500	2,500	2,500	2,500	2,500
Utilities	800	800	800	800	800
Telephone	700	700	700	700	700
Office Equipment	700	700	700	700	700
Insurance	500	500	500	500	500
Advertising	700	700	700	700	700
Accounting	300	300	300	300	300
Fees for electronic payment system	300	300	300	300	300
Miscellaneous	1,000	1,000	1,000	1,000	1,000
Total Fixed Expenses	11,000	11,000	11,000	11,000	11,000
Net Profit (Loss)	$ 4,360	$ 6,920	$ 6,920	$ 6,920	$ 6,920

June	July	Aug	Sept	Oct	Nov	Dec	Year Total
$ 35,000	$ 35,000	$ 35,000	$ 35,000	$ 35,000	$ 35,000	$ 40,000	$ 420,000
17,920	17,920	17,920	17,920	17,920	17,920	20,480	$ 215,040
3,500	3,500	3,500	3,500	3,500	3,500	3,500	$ 42,000
2,500	2,500	2,500	2,500	2,500	2,500	2,500	$ 30,000
800	800	800	800	800	800	800	$ 9,600
700	700	700	700	700	700	700	$ 8,400
700	700	700	700	700	700	700	$ 8,400
500	500	500	500	500	500	500	$ 6,000
700	700	700	700	700	700	700	$ 8,400
300	300	300	300	300	300	300	$ 3,600
300	300	300	300	300	300	300	$ 3,600
1,000	1,000	1,000	1,000	1,000	1,000	1,000	$ 12,000
11,000	11,000	11,000	11,000	11,000	11,000	11,000	$ 132,000
$ 6,920	$ 6,920	$ 6,920	$ 6,920	$ 6,920	$ 6,920	$ 9,480	$ 83,040

Start-Up Cost Estimate

If your profit/loss forecast shows your projected income will be higher than expenses each month, that's a positive sign. But you haven't yet accounted for an important category of expenses: business start-up costs. The worst part about start-up costs is that you need to pay them before your business is actually making any money. That's why you should have a firm grasp on what you really need to spend to successfully start your business and a plan for where that money will come from. Of course, potential lenders or investors will want to see that you've accounted for these costs in your planning. But it's also important that you understand for yourself how high this initial financial hurdle will be so that you can figure out how to clear it. Obviously, you don't want to start a business with high start-up costs but low projected profits, since it will take you far too long to recover your initial investment.

CAUTION

Buy only what your business really needs. Too many new small business owners weigh down their new enterprises with unneeded start-up costs. Unless a particular item is absolutely necessary to generate revenue, don't buy it—or, if you do, spend as little as possible on it. Sure, you need a desk, but unless customers will see it (and sometimes even if they will), repainting a door and laying it across a couple of secondhand filing cabinets at a net cost of $40 makes a lot more sense than paying $800 for a new desk.

Compared to the projections explained earlier, estimating your start-up costs is a breeze—just list them and add them up. Include items like business registration fees and tax deposits you need to pay up front, rent and security deposits you'll have to pay before business starts, costs of any initial inventory, office supplies, equipment, and anything else you'll have to cover before your business starts bringing in money.

EXAMPLE: Inga makes a list of the start-up expenses she expects to pay before she'll start selling books.

Initial inventory	$ 20,000
Rent deposit (security deposit and last month's rent)	7,000
Office supplies, stationery	500
Fax machine	500
Business registration fees	200
Total start-up expenses	$ 28,200

If you don't have enough cash to pay all of your start-up costs out of pocket, you'll either need to come up with the money or figure out a way to spread the costs over the first few months of business when you'll have at least some cash flowing in. For instance, maybe you could lease, rather than buy, needed equipment.

The next and final financial projection you'll need to do as part of your business plan—a cash flow projection—will help you plan and manage your incoming and outgoing cash so that you can cover needed expenses when they come due.

Cash Flow Projection

To round out the collection of financial information in your business plan, you should include a cash flow projection. Though your profit/loss forecast may show that your business should make enough sales at a high enough price to cover your estimated expenses, a cash flow projection analyzes whether the cash from those sales, as well as from other sources, such as loans or investments, will come in fast enough to pay your bills on time. Cash flow management is important once your business is up and running, especially if you plan to stock a good-sized inventory or extend credit to customers. A high sales volume won't be enough to cover your expenses if your customers are slow to pay you and your checking account is empty.

FORM ON CD-ROM

Cash Flow Projection Worksheet. On the CD-ROM that comes with this book, you'll find an interactive worksheet to help you do a cash flow forecast. The file name of the worksheet is CashFlow.xls. For the automatic calculations in the worksheet to be active, you'll need to open the worksheet in a spreadsheet program such as Microsoft *Excel*.

To use the worksheet, follow the steps outlined below. Each step is explained in greater detail later in this section. You should read the detailed information before using the worksheet. Enter figures only into white cells; do not enter anything in blue cells.

Step 1: Enter any cash you expect to have in the bank at the beginning of the period for which you are doing a cash flow forecast. You may change the months to begin with a month other than January. For most start-up businesses, the amount you enter here will be zero. Do not enter any amounts beyond the first month. The worksheet will automatically add any estimated cash available at the end of each month to your cash available for the next month.

Step 2: In the "Cash Ins" section, enter any estimated paid sales (not credit sales) you expect, plus any loans or other money you intend to put into the business.

Step 3: In the "Cash Outs" section, enter the amounts you expect to pay out from your business, in the month you expect to make the payments. The worksheet uses common categories and contains some rows you may customize for expenses specific to your business. If you do not anticipate a certain type of expense, you may leave cells blank.

Result: When you have entered all anticipated cash-ins and cash-outs, the worksheet will display your projected cash flow.

Cash flow projection is also important in your planning stages to show how you intend to survive the first few lean months of business—particularly after you figure in your start-up expenses. If you'll have more than enough cash to cover your expenses for the first months of business, then you're one of the lucky few. More likely you'll be pressed to figure out how to cover a cash deficit for at least the first few months, and maybe longer. One way to do this is to put off or cut some expenses. Another is to hit up your family or friends for a loan, find a bank or other lender willing to provide a start-up loan (which is much easier said than done), or sell part of your business to investors. The important thing is to do

your best to predict your cash needs in advance, both to give yourself ample time to come up with a plan for getting the cash and to inspire more confidence in lenders or investors.

Your cash flow projection will use many of the figures you developed for your profit/loss forecast. But here you'll include all cash inflows and outflows, not just sales revenues and business expenses. Also, you'll record costs in the month that you expect to incur them, rather than spreading annual amounts equally over 12 months. Inflows and outflows of cash that belong in your cash flow analysis include loans, loan payments, and start-up costs. Once you're turning a profit, you'll also include tax payments in your cash flow analysis, but for now let's assume that you'll be free from taxes for your first year.

For each month, start with the actual amount of cash your business will have on hand. Next, fill in your projected cash-ins for the month, which should include sales revenues, loans, transfers of personal money—basically any money that goes into your business checking account. Add these together along with the cash you have at the beginning of the month to get your total cash-ins for the month.

Next enter your projected cash-outs for the month, such as your fixed expenses and any loan payments, and the costs of products and materials you use in your products or services—your variable costs. Add together all your cash-outs to obtain a total for the month. Subtract total monthly cash-outs from total monthly cash-ins and the result will be your cash left at the end of the month. That figure is also your beginning cash balance at the start of the next month; transfer it to the top of the next month's column, and do the whole process over again.

EXAMPLE: Inga projects her cash flow for her first year in business. She starts her projection one month early to account for the money she must spend before she opens her bookstore. In her cash-in section, she figures in $15,000 that she will put into the business: $9,000 of her own savings and an interest-free loan from her sister of $6,000. In her cash-out section, she includes what she'll pay for the initial setup of the business, as well as that month's rent and a $500 allowance for unexpected expenses. Inga

Inga's Book Haus Cash Flow Projection: Year One

	Dec	Jan	Feb	Mar	April
Cash at Beginning of Month	$ 0	$ (17,200)	$ (16,540)	$ (8,920)	$ (3,400)
Cash-Ins					
Sales Paid	0	30,000	35,000	35,000	35,000
Loans and Transfers	15,000	0	0	0	0
Total Cash-Ins	15,000	12,800	18,460	26,080	31,600
Cash-Outs					
Start-up Costs	28,200	0	0	0	0
Books & Other Products	0	14,640	17,080	17,080	17,080
Rent	3,500	3,500	3,500	3,500	3,500
Salaries	0	2,500	2,500	2,500	2,500
Utilities	0	800	800	800	800
Telephone	0	700	700	700	700
Office Equipment	0	1,400	0	2,100	0
Insurance	0	3,000	0	0	0
Advertising	0	700	700	700	700
Accounting	0	300	300	300	300
Electronic Payment System Fees	0	300	300	300	300
Loan Payments	0	500	500	500	500
Miscellaneous	500	1,000	1,000	1,000	1,000
Total Cash-Outs	32,200	29,340	27,380	29,480	27,380
Cash at End of Month	$ (17,200)	$ (16,540)	$ (8,920)	$ (3,400)	$ 4,220

May	June	July	Aug	Sept	Oct	Nov	Dec
$ 4,220	$ 11,840	$ 17,360	$ 21,980	$ 29,600	$ 34,420	$ 42,040	$ 49,660
35,000	35,000	35,000	35,000	35,000	35,000	35,000	40,000
0	0	0	0	0	0	0	0
39,220	46,840	52,360	56,980	64,600	69,420	77,040	89,660
0	0	0	0	0	0	0	0
17,080	17,080	17,080	17,080	17,080	17,080	17,080	19,520
3,500	3,500	3,500	3,500	3,500	3,500	3,500	3,500
2,500	2,500	2,500	2,500	2,500	2,500	2,500	2,500
800	800	800	800	800	800	800	800
700	700	700	700	700	700	700	700
0	2,100	0	0	2,800	0	0	0
0	0	3,000	0	0	0	0	0
700	700	700	700	700	700	700	700
300	300	300	300	300	300	300	300
300	300	300	300	300	300	300	300
500	500	500	500	500	500	500	500
1,000	1,000	1,000	1,000	1,000	1,000	1,000	1,000
27,380	29,480	30,380	27,380	30,180	27,380	27,380	29,820
$ 11,840	$ 17,360	$ 21,980	$ 29,600	$ 34,420	$ 42,040	$ 49,660	$ 59,840

also includes in her cash-out section a $500 payment each month to her sister for the loan.

Notice that Inga's cash-outs look a bit different than her expenses in her profit/loss forecast, even though they add up to the same totals. There are a few reasons for this. One is that Inga includes her inventory costs in the cash-outs section, instead of accounting for those costs in the gross profit calculation, as in her profit/loss forecast. Also, Inga's cash-outs section of the cash flow projection reflects that some expenses are not paid equally every month. For instance, her insurance is paid twice a year, and she plans to buy office equipment in a few chunks.

Also notice that Inga's estimated paid sales (as opposed to sales on credit) for the year come to the same total as her estimated annual sales revenue. That's because, for her first year at least, Inga doesn't plan to take credit cards or checks, only cash and ATM purchases. That way, all her sales will be paid immediately.

Inga's happy to see that by the end of April, she should have cash left in the bank after all her expenses are paid (though she hasn't yet provided for money for her living expenses). Still, she needs to close the cash deficits that she predicts for her first three months in business. Based on her cash flow projection, an extra $17,200 up front would keep her cash flow (barely) in the black. She decides to apply for a loan of $15,000 and try to juggle expenses to cover the remaining $2,200 shortfall.

Once you've completed a year's worth (or more, if you want) of a cash flow projection, you'll have a blueprint for your business's financial situation from month to month. If any months are projected to have a cash deficit, you'll need to tweak your plan to make sure you can cover all of your important expenses. As usual, this means you'll have to juggle, reduce, or cut costs. A cash flow projection that shows difficulty in paying all your bills won't only scare investors away, it may mean that your plan needs serious revision. On the other hand, if your cash flow projection shows that you'll be in the black every month, then you'll be in a good position to show your numbers to potential sources of money—and to get your business under way.

 CAUTION

Credit transactions complicate the picture. Cash flow analysis is concerned with when your business receives or spends money, not when sales or purchases are made. This means that you'll need to account for delayed payments if you do any sales or purchases on credit.

Putting It All Together

Congratulations! You've finished the descriptive and financial aspects of your business plan. While you kick back and enjoy a cold one, think about how you want to put all the information together. If you put the plan together for your own information, then you might want to simply review it, edit anything that needs fixing, print it out, and put it into a binder for your reference. If you plan to present the information as part of a loan request or as a package for investors to review, you might want to do some extra polishing. As mentioned earlier, consider hiring a writer to help you develop the information into a well-written, persuasive document. The bottom line is to package the information as needed for your specific purposes. One of those purposes may be to raise start-up money.

Using Your Plan to Raise Start-Up Money

With a solid business plan in place, you're well positioned to seek start-up funds. Before you start your quest for cash, however, you'll need to understand the types and sources of financing generally available to start-up businesses. This section provides an overview of key concepts you need to know and common lending sources to consider.

The reality is that it's much harder for start-up businesses to secure financing than for existing businesses, for the simple reason that start-ups lack any history of success or creditworthiness.

And it's also tough for them to secure funds from conventional lenders such as banks. But your chances will be improved by understanding some basics about how financing works and by knowing where to look beyond the traditional funding sources.

RESOURCE

For more on business planning and start-up financing. See *How to Write a Business Plan*, by Mike McKeever (Nolo). It offers in-depth information on preparing a business plan to submit to financiers and includes up-to-date information on funding sources.

Basic Types of Financing

An initial, fundamental distinction you should understand is the difference between debt financing and equity financing. The concepts are simple. With debt financing, you borrow money that needs to be repaid; equity financing involves receiving money in exchange for an ownership share, or equity, in your business. Debt financing involves a repayable loan; equity financing means acquiring new owners who invest cash in your business.

Unless you originally planned to get money by acquiring investors, chances are that a business loan is a more practical option for your business. Not only will bringing new owners into your business involve potentially complicated issues related to the legal structure of your business, but it will dilute the shares that you and any other original partners own. This means your share of business profits will be reduced, and—potentially even more troubling—you may have to share management control and decision-making authority with the new owners, raising the distinct possibility of conflict.

One way to avoid this is to bring on investors as limited partners who will have no authority over business decisions. (See "Partnerships," in Chapter 1, for more on this arrangement.) Still, equity financing involves more structural complexities than raising money via a loan.

What Attracts Funders

In addition to making sure you have a solid business plan that shows your business idea to be a winning one, funders will want to know other specific details of your financial situation. One of the most common measures that funders will examine is whether your business has a healthy balance between debt and equity—a relationship that is called a debt-to-equity ratio. Your debt-to-equity ratio is the extent to which your business is in debt to lenders, versus how much you and any other owners have invested in the business. The ratio is calculated simply by dividing outstanding debt by the owners' equity in the business.

EXAMPLE: Sara is considering financing options for her sole proprietorship, which has been in operation for about two years. So far, she has invested $50,000 of her own money into the business and obtained one loan for $15,000, of which she has paid back $5,000. Her debt-to-equity ratio is calculated as follows:

Outstanding debt	$ 10,000
÷ Owner's equity	50,000
= Debt-to-equity ratio	20%

In the most basic terms, lenders want to see a low ratio of debt to equity to make sure your business is not overextended and has sufficient assets to repay the loan. Commercially acceptable debt-to-equity ratios generally range from 50% to 150%—but because any ratios over 100% reflect more debt than equity, they should be viewed with caution. Conversely, if you have nearly no debt, lenders may take it as an indication that your business is not leveraging its assets to make the most of business opportunities.

Of course, when you're seeking a loan for the first time, your debt-to-equity ratio will be zero. The point is to understand the ratio and how lenders view it so that you can keep it in the right range as your business grows.

Sources of Funding

A fact that surprises many entrepreneurs is that the most popular source of start-up funding is the source closest to home: personal savings. A 2005 study by the United States Chamber of Commerce reports that 81% of the small businesses participating in the study used their personal savings to start their businesses. Contrast this with the 2% reporting receiving venture capital or 3% receiving a Small Business Administration (SBA)-guaranteed loan. (See "Sources of Start-Up Funding," below, for more results from this study.)

Statistics aside, start-ups need to be creative when looking for funds. Traditional funders, such as commercial banks, often won't consider your business until you have a successful track record. Happily, alternative sources of funds, such as microlenders and small business incubators, tend to be incredibly helpful, since they give not only money, but support and expertise to nurture your fledgling business. Of course, these sources may not be available in a certain region or may be overflowing with hopeful applicants. Possible sources for start-up funds are discussed below.

Sources of Start-Up Funding

A survey by the U.S. Chamber of Commerce Statistics and Research Center asked business owners to report where they obtained start-up funding. The figures below reflect the percentage of business owners that reported receiving start-up funds from that source.

Venture capital	2%
Revolving credit	3%
SBA loan	3%
Home equity loan	8%
Friend/family loan	15%
Credit card	15%
Bank loan	18%
Personal savings	81%

Source: "Access to Capital: What Funding Sources Work for You?" published by the U.S. Chamber of Commerce Statistics and Research Center, 2005. Available for download at www.uschamber.org.

> **TIP**
>
> **Establish a relationship with a bank.** It's smart to establish a relationship with a bank early in the life of your business, even if you don't need start-up funding. Open an account and use the services it offers to small business owners to establish your business as a trustworthy and reputable customer. With a solid relationship in place, you'll be in a better position to apply for funding down the road—say, via a loan or a line of credit—when your business is growing and needs money to expand.

Community Development Financial Institutions

It's a smart idea to start your search for start-up funding at alternative sources, such as community development financial institutions (CDFIs) in your community. CDFIs, which are certified by the U.S. Treasury, are a fast-growing segment of the business financing market specializing in loans to underserved communities and populations. Sometimes CDFIs are known in a community as a microlender or small business incubator. These funding organizations can be especially helpful for start-ups, businesses with poor credit, and businesses seeking relatively small loans, generally up to $100,000.

CDFIs usually, but not always, have a specific focus, such as improving economic opportunities in blighted communities, or supporting businesses owned by women or minorities. But many of these organizations offer assistance broadly, not just to specific populations or communities. Even better, CDFIs often offer guidance and expertise to your business in addition to financing, which will help your chances of success.

 RESOURCE
For help in finding a CDFI. To find a certified CDFI in your area, go to the CDFI Fund website at www.cdfifund.gov and click "What We Do," then click "Information for the General Public." From that page you will be directed to the lists of certified CDFIs, which can be downloaded in PDF format.

Bank Loans

As mentioned earlier, start-up businesses have a notoriously hard time getting financing from commercial banks. If, however, you are fortunate enough to find a bank willing to finance your start-up, you should understand the basics of how bank loans operate.

Loans can be secured or unsecured. When you obtain a secured loan, you give the creditor an interest in some kind of asset—such as business equipment, real estate, inventory, or receivables—in case you default on the loan. An asset used to secure a loan is called collateral. Lenders tend to be conservative when appraising the value of the collateral and will only lend a percentage of that value. The loan amount compared to the value of the collateral is called a loan-to-value ratio. An unsecured loan is a loan that is not backed by any collateral.

Because a strong credit history or an established cash flow is essential in obtaining an unsecured loan, most start-ups aren't in a good position to obtain one. Also, banks usually require start-up business owners to personally guarantee the loan, which puts your personal assets at risk—even if you are incorporated or have formed an LLC. A personal guarantee can sometimes be avoided if you put up sufficient collateral, but personal guarantees are a necessity for most loans to start-up businesses.

Certain details regarding your loan are obviously crucial, such as the length of time over which you'll pay it off (the term), the interest rate, and any fees you'll need to pay. Most small business loans are short term, from one to three years. And as with most other loans, the longer the loan, the higher the interest rate. Interest rates can be variable or fixed, usually a little higher for a fixed rate. In addition, you may have to pay points or other fees for various aspects of the application process, such as document reviews or credit checks. Find out if there will be any fees for prepayment of the loan.

Small Business Administration

The Small Business Administration, or SBA, has developed programs to help solve the problem of banks being reluctant to lend to small businesses. The SBA does not provide loans itself, but helps businesses secure loans from banks by guaranteeing them—in other words, the SBA promises to repay the loan if the business defaults. To find out about the SBA's guarantee programs and the application process, contact your local SBA office or visit the SBA online at www.sba.gov.

Thinking Locally

Besides using the SBA programs to help secure funding from banks, start-up owners should be savvy about which banks offer the best chances of success. Local community banks that have a vested interest in the health of the local economy tend to be much more supportive of local businesses than big chain banks. And often, the application processes and criteria are softer at the smaller banks.

Similarly, be sure to look into credit unions, savings and loans, and other financial institutions in your area that may have financing programs for small businesses.

Family and Friends

Because start-ups are so commonly turned down by banks and other traditional funders, entrepreneurs often turn to friends and family for an injection of cash. But as you surely know, you must be careful when mixing money, blood, and friendship.

The best way to proceed is to be as businesslike as possible when getting money from family or friends. Draft a promissory note outlining the amount of the loan, the interest rate, and its repayment terms. Make it clear to the person who is lending you the money that you will treat the loan just like a commercial loan from a bank. And follow through with that promise by generating financial reports at least quarterly—and paying back the loan according to the agreed-upon terms.

RESOURCE

Recommended reading on borrowing money from family and friends. For all the information and legal forms you need to raise business capital through loans and gifts, see *Business Loans From Family & Friends: How to Ask, Make It Legal & Make It Work*, by Asheesh Advani (Nolo).

Credit Cards and Personal Financing

If all other options have failed, many tenacious entrepreneurs turn to credit cards and home equity loans to get their ventures off the ground. This route may work, but you must watch for serious potential pitfalls. Credit cards often charge much higher interest rates than business loans and require minimum payments set at such a level that it could take decades to pay off your debt. If you keep high balances on the credit cards and pay just the minimum, your debt can quickly spiral out of control.

Another issue is that a business owner who resorts to credit cards to finance the business may not be as disciplined in managing the debt and spending. While bank lenders typically require financial reports and other proof of solid financial management, credit cards do not—potentially allowing you to get sloppy with your finances. Don't make this mistake. If you use credit cards as start-up funding, be just as serious about your bookkeeping and financial management as if you had a big bank looking over your shoulder.

Home equity loans will usually offer better interest rates than credit cards, but of course, they require you to put your home at risk. If your business fails and you are unable to pay your home loan, you may face foreclosure. Be sure you evaluate this sobering possibility before taking out a loan against your home to finance your new business.

Chapter 4 Checklist: Drafting an Effective Business Plan

☐ Decide how you will use your business plan: to attract investors or for your own use as a blueprint for your business.

☐ Draft narrative sections of your business plan that describe your business in detail.

☐ Put together financial projections for your business, including a break-even analysis, a profit/loss forecast, and a cash flow analysis.

☐ Have a friend or business associate look over your plan—both the descriptive elements and the financial analysis—and make edits or suggestions.

☐ Edit your plan and prepare a final draft. Assemble the various sections of the plan into a final document, and package it as necessary for however you intend to use the plan.

☐ Evaluate your need for financing. If you decide to apply for a loan or to solicit investors, research the institutions in your area that offer potential sources of funds. Even if you decide not to seek financing right away, establish a relationship with a community bank to help your chances of obtaining a loan later.

Pricing, Bidding, and Billing Projects

Pricing is a crucial factor in any business strategy, yet many fledgling business owners have little idea how to go about setting prices that are both competitive and profitable. This chapter explains how to develop your pricing strategy and introduces you to some standard methods for setting prices, whether your business sells services or products.

In addition, this chapter offers guidance for business owners who need to make bids to get work. Service businesses typically fall into this category, though sometimes product-based businesses also need to bid for jobs. This chapter also includes some general tips for the process and an outline for what typical proposals include.

On a cautionary note, be aware that antitrust laws forbid business competitors to fix, or even merely discuss, prices. For this reason, you won't find newsgroups or bulletin boards online where other businesses in a certain industry offer specific information on their pricing. Both online and off, pricing discussions among businesses in the same industry are not just taboo, they're illegal.

Directly sharing pricing information with competitors is illegal, but publishing general information about pricing guidelines is not. Good thing, since pricing is discussed below.

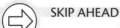

SKIP AHEAD

Product sellers can skip ahead. Business owners who plan only to sell products don't need to deal with service-pricing or service-billing issues. If you don't plan to offer services, skip ahead to "Pricing for Businesses Selling Products."

Pricing and Billing for Service Businesses

Two major components of running a service-based business are setting prices and figuring out how to bill clients. Having rates that are well thought out is a key factor in soliciting clients with confidence. And if you know the best way to bill clients, you can manage your projects for maximum profitability and establish yourself as a true professional. This section explains these two essential tasks for service businesses. Once you understand what drives the pricing and billing processes, you'll find them much easier.

Setting Hourly Rates

Those who work as freelancers or own service-based businesses often find it difficult to figure out what rates to use. Many people struggle with assigning value to their time. Remember that your service rates are not just a measure of the value of your time—they also need to cover your overhead and yield your profits.

There's no single formula to put a price on your services, but there are a couple of common approaches. One formula is based on adjusting the number of billable hours so that revenue equals salary, overhead, and profit. And some businesses base their rates on what the market will bear. Each of these approaches is described in more detail below.

Billable Hours Formula

Many service businesses use a fairly simple formula to calculate their hourly rate. To keep it simple, look at this formula as if you're a solo freelancer without any employees:

> Desired annual salary
> + Annual fixed costs (or overhead)
> + Desired annual profit
> ÷ Annual billable hours
> = Hourly rate

The gist of the formula is that it adds together all the money you want to bring in each year and divides that total by the number of hours you plan to work each year. The result is the hourly rate. This simple formula can be adjusted depending on the specifics of your business.

But first it's a good idea to get a solid grasp on the concepts behind the formula.

- **Desired salary:** This is straightforward. How much would you like to earn annually? Include only salary here; desired profit comes later.
- **Fixed costs:** This is also a simple concept. How much will you spend each year on

rent, utilities, office equipment, computers, and other items of overhead? As discussed in Chapter 4, fixed costs are independent of individual projects or services. You pay them regardless of how much business you're doing.

- **Desired profit:** You're in business to make a profit, not just to bring home a paycheck. A typical profit goal is 20% above salary and overhead (or fixed costs).
- **Billable hours:** There's no single way to estimate this. Basically, the fewer billable hours you estimate, the higher your hourly rate will be; the more billable hours, the lower your hourly rate. A common way to approach this estimate is by calculating the number of potentially billable hours in a year. With 52 weeks in the year and a 40-hour workweek, there are 2,080 potentially billable hours each year. Reduce that total by the number of nonbillable hours you expect to have—vacation, administrative work, or selling, for example. Just use your best estimate here. Very generally, the percentage of your time that is billable will probably be 50% to 80%. Much below that won't be very profitable, and higher than that usually isn't realistic. Use this percentage to determine how many billable hours you'll probably have each year. For instance, if 70% of your time will be billable, you will have 1,456 billable hours (2,080 hours x 70%).

Now add together your desired salary, fixed costs, and desired profit. Then divide that total by your billable hours. The result will be the hourly rate you'll need to charge to cover your fixed costs and bring in your desired salary and profit.

EXAMPLE: Samantha is starting a translation service and wants to figure out her hourly rate. She sets a salary for herself of $30,000 per year and estimates her annual fixed costs to be approximately $25,000. This totals $55,000 for salary and overhead. A 20% profit brings the total to $66,000. Samantha thinks she'll have to spend a good amount of time doing sales and getting her business off the ground, so she figures only about 60% of her time will be billable, resulting in 1,248 available billable hours. By dividing her salary, fixed expenses,

and profit ($66,000) by 1,248 billable hours, Samantha sees that her hourly rate should be $52.88. She rounds that up to $55 per hour.

	Salary	$ 30,000.00
+	Fixed costs	25,000.00
	Total salary and fixed costs	55,000.00
+	20% profit	11,000.00
	Total salary, fixed costs, and profit	66,000.00
÷	Billable hours	1,248
=	Hourly rate	$ 52.88

Setting Market-Based Rates

Another way to set your hourly rate is to throw the formula out the window and simply set your rate for what the market will bear. Be aware that this might not yield a profitable hourly rate, because you're not basing your rate on the actual numbers you'll need to achieve. On the other hand, this approach may be more likely to deliver a rate that customers will accept.

If you base your rates on the market, use any market information you can get to guide you—including what competitors charge, industry standards, and your own experience of using various rates. If you constantly fail to snag clients once you provide a quote, that's a sign your rates may be too high. On the flip side, if you get every job you bid on, you could probably get away with nudging, or even shoving, your rates upward.

  TIP

It is legal to research and use competitors' rates. The antitrust laws mentioned earlier are intended to protect consumers by maintaining competition in the marketplace. The laws are supposed to prevent anticompetitive agreements among competitors to set prices at a certain level. On the other hand, setting your rates to position your business among similar businesses is perfectly legal, so long as you obtained your competitors' pricing information from another source, not directly from them. After all, researching the market and setting prices accordingly is the essence of competition.

FORM ON CD-ROM

Billable Rate Worksheet. On the CD-ROM that comes with this book, you'll find an interactive worksheet to help you calculate an hourly rate for your service business. The file name of the worksheet is BillableRate.xls. For the automatic calculations in the worksheet to be active, you'll need to open the worksheet in a spreadsheet program such as Microsoft *Excel*.

To use the worksheet, follow the steps outlined below. Each step is explained in greater detail later in this section. You should read the detailed information before using the worksheet. Enter figures only into white cells; do not enter anything in blue cells.

Step 1: Enter your desired annual salary. This is your take-home pay, not your overall business profit.

Step 2: Enter your estimated annual fixed costs. (For more on estimating fixed costs, see Chapter 4.)

Step 3: Enter a profit goal for your business, as a percentage you want to exceed salary and fixed costs. A 20% profit goal is typical.

Step 4: If you know how many billable hours you plan to perform in a year, enter that amount. Or, if you're not sure how many billable hours you plan to work in a year, you can work backward by estimating the number of *nonbillable* hours you plan to spend—such as vacationing or doing administrative work—and subtracting those hours from the total number of possible billable hours in one year (2,080). The worksheet asks for your estimated nonbillable hours of various types for time periods that are easiest to estimate (for instance, vacation is estimated in weeks, while administrative work is estimated in hours per day), then converts those figures into annual hourly amounts. If you enter figures both for your estimated billable hours and estimated nonbillable hours, the calculator will use the first figure, estimated billable hours.

Result: The worksheet will show you what hourly rate you should charge in order to make your desired salary, cover your fixed costs, and make your desired profit, assuming you work the number of billable hours you estimated.

It's not a bad idea to use a combination of the formula-based and market-based approaches. Using the formula will help ensure that you set a rate that is profitable, and using the market to adjust the rate up or down will help you stay competitive. For example, if the formula yielded an hourly rate of $45, but other similar businesses charged $65 to $75 per hour, you could feel comfortable increasing your rate to $55 per hour, making your business a bargain while still turning a profit.

Billing Options

Service business owners and freelancers typically use a variety of billing options to accommodate different types of projects and clients. Common billing options include flat fees, hourly billing, or retainer arrangements. Each of these options is discussed below.

Flat Fees

With flat-fee billing, you and your client agree to a total fee for a specific project. In the right situation, it is efficient and professional to charge your client a flat fee for your services. The fee should reflect roughly the number of hours you'll work multiplied by your hourly rate. Contractors typically discount their hourly rates for larger projects.

Billing per project usually makes clients happy because they know up front what their costs will be. Project-based billing can also benefit you. A flat fee encourages efficient project management and reduces the hassle of tracking and billing for your hours (though you should always keep track for your own records).

However, flat fees aren't the best idea for every project. You will feel underpaid if it takes much more work to finish a project than you expected, and the customer will feel overcharged if a project takes much less time than you estimated. If you want to bill per project, it's crucial that you and the client both understand and agree on the project's exact scope. In fact, you should reach this agreement even before you quote a fee. Once the client accepts your fee, the project details should be outlined in a contract. Payment terms can vary, but contractors typically require a deposit of up to one-half of the total fee on signing the project contract.

Sometimes it's not possible to pin down a project with specificity at the outset. Some clients simply don't want to hammer out all details. Other times, a short deadline makes it difficult or impossible to carefully consider all aspects of the project before you start work. In these cases, you're asking for trouble if you set a flat fee.

Suppose, for instance, that a client calls and needs a new section developed for a website ASAP. The owners of the site desperately want you to start immediately, but you have only a vague idea of the work involved. A flat fee here would be a really bad idea. The project could take much longer than you expect, leaving you to do the work for an unfairly low flat rate.

If the project isn't carefully outlined before you start, forget the flat fee; hourly billing is probably the safest way to go.

Hourly Billing

Billing clients by the hour is pretty straightforward: You keep track of how many hours you work and bill the client accordingly. As explained above, you should use this type of billing—also called "time and materials billing"—in situations in which the project isn't well defined.

While billing by the hour will protect you from being underpaid for a poorly defined project that takes more time than you thought it would, the client will never be happy if you present a huge, unexpected bill. Even when you choose hourly

Charging for Outsourced Services

Sometimes service businesses need to hire another contractor (typically called a subcontractor) to get a job done for a client. You can charge your client for the subcontractor's work in different ways. You can simply charge your standard hourly rate for all work completed, whether your company did the work or a subcontractor did. This approach can work for or against you, depending on what you pay the subcontractor. Under a common second approach, businesses mark up the cost of the subcontractors by 15% or 20% or more and bill the client accordingly.

Sometimes the client will hire and pay the sub directly, without a markup. This can work if that piece of the work is discrete, or distinct from the rest, and if the client is responsible for supervising the sub's work and has appropriate liability insurance. However, many contractors prefer to choose and supervise all workers on the same project, for many reasons: They like to have total control over the project, they like to choose subcontractors whose work they trust, they usually make a fair profit on the subcontractor, and it may simplify the project as well as the contractor's potential liability to the subcontractor and the client.

In any case, let your client know in advance whether you plan to use a subcontractor on a project, especially if the subcontractor is a highly skilled specialist and the rate you bill for the subcontractor will be higher than your standard rate.

EXAMPLE: Glenn is a construction contractor with a standard hourly rate of $55 per hour. When hired for a remodeling project, Glenn tells his client he will need to hire a few subcontractors over the course of the project who may have rates higher or lower than his. Glenn and the client come to the understanding that they'll agree to all subcontractors and their rates before Glenn hires them. When it's nearly time to bring in a plumber, Glenn tells his client he'd like to hire Khalsa, whose rate to the client will be $69 per hour. Khalsa's own rate is $60 per hour, but Glenn marks up the rate by 15% to $69 so that he can make a reasonable profit for managing Khalsa on the project.

billing for a project without a clear scope, do your best to work efficiently, communicate with the client, and avoid handing over a surprising bill.

Keep in mind that it's up to you to demonstrate your value to the client—including explaining why your hourly rate is justified and how you spent your hours. Even if you can't define the project specifically enough to set a flat rate, do your best to estimate how long the project will take, and try to keep your hours within your estimates.

TIP

Set reasonable increments when billing.
For instance, will you bill the client a full hour for work that takes you 20 minutes to finish or for a five-minute phone conversation? This approach is generally not recommended because clients think it's unfair. Many people use increments of 15 or 30 minutes for billing purposes. It can be good public relations to show some short phone calls on the bill with no charge attached. That makes the client feel better about the times you round up to the nearest 15 minutes for other tasks.

Retainer Arrangements

In a traditional retainer arrangement, the client pays an ongoing fee, usually monthly, to keep the contractor "on call" for certain services. Retainer arrangements are usually best for clients with predictable needs—for example, regularly updating a law firm's website, providing maintenance services for an apartment building, sewing and tailoring costumes for a theater, or doing public relations for a ski resort. As with flat-rate billing, always define the amount and scope of services expected of you under a retainer arrangement.

In some professional businesses, especially law offices, a "retainer" is requested at the outset that is really a deposit, or a prepayment of fees and costs, usually under a written fee agreement. Lawyers also sometimes use the traditional monthly fee retainer described above.

Jennifer F. Mahoney, owner of an illustration service in Northern California:
It's helpful to learn about the accounts payable process for each client and to understand who in the company releases checks. It's often an entirely different person or department from the one who calls you to offer work. You don't necessarily want to strain your relationship with the person who calls offering you work just because a different department of the business doesn't pay on time. Pave the way for timely payments as much as possible by getting to know the correct procedure, and when it's time to press for payment, you'll know the right person to call.

Bidding and Creating Proposals

Sometimes it is not possible to sell a service or product just by offering it to the public for a certain price. Many service businesses (and some businesses selling products) must submit a bid or a proposal on a project to be considered for the job. (The terms "bid" and "proposal" are often used interchangeably.) If the client accepts the bid, then a contract is typically written and signed to confirm the sale.

Because bids can make or break a sale, you should take care when putting one together, both with the contents of the bid and its physical appearance. Often, the hardest part of bidding is breaking down the project into smaller parts so that you can make good estimates of how much work, time, and materials it will require. Once that's done, it is usually quite easy to write the proposal. This section outlines how to put together a bid to help ensure your chances of success.

SKIP AHEAD

When you don't need to get it in writing.
Businesses selling products usually don't need to worry about bids or proposals. If you don't need to learn about the bidding process, skip ahead to "Pricing for Businesses Selling Products."

TIP
When a proposal becomes a contract. A proposal usually converts to a contract when a client accepts your terms. In practice, however, you should suggest that you sign a separate contract to finalize the agreement with the client. This is partly because it's an opportunity to make sure the client truly understands what you said in your proposal. It's also a good idea because there are things you should cover in a contract that you wouldn't necessarily put in a proposal, such as who provides the insurance, how you will handle extras or change orders, specifics of each side's remedies for breach of contract, which state's laws apply, and whether you will mediate or arbitrate any disagreements. (See Chapter 10 for an in-depth look at how to use contracts in your business.)

Get All the Information You Need

You won't be able to make an effective bid on a project until you thoroughly understand all the details involved. Ask the prospective client as many questions as necessary to flesh out the full scope of the project. A prospective client who's putting a project out to bid among competitors may already have a sheet of specifications, but if you have any questions, be sure to ask them.

Often, the client will want to be involved in certain aspects of the project, so it's important you both agree who will take a primary role in various tasks or duties. Hash out the breakdown of duties and the workflow right at the beginning.

Break Down the Project and Make Estimates

Next, break down the project into manageable components and estimate how much time, labor, and materials you'll need for each one. This is generally the best way to make accurate estimates.

For instance, your head will spin if you try to estimate how long it will take you to complete an entire landscape design project. But once you break the project into parts—grading, spreading gravel, paving, planting trees, and so on—making estimates for the individual bits won't seem nearly as overwhelming.

Multiply the number of hours you expect the project to require by your hourly rate. It's common for freelancers to lower their hourly rates a bit if the project is a large one. This is reasonable, because it's usually more profitable for a freelancer to work consistently on one project than to work piecemeal on several smaller projects.

Sometimes, however, freelancers are tempted to lower their estimates out of fear. After adding up all the hours needed for a large project and multiplying this by their normal hourly rate, they think the fee looks too high and start slashing it to make it more acceptable to the client. Guard against this temptation. It's fine to reduce your hourly fee slightly when you anticipate efficiencies on a large-scale project, but don't sell yourself short just to get the job. Not only will you regret it after you've worked long hours on the project for an unreasonably low fee, but you'll fail to earn respect from clients if you don't ask for the compensation you are worth.

Consider Expenses

Who will be responsible for expenses incurred during the project? The answer varies from project to project; there are no hard and fast rules. Typically, contractors are responsible for covering their own normal expenses of doing business. (However, this is not always true. Attorneys, for example, commonly bill clients for copies and telephone calls.) Clients usually bear printing and production costs, as well as any costs that aren't typical to the contractor's business—such as travel, international phone calls, or equipment rental fees.

In any case, you and the client should agree in advance who will cover which expenses. In addition, make sure to address whether there are any limits on reimbursable expenses or whether the client must approve expenses in advance.

Also nail down the matter of how you will bill the client for expenses. For example, travel expenses are quite often billed to clients. It's wise to make a specific breakdown of the expenses that will be covered—such as airfare, rental car, lodging, taxi, train, parking, and food.

TIP

Proposing reasonable limits on client expenses. Even if your client has deep pockets and seems willing to cover whatever expenses you incur, you should offer some limits on reimbursable expenses. This will help to head off any potential conflicts or unpleasant surprises over reimbursement bills. It also shows the client that you care about giving a good deal.

You can handle payments for expenses a number of different ways. A few possibilities are discussed here.

- **Set an amount that the client will pay, regardless of the amount actually incurred.** For instance, you and the client can agree that the client will pay $1,000 to cover all travel costs. If your actual costs are lower, the extra money will be yours; if higher, you'll eat the difference.
- **Bill the client for actual expenses incurred.** You can do this with or without a cap. For instance, you could agree that the client will reimburse you for all actual travel costs. Or you could agree the client will reimburse you for actual travel costs up to $500.
- **Set a per diem rate for certain expenses.** "Per diem" simply means "per day." Food is typically billed at a set per diem rate—say, $35 or $50 per day.

EXAMPLE: Samantha is working on a bid for a translation project that will require her to travel to Brazil three times during the course of the project. Her client, Bahia Travel Company, says it will cover travel expenses and asks Samantha to draft a proposal specifying the terms. Samantha drafts the following terms regarding travel expenses that she will include in her proposal:

"Samantha will be responsible for all expenses involved in the project, except for travel-related expenses, which Samantha will bill to Bahia Travel Company monthly, as follows:

Airfare: Billed as actually accrued, including all taxes, not to exceed $1,500 per round-trip ticket. Tickets will be economy class.

Rental car: Billed as actually accrued, including insurance and taxes, not to exceed $50 per day.

Lodging: Billed as actually accrued, including all taxes, not to exceed $75 per night.

Food: Billed at $40 per day.

Taxi: Billed as actually accrued.

Parking: Billed as actually accrued."

Write Your Proposal

Once you've finalized all the important details of the project, it's time to put together your proposal. Your goal is to present all important information clearly and professionally and to demonstrate you have a solid plan for getting the job done right. Proposals should always be professional and somewhat formal in tone, but do not be afraid to let your personality show. If you feel stiff, you won't usually have a better bid, just a more stilted one.

Some project proposals are two to three pages long, some exceed 20 pages. There's no hard and fast rule here. You should use as much space as it takes to outline the project details with adequate—but not excruciating—detail. An outline for a project proposal might go something like this:

- **Project overview.** Describe the big picture of the project, including a description of the client and an overview of the project.
- **Project objectives.** Include detailed information about the project, including all the different components of the project and how they fit together.
- **Proposed approach.** Describe how you would approach the project and how you would achieve the client's goals. Be specific, and don't assume that the client knows anything about how you do your work.
- **Specific responsibilities.** Outline your understanding of your specific responsibilities.
- **Deliverables.** This is a term for the specific products that your work will yield. For instance, deliverables might include a 20-page written report, a set of tax documents, or a 100-page travel guide.
- **Timetable.** Scheduling is always an important part of project management, so you should

always outline when you expect certain parts of the project will be completed.

- **Fee and payment terms.** In stating your fee, you don't have to explicitly state your hourly rate or how you arrived at your amount. Simply make it clear that your fee is based on your understanding of the project requirements as outlined in the rest of the proposal.

- **Expenses.** Outline whatever agreement you and the potential client have regarding who will cover which expenses.

- **Conclusion.** Wrap up the proposal. Strive for a professional tone that expresses your enthusiasm for the project. Though some proposals serve as the project contract once the client has accepted them, you will usually state here that you expect to sign a separate formal contract.

Pricing for Businesses Selling Products

As with pricing services, there are different ways to figure out what to charge for the products that your business sells. Of course, your cost of acquiring or making the products will play a big part in your pricing decisions. But you may have difficulty deciding on an appropriate markup. This section walks you through a few issues to consider when pricing goods.

 CAUTION

Don't discuss pricing strategy with competitors. Antitrust laws forbid you to fix prices with your competitors and even to share price information or discuss prices with them. Steer clear of this potentially serious legal trouble.

Establish an Overall Strategy

Before deciding how much you'll charge for your widgets, think about and adopt an overall pricing strategy for your business. Keep in mind that the very same widget might be sold for 99¢ at your local 99¢ store, $5 at a chain retailer, and $25 at a swank boutique. The price can vary so much because each of these stores has its own pricing strategy—and you should, too.

The concept is simple: Will your business use a high-end, middle-end, or low-end strategy? Each strategy can be profitable if you work within its logic. Here's a quick description of how each strategy typically works.

- **High-end** shops can charge high prices so long as they offer something in return, such as a great selection of hard-to-find or highly specialized products, extraordinary customer service, an exclusive atmosphere, or simply top-notch quality.

- **Middle-range** shops charge average prices and succeed on the basis of other factors, such as selection, customer service, and convenient hours and locations. None of these factors are exceptional enough to justify high-end prices, but they're attractive enough to draw customers who aren't necessarily looking for the very lowest price.

- **Low-end** shops succeed by forgoing some amenities, such as a reliable selection or a convenient location. They attract customers by offering the lowest prices. Customers might have to paw through bins of merchandise or drive across town to a cold, cheerless warehouse store, but they'll do it because they know they'll get a bargain.

Whichever strategy you choose, it's important that you stick with it and use it consistently. You will confuse customers and push them to your competitors if you offer a confounding mix of high-end and low-end items in the same store.

Research Markup Data

Once you've got a pricing strategy in place, decide how much you'll mark up your products for sale. You can set your prices appropriately after you do some research to figure out how much other similar businesses mark up their goods.

One easy source of markup information is simply the manufacturer's suggested retail price or MSRP, also called the suggested list price. If you buy a line of floor lamps that cost you $15 per unit and the

MSRP is $45, then you know the manufacturer is recommending a markup of 200% of cost. You don't have to follow the recommendation—the days of strict adherence to MSRPs are over—but you'll get a good idea of what may be typical in the marketplace for that item.

In addition to using MSRPs, ask your manufacturers and suppliers for information they may have on average markup rates. Your suppliers can be a valuable source of this kind of information, beyond setting MSRPs for each product.

You can find good information about industry standard markup rates in many sources. Trade associations and journals may give you valuable data. Directories and guidebooks are also available on many industries. These books tend to be expensive (easily $100 and up) but are often treasure troves of valuable industry info. Hoover's Inc. is a company that specializes in providing comprehensive market data; its website (www.hoovers.com) offers a wealth of information and publications for sale. Many of the titles offered at Hoover's are from Plunkett Research, another firm specializing in market data. Plunkett has its own website at www.plunkettresearch.com.

Don't stop there. Do your own research, and look specifically for info pertaining to your type of business. Search online, visit the library of a local business school, ask local trade associations, and generally do some sleuthing to turn up the data you need.

What's Up With Markup?

Markup is the amount that's tacked on to the cost of an item to arrive at its selling price. For instance, a wristwatch that cost $25 to the retailer may be marked up by $37.50 for a selling price of $62.50. What can be confusing is that markup rates are sometimes expressed as a percentage of cost and other times as a percentage of selling price.

For example, the markup percentage for the wristwatch is 150% of cost or 60% of selling price. What does this mean? The percentage of cost calculation works like this: The cost of the watch ($25) is multiplied by 150%, resulting in a $37.50 markup, which is added to its original cost ($25) to arrive at the selling price of $62.50.

Here is the percentage of selling price calculation: The selling price ($62.50) is multiplied by 60%, resulting in the same $37.50 markup arrived at with the percentage of cost calculation. As you can see, these two different ways of expressing a markup percentage yield the same result.

When you search markup rates, be sure you know which type of percentage you're dealing with, percentage of cost or percentage of selling price. If you apply a percentage of selling price markup rate to the item cost, or use the percentage of cost markup with the item's selling price, you'll end up with the wrong result. For instance, if you mistakenly calculate the wristwatch markup by multiplying the item cost ($25) by the percentage of selling price markup rate (60%), you'll end up with a markup of $15, and a selling price of just $40.

Chapter 5 Checklist: Pricing, Bidding, and Billing Projects

☐ Never discuss the topic of pricing with competitors—basically, anyone in the same industry as you.

☐ Service business owners should set hourly rates carefully, by using a formula, basing their rates on market conditions, or a combination of these approaches. However you set your rates, remember that you'll not only need to earn a salary but also pay for your overhead and make a profit.

☐ If in a service business, you should also become familiar with various ways to bill clients and understand which methods are best for specific situations.

☐ Any business owners who will have to bid for work should learn how to put together a professional proposal.

☐ Those who sell products need to develop an overall pricing strategy to guide their pricing decisions.

☐ Owners of businesses who sell products should research the market to understand what typical markup rates are used by others in the same industry.

Federal, State, and Local Start-Up Requirements

By now you've finished hammering out the details of how you plan to operate your business. In a perfect world, you could hang up your "Open" sign and start selling your products or services at a nice profit. Sorry! In the real world of California business, things are not quite that easy. Before you can legally begin your business, you need to take care of a number of pesky requirements with government agencies from the city to the federal level. Although none of these requirements are difficult or even terribly time consuming, lots of entrepreneurs get stymied at this point because it's so hard to find one centralized source of information that explains what to do. They're left to ferret out each bureaucratic requirement one by one and hope they've found all of them by the time they start doing business.

For example, your city tax office can tell you what forms you must file there, but won't tell you how to obtain a California seller's permit in order to sell retail goods. And while the state Board of Equalization can tell you everything you need to know about getting a seller's permit, it won't explain how to obtain a federal employer identification number, which is required for most businesses. The process of finding out what you need to do and how to go about doing it can feel like putting together a jigsaw puzzle without knowing how many pieces it should have or how it should look when completed.

To help you figure out what you need to do and where you need to do it, all the basic start-up requirements for California businesses are discussed here in this chapter. It guides you through the bureaucratic maze and explains the typical registration requirements that apply to most businesses. (Businesses with employees have to meet a few extra requirements—explained in Chapter 15.) There are far more regulations for specific small businesses than we could possibly cover here—particularly at the state and city levels. But this chapter explains the basic regulatory structure that every businessperson will have to deal with and points out which agencies typically deal with certain types of requirements. By the time you finish reading this chapter, you'll know a number of registration requirements that you will have to meet, plus you'll have a good idea of where to check for other requirements that may apply to

you, depending on what type of business you're starting and where you'll be conducting it.

Sure, dealing with city and state bureaucrats can be a mind-numbing endurance contest. But once the mystery is taken out of the registration process and you have a clear idea of which requirements may apply to you, you'll be able to tackle the bureaucracy with a minimum of time and stress.

One-Stop Shopping for Information on Government Requirements

One of the few centralized sources of small business start-up information is an online clearinghouse called CalGOLD. It's maintained by the California Environmental Protection Agency (CalEPA), but the information it offers isn't restricted to environmental permit issues. When you enter your type of business and the city and county in which it's located, this interactive site will pull up a comprehensive list of registration requirements and contact information for the agencies that administer them. The Web address is www.calgold.ca.gov.

Jennifer Mahoney, owner of an illustration service in Northern California:

I'm lucky enough to have a technical skill to combine with a regular drawing skill that puts me in a market niche among illustrators. Lacking any entrepreneurial "uncles," it took me a while to get a clue about the business world, like finding untapped markets, understanding agreements, getting paid, handling copyright issues, and finding out how many regulatory bodies need a portion of my modest income. It all felt like groping in the dark: Where are all the rules written down? I'm doing well for myself now, supporting my family, but I wish it hadn't taken me so long to figure out.

CAUTION

Slower going for corporations, LLCs, or limited partnerships. Although starting up a company that offers limited liability—a corporation, LLC, limited partnership, or limited liability partnership—isn't rocket science, the process is more complex than starting a sole proprietorship or general partnership. While this chapter outlines the basic start-up requirements for businesses that offer limited liability, you will also need to understand some additional formalities and requirements. For example, if you plan to create one of these types of businesses, you may need to comply with federal and state securities laws. Step 1, below, gives you a brief overview of the extra formation step you'll have to take to set up a business with limited liability. Once you have formed your corporation, LLC, or limited partnership, you'll be ready to use the information in this chapter on permits, licenses, and tax-filing requirements.

Here are the general start-up steps discussed in this chapter:

Step 1: File organizational documents with the California Secretary of State (corporations, LLCs, and limited partnerships only).

Step 2: Obtain a federal employer identification number (FEIN).

Step 3: Register your fictitious business name with your county.

Step 4: Obtain a local tax registration certificate (also known as a business license).

Step 5: Obtain a State of California seller's permit.

Step 6: Obtain specialized vocation-related licenses or environmental permits, if necessary.

Step 1: File With the Secretary of State

SKIP AHEAD

Sole proprietors and partnerships can skip this step. Only corporations, LLCs, limited partnerships, and limited liability partnerships need to file organizational documents with the state. If you're starting a sole proprietorship or partnership, skip ahead to Step 2.

Unlike sole proprietorships or partnerships, businesses with limited liability don't just pop into existence as soon as their owners start selling products or

---

"Why Am I Filling Out All These Forms?"

Why do you have to sort your way through a tangled bureaucracy to start a small business? At the most basic level, there are three purposes to the various business permit and license requirements.

- **To identify you.** No matter what kind of business you run, society has an interest in making sure that you are accountable for your actions. That's why businesses that don't use their owners' names as part of their business names must register a fictitious business name statement with the county in which their business is headquartered. That way, a member of the public who has a problem with Racafrax Designs or Acme Sandblasting can easily find out who the owners are, complain to them, and, if necessary, sue them.

- **To protect the public.** Government agencies issue permits and licenses to ensure that your business offers safe products or services that won't harm people or the environment. For example, if you open a food service business, your city's department of health understandably wants to make sure that your kitchen is sanitary and will likely require that you obtain a permit, license, or other official approval before you can start serving snacks.

- **To keep track of your finances for tax purposes.** Several of the registration requirements are based on the government's nasty habit of taxing everything that moves (and lots of things that don't). To be sure that they collect every possible tax and fee, local, state, and federal governments use various registration requirements to keep tabs on your business.

services. You need to take the first step of explicitly creating a corporation, an LLC, a limited partnership, or limited liability partnership by filing registration papers with the California Secretary of State. For corporations, the necessary papers are called Articles of Incorporation; for LLCs they're called Articles of Organization. Limited partnerships must file a *Certificate of Limited Partnership* (LP-1). Limited liability partnerships file a *Limited Liability Partnership Registration* form. Samples of all four types of organizational documents appear in Appendix C, but this book does not contain the rest of the forms or information necessary to create one of these business types. The samples are for your reference only; to create these business forms you'll need to do additional reading or consult other resources. (See "Additional Resources From Nolo," below.)

When you file your organizational documents with the Secretary of State, you will be registering your corporate, LLC, or limited partnership name at the same time. Before your name can be registered, however, it must be approved by the Secretary of State. Your name won't be approved if another California business of the same legal structure (corporation, LLC, or limited partnership) has already taken that name. A California corporation may not use a name that's used by an existing corporation, an LLC may not use a name that is used by another California LLC, and so on.

If you file your organizational papers without checking on your business name, you run the risk of having to redo the papers with a new name and refile them. To save time and headaches, before you file your papers, check your potential names with the Secretary of State to see if they are available, then reserve one of them. That way, when you file your organizational documents, your business name is sure to be accepted.

Checking and reserving a name by phone both involve a small fee—in 2009, the charge was $4 to check availability and $10 to reserve—and require a prepaid account. The Secretary of State's phone number is 916-653-6814; follow the prompts for each division. More information is available online at www.sos.ca.gov.

Generally, the office will reserve for 60 days the first name on your list that is available.

You may also be able to do a name search in person at one of the California Secretary of State offices (addresses appear below). Call ahead to find out if that office will allow you to search in person. No matter how you search, it is best to reserve a name once you find one that's available.

California Secretary of State Offices	
Sacramento Headquarters 1500 11th Street Sacramento, CA 95814	916-653-6814
Los Angeles Branch 300 S. Spring Street, Room 12513 Los Angeles, CA 90013-1233	213-897-3062
San Diego Branch 1350 Front Street, Suite 2060 San Diego, CA 92101	619-525-4113

Just because your name is accepted by the Secretary of State doesn't mean you're free to use it. As discussed in Chapter 2, trademark and unfair competition laws may prevent you from using a name used by another business, including businesses that aren't included in California's corporate, LLC, or limited partnership name databases. For instance, the name of a general partnership wouldn't be registered in California's corporate name database, but may have been in use for years. Or the name you've chosen may have been taken by a corporation in another state, which means it would not appear in California's database. To avoid running afoul of trademark and unfair competition laws, it's a good idea to do a trademark search before choosing any name for your business, or for its products or services. (Be sure to read Chapter 2 for a full discussion of the legal issues surrounding business names.)

Additional Resources From Nolo

Nolo's Quick LLC: All You Need to Know About Limited Liability Companies and *Form Your Own Limited Liability Company* (includes forms on disk), by Anthony Mancuso, offer guidance on creating an LLC and legal and tax information about this form of business. Also, a software package, *LLCMaker*, and *Your Limited Liability Company: An Operating Manual*, both by Anthony Mancuso, offer detailed information on how to manage LLCs in compliance with various state and federal laws.

On the corporate side, *How to Form Your Own California Corporation*, by Anthony Mancuso, takes you step by step through the requirements for forming a corporation in California. It also explains limited liability partnerships. And *The Corporate Records Handbook: Meetings, Minutes & Resolutions*, also by Anthony Mancuso, provides forms and instructions for running a corporation and handling corporate meetings and documentation.

For more information on limited partnerships, see *Form a Partnership: The Complete Legal Guide*, by Denis Clifford and Ralph Warner.

Step 2: Obtain a Federal Employer Identification Number

Sole proprietors and partners don't need to explicitly "create" their business by registering with any state office; once they're engaged in business activity, their businesses more or less exist by default. (See Chapter 1 for more information about creating all types of businesses, including sole proprietorships and partnerships.) If you're starting a sole proprietorship or a partnership, getting a federal employer identification number from the Internal Revenue Service should be your first registration task, mainly because you can get one before you've registered with any other agency or filled out any other forms.

Corporations and LLCs must also apply for a federal employer identification number, but they have to file their organizational documents with the state first. (See Step 1, above.)

What an FEIN Is and Who Needs One

A business's federal employer identification number (alternately called an FEIN, an EIN, or an employer ID) is roughly equivalent to a Social Security number for an individual. It's a number the government uses to identify your business, and you'll use it over and over again on most of your important business documents, including your business's local tax registration forms, your federal tax return, and any applications for business licenses.

Some of you are probably saying, "But I don't plan to have employees. Why do I need an employer ID number?" Blame the IRS for the confusing terminology. Although it's called an "employer" ID number, FEINs are required for most businesses, even those that don't have employees. The one exception is sole proprietors with no employees, who can use their own Social Security number instead of an FEIN. Partnerships, LLCs, and corporations need FEINs whether they have employees or not.

Applying for an FEIN

Thanks to a mail-in, fax, and phone system, getting an FEIN is easy—and free. Simply fill out and submit IRS Form SS-4, according to the instructions just below. (This book contains two copies of Form SS-4: one in Appendix C, which you can tear out and use, and one on the CD-ROM, along with the IRS's instructions for completing the form.) If you submit the form by mail you'll get your FEIN in about four weeks.

Better yet, by using the IRS's free Tele-TIN phone-in system you can file by phone, get your number the same day, and then send in Form SS-4. To do this, simply call the appropriate Tele-TIN number for your location (listed on the SS-4 form instructions) and relay the information from your completed SS-4 form to the IRS representative, who will then give you your FEIN over the phone. Enter the FEIN in the upper right corner of the SS-4, sign and date the form, then mail or fax it to the Tele-TIN service center within 24 hours of the phone call.

A blank copy of Form SS-4 appears below.

Form **SS-4**
(Rev. January 2009)
Department of the Treasury
Internal Revenue Service

Application for Employer Identification Number

(For use by employers, corporations, partnerships, trusts, estates, churches, government agencies, Indian tribal entities, certain individuals, and others.)

▶ See separate instructions for each line.   ▶ Keep a copy for your records.

OMB No. 1545-0003

EIN

Type or print clearly.

1 Legal name of entity (or individual) for whom the EIN is being requested

2 Trade name of business (if different from name on line 1)

3 Executor, administrator, trustee, "care of" name

4a Mailing address (room, apt., suite no. and street, or P.O. box)

5a Street address (if different) (Do not enter a P.O. box.)

4b City, state, and ZIP code (if foreign, see instructions)

5b City, state, and ZIP code (if foreign, see instructions)

6 County and state where principal business is located

7a Name of principal officer, general partner, grantor, owner, or trustor

7b SSN, ITIN, or EIN

8a Is this application for a limited liability company (LLC) (or a foreign equivalent)? . . . . ☐ Yes ☐ No

8b If 8a is "Yes," enter the number of LLC members . . . . ▶

8c If 8a is "Yes," was the LLC organized in the United States? . . . . ☐ Yes ☐ No

9a **Type of entity** (check only one box). **Caution.** If 8a is "Yes," see the instructions for the correct box to check.

☐ Sole proprietor (SSN) _____
☐ Partnership
☐ Corporation (enter form number to be filed) ▶ _____
☐ Personal service corporation
☐ Church or church-controlled organization
☐ Other nonprofit organization (specify) ▶ _____
☐ Other (specify) ▶

☐ Estate (SSN of decedent) _____
☐ Plan administrator (TIN) _____
☐ Trust (TIN of grantor) _____
☐ National Guard   ☐ State/local government
☐ Farmers' cooperative ☐ Federal government/military
☐ REMIC   ☐ Indian tribal governments/enterprises
Group Exemption Number (GEN) if any ▶

9b If a corporation, name the state or foreign country (if applicable) where incorporated

State

Foreign country

10 **Reason for applying** (check only one box)

☐ Started new business (specify type) ▶ _____
☐ Hired employees (Check the box and see line 13.)
☐ Compliance with IRS withholding regulations
☐ Other (specify) ▶

☐ Banking purpose (specify purpose) ▶ _____
☐ Changed type of organization (specify new type) ▶ _____
☐ Purchased going business
☐ Created a trust (specify type) ▶ _____
☐ Created a pension plan (specify type) ▶ _____

11 Date business started or acquired (month, day, year). See instructions.

12 Closing month of accounting year

13 Highest number of employees expected in the next 12 months (enter -0- if none).

Agricultural	Household	Other

14 Do you expect your employment tax liability to be $1,000 or less in a full calendar year? ☐ Yes ☐ No (If you expect to pay $4,000 or less in total wages in a full calendar year, you can mark "Yes.")

15 First date wages or annuities were paid (month, day, year). **Note.** If applicant is a withholding agent, enter date income will first be paid to nonresident alien (month, day, year) . . . . ▶

16 Check **one** box that best describes the principal activity of your business.
☐ Construction ☐ Rental & leasing ☐ Transportation & warehousing ☐ Health care & social assistance ☐ Wholesale-agent/broker
☐ Real estate ☐ Manufacturing ☐ Finance & insurance ☐ Accommodation & food service ☐ Wholesale-other ☐ Retail
☐ Other (specify)

17 Indicate principal line of merchandise sold, specific construction work done, products produced, or services provided.

18 Has the applicant entity shown on line 1 ever applied for and received an EIN? ☐ Yes ☐ No
If "Yes," write previous EIN here ▶

Third Party Designee

Complete this section **only** if you want to authorize the named individual to receive the entity's EIN and answer questions about the completion of this form.

Designee's name

Designee's telephone number (include area code)
(   )

Address and ZIP code

Designee's fax number (include area code)
(   )

Under penalties of perjury, I declare that I have examined this application, and to the best of my knowledge and belief, it is true, correct, and complete.

Name and title (type or print clearly) ▶

Applicant's telephone number (include area code)
(   )

Signature ▶   Date ▶

Applicant's fax number (include area code)
(   )

For Privacy Act and Paperwork Reduction Act Notice, see separate instructions.   Cat. No. 16055N   Form **SS-4** (Rev. 1-2009)

Keep Your Business Names Straight on Form SS-4

Although most of the information you'll have to put on the form is pretty basic, you need to be careful—and consistent—about names. Here are some tips to help you get the job done.

Line 1 asks for the legal name of the entity that is applying for the FEIN. Sounds simple enough, but it can get a little tricky.

Sole proprietors should enter their full individual name—first, last, and middle initial. Do not enter any fictitious business name (FBN) you use or plan to use. (A fictitious business name is a name you use for your business that doesn't contain your legal name. FBNs are explained in more detail in the next section in Step 3.)

A partnership should use the legal name of the partnership as it appears in the partnership agreement. For example, say Gene Cook and Beth Lynch own a partnership that they refer to as "Cook and Lynch, Partners" in their partnership agreement. This is the name they should write on Line 1. If you own a partnership but don't have a written partnership agreement, insert the name you plan to use for all official business and on all government forms—either a business name that contains each partner's last name or the trade name that you will present to the public (also known as your fictitious business name or your "DBA name," discussed below). (See Chapter 2 for the full spiel on the various types of business names.)

An LLC should enter the official company name as it appears in its Articles of Organization. A corporation should use its legal name as it appears in its Articles of Incorporation.

Line 2 asks for the trade name of the business. This is the same as asking for your fictitious business name or your "doing business as" (DBA) name.

You can leave this line blank if you plan to do business under the name you entered in Line 1. For example, if Gene Cook and Beth Lynch plan to do business under the name Cook and Lynch, Partners, and they entered that name in Line 1, they can leave Line 2 blank. Similarly, if a sole proprietor named Stacey Stickler will use just her name to identify her landscape design services, she, too, can leave Line 2 blank.

But when your company's legal name doesn't match its trade name, you should enter the trade name on Line 2. For example, if Stacey Stickler decides to do business as Stickler's Landscape Design—she should enter that on Line 2. And a partnership that wants to do business under any name other than its legal name would do the same thing. For example, if "Cook and Lynch, Partners" want to do business under the trade name "CooLyn Enterprises," they will enter "Cook and Lynch, Partners" on Line 1 and "CooLyn Enterprises" on Line 2. (You'll find more on trade names and fictitious business names just below in Step 3.)

While it may seem like splitting hairs, your trade name is actually quite important. Think about it: The FEIN form introduces you and your business to the IRS and identifies you in an official way. Using the correct name will help you avoid snafus with the IRS and other government agencies. For example, if the Cook and Lynch partnership goes back and forth between calling its business "Cook and Lynch" and "CooLyn Enterprises" on government documents, then Cook and Lynch will almost surely experience a raft of bureaucratic headaches.

Line 3 to the end of form asks for fairly straight-forward information. For advice, see the Instructions for Form SS-4, included in Appendix C and on the CD-ROM that comes with this book.

Step 3: Register Your Fictitious Business Name

As discussed in Chapter 2, any trade name that doesn't contain the legal names of the owners (for sole proprietorships or general partnerships) or doesn't match the company's corporate, limited partnership, or LLC name on file with the state is called a fictitious business name (FBN). Fictitious business names are sometimes called assumed names or "DBAs" for "doing business as"—as in, "Spikey Andrews, doing business as Coffee Corner" or "Alibi Corporation, doing business as Ferryville Bait and Tackle." In this chapter and the rest of the book, the term fictitious business name will be used for any business name that doesn't contain the legal name of the business owner.

California requires every business that uses a fictitious business name to file a fictitious business name statement with the county clerk in the county in which its primary business site is located.

Counties keep track of business names for a couple of reasons. One is to prevent customer confusion between two local businesses that use the same name. (Before a business owner can register a fictitious business name, the owner will be required to search the county database of registered names to make sure the name isn't already being used.) Another reason is to give customers a quick way to find out who the owner of a company is without having to hire a private investigator. This allows customers to easily contact the owners to make a complaint or to take legal action against them. Requiring owners to register their business names makes it harder for fly-by-night businesses to operate anonymously and defraud customers.

The Importance of Filing an FBN Statement

Do not neglect or put off registering your fictitious business name. Without proof of registration, many banks will not open an account under your business name. Also, if you don't register your name, it won't appear in any county fictitious name databases. This means that another business will be less likely to find out you're using it—and may start using

the name itself. Even though you have other legal avenues to stop another business from using a name that you used first (see Chapter 2), you don't want to create customer confusion between the two businesses and get into a name dispute with another business. If you lose a dispute over a name, at the very least, you'll have to redo stationery, signs, and anything else that contains the name, such as T-shirts or maybe even your company logo.

Who Needs to Register?

The rules for registering fictitious business names depend on which business structure you use:

Sole proprietorships. A sole proprietor who includes his or her last name in the business name—such as O'Toole's Classic Cars—does not need to file an FBN statement. But it is not enough to include only initials, a nickname, or part of a name. For example, a business called J.R.'s Classic Cars would have to file a fictitious name statement indicating that it really is John O'Toole's business.

If your business name falsely implies that additional owners are involved, you must file a fictitious business name statement. If Jason Todd were a sole proprietor, for example, and named his business Jason Todd and Sons, or Jason Todd & Associates, he would have to file an FBN statement, even though he included his last name in his business name.

Partnerships. If a partnership includes the last names of all the partners—for example, Lawrence Anderson and Nancy Fawcett name their business "Anderson and Fawcett Metal Designs"—they don't have to file a statement. Otherwise, an FBN statement will be required. For example, if three partners—Lynch, Cook, and Briggs—did business only under the name "Lynch & Cook," they would have to file an FBN statement.

Corporations, LLCs, and limited partnerships. A corporation, LLC, or limited partnership does not need to file an FBN statement unless it operates under a name different from its official name as stated in its Articles of Incorporation, Articles of Organization, or *Certificate of Limited Partnership*. For example, an LLC that registered with the Secretary of State under the name "Landmark Lanes, LLC" wouldn't have to file an FBN statement as long as it conducted business under that name. Any other trade name, "Landmark Bowl," for instance—or even "Landmark Lanes" without the "LLC" tacked onto the end—would be considered fictitious and would have to be registered. The same is true for corporations: If "Inc." is included in the corporation's name in the Articles of Incorporation, but not in the company's trade name, an FBN statement must be filed.

Filing With Your County

The law governing fictitious business names (Cal. Bus. & Prof. Code §§ 17900 to 17930) applies to the whole state, but is administered by each county. The result is a mammoth exercise in governmental inefficiency, with each county in California issuing different forms and charging different fees for registering an FBN. (In Appendix C and on the CD-ROM, we provide a form that includes all the information required by state law for FBN statements.) Logically, each county should accept this form, but, of course, some clerks will insist that you use specific forms provided by their offices.

Your first step should be to call your county clerk's office to find out its requirements and fees. Many counties allow you to order the FBN registration form by phone; others require you to request it in writing, with a self-addressed stamped envelope. Unless you live a good distance from the nearest county clerk, it may be easiest just to go to the office and complete the form in person. If you'd rather handle the process by mail, call and ask if the office will accept our standard form and, if so, how many copies you must submit and what fees you must pay. If the clerk's office requires filers to use a specific county form, use that form. The clerk will tell you how to obtain one. (You'll find a list of county clerks' websites in Appendix A.)

Searching the County Database

In most counties, you'll be instructed to search the county database of registered fictitious business names before submitting your statement, to make sure no one else has already registered the name you want to use. Typically, you can search a county's database (often an easy-to-search computerized system) for free if you go to the office in person. Sometimes, you can pay a fee for a staff person to do

the search for you. If you want the clerk's office to do the search, you must usually submit the request and fee by mail.

CAUTION

County databases won't tell you if a name is trademarked. Ironically, the county clerk's requirement that you search its database of registered FBNs may well do more harm than good. Why? Because lots of people who find that no one in the county has registered a certain name are misled into believing that the name is free to use.

The truth of the matter is that only the tiniest of businesses can feel safe after doing only a county-wide search of a name they want to use. If someone else is using the name in a neighboring county, or even in a different state or country, you may well run into legal trouble, depending on your geographical scope and the products or services you sell. Particularly with the explosion of e-business, geographical distance is becoming irrelevant as the World Wide Web turns businesses on opposite sides of the globe into neighbors.

To avoid being accused of unfair competition or trademark infringement, it is wise to check neighboring counties' FBN databases, look into California and other state registries of corporate and LLC names, or even do a full international trademark search. Failing to do an appropriate search puts you at risk not only of lawsuits, but also of having to change your name after you start your business when you may already have stationery, business signs, and invoices printed up. Be sure to read Chapter 2 on trademark and business name issues for more information on choosing and researching a name that won't get you into legal trouble.

Completing and Submitting an FBN Statement

If the name you've chosen is free to use, simply fill out the FBN statement and submit it to your county clerk along with the appropriate fees. The following instructions are for the standard form (that follows and is) included in Appendix C and on the CD-ROM with this book.

Item 1: Insert the fictitious business name or names you will use. If you enter more than one, such as "Loaded for Bear Publishing" and "Bear Bones Comics," be sure to number them to make it clear that they're separate names. You're only allowed to register business names used at the same address on a single FBN statement. For instance, if the same owners use more than one fictitious business name at the same location, such as "Snak Central Cafe" and "Turtle Tavern" all under one roof, both names can be registered on one statement. Business names used at different locations—or by different owners at the same location—must be registered on separate FBN statements.

Item 2: Enter the street address of the business. P.O. boxes aren't acceptable. If you're working from home, just enter your home address.

Item 3: Enter the legal name and residence address of the person, people, LLC, or corporation that's registering the fictitious business name. Partnerships should enter this information for each general partner. For LLCs and corporations, use the name in the Articles of Organization or Incorporation that were filed with the Secretary of State and the business's principal address (again, no P.O. boxes). LLCs and corporations should also indicate the state in which they organized or incorporated (probably California) and enter their Articles of Organization or Incorporation number.

Item 4: Indicate what type of business entity you are operating—most likely a sole proprietorship, general partnership, LLC, or corporation. For corporations and LLCs, some counties require you to attach a certified copy of the Articles of Organization or Incorporation. Check with your county for its requirements.

Item 5: Enter the date you started your business or check the box that indicates you haven't opened for business yet. State law requires you to file an FBN statement within 40 days of using a fictitious business name, though this rule isn't strictly monitored.

Item 6: Enter the appropriate signatures. The following people may sign for each specific business type:

Sole proprietorship:	Sole proprietor
Partnership:	General partner
LLC:	Officer or manager
Corporation:	Officer

Whoever signs for an LLC or corporation must indicate his or her title.

You can submit the form in person or by mail. Depending on the county, the fee is generally between $10 and $40 for registering one business name and one business owner. You can also pay an additional fee, around $5 or so, to register additional business names to be used at the same business location or additional owners. In other words, the more owners a business has, the more expensive it is to file an FBN statement.

Publishing Notice of Your FBN Statement

Once you've filed your name and paid the necessary fees, you are free to start doing business under that name—but there is one more catch. Within 30 days of your filing date, you must have your FBN statement published in an approved newspaper in the county in which you filed it. Most county clerks will provide a list of acceptable publications for posting your FBN statement, though by state law any newspaper of general circulation in the county will suffice. (Really, no one reads these notices anyway.) Publishing your statement is dead simple; just take a copy of your completed statement to your publication of choice, which will have a standard format to present the required information.

> **TIP**
>
> **Obscure publications are cheapest.** As long as a newspaper is on the approved list or doesn't otherwise violate your county's rules, there's nothing wrong with picking the cheapest one.

The published notice must run once a week for four consecutive weeks. Within 30 days after the last publication, an affidavit (sometimes called proof of publication) must be filed with the county clerk to show that publication has been completed. Many newspapers that provide publication services will automatically send in the affidavit for you after your ad has completed its run. Make sure to find out whether the publication you use will do this (and double-check after four weeks to make sure it actually has done it). If not, you'll have to get the affidavit from the publication yourself and submit it to the county clerk within the 30-day deadline. If the affidavit isn't filed in time, you may have to start the process all over again.

Office of the County Clerk	**Fees**	**FILING STAMP ONLY**
Address _____ City _____ ☐ First Filing　　☐ Renewal Filing	$ _____ for 1 FBN and registrant $ _____ for each additional FBN filed on same statement and doing business at same location $ _____ for each additional registrant	 **File Number:** _____

FICTITIOUS BUSINESS NAME STATEMENT

THE FOLLOWING PERSON(S) IS (ARE)

1

Fictitious Business Name(s)
1

3.

2

Articles of Incorporation Number (if applicable)
AL#

2 Street Address & City of Principal Place of Business in California (P.O. Box alone not acceptable)　　Zip Code

3 Full Name of Registrant　　　　　　　　　　　if corporation—incorporated in what state

Residence Street Address　　　City　　　State　　　Zip Code

3a Full Name of Registrant　　　　　　　　　　if corporation—incorporated in what state

Residence Street Address　　　City　　　State　　　Zip Code

3b Full Name of Registrant　　　　　　　　　　if corporation—incorporated in what state

Residence Street Address　　　City　　　State　　　Zip Code

4 This Business is conducted by:

( ) an individual　　( ) a general partnership　　( ) joint venture　　( ) a business trust
( ) co-partners　　( ) husband and wife　　( ) a corporation　　( ) a limited partnership
( ) an unincorporated association other than a partnership　　( ) other—please specify _____

5 ( ) The registrant commenced to transact business under name or names listed on (date): _____
( ) Registrant has not yet begun to transact business under the fictitious business name or names listed herein.

6 If registrant is not a corporation or a limited liability company sign below:

SIGNATURE	TYPE OR PRINT NAME
SIGNATURE	TYPE OR PRINT NAME
SIGNATURE	TYPE OR PRINT NAME

6a If registrant is a corporation or a limited liability company sign below:

COMPANY NAME

SIGNATURE & TITLE

TYPE OR PRINT NAME AND TITLE

This statement was filed with the County Clerk of _____ County on date indicated by file stamp above.

NOTICE—THIS FICTITIOUS NAME STATEMENT EXPIRES FIVE YEARS FROM DATE IT WAS FILED IN THE OFFICE OF THE COUNTY CLERK.

A NEW FICTITIOUS BUSINESS NAME STATEMENT MUST BE FILED PRIOR TO THAT DATE. The filing of this statement does not of itself authorize the use in this state of a fictitious business name in violation of the rights of another under federal, state, or common law (SEE SECTION 14400 et seq., Business and Professional Code).

*This form should be **typed** or **printed** legibly in **black ink**.*

TIP

Save your ad receipt. For practical reasons, you may need to prove that you completed your fictitious business name filing requirements, including publication, before your ad has actually run for four weeks. Banks, for instance, want to see that you have met fictitious name rules before they allow you to open an account in that name. Fortunately, a receipt from the newspaper showing that you have paid for publication, along with a copy of the FBN statement certified by the county clerk, is generally sufficient to prove that you've met all the registration requirements, even though the ad hasn't yet run for four weeks. So be sure to get a certified copy of your FBN statement back from the county clerk when you submit it, as well as a receipt from the newspaper when you pay for publishing the statement.

After You File

Legally, your FBN statement must be renewed every five years. You (or someone at your business) should keep track of your expiration date—five years after the date of initial filing. The county clerk will not notify you when your renewal date approaches. Also, you must renew your FBN statement if there is any change in the facts in the statement (except for changes of residence of an owner). If you don't file a new FBN statement when facts change, your FBN statement will expire in 40 days. If you no longer want your FBN registered, your FBN statement will expire as soon as you file a statement of abandonment, which usually costs anywhere from $10 to $40.

Changes to Your Business That Require a New FBN Statement

You'll have to file a new FBN statement in these circumstances:

- business name change
- business address change
- change of business ownership (unless a withdrawing partner files a statement of withdrawal), or
- change of business type (for example, you change your partnership to an LLC).

Step 4: Obtain a Local Tax Registration Certificate

Most cities in California require all businesses (including home businesses) to register with that city's tax collector, regardless of business type, structure, size, or name. Businesses located in rural, unincorporated areas must usually register with the county clerk rather than a city tax collector.

Depending on where you register, the locality may use different names for the process: tax registration, business tax application, business license application, or tax certification, for example. In this book, the terms "tax registration" and "tax registration certificate" are used—and it's best if you don't use the term "business license" when you really mean "tax registration certificate" (or whatever term is used in your locality for tax registration). True licenses, which are discussed in Step 6, below, are typically administered at the state level. Certain businesses must obtain them if they engage in regulated activities, such as selling alcohol or cutting people's hair. Getting such a license often involves taking a test or otherwise proving you're qualified to do a certain activity.

TIP

Some businesses need to satisfy more requirements. Your tax registration certificate is not the same as a specialized license your business might need—such as a permit from the local health department for handling food, from the Federal Communications Commission for broadcasting over the radio waves, or from a regional air management district for emitting particles into the air. (Step 6, below, discusses these specialized licenses and permits.) Whether or not you need one of these licenses or permits, you'll still need to get a tax registration certificate.

The reason you need to register with your local tax collector is that just like the federal and state governments, your local government wants a cut of your business income. The tax registration requirement is basically your local government's way of keeping track of your business so that it will be able to collect any taxes due.

Cities and counties have been known to tax businesses with even more flair and creativity than the feds or the state. Localities tax businesses based on criteria such as net profit, gross income, number of employees, total payroll, number of vehicles, number of machines, and sometimes even seating capacity. In addition, most cities categorize businesses and use different tax structures for each category. Oakland, for instance, taxes media firms at $1.20 per $1,000 of gross receipts, recreation/entertainment businesses at $4.50 per $1,000 of gross receipts, and limousine companies at $75 per vehicle.

For the privilege of registering to pay local taxes, you'll generally have to pay an annual fee, which varies a lot from city to city. Usually the annual fee depends partly on how much tax your business is expected to owe the following year, based on city (or county) tax rates. If the fee is based on estimated taxes, at least part of the registration fee may be a nonrefundable administrative fee—in that case, the other part of the fee will go toward paying your estimated taxes or will be returned to you if your taxes turn out to be lower than expected. In Oakland, for instance, registering your business with the city costs $30, but you must also pay your estimated tax based on your business category and your estimated income for the next year. The estimated tax portion—but not the $30 fee—will be credited towards your tax bill for the next year.

For your city's requirements, call your city tax collector; look under "Tax Collector" in the city government section of your white pages. The tax collector's office will be able to provide you with the forms necessary to register in your city, as well as any breakdown of business categories and tax tables. If you're doing business outside city limits, call your county clerk, usually listed under "County Clerk" in the county government section of the phone book.

Step 5: Obtain a State Seller's Permit

Those who sell merchandise must get a seller's permit from the California Board of Equalization (BOE), which is in charge of collecting taxes from businesses that do retail sales. The permit allows your business to collect sales taxes from customers to cover any sales tax that you'll owe to the BOE. You'll pay any taxes you owe annually, quarterly, or monthly, depending on your sales volume. (See Chapter 8 for a detailed discussion of collecting, reporting, and paying state sales taxes.) This section explains how to get a seller's permit, so you can get on with your business.

Who Needs a Seller's Permit?

Any business—whether it's a sole proprietorship, an LLC, a corporation, or any other type—must have a seller's permit if it sells any tangible goods to the public. Tangible goods are things you can touch, such as furniture or food. Businesses that sell only services are exempt from the seller's permit requirement.

If you plan to sell tangible goods, you'll need a seller's permit whether or not those sales will be taxable. While a seller's permit is required if you sell tangible goods, taxes are due on those sales only if the tangible goods are sold to a final user within the state. In other words, you'll need a seller's permit even to conduct nontaxable sales of tangible goods—such as to a wholesaler or to an out-of-state customer. This means you need to get a sales permit before you begin to sell tangible goods; when the sales are made, you'll distinguish the taxable ones from the nontaxable ones. When it comes time to report and pay sales taxes to the state, you'll be taxed only on the taxable sales. (Reporting and paying sales taxes is covered in more depth in Chapter 8.)

Unfortunately, it's sometimes tricky to figure out whether a permit is required (or whether a sale is taxable), mostly because distinguishing service sales (no permit required) from product sales (permit required) can be tough. For instance, graphic designers were for years subject to confounding BOE rules that treated their work as tangible merchandise. Many designers assumed that they operated a service, not a retail business, and thus never collected or paid sales tax. Several were socked with hefty back taxes and fines because the BOE considered them to be selling tangible goods, rather than providing services. After years of efforts by the Graphic Artists Guild and other groups, the BOE finally clarified the sales tax regulations in 2002, resulting in clearer—and, many say, fairer—treatment of the intangible nature of many graphic artists' work.

As you can see, the rules don't always comply with common sense, so you shouldn't make assumptions about how the BOE will treat your business when it comes to seller's permits and sales taxes. If you can't figure out whether your business needs a seller's permit, check out the BOE's pamphlets (listed below). Or, check out the regulations themselves, which you'll find at the BOE's website at www.boe.ca.gov.

If you want a more definitive answer as to whether your specific business needs a seller's permit, call the BOE at 800-400-7115 and speak with an agent. When describing your business to an agent, give as much detail as you can about what you'll be doing—but not so much information that you invite an audit. It's a good idea not to identify yourself or arouse too much bureaucratic interest in your business.

TIP

Keep track of service and product sales separately. Many businesses both perform services and sell products. A metalsmith, for instance, both repairs jewelry and sells raw materials, such as precious metals and gemstones. If a business sells both labor and goods, it will need a seller's permit. Plus, to assure proper tax reporting, that business will need to keep its labor sales separate from sales of goods, since sales of services aren't taxed. (Chapter 11 explains simple bookkeeping and how to account for taxable sales separately from tax-exempt sales.)

Commonly Requested BOE Publications

In addition to the application forms for seller's permits, the BOE offers hundreds of free publications, including regulations and tax tips for particular businesses.

Some of the more popular BOE pamphlets are:

Pamphlet 22, *Tax Tips for the Dining & Beverage Industry*

Pamphlet 24, *Tax Tips for Liquor Stores*

Pamphlet 25, *Tax Tips for Auto Repair Garages and Service Stations*

Pamphlet 32, *Tax Tips for Purchasers from Mexico*

Pamphlet 35, *Tax Tips for Interior Designers and Decorators*

Pamphlet 37, *Tax Tips for the Graphic Arts Industry*

Pamphlet 76, *Audits and Appeals*

Pamphlet 80B, *Electronic Funds Transfer Program*

Commonly requested regulations include:

Regulation 1501, *Service Enterprises Generally*

Regulation 1502, *Computers, Programs, and Data Processing*

Regulation 1574, *Vending Machine Operators*

Regulation 1602, *Food Products*

Regulation 1668, *Resale Certificates*

Many of these publications are available in Chinese, Spanish, Korean, and Vietnamese.

There are a number of different ways to get BOE publications.

- You can use one of the BOE's order forms to order information by mail. An order form is included in Appendix C; you can also download it from the BOE's website at www.boe.ca.gov.

- If you already know which publication you want, you can call the BOE at 800-400-7115 and order it 24 hours a day by leaving a message. Or call during business hours so that you can ask an agent which publication you need.

- All publications are also available in person at any of the BOE's field offices, which are listed in Appendix C, in the California Seller's Permit Application.

- Finally, a limited selection of the BOE's publications can be downloaded directly from the Web, at www.boe.ca.gov.

Obtaining a Seller's Permit

To obtain a seller's permit, a business must submit Form BOE-400-SPA to the Board of Equalization. A sample copy of BOE-400-SPA appears on the next two pages, and this book contains a tear-out and a digital form for you to fill out and use. (Tear-out forms are in Appendix C; digital copies are on the CD-ROM.) The BOE's instructions are included with the form.

You'll need a seller's permit for each location where you sell goods, but you don't need to apply separately for each one. If you'll sell goods from more than one location, just include the address of each location with your application, and the BOE will issue as many permits as you need from the single application.

Most of the items on the BOE-400-SPA form are self-explanatory, but we'll go through a few tips, below.

Note that if you mail in your application (rather than handing it over in person), you will need to include a photocopy of each owner's driver's license or California ID card with your application. Generally, this rule applies to everyone who signs the application, including sole proprietors, general partners, LLC members, and corporate officers. In addition, partnerships are required to include a copy of the partnership agreement along with the seller's permit application.

When indicating business type, if you and your spouse are co-owners—either as a partnership or as a sole proprietorship at which one spouse occasionally works without pay—the BOE wants you to check the "Married Co-ownership" box. If, instead of being married, you are domestic partners registered with the Secretary of State, check the "Registered Domestic Partnership" box. But if one spouse is a sole proprietor and the other is either an official employee or not involved in the business at all, check the "Sole Owner" box. (See Chapter 1 on different business structures and how a business owner's spouse can sometimes participate in a sole proprietorship.)

EXAMPLE 1: Chris and his wife Amy are starting a small business selling chili peppers that they grow on their ranch in the Central Valley. Since they will both actively work in the business, they will be partners for tax purposes. When filling out their application for a seller's permit, they check the "Married Co-ownership" box.

EXAMPLE 2: Tim is starting a business selling imports from Brazil and other South American countries. His partner, Dan, will do some work for the business, but won't share in management decisions. If Tim decides to hire Dan as an employee and pay employment taxes, he should check the "Sole Owner" box on his seller's permit application. But if he doesn't want to pay employment taxes, he could simply allow Dan to volunteer for the business without being classified as an employee. In that case, Tim would check the "Registered Domestic Partnership" box on the seller's permit application.

The form asks for an estimate of monthly gross sales and taxable sales. Gross sales include all sales, whether taxable or not. Taxable sales generally include sales of tangible products sold to a final user. Nontaxable sales include sales of services and sales of tangible goods to resellers. See Chapter 8 for a discussion of sales taxes in general and of which transactions are subject to sales tax.

The form asks whether you are selling "covered electronic devices," or CEDs, in order to help determine whether you will need to pay an electronic waste recycling fee. CEDs are generally defined as follows:

- televisions that contain cathode ray tubes
- computer monitors that contain cathode ray tubes or use liquid crystal displays (LCD)
- laptop computers
- "bare" cathode ray tubes or any other product that contains a cathode ray tube
- televisions containing LCD screens, which includes any device containing an LCD display greater than 4 inches measured diagonally (viewable size) that has television tuner capability and can process a broadcast, cable, or satellite-transmitted television signal
- plasma televisions, and
- portable DVD Players with LCD screens.

BOE-400-SPA REV. 3 (FRONT) (7-08)

APPLICATION FOR SELLER'S PERMIT

STATE OF CALIFORNIA
BOARD OF EQUALIZATION

1. PERMIT TYPE: *(check one)* ☐ **Regular** ☐ **Temporary**

FOR BOE USE ONLY			

2. TYPE OF OWNERSHIP *(check one)*   * Must provide partnership agreement

☐ Sole Owner   ☐ Married Co-ownership
☐ Corporation   ☐ Limited Liability Company (LLC)
☐ General Partnership   ☐ Unincorporated Business Trust
☐ Limited Partnership (LP)*   ☐ Limited Liability Partnership (LLP)*
(Registered to practice law, accounting or architecture)
☐ Registered Domestic Partnership
☐ Other *(describe)* _____

TAX	IND	OFFICE	PERMIT NUMBER
S			

NAICS CODE	BUS CODE	A.C.C.	REPORTING BASIS	TAX AREA CODE

PROCESSED BY	PERMIT ISSUE DATE ___/___/___	RETURN TYPE ☐ (1) 401-A ☐ (2) 401-EZ VERIFICATION ☐ DL ☐ PA ☐ Other

3. NAME OF SOLE OWNER, CORPORATION, LLC, PARTNERSHIP, OR TRUST

4. STATE OF INCORPORATION OR ORGANIZATION

5. BUSINESS TRADE NAME/"DOING BUSINESS AS" [DBA] *(if any)*

6. DATE YOU WILL BEGIN BUSINESS ACTIVITIES *(month, day, and year)*

7. CORPORATE, LLC, LLP OR LP NUMBER FROM CALIFORNIA SECRETARY OF STATE

8. FEDERAL EMPLOYER IDENTIFICATION NUMBER (FEIN)

CHECK ONE ☐ Owner/Co-Owners ☐ Partners ☐ Registered Domestic Partners ☐ Corp. Officers ☐ LLC Officers/Managers/Members ☐ Trustees/Beneficiaries

Use additional sheets to include information for more than three individuals.

9. FULL NAME *(first, middle, last)*

10. TITLE

11. SOCIAL SECURITY NUMBER *(corporate officers excluded)*

12. DRIVER LICENSE NUMBER *(attach copy)*

13. HOME ADDRESS *(street, city, state, zip code)*

14. HOME TELEPHONE NUMBER ( )

15. NAME OF A PERSONAL REFERENCE NOT LIVING WITH YOU

16. ADDRESS *(street, city, state, zip code)*

17. REFERENCE TELEPHONE NUMBER ( )

18. FULL NAME OF ADDITIONAL PARTNER, OFFICER, OR MEMBER *(first, middle, last)*

19. TITLE

20. SOCIAL SECURITY NUMBER *(corporate officers excluded)*

21. DRIVER LICENSE NUMBER *(attach copy)*

22. HOME ADDRESS *(street, city, state, zip code)*

23. HOME TELEPHONE NUMBER ( )

24. NAME OF A PERSONAL REFERENCE NOT LIVING WITH YOU

25. ADDRESS *(street, city, state, zip code)*

26. REFERENCE TELEPHONE NUMBER ( )

27. FULL NAME OF ADDITIONAL PARTNER, OFFICER, OR MEMBER *(first, middle, last)*

28. TITLE

29. SOCIAL SECURITY NUMBER *(corporate officers excluded)*

30. DRIVER LICENSE NUMBER *(attach copy)*

31. HOME ADDRESS *(street, city, state, zip code)*

32. HOME TELEPHONE NUMBER ( )

33. NAME OF A PERSONAL REFERENCE NOT LIVING WITH YOU

34. ADDRESS *(street, city, state, zip code)*

35. REFERENCE TELEPHONE NUMBER ( )

36. TYPE OF BUSINESS *(check one that best describes your business)*
☐ Retail ☐ Wholesale ☐ Mfg. ☐ Repair ☐ Service ☐ Construction Contractor ☐ Leasing

37. NUMBER OF SELLING LOCATIONS *(if 2 or more, see Item No. 66)*

38. WHAT ITEMS WILL YOU SELL?

39. CHECK ONE ☐ Full Time ☐ Part Time

40. BUSINESS ADDRESS *(street, city, state, zip code)* [do not list P.O. Box or mailing service]

41. BUSINESS TELEPHONE NUMBER ( )

42. MAILING ADDRESS *(street, city, state, zip code)* [if different from business address]

43. BUSINESS FAX NUMBER ( )

44. BUSINESS EMAIL ADDRESS

45. BUSINESS WEBSITE ADDRESS
www.

46. DO YOU MAKE INTERNET SALES? ☐ Yes ☐ No

47. NAME OF BUSINESS LANDLORD

48. LANDLORD ADDRESS *(street, city, state, zip code)*

49. LANDLORD TELEPHONE NUMBER ( )

50. PROJECTED MONTHLY GROSS SALES
$

51. PROJECTED MONTHLY TAXABLE SALES
$

52. ALCOHOLIC BEVERAGE CONTROL LICENSE NUMBER *(if applicable)*
___ ___ - ___ ___ ___ ___ ___ ___

53. SELLING NEW TIRES AT RETAIL? ☐ Yes ☐ No

54. SELLING COVERED ELECTRONIC DEVICES? ☐ Yes ☐ No

55. SELLING TOBACCO AT RETAIL? ☐ Yes ☐ No

(continued on reverse)

BOE-400-SPA REV. 3 (BACK) (7-08)

56. NAME OF PERSON MAINTAINING YOUR RECORDS	57. ADDRESS *(street, city, state, zip code)*	58. TELEPHONE NUMBER ( )
59. NAME OF BANK OR OTHER FINANCIAL INSTITUTION *(note whether business or personal)*		60. BANK BRANCH LOCATION
61. NAME OF MERCHANT CREDIT CARD PROCESSOR *(if you accept credit cards)*		62. MERCHANT CARD ACCOUNT NUMBER
63. NAMES OF MAJOR CALIFORNIA-BASED SUPPLIERS	64. ADDRESSES *(street, city, state, zip code)*	65. PRODUCTS PURCHASED

ADDITIONAL SELLING LOCATIONS (List All Other Selling Locations)

66. PHYSICAL LOCATION OR STREET ADDRESS *(attach separate list, if required)*

OWNERSHIP AND ORGANIZATIONAL CHANGES (Do Not Complete for Temporary Permits)

67. ARE YOU BUYING AN EXISTING BUSINESS?

☐ Yes ☐ No   If yes, complete items 70 through 74.

68. ARE YOU CHANGING FROM ONE TYPE OF BUSINESS ORGANIZATION TO ANOTHER (FOR EXAMPLE, FROM A SOLE OWNER TO A CORPORATION OR FROM A PARTNERSHIP TO A LIMITED LIABILITY COMPANY, ETC.)?

☐ Yes ☐ No   If yes, complete items 70 and 71.

69. OTHER OWNERSHIP CHANGES *(please describe)*:

70. FORMER OWNER'S NAME	71. SELLER'S PERMIT NUMBER
72. PURCHASE PRICE $	73. VALUE OF FIXTURES & EQUIPMENT $

74. IF AN ESCROW COMPANY IS REQUESTING A TAX CLEARANCE ON YOUR BEHALF, PLEASE LIST THEIR NAME, ADDRESS, TELEPHONE NUMBER, AND THE ESCROW NUMBER

TEMPORARY PERMIT EVENT INFORMATION

75. PERIOD OF SALES FROM: ___ / ___ / ___ THROUGH: ___ / ___ / ___	76. ESTIMATED EVENT SALES $	77. SPACE RENTAL COST *(if any)* $	78. ADMISSION CHARGED? ☐ Yes ☐ No
79. ORGANIZER OR PROMOTER OF EVENT *(if any)*	80. ADDRESS *(street, city, state, zip code)*		81. TELEPHONE NUMBER ( )

82. ADDRESS OF EVENT *(If more than one, use line 66, above. Attach separate list, if required.)*

CERTIFICATION

All Corporate Officers, LLC Managing Members, Partners, or Owners must sign below.

I am duly authorized to sign the application and certify that the statements made are correct to the best of my knowledge and belief.
I also represent and acknowledge that the applicant will be engaged in or conduct business as a seller of tangible personal property.

NAME *(typed or printed)*	SIGNATURE	DATE
NAME *(typed or printed)*	SIGNATURE	DATE
NAME *(typed or printed)*	SIGNATURE	DATE

FOR BOE USE ONLY

SECURITY REVIEW

☐ BOE-598 ($ _____) or ☐ BOE-1009

REQUIRED BY _____ APPROVED BY _____

FORMS

☐ BOE-8   ☐ BOE-400-Y
☐ BOE-162   ☐ BOE-519
☐ BOE-467   ☐ BOE-1241-D

REGULATIONS

☐ REG. 1668   ☐ REG. 1698
☐ REG. 1700   ☐ _____

PUBLICATIONS

☐ PUB 73   ☐ PUB DE 44

_____
_____

RETURNS

_____
_____

If your business will sell any of the above products, indicate "Yes" on your seller's permit application. Note, however, that not all sales of CEDs will incur the electronic waste recycling fee; there are a number of exceptions. For more detailed information, go to the BOE website at www.boe.ca.gov and search for "electronic waste recycling fee."

BOE-410-D (for Swap Meets, Flea Markets, and Special Events)

Swap meet and flea market vendors need seller's permits too. Even though you're only selling junk from your backyard or garage, you're not exempt from seller's permit requirements. The BOE requires a flea market vendor to get a seller's permit unless the vendor is an "occasional seller," who is defined as follows: "A person who has cleared their garage of used items *accumulated for their own use* and who sells *only* those items would usually qualify as an occasional seller, provided they make sales no more than twice in a 12-month period."

The BOE requires flea market operators to ask individual vendors, including you, for your seller's permit number and other information. (The BOE form for this purpose, BOE-410-D, is included in Appendix C and on the CD-ROM.) If you're a vendor, fill it out and give it to the coordinator of whatever sale you're participating in; don't send it to the BOE.

Step 6: Obtain Special Licenses or Permits

Depending on the nature of your business, you might be finished with your list of bureaucratic tasks. But before you run off to rev up your cash register, cool your jets—you may be surprised to find out that even your simple little business is subject to an extra regulation or two. Some business activities are prohibited until you obtain a license or permit to engage in them, and some business locations require special approval from the local planning department. These extra requirements are especially likely to apply to your business if it has any potential for harming the environment or hurting the public, but they also apply in lots of seemingly risk-free situations.

Figuring out what additional permits or licenses you might need can be confusing, because there are literally hundreds of independent agencies from the local to the federal level that regulate various businesses. Obviously you don't want to waste your time calling each and every one of them to find out whether your business is subject to its rules. This section will help streamline the process by first outlining the basics on what types of activities are generally regulated, and by whom. This should help you figure out whether your business is likely to face a special regulation. Then you'll find here a few resources that will help you make sense of the crazy patchwork of local, state, and federal regulations that might apply to your business.

> **TIP**
> **Regulations have different focuses.** Very generally speaking, local regulations tend to focus on the location of your business and whether it poses a nuisance or a threat to public safety. State and federal regulations typically focus more on the type of work you do and your qualifications to do it.

Zoning and Local Permits

Local business regulations usually deal with the physical location of the business and the safety of the premises and equipment. City zoning laws, for instance, regulate which activities are allowed in particular locations. If a certain location is zoned exclusively for residential use, there isn't enough parking to support your business, or there are too many similar businesses nearby, the zoning board might not approve your business location. Even if your business activities are acceptable for the time being, you might not be allowed to put up the sign you want or put in additional seating once your business takes off.

If your business doesn't comply with zoning laws, you'll either need to get a permit known as a conditional use permit or be granted an exception to the law, sometimes called a variance. Your city or county planning department is generally in charge of zoning laws. Contact them to find out whether your business complies with local rules, and, if not, how to request a conditional use permit or a zoning variance. (Chapter 3 discusses zoning laws and picking a business location.)

Audrey Wackerley, owner of RetroFit, a vintage clothing store in San Francisco:

Getting the right permits turned into a total hassle for our clothing store. After we'd been in business for a year and a half, a cop walked in our store and said we needed a "second-hand" permit. We had never even heard of one! It's not like we hadn't really made an effort to get all the permits we needed. Before we opened, we spent hours in all these different buildings downtown, waiting in endless lines (it's a lot like going to the DMV), asking a million questions to find out what permits we needed to open our store. We had a business license, a seller's permit, a sign permit ... we thought we had everything we needed. But all of a sudden this cop said he'd shut us down if we didn't get the second-hand permit within five days. Five days! The permit cost $700, which was a real stretch for us right then. But what could we do? We had to scramble to get the money together and buy that stupid permit. The cop also let us know that we needed a separate jewelry permit to sell jewelry, but getting the second-hand permit was enough of an ordeal. We just decided to stop selling jewelry.

San Francisco's Permit Agencies

To give you an idea of the types of local regulations that apply to businesses, here's a partial list of agencies in San Francisco and the types of businesses that they regulate:

- **Health Department:** preparers, servers, manufacturers, and marketers of food; laundries
- **Police Department:** billiard parlors, dance halls, massage parlors, street peddlers, taxicabs, valet parking services
- **Fire Department:** garages, storage facilities, service stations, theaters, handlers of hazardous chemicals or gases and
- **Public Works Department:** apartments and hotels.

Assuming your business has met zoning requirements, it still might need to be approved by other city agencies, such as the fire or police departments, the building inspector, or the department of public health. To ensure compliance with local laws, such as health and fire codes, noise laws, and environmental regulations, you may need one or more permits from these agencies. When you register with your local tax collector, you may receive information on these agencies and which types of businesses need to contact them. Your county clerk might also be able to direct you to information about regulatory agencies in your area.

State and Federal Regulations

The State of California keeps track of how you conduct your business. For instance, the state wants to make sure that your cosmetologists are competent and that your carpenters do safe work. The state regulates these business activities through licensing. Businesses are more likely to need a state license or permit if they are highly specialized or if they affect the public welfare. In other words, if there's a risk that poor handling of your business activities might harm the public, chances are good that a state license is required. Common examples of state-licensed businesses are bars, auto shops, health care services, and waste management companies.

Don't assume that your business is so simple or straightforward that you don't need a special license. You'd be amazed at how many activities the state regulates; to name a few, locksmiths must be licensed by the Bureau of Security and Investigative Services; people who train guide dogs must be licensed by the State Board of Guide Dogs; and furniture makers must be licensed by the Bureau of Home Furnishings. If you think some of these regulations sound far-fetched, take a look at a list of California's regulatory agencies.

The federal government doesn't regulate as heavily as local and state offices, but you may need a federal permit or license to engage in certain activities, including:

- operating a common carrier such as a trucking company (Interstate Commerce Commission)
- constructing or operating a radio or television station (Federal Communications Commission)

- manufacturing drugs or meat products (Food and Drug Administration)
- manufacturing alcohol or tobacco products, or making or selling firearms (Bureau of Alcohol, Tobacco and Firearms), and
- providing investment advice or counseling (Securities and Exchange Commission).

License and Permit Information Resources

Fortunately, there are resources that offer help with license and permit questions. Unfortunately, recent budget cuts forced several business assistance offices to close. Note that many of the phone numbers and other contact information you'll find at California government websites are no longer in service.

If you aren't sure what regulations might apply to your business, consult the resources listed below for help figuring out what you need to do to keep your business in full compliance:

- **CalGOLD.** The state Environmental Protection Agency (CalEPA) has an impressive interactive website that offers information on all the government requirements—not just environmental ones—a start-up business needs to know about. The site, located at www.calgold.ca.gov, requires you to enter your business type and location (city and county), then returns a list of all the licenses and permits you'll need from the local to the federal level, as well as contact information for the agencies that administer them. You won't find any detailed information about these requirements, but it still is very helpful to see them all at a glance. On the down side, this website is like any other automated information source in that it can only handle very standard information requests. For example, if you're not sure how to categorize your business, this site won't be of much help.

- **Small Business Development Centers (SBDCs).** In California—and nationwide—networks of SBDCs offer valuable and free assistance to small businesses on a range of issues, including permit and license questions. For a list of SBDCs around the state, go to the California Business Portal website at www.calbusiness.ca.gov, and click the "Grow" tab.

Keep in mind that while the Web is a potentially awesome resource for navigating the permit requirements in your area, many state agencies and local governments are still lagging in posting this kind of practical information. Don't waste your precious time searching endlessly through a government website trying to find the information you need. If it's not readily available at the site, chances are it's either not there or is so hopelessly buried that it's not worth your time to ferret it out. In these situations, it may well be better to just get on the phone or even go to the state office in person.

Chapter 6 Checklist: Federal, State, and Local Start-Up Requirements

☐ File organizational documents with the California Secretary of State (corporations, LLCs, limited partnerships, and limited liability partnerships only).

☐ Obtain a federal employer identification number (FEIN).

☐ Register your fictitious business name with your county.

☐ Obtain a local tax registration certificate.

☐ Obtain a seller's permit from the California Board of Equalization to sell retail goods and collect state sales tax.

☐ Obtain specialized vocation-related licenses or environmental permits if necessary.

Risk Management

Chapter 1 explained the different business structures that exist and how they relate to liability issues. As discussed, creating a corporation or an LLC generally protects business owners from personal liability. If the corporation or LLC loses a lawsuit or otherwise finds itself in debt, only the business will be liable for that debt, not the owners. But in a partnership, each partner is 100% personally liable for all the business's debts and obligations. True, these debts should normally be shared among the partners, and one partner can sue the others to force them to pay up. But this not a very satisfying option if the other partners are broke or have disappeared.

Shielding owners (or employees, as discussed below) from personal liability is a totally different issue from shielding the business itself. In fact, when an individual owner or employee avoids personal liability, you can usually assume that the business will be stuck with it. The owners and employees might be happy they are not personally liable, but there's not much to cheer about when the business assets are wiped out to satisfy a judgment.

The bottom line is that a successful lawsuit against a business can be devastating, whether or not the owners are personally liable for the damages. No matter who ultimately faces liability, every business should consider where risks lurk and how to avoid them. In our litigious society, you must take liability issues seriously and take active steps to protect your business and yourself.

Though the world of possible lawsuits is limited only by lawyers' imaginations, most claims arise from predictable—and often preventable—situations. If you analyze the true risks that face your business and employees, you can learn to recognize where your business is truly vulnerable and reduce the likelihood of ending up in court.

This chapter outlines the typical risks your business might face, and offers guidance on how to reduce them. It also discusses who and what may be at risk—including the owners, the staff, and the business itself. Then it offers risk management strategies and techniques to reduce your exposure to liability.

The encouraging news is that there are things you can do to protect yourself and your business.

Hiring carefully, training thoroughly, having solid personnel policies in place, maintaining a safe working environment, and purchasing insurance are important risk management techniques that all businesses should use. It's crucial to do as much as you can before any legal issues arise.

SEE AN EXPERT

Get advice on possible liability claims. Liability issues typically involve gray areas, so the only way to absolutely determine whether someone will be held responsible for a particular act is to find out in court—an expensive way to get an answer. Use the information in this chapter as a foundation for understanding what can go wrong, and do your best to reduce your risks, but consult an attorney if you fear possible legal trouble. And run, don't walk, to an attorney if you receive an official document, such as a court order, a subpoena, or a written complaint that signals the start of a lawsuit. (See Chapter 16 for advice on finding and working with an attorney.)

Who Might Sue or Be Sued?

Pretty much anyone you deal with in your business can sue you or the business, and vice versa. What you want to do is ward off claims by understanding your risks and taking steps to avoid problems. This section lists what could possibly go wrong for a business, divided according to which people are involved. You can read it as a checklist now, or come back later to make sure you've covered the most likely risks for your business.

The most likely kind of claim or lawsuit that could be brought by or against your business will be over a contract or agreement of some sort. That's because businesses routinely buy, rent, make, sell, or provide products or services—and all of those transactions involve contracts, whether written or oral. Most small businesses find their main problems are money related, whether it's not getting paid by reluctant customers or insurers or not meeting their own financial obligations by paying their suppliers, landlord, or employees. Problems like these are called "contract" claims, because they stem from contractual agreements.

A less likely but extremely serious risk can also arise when someone in or around your business gets injured—financially or personally—by some act not related to a contract. For example, if one of your employees injures someone by being negligent, typically, the business will be liable. A lot of your risk management efforts will be directed at preventing these kinds of claims—called "torts" in legalese—because they can be very costly to you and your business.

Co-Owners

If you are a co-owner of your business, you and the other co-owners have many obligations to one another. That's because mismanaging the business, whether on purpose or unintentionally, can damage the owners' investment and may expose all owners to liability.

Claims between and among owners can arise from one owner:

- lying—for instance, about cash flow or complaints
- self-dealing—working for personal interests instead of the business's
- stealing the business's money or taking business assets for personal use
- handing out profits incorrectly
- selling property for less than it's worth
- conspiring—for example, to defraud or push out one of the co-owners
- failing to live up to the business agreement—for instance, by not contributing the amount of time and money agreed
- mishandling company funds
- mistreating the employees
- making bad deals
- producing bad products or providing poor service
- defrauding lenders, customers, landlords, or suppliers
- failing to pay payroll and income taxes
- violating laws and regulations of various kinds: safety or securities regulations, local ordinances, employment laws, and antitrust laws
- failing to properly hire, train, and supervise employees, or

- failing to observe formalities, such as recording corporate minutes or keeping personal money separate from business money.

There are many possible claims involving those who venture into business together. For example, even if you've done nothing wrong personally, a partner could sue you for your share of partnership debts, which may result in an expensive verdict or settlement. If your co-owner is your spouse and you get divorced, the business could get mired in the tussle over marital assets. Or if you and your co-owners decide to stop being in business together, you could sue each other over mismanagement, unfair competition, wrongfully expelling a partner, or other irregularities in splitting up.

Landlord, Customers, and Other Parties to Business Contracts

As mentioned above, business contracts are a common source of claims and problems. Lenders, suppliers, landlords, and customers could sue you—just as you could sue them—over contracts. For instance, your landlord could claim rent was in arrears or that you damaged the premises. Or you could sue your landlord for failing to make promised repairs or improvements. You could take over a lease or a contract and find that you are obligated for more than you agreed to take on. Customers could claim that your goods are shoddy and your return policy inadequate. Or you could have a supplier who gives you substandard goods.

Injuries outside of contractual agreements are the other main risk. Claims can be based on acts that were either intentionally bad or just unintentionally unfortunate. Customers could be accidentally injured on your premises or by your products. You or another partner could physically assault, harass, or make racially derogatory remarks about a supplier or customer. Your customers could claim that you were not careful enough in hiring, training, and supervising the employees—who subsequently hurt someone or something. You could have a claim if a business contact assaults your employee or steals your property. The people who hire your former employee could claim you gave a falsely positive recommendation.

Employees

Many businesses simply can't operate without employees to help. But while these extra minds and bodies may be essential to the business, they can also be the targets and sources of liabilities and lawsuits.

Owner's Claims Against Employees

A business owner may sometimes be compelled to sue an employee. Theft and property damages are common impetuses—although it may not be cost-effective to take a pilfering employee to court for small reimbursements or money owed for small repairs.

In almost every case, someone who is injured by your employee will choose to sue you—not the employee. An injured person nearly always looks for a way to sue the employer, who usually has assets, including insurance. An employer who has to pay an injured person for harm caused by an employee could theoretically sue the employee for reimbursement, but it's not worth the trouble if the employee has no money.

A rare but important problem is that employees sometimes steal customer lists or a secret process or invention and then go into business in competition with their former bosses. An employee with a head full of business information and years of experience in the field can be a formidable competitor, even without stealing trade secrets or a customer list.

 RESOURCE

For more information on restricting competition. The laws controlling how much and how long you can effectively restrict a former employee or associate from going into competition with you can be tricky. For guidance, see the article on nondisclosure agreements in the Legal Encyclopedia at www.nolo.com.

Owner's Responsibility for Claims Against Employees

A business owner's responsibility for harm done by an employee is an area of potentially very serious liability. There are two different ways an employer may be held responsible for the harmful acts of an employee: when the employer is at fault in some way, and when the employer isn't at fault at all. This is surprising, but unfortunately true.

In general, an employer is liable for everything an employee does "within the course and scope of employment," because the employee acts as the employer's agent. This means that for legal purposes, it is as if the employer directed an employee's every move, simply by authorizing the employee to act. For instance, the U.S. Supreme Court held that a real estate corporation was "vicariously liable" for its salesman's illegal discrimination when he refused to accept a biracial couple's offer to buy a house. (*Meyer v. Holley*, 537 U.S. 280 (2003).) The ruling expressly held that the corporation's sole owner was not personally liable. This effectively protected the corporation owner's other assets by limiting liability to the corporation itself—exactly why some business owners choose to incorporate.

An employer obviously should be held responsible when the employer tells the employee to do something, and the employer knows that act will probably cause harm. An employer who knows or should know that the employee is harming someone or something will also be held culpable.

In addition, an employer is often legally responsible for an employee's acts—even when the employer did not direct the employee to do the act that caused the trouble and didn't know that the employee was doing it—if the employer should have done something to prevent the situation from arising. For example, an employer may be liable for carelessness in hiring, training, or supervising an employee who causes some harm on the job. This can be true even when the harm happens after work hours or away from the work premises, as long as there is some connection to the job.

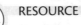 **RESOURCE**

For more in-depth information on employers' potential liabilities. See *The Employer's Legal Handbook*, by Fred S. Steingold, and *The Manager's Legal Handbook*, by Lisa Guerin and Amy DelPo (both published by Nolo).

Risks Facing Employees

Employees may have to pay an injured person for damages for injuries they cause at work by:

- failing to act reasonably and carefully—for example, working without enough sleep when they need to stay alert
- acting with reckless disregard for the safety or interests of others—for example, removing safety equipment from a machine or ignoring warnings on it, or
- hurting someone deliberately or breaking the law.

If the person injured is a coworker, the legal relief is usually limited to workers' compensation benefits.

Liability for Independent Contractors

An independent contractor is someone who works for you but is not a regular employee. (For a discussion of the differences between an independent contractor and an employee, see Chapter 15.)

Employer liability for an independent contractor's acts is a complex area. Because a typical independent contractor works off-site using his or her own equipment and without direct supervision, a business owner usually has little control over how the work is done. Nonetheless, the employer may still be liable to anyone who is hurt by the finished product that the independent contractor produces —for instance, if the employer uses the product at the business site or sells it to the public.

Fortunately, independent contractors often have insurance, so an employer who is sued can in turn sue the independent contractor for mistakes. For more information, see *Consultant & Independent Contractor Agreements*, by Stephen Fishman, and *The Employer's Legal Handbook*, by Fred S. Steingold (both published by Nolo).

Claims by Employees Against Owners

Employment-related claims may pose a major liability risk to businesses with employees. Lawsuits alleging wrongful termination, sexual harassment, or other types of illegal discrimination are a serious risk to all businesses—and possibly to individual owners, managers, and employees. Here's an extremely brief and simplified outline of the types of workplace-related suits commonly faced by businesses.

 RESOURCE

For more information on employee lawsuits. See *The Employer's Legal Handbook*, by Fred S. Steingold; *Dealing With Problem Employees: A Legal Guide*, by Amy DelPo and Lisa Guerin; *The Manager's Legal Handbook*, by Lisa Guerin and Amy DelPo; and *The Essential Guide to Federal Employment Laws* by Lisa Guerin and Amy DelPo (all published by Nolo). You can also get lots of free information online from Nolo's website at www.nolo.com under the heading "HR & Employment Law."

Wrongful Termination

In California, every employee without a written employment contract has a job only as long as both the employer and the employee agree to continue the employment. An employee can quit at any time, for any reason or no reason, and the employer can fire the employee any time, for any or no reason. This is a legal doctrine called "employment at will."

There are major qualifications to that general rule, however, that may open an employer to a lawsuit for firing a worker. For instance, an employer can't fire someone for an illegal reason, such as wrongful discrimination (discussed below), in retaliation for union organizing, or whistleblowing—reporting the employer's wrongdoing to a government agency. In these cases, the employees could sue their former employers for wrongful termination.

And employees who have written contracts setting out conditions of termination—an increasingly rare breed—can sue a business on a claim that the company did not have "good cause" to terminate the employment. This is a "breach of contract" claim.

Most businesses avoid these claims by making it clear in writing that all their employees are at will.

RESOURCE

For more on potential liability for firing workers. See *The Manager's Legal Handbook*, by Lisa Guerin and Amy DelPo (Nolo).

Defamation

A business that gives out false and damaging information about a former employee may be sued for harming that individual's reputation—also called defamation.

Defamation may rear its head when business owners and managers are asked to give references for former employees. In California, there is a legal defense called a "privilege" that protects people who give job references in good faith or when negative information is true. However, if you were sued for defaming a former employee, it would still cost time and money to defend yourself in court.

Another problem is that, while you may believe something to be true, it is always possible to argue about the truth of subjective evaluations and personal experiences. To combat this, some managers refuse to comment at all about any former employee, except to confirm that the employee worked for the business and when. Though this may be a wise policy for commenting on problem former employees, it also limits the opportunity to pass along good information about good workers. It's best to use discretion.

Another time for business owners and managers to beware of the possibility of defaming a worker is during the firing process, when emotions often run high. It's always wise to keep termination discussions brief—and tied to specifics about an individual's work performance.

Sexual Harassment

Sexual harassment is any unwelcome sexual conduct on the job that creates an intimidating, hostile, or offensive work environment—and by now you're surely aware that it can expose a business to liability. Some courts categorize harassing behavior as either "quid pro quo" or "hostile environment."

In quid pro quo harassment—literally, "do this for that"—a worker is confronted with demands for sexual favors to keep a job or get a promotion. Hostile environment harassment is found when sexual jokes, pictures, innuendoes, or comments are allowed to persist in the workplace.

A business can help avoid these types of claims by putting a strong sexual harassment policy in place and strictly enforcing it—along with offering periodic training for all employees on how to recognize and report sexual harassment on the job.

RESOURCE

For more on sexual harassment in the workplace. See *The Essential Guide to Handling Workplace Discrimination & Harassment*, by Deborah C. England (Nolo).

Illegal Discrimination

Federal law prohibits discrimination in employment based on race, skin color, gender, religious beliefs, national origin, disability, or age. And state and local ordinances may also protect additional characteristics, such as medical condition, political activities and affiliations, and sexual orientation. That makes it illegal to use any of these factors in decisions about hiring, promoting, making job assignments, firing, or paying workers. It is even a bad idea to ask questions about those parts of an applicant's background before the business gives the offer to hire. Most businesses use clear job descriptions, review standards, and termination guidelines to avoid claims of discrimination. And, of course, epithets or hostility on the job based on these protected characteristics should not be tolerated.

But discrimination law can get more subtle and complicated, making it necessary to pay attention to reality rather than blindly enforce workplace policies. An apparently neutral job requirement may disproportionately harm members of a protected group. For instance, in California, black male employees have successfully challenged grooming codes requiring all workers to be clean-shaven, on the basis of medical evidence that black men are disproportionately likely to suffer from a skin disorder giving them painful ingrown hairs after shaving.

A growing number of discrimination complaints these days are filed by employees who have disabilities. A federal law, the Americans with Disabilities Act, requires an employer to make "reasonable accommodations" for an employee who has a disability but is otherwise able to do the job— as long as the employee requests an accommodation and the business can provide it without suffering hardship. The accommodation may be buying a special chair, computer, or other equipment, or installing a safety bar in the restroom. It may be allowing the employee to reduce work hours to undergo chemotherapy or reassigning an employee to a job that requires less lifting or standing.

How far the employer must go to accommodate the employee varies on the facts of each situation. The employer need not always provide the most expensive accommodation or the one the employee requests first or most stridently. At a minimum, the employer and the employee should discuss and negotiate what accommodations are possible and reasonable.

The Americans with Disabilities Act also requires many businesses and buildings to be made accessible to people with disabilities. Not complying with that law is another form of illegal discrimination.

Another growing area of discrimination claims arises from bringing religion into the workplace. Employees may complain that they are being harassed by evangelical coworkers or upset by required prayers at business meetings. But if the business forbids all religious practice, employees may claim that they have a right to practice their religion at work, including praying and proselytizing. Employers often handle this by restricting religious and personal postings to a designated bulletin board and prayer groups to nonwork times. However, a business should generally accommodate employees' religious practices, including religious garb and religious holidays.

RESOURCE

For more on illegal discrimination in the workplace. See *The Essential Guide to Handling Workplace Harassment & Discrimination*, by Deborah C. England (Nolo).

Privacy

The flip side of bringing an employee's personal beliefs into the workplace is that many employees do not want an employer to know about their lives outside the office. A manager who inquires about whether an employee went to church on Sunday may be both invading privacy and appearing to discriminate based on religious beliefs.

Various forms of employer testing may also involve privacy concerns for workers. In California, a business may legitimately require a drug test prior to offering a job. The employer may also require drug testing on the job if there are specific and significant reasons why drug testing is necessary, such as when employees handle dangerous machinery or drive on the job. However, many potential legal hazards can be addressed simply by having a rule that forbids being "under the influence" of any substance at work. An employee can be held responsible for truly dangerous or inappropriate behavior without requiring an invasive or humiliating test. Keep in mind that some prescription and over-the-counter drugs also may temporarily affect an employee's mood or concentration.

RESOURCE

For more on drug testing and privacy issues in the workplace. See *The Manager's Legal Handbook*, by Lisa Guerin and Amy DelPo (Nolo).

Personal Injuries

An employee who is injured on the job cannot usually sue the employer or another employee for damages because state workers' compensation laws provide insurance benefits to cover those injuries. State or private disability insurance may also help compensate an injured employee.

RESOURCE

For more information on workers' compensation laws and disability insurance. See *The Employer's Legal Handbook*, by Fred S. Steingold (Nolo).

Outsiders

People you never expect to come into contact with your product or service could be injured by it. And you or your employee might get into an auto accident in a company car, or on company business, and sue or be sued. You might also commit a crime that results in harming someone.

Risk Management Strategies

"Risk management" refers to actively addressing, managing, and reducing risks for any business. It is a rapidly growing field, partly because of the widespread and realistic fear of lawsuits. Your first goal is not to win a lawsuit, but to avoid a claim altogether. Your second goal is to resolve any claim as quickly and cheaply as is appropriate, without a lawsuit. Only as a last resort should you venture to court, because that is usually very expensive and the outcome is always a gamble.

Insurance is part of a risk management program, but be aware that it does not in itself constitute risk management. Sometimes the protection of insurance is adequate, but in some cases insurance may be either too expensive or simply unavailable for particular activities. (See "Insurance and Warranties," below, for more specifics on insurance.)

Here's one example of risk management: Many commercial and industrial sites have residual contamination from solvents, metals, and chemicals. If you buy the property, you may legally have to pay for environmental cleanup, even though the mess wasn't your fault. So, before you purchase, you should consider some ways to manage your risk.

Here are some possibilities.

- You could evaluate the likelihood and extent of contamination with scientific sampling by an engineering firm that also provides an estimate of the probable cost of cleanup. Then you would weigh whether the purchase is worth the additional costs.
- You could try to get protection through contracts—for instance, you could try to purchase insurance directly or to negotiate a reimbursement agreement or an agreement to purchase environmental insurance from the seller.

- You could ask the relevant government agencies for a "comfort letter," in which they promise—or at least come close to promising—that their lawyers will not go after innocent landowners. Your bank may require this letter as a condition of a loan.
- You could look into a federal "brownfields" program, which gives you certain immunities from future surprise liability if you clean up urban industrial land.

As you can see, many options are available to manage that one potentially expensive risk.

Liability Lurks All Around You

There is a sea of laws and regulations controlling safety, land use, business, employment, and other matters that business owners must abide by—and ignorance of them is no excuse. You never know when you will be hauled up short for parking too many cars on the street, having an unsafe workplace, or causing an environmental disaster. You should have a pretty good idea, though, of the kinds of laws that apply to you, especially if you are in a heavily regulated industry, such as manufacturing, food preparation, or professional services. There can be harsh penalties (including prison time) if, for example, you fail to report a workplace death to the appropriate agency.

Finally, it should be no surprise that you can also get in trouble by breaking various criminal laws. Businesses traditionally have special problems with failing to pay taxes, with property crimes such as theft, fraud, and arson, and with antitrust laws that prohibit forming monopolies.

Find Out What Can Go Wrong

A good place to start your risk management program is to outline what you are trying to protect. Most businesses will have a similar list: its people, its physical and financial assets, and its reputation. Keeping these items in mind, you can move ahead to anticipating potential threats to them.

In addition to general risks, find out what can go wrong in your field. Talking with an insurance agent who is familiar with your type of business is one of the best ways to assess the possible risks you face. Talking with people who own or work in similar businesses is also useful, especially outside your local area; if they don't compete with you, it's more likely you can trust what they tell you. Reading trade magazines and the newspapers will keep you abreast of the kinds of lawsuits being brought. And finally, ask your employees what risks they see and what problems are waiting to happen. They may be one of your best sources for ideas to prevent problems.

Focus on Prevention

Once you've identified the main ways that your business is vulnerable, brainstorm ways to protect against these risks.

Setting a Solid Foundation

Most obviously, you should choose your partners, lenders, landlords, business sites, vendors, agents, and employees carefully. In particular, investigate in depth any deal that seems too good to be true—including the sales pitches of people who encourage you to set up in a franchise or buy expensive equipment.

Next, if you will be a joint owner of the business, get a clear understanding with your co-owners about all aspects of your business: what you want to accomplish, what you expect from one another, and how or when you might split up or buy out a co-owner. Agreements known as buy-sell agreements outline how the business will handle transfers of ownership. (Buy-sell agreements are discussed in Chapter 14.)Money is usually the first big issue; control is next. You would be wise to have your business formation agreement in writing, whether it's a simple one-page partnership agreement or a detailed operating agreement for an LLC. If possible, co-owners should agree to mediate disputes that do arise. Mediation is generally quicker, simpler, and cheaper than a lawsuit, which is why the business community has adopted it enthusiastically.

It goes without saying that you should operate your business on the up-and-up. That includes:

- filing all the required papers and getting the right permits
- telling the truth on all documents and to everyone with whom you deal
- keeping track of company funds, inventory, and important documents
- paying your debts
- delivering what you promise
- observing business formalities, such as keeping your personal money separate from business accounts
- putting important agreements into written contracts
- maintaining safety standards, and
- complying with all applicable laws, especially by paying your income and payroll taxes quarterly.

Owners must make sure their businesses comply with bureaucratic requirements. Applying for permits and licenses, filing reports, paying taxes, and so on are necessary evils for all businesses, and failing to do so may, in some cases, expose the owners to personal liability. (Permits, licenses, and other bureaucratic hurdles are covered in detail in Chapter 6.) Even if a manager or another employee is in charge of filling out and filing the paperwork, ultimately it's your responsibility as an owner to make sure your business is in compliance. Check in regularly to make sure that paperwork is getting done.

Risk management can affect your decisions about what your business actually does. You may need to change or eliminate certain activities that are uninsurable or too risky. What is too risky may depend on the law and the availability of insurance—especially for construction, manufacturing, and professional services.

Covering Employee Issues

Employees make businesses vulnerable. Every business owner who hires employees should be very concerned about workplace-related liability issues and take steps to decrease the risks from possible claims and lawsuits. Lay the groundwork to hire carefully, train thoroughly, supervise adequately, have solid personnel policies in place, and maintain a safe working environment.

If you are unsure what your employment policies should be and what laws you must follow, check the Small Business Compliance section of the U.S. Department of Labor website (www.dol.gov) and the California Department of Industrial Relations by phone at 800-963-9424 or at its website at www.dir.ca.gov.

You can also consult a personnel specialist or an HR manager or review other employers' personnel manuals to see what's covered. Nolo (www.nolo.com) also provides good, free information online.

RESOURCE

For in-depth information on employment matters. See *The Employer's Legal Handbook*, by Fred S. Steingold; *Dealing With Problem Employees: A Legal Guide*, by Amy DelPo and Lisa Guerin; *The Manager's Legal Handbook*, by Lisa Guerin and Amy DelPo; *Create Your Own Employee Handbook*, by Lisa Guerin and Amy DelPo; and *The Essential Guide to Federal Employment Laws*, by Amy DelPo and Lisa Guerin (all published by Nolo).

With many workplace issues, the most effective risk management technique is to implement effective policies and training programs. For instance, straightforward hiring and firing policies, including a written policy that employment is "at will," help protect you against claims of discrimination and wrongful termination. A solid orientation and annual training program for employees on sexual harassment and other discrimination issues will significantly reduce your liability exposure in those areas. Every business with employees should have written, posted policies to clarify what behavior is expected and what will not be tolerated.

Similarly, workplace safety issues can be addressed through training programs and posted materials. You can ask consultants who know your type of business to evaluate your workplace for compliance with the Occupational Safety and Health Administration (OSHA)—the agency that establishes and oversees workplace safety standards. Workplace safety will be an ongoing consideration and expense.

Beyond establishing and communicating personnel and other policies, your business needs to have enforcement mechanisms in place. The toughest written sexual harassment or safety policy won't protect a business from a major lawsuit if there's no one to complain to who has power to change the situation, or if complaints go uninvestigated and policies unenforced.

An "open door" policy and a safe channel to launch complaints are very helpful. Employees who understand that their employers are taking care of their concerns are less likely to become frustrated and sue.

Deal With Problems

When a problem does arise, stay as calm as possible while you get as much information as you need to decide what to do. You won't do yourself or your business any good with an unconsidered response.

If a problem comes up in an area that is addressed in a written contract, a calm meeting or phone call is a good idea, followed up by a letter summarizing the meeting or conversation. Any meeting with a problem employee should be witnessed by at least one person who is neutral. If you are out of your depth, contact an expert, such as an accountant, a lawyer, a doctor, an employment law specialist, or a mediator. Keep employment matters confidential.

RESOURCE

For in-depth information on many business problems. See *Legal Guide for Starting & Running a Small Business* and *The Employer's Legal Handbook*, by Fred S. Steingold; *Dealing With Problem Employees: A Legal Guide*, by Amy DelPo and Lisa Guerin; and *Tax Savvy for Small Business*, by Frederick W. Daily (all published by Nolo). There are also numerous articles on lawsuits and personal injuries at Nolo's website at www.nolo.com.

You can ask the employee to agree in advance to refer serious issues to a mediator and then, if they can't be resolved within a reasonable time, to an arbitrator. A mediator is someone who helps people come to an agreement, while an arbitrator makes a binding decision. Many employers have such an agreement in their personnel manuals, which every new employee reads and signs.

It helps morale if the employer pays the costs of mediation and arbitration. After all, the employee probably has very little spare money, and a one-day mediation can commonly cost anywhere from $500 to $3,000. Some community mediation groups will take on small business claims for free or a nominal cost.

Finally, realize that you might end up paying something to settle a claim or to defend yourself, whether or not you feel responsible for what went wrong. As discussed in Chapter 1, owners of sole proprietorships and partnerships are personally liable for all business debts, including damages stemming from a lawsuit against the business. It doesn't matter much whether these owners are personally named or found liable in a lawsuit, or whether only the business itself is—either way, they'll be personally responsible for paying the damages. This fundamental rule regarding sole proprietorships and partnerships is a major reason why many business owners choose to create an LLC or a corporation.

If your small business is an LLC or a corporation (or if you are a limited partner in the business), then you, and owners like you, will ordinarily not be personally responsible for any damage awards against the business. Only business assets can be used to satisfy those debts. Of course, that could wipe out your business.

CAUTION

Personal guarantees may bind you. As a practical matter, most suppliers and banks require a personal guarantee from small business owners on contracts and loans. This means that there will be personal, individual liability on claims arising from those contracts. Similarly, business owners will personally sign the document that creates their business, so the co-owners can sue one another personally on claims that arise out of starting, running, or winding up the business.

All business owners—even owners of corporations and LLCs—may face personal liability in certain situations. Those who recklessly or intentionally cause harm may be found personally liable for injuries caused by their actions. The same is true for business owners who don't carefully investigate a deal before making a business decision.

Paying for What Goes Wrong

If you have been prudent, and if the business is reasonably successful, there will be some extra money in the bank for emergencies. There may be business assets, such as machinery or a building or inventory, that you can sell or pledge to raise money—subject, of course, to agreement by your co-owners. You may also have some insurance that applies. An insurance company has to pay for an attorney to defend you against a claim your policy covers. It will likely also pay some, maybe most, of any eventual settlement or judgment against you if the claim is covered by your policy. (Insurance is discussed in more detail below.)

Insurance and Warranties

Insurance coverage is a powerful tool in risk management. However, there's no requirement that you obtain property or liability insurance for your business, unless:

- you or your employees use a company or personal vehicle for business purposes, in which case California law requires you to have liability coverage
- you have one or more employees, which in California means you must purchase workers' compensation and unemployment insurance (see Chapter 15)
- a contract job (usually with a government agency) requires the contractor (your company) to have a certain amount of insurance, or
- your lender requires it as a condition for getting a loan.

But just because you don't have to get insurance doesn't mean you shouldn't. Even if you form a corporation or an LLC, which shields your personal assets from business liabilities (see Chapter 1), it won't protect you from losing your business if disaster strikes. Careful as you may be, fate sometimes deals an unforeseen blow. If you face unexpected trouble, you'll be thankful you've taken steps to protect yourself.

CAUTION

Employers are subject to special insurance requirements. Employers must typically pay for workers' compensation insurance and unemployment insurance. A handful of states also require employers to pay into a state disability insurance fund. All of these insurance programs are specifically set up for employers and are largely regulated by state agencies. (See Chapter 15 for some of the special rules governing employers' and employees' contributions to these insurance programs.)

There is an art to insuring your business: You want to get the maximum protection from insurance without blowing your whole bankroll on policies for every conceivable risk. Once you start to look, you'll find every imaginable type of insurance policy out there, although your business will probably need only a few of them at most. The two most common and generally useful types of policies are property insurance and liability insurance. The basics of these and many other kinds of policies that cover specific risks involved in your business are covered in this section. It also shines some light on the process of shopping for and buying the policies you need.

TIP

Caring for your policy. Treat your insurance policy just as the precious, and possibly irreplaceable, document that it is. Store it carefully. Keep an old policy even after you change insurance providers. A claim could come up that arises from a long-ago event, and that document may be your only way to track down an insurer that you had in the past. Believe it or not, if the insurance company or its successor is still in business and you have a copy of the old policy to prove it covered that event, the insurance company should provide the protection you paid for at the time.

Property Insurance

This chapter concentrates mostly on liability issues, but other types of losses can also be devastating to a business. Property insurance can cover your business for damages or loss to your business property due to theft, fire, or other causes. There is a good deal of variation among policies on what property and what risks are covered and what the coverage is. Be sure you're absolutely clear on these terms when you choose a policy.

You'll want to make sure that your property insurance covers the premises themselves as well as the business's assets that are kept there, including:

- the property's fixtures, such as lighting systems or carpeting
- equipment and machinery
- office furniture
- computers, telephones, and other office machines, and
- inventory and supplies.

Most basic property insurance policies will cover these items.

TIP

If you rent your business space. Your lease may require you to get a specific amount or type of property coverage. Be sure to check your lease for any insurance requirements before you purchase a policy.

If you purchased your business property. You almost certainly paid for title insurance, which protects you from challenges to your ownership of the property. You may also want to purchase a life insurance policy that is dedicated to paying the mortgage if anything happens to you. You usually get the best deal if you buy this on your own, not from your mortgage lender or broker.

You'll need to understand not only which property is covered by your policy but what types of losses will be covered. Read it carefully to determine what causes of damage are insurable. Most general business property insurance policies will provide basic, broad, or special coverage—with special offering the broadest coverage and basic the narrowest.

A basic form policy will normally cover fire, explosions, storms, smoke, riots, vandalism, and sprinkler leaks. A broad form policy typically covers damage from broken windows and other structural glass, falling objects, and water damage. With both basic and broad form policies, certain risks may be listed as excluded—that is, not covered. Note that theft isn't typically covered under either a basic or broad form policy, a fact that surprises many business owners. (See "Theft Insurance," below.)

Special form coverage offers the widest range of protection, as it typically covers all risks—including theft—except for those risks that are specifically excluded. Although premiums for special form policies are more expensive, they may be worth the added expense if your business faces unusual risks— or simply to make sure you're covered against theft.

A basic policy may not cover the other property that you have at your business premises—for instance, if you rent a laptop or other equipment, or if customers leave their goods with you as happens at a jeweler, dry cleaner, or repair shop. If you expect to regularly have property that belongs to others at your business, get a policy that covers it.

If the policy you're considering excludes one or more items that you want covered, find out whether it can be included and at what cost. You may have to purchase what's commonly called a "rider" or an "endorsement" to add special coverage to the policy. For example, accounting records, cash, and deeds are often excluded from standard property insurance policies but can usually be covered with some extra paperwork—and an additional premium.

You may find other ways to bring the property you want covered under the scope of the policy. For example, if you want the policy to cover your personal stereo that you keep at the office, but the policy only covers business property, one option is to transfer title of the stereo to the business.

Be sure that you clearly understand the dollar limits on your policy and any deductibles or co-payments you'll have to make. Also, make sure the policy covers the replacement cost of the property, not merely its depreciated value. Computer equipment, for example, loses value incredibly fast. If you lost your two-year-old computer to theft, you'd definitely want your insurance to pay for a new computer rather than the value of the stolen one, which might be barely enough to cover the shipping costs of a new machine.

CAUTION

Possible policy adjustments for home-based businesses. Owners of home-based businesses should figure out whether their homeowner's or renter's policies forbid business use of the home or exclude coverage of business-related claims. Make sure that your policy won't be limited or voided entirely by running a business out of your home. It's better to come clean with your insurance company about your home business and maybe spend some extra premium dollars than to find out after a catastrophe that you had no insurance after all.

Liability Insurance

Find out what an available "commercial general liability" (CGL) insurance policy will cover. Ask, for instance, whether it covers negligence—that is, carelessness or recklessness. Most CGL policies do not cover certain employment law claims, such as harassment, discrimination, and wrongful termination. And all insurance companies will refuse to insure you against bad business decisions, criminal acts, or intentional acts of harm.

Personal Injury Liability Insurance

Say, for instance, that someone—a customer or supplier—puts a foot through a floorboard weakened by dry rot, trips on an electric cord, or is hit by a shelving unit that falls over. One accident like that could result in a verdict against your business for tens of thousands or even millions of dollars, even if you were only marginally at fault. For this reason, liability insurance is probably a wise investment for any business that has even minimal contact with the public.

Liability coverage insures you against the notorious slip-and-fall situation, when someone gets injured on your premises and sues you for the ranch. A general liability policy (versus a product liability or vehicle liability policy, discussed below) will cover damages that your business is ordered to pay to an individual such as a customer, supplier, or a business associate who was injured on your property.

Product Liability Insurance

A related, though technically different, type of insurance is product liability insurance, which protects you from lawsuits by customers claiming to be hurt by a product you made, sold, or provided. If your business has a product that has a risk of harming anyone, no matter how far-fetched that risk, you might consider this type of insurance. Plaintiffs have won product liability lawsuits even when they were ignoring warnings or misusing the product. An insurance premium will be less expensive than a big award to a tragically injured plaintiff.

Auto Insurance

Auto liability coverage will not be provided by a general business liability policy, but it is legally required in California. Even if it weren't required by law, it's foolish not to protect yourself against this potentially devastating risk. Insurance coverage for employees' personal cars that are used for business is known as "nonowned auto" liability insurance. This protects your business if an employee hurts someone or damages property while driving his or her car on the job. If your employees will use their own cars for business activities, it's important that you get this type of coverage. Many nonowned auto liability insurance policies do not protect employees themselves, just the business; employees usually need to get their own coverage.

In California, as in most other states, you must by law purchase a minimum level of insurance. California's liability minimums are 15/30/5, which means $15,000 per person for injuries you cause to another person, up to $30,000 for all injuries you cause, and $5,000 for damage you cause to another party's property. Keep in mind that these minimums are quite low, and car accidents can easily cause damages that far exceed these amounts. The extra premium cost for a policy with higher protection levels may be well worth it.

Specialized Insurance

Property and liability insurance are the two most important types of coverage for small businesses, but there are many other kinds of policies. Some of the more common ones are listed below. Keep in mind

that a broad property or liability policy might already cover one or more risks listed here. For instance, if you have special form property insurance (discussed above), you'll probably be insured against theft.

Employment Practices Liability Insurance

This is a relatively new kind of insurance. It can protect you against a number of employee claims, including harassment, discrimination, and wrongful termination. It can be a very useful supplement to commercial general liability insurance.

Business Interruption Insurance

This type of insurance will cover you if your business is forced to close for a period of time for a reason covered under the policy, such as damage from a fire or earthquake. In that case, your policy will pay approximately what you would have earned if you had been open as normal.

"Key Man" Insurance

This is a life insurance policy that the business owns, pays for, and collects on. It protects the business when a crucial person dies unexpectedly and the business grinds to a halt. The "key" person whose life is insured can be the founder, the owner, or an employee—the person who knows everything and holds things together, especially in a small business. This insurance gives the business some extra cash that buys time to decide what to do: whether to hire a replacement, sell the business as a going concern, or wind down gracefully. It is similar in effect to business interruption insurance.

Malpractice Insurance

Often expensive, this type of insurance protects you from lawsuits arising from professional mistakes. Doctors, lawyers, real estate agents, accountants, and a number of other professionals typically need malpractice insurance. It is also known as "errors and omissions" (E & O) insurance.

Theft Insurance

Because many basic policies do not cover losses due to theft, you may want to purchase specific insurance to cover you in case office equipment is stolen. Be sure to find out whether the policy covers employee theft as well as ordinary burglary and robbery. If not, you can usually purchase that type of coverage separately.

Special Coverage

Other types of insurance include credit insurance for accounts receivable, insurance for intellectual property, such as trade secrets or patents, and disability insurance for owners of the business. (This is not the same as state-mandated insurance for employees, discussed in Chapter 15.) Some businesses need insurance for issues that arise out of advertising, while others might need to guard against a big bill for environmental cleanup of purchased real estate. If you are an importer and travel frequently to dangerous foreign locations, you might want kidnap and ransom insurance. Talk with an insurance agent or broker about whether your specific business activities might warrant one or more of these special types of coverage.

Many corporations have special liability insurance called "directors and officers" (D & O) insurance, because there are occasions when directors and officers are sued individually for making employment and other decisions. This comes up, for example, in sexual harassment cases. An insurance agent can tell you when a small corporation needs this type of coverage.

Investigating and Purchasing a Policy

You have to do your homework to make an intelligent and cost-effective insurance purchase. And you must understand both the large and fine print so you can compare policies and purchase the best one for your business. For example, when comparison shopping among different insurance companies, it's useless to compare two policies unless they cover the same types of property, the same risks, and the same payouts and deductibles. You can't make an informed decision until you understand all these details.

Insurance brokers who gather information from different insurance companies can help you decipher policies and figure out your best deal. Make sure any broker you consult understands all the nooks and crannies of your specific business activities and the risks that may be involved. Try to find one who specializes in policies for your type of business. You may be surprised to learn that specially tailored policies already exist that cover your particular needs. For instance, a "producer's package policy" for filmmakers covers several risks unique to the film business, such as the costs of production—often in the tens or hundreds of thousands of dollars—in case your negatives are destroyed. An insurance broker who knows your type of business will be able to direct you to these specialized policies, while a run-of-the-mill broker may not. Check trade magazines for the ads of specialized brokers, and ask other business owners who they use and what they buy.

You'll probably encounter insurance companies that offer package deals that are cheaper than buying several individual policies separately. As long as all your needs are met—and not exceeded—these deals can be a good way to go. As always, be sure you understand the extent of coverage in each area rather than relying on any general promises that the package covers "all your business needs."

RESOURCE

Finding help on the Internet. A couple of websites that may be helpful are IRMI.com, the website of the International Risk Management Institute and the Insurance Information Institute at www.iii.org.

Manufacturer's and Extended Warranties

While insurance can protect you when property is damaged or stolen, product warranties can protect you in case equipment malfunctions for various reasons. Don't overlook the value of warranties when considering ways to reduce risks and potential losses related to your equipment.

Most products come with a standard manufacturer's warranty against defects for a certain period of time. Warranties generally range from 90 days to one year of coverage. It's not uncommon for the warranty to cover parts and labor for different time periods—for example, parts might be covered for one year and labor for 90 days.

In addition, you can purchase extended warranties that offer coverage for longer periods for most equipment, generally from two to five years. Though some manufacturers offer extended warranties to supplement the standard manufacturer's warranty, many extended warranties are sold by companies other than the manufacturer. These companies make big profit margins on extended warranties, leading many consumer advocates, including *Consumer Reports* magazine, to generally advise people against purchasing an extended warranty. However, a *Consumer Reports* article from September 2005 advises that extended warranties might be a good safety net for products such as laptops and plasma TVs due to their high cost and relatively high repair rates.

The truth is there may be some situations in which purchasing an extended warranty makes sense for your business. Generally speaking, the more expensive and important a piece of equipment is to your business, the more an extended warranty might be a smart idea. For example, if your business cannot live without a certain piece of equipment, such as a computer, and would be financially hard-pressed to replace it if it went south, an extended warranty might be a godsend—but always account for the repair time during which you won't be able to use the equipment.

When considering whether to buy an extended warranty, be sure to consider the following factors.

Be clear about when the extended warranty coverage begins and how long it lasts. In particular, don't pay for extended coverage that overlaps with the original manufacturer's warranty. If coverage begins as of the date of purchase of the extended warranty, as opposed to the date of purchase of the equipment, then wait until the original warranty is about to expire before purchasing the extended warranty. Most warranty companies allow this—but be aware that you will usually not be able to purchase an extended warranty if the original warranty has expired. Find out in advance what deadlines apply to the extended warranty purchase.

Make sure you trust the warranty company. Particularly if the warranty is being sold by a third-party warranty company, evaluate the reputation and reliability of that company. If the extended warranty is being sold through a major national retailer, chances are that it is not a fly-by-night scam—though it still may not be worthwhile. But be aware that scam warranty companies do exist.

Evaluate the value of the extended coverage. Weigh the cost of the extended warranty and what it will cover against the cost of the equipment and the likelihood it will need repair. Just as with insurance, warranties generally exclude certain types of damage from coverage. The more limitations on coverage, the lower the value of the warranty.

When you do have warranty protection, whether from an original manufacturer's warranty or an extended warranty, it's crucial to keep track of important warranty details—especially the expiration dates so that you can purchase extended coverage if you so choose. As mentioned above, you will usually not be allowed to purchase an extended warranty if the original or previous extended warranty has expired—so be careful not to let those important dates slip by if you intend to purchase extended coverage.

FORM ON CD-ROM

On the CD-ROM that comes with this book, you'll find a worksheet to help you track your warranty information. The file name of the worksheet is Warranty.xls. The file is meant to be used with a spreadsheet program such as Microsoft *Excel*, but it may also be opened in Microsoft *Word*. Note that sorting and other features will be affected if you do not use *Excel* or another spreadsheet program.

Simply enter all relevant information into the worksheet about warranty coverage for every piece of business equipment you buy. If you don't have information for every column, it's okay, but be sure to include the warranty expiration date. Keep the list sorted by "warranty expiration date" (Column C) in ascending order, so that the warranties about to expire will be at the top of the list. Make it a habit to enter this information as soon as you purchase any equipment, and to review and update the worksheet periodically so that you don't miss any expiration dates and the chance to purchase extended coverage.

Chapter 7 Checklist:
Risk Management

☐ Have active risk management strategies. Start by evaluating your risks and identifying specific ways to reduce them.

☐ If your business has employees, establish personnel policies, including hiring and firing guidelines, policies prohibiting sexual harassment and other discrimination, and effective enforcement mechanisms.

☐ Research and purchase appropriate insurance for your business. Contact an insurance agent or broker familiar with your business to answer your questions and to price out various policies.

☐ Get a property insurance policy that covers against all the types of losses that your business may face, such as theft, fire, and water damage.

☐ Get a liability insurance policy if your business will have any contact with the general public or if you determine there's a significant risk that someone could sue your business for injuries or other damages.

☐ Get auto liability coverage for any vehicles used for business, including the personal cars of employees that are used for business.

Paying Your Taxes

It's no fun for any profitable business to share its hard-won earnings with the government. But like it or not, as soon as your business is in the black, everyone, from your city and county to the State of California and, of course, the IRS, will demand a piece of the action. Although it's not necessary to become a tax expert before going into business, you do need to know what taxes you'll have to pay and how to pay them. Understanding your tax liability will help you be better able to:

- plan your finances, including whether you'll have enough cash to stay in business
- avoid reporting and deposit errors, which can result in hefty (sometimes even business-threatening) penalties, and
- make good business decisions that will reduce your tax burden.

Even if your business won't make a fast profit, you may owe taxes. Lots of new businesspeople believe that if there is no profit, there is no tax. Sadly, this is not the case—local taxes on gross receipts and taxes on sales of retail goods (sales taxes) are but two examples of taxes that need to be paid regardless of whether a business is turning a profit. So even if your business may not be profitable for a year or two, you need to prepare for the possiblity of owing some taxes.

This chapter gives you simple, straightforward information on the taxes that owners of sole proprietorships, partnerships, and LLCs will face. It also provides basic instructions for filing the necessary forms and paying correctly and on time. After covering the basics, it offers the specific tax rules that apply to each business type; there's a separate section for sole proprietorships, partnerships, and LLCs. Simply read the section that's appropriate for your business form and skip the others. Then, the last three sections cover estimated taxes, local taxes, and sales taxes—all of which apply more or less evenly to all business types. If your business is home based, see the section on home business tax deductions in Chapter 9, "Laws, Taxes, and Other Issues for Home Businesses." If your business has employees, refer to Chapter 15 for information on the special taxes employers face.

> **CAUTION**
>
> **Help with corporate taxation issues.** This chapter offers only some broad outlines of corporate taxation. The full maze of corporate tax rules is far too complicated to cover here in detail. If you're thinking about incorporating, keep in mind that doing so will subject you to more complicated (and occasionally unpleasant) tax rules. See the "Corporations" section in Chapter 1 for an overview of the potential tax advantages and disadvantages of corporations. If you need more detailed information, take a look at *Tax Savvy for Small Business*, by Frederick Daily, or *How to Form Your Own California Corporation*, by Anthony Mancuso (both published by Nolo).

> **SEE AN EXPERT**
>
> **Having an accountant handle your federal and state taxes is almost always well worth the expense.** Income tax rules and filing procedures can get complicated quickly, even for a relatively simple business. While it's wise to learn the basics as outlined in this chapter, it's almost always a good idea to turn over the task of preparing federal and state income tax returns to a professional accountant. If you have well-organized records (see Chapter 11 on bookkeeping), annual tax prep for a small to medium-sized business will probably cost less than $1,000. For really small operations it might even be less than $500. Considering the importance of competent tax preparation, you should accept early on that this is an unavoidable cost of running any business. (See Chapter 16 for advice on finding and working with professionals like accountants.)

Tax Basics

One of the first things you should understand is that there's little rhyme or reason to the world of taxes. Don't drive yourself nuts by trying to figure out the logic of a system that has virtually none. The bottom line is that in the United States—and especially in California—governments tax everything they legally can. And this includes virtually every aspect of a business that can be quantified. For example, depending on the type of business and its location, a business might have to pay taxes based on its

Talking About Income—Key Terms Defined

A lot of different jargon is used to describe the money that comes into and flows out of your business. These financial terms are discussed in more detail elsewhere in the book, where we discuss financial projections and accounting (Chapters 4 and 11). Because these concepts are also important in understanding your taxes, here are some brief definitions.

- **Gross versus net.** It's crucial to understand this distinction. "Gross" generally refers to total revenue, before deducting expenses such as salaries, rent, product costs, or office supplies. "Net" means what's left over after subtracting costs and expenses. (As you can see, a "gross" figure will be higher than a "net" figure, because deductions come out of the "gross" and result in the "net.") Thus "gross income" (sometimes called "gross receipts" or "gross sales") refers to the total money your business brings in, before you've begun to cover any of your costs. "Net profit" refers to your income after deducting costs and expenses. In some contexts, "net" may refer to your after-tax profit. In other words, it may reflect not only your costs and expenses, but also any taxes you owe on your income. Be aware that the terms "gross" and "net" are often bandied about loosely. It's important to understand which deductions are included when using these terms.

- **Fixed versus variable expenses.** Fixed expenses are the ones that will be more or less the same regardless of how well your business is doing. They include rent, utility bills, insurance premiums, and loan payments. Variable expenses are the costs of the products or services themselves and anything that goes along with your product, including packaging or shipping. Variable expenses increase or decrease depending on how much business you're doing.

- **Gross profit** refers to how much money you make on each sale above the cost of the item itself (its variable cost). Unlike the term "gross income," which refers to all the money your business brings in before expenses are accounted for, the term "gross profit" does take into account the cost of the product or service you're selling. For example, if a widget costs you $3 and you sell it for $5, your gross profit is $2. The term "profit margin," or "gross margin" is sometimes used to mean the same thing. The key thing to remember about gross profit is that fixed expenses, such as rent or utility bills, are not deducted—only the cost of the product or service itself.

- **Net profit** is what's left over after subtracting fixed expenses from gross profit. Put another way, net profit means the amount of money you have left over after subtracting all expenses—fixed and variable—from your gross income. Sometimes the term "net income" is used to mean the same thing as net profit.

- **Current versus capital expenses.** Current expenses include ordinary, day-to-day business expenses, such as office supplies and salaries. For tax purposes, you can deduct them from your business income in the year that you pay for them. Capital expenses, on the other hand, include payments for business assets (also called "capital," "fixed," or "depreciable" assets) that have a useful life of one year or more, such as computers or office furniture. Capital expenses generally can't be fully deducted in the year they are incurred, but must be deducted over a number of years—a process known as depreciation, capitalization, or amortization.

gross income, net profit, gross retail sales, number of employees, how much employees are paid, how much property it owns or leases, its seating capacity, or how many vehicles it owns—and the list goes on and on.

To complicate matters further, the many different taxes are administered by different government agencies, each with its own rules, forms, and filing procedures. It's little wonder that the mere mention of taxes often induces anxiety and sometimes even panic in otherwise well-adjusted businesspeople.

The Agencies Behind the Taxes

The first step in understanding small business taxes is to recognize who levies which taxes. Here's a quick breakdown:

- **Federal taxes.** The United States Internal Revenue Service, the top dog of tax agencies, collects the following taxes from small businesses and their owners: taxes on individual or corporate income, self-employment taxes (which go to the Social Security and Medicare systems), and payroll taxes. (See Chapter 15 for information on payroll taxes.)

- **California taxes.** The State of California collects the following taxes: taxes on personal or corporate income, franchise taxes on corporations, LLC taxes on LLCs, limited partnership taxes on limited partnerships, sales taxes on sales of retail goods (after the business has collected the sales tax from its customers), and payroll taxes. (See Chapter 15 for information on payroll taxes.) California also collects special taxes (called "excise taxes") on certain types of business activities, such as distributing alcohol, cigarettes, or gasoline.

- **County and city taxes.** Cities, counties, or both typically impose taxes on businesses, based upon several factors. Most cities assign businesses to categories (for example, retail businesses, wholesalers, or services) then tax each category based on certain criteria, such as gross receipts, gross payroll, or number of employees. Counties in California assess and collect property taxes on real and personal property owned by businesses within the

county. Cities and counties also impose a sales tax. This tax may be collected by the state along with the state sales tax.

> **CAUTION**
>
> **A tax by any other name is … a fee.** In addition to the taxes listed above, your business may have to pay additional fees for business licenses and tax registration. For instance, many California cities and counties require all businesses in the area to register with the local tax collector and pay a registration fee. And if your business needs to obtain a special license, such as a permit to handle food or a cosmetology license, you'll usually have to pay for it. While these fees arguably could be called taxes, we don't deal with them as such in this chapter. The various registration, permit, and license requirements—including their associated fees—for California small businesses are covered in Chapter 6.

Forms and Schedules and Returns, Oh My!

This chapter makes many mentions of tax forms, tax schedules, and tax returns. Basically, these are simply different names for the papers you have to fill out and submit to your federal, state, and local tax agencies.

Technically, a "tax form" is the principal document that businesses and their owners must use to report all the basic information about the business's or individual's income. For instance, every individual who earns income must fill out Form 1040, *Individual Income Tax Return,* and all partnerships and LLCs must file Form 1065, *U.S. Return of Partnership Income.*

A "schedule" is an additional sheet of information that the IRS requires businesses and business owners to attach to their tax forms. For instance, sole proprietors must submit Schedule C with their Form 1040 to report their income from their businesses, and partners and LLC owners usually need to report their business income on Schedule E. Partnerships and LLCs also have to include various schedules with their Form 1065s.

Finally, a "tax return" is simply a general term for the whole package you send off to the IRS and the state: your tax form and any attached schedules and other documents.

Understanding Deductions

Increasing profits while keeping taxes as low as possible is the name of the game in any business. The main way to do this is by claiming business deductions. When you deduct an expense, you subtract it from your taxable income—which means you'll have less income to report and pay taxes on. Of course you can't deduct just any old expense you want. To stay out of tax trouble, you need to understand which deductions are allowed and which are not. (Note that deductions are often irrelevant for local and sales taxes, which tend to be based on gross income—also called "gross receipts"—without taking any deductions into account.)

What Expenses Are Deductible?

Allowable deductions are outlined in great length (to put it mildly) in the Internal Revenue Code; the basic guidelines are summarized below. You'll need to follow these rules when filling out your federal tax return, which you use to report your business income and deductions. When you file your state income tax return, you'll fill out a form (Schedule CA) that uses the information from your federal return, with a few adjustments to reflect California's rules on deducting business expenses. As far as local taxes go, they're often based on gross income (also called gross receipts) without taking any deductions into account. In short, your main concern should be the federal rules on deductions.

The Internal Revenue Code (IRC) states that any "ordinary and necessary" business expenses can be subtracted from your business income for federal tax purposes (IRC § 162). Figuring out whether most expenses qualify is a no-brainer. Product costs, office rent, equipment and machinery, office supplies, your business computer system, business insurance, and office utility bills are just a few examples of costs that easily count as deductible expenses. As long as an expenditure is, in fact, made for business—not personal—purposes, the general rule is that you can deduct it from your business's gross income.

It gets a little more complicated when expenditures aren't made clearly for business reasons. The IRS has special rules for expenses that border on the personal, such as travel, entertainment, and vehicle expenses. These costs are deductible, but only according to special IRS rules.

> **CAUTION**
>
> **Resources for the details on expenses.** The rules on allowable travel and entertainment expenses are fully explained in Nolo's *Deduct It! Lower Your Small Business Taxes,* by Stephen Fishman (Nolo), and in IRS Publication 535, *Business Expenses,* available online at www.irs.gov.

How Are Expenses Deducted?

In addition to figuring out whether an expense is deductible, you need to understand how particular expenses may be deducted. First, you need to know that there's a major distinction between current and capital expenses. Current expenses can best be described as your everyday costs of doing business, such as rent, supplies, utility bills, and the like. These expenses are fully deductible in the year they occur. Capital expenses, on the other hand, are not. You incur a capital expense when you purchase an item with a useful life of at least one year—called a "business asset." Business assets include items such as vehicles, furniture, heavy equipment (like a forklift or printing press), and real estate.

Rather than fully deducting a capital expense in the year it was made, you must spread out the deduction over a number of years. This process is variously called "depreciation," "amortization," or "capitalization." Different types of assets have different depreciation rules, and the number of years over which the cost of an item must be depreciated varies. Depreciation rules are explained in IRS Publication 946, *How to Depreciate Property,* available online at www.irs.gov, as well as in other IRS publications that cover specific types of assets.

Note also that start-up expenses—those incurred before you actually launch your business—are subject to special tax rules. Since 2004, the general rule is that businesses may write off up to $5,000 of their start-up costs in the first year of business. If you spend more than $5,000 in start-up costs, you'll have to deduct that excess amount in equal amounts—a process called amortization—over the next 15 years.

This introduction to tax deductions only begins to scratch the surface of a huge and complex body of information. *Deduct It! Lower Your Small Business Taxes,* by Stephen Fishman (Nolo), does an excellent job of leading you through the maze, and includes detailed advice on how to write off your start-up costs. Especially as your business grows and its finances become more complicated, you may well want to hire a tax advisor to help you use the tax rules to your best advantage. (See Chapter 16 for information on hiring and working with tax professionals.)

The Section 179 Deduction

The IRS allows every business to treat a certain amount of capital expenditures as current expenses—and fully deduct them in the year they were made. This major exception is known as a "179 deduction," because it's established by Internal Revenue Code § 179.

Tax law changes since 2003 have dramatically increased the limit from $25,000 in 2003 to $250,000 in 2009—allowing businesses to write off up to $250,000 in expenditures that would normally qualify as capital expenses.

Whether and to what extent you should take advantage of a 179 deduction depends on your circumstances. Generally, you should take this deduction only when your taxable income is high enough that the deduction will give you a decent tax benefit right away. Businesses with low incomes might want to depreciate assets instead—taking their deductions slowly—so that they'll have more deductions available in future years when income is likely to be higher.

Where to Get Tax Forms and Schedules

Although this book provides several tax forms in Appendix C and on the CD-ROM (a list is included at the beginning of Appendix C), many federal and state tax forms are not included here because they change from year to year and are readily available from other sources. Besides the flood of tax forms that are available at post offices and libraries as April 15 draws near, you can always obtain the most current forms, schedules, and publications by ordering them over the phone or downloading them off the Web. Here's where to order them.

- Order federal tax forms and other publications from the IRS by calling 800-829-3676. Or download them from the Web at www.irs.gov. Click the "Businesses" tab on the IRS website home page for an organized list of tax-related articles, forms, and publications for businesses of all types and sizes.
- California Franchise Tax Board (FTB) forms can be ordered by phone at 800-338-0505 or downloaded from the Web at www.ftb.ca.gov.
- Order forms from the California Board of Equalization (BOE) by calling 800-400-7115 or download them from the Web at www.boe.ca.gov.
- Local tax forms and instructions are generally sent to businesses automatically once they've registered with their city or county. Otherwise, contact the agency in charge of business taxes in your city or county (depending on where your business is located) for more information on how to obtain local tax forms. To find your local tax agency, look in the city government section of your white pages under "Tax Collector," "Business Tax Division," or "City Clerk."

Hobby Businesses

For many small business owners, their "business" is more a labor of love than a reliable source of income. This is most often the case when an owner has other means of financial support—such as a regular job or a spouse who brings home wages or other income—that allow a microbusiness to continue even though it makes little or no money. These types of tiny businesses are usually operated from the home (renting an office would be too expensive) and are often based on activities near and dear to the owner, earning them the nickname "hobby businesses."

There is no one type of hobby business. Examples might include a basement jewelry studio, a jazz band for hire, or an antique-refinishing business. The owners would probably keep on making jewelry, playing jazz, or restoring antiques even if they never made a penny, but are making a go of turning their hobbies into profitable businesses.

Often, profits fail to materialize. For most regular businesses, spending more than a year or so losing money is a cue to close up shop. But if you love what you're doing, it might make sense for you to stick with your losing business rather than fold it up. This is true because if you have another source of income (as many owners of hobby businesses do), the losses from your hobby business can be used to offset that income. Deducting business losses—including everyday expenses and depreciation on assets such as computer equipment—not only lowers the amount of income upon which taxes are calculated, but also may drop you into a lower tax bracket. This is what is commonly referred to as a tax shelter: an unprofitable business whose losses offset the owner's taxable income from other sources.

Of course, most entrepreneurs would much rather earn a healthy profit than lose money. And the savings made possible by a tax shelter do not always justify continuing a marginal or losing business. But they definitely can make a difference in deciding whether it's worth it to keep your unprofitable—but enjoyable!—business going.

> **EXAMPLE:** Kay and Reza are married and file joint tax returns. Reza earns a salary as a chef in a local restaurant, and Kay is a magazine editor. Kay has a passion for plants and decides to try to make a business of selling some of the hundreds of plants she grows and propagates in her backyard greenhouse. After she's spent thousands of dollars on exotic plants and better lighting equipment, the greenhouse heater goes on the fritz and over 300 of Kay's expensive, exotic plants die. Her expenses for the year total nearly $10,000, and she has not yet sold any plants. The silver lining for Kay and Reza comes at tax time, when they deduct the $10,000 loss from their joint taxable income of $105,000. This not only reduces their taxable income, but—depending on their income level and any other deductions they take—might drop them into a lower tax bracket as well.

On the down side, if you consistently use your unprofitable business as a tax shelter, deducting your losses from your other income year after year, you'll likely attract the attention of the IRS. One issue that often arises with hobby businesses is whether the venture is really a business at all. To deduct expenses from your taxable income, those expenses must have been incurred by a legitimate profit-motivated business—not merely a personal hobby. As you might expect, not every hobby counts as a business. If you claim a loss from your hobby business and you're audited, you'll have to prove to the IRS that your hobby is in fact a legitimate business.

Proving Your Hobby Is a Business

Before you start claiming deductions for the costs of your favorite art projects or toy car collections, make sure your venture will pass IRS scrutiny and qualify as a real business. Thankfully, the IRS's definition is fairly broad. Basically, any activity that you undertake to make a profit counts as a business. In other words, you need only prove to the IRS that you're trying—not necessarily succeeding—to make a profit with your venture. The IRS uses a few different criteria to decide whether your business truly has a profit motive.

The main test for profit motive is called the "3-of-5" test. If your business makes a profit in three out of five consecutive years, it is legally presumed to have a profit motive.

While the IRS gives a lot of weight to the 3-of-5 test, it is not conclusive. In other words, if you flunk the 3-of-5 test, you still may be able to prove that your business is motivated by profit. You can use virtually any kind of evidence to prove this. Business cards, a well-maintained set of books, a separate business bank account, current business licenses and permits, and proof of advertising will all help to persuade an IRS auditor that your activity really is a business.

Watch Out for Local Tax Rules

When planning your hobby business, don't forget that local requirements and taxes will increase your costs of doing business, both in time and money.

Owners of lots of small businesses are surprised to find out that state and local tax regulations for small businesses can be more of a bear than IRS rules. For example, if you sell tangible products, you may be subject to state sales taxes. Plus, many cities impose taxes or fees on small businesses and require them to go through some sort of registration process, and counties often have similar requirements for businesses in rural areas. Generally speaking, these rules apply to any money-making activity within the locality—even if the hobby business doesn't intend to claim any federal or state tax deductions.

In practice, many tiny hobby businesses—so tiny that the word "business" even seems excessive—might be able to get away unnoticed, assuming you don't deduct business losses on your tax return. Even so, you should be aware that, depending on your local rules, you may be penalized if you're caught doing business without the permits or licenses required by the state or your local government. These penalties may include fines and back taxes.

Income Taxes for Sole Proprietors

As mentioned throughout this book, a sole proprietorship is one and the same as its owner (the sole proprietor) for most legal and tax purposes. It follows that the sole proprietor must report and pay federal and state income taxes on all business profits, including any profits the sole proprietor leaves in the business for expansion. In other words, the business itself does not file tax returns or pay income taxes.

Federal Income Taxes

You're probably already familiar with the process of filing IRS Form 1040, based on income you earned at a job. Good—this means much of the process of filing federal income taxes as a sole proprietor will already be familiar to you. That's because income from your business will be treated as personal income, which you report on Form 1040 much as you report wages or returns on investments. But there are two additional steps you'll have to take: You'll have to use a separate sheet (called Schedule C) to report your business profit, and you'll also have

to pay self-employment taxes based on your income, reported on Schedule SE.

Income Tax

You report business profits or losses on Schedule C, *Profit or Loss from Business,* which you submit once a year with your 1040 return, usually by April 15. A sole proprietor who owns more than one business must file a separate Schedule C for each business.

Simplified Tax Schedule for Super-Small Sole Proprietorships

Extra-small sole proprietorships may be able to use a simplified schedule to report their incomes, Schedule C-EZ. (This schedule may only be used by sole proprietors.) To use this simplified form, which works just like Schedule C, you must:

- claim less than $5,000 in business expenses
- have had no inventory during the year
- have had no employees during the year
- use the cash method of accounting (see Chapter 11 for an explanation of the difference between the cash and accrual methods of accounting)
- own and operate only one sole proprietorship during the year
- not deduct expenses for business use of your home, and
- not report a net business loss.

If you depreciate assets or have unallowed passive activity losses from previous years, you may not be able to use this schedule. See the IRS instructions for details on who may use Schedule C-EZ.

Though Schedule C-EZ is easier to fill out than Schedule C, you won't save enough time or trouble to warrant trying to squeeze a too-large business into its parameters. Don't, for example, neglect to claim more than $5,000 in business expenses or to claim depreciation expenses just so you qualify to use the schedule. The marginal convenience of the simplified schedule just isn't worth it.

You're not required to file Schedule C if your sole proprietorship doesn't make at least $400 profit in the business year, though it's a good idea to file one anyway. If your business loses money in any year, filing Schedule C allows the loss to be deducted from any other income you make for that year, reducing your total taxable income. Or you can carry over the loss into a future profitable year to offset those profits and thereby reduce your taxes. Another reason to report losses or profits under $400 on Schedule C is that doing so triggers the beginning of the time window during which the IRS can audit you. Otherwise, the IRS can audit you virtually forever.

There's also an important procedural difference between reporting and paying taxes on income from a job and income from a sole proprietorship: Regular employees are subject to tax withholding by their employers, but sole proprietors usually have to estimate their taxes for the year and pay them in quarterly installments. The IRS is a stickler when it comes to making these quarterly payments and won't hesitate to fine you for doing it incorrectly or late—and especially for not doing it at all. Even if you pay your taxes in full by April 15 (or whenever your business year ends), failure to make quarterly payments means you'll be charged a penalty, typically about 9%. (See "Estimating and Paying Your Taxes Quarterly," below.)

Self-Employment Taxes

Sole proprietors must also make contributions to the Social Security and Medicare systems, called "self-employment taxes." Regular employees contribute to these two programs through deductions from their paychecks. Sole proprietors must make their contributions when paying their other income taxes. And they have to pay more than employees do—employees only have to pay half as much into these programs because their contributions are matched by their employers. Sole proprietors must pay the entire amount themselves.

The self-employment tax rate is 15.3%, of which 12.4% goes towards Social Security and 2.9% goes towards Medicare. While the Medicare portion is calculated based upon a sole proprietor's total profits, the Social Security portion is capped at a certain amount that changes each year ($106,800 for 2009).

In other words, profits of $106,800 and less will be taxed at 15.3% (both Social Security and Medicare), and profits above that will be taxed at 2.9% (Medicare only). In comparison, regular employees only pay a 7.65% tax on wages of $106,800 or less, and a 1.45% tax on wages above that.

Fortunately, there is a small silver lining to this dark tax cloud: Half of the total self-employment tax you'll pay can be deducted from your taxable income at year-end. And if your sole proprietorship makes less than $400 profit in the business year, you don't have to pay self-employment taxes.

> ### Reporting and Paying Are Not the Same
>
> As you read about the often complex rules of taxes, you'll see that having to report income does not necessarily mean that you'll have to pay tax on that income. Sometimes, a tax agency, such as the IRS or the California Franchise Tax Board, requires you to submit a tax return even if you don't owe any taxes. Generally, a "filing" or "reporting" requirement means simply that you need to provide income and expense information, which may or may not create an actual tax obligation.

Self-employment taxes are reported on Schedule SE, which, like Schedule C (*Profit or Loss from Business*), is submitted yearly with your 1040 income tax return. Once you determine the amount of self-employment taxes you owe on Schedule SE, you enter the result on your 1040 form in the "Other Taxes" section and add it to your personal income tax obligation. Remember, however, that most sole proprietors must estimate their total taxes for the year and pay them in quarterly installments. (See "Estimating and Paying Your Taxes Quarterly," below, for more information.)

California Income Taxes

You must report and pay California income tax in much the same way as federal income tax. Any profit generated by a sole proprietorship is treated as personal income of the sole proprietor and reported on Schedule CA, which is submitted with Form 540,

California Resident Income Tax Return. Unlike with the federal system, you must file Schedule CA even if your business loses money or makes less than $400 profit. Obviously, you won't owe any taxes unless you've made a profit, but you must file the form in any case.

California law, like federal law, requires many businesses to estimate and pay their income taxes in quarterly installments. (See "Estimating and Paying Your Taxes Quarterly," below.)

Income Taxes for Partnerships

Although a partnership itself does not pay taxes (its owners do), it does need to submit an annual informational return to the IRS and to the California Franchise Tax Board to report its income. As is true for sole proprietorships, taxes are paid only by the partners (business owners), not the business itself, and the partners have to pay taxes on all business profits, whether or not they take any money out of the business. This section explains what partnerships need to do to comply with the rules of the IRS and California's FTB.

Federal Income Taxes

Partnerships are called "pass-through tax entities," which means that profits pass right through the business to the owners, who report them on their individual income tax returns. The partnership itself is not taxed, though it must report its income and losses each year. (Although few do, a partnership can also elect to be taxed as a corporation, by submitting Form 8832 and electing corporate tax status.) In addition to income taxes, partners must also file and pay self-employment taxes.

Income Tax

Even though the partnership itself does not pay taxes on profits, it must report profits and losses on an informational return, Form 1065, *U.S. Return of Partnership Income.* No tax is due with this return, which is generally due by April 15.

Along with Form 1065, the partnership must also submit a Schedule K-1, *Partner's Share of Income,*

Deductions, Credits, etc., for each partner, reporting each partner's share of profits or losses. The K-1 schedule is used to inform the IRS of the partners' chosen profit division. Often, partners own equal shares of the business, which normally means they will choose to share profits and pay taxes equally —such as four partners each getting one quarter of a business's profits and paying one quarter of its taxes. But if they choose, partners can divide profits and losses unequally. (See Chapter 1 for more on partnerships.) A copy of the completed K-1 must also be given to each partner on or before the date that the partnership return is due to the IRS.

As mentioned above, profits earned by a partnership are taxed as personal income of the individual partners. Each partner reports an allocated share of business income or losses on his or her individual federal income tax return (Form 1040) using Schedule E, *Supplemental Income and Loss.* Schedule E repeats the income information reported on Schedule K-1 (which each partner should have received from the partnership). Since the partnership already filed Schedule K-1 with the IRS, partners do not need to submit this schedule with their individual tax returns.

Partners who earn income from a profitable partnership often must estimate their taxes and pay the total in quarterly installments.

Self-Employment Taxes

Partners and other self-employed individuals who earn more than $400 profit during the business year must contribute to Social Security and Medicare through federal self-employment taxes. The self-employment tax rate is 15.3%, of which 12.4% goes towards Social Security and 2.9% goes towards Medicare. While the Medicare portion is calculated based upon the partner's total share of profits, the Social Security portion is capped at a certain amount that changes each year ($106,800 for 2009).

Put another way, profits of $106,800 and less will be taxed at 15.3% (both Social Security and Medicare), and profits above that will be taxed at 2.9% (Medicare only).

On a brighter note, a partner can deduct half of the total self-employment tax from his or her taxable income at year-end. And if the partner makes less than $400 in profit, no self-employment taxes need be filed or paid.

Self-employment taxes are reported on Schedule SE, which, like Schedule E, *Supplemental Income and Loss,* is submitted yearly with a partner's 1040 return. Once you determine your self-employment tax with Schedule SE, enter the result on your 1040 form in the "Other Taxes" section, which you must add to your personal income tax obligation. But don't forget about estimating and paying taxes quarterly; most partners of profitable businesses must do so, or face the IRS's penalties. Ouch.

California Income Taxes

Like the federal government, the state of California requires partnerships to file informational returns reporting business income and losses. Fortunately, California Form 565—which is filed with the state Franchise Tax Board (FTB)—is almost identical to the federal Form 1065. Also like the federal system, a partnership must submit to the FTB a Schedule K-1 for each partner, indicating the partner's share of the business profit or loss. The partnership must give each partner a copy. The California version of this form, Schedule K-1 (565), is similar to the federal version, but accounts for differences between California and federal tax laws. No tax is due with the partnership return or schedules.

Any partnership profit is taxed as personal income of the partners, who report their shares on Schedule CA, which should reflect the information from California Schedule K-1 (565). Schedule CA is submitted with Form 540, *California Resident Income Tax Return.* Partners do not submit the state Schedule K-1 (565) with their state returns. Unlike the federal rule for partners, a partner must file Schedule CA with the FTB even if the partnership loses money and no taxes are due.

Finally, like federal taxes, California income taxes must often be paid in quarterly installments.

Income Taxes for LLCs

The limited liability company or LLC (explained in greater detail in Chapter 1) is a relatively new business ownership structure. LLCs combine several key attributes that distinguish the traditional partnership and corporation, allowing LLC owners (usually called "members") to enjoy the protection from personal liability that a corporation offers, yet avoid the complicated and often expensive corporate tax system. LLC profits are taxed to the owners as individuals (like a sole proprietor or owners of a partnership). Although LLC members can instead choose to be taxed like a corporation, this choice is somewhat unusual. (But see Chapter 1 for reasons why some LLCs may want to be taxed like a corporation.) In this section, assume your LLC will stick with pass-through tax status.

Federal Income Taxes

Like owners of partnerships, most LLC owners will report business profits on their individual federal income tax returns. Although this means the LLC itself is not taxed, it must still report its income and losses to the IRS each year if it has two or more members. In addition to regular income taxes, members may be obligated to pay self-employment taxes, which are also based on business income.

Income Tax

LLCs with only one member are treated as sole proprietorships for tax purposes, so that business profits and losses are reported on Schedule C, to be submitted with the member's regular individual income tax return. If the LLC has two or more members, it must file an annual informational return with the IRS, similar to the requirement faced by partnerships. Since the IRS hasn't yet come up with tax forms specifically for LLCs, LLC profits and losses are reported on Form 1065, *U.S. Return of Partnership Income.* No tax is paid with this return, which is generally due by April 15.

Along with Form 1065, an LLC must also submit a Schedule K-1 (again, the same schedule used by partnerships) to the IRS for each member, reporting that member's share of profits or losses. The K-1 schedule is used to inform the IRS of the members' chosen profit division. A copy of the completed K-1 must also be given to each member on or before the date that the LLC return is due to the IRS.

Often, members own equal shares of the business, which normally means they will choose to share profits and pay taxes equally—such as four members each getting one quarter of a business's profits and paying one quarter of its taxes. But if they choose, LLC members can divide profits and losses unequally. (See Chapter 1 for more on LLCs and profit allocations.)

Profits earned by an LLC are taxed as personal income of the individual members. Members use the information from Schedule K-1 to report business income or losses on their individual federal income tax returns (Form 1040) using Schedule E, *Supplemental Income and Loss*. Since the LLC already filed Schedule K-1s with the IRS, members do not need to submit this form with their returns.

Like sole proprietors and partners, LLC members will have to estimate their taxes for the year and pay them in quarterly installments.

Self-Employment Taxes

LLC members who earn more than $400 profit during the business year must contribute to Social Security and Medicare through federal self-employment taxes. The self-employment tax rate is 15.3%, of which 12.4% goes towards Social Security and 2.9% goes towards Medicare. While the Medicare portion is calculated based upon the member's total share of profits, the Social Security portion is capped at a certain amount that changes each year ($106,800 for 2009).

This translates into a 15.3% tax on profits up to $106,800 (Social Security and Medicare combined), and a 2.9% tax on profits above that amount (Medicare only). In comparison, regular employees pay only a 7.65% tax on wages of $106,800 or less, and a 1.45% tax on wages above that.

> **CAUTION**
>
> **There are some gray areas in the rules on self-employment taxes for LLC members.** Since LLCs are partnership-like in some respects, corporate-like in others,

the rules on whether LLC members are subject to self-employment tax are not fully settled. Generally speaking, an LLC member who is actively involved in the business must pay self-employment taxes, while an LLC member who is nonactive and merely invests in the company may be exempt from the self-employment tax obligation. If you're not sure whether this tax would apply to you, it may be wise to consult an accountant to get a definitive answer for your situation. (Chapter 16 gives information on finding professionals to advise you.)

Fortunately, if self-employment taxes are due, you can deduct half of your total self-employment taxes from your taxable income at year-end. And if an LLC member either earns less than $400 profit in the business year or loses money, he or she will be totally exempt from having to pay self-employment taxes.

Self-employment taxes are reported on Schedule SE, which, like Schedule E, *Supplemental Income and Loss,* is submitted yearly with an LLC member's 1040 return. Once you determine the self-employment taxes you owe on Schedule SE, enter the result on your 1040 form in the "Other Taxes" section, which is added to your individual income tax obligation. If the LLC member is required to pay advance quarterly tax installments, however, any self-employment taxes will be included in those payments.

California Taxes: Special LLC Tax and Fee

Though the federal government treats LLCs with pass-through tax status almost exactly like partnerships, the State of California's tax treatment is annoyingly inconsistent. Like an owner of a partnership, an LLC member is subject to California income taxes on any share of business profits. However, California also imposes special taxes on LLCs themselves, despite treating them as pass-through tax entities in most other respects.

LLC Tax and Fee

LLCs need to make two payments to the Franchise Tax Board (FTB): One is called an LLC tax, the other, an LLC fee. To make matters more confusing, the LLC tax is really more like a fee, and the LLC fee seems much more like a tax. Here's how this screwy system works.

The LLC tax is an $800 annual payment (it may help you to think of it as a prepaid minimum tax) that the FTB collects, in its words, "for the privilege of doing business in California." It applies to all LLCs, even if they're losing money. For newly formed LLCs, the tax is due within three months and 15 days after the LLC is formed. For ongoing LLCs, this tax is due each year within three months and 15 days after the beginning of the business year. On the plus side, the $800 can be credited toward the other tax the LLC may owe at year-end. The LLC tax is paid with Form 3522, *Limited Liability Company Tax Voucher.* A blank copy of Form 3522 appears on the next page.

The other tax that California imposes on LLCs is the LLC fee. This fee has been challenged in court and ruled unconstitutional, which led to legislative amendments to the fee and how it is applied. While in the past it applied to an LLC's total income, since 2007, it has been assessed only against an LLC's income from sources "derived from or attributable to the state of California." In other words, income derived from business in other states would not be subject to the LLC fee. If your business is entirely conducted within California, then you'll likely be subject to the fee. If you do some business out of state, you should check with your accountant or lawyer about whether and what income may be subject to the fee.

Any LLC fee owed is due the fifteenth day of the sixth month of the taxable year. For businesses using a calendar year, this falls on June 15. The fee is reported and paid with Form 3536, or Form 3588 for electronically filed returns.

The LLC fee varies according to the LLC's total income. The annual fee for taxable years beginning on or after January 1, 2001, is as follows:

Total Income*	LLC Fee
0 to $249,999	$0
$250,000 to $499,999	$900
$500,000 to $999,999	$2,500
$1,000,000 to $4,999,999	$6,000
$5,000,000 and over	$11,790

*Fee is assessed upon total income from all sources derived from or attributable to California.

> **CAUTION**
>
> **The LLC fee has been ruled unconstitutional, and some LLCs may be entitled to refunds of LLC fees they've already paid.** A couple of lawsuits challenging the constitutionality of the LLC fee have been successful, and LLCs with similar factual situations may be entitled to a refund of LLC fees paid. The cases of *Northwest Energetic Services LLC v. California Franchise Tax Board* and *Ventas Finance I, LLC v. Franchise Tax Board* established situations in which an LLC's income is not subject to the LLC fee (in a nutshell, income earned from out-of-state sources may be exempt from the fee). The Franchise Tax Board has implemented procedures for businesses to use to file for refunds of LLC fees already paid, if they believe they have factual situations substantially similar to the *Northwest* or *Ventas* cases. For more information, go to the FTB website (www.ftb.ca.gov) and search for "LLC fee."

All LLCs doing business in California (and classified as partnerships) must file Form 568 regardless of how much or little income they have made. On that return, you'll subtract the $800 tax that you prepaid for the year, but since you'll also need to prepay for the next year, you'll always be $800 behind (until you dissolve your LLC).

EXAMPLE: Chad plans to open his restaurant, Kitty B's Catfish Shack, as a limited liability company. He files his Articles of Organization on May 31, 2009, which means his $800 minimum tax for the year is due September 15, 2009. When Chad reports taxes for the Catfish Shack the following April in the year 2010, he can count the $800 he prepaid toward any LLC taxes the restaurant owes. However, he'll have to pay another $800 minimum tax by April 15, 2010, as prepayment for that year of business.

Regular State Income Taxes for Members

Aside from these special rules for the LLC tax and fee, LLCs file state income taxes much like federal income taxes. An LLC must file Form 568, *Limited Liability Company Return of Income,* accompanied by Schedule K-1 (565) for each LLC member, reporting that member's share of profit or losses. The LLC also needs to supply each member with a copy of the Schedule K-1 (565) submitted to the FTB.

Instructions for Form FTB 3522
LLC Tax Voucher

General Information

Use form FTB 3522, LLC Tax Voucher, to pay the annual limited liability company (LLC) tax of $800 for taxable year 2009. An LLC should use this form if any of the following apply:

- The LLC has articles of organization accepted by the California Secretary of State (SOS).
- The LLC has a certificate of registration issued by the SOS.
- The LLC is doing business in California.

You can download, view, and print California tax forms and publications from our website at **ftb.ca.gov**.

Access other state agencies' websites through the State Agencies Directory on California's website at **ca.gov**.

Round Cents to Dollars – Round cents to the nearest whole dollar. For example, round $50.50 up to $51 or round $25.49 down to $25.

Who Must Pay the Annual LLC Tax

Every LLC that is doing business in California or that has articles of organization accepted or a certificate of registration issued by the SOS **is subject to the $800.00 annual tax.** The tax must be paid for each taxable year until a certificate of cancellation of registration or of articles of organization is filed with the SOS.

For taxable years beginning on or after January 1, 2003, an LLC as described in Internal Revenue Code Section 501(c)(2) and 501(c)(25) and California Revenue and Taxation Code Sections 23701h and 23701x is exempt from the annual LLC tax.

How to Complete Form FTB 3522

Enter all the information requested using blue or black ink. To ensure the timely and proper application of the payment to the LLC's account, enter the SOS file number (assigned upon registration with the SOS), and the federal employer identification number (FEIN).

Series LLC – After the name for each series, write "Series LLC # ___." In addition, write "Series LLC" in red on the top right margin of the form. Only the first series to pay tax or file a return may use a California SOS number. For all other series, enter zeroes in the Secretary of State (SOS) file number field. We will assign a number and notify each series. See FTB Pub. 3556, Limited Liability Companies, for more information.

Private Mail Box
Include the Private Mail Box (PMB) in the address field. Write "PMB" first, then the box number. Example: 111 Main Street PMB 123.

Where to File

Make a check or money order payable to the "Franchise Tax Board." Write the SOS file number, FEIN, and "2009 FTB 3522" on the check or money order. Detach the payment form from the bottom of the page. Enclose, but do **not** staple, your payment to the form and mail to:

FRANCHISE TAX BOARD
PO BOX 942857
SACRAMENTO CA 94257-0631

Make all checks or money orders payable in U.S. dollars and drawn against a U.S. financial institution. **If no payment is due, do not mail this form.**

When to Pay the Annual LLC Tax

The annual LLC tax is due and payable **by the 15th day of the 4th month** after the **beginning** of the LLC's taxable year (fiscal year) or April 15, 2009 (calendar year).

The first taxable year of an LLC that was not previously in existence begins when the LLC is organized or registered with the California SOS.

If the 15th day of the 4th month of an existing foreign LLC's taxable year has passed before the foreign LLC commences business in California or registers with the SOS, the annual LLC tax should be paid immediately after commencing business or registering with the SOS.

Example: LLC1, a newly-formed calendar year taxpayer, organizes as an LLC in Delaware on June 1, 2009. LLC1 registers with the SOS on August 13, 2009, and begins doing business in California on August 14, 2009. Because LLC1's initial taxable year began on June 1, 2009 the annual LLC tax is due by September 15, 2009 (the 15th day of the 4th month of the short period taxable year). LLC1's short period (June 1, 2009-December 31, 2009) tax return is due by April 15, 2010. The annual tax payment for taxable year 2010, with form FTB 3522 also is due by April 15, 2010.

Penalties and Interest

If the LLC fails to pay its annual tax by the 15th day of the 4th month after the beginning of the taxable year, a late payment penalty plus interest will be assessed for failure to pay the annual LLC tax by the due date. The FTB may waive the late penalty, based on reasonable cause, where the greater of the annual tax or 90% of the tax shown on the return is paid by the original due date of the return. The penalty and interest will be computed from the due date of the tax to the date of payment.

Late Payment of Prior Year Annual LLC Tax

If a prior year LLC tax of $800 was not paid by the 15th day of the 4th month after the beginning of the taxable year, the tax should be paid as soon as possible, using the **appropriate taxable year** form FTB 3522. **Do not** use any other form for payment of the tax. This will assure proper application of the payment to the LLC's account.

✂ DETACH HERE IF NO PAYMENT IS DUE, DO NOT MAIL THIS FORM DETACH HERE ✂

Fiscal year: File and Pay by the 15th day of the 4th month after the beginning of the taxable year.
Calendar year: File and Pay by APRIL 15, 2009.

TAXABLE YEAR   CALIFORNIA FORM

2009 LLC Tax Voucher   3522

For calendar year 2009 or fiscal year beginning month_____ day_____ year_____, and ending month_____ day_____ year_____.

Limited liability company name | Secretary of State (SOS) file number

DBA | FEIN

Address (including suite, room, PO Box, or PMB no.).

City | State | ZIP Code

Contact Telephone no. | Amount of payment
(   ) | _____.00

6111093 | FTB 3522 2008

All profits or losses that pass through the LLC to its owners must be reported on their personal California income tax returns, Form 540, using Schedule CA. Schedule CA should reflect the profit or losses reported on the state K-1 (565) return that the LLC provided to each member. Unlike the federal government, California requires an LLC member to file Schedule CA with Form 540 even if the LLC loses money. The member won't owe any taxes unless the LLC made a profit, but the form must be filed in any case.

Like federal taxes, California income taxes for LLC members must generally be paid in quarterly installments.

Estimating and Paying Your Taxes Quarterly

Anyone who earns income from a business must generally pay income taxes in quarterly installments over the course of the business year. Some business-people who expect to owe little or no tax are exempt from these estimated payment requirements. At year-end, if you've paid more than what you owe, you'll get a refund. On the other hand, if you didn't pay enough in your quarterly installments, you will owe more.

This system isn't all that different from the way taxes on employment wages are handled. From each paycheck, the state and federal governments require an employer to withhold income taxes based on the employee's expected annual salary or hourly pay. At year-end, the employee calculates and reports the individual tax obligation based on how much money was actually earned during the year. Depending on the dollar amount of the tax obligation, the employee will either owe more money (if the employer didn't withhold enough) or be due a refund (if the employer withheld too much).

The IRS and California's FTB require tax withholding or advance payment of estimated taxes for a simple, practical reason: They know that a sudden multithousand-dollar bill on April 15 can be difficult for anyone. Spreading out payments by wage withholding or estimated payments is the tax

agencies' way of making your life a little easier—and making sure they get their money.

Unfortunately, it's much easier for an employer to figure out an employee's estimated tax burden based on yearly salary or hourly wage than it is for a small business owner to estimate taxes based on future income from a new and unproven business. If you're wondering how you can estimate taxes on business income that hasn't come in yet, you're not alone. Projecting future income in order to estimate your tax obligation can be a dicey task, especially for brand-new business owners whose income hasn't yet evened out into any predictable rhythm. To make matters worse, you'll be socked with a penalty if your estimates are off and you don't pay enough each quarter.

But here's the good news: You don't need to start making estimated tax payments until you earn enough income to subject you to a threshold quarterly payment requirement. This should give you enough time to get a pretty good feel for how much and how quickly money—and, by extension, taxable profits—are coming into your business. And even if you do underestimate your taxes and face a penalty of a few hundred dollars, you can at least take heart that you owe extra only because your business has become profitable sooner than you anticipated.

Who Must Pay Estimated Taxes?

In a nutshell, business owners have to pay federal estimated taxes if they expect to owe at least $1,000 in federal taxes for any particular year (including income taxes and self-employment taxes). Generally, this means you'll have to make estimated payments if your adjusted gross income (taxable net profits minus tax exemptions, deductions, and credits) will be between $3,000 and $6,000, depending on your tax bracket. If your business is at all profitable, count on estimating and paying your taxes quarterly. On the other hand, if you're operating at a net business loss or making next to nothing, you may not have to make estimated payments.

EXAMPLE: On December 31, as part of a New Year's resolution, Jason quit his job as computer salesman and opened a river-rafting outfit called the Rapids Transit Company. For the first few months of the next year, every dollar he takes in pays for equipment, insurance, and marketing. At the rate he's going, he doesn't know if he'll make a profit at all that year, so he doesn't worry about estimated taxes. However, starting in June with the heavy tourist season, he starts clearing about $1,300 per month, after all deductions. He thinks he may have at least four more months like that before winter slows business down. If so, his annual profit will be about $6,500 ($1,300 x five months). Depending on his tax status, he'll probably owe between $1,000 and $2,000 in taxes at the end of the year. He realizes he'd better start making estimated quarterly payments—or risk a penalty.

Your Day Job May Help You Avoid Estimated Taxes

If, in addition to the business you own, you work at a job that withholds taxes from your income, you might not have to pay estimated taxes if your income from your business is not a significant part of your total income. This is because the taxes withheld from your job may cover any estimated taxes owed on your business income. In other words, the IRS wants to make sure that a certain portion of the total taxes you'll owe are paid in installments over the year, but it doesn't care whether those taxes are withheld from your paycheck or paid as estimated taxes. It's possible that the taxes withheld from your paycheck will be enough to meet your entire tax obligation. On the other hand, if your business is bringing in significant income, your wage withholding probably won't cover your tax bill.

Now for the nitty-gritty. The IRS has a relatively straightforward formula (okay, that may be stretching this just a bit) for determining whether you need to estimate and pay your taxes in installments. You'll have to pay estimated taxes if you expect:

- to owe at least $1,000 in federal taxes (including income taxes and self-employment taxes) for the current year, after subtracting any withheld taxes, and
- your withheld taxes are likely to be less than the smaller of:
  - 90% of your total tax obligation for the current tax year, or
  - 100% of your total tax owed for the previous tax year.

This formula sounds complicated, but it's not. First, it requires you to make estimated payments only if you expect to owe at least $1,000 to the IRS at year-end above and beyond any taxes withheld from wages. This translates to about $3,000 to $6,000 in adjusted gross income from your business, depending on your tax bracket. So if your business is barely breaking even, you probably won't have to make estimated payments.

Second, if you do expect to make at least that amount from your business, you may not have to pay estimated taxes on your business income if enough taxes are withheld from any paycheck you receive. If the taxes that are withheld from your paycheck in the current year will come out to be more than 90% of what you'll owe in taxes, you won't have to make estimated payments. Or, if that's not true, there's one more way you can escape paying estimated tax payments. If the taxes withheld in the current year will add up to at least what your entire tax bill was for the previous year, you're free of the estimated tax requirement.

EXAMPLE: Nels works as a manager of an auto parts store, which pays him a salary and deducts federal and state taxes from each paycheck. He starts a sole proprietorship called Falcon's Auto Tow. In the first few months of his auto-towing business, Nels operates at a loss. Since his only taxable income during those months is from his paychecks, on which taxes are withheld, he doesn't have to worry about estimated payments. In the fifth month, he starts to turn a profit, at which point Nels starts to pay attention to whether he must pay estimated taxes. If he thinks his wage withholding will account for at least 90% of his total tax bill at the end of the year, he doesn't need to file and pay estimated taxes. In other words, if he thinks that taxes on his small business income will account for less than 10% of his total tax bill, he'll just file his taxes at year-end like most people whose entire income is subject to wage withholding.

Most businesspeople, of course, anticipate becoming profitable eventually—preferably sooner than later—so at some point, you'll need to start paying estimated taxes. In the real world, what usually happens is that once you become profitable and owe income taxes for the first time, your accountant will calculate the next year's estimated tax payments based upon what you owed the previous year. The accountant will likely even prepare the vouchers for you, so all you have to do is send in the payment with the voucher stub by the applicable deadline.

California Estimated Taxes: Who Must Pay?

The state follows the same general rule as the federal government. You must pay estimated state taxes if you expect:

- to owe at least $200 in state taxes after any wage withholding is taken into account, and
- your withholding and credits are likely to be less than the smaller of:
  - 90% of your total tax obligation for the current year, or
  - 100% of your total tax owed the previous year.

> **CAUTION**
>
> **Estimated tax rules vary.** At the federal level, if your adjusted gross income is more than $150,000 ($75,000 if married filing a separate return), you will have to pay as estimated taxes 90% of your expected tax for the current year or 110% of the tax for the previous year, whichever is less, to avoid an estimated tax penalty. In California, an individual whose adjusted gross income is more than $150,000 (or $75,000 if married filing separately) must pay as estimated taxes a minimum of 90% of his or her tax for the current or 110% of that tax for the previous year, whichever is less. Note that these figures vary slightly from the general federal and state rules for estimated taxes. Your accountant will be a big asset in making sure your estimates are correct.

When to Make Estimated Tax Payments

As just discussed, you become subject to estimated tax payment requirements when you expect to earn enough profit during a business year to trigger the payment requirement. Once you expect to earn that much income, you need to do your best to estimate your income for the year and pay a quarterly installment based on the taxes due. Each quarterly payment must be filed a half-month after the end of the quarter. For both federal and state estimated taxes, the quarterly due dates are as follows:

Income made during:	Tax installment due:
Jan. 1 through Mar. 31	April 15
Apr. 1 through May 31	June 15
June 1 through Aug. 31	September 15
Sept. 1 through Dec. 31	January 15 of the next year

If your business uses a fiscal rather than a calendar year, your payments will be due on the 15th day of the fourth, sixth, and ninth months of your fiscal year and the first month of the following fiscal year.

For more state estimated tax information, call the Franchise Tax Board at 800-852-5711.

Defining Your Business Year

Except for C corporations, a business must use the calendar year as its business year unless it gets permission from the IRS to choose a different starting and ending point. It's important to understand a bit of tax jargon. Any one-year period other than the calendar year (ending on December 31) that a business uses for tax purposes, is called a "fiscal year," a "tax year," or an "accounting period." The IRS allows sole proprietorships, partnerships, LLCs, and S corporations to use a fiscal year only if there is a valid business reason for it, such as significant seasonal fluctuations in business. Fiscal years must begin on the first day of a month and end on the last day of the previous month one year later. An unincorporated business that wants to use a fiscal year must submit Form 8716, *Election To Have a Tax Year Other Than a Required Tax Year*, to the IRS and have it approved. (This form is included in Appendix C and on the CD-ROM.)

 CAUTION

Don't overlook your self-employment taxes. Self-employment taxes, like income taxes, are subject to the estimated tax payment requirement. Be sure to include them when figuring your estimated tax burden for the year.

City and County Taxes

Unlike the federal or state governments, most cities and counties in California impose taxes directly on your business, even if your business is a pass-through entity such as a sole proprietorship, partnership, or limited liability company. Of course, you, as the owner of the business, are personally liable for these financial obligations, but the difference is that your business itself—not merely the profits that flow through to you and any other owners—incurs taxes by local governments. Often,

these taxes can be more of a burden than federal or state ones because many of them are based on your business income before you deduct business costs and expenses. Some areas, for instance, impose a gross receipts tax, which calculates the tax based simply on how much total income your business brings in, without regard for your expenses.

Local taxes vary a lot from one area to the next, but your business can always expect to face some sort of "business taxes" from your city or county, as well as property taxes imposed by your county.

Business Taxes

The vague term "business taxes" simply refers to the tax your local government imposes on all businesses within the city or county limits. Businesses in rural areas will probably only deal with the county tax authority. Whether the tax is imposed by a city or a county tax authority, the information about business taxes provided in this section generally applies.

Unlike the IRS and the California FTB, which simply collect taxes after they're incurred, most local tax collectors require you to go through a tax registration process before you start your business. (Information on this process is provided in Chapter 6, Step 4). Once you've registered, you'll obtain what's commonly called a "tax registration certificate" (or sometimes, inaccurately, a "business license"). Registration gives notice to your local tax authorities that your business exists and allows them to tax it, based on whatever method your locality has adopted for your type of business.

The schemes used to tax your business in various California cities and counties are usually based on certain attributes of your business. Most localities divide businesses into a number of different categories or types, such as retail sales, wholesale sales, hotels/apartments, and service businesses. Each category uses a certain criterion to calculate taxes on, also called a tax base. A common tax base, for example, is "gross receipts" (total income, before expenses). Each category also has a certain tax rate for each tax base. Other criteria used as tax bases include total payroll, number of employees, or number of company vehicles.

In Oakland, for example, retail sales businesses pay $1.20 per $1,000 of gross receipts, while limousine companies pay a tax rate of $75 per vehicle. And San Jose charges all businesses a basic rate of $150 for up to eight employees and adds $18 for each additional employee. Other tax bases exist as well. In Sacramento, for instance, certain professionals, such as accountants, attorneys, and podiatrists, are taxed based on the number of years they have been licensed in the state of California.

In many cities and counties, you start paying your local taxes when you purchase your business license or registration certificate. Often, a locality will base its registration fee on your expected local tax for the year. In some localities, your registration fee is like a prepaid tax that can be applied toward your total year-end tax. In other places, the registration cost is purely an administrative fee and cannot be applied to your tax bill. And in still other areas, part of the registration cost is a prepaid tax that can be credited toward your tax bill, and part is an administrative fee.

Because rules vary widely from city to city and county to county, you'll need to check with your local tax agency to find out how it will tax your business. When searching for the appropriate tax agency, look in the government section of your white pages under "City Government" (or "County Government" if you live in an unincorporated area) for names such as "Tax Collector," "Business Licenses and Permits," or "Business Tax Division." And since local taxation of businesses is usually closely tied to start-up registration requirements, most businesses will automatically receive tax information either when they register or soon thereafter by mail. (For more information on start-up registration requirements, see Chapter 6.)

Property Taxes

Under state law, each county is responsible for assessing and collecting tax on certain kinds of property within the county. For businesses, this includes real estate and business equipment (sometimes called "business personal property"). An important exception is that business inventory (or items that will go into making a product or providing a service) is *not* subject to property tax.

Real estate is appraised by the county assessor only when it changes ownership or when construction is completed. Business personal property, on the other hand, is assessed every year. Some businesses must send the assessor a property statement each year, with information on the cost of all supplies, equipment, and fixtures at each business location.

The tax rate is 1% on the assessed value of the property, plus any additional tax that may have been approved by voters in your county. For specific information on your county's property tax system, call your county assessor's office, which is often part of the county clerk's office.

Sales Taxes

In California, retail sales are subject to state, county, and local district sales taxes. They are often simply referred to as state sales taxes, since they're filed and paid to the California Board of Equalization (BOE) on one return. It's up to the BOE to distribute the collected taxes to the counties and districts across the state.

CAUTION

Sales tax and seller's permits are related. Recall that all businesses that sell tangible goods must apply for a seller's permit. All businesses that have a seller's permit must file a sales tax return, even if the business ultimately makes no taxable sales—for instance, if all sales fall into a tax-exempt category, such as groceries. (Refer to Chapter 6 for help figuring out whether your business needs a seller's permit.)

Taxable Versus Nontaxable Sales

For a sale to be taxable, it must:
- involve the sale of a tangible item, and
- be made to the final user of the item.

Tangible items are things you can touch, such as books, toys, or furniture. Nontangible items might include services, downloadable books, software, or intellectual property items such as patents or copyrights. (See Chapter 6 for more information about what constitutes a tangible item.)

A final user is a consumer—either an individual or a business—rather than a reseller (a wholesaler or distributor). Sales that are made directly to end users (consumers) are retail sales (taxable). Sales to resellers are wholesale sales (nontaxable). If you operate as a wholesaler and sell tangible goods to resellers, who will in turn sell them to consumers, you probably won't have to pay sales tax.

Sales Tax Exemptions

The rules on sales taxes are clouded by swarms of exceptions and exemptions. Here are several examples of common exemptions from sales tax—that is, sales transactions that are generally not taxed:

- most groceries (but not restaurant or take-out food)
- sales to out-of-state customers
- sales to the U.S. government, and
- some sales related to the entertainment industry.

CAUTION

You may need a seller's permit. As discussed in Chapter 6, businesses that sell tangible goods must obtain a seller's permit from the California BOE before sales begin, even if the sales aren't taxable. Selling tangible goods without a seller's permit is technically a misdemeanor crime, but typically, the BOE will give you the opportunity to comply by getting a permit before it files any criminal charges. If you made any sales that were taxable before you got your seller's permit, the BOE will require you not only to get a permit, but also to pay all back taxes that are due.

The Nexus Requirement

Not all sales of tangible goods to end users are subject to sales tax. One additional requirement applies: A sale is taxable only if it is made to a customer who is a resident of the state in which you're doing business. In other words, sales to out-of-state customers (such as by mail order) are not subject to sales tax.

The general rule—established by the U.S. Supreme Court in *Quill v. North Dakota*, 504 U.S. 298 (1992)—is that your business has to collect sales taxes only on sales conducted within the states in which your business is physically located. In legal terms, this is known as having a "nexus," which essentially means a physical presence. For instance, if your business has a store in California and warehouses in Texas and Illinois, then your business would have a nexus in those states and would need to collect sales taxes from customers there. On the other hand, orders shipped to customers in Wisconsin, where your business has no physical presence, would not be taxed. This explains why mail-order forms often contain language such as "California residents add 8.5% sales tax." When you see such language, you can infer that the business is located in California and must collect sales tax from customers in the state, but not from residents of other states.

Your business is likely to be deemed to have a nexus with a state if:

- you operate a retail store in the state
- your company's salespeople conduct business within the state, or
- you own or lease a warehouse or office in the state, even if it's not open to the public.

Generally, simply shipping a product or a catalogue to a customer in a certain state isn't enough to establish a nexus there (assuming that you use a third-party shipper such as UPS or the U.S. Post Office).

Once a nexus exists with a given state, your business will be subject to all of that state's sales tax laws, including any seller's permit and sales tax collecting and reporting requirements. For this reason, many businesses limit their physical presence to one or two states and conduct nationwide business by mail-order or e-commerce. This approach is sound in theory, but the explosion of e-commerce has created a number of wrinkles you should know about. (These are discussed in the next section.)

Sales Taxes Online

While the Web can help you leap geographical boundaries and bring the world into your living room, it also makes a quagmire out of state and local laws that are supposed to apply only to specific areas on the map. Sales tax laws have had a particularly hard time adapting to the world of e-commerce.

As more and more companies have started selling products online, there's been increasing confusion over which of these sales are subject to sales tax and which state's rules apply. Online businesses charge sales tax in a seemingly random manner, causing many lawmakers and businesspeople to call for the reform of sales tax laws. In particular, brick-and-mortar businesses are bitter that many online businesses unfairly escape paying sales taxes, giving them a competitive advantage over the real-world stores. Before going into any details, simply keep in mind that online sales tax rules are still emerging and highly controversial. Expect a good deal of development and change over the next few years.

Currently, the rules that apply to businesses that sell products online are no different than those for non-Web retailers. Businesses that sell products over the Web are subject to the sales tax laws in the states in which the business has a physical presence. And even for online businesses, only a traditional physical presence counts with regard to sales taxes; the fact that customers can access your website from a particular state currently isn't enough to create a nexus with that state. So online retailers don't need to pay sales taxes for transactions in every state where the website appears (which, of course, is everywhere). E-tailers need only to pay sales taxes on sales in states where the business has an office, salespeople, or other type of physical presence. Of course, if the business has a nexus with a state that doesn't charge sales taxes, then transactions there are tax free.

EXAMPLE: Killer Computers sells computers and related accessories from its website, killercomputers.com. Killer Computers has a main office in California, a phone bank in Nebraska, and warehouses in Oregon, Texas, and New Hampshire. Because of its physical presence in these five states, Killer Computers will need to comply with those states' sales tax laws. This means that when killercomputers.com sells computers to customers in California, Nebraska, Oregon, Texas, and New Hampshire, the sales tax laws of those states will apply to transactions within their borders. Because Oregon and New Hampshire don't charge sales taxes, Killer Computers doesn't have to worry about paying sales taxes when it sells computers to customers in those two states. California, Nebraska, and Texas, on the other hand, do charge sales taxes on retail sales, so when killercomputers.com sells to California, Nebraska, or Texas residents, those sales will be subject to sales taxes.

It's tough to say what the future holds. The e-business boom in general is being blamed for billions of dollars in lost sales tax revenues each year. A number of states have begun to enact or consider legislation specifically subjecting e-tailers to state sales taxes. State revenue departments as well as brick-and-mortar companies are lobbying heavily for sales tax reform to make the system more fair for everyone.

It may be a while before any significant reform takes place. If online sales are part of your business plan, you'll want to monitor developments in this rapidly evolving area.

Sales to Final Users Versus Sales to Resellers

As mentioned above, states generally tax only sales to the final user. The idea behind this rule is to make sure that items are taxed only once. Rather than taxing the sale of a lamp, for instance, each time it is sold—from its manufacturer, to the wholesaler, to the final customer—it is taxed only when it is sold to the final consumer. (Some transactions that are exempt from sales tax, however, may be subject to a nearly identical tax. See "Use Taxes," below.)

How can you be sure that a customer is a final user? Customers who intend to resell your product should present you with a "resale certificate," which states that the product is being purchased for resale. The certificate must contain certain information, including:

- the purchaser's name and address
- the number of the purchaser's seller's permit
- a description of the property to be purchased
- a statement that the property is being used for resale, in terms such as "will be resold" or "for resale" (language such as "nontaxable" or "exempt" is not enough)

- the date of the sale, and
- the signature of the purchaser or an authorized agent.

If you are not presented with such a certificate, you should assume the customer is the final user and treat the sale as taxable. If you sell to the same customer repeatedly, you need only collect one resale certificate, which you should keep on file at your office. From then on, whenever you sell items to that company, there is no need to collect another resale certificate.

Using Resale Certificates

Just as your customers can escape paying you sales taxes by presenting a resale certificate, you can use one to purchase goods and supplies free of sales tax, as long as the goods and supplies are for legitimate resale. This applies whether you'll resell purchased goods as is, or whether you'll incorporate purchased supplies into your products. If you buy regularly from the same supplier, you should only have to present your resale certificate once.

Appendix C and the CD-ROM that comes with it contain blank resale certificates approved by the BOE. Simply give a completed resale certificate, with your valid seller's permit number and the other information listed above, to any company from which you buy goods in order to be exempt from sales tax. There is no need to file a copy of the form with the state.

This exception doesn't apply to goods and supplies that you don't plan to resell or use in manufacturing products. You must pay sales taxes on all items that you'll use in your business and not pass on to a customer. In other words, when you are actually the final user, you have to pay sales tax like anyone else. This includes sales tax on goods and supplies you use to perform services or operate your business. For example, a hairdresser must pay sales tax on the shampoo used to wash people's hair, but not on shampoo offered for sale to salon customers. Similarly, if you purchase a computer to keep track of your sales, you should pay the sales tax on that purchase. When purchasing a combination of goods, only some of which you intend to resell, you must clearly indicate which items are for resale and pay sales taxes on the rest.

Use Taxes

Before you get too excited about sales tax exemptions and exceptions, you should know that California usually finds a way to get a piece of the action, even on sales that aren't subject to sales tax. Although some sales of tangible goods are exempt from sales tax, many of these transactions are actually subject to a use tax. In keeping with its name, a use tax is due when you use a tangible good in the state of California, but didn't pay sales tax for it. The use tax rate is the same as the sales tax rate in that county.

Use taxes commonly apply to purchases of tangible goods from out of state that are used in California. For instance, if you order 20 computers, 20 chairs, and 20 desks for your office from an out-of-state mail order catalogue, you probably didn't pay sales taxes on those items, because most states don't require businesses to collect sales tax from out-of-state purchasers. But under California's use tax law, the state can collect use taxes from you, the buyer, to make up for the revenue it would have gotten if you had bought the equipment within the state. In that way, California collects taxes from the purchaser that it can't collect from the out-of-state seller.

Other transactions subject to use tax include purchases of items you originally intended to resell (and bought tax free because you used your resale certificate), but used for another purpose. Also, items used in manufacturing are subject to use tax (unless they become a physical part of the final product sold), as are items you lease, if the items were bought or leased tax free with a resale certificate. Inventory that you store for future resale is not subject to use tax. (See BOE Publication 110, *California Use Tax Basics,* for more information.)

You report the use taxes you owe at the same time you report sales taxes, on Form BOE-401, *California State, Local and District Sales and Use Tax Return.* If you are confused about how the sales and use tax laws apply to your specific activity or transaction, call the State Board of Equalization office at 800-400-7115.

There's a high blow-off factor when it comes to use taxes. Use taxes have largely been ignored by individuals and businesses, and the inherent difficulty of enforcing this tax allows virtually everyone to get away with it. However, many states that have traditionally been lax in enforcing and collecting use taxes are now stepping up their efforts to collect them. Particularly in today's environment of thriving e-commerce, sales taxes on out-of-state purchases are becoming a burning issue. Keep an eye out for developments in this area, and don't get caught with your use taxes down.

Keeping Track of Your Sales

When you obtain a seller's permit, you obligate yourself to file a sales (and use) tax return. This means that you'll need to keep careful records of both your sales and purchases. The BOE requires that you keep:

- books or computer files recording your sales and purchases
- bills, receipts, invoices, contracts, or other documents (called "documents of original entry") that support your books, and
- schedules and working papers used in preparing your tax returns.

In addition, if you conduct business in more than one county, you'll need to keep separate records of sales made in each county.

Finally, your records should show all sales your business makes, even sales that aren't taxable.

Calculating, Paying, and Filing Sales Taxes

As of late 2009, the standard statewide sales tax rate is 8.25%, which is the total of a 7.25% state tax and a 1% local (city/county) tax. However, if you conduct business in an area that has imposed an additional tax, your sales in those areas will be subject to the higher rate. Individual counties often impose their own additional taxes, which apply to sales throughout the county. Further, cities within those counties may impose their own sales taxes which apply to sales in those cities.

For example, Contra Costa County currently imposes an additional 1% tax (actually, it's two .5% taxes, but let's not split hairs), bringing the sales tax rate throughout Contra Costa County to 9.25%. And the City of Richmond within Contra Costa County imposes its own .5% tax as well, bringing the sales tax rate in Richmond to 9.75%.

To find out what rate applies to specific cities and counties in California, go to the Board of Equalization website at www.boe.ca.gov. Click on the "Taxes & Fees" tab, then the "Sales & Use Tax" section, then "Find the Tax Rate."

Fortunately, you can report and pay all of your sales taxes on one form: BOE-401, *California State, Local and District Sales and Use Tax Return*. (Many small businesses can fill out a shortened version of that form, BOE-401-EZ. See "Simplified Sales Tax Return," below.) All types of businesses, including sole proprietorships, partnerships, LLCs, and corporations (for-profit as well as nonprofit), use the same form and are subject to the same sales tax rules.

Businesses that have been issued a seller's permit will automatically receive Form BOE-401 in the mail, along with an account number, due date, and filing instructions. Depending on your sales volume, you'll need to submit your sales tax return yearly, quarterly, or monthly.

CAUTION

Sellers may be required to file sales tax returns. If you applied for and received a seller's permit because you anticipated selling goods, you'll need to submit Form BOE-401 even if you never made a sale. If you didn't make any taxable sales, you won't owe any taxes, but you still need to submit the form. If you don't, you risk losing your seller's permit, which means you couldn't legally make any retail sales at all.

Simplified Sales Tax Return

Some businesses can fill out a simplified sales tax return, Form BOE-401-EZ. Your business can use the simplified form if you:

- sell in only one county
- do not sell fixed-price contracts or leases
- do not sell fuel, cars, boats, or aircraft, or sell to aircraft common carriers
- do not claim sales tax exemptions for discounts, returned items, or bad debts, and
- do not claim a credit for sales tax paid to another state.

Chapter 8 Checklist: Paying Your Taxes

☐ Become familiar with the general scheme of taxes faced by small businesses.

☐ Remember that you may have to pay estimated taxes in quarterly installments. Other taxes may also have to be paid more often than once a year, such as your California sales tax. Make a calendar of important tax dates so you don't miss them and incur penalties.

☐ Keep careful track of your expenses so that you may deduct them.

☐ Consult a tax professional at least once a year to help you organize your books and reduce your taxes.

☐ File and pay your annual taxes each year and other taxes as they become due.

Laws, Taxes, and Other Issues for Home Businesses

It's not an exaggeration to say that the explosion of home-based businesses has radically reshaped the small business landscape. By most accounts, the number of home-based businesses in the United States exceeds 30 million and is growing strong. Along with the boom in home businesses, whole new industries have emerged, such as major office supply chains; home office networking equipment dealers; home business consultants; and a host of magazines, websites, and other media dedicated to home business issues. No question about it, home businesses—and the industries that have grown around them—are here to stay.

The home business sector has achieved a new level of respect in recent years. Entrepreneurs of all stripes and funding levels have discovered that setting up shop in a home can be a cost-efficient, flexible way to get a business venture off the ground. And an increasing number of home-based businesses are staying put at their founders' homes rather than moving into company digs. "Home business" no longer means Tupperware parties or shady multilevel marketing schemes. Even the most professional, reputable, and aggressively growth-minded companies are joining the ranks of home-based businesses.

It's no secret why the idea of starting a business from home is so attractive to so many. The convenience of working at home is a major draw, especially to parents who want to cut commute times and increase time with the family. Not having to pay rent for an external office helps the bottom line of any business—especially important in the start-up days. And thanks to fast, affordable Internet connections and wireless networks, it's never been easier to exchange documents, do research, send emails, teleconference, and otherwise be connected to the world from home.

In addition to communications and networking, a number of other technologies have advanced by leaps and bounds to help home businesses get firmly established. Prosumer—a hybrid of professional and consumer—imaging products, such as digital cameras, scanners and printers, and easy-to-use Web development software, allow home businesses to create professional-looking brochures, websites, and other marketing materials. With all this new technology, a home business can develop a much more professional image than was possible a decade ago.

Before you hang out your shingle, however, it's important to realize that a home business isn't immune from a number of the requirements that affect businesses in general. Similar to a business operated from a commercial office space, a business run from home must comply with zoning requirements in your area. And there are several special tax rules for home businesses, as well as insurance issues, that you should understand. All of this is discussed in this chapter.

Is a Home-Based Business Right for You?

Not all businesses lend themselves to being run out of a residence. Make sure you've considered whether using your home as your office is a good idea. Ask yourself the following questions:

- How will you deal with customers and suppliers? Will they be able to easily park and pick up or unload material if necessary?
- Will customers take you and your company seriously if you work out of your house?
- Will your business require a lot of space for performing services or storing supplies?
- Can you work productively in your home, considering potential distractions, such as kids, the couch, the refrigerator, and the TV?
- If you rent, will your landlord give your business the okay?

Businesses that require nothing but a small office and don't generate much traffic coming and going —such as graphic design, accounting, and Web development—and those in which most of the dirty work is routinely done offsite—such as construction and plumbing—are particularly well suited for home businesses.

Zoning Restrictions

As with leased office spaces, you need to make sure that the business activities you plan to carry on in your home are within the letter of your local zoning laws. You may also have to apply for a special "home occupation permit" before you begin. (Zoning laws typically refer to home businesses as "home occupations.")

If your home is in an area that's zoned for residential use only (some loft-type or urban apartments might be zoned for mixed use), the types of businesses allowed in your neighborhood will probably be pretty limited. A few areas actually forbid home businesses altogether. But most cities and counties allow home businesses that have little likelihood of causing noise or pollution, creating traffic, or otherwise disturbing the neighbors. Writers, artists, attorneys, accountants, architects, insurance brokers, and piano teachers are examples of businesspeople commonly allowed to work from home. Typically not allowed are retailers, automotive repair shops, cafes and bars, animal hospitals and breeders, or any type of adult-oriented businesses.

 CAUTION

Watch out for private land use restrictions. If you live in a condo, co-op, planned subdivision, or rental property, you are likely subject to private land use restrictions in addition to your local laws. Condo regulations, for instance, often contain language restricting or sometimes even prohibiting business use of the premises. Or your apartment lease might prohibit business on the property. Check the documents governing your property to see if you are bound by any such rules.

Check With the Planning Department

To find out how your city or county deals with home businesses, call the planning department or visit its website if it has one. Ask or look for any information available on home businesses. Some areas have websites or pamphlets with information explaining home business restrictions and how to obtain any necessary permits. In other places, all that's available

might be a grainy photocopy of the municipal code, which you'll have to decipher yourself. If there's no approval or permit process for home businesses in your area, it's generally up to you to comply with the local zoning codes. And those codes are subject to change; be sure to check with the local zoning offices for updates.

The most foolproof way to avoid trouble with zoning officials is to do your best to keep down your business's impact on the neighborhood. As long as you're not in flagrant violation of the zoning laws regarding home businesses and your neighbors are happy, you'll probably be fine.

 TIP

Let your neighbors in on your business plans. Getting to know your neighbors can be a huge help in avoiding problems with zoning officials. For instance, if your business requires people to come and go from your house or packages to be delivered daily, your neighbors might jump to the nutty conclusion that you're a drug dealer and report you to the city. Even though you can show your drug of choice is vitamin C, the city might unearth technical zoning violations that never would have otherwise turned up. As preventive measures, communicating with your neighbors and dealing with their concerns about issues such as parking and noise will greatly reduce the likelihood that the zoning police will come knocking on your door.

Understand Common Restrictions

Assuming that your local zoning laws do allow your type of home business, they are likely to impose some restrictions, such as allowing only residents of your home to be employees, restricting the number of customers that may come to your house, limiting the percentage of your home's floor space that can be used for business, or prohibiting signs outside of your house that advertise the business. In Sacramento, for example, home businesses may have only three employees, of which two must be residents of the home, and home businesses are not allowed to use any trucks larger than one ton.

In addition to these general limitations, cities often impose restrictions on specific types of home businesses. For instance, a city might forbid any type of home business from having a neon sign, or it might have a special rule for landscapers that prohibits landscaping supplies from being kept at the home office. Be sure to find out from zoning officials or the local city hall whether there are special rules for your type of business.

Comply With Local Requirements

If you find out that your city does allow your type of home business in your area, you may have no further need to contact the zoning office. Many cities do not require any special permits, as long as a home business complies with all of the rules and restrictions contained in its planning code (as discussed above). Some cities, however, require all home business owners to get a home occupation permit. Obtaining such a permit is usually a simple matter of filling out a form provided by the planning department and paying whatever fee may be required. If your business meets the restrictions your city imposes, your permit will be issued.

If you don't meet all of your city's rules for having a home occupation, or your area isn't zoned for your type of home business, you may be out of luck and simply not allowed to run your business from home. In some locales, however, a home business that meets most but not all of the city's restrictions may be allowed to operate, but only after obtaining a home occupation permit. In San Diego, for instance, no permit is required for home businesses that meet all of the city's criteria: no business signs, no employees on the premises, and so on. If the home business deviates from the criteria, the city may allow the business to proceed, but only with a home occupation permit. Acceptable deviations in San Diego include having one employee, having one client who visits your home office by appointment, and using more than one vehicle for business.

Keep in mind that the zoning agency is probably not the only land use regulatory agency in your area. Even though your activity might be okay with zoning officials, operating out of your home may not pass other departments' requirements. For example, if you're starting a catering business, chances are your county health department won't let you work out of your home kitchen. You may be allowed to convert your garage or another separate structure into a professional kitchen—but, of course, that is likely to necessitate securing building permits and passing county health inspections, in addition to zoning compliance or permission. (For more information on permits for your specific business activities, see Chapter 6 on start-up requirements.)

Some home occupation restrictions and permit fees for a few of California's cities are listed in the chart "Local Regulations for Home Offices," below. They will give you a general idea of the types of regulations home businesses face across the state. There are, of course, exceptions to these rules and they are subject to change, so be sure to check with your city or county for its specific laws regulating home occupations.

The Home Business Tax Deduction

If your office is located in your home, you may be able to claim a portion of your home expenses—such as rent or depreciation, property taxes, utilities, and insurance—as a special deduction when reporting federal taxes. (This deduction will also flow through to your state return.) The IRS's general rule is that if your business qualifies (see "IRS Requirements," below), you can deduct a pro rata share of home business expenses. "Pro rata" simply means a share that's proportional to the percentage of home space that you use for your business.

This section explains which businesses may qualify for the home business tax deduction, how the deduction is calculated, and other tax issues that apply. (For information on how businesses in general are taxed, see Chapter 8.)

 TIP

Many expenses are automatically fully deducted. Many taxpayers mistakenly believe that they need to qualify for the home business deduction before they can claim any expenses associated with a home-based business. But, in fact, you can deduct business expenses necessary for your business whether they're incurred in your home or anywhere else, even if you don't qualify for

Local Regulations for Home Offices			
City	**Restrictions**	**Required Permit**	**Fees**
Fresno	• All employees must be residents of the home. • Business may not use more than one room of the home. • Business may not use space outside the main home structure—for example, no business activities in the garage. • Business vehicle may not weigh more than one ton and must be stored in an entirely enclosed garage.	None	None
Oakland	• All employees must be residents of the home. • Signs may not be larger than one square foot, must be nonmoving, and may be lit only if indirectly without flashing lights. • If business is conducted in the garage, garage door must be closed. • Any vehicle with a sign advertising the business may not be visible from the edge of the property.	Same zoning approval requirements as for other businesses; $27.54 fee for zoning clearance	$27.54 fee for zoning clearance—applies to all businesses, not just home occupations
Sacramento	• Only three employees or partners are allowed; two must be residents of the home. • Only one customer or client allowed per hour. • Only one truck weighing up to one ton allowed. • No signs allowed.	Home Occupation Permit	$54 one-time fee
San Jose	• All employees must be residents of the home. • Only two clients allowed on premises at one time. • Clients allowed only between 9 a.m. and 9 p.m. • Only one vehicle under 10,000 pounds may be kept at residence.	None	None
San Diego	• Any products produced for sale must be handmade or grown on the premises. • No business signs allowed. • Advertising may not include the home business. • Indoor storage of materials or products may not exceed 1,000 cubic feet.	None	None

the home business deduction. For instance, you can always deduct the portion of your home long-distance phone bill that you spend on business-related calls. Other deductible business expenses might include office supplies, furniture, and equipment that you use in your home office, and the cost of bringing a second telephone line into your home for business use. As used in this chapter, "home business expenses" will refer to expenses that can only be claimed with the home business deduction.

IRS Requirements

Before tackling the nitty-gritty requirements, let's look at a couple basics. First, the IRS definition of "home" is pretty broad, generally including any type of dwelling in which you can cook and sleep. This includes houses, condos, apartment units, mobile homes, boats, and wherever else you reside. Both renters and owners are eligible to take the home tax deduction.

Moving on to the meat of the criteria, the IRS has two requirements for any business owner who wants to deduct expenses for using part of a home as a business:

1. You must regularly use part of your home exclusively for a trade or business.
2. You must be able to show that you:
   - use your home as your principal place of business, or
   - meet patients, clients, or customers at home, or
   - use a separate structure on your property exclusively for business purposes.

Each of these criteria is examined a bit more closely below.

Exclusive and Regular Use for Business

The IRS will allow you to deduct home business expenses only for space in your home that is 100% dedicated to business use. For example, a graphic designer who sometimes sits at the kitchen table to do illustrations can't claim business deductions for using the kitchen—assuming the kitchen is also sometimes used for nonbusiness purposes, such as cooking and eating. A spare room, however, that's set up as an office space and used only for business

would probably meet the exclusive-use test. But if the room contains a bed for the occasional overnight guest or doubles as storage space for clothing, then, technically, it wouldn't qualify.

The regular-use test is generally pretty easy to pass. As long as you use your home business space for business on a frequent, continuing basis, rather than for a once-in-a-while garage sale or other sporadic business activity, you'll probably make the cut.

EXAMPLE 1: Stacey runs a hat-making business. She makes the hats in an extra room of her house in which she has a sewing machine and all her supplies, as well as a computer and a file cabinet containing her sales and other financial information. Because the only use of that room is for the hat-making business, it will meet the IRS's criteria of exclusive use. And because Stacey has made and sold hats for a couple of years, with consistent monthly sales, she'll have no trouble proving that she uses the space regularly for business.

EXAMPLE 2: Parisha has a full-time job at a plant nursery, but also does occasional free-lance photography work. She has a darkroom in her basement that she uses to develop photos for her assignments. Her darkroom is dedicated to her photography business, but she spends most of her time working at the plant nursery and has only done one photo shoot in the last six months. Parisha would be ill-advised to claim her darkroom expenses as a home business deduction, because she doesn't regularly use it for business.

There are two exceptions to the exclusive use rule: If your business use is either storing inventory or product samples, or running a qualified day care center, you don't have to meet the exclusive use test. In these two cases, the parts of the home you use for business—say, a closet for inventory storage or a living room for the day care center—may also be used for personal activities, and you will still qualify for the home business tax deduction. (See IRS Publication 587, *Business Use of Your Home,* for details. It's available online at www.irs.gov.)

Exceptions to the Home Storage Exception

In its inimitable fashion, the IRS has created two exceptions to the home storage exception. First, you won't qualify for the deduction if you have an office or other business location outside your home. Second, you must store the products in a specific, identifiable space such as your garage, a closet, or extra room—not just stacked against the wall of your garage or in the corner of your basement. It's okay to use the storage space for other purposes as well, as long as you regularly use it for storing inventory or samples.

EXAMPLE: Mariana teaches ballet lessons to children at a studio in her home. She also sells instructional dance videos and regularly stores the inventory of DVDs in a large closet in her basement. Because Mariana has no other business location away from her home, she can claim a home business deduction for the basement closet. This is true even though she also stores other things in that closet, such as skis and boxes of books. However, if Mariana ever opens a studio outside her home, she will not be able to deduct the expenses of the storage space.

Principal Place of Business

In addition to fulfilling the exclusive and regular use requirements, your home business space must also be the main place where you do business—with two exceptions, as explained in "Meeting Clients or Customers" and "Home Business in a Separate Structure," below. Thankfully, since 1999, the principal place of business rule has been fairly easy to satisfy. Before 1999, business owners often had to use an imprecise formula to balance how "primary" their places of business were. Now, however, the rule is simple. Your home office will qualify as the principal place of business if you:

- use the office to conduct administrative or management activities, and

- do not have an office or other business location outside your home set up to conduct these activities.

This rule is just as straightforward as it sounds. As long as you use your home office to keep track of your business files, do your bookkeeping and accounting, maintain your client databases, or conduct whatever other type of administration is required, and you don't have a space away from home set up for these activities, your home office will be considered your principal place of business.

Meeting Clients or Customers

If your home office doesn't qualify as your principal place of business under the test described above, you can still qualify for the home business deduction if you regularly and exclusively use your space to meet with clients or customers. As long as you regularly use the home space to meet clients—say, once or twice a week—and don't use the space for nonbusiness purposes, you can claim the deduction for the space even if you have an office away from home.

Home Business in a Separate Structure

Finally, another way to qualify for the home business deduction is to use an external structure on your property—a detached garage, shed, or an in-law unit, for example—regularly and exclusively for your business. Again, this rule applies even if you have another business space such as a storefront or office, and regardless of whether you meet clients or customers there. If the space is used regularly and exclusively for business and is not physically connected to your house, you can deduct expenses for it.

CAUTION

Tax concerns for separate structures. If you use a separate structure on your property for your home business, beware of possible tax repercussions when you sell your home. When a separate structure is used, the business portion of the home will be subject to capital gains tax when sold. (See "Tax Issues When You Sell Your Home," below.)

Tips on Establishing Home Business Use

Home business owners should make an effort to clearly establish their home offices as places of business. Here are some ways you can accomplish this.

- Take pictures of your home office that show its business character.
- Draw a diagram showing the floor plan of the house with the home office clearly defined. Include room dimensions if possible.
- Keep a log of the times you work in the office.
- Keep a record of all client meetings at your office, including whom you met, when, and the subject of the meeting. Recording client visits to your home office is especially important if you also have an outside office.
- Have your business mail sent to your home.
- Get a separate phone line for the business.

Figuring Deductible Home Business Expenses

Once you've determined that you do in fact qualify for the home business tax deduction, you'll need to figure out exactly how much you can deduct. Obviously, you can't deduct all of your housing costs—only the expenses attributable to business purposes qualify.

At the outset, you'll need to determine a "business percentage" for your home—simply, the percentage of your home that is used for business. Then you'll need to look at your home expenses and figure out to what extent they may be deducted.

Calculating Business Percentage

You can calculate the percentage of your home used for business in one of two ways: the "square footage" method or the "number of rooms" method. Either approach is acceptable to the IRS.

The square-footage method simply divides the square footage of the business space by the square footage of the whole house. For instance, if you use 250 square feet for business, and your entire house takes up 1,000 square feet, then your business space uses 25% (250 ÷ 1,000) of your home.

The number-of-rooms method is just as simple: If your house has five similarly sized rooms, and you use one of them for business, then the business uses 20% (1 ÷ 5) of your home.

Categorizing and Deducting Expenses

Once you have calculated a space percentage for your business, use it to calculate the portion of your home expenses that is deductible to the business. Home expenses fall into one of three categories, with different deductibility rules for each.

Unrelated expenses. Expenses that are unrelated to your business space are not deductible at all. For example, you can't deduct the cost of repainting your bedroom or replacing your dining room window.

Direct expenses. You can fully deduct expenses that directly affect your business space, such as the cost of installing new carpeting, replacing a broken window, or repairing the heating vent in your office space. Note that direct expenses for a day care center may not be fully deductible. (For more information, see IRS Publication 587, *Business Use of Your Home,* available online at www.irs.gov.)

Indirect expenses. Expenses that affect the whole house—called indirect expenses—are deductible, but only partially so, based on the percentage of your home that is used for business. For instance, you can deduct a percentage of the cost of plumbing services, roof repairs, mortgage interest, real estate taxes, and utility bills.

To calculate the portion of indirect expenses attributable to your business, you generally multiply the indirect expense by your business percentage. Rent, for example, is an easy expense to prorate. If your business uses 25% of your home, and your rent is $800 per month, then $200 per month is a deductible home business expense (25% x $800). The same simple approach generally works for calculating the deductible business portion of many other indirect expenses such as homeowners' insurance, mortgage interest, home utilities, and repairs.

CAUTION

Repairs are generally deductible; permanent improvements are not. The IRS won't let you deduct the cost of major projects it considers "permanent improvements"—those that increase the value of property, add to its life, or give it a new or different use. The cost of repairs, on the other hand, may be deducted—either fully if a direct expense or partially if an indirect expense. The IRS defines "repairs" as those that "keep your home in good working order over its useful life." (For more details on the IRS's distinction between repairs and permanent improvements, see IRS Publication 587, *Business Use of Your Home*, available online at www.irs.gov.)

RESOURCE

For more on the home office deduction. For more detailed information on tax deductions for home businesses, read *Home Business Tax Deductions*, by Stephen Fishman (Nolo).

Calculating a Depreciation Deduction

If you own your home and you qualify for the home business tax deduction, an indirect expense that you may deduct is the depreciation of your home. Depreciation of your home is an allowance for the wear and tear inflicted upon it. And the home business depreciation deduction is simply a deduction for the business portion of this. Calculating this deduction is slightly more involved than the indirect expense deductions mentioned above. This section offers an overview below of how to calculate the depreciation deduction; detailed instructions are included in IRS Publication 587, *Business Use of Your Home*, available online at www.irs.gov.

Keep in mind that depreciation is calculated for the building only—not the land. Property tax assessments usually show the breakdown of home value versus land value.

In a nutshell, calculating the depreciation deduction works like this:

1. Figure out the adjusted basis of your home (don't include land value) at the time you started using it for business. The adjusted basis of your home is generally its cost, plus the cost of any permanent improvements, minus any casualty losses (sudden losses from accidents, such as a fire or damages from a falling tree) or depreciation deducted in earlier tax years. (The IRS explains adjusted basis in its Publication 551, *Basis of Assets*, available online at www.irs.gov.)

2. Figure out the fair market value of the home (again, not the land) at the time you started using the home office. The IRS defines fair market value as follows: "the price at which the property would change hands between a buyer and a seller, neither having to buy or sell, and both having reasonable knowledge of all necessary facts." Information such as appraisals or the selling price of similar homes in your area when you started using yours for business will help you determine its fair market value.

3. Calculate the portion of the cost of your home that can be depreciated. This amount is called the "depreciable basis." Calculate the depreciable basis by multiplying the percentage of your home used for business by the smaller of:

   - the adjusted basis of your home (excluding land) on the date you began using it for business, or
   - the fair market value of your home (excluding land) when you began using it for business. The result of this calculation—the depreciable basis—is the portion of the home's value attributable to the business.

4. Calculate the actual deduction that your home business will be able to claim. To oversimplify, this deduction is calculated by multiplying your depreciable basis by a certain percentage, set by the IRS. The percentage and specific depreciation method to use will depend on when you started your home business.

There are many more details involved than this book can cover, so you would be wise to at least consult the IRS publications mentioned here before tackling the depreciation deduction on your own. Or consider handing the job over to an experienced business accountant. (See Chapter 16 for more on working with accountants and other professionals.)

Tax Issues When You Sell Your Home

Homeowners with home businesses face a couple of tax issues if they end up selling their homes: capital gains taxes and depreciation recapture. These concepts are widely misunderstood, with the result that many home business owners don't claim their rightful share of deductions for fear of the tax implications. Don't make this mistake. Not only are the rules relatively easy to understand, they're quite favorable to home business owners.

No Tax on Proportional Gain

Before 2002, a home business owner who sold a home at a profit had to pay capital gains tax on the portion of the home used by the business. This was a widely cursed exception to the general IRS rule that exempted home sellers from capital gains taxes on gains up to $250,000 ($500,000 for married couples), as long as they owned and lived in the home for at least two of the last five years. For home business owners, even if the profit from the home sale was within the exempt limits, capital gains taxes would be due on the portion allocated to the home business. One way around this was to stop claiming home business deductions—which is exactly what many home business owners did, kissing goodbye hundreds or thousands of dollars in potential tax savings.

Mercifully, in December 2002, the IRS reversed itself with a new regulation. Now, when you sell your home at a gain, you do not need to allocate a portion of that gain to your home business. You can go ahead and claim all the home business tax deductions you're entitled to, without worrying that you'll be stuck with capital gains taxes for your home business portion. You'll only have to pay capital gains taxes if you exceeded the limits of $250,000 gain ($500,000 for married couples), which would apply whether or not you had a home business.

An important exception to the IRS's 2002 rule is that home businesses located in a separate structure will continue to be subject to capital gains taxes. So if you run your business from a separate, freestanding garage or shed, for example, you'll be stuck paying the gains taxes when you sell your home. To avoid this, stop claiming the home business tax deduction two years before you sell your home.

Recaptured Depreciation Tax

The IRS's 2002 rule change does not change what's known as "depreciation recapture," however. As in the past, home business owners who sell their homes must still pay taxes on the depreciation deductions they've taken over the years. In other words, if you claim depreciation deductions for a home business, the total of those deductions will be taxed—"recaptured," if you will—when you sell your house.

> **EXAMPLE:** Patrice, a yoga instructor, sells her house at a gain of $200,000. Her home studio takes up 10% of her home. Under current IRS rules, she will not be subject to capital gains taxes for the 10% of her home used for business activities. However, Patrice must pay depreciation recapture tax on the total depreciation deductions she's taken in the five years of operating her home teaching studio.

This rule isn't really so bad when you consider the depreciation recapture rate is only 25%. Most business owners pay much more than this on income—self-employment tax at a rate of 15.3%, plus their federal personal tax rate of 15%, 28%, or higher, plus state tax rates—so that depreciation deductions can easily offer savings of 40% or more each year. The bottom line is that it's worth it to take the depreciation deductions, since you'll almost certainly save more in cumulative savings over the years than you'll end up paying when you sell your home.

Risks and Insurance

Just because you run a business from your home, don't make the mistake of taking risk management and insurance issues lightly. Home businesses are often just as vulnerable to theft, fire, personal liability claims, and other risks as businesses based in storefronts or office buildings—sometimes even more vulnerable. It can be a real catastrophe if your computer system is stolen or destroyed, or if a client trips and falls over your garden hose on the way up your front walk.

If you assume that your homeowners' policy will protect you against these risks, you may well find out the hard way that you're horribly wrong. Potentially even more important, home business owners need to make sure that none of their business pursuits jeopardize their regular homeowners' policy for nonbusiness-related claims.

This section discusses the insurance and risk management issues particular to home businesses. (Chapter 7 offers a full discussion of these topics as they apply to all businesses. Be sure to read that chapter in addition to the material below.)

RELATED TOPIC

Start by evaluating your risks. All risk management and insurance decisions must begin with a realistic assessment of what risks your business faces. Only after you do this assessment will you be able to decide how to reduce your risks with insurance or other strategies. While some basic insurance protection for your business assets is never a bad idea, some home business owners may sensibly conclude that insurance is not necessary. (See Chapter 7.) Much of the discussion in this chapter presumes that you've decided some insurance is necessary.

Limitations of Homeowners' Policies

A common mistake among owners of home-based businesses is to assume that business losses will be covered by their homeowners' or renters' policies. This is a very dangerous assumption. While many insurance companies will extend homeowners' coverage to a home business, they'll often require an endorsement—sometimes called a "floater" or "rider"—to a policy that specifically authorizes the coverage. You'll generally have to pay an extra premium for such an endorsement. Without one, the insurance company may deny claims related to a home business.

TIP

Honesty is the best insurance policy. You might wonder how an insurance company would find out that you are quietly operating a home business. Apart from the fact that trying to deceive your insurance company is just a foolish idea, the insurance company's suspicion can easily be aroused by claims involving major business assets such as high-end computer systems, machine equipment, or inventories that seem unsuited for home use. All it could take is a few questions or a visit from an insurance adjuster to blow your cover. When it comes to communicating with your insurer, the best advice is not to mess with the truth.

In addition to requiring home businesses to jump through extra hoops, some insurance companies exact harsh consequences if you run a business from home without informing them first. In some cases, an insurance company may terminate your coverage altogether—even for nonbusiness claims—if it discovers that you've been running a business from your home without its authorization. This is a sobering possibility.

And even when homeowners' policies do cover home businesses—either with or without an endorsement—the coverage may be only for property loss, not for other claims such as liability or business interruption. If a client is injured on your slippery floor, your business may have to pay for any damages awarded in a personal injury lawsuit without any coverage from the homeowners' policy. And if your business records are destroyed in a fire, it's highly unlikely that your homeowners' policy would cover your inability to collect accounts receivable or your lost income from business downtime.

The bottom line is that no home business owner should make the mistake of finding out what is or isn't covered the hard way. If you have homeowners' or renters' insurance, contact the providing company and find out specifically how it deals with home businesses and what kinds of claims are covered. If you're like many home business owners, you'll likely find that your coverage isn't quite what you hoped it might be. Your next step will be to fill in those gaps, either by getting an endorsement to your existing homeowners' policy or purchasing separate coverage.

Finding and Purchasing Coverage

An increasing number of insurance companies are willing to insure home businesses, no doubt due to the massive growth of this market. And despite what you might fear, costs are generally not prohibitive. An endorsement for a home business is typically no more than $1,000 a year—and sometimes much less. Another option is a home business-type policy that's becoming more common. These are distinct from homeowners' policies but aren't quite as robust as full commercial policies, and as a result are generally a good value. Larger businesses with significant assets or risks may need to look at full commercial policies, which may be somewhat more expensive.

If you have a homeowners' or renters' policy, start your search by contacting your current insurance provider. If an endorsement is required, the process is generally a simple matter of paying an extra premium and having documents drafted reflecting the home business coverage. Of course, you'll need to check that the coverage limits are sufficient to cover the value of your business equipment. Also find out whether liability or loss-of-income claims are covered. If not, and if these risks are a concern, you may need to purchase additional coverage.

If your current insurer doesn't offer the coverage you need, one possibility is to find a policy with a different company that meets your requirements. Another option, whether or not you have existing home coverage, is to look for a separate business policy. Business policies can get complicated and expensive, so it's a good idea to use a broker who can present you with options from a range of companies. (See Chapter 7 for general tips for buying insurance.)

Home business owners sometimes can get good deals through trade associations or other organizations that offer coverage options for their members. Organizations tend to get favorable group rates from insurance companies, so these resources are definitely worth a look.

Chapter 9 Checklist: Laws, Taxes, and Other Issues for Home Businesses

☐ Evaluate whether your business activities can be run well from your home.

☐ Find out whether any city or county restrictions—commonly called home occupation regulations—apply to running a business at home and obtain any necessary permits.

☐ To satisfy IRS requirements for the home business tax deduction, use your home business space exclusively for business and not for any personal uses. Review other IRS rules such as the "principal place of business" rule to make sure your home business qualifies for the tax deduction.

☐ Take photos of your home business space to establish its business use.

☐ Do not rely on homeowner's insurance to protect you against losses related to your home business. Even more important, make sure your homeowner's policy is not voided entirely—even for personal claims—by running a business from home.

Entering Into Contracts and Agreements

As a business owner, you'll often have to enter into contracts—legal agreements—with other businesses and people: suppliers, customers, creditors, and landlords, for example. While a few of these transactions will be simple enough to complete with a handshake, most will be sufficiently complicated, long-term, or financially important to require a written contract.

Thankfully—and contrary to what many people believe—a contract is often a fairly simple legal document. A contract usually consists of mutual promises to do specific acts: "A promises to pay B $1,000 if B delivers 50,000 twist-ties to A's warehouse on or before March 1, 20xx." A written contract usually includes the main terms of the agreement: the price of goods, important dates, and the time and place of delivery. For most contractual agreements, standard forms are readily available. Except in the relatively few instances in which lots of money or cutting-edge legal issues are involved, you probably won't need a lawyer to complete your contract.

Simple as some types of contracts may be, you must remember that they are legally enforceable. If you fail to keep your end of the bargain, you can be sued and forced to pay monetary damages to the other party or, in some circumstances, to do the things you promised in the contract.

This chapter explains some contract basics, including what makes a contract enforceable and which contracts are legally required to be in writing.

Contract Basics

Although lots of contracts are filled with mind-bending legal gibberish, there's no reason why this has to be true. For most contracts, legalese is not essential or even helpful. On the contrary, the agreements you should put into a written contract are best expressed in simple, everyday English.

TIP

Don't be afraid to redraft. When reading a contract that has been presented to you, your first task is to make sure you understand all of its terms. It is just plain foolish to sign a contract if you're unclear on the meaning of any of its language. If a clause is poorly written, hard to understand, or doesn't accomplish your key goals, rewrite it to be clear. By refusing to sign at the "X" unless your goals are clearly met, you'll be less likely to find yourself in a breach-of-contract lawsuit later on. A breach of contract occurs when one party fails to live up to the terms or promises in the contract. (For more on changing contract language, see "Reading and Revising a Contract," below.)

Elements of a Valid Contract

A contract will be valid if:

- all parties are in agreement (after an offer has been made by one party and accepted by the other), and
- something of value has been exchanged, such as cash, services, or goods, for something else of value (or there is a promise to make such an exchange).

In a few situations, such as the sale of real estate, the agreement must also be in writing. (See "Oral Versus Written Contracts," below.) Of course, because oral contracts can be difficult or impossible to prove, it is wise to write out most agreements.

Each of these elements is described below in more detail.

Agreement Between Parties

Although it may seem like stating the obvious, an essential element of a valid contract is that all parties really do agree on all major issues. In real life there are plenty of situations that blur the line between a full agreement and a preliminary discussion about the possibility of making an agreement. To help clarify these borderline cases, legal rules have been developed to define when an agreement legally exists.

The most basic rule of contract law is the "offer and acceptance rule" that a legal contract exists when one party makes an offer and the other party accepts it. For most types of contracts, this can be done either orally or in writing. (For a few, discussed in "Oral Versus Written Contracts," below, the offer and acceptance must be made in writing.)

Let's say, for instance, you're shopping around for a print shop to produce brochures for your business. One printer confirms, either orally or in writing, that he'll print 5,000 two-color flyers for $200. This constitutes his offer. If you tell him to go ahead with the job, you've accepted his offer. In the eyes of the law, when you tell the printer to go ahead, you create a contract, which means you're liable for your side of the bargain (in this case, payment of $200). But if you tell the printer you're not sure and want to continue shopping around (or don't even respond, for that matter), you clearly haven't accepted his offer and no agreement has been reached. Or if you say his offer sounds great, except that you want three colors instead of two, no contract has been made, since you have not accepted all of the important terms of the offer—you've changed one. (Depending on your wording, you may have made a "counteroffer," which is discussed below.)

Advertisements as Offers

Generally, an advertisement to the public does not count as an offer in the legal sense. In other words, if you advertised your catering services in your local weekly newspaper and included a price quote of $300 for your standard menu serving 20 people, you would not be legally bound to live up to that service if someone called you and said, "I accept!" If, for instance, you were too busy with other catering jobs and unable to do the job for the eager caller, you could decline. Because your ad wasn't, legally speaking, an offer, the caller couldn't claim a legal acceptance to create a binding contract.

Despite this rule, however, you do need to watch what you say in your advertisements. Generally, you must stock enough of an advertised item to meet reasonably expected demand, or else your ad must state that stock is limited.

Of course, false or misleading advertising is always a bad idea. Federal laws regulating trade and state consumer protection laws prohibit deceptive advertising, even if no one was actually misled. And check your ad's facts—false advertising is illegal, even if you believed the ad to be truthful when you ran it.

In real, day-to-day business, the seemingly simple steps of offer and acceptance can become quite convoluted. For instance, sometimes when you make an offer, it isn't quickly and unequivocally accepted; the other party may want to think about it for a while or try to get a better deal. And before your offer is accepted by anyone, you might change your mind and want to withdraw or amend it. Delaying acceptance of an offer, revoking an offer, and making a counteroffer are common situations in business transactions that often lead to confusion and conflict. To cut down on the potential for disputes, make sure you understand the following issues and rules.

- **How long an offer stays open.** Unless an offer includes a stated expiration date, it remains open for a "reasonable" period of time. What's reasonable, of course, is open to interpretation and will depend on the type of business and the particular situation. Because the law in this area is so vague, if you want to accept someone else's offer, the best approach is to do it as soon as possible, while there's little doubt that the offer is still open. Keep in mind that until you accept, the person or company who made the offer—called the offeror—may revoke it.

  If you are the offeror, be very clear about how long your offer will remain open. The best way to do this is to include an expiration date in the offer. But to leave yourself room to revoke the offer, don't promise that an offer will remain open until a certain date. Instead, state that the offer will expire on that date.

 TIP

Include an expiration date clause in all bids. In many types of businesses, from replacing roofs to redesigning websites, it is common to bid (in other words, to make an offer to create a contract) on lots more jobs than you really need or want. But sometimes this strategy can backfire. With lots of offers floating around, there is always the chance that too many will be accepted, raising the embarrassing possibility that you won't be able to deliver on all the work. One easy way to minimize this problem is to print right on your bid or offer form that all offers are good for only ten days (or some other relatively short period) unless extended in writing.

- **Revoking an offer.** Anyone who makes an offer can revoke it as long as it hasn't yet been accepted. This means if you make an offer and the other party needs some time to think it through, you can revoke your original offer. If your offer is accepted while it is still open, however, you'll have a binding agreement. In other words, revocation must happen before acceptance.

- **Options.** Sometimes the offeror promises that an offer will remain open for a stated period of time—and that it cannot and will not be revoked during that time. This type of agreement is called an option, and options don't usually come free. Say someone offers to sell you a forklift for $10,000, and you want to think the offer over without having to worry that the seller will revoke the offer or sell the forklift to someone else. You and the seller could agree that the offer will stay open for a certain period of time, say 30 days. Often, however, the offeror will ask you to pay for this 30-day option—which is understandable, since he or she can't sell to anyone else during the 30-day option period. But payment or no payment, when an option agreement exists, the offeror cannot revoke the offer until the time period ends.

- **Counteroffers.** Often, when an offer is made, the other party will not accept the terms of the offer right off, but will start bargaining. Of course, haggling over price is the most common type of negotiating that occurs in business situations. When one party responds to an offer by proposing something different, this proposal is called a "counteroffer." When a counteroffer is made, the legal responsibility to accept or decline the offer or make another counteroffer shifts to the original offeror. For instance, if your printer (here, the original offeror) offers to print 5,000 brochures for you for $300, and you respond by saying you'll pay $250 for the job, you have not accepted his offer (no contract has been formed), but

instead have made a counteroffer. It is then up to your printer to accept, decline, or make another counteroffer. If your printer agrees to do the job exactly as you have specified for $250, he's accepted your counteroffer and a legal contract has been formed.

Exchange of Things of Value

Even if both parties agree to the terms, a contract isn't valid unless the parties exchange something of value in anticipation of the completion of the contract. The "thing of value" being exchanged—called "consideration" in legal terms—is most often a promise to do something in the future, such as a promise to perform a certain job or a promise to pay a fee for that job. Returning to the example of the print job. Once you and the printer agree on terms, there is an exchange of things of value (consideration): The printer has promised to print the 5,000 brochures and you have promised to pay $250 for them.

This requirement helps differentiate a contract from generous statements and one-sided promises, neither of which are enforceable by law. If a friend offers to do you a favor, for instance, such as helping you move a pile of rocks, without asking anything in return, that arrangement wouldn't count as a contract because you didn't give or promise him anything of value. If your friend never followed through with the favor, you would not be able to force him or her to keep the promise. If, however, in exchange for helping you move rocks on Saturday, you promise to help your friend weed a vegetable garden on Sunday, the two of you have a contract.

Although the exchange of value requirement is met in most business transactions by an exchange of promises ("I'll promise to pay money if you promise to paint my building next month"), actually doing the work or paying the money can also satisfy the rule. If, for instance, you leave your printer a voice mail message that you'll pay an extra $100 if your brochures are cut and stapled when you pick them up, the printer doesn't have to respond; he can create a binding contract by actually doing the cutting and stapling. And once he does so, you can't weasel out of the deal by claiming you changed your mind.

Oral Versus Written Contracts

Before you learn more about which contracts have to be in writing to be legally enforceable, here's some advice: Put all of your contracts in writing, regardless. For compelling practical reasons, all contracts of more than a trivial nature should be written out and signed by both parties. Here is why:

- Writing down terms tends to make both parties review them more carefully, eliminating misunderstandings and incorrect assumptions right from the start.
- An oral agreement—no matter how honestly made—is hard to remember accurately.
- Oral agreements are subject to willful misinterpretation by a not-so-innocent party who wants to get out of the deal.
- Oral contracts are sometimes difficult and often impossible to prove, making them hard to enforce in court.

EXAMPLE: Kay opens a plant shop called The Green Scene. Because she needs specialized grow lights for her extensive line of tropical plants, she checks with several contractors who install lighting systems. One company, Got a Light, says it will install a system for $3,000, including the cost of the lights themselves and installation charges. That quote is the lowest among the companies Kay has checked, so she tells Got a Light she'll accept the offer—but only with a written contract.

When Got a Light sends Kay a contract, she notices that it doesn't address rewiring her shop. She calls Got a Light and talks with Dan, who tells her that she needs to have an electrician add several new circuits and provide six specialized outlets before Got a Light can install the lighting system. Based on this discovery, Kay and Dan discuss exactly what needs to be done before Got a Light's work begins, and they include this new agreement in an additional contract clause. Dan recommends an electrician, whom Kay hires to do the rewiring. She also manages to negotiate a lower price with Got a Light, based on the fact that the rewiring will be done according to Got a Light's specifications, making the installation much easier.

The best advice is to get every contract in writing. Now here's what the law says: California has a law called the Statute of Frauds that requires certain contracts to be in writing. (Cal. Civ. Code § 1624.) The Statute of Frauds typically requires the following types of contracts to be in writing:

- An agreement that by its terms can't be completed in a year or less. For example, a contract for a bakery to provide fresh bread to a restaurant for two years must be in writing. On the other hand, if the contract might take longer than a year to complete but could be completed within a year, it doesn't need to be in writing. For example, a contract for a gardener to landscape five big properties would not need to be written, because it is quite possible that the gardener would finish the work within one year. Similarly, a contract for a bakery to bake bread for a restaurant with no time period stated would not need to be in writing.
- A lease with a term longer than one year, or an agreement authorizing an agent to execute such a lease on your behalf.
- Any sale of real estate (or of an interest in real estate), or an agreement authorizing an agent to purchase or sell it on your behalf.
- An agreement that by its terms will not be completed during the lifetime of one of the parties. This includes a promise to leave someone your business when you die.
- A promise to pay someone else's debt, such as a business partner's promise to pay your car payments or an agreement that the person who prints your brochure will also pay the cost of photographic work done at another shop.

In addition to the Statute of Frauds law, California has a special body of law on commercial issues called the Uniform Commercial Code (UCC). (California Commercial Code §§ 1101 et seq.) Under the UCC, a sale of goods for $500 or more requires at least a brief written note or memo indicating the agreement between buyer and seller. The note can be much less detailed than a normal contract; it only has to show an agreement between the parties and the quantity of goods being sold. Other terms that are typically covered in contracts, such as the price of goods or the time and place of delivery, aren't required. This written memo usually has to be signed, although if one party doesn't object to the memo within ten days of receiving it, then his or her signature isn't required.

Using Standard Contracts

By now, you should understand that your contracts should be written, but you may still have no idea how to write the ones you'll need. Luckily for you and most other businesspeople, virtually every type of business transaction is covered by a readily available standard contract. Service contracts, rental agreements, independent contractor agreements, contracts for sales of goods, and licensing agreements are just a few examples of blank-form contracts you should easily be able to find.

Anyone who has ever picked up a fill-in-the-blanks lease or promissory note from an office supply store, torn one out of a self-help law book, or downloaded one from a website is familiar with how this works. Blank rental agreements, for example, are widely available at office supply stores, through landlords' associations, at most public libraries, in Nolo's *LeaseWriter* software, and from many other sources. Once you find the blank contract you need, you simply fill it in and, if necessary, modify it before signing.

If you can't easily find a blank-form contract that meets your needs, try the sources mentioned here.

- Trade associations are excellent resources for fill-in-the-blanks contracts.
- Your competitors might be less than willing to share their contracts with you, but similar businesses in faraway locations (which you won't be competing with) might be willing to show you theirs.
- The Web has oceans of information for small businesses, including sample contracts. Try searching for terms particular to your type of business to find specific contracts you need.
- Nolo books offer many different blank-form agreements, and www.nolo.com includes

Special Requirements for Certain Contracts

Other state laws impose additional requirements for contracts involving particular businesses or certain kinds of transactions. For instance, contracts for weight-loss services, dating services, and fitness services must be in writing, regardless of the dollar value or length of time covered by the contract. Plus, these contracts must include the following special language in at least ten-point boldface type:

"**You, the buyer, may cancel this agreement, without any penalty or obligation, at any time prior to midnight of the original contract seller's third business day following the date of this contract, excluding Sundays and holidays. To cancel this agreement, mail or deliver a signed and dated notice, or send a telegram which states that you, the buyer, are canceling this agreement, or words of similar effect.**" (Cal. Civ. Code §§ 1694 & 1812.)

Unfortunately, there's no centralized place where a business owner can learn about any special contract laws that apply to a particular type of business.

You can always search through California's business statutes for any mention of your type of business. However, if doing legal research is too time consuming or overwhelming for you, a good alternative is to use the limited help of a lawyer who's generally familiar with small business issues and, if possible, already works with businesses in your field (other plant nurseries, website designers, or restaurants, for example). Many small business lawyers are now more flexible in offering just as much or as little help as clients need, and offer coaching services to those who want to handle their simple legal affairs themselves. Using a legal coach is especially useful for small business owners who often need answers to simple legal questions, rather than full-blown attorney services. (Chapter 16 discusses working with lawyers and finding one who's willing to coach you through simple legal matters.)

many single-copy forms, such as promissory notes. For general business contracts on paper and CD-ROM, a great resource is *Legal Forms for Starting & Running a Small Business,* by Fred S. Steingold (Nolo).

Once you've found a contract that generally fits your needs, you can amend it for your particular situation. It's entirely appropriate and often necessary to change the clauses of a fill-in-the-blanks contract to suit your needs. Of course, it's crucial that you understand what you're doing. Don't just strike a clause because you don't understand what it means, or add a clause without fully knowing the consequences of including it. To help you educate yourself about typical contract language, the next section explains some of the clauses that commonly appear in contracts.

How to Draft a Contract

If you can't find a form agreement or if you find one that needs a load of revisions, you may need to draft a clause or two—or possibly even a whole contract—from scratch. Don't be intimidated. Either way, your goal is simple: to state clearly what each party is agreeing to do and the specifics of how they'll do it (usually called the terms of the contract). Put another way, your written contract should be the most accurate reflection possible of the understanding you have with the other party. This section explains the important terms you'll need to include in most contracts and alerts you to situations that might require more specialized provisions. The information provided will help you edit or draft amendments to a standard contract, or draft a contract from scratch if necessary. You'll also find examples of how to state certain terms—although, as mentioned above, clear English is usually all that's necessary.

TIP

Don't get too specific. Although a good contract covers all the important aspects of a deal, don't be too anal specifying every minute detail. For instance, if you hire a cleaning service, you probably don't need

to specify what type of brushes it will use to scrub your floors. Better to put your energy into picking the right person or company to do the job and leave some of the specifics of the actual work up to those who will do it. In deciding how much detail is enough, you'll simply have to judge for yourself which nitpicky details are so important that they should be covered in your contract and which ones you can safely ignore. For example, if you need fresh salmon for a party at 6 p.m., the time of delivery and quality of the fish are extremely important points, but the exact weight of each fish or the method of delivery may be a lot less so.

Contract-Writing Basics

Here are some tips for writing contracts.
- Avoid the use of "he," "she," "they," or other pronouns in your contracts, as they can easily lead to confusion over whom you're talking about. Use either the actual names of the parties or their roles, such as Landlord and Tenant. It might seem repetitive or clumsy to write this way, but your goal is to be clear—not to write beautiful prose.
- Stay away from legalistic words, such as wherefore, herewith, or hereinafter. Far from making your contract sound more impressive, this type of language is simply unnecessary, outdated, and confusing. Stick to modern, clear English. Likewise, don't include legal expressions you think you may have heard elsewhere. Legal-sounding jargon will not make your contract more binding—and if you get it wrong, you may be bound to terms you didn't want, or your contract may be void.
- Make at least a couple of drafts of your contract. After the first draft, let it rest a day or so and then reread it. Does it leave any questions in your mind? If it does, fill in the gaps on your second try.

What to Include in a Basic Contract

So you've reached an agreement with another party and are ready to put it into writing. Before you start editing a form contract or writing one on your own, step back a moment to consider that the goals of all contracts are to:

- clearly outline what each party is agreeing to do (including timelines and payment arrangements)
- anticipate areas of confusion or points of potential conflict, and
- provide for recourse (remedy) in case the agreement is not followed through to completion.

The more you have at stake, the more carefully you'll have to approach the task of putting together your contract. For example, if you're entering into a contract to buy a truckload of bicycle tires for $1,000, you won't need your agreement to be outlined nearly as meticulously as you would in a contract for the construction of a building.

SEE AN EXPERT

For complex agreements, you may need an attorney. More complex contracts—especially those in areas unfamiliar to you—are often best handled with the help of a lawyer. Certainly, if a transaction is so huge or elaborate that it makes your head spin, you shouldn't go it alone. First, decide how much help you need. Rather than having an attorney draft your contract from start to finish, you could simply have an attorney review a contract that you or the other party has written. Ideally, you should hire a lawyer with some experience with small business, preferably your type of business. Even better would be an attorney who knows the ins and outs of your business, based on a long-term working relationship. (See Chapter 16 on getting legal assistance.)

Let's look at the information most contracts include to fulfill these three goals. Except where noted, you don't need to use any special language to get the following information across:

- **Title.** Generally a contract will have a simple, to-the-point title such as "Contract for Printing Services" or "Agreement for Sale of Ball Bearings."
- **The names and addresses of all the parties.** It should be clear what role each party has in the contract, such as seller or buyer; landlord or tenant; client or service provider.

The addresses of the parties generally appear at the end of the contract in the section with the signature.

EXAMPLE: Christopher Johnson ("Client") desires to enter into a contract with Virgil's Printing ("Printer") for printing services for Client's newspaper.

- **A brief description of the background of the agreement (called "recitals").** While not always included, this type of information is often necessary to frame the contents of the agreement. Typically this section includes a brief description of what kinds of businesses the parties run and the nature of the transaction covered in the contract.

EXAMPLE: Client prints and distributes a free, weekly, 24-page newspaper, called *El Norte*, with a circulation of 40,000. Printer operates a full-service print shop with three printing presses. The subject of this contract is an agreement that Printer shall print Client's newspaper each week in exchange for payment.

- **A full description of what each party is promising to do as part of the agreement.** This section, sometimes called the "specifications," or just "specs," describes the terms of the deal. If a product is being sold, describe the product and delivery terms. If a service is being performed, describe the job and then state when it will be completed, including any intermediate deadlines that must be met before the final completion date. Indicate whether strict compliance with deadlines is necessary by throwing in the phrase, "Time is of the essence." This is a standard phrase used in contracts—it simply means that deadlines will be enforced strictly.

If specifications are complicated (for example, intricate performance details for a software contract), they should normally be set out in attachments to the contract, which may include scale drawings, formulas, or other detailed information about the transaction.

EXAMPLE: Client promises to upload PDF files ("Files") for printing to Printer's shop no later than 10 a.m. each Wednesday morning. Printer promises to print, fold, and bundle 40,000 copies of Client's newspaper and have them ready for Client to pick up from Printer's shop by 8 p.m. that same Wednesday. Time is of the essence regarding this contract. If, however, Client fails to upload Files to Printer by 10 a.m. Wednesday morning, Printer may take extra time to complete the job. The amount of extra time will depend on how late Client is in uploading the Files and on Printer's schedule of other jobs, but in no case shall be longer than 24 hours after uploading of the Files.

- **The price of the product or service.** This section states how much one party will pay for the other party's goods or services. If the price may vary (say, based on the time or quality of performance) or if it will be established later, a description of how it will be calculated should be included.

EXAMPLE: Client will pay Printer $1,000 for every 10,000 24-page newspapers printed, up to 50,000 newspapers. The price will be renegotiated if Client orders more than 50,000 newspapers, or if the number of pages per newspaper changes.

- **Payment arrangements.** This section should explain when payment is due, whether it will be paid all at once or in installments, and whether interest will be charged if payments are late. Also include any other special requirements, such as whether payment must be by certified or cashier's check. Otherwise, a garden-variety check will normally suffice. Again, if strict compliance with payment deadlines is necessary, use the phrase "Time is of the essence."

EXAMPLE: Client will pay Printer the full amount of each week's printing cost within three days of picking up the completed newspapers.

- **A statement of any warranties made by either party regarding the product or service being provided.** A warranty is essentially a guarantee made by one party to another that a product or service will meet certain standards. If either party gives a warranty, the contract should state what will happen if the guarantee isn't satisfied—for instance, if certain standards aren't met, the party who got the raw end of the deal will be given a refund or may give the other party another chance to do the job right.

EXAMPLE: Printer warrants that the completed newspapers shall be free from printing defects or errors attributable to Printer. In case such errors do occur, Printer and Client may negotiate a discount not to exceed actual damages suffered by Client.

Automatic Warranties

Under California's Uniform Commercial Code (UCC), all sales of products are automatically covered by some warranties whether or not the seller promised anything to the buyer. These warranties are called "implied warranties" and include two guarantees: that the product is fit for its ordinary use and that it is fit for any special purpose for which the seller knows the buyer wants to use it. For example, the sale of a kitchen knife comes with an implied warranty that the knife will work in ordinary kitchen uses. If the buyer asked the retailer to help pick out a knife that would cut through heavy beef bones, then whatever knife the retailer sold would come with a warranty that it would work for cutting heavy beef bones. This is true regardless of whether or not the knife came with an express, written warranty that it could be used for heavy butcher work.

Be aware of the existence of implied warranties when drafting your contracts. Even if you don't make specific promises in your contracts, you will still be legally bound by the two kinds of implied warranties described above: fitness for ordinary use and fitness for a particular purpose. The law regarding warranties can be complex. You may want to consult an attorney for more detailed information about your obligations as a seller.

- **A statement whether either party may transfer the contract to an outside party.** Transferring contract rights is also called assigning. If you have chosen a company to provide products or services because of particular characteristics, such as good personal service or artistic detail, you may not want that company to be able to hand off the job to someone else, who may not do as good a job.

  EXAMPLE: Neither Printer nor Client may assign this contract or any part of it to another party.

- **The contract term.** This section, usually only one sentence, establishes how long the contract will be in effect.

  EXAMPLE: This contract will remain in effect for a period of one year, or until it is terminated by one of the parties, whichever is first.

- **A description of any conditions under which either party may terminate the agreement.** For some types of contracts (for example, contracts to provide an ongoing service), a termination clause often states that either party must give a written termination notice to end the contract, often 30 or 60 days in advance.

  EXAMPLE: Upon written notice of at least 30 days to the other party, either Printer or Client may terminate this agreement.

  But you may not want the parties to be able to terminate the contract, even with advance notice, just on a whim. In this case, you can specify a limited number of certain events that might allow a party to end a contract. For instance, say you want to be able to rely on using your website hosting service for at least a year, so you include a clause in your contract that neither party can terminate the contract for the next 12 months except if either party goes bankrupt, in which case either party would have the right to terminate the contract.

On the other hand, there may be situations in which you want to be able to terminate a contract yourself. For instance, say you own a rock shop that sells lots of agate, so you contract with a supplier to sell you a half-ton of agate each month for a year. To protect yourself, you could include a clause in your contract stating that if you resell less than a quarter-ton of agate in any calendar month, you may terminate the agreement.

- **An outline of how you will deal with a breach.** Though signing a contract may not head off a subsequent dispute, it can channel the dispute in ways that will allow it to be resolved as quickly and cheaply as possible. There are a number of different approaches you can take if someone fails to abide by the contract—or breaches it.

  You can decide, in advance, the amount of damages (financial compensation) a breaching party will have to pay. This will help you avoid the often lengthy and contentious process of calculating a party's damages after the other party breaches the contract. When damages are preset in a contract, they are called liquidated damages. In order for a liquidated damages clause to be valid, the dollar amount of damages that you set must be a reasonable estimate of what actual damages would be, not merely a preset penalty for breaking the contract.

  Another option is for both parties to agree in the contract to try mediation and, if that fails, arbitration to settle a dispute as an alternative to going to court.

  EXAMPLE: If any dispute arises under the terms of this agreement, the parties agree to select a mutually agreeable, neutral third party to help them mediate it. The costs of mediation will be shared equally. If the dispute is not resolved after 30 days in mediation, the parties agree to choose a mutually agreeable arbitrator who will arbitrate the dispute. The costs of arbitration will be assigned to the parties by the arbitrator. The results of any arbitration will be binding and final.

If one or both of you prefers going to court, you can provide in the contract that the losing party in a dispute must pay the other party's legal fees, or you can establish that each party is responsible for their own legal fees regardless of who prevails. Note that, for some commercial transactions, neither party in a lawsuit can collect attorney's fees from the other unless it is provided for in a written contract.

- **For contracts with out-of-state entities, a statement of which state's laws apply.** Although contract law in all states is very similar, using California law will generally be the simplest for you, since you'll have more resources at your disposal, including law libraries and local attorneys.

  EXAMPLE: This contract shall be governed by and interpreted according to the laws of California.

- **Signatures, dates, and addresses.** Your signature section should always include room for the date the contract was signed, as well as the addresses of the parties.

Jennifer F. Mahoney, owner of an illustration service in Northern California:
My creativity is exercised just as much by drawing up a good agreement with a client as it is by the way I create art for that client.

Putting Your Contract Together

In addition to making sure your contract includes all the necessary information, you'll need to present it in an easy-to-follow, professional format. Generally, contract clauses are organized in a series of numbered paragraphs for easy reference to specific terms.

If your agreement includes any hard-to-articulate details, such as the specifications of a software product, drawing a company logo, or originating architectural blueprints, you can include them as attachments to the main contract. If you do include an attachment, be sure to label it and refer to it in the main contract. To officially make it a part of the contract, state somewhere in the main contract that you "include the Attachment in the contract," or that you "incorporate the Attachment into the contract."

EXAMPLE 1: Company agrees to pay artist $100 for use of logo. Logo is attached to this contract as Attachment A and is hereby included in this contract.

EXAMPLE 2: Contractor agrees to complete remodeling within one year. The final plans are attached to this contract as Exhibit B and are incorporated into this contract.

Reading and Revising a Contract

If you don't like certain terms of a contract that's presented to you, you can propose changes. By doing this, you are technically making a counteroffer. Contracts are commonly negotiated back and forth (offer and counteroffer) this way until all the terms are accepted by both parties. Remember, if the parties aren't in agreement, there's no contract—oral or otherwise.

Changes to a contract—whether to a form contract or one drafted from scratch—can be made in a number of ways. You can simply cross out language and fill in new language directly on the contract itself. Both parties should initial any such changes to show that they approve of them, then sign the contract as a whole.

In today's world, however, it's more than likely that there will be an electronic copy of the contract on someone's computer. If so, it makes much more sense to make the necessary changes on the computer and then print out a clean copy for both parties to sign. However, some industries (such as the real estate industry) when making a counteroffer commonly use a separate document that states the desired changes and refers back to the original offer. In that case, the original offer and the counteroffer together form the contract.

A contract can also be amended at a later date with a separate document called an addendum. The addendum should state that its terms prevail over the terms of the original contract, especially if the terms are in direct conflict, as would be the case if the price or completion time for a job is changed. Both parties should sign the addendum.

Electronic Contracts

While the basics covered so far generally apply to any contract regardless of form—whether the contract is printed in a formal document, scratched on a cocktail napkin, or just spoken and sealed with a handshake—there are new and emerging rules that apply specifically to contracts created online. Before you read the very general overview of the special issues involved in electronic contracts, keep in mind that law in this area is rapidly evolving—scrambling, in fact—to catch up with fast-evolving technology.

What Is an Electronic Contract?

An "electronic contract" is essentially any agreement that is created and executed in electronic form—in other words, no paper or other hard copies are used. Typically, electronic agreements are created either via email or on interactive Web pages. For instance, many companies use interactive forms at their websites that users must complete to purchase goods or software, join a membership organization, participate in a mail listserv, or do whatever else the company is offering. In addition to asking the user to enter various items of personal information, these forms typically display the terms of the contract between the company and the user, and ask the user to agree to the terms by clicking on a button such as "I Accept."

Here's another example of an electronic contract: A business associate of yours emails you a request to purchase a specified number of items you sell, at a named price, for immediate delivery. If you email back that you agree to all the proposed terms, you've probably just entered into a legally enforceable electronic contract. Why "probably"? Because there is no way for you to sign the contract with pen and ink, and states vary in how they treat digital signatures. Read on.

Taking Traditional Contract Principles Online

As mentioned above, contract law is only beginning to grapple with the details of paperless agreements. When electronic contracts have been challenged, courts have had a difficult time determining whether an actual binding contract existed, since it can be unclear whether all the traditional elements of contract formation were met.

Shortcut Contracts for E-Commerce

When it comes to small transactions in which you pay for goods by credit card, most sites get around the issue of whether a valid contract has been formed by noting that if you are dissatisfied for any reason, they will give you your money back. This is another way of saying that if you don't want a contract to exist, it doesn't. Or put another way, the company concedes in advance that it won't try to enforce the contract. This trust-the-customer approach works well for small transactions, but has obvious limitations when it comes to major purchases—a car, for example, or significant business-to-business transactions. In these situations, a real signature on an enforceable contract is needed.

Clickwrap Agreements

Businesses have traditionally used standard contracts that aren't open to negotiation; customers have to either accept the contract as is or not complete the transaction. Examples might include a car purchase contract or an agreement to rent a moving truck, in which a consumer who insisted on changing any of the terms of the company's standard contract would not be able to buy the car or rent the truck. Over the years, these types of contracts have been challenged on the grounds that they are not fair to the consumer because they are typically presented in a take-it-or-leave-it manner, giving the consumer little or no power to amend a contract that is often highly favorable to the seller. Whether or not these types of contracts (sometimes called contracts of adhesion, because consumers are forced to "adhere" to the contract) are valid has long been a contentious area of contract law. Generally, adhesion contracts are held to be valid, as long as the terms are clear to the consumer and not grossly unreasonable.

Today, Internet click-to-agree contracts—often called clickwrap, webwrap, or browsewrap agreements—are facing similar challenges. So are other nonnegotiated agreements, such as the software licenses included with packaged software, sometimes called shrinkwrap agreements. While these types of agreements have generally been found valid, courts have refused to enforce certain terms that are deemed too burdensome or unfair to the consumer.

A federal case decided in 2002 sheds some light on the question of when a clickwrap agreement may be deemed invalid. In that case, an Internet user who downloaded software from a website operated by the Netscape company later sued Netscape, claiming that the software license was not binding. To download the software, the user had simply clicked a "Download" button and was not required to view the software license or click any button such as "I Agree" to indicate consent to license terms. To view the license, the user would have had to scroll below the "Download" button and click on another link to a separate page where the license terms were posted.

The U.S. Court of Appeals for the Second Circuit ruled in favor of the user, based on the principle that for a contract to be binding, both parties must assent to be bound. The court found that the structure of Netscape's software download page "with license terms on a submerged screen" and no button to clearly indicate consent was not sufficient to create a binding contract with the user. (*Specht v. Netscape Communications Corp.*, 306 F.3d 17 (2d Cir. 2002).)

The *Netscape* case establishes that downloading alone does not indicate acceptance of license terms. To make sure a clickwrap agreement is binding, the site must be set up to ensure that a user can clearly indicate consent to the license terms of any downloads. Keep this in mind if you plan to use any clickwrap agreements with your business.

Legislative Attempts to Solve Clickwrap Issues

Over the past few years, there have been a number of state legislative efforts to deal with the issues and problems raised by clickwrap agreements. However, state laws governing electronic contracts are not consistent, which has actually done more harm than good. And the state courts that have heard and ruled upon electronic contract cases have come up with different decisions, with the result that checking an "I Accept" box may create a contract in one state, but not in another. No question, this lack of uniformity has been a real thorn in the side of e-commerce, which of course recognizes no state boundaries.

In response, the National Conference of Commissioners on Uniform State Laws (NCCUSL) decided to tackle the problem by drafting model legislation for adoption by the states. One of these proposed laws, the Uniform Computer Information Transactions Act (UCITA), addresses the issue of clickwrap and shrinkwrap agreements, essentially making these types of contracts valid and binding. California has not adopted the UCITA—and doesn't seem likely to do so in the future.

In fact, few states have adopted the UCITA in the years since it was drafted. One reason may be that many consumer advocates, as well as over 25 state attorneys general, argue that the UCITA is biased in favor of software vendors and information services providers, leaving consumers with significantly less protection than they have under current law. An online search of the term "UCITA" will lead you to many sites with updated information on the act—and an almost universally negative take on it.

Electronic and Digital Signatures

One of the stickier issues involving electronic contracts has to do with whether agreements executed in a purely online environment have been "signed" (outside of clickwrap agreements, discussed above). For many centuries, the traditional way to indicate your acceptance of a contract (and most other binding documents) has been to sign it with your unique signature. But electronic contracts can't be signed this way. Instead, people use other means to indicate they accept the terms of a contract, such as simply typing their names into the signature areas of the documents. But increasingly, better technological approaches to the problem of signing contracts online are being developed, such as fingerprint and iris scanning, in addition to a cryptographic technology known as Public Key Infrastructure (PKI). These methods are collectively known as electronic signatures. The term "digital signature" refers specifically to cryptographic signature methods such as PKI.

What Is PKI?

Security experts currently favor the cryptographic signature method known as Public Key Infrastructure (PKI) as the most secure and reliable method of signing contracts online. Without going too deep into the technical details, PKI involves using an algorithm to encrypt the document so that only the parties will be able to modify it or "sign" it. The process of encrypting the document is known as creating a digital signature. Each party will have a "key" allowing him or her to read and sign the document, ensuring that no one else will be able to sign it fraudulently. PKI standards are still evolving, but the technology is already widely accepted as the best electronic signature method available. A good source for more information on PKI technology is the Information Assistance Support Environment's Public Key Infrastructure (PKI) page at http://iase. disa.mil/pki.

Until relatively recently, most states didn't have any laws stating which of these ways to sign an electronic document was legally acceptable. In response, the NCCUSL drafted another model law, the Uniform Electronic Transactions Act (UETA), which specifically addresses electronic signatures. In a nutshell, the UETA provides that electronic signatures (in all their forms) and contracts are just as valid and legally binding as their paper counterparts. As of late 2009, all states except Illinois, New York, and Washington had enacted the UETA—making it easier for California businesses to operate nationally.

Federal Law on Electronic Signatures

Fortunately, as the states were mulling over whether to adopt the UETA, the UCITA (see "Legislative Attempts to Solve Clickwrap Issues," above), or both, the U.S. Congress forged ahead and passed federal legislation establishing the validity of electronic signatures nationwide. This bill, known as the Electronic Signatures in Global and National Commerce Act, was signed into law in June 2000 and became effective on October 1, 2000. The law applies to all states that had not already adopted the UETA or a similar electronic signature law by mid-2000. In states such as California that have already adopted essentially the same legislation, state law will govern electronic signatures; the other states will be bound by the federal law. In this way, the law finally gives some much-needed consistency to the way states treat electronic signatures in online transactions.

This law is similar to the model UETA in that it makes electronic signatures and contracts (including clickwrap agreements) just as valid as paper ones. While certain transactions are exempt from this law and must still be completed on paper (wills, cancellation of utility services, court orders, and other official court documents, among others), the law allows an enormous range of business and consumer transactions to be completed totally online. In essence, it throws the door wide open for all types of e-commerce, allowing businesses and consumers to create (in theory at least) reliable, binding contracts online, without the inconvenience of shuttling paper documents back and forth.

Tips for Creating Contracts Online

While the federal e-signature law, along with the UETA, create a solid legal framework for online contracts, electronic signature technology is still evolving, which means the reality of online contracts still falls somewhat short of its promise. Like the UETA, the e-signature law does not specify any particular technology for electronic signatures, leaving that up to software companies and the free market to establish. As mentioned above, PKI technology is currently favored by security experts, though its standards aren't completely nailed down or ready for common use. As developments in PKI and other electronic signature methods create solid, worldwide standards, e-commerce will only become more efficient and widespread.

While waiting for reliable standards to develop, it will be important to approach online contracts carefully. Of particular concern is the possibility for fraud, especially since there is no set standard for what constitutes a valid electronic signature. Until the technology is airtight, make sure that you trust the other party to an online contract and are comfortable with the type of electronic signature that you're using. If you're not comfortable creating a contract online, you may want to stay low tech and stick with paper contracts, either faxed back and forth or sent by overnight mail.

The nonprofit Consumers Union, which publishes *Consumer Reports* magazine, has issued a set of tips to follow when using electronic signatures and creating online contracts.

- Don't consent to using an online contract if you are uncomfortable using a computer or do not understand how to use email.
- Don't agree to use an online contract or to receive electronic documents until you are sure that your computer's software and hardware will be able to read and use the documents provided by the company.
- Remember that the electronic signatures law allows you to opt to receive documents on paper instead of electronically if you prefer.
- Keep back-up paper copies of the electronic documents you receive, and keep a list of the businesses with which you agree to create electronic documents.
- Notify the businesses of any changes that may affect your ability to receive and read email and attachments, such as changing your email address, your hardware, or your software.
- Close any unused email accounts.
- Don't give out your email address to any business if you don't want to receive email notices from it.

- Notify the business right away if you have any problems receiving its emails or opening its documents.

You can find these tips and other information about online contracts at the Consumers Union website at www.consumersunion.org.

⚠ CAUTION

Beware of e-viruses. Never open attachments to email if you aren't expecting the email or don't know who it's from. Nasty viruses are often spread through email attachments, so it's good policy to just throw away suspicious mail as soon as you see it. Even when you know the sender of the email, you need to be cautious. Some viruses use a computer user's email address book to replicate themselves, by sending themselves out to everyone in the book. This means that if you get an email with an attachment from your friend Steve Smith, there's a chance that Steve Smith didn't actually send the email. For this reason, you shouldn't open attachments unless you're expecting them.

Chapter 10 Checklist: Entering Into Contracts and Agreements

☐ Become familiar with the legal basics of contracts.

☐ Put all your contracts into writing whenever possible. (Contracts created online or by email are considered to be "in writing.")

☐ Try to respond to offers promptly, and when making an offer, include an expiration date.

☐ When you need to draft a contract from scratch, try using standard form contracts to get started.

☐ Be thorough in your contracts. Make sure that any points of potential conflict are clearly spelled out.

☐ Use caution when entering into electronic contracts (also called online contracts or digital contracts). If you're uncomfortable creating a contract online or by email, don't do it—opt for a paper contract.

Bookkeeping, Accounting, and Financial Management

Perhaps the hardest part of accounting is getting over the psychological hang-up that most people seem to have about it. Many of us hate to balance our checkbooks on a regular basis, much less keep detailed accounts of how our money comes and goes. In truth, you don't need to be a financial wizard to start a small business; you just need a comfortable working knowledge of the basics.

If you read Chapter 4, "Drafting an Effective Business Plan," some of this material may be a review. That chapter explained how to generate financial projections using sales and expense estimates to see if your business is likely to turn a profit. The financial tools used in business planning —particularly profit/loss analysis and cash flow projection—are the same tools used in accounting, just employed slightly differently. Instead of making financial projections, we'll focus on how to track actual, current financial data for your business.

This chapter will give an overview of what's involved in bookkeeping and the basic concepts business owners need to understand. We'll explain what receipts and records your business should keep and describe simple ways to organize them. We'll also explain how bookkeeping software works, including setting it up, entering your income and expense data, and generating reports showing how well (or poorly) your business is doing financially. Generating reports from your income and expense data will also help you manage the cash that flows through your business so that you can pay your important bills on time.

While this chapter provides important, basic financial management information that every business owner should understand, keep in mind that it often makes sense to use a professional bookkeeper to handle data entry and financial management tasks. Retail stores, for example, with dozens or hundreds of transactions every day would likely want to have a part- or full-time bookkeeper on staff to keep the books continually updated. Smaller businesses, like consultants or freelancers, might simply do the data entry themselves, or contract with a bookkeeper to do data entry once a month. And even if you plan to do all the data entry and financial management yourself, it's still a good idea to have at least a consulting session or two with an experienced bookkeeper when you start your business to make sure you set up a solid financial management system from the very beginning. An experienced bookkeeper can be a huge help in getting off on the right foot, from clarifying what records you should keep, to setting up your bookkeeping software and understanding how to use it.

Fortunately for today's entrepreneurs, inexpensive, powerful, and easy-to-use software is available that vastly simplifies financial management tasks. Programs such as *Quicken, QuickBooks,* and *MYOB* have several different versions to meet the needs of all sizes and types of businesses, making this once-unsavory task much more palatable. Once your income and expenses are entered into the software, you can easily generate sophisticated financial reports that would have taken many hours and considerable skill to create just a decade ago. In fact, these programs are so affordable (generally under $400, and often far less or even free) and user friendly, it really doesn't make sense to track your finances by hand, which is not only much more time-consuming but more prone to errors.

TIP

Don't expect software to do your accounting. You shouldn't simply rely on the numbers that your software program spits out if you don't fully understand them. The accounting concepts and processes described in this chapter are the same whether done manually or by accounting software—and you should take the time to learn them. Though accounting software makes it much easier to manipulate the numbers you've entered and to generate informative financial reports, you still need to understand what all the numbers mean in order to use them to make meaningful business decisions.

Bookkeepers and Accountants: What Is the Difference?

In a nutshell, bookkeepers specialize in the day-to-day tasks of tracking a business's income and expenses, often being in charge of data entry and generating reports such as monthly profit/loss statements (explained later in this chapter). In addition, bookkeepers are often hired to prepare payroll (including determining how much tax to withhold from employee's checks, issuing the checks, and managing payroll tax deposits), file statements for property or unemployment taxes, and related bureaucratic tasks.

Accountants, on the other hand, specialize in making sense of your financial data and handling tasks such as filing tax returns and managing tax-savings strategies for businesses. Accountants can analyze your financial data and give advice on questions such as whether it's a good time to expand your business or how to set up employee benefits to maximize tax savings. Since accountants typically have deeper knowledge of tax rules than bookkeepers, they are usually in the best position to answer any gray-area tax questions, such as whether certain types of transactions are subject to state sales tax. (See Chapter 16 for more information on different kinds of accountants, such as certified public accountants.)

There's typically a big cost difference between accountants and bookkeepers—accountants usually charge significantly more—so you'll want to hire the right one for the right tasks. It's generally advised for all small businesses to hire an accountant at least once a year to prepare your business's tax return. (Tax basics are discussed in Chapter 8.) For smaller, day-to-day tasks and routine filings, you'll be better off hiring a bookkeeper. Bookkeepers can also be a big help in establishing an effective recordkeeping system, including choosing the best financial management software for your business, setting it up, and showing you how it works.

CAUTION

Avoid money laundering. Someone in a trade or business has 15 days to report receiving more than $10,000 in cash in one transaction or related transactions. A "transaction" includes the purchase of property or services, the payment of debt, and even holding cash for someone for more than 15 days as part of a deal. "Cash" includes any combination of U.S. and foreign coins and bills and a cashier's check, money order, bank draft, or travelers' check (but not a personal check) with a face amount of $10,000 or less—unless it comes from a bank loan. To report, the business owner must file Form 8300 with the IRS and the Financial Crimes Enforcement Network (FinCEN). Breaking up one transaction into many little ones to avoid this reporting requirement can lead to prison and heavy fines. Check with your accountant or lawyer if you are in this league.

Accounting Basics

For anyone intimidated or just plain overwhelmed by the prospect of managing your business's finances, it can be helpful to get back to basics and consider the big picture. Carefully tracking income and expenses helps you in the following two primary ways:

- **You'll improve your chances of making a profit.** Having a firm handle on your income and expenses is essential to making smart business decisions that lead to profitability.
- **You'll have well-organized financial information that is necessary to file your various tax returns and local tax registration papers.** There's no worse nightmare than facing a tax deadline and having months' worth of unorganized receipts that haven't been entered into your recordkeeping system (or worse yet: not having a recordkeeping system in place at all).

Sounds pretty simple, no? All the intricacies of financial management basically boil down to these two points. You should also be reassured to know that there is no requirement that your records be kept in any specific organizational system. There is a requirement, however, that some businesses use a certain method of crediting their accounts. (See "Cash Versus Accrual Accounting," below.) In other words, there's no official system or format

Accounting Glossary

A big part of understanding the financial side of your business consists of nothing more than learning the language of accounting. Once you're familiar with some common terms, such as the ones listed below, you'll be better able to make sense of basic written reports and to communicate with others about important financial information. And you'll also be well positioned to cope with a common business problem: people who use key financial terms imprecisely or even incorrectly, needlessly confusing themselves and others.

- **Accounting** refers to the process of tracking your business's income and expenses, then using these numbers in various calculations and formulas to answer specific questions about the financial and tax status of the business.
- **Bookkeeping** refers to the task of recording the amount, date, and source of all business revenues and expenses. Bookkeeping is essentially the starting point of the accounting process. Only with accurate bookkeeping can there be meaningful accounting.
- An **invoice** is a written record of a transaction, often submitted to a customer or client when requesting payment. Invoices are sometimes called "bills" or "statements," though statement has its own technical meaning.
- A **statement** is a written summary of an account. Unlike an invoice, a statement is not generally used as a formal request for payment, but is used to outline the details of an account.

- A **ledger** is a collection of related financial information, such as revenues, expenditures, accounts receivable, and accounts payable. Ledgers used to be kept in books preprinted with lined ledger paper (which explains why a business's financial information is often referred to as the "books"), but are now commonly kept electronically using various software programs.
- An **account** is a collection of financial information grouped according to customer or purpose. For example, if you have a regular customer, your information regarding that customer's purchases, payments, and debts would be called his or her "account." A written record of an account is called a "statement."
- A **receipt** is a written record of a transaction. A buyer receives a receipt to show that he or she paid for an item. The seller keeps a copy of the receipt to show that he or she received payment for the item.
- **Accounts payable** are amounts that your business owes. For example, unpaid utility bills and purchases your business makes on credit are included in your accounts payable.
- **Accounts receivable** are amounts owed to your business that you expect to receive, including sales your business makes on credit.

to organize your books. As long as your records accurately reflect your business's income and expenses, the IRS will find them acceptable.

TIP

Organization is everything. One thing that all good bookkeeping systems have in common is organization. A well-organized system with accessible, reasonably neat files (including both hard-copy and electronic records) not only will be a godsend in the event of an audit, but will help you keep track of your business as well.

Benefits of Well-Maintained Financial Records

Are you beginning to believe that you don't need to be afraid of accounting? Good, because it's something you absolutely need to embrace as part of running any business. Failing to keep track of income and expenses is one of the surest ways to run any business off a cliff. Here are a few more details on how a well-maintained bookkeeping system will help your business.

- **You'll be able to price your goods and services more competitively.** Only by staying on top of your business's income and expenses will you know how much money you'll need to bring in each week, month, or year to make a profit. This knowledge is essential to allow you to price your goods and services appropriately. For instance, if you don't know your break-even point, you will only be able to guess at how much you should charge your customers for products or services, with the likely result that you'll charge too little (and make an inadequate profit) or too much (and alienate customers).

- **You'll be able to trim costs strategically.** Having updated and categorized expense data will allow you to see your spending patterns and spot areas where you can reduce your costs to improve your bottom line. For example, you may see the need to cut back on travel expenses or on outsourced services that aren't sufficiently helping generate income.

- **You'll be able to pace your growth more effectively.** A good set of books will give you the information you need to decide when and how to expand your business. If your numbers tell you that sales and profits have been growing consistently for several months, that may be a signal that it's time to hire additional employees or enter into a new market—or both. Without meaningful financial numbers, making any decisions about growth can be a gamble. For example, just because your business has a lot of money in its checking account doesn't necessarily mean you're making good money. (You might have received several big payments from past sales, while current sales are actually slowing down.)

- **You may be able to reduce taxes.** Knowing your company's finances inside and out will help you save money when tax time comes around. For example, if the end of the year is nearing and your up-to-date records clearly show the year to be profitable, you can purchase needed supplies or equipment before the end of the year and write off these expenses, reducing your taxable income. Also, keeping careful track of your expenses will remind you to claim them as deductions at year-end. Businesses that are sloppy about bookkeeping

often miss opportunities for saving tax dollars. Don't be one of them.

- **You'll avoid tax penalties.** In addition to helping you legally save tax dollars, responsible bookkeeping will help you avoid errors in your tax returns that can subject you to fines and other penalties. If your business is audited, the IRS can be really nasty if it finds your books in bad shape. In extreme situations, it may even refuse to recognize perfectly legitimate expenses. In short, neglecting your responsibility to maintain basic, accurate records is likely to result in the kind of trouble with the IRS that you might not wish on even your worst enemy.

The Financial Management Process

At the most basic level you can break down the process of financial management into three broad steps. We'll discuss these in more detail later in the chapter; for now let's just look at an overview.

1. The process starts with keeping records (basic receipts, usually) of all the money the business spends (expenses) and all the money it earns (income). This means carefully keeping and organizing your expense receipts (that is, receipts from the office supply store, bills from your accountant and lawyer, records of payments to your employees and freelancers, and so on) and your income receipts (such as a cash register tape of your clothing store's income, check stubs from your client's payment checks, or your invoices to clients marked "Paid").

2. Next, on some periodic basis—say monthly for a small consulting business, or daily for a busy retail store—you'll enter the information from the income and expense receipts into a bookkeeping system. More often than not this will be some sort of financial management software such as *QuickBooks*. (In the old days, this was done by entering the income and expenses into a hardbound book called a ledger.)

3. Finally, with up-to-date information entered into your bookkeeping system, you'll generate reports such as a profit/loss report or an

accounts receivable report to reveal how your business is doing. These reports summarize the data you've entered to show you different aspects of your business's financial situation. For example, a profit/loss report shows whether you made a profit in a given time period (usually monthly), while an accounts receivable report shows how much your clients owe you at any given time. Generating reports should be done on some periodic basis, with some reports following different schedules than others. For example, most businesses should generate a profit/loss report each month, as well as quarterly and annually.

! **CAUTION**

Do not neglect to open a business bank account! Using your personal bank account for business deposits and expenses is a huge mistake for a number of reasons. One is that if you hoped to protect your personal assets by creating an LLC or a corporation, you'll basically throw any such protection out the window by comingling personal and business funds. And on a more important day-to-day level, mixing your business transactions with personal transactions will make it impossible to do the types of simple financial management described in this chapter. Run, do not walk, to your local community bank and open a business bank account as soon as you're ready to launch.

Cash Versus Accrual Accounting

Before turning to several simple systems for keeping your records, you need to understand the two principal methods of keeping track of a business's income and expenses: cash method and accrual method accounting (sometimes called cash basis and accrual basis accounting). In a nutshell, the difference between these methods has to do with the timing of when transactions—both sales and purchases—are credited to or debited from your accounts. In short:

- Under the cash method, income is counted when cash (or a check) is actually received, not necessarily when the sale occurs; expenses are counted when they are actually paid, not necessarily when you made the purchase.
- Under the accrual method, transactions are counted when they happen—for example, when you complete a sale, or make a purchase—regardless of when the money is actually received or paid. You don't have to wait until you receive the money, or until you actually pay money out of your checking account, to record the transaction.

For example, say you purchase a new laser printer on credit in May and pay $2,000 for it in July, 60 days later. Using cash method accounting, you would record a $2,000 expense for the month of July, the month when the money was actually paid. But under the accrual method, the $2,000 payment would be recorded in May, when you took the laser printer and became obligated to pay for it. Similarly, if your computer installation business finished a job on November 30, 2010, and didn't get paid until January 10, 2011, you'd record the payment in January 2011 if you used the cash method. Under the accrual method, the income would be recorded in your books in November of 2010.

💡 **TIP**

Timing can be tricky. Some sales aren't completed all at once. If you use accrual accounting, you may sometimes wonder exactly when you can enter the transaction into your books. For instance, say someone buys two CDs from your record store but also makes a special order for another CD, and pays for all three at once. Or, say your landscaping company finishes a large project, except for the last step of applying a final lawn fertilizing treatment two weeks after laying the sod. The key date here is the job completion date. Don't count the transaction until you deliver all of the goods, finish all parts of a service, or otherwise meet all terms of a contract. If a job is mostly completed but will take another few days to add the finishing touches, it doesn't go on your books until it is completely done. In situations like these, the help of an experienced bookkeeper can be a godsend.

TIP

Both methods can produce the same results. As you can see, the results produced by the cash and accrual accounting methods will only be different if you do some transactions on credit. If all your transactions are paid in cash as soon as completed, including your sales and purchases, then your books will look the same regardless of the method you use.

Accounting Methods and Taxes

The most significant way your business is affected by the accounting method you choose involves the tax year in which income and expense items will be counted. (See "Tax Years and Accounting Periods," below.) For instance, if you use the cash method, and incur expenses in the 2011 tax year but don't pay them until the 2012 tax year, you won't be able to claim them on your 2011 tax return. But you would be able to claim them in 2011 if you use the accrual method, since that system records transactions when they occur, not when money actually changes hands.

> **EXAMPLE 1:** Zara runs a small flower shop called ZuZu's Petals. On December 22, 2010, Zara buys a number of office supplies for which she will be billed $400. She takes the supplies that day but, according to the terms of the purchase, doesn't pay for them for 30 days. Under her accrual system of accounting, she counts the $400 expense during the December 2010 accounting period, even though she didn't actually write the check until January of the next year. This means that Zara can deduct the $400 from her taxable income of 2010.

> **EXAMPLE 2:** Scott and Lisa operate A Stitch in Hide, a leather repair shop. They're hired to repair an antique leather couch, and they finish their job on December 15, 2011. They bill the customer $750, which they receive on January 20, 2012. Because they use the accrual method of accounting, Scott and Lisa count the $750 income in December 2011, because that's when they earned the money by finishing the job.

This income must be reported on their 2011 tax return, even though they didn't receive the money that year.

Tax Years and Accounting Periods

Income and expenses must be reported to the IRS for a specific period of time, alternately called your "tax year," "accounting period," or "fiscal year." Unless you have a valid business reason to use a different period, or unless your business is a corporation, you'll have to use the calendar year, beginning on January 1 and ending on December 31. Most business owners do use the calendar year for their tax years, simply because they find it easy and natural to use. But if you want to use a different period, you must request permission from the IRS by filing Form 8716, *Election To Have a Tax Year Other Than a Required Tax Year.* (A copy of this form is included in Appendix C and on the CD-ROM that comes with this book.) Also, your fiscal year can't begin and end on just any day of the month; it must begin on the first day of a month and end on the last day of the previous month one year later.

Which Method to Use

In choosing a method, first consider the IRS rules that may dictate your choice. The general rule is that businesses that have inventories (retail businesses, for example) must use the accrual method, but there are exceptions. Businesses that have sales of less than $1 million per year are generally free to adopt either accounting method even if inventories are involved—but note that other rules may apply regarding tracking inventories in your books. For businesses with gross sales of more than $1 million but less than $10 million annually, there are more rules and exceptions that may allow a business to use the cash method. Broadly speaking, businesses with gross sales in this range can use the cash method if the principal business activity is not mining, wholesaling, manufacturing, retailing, publishing, or sound recording. Another requirement is that the business must primarily be service oriented, though it's acceptable for some products to be provided if they are incidental to the business. If your business doesn't meet these requirements, it will generally be required to use the accrual method. The rules are a bit squirrely, so you should ask an accountant for advice.

Perhaps even more important than the IRS rules is to consider which method will give you the most control over your business's finances. In general, the cash method is simpler and may be the best route for freelancers and small firms. However, the cash method does not give as accurate a picture of your operational profitability as does the accrual method. Under the cash method, for instance, your books may show a three-month period to be spectacularly profitable because a lot of credit customers paid their bills in that period, when actually sales have been slow. Because accrual method shows the ebb and flow of business income and debts more accurately, it is generally recommended for all but the smallest businesses.

Whichever method you use, it's important to realize that either one gives you only a partial picture of the financial status of your business. To have a true understanding of your business's finances, you need more than just a collection of monthly totals; you need to understand what your numbers mean and how to use them to answer specific financial questions, as discussed in the rest of this chapter.

Step 1: Keeping and Organizing Receipts

Comprehensive summaries of your business's income and expenses are the heart of the accounting process. But unless you want to flirt with tax fraud, you can't just make up the information in your books. Each of your business's sales and expenditures must be backed up by some type of record containing the amount, the date, and other relevant information about that transaction. The best way to stay organized is to have a system in place—in other words, a set of files, folders, cash registers or whatever else that you use consistently over time so

that you always know where to find the information you need.

From a legal point of view, your method of keeping receipts can range from slips kept in a cigar box to a sophisticated cash register-based system; this may include point-of-sale (POS) software which typically goes beyond tracking transactions to managing categories and subcategories, inventory, and more. Practically, you'll want to choose a system that fits your business needs. For example, a small service business that handles only relatively few jobs may get by with a bare-bones approach. But the more sales and expenditures your business makes, the more sophisticated your system needs to be. Whether your needs are simple or complex, the important thing is to make sure that you and any staff know the system and use it consistently. If your records aren't accurate, the financial statements you make from them won't be, either.

This section discusses common ways of keeping your receipts. The bottom line is to choose or adapt one to suit your needs.

Income Receipts

Every time your business brings in money, you need a record of it. Most of your revenue will come from sales of your products or services, but keep in mind that some may come from loans or capital contributions. How you keep track of sales will vary a great deal, depending on what type of business you run and how many sales you make. Businesses such as grocery stores that make hundreds or even thousands of sales a day will likely need a cash register (and possibly an integrated POS system) to record each sale. Other businesses with slower sales, such as hair salons or auto shops, may get by simply writing out a receipt for each sale from a receipt book. Freelancers and consultants generally use their invoices marked "Paid" as income receipts.

Regardless of how you generate income receipts, they should always include the date, a brief description of the goods or services sold, an indication of how payment was made, whether the sale was subject to sales tax, and if so, the amount of sales tax separate from the total.

If any of your sales are subject to sales tax, it's critical that your income receipts distinguish a pretax total from the amount of sales tax charged (if any). As discussed in more detail under "Sales Taxes" in Chapter 8, many sales of goods are subject to sales tax, which retailers must pay to the state. But other large categories of sales are often exempt from sales tax, such as sales of services, sales to out-of-state residents, or sales to resellers. So, some sales income is taxable, and some is not. Your income records must reflect whether a sale is taxable, and if so, the amount of sales tax. If any of your sales are subject to California sales taxes, you'll need this information to compute and file your state sales tax returns with the California Board of Equalization (BOE).

In addition, the BOE requires that you keep records of nontaxable sales in separate categories, such as food sales, sales to retailers, and sales to the U.S. government. The required categories may vary depending on what kind of business you run. Contact the BOE for information on the specific categories your particular business must use. The BOE has a number of publications and tax tip pamphlets that explain the bookkeeping requirements for various businesses. Check the BOE's website at www.boe.ca.gov for its list of publications.

If you use a cash register, taxable sales will generally be marked as such by the push of a button at the time of each sale, and tax amounts will be shown separately. If you write out a receipt of each sale by hand, be sure to show any sales tax separately, not just as part of a total. If the sale is nontaxable, make that clear by writing "no tax," "nontaxable," or the like. Most cash registers will also allow you to set up categories to track, which will help you meet the Board of Equalization's requirements as mentioned above.

Finally, make sure to document any income your business receives from sources other than sales and keep these receipts separate from your sales receipts. If you get a loan or contribute your own personal money to the business, record this fact with some sort of receipt or promissory note. Be sure your written records adequately describe the source of income so you'll know whether to count it as taxable income or not (see "Taxable Sales Versus Taxable Income" below). Most income generated from sales of your products or services, for example, will be taxed at the end of the year, while income that you personally contribute to the business will not.

TIP

While it's good business practice to give receipts to customers who purchase goods or services, it's a legal requirement that you keep a copy for yourself. Therefore, if you write out your own receipts, you'll need to make two copies—one for you, and one for the customer. Cash registers and most receipt books make each record in duplicate.

Taxable Sales Versus Taxable Income

As discussed in this section (and in more detail under "Sales Taxes" in Chapter 8) many sales of goods are subject to California sales tax, which retailers must pay to the state. But other large categories of sales are often exempt from sales tax, such as sales of services, sales to out-of-state residents, or sales to resellers. So some sales income is taxable, and some is not.

However, whether a sale is taxable for *sales tax* purposes is a different issue from whether income is taxable or not for *income tax* purposes. Generally, taxable income—that is, money you take in that is subject to income taxes at the end of the year—includes any money earned by your business, minus certain deductions. All of this income must be reported on your year-end income tax return, whether or not it is subject to state sales tax.

Expenditure Receipts

Ever hear the business wisdom that the key to small business success is to keep your costs down? Though this isn't the only thing a successful business owner needs to do, watching those pennies is always a good idea. The first step in keeping costs down is keeping accurate track of what they are. Just as you keep a record of each individual sale, you need to keep a record each time you spend money for your business. Business expenditures include paychecks to employees; money spent on supplies, office rent, and telephone bills; payments on loans; and all other costs associated with your business. Legally and practically, each and every one of these expenses must be recorded.

The easiest way to ensure you track every expense is to make sure to get a written receipt for every transaction in which you spend money for the business. Each expenditure receipt should include the date, the amount, the method of payment, who was paid and—most important—a description of what type of expense it was, such as rent, supplies, or utilities. The description is important because later, when you enter your expenses into your bookkeeping software, you'll need to assign one or more categories to each expense. These categories— such as rent, advertising, supplies, utilities, meals, travel, and taxes—are important for tax purposes, because different types of expenses have different rules for deductibility. If any important information isn't included on the receipt, write it in. Later, when entering receipts into your bookkeeping system, you'll be glad you made sure to note the important information.

Bear in mind that you'll often have a number of receipts for just one purchase: a credit card slip, a register receipt, and an itemized statement, for example. If you throw all three receipts into your files to be posted later, you run the risk of counting all three separately. Ditto if you have a checkbook register entry plus a register receipt. To avoid counting transactions more than once, either discard multiple copies of receipts immediately after the transaction or staple them all together. It's also a great idea to write the check number on the cash register receipt so you can easily cross check when entering receipts into your software.

Step 2: Entering Receipts Into Bookkeeping Software

On some regular basis—every day, once a week, or once a month at a minimum—you should transfer ("post") the amounts from your income and expenditure receipts into your bookkeeping software. (Entering income and expense receipts could also be described as entering transactions.) Later, you'll use the data you've entered to answer specific financial questions about your business, such as whether you're making a profit and, if so, how much.

Generally speaking, the more sales you make, the more often you should enter your receipts. A busy retail operation that does hundreds of sales every day should post daily, while smaller, slower businesses with just a few large transactions per month would probably be fine posting weekly or even monthly. With a high sales volume, it's particularly important to see what's happening every day and not to fall behind with the paperwork. For this reason, most busy, high-volume businesses will have a modern cash register that's programmed to automatically "dump" the day's information into the bookkeeping software at the end of each day.

When entering information into your bookkeeping software, remember the adage "garbage in, garbage out." If the information you enter isn't accurate or the software isn't set up correctly in the first place, you won't be able to generate the meaningful financial reports that are so crucial to any business. Take the time early on to learn how your software works, configure it correctly, and enter data carefully to minimize errors.

Let's take a look at some of the details involved in setting up your bookkeeping software and entering transactions. Remember, once the transactions are entered, accounting software makes preparing monthly and yearly financial reports incredibly easy.

 TIP

Learn the concepts behind the numbers. Even though bookkeeping software allows you to generate sophisticated financial reports with a few mouse clicks, you should still take the time to understand how the numbers fit together and what they mean. The more you know about your numbers and the relationships between various figures, the better able you'll be to make positive and profitable business decisions.

Creating Accounts

When setting up your bookkeeping software, one of the first things to do is set up accounts to mirror the business accounts you have in real-life: a checking account and a credit card account, for instance. It's critical to post transactions to the appropriate accounts, so that you can reconcile your bookkeeping records against the bank or credit card statements. Reconciling each month is an important way to make sure your records are complete and accurate; we'll describe the reconciling process in a bit more detail below.

> **TIP**
>
> **Create a "catch-all" account for business expenses paid for with personal accounts.** Inevitably, business owners occasionally spend money from their personal accounts (either using cash or a debit or credit card) on business expenses. While you should strive to avoid this, it just happens from time to time—for example, you bought some business books among a bunch of personal books paid for with your personal debit card; or you bought a business suit along with personal clothes and paid for it all with your personal checking account. One good way to account for these stragglers is to create a "general register" account in your bookkeeping software as a catch-all account that will include any transactions (usually expenditures, not income) that for whatever reason weren't made from an official business checking or credit account.

Depending on your circumstances and how your accountant or bookkeeper advises you, there are other accounts you can create to track your business's finances. Common examples include separate accounts for receivables (amounts owed to you) and payables (amounts you owe to others), or accounts to track depreciable assets, such as computers or vehicles. Again, a bookkeeper can be quite helpful in figuring out which accounts to set up.

Creating Income and Expense Categories

Besides creating accounts, an important part of setting up your bookkeeping software is creating categories for income and expenses. As mentioned above, different types of income and expenses are treated differently for tax purposes, so it's essential that they are tracked separately in your bookkeeping system. As we discuss in more detail in Chapter 8, some expenditures can be deducted right away in full, others may be deducted only over several years (referred to as "depreciating expenses"), while other costs may not be deductible at all.

Income categories will typically include "taxable sales," "sales tax," and "nontaxable sales" categories and possibly others—say, "travel reimbursement," "loan," or "interest income." Businesses typically have many different categories for expenses such as rent, utilities, computer equipment, employee wages, legal fees, postage, or travel, to name a few.

> **RESOURCE**
>
> **The IRS has oceans of rules.** For more information on different types of business expenses and their deductibility, read *Deduct It! Lower Your Small Business Taxes*, by Stephen Fishman (Nolo). Reading the rules issued by the IRS isn't a bad idea, either. IRS Publication 334, *Tax Guide for Small Business*, is a good place to start. It's available at www.irs.gov.

Besides categorizing income and expenses to account for different tax treatment, there's another essential reason to categorize expenses: Careful, strategic categorization will allow you to generate financial reports that reveal which aspects of your business contribute the most (or least) to your bottom line, which in turn will allow you to make adjustments to maximize profits. We'll discuss the details of financial reports in the next section, but the point here is that the categorization is essential. Without tracking income and expenses by category, you won't be able to generate meaningful financial reports later on.

EXAMPLE: Shane is launching a photography studio that will focus on weddings, baby portraits, and professional head shots. When setting up the bookkeeping system (with the help of a trusted bookkeeper), Shane makes sure to include separate categories for income from these three separate services. This way, he will be able to generate reports showing which services bring in the most gross income. In addition, Shane makes sure to categorize expenses so that he will be able to generate reports showing the expenses associated with each of the services, as well as reports comparing income to expenses for each service.

After six months in business, the financial reports show that the weddings consistently generate the most gross income. The profitability picture is different, however. When expenses associated with each service are factored in, Shane sees that baby portraits are actually the most profitable service, because there are much lower costs associated with them than with the weddings. Shane decides to put some effort into lowering the costs associated with weddings in order to make them more profitable. If Shane had not created separate income and expense categories for weddings, baby portraits, and professional head shots, the financial records would not have revealed the revenue and profit trends, and Shane would have missed out on the opportunity to tweak his marketing and pricing in order to boost profits.

When deciding what categories to create and track, keep in mind the distinction between fixed costs and variable costs. Variable costs, you may remember from Chapter 4, are tied to your products or services, while fixed costs (overhead) more or less stay the same regardless of your production and sales volume. Without keeping careful track of variable costs, you won't know how profitable your individual products or services are, or whether your pricing is too high, too low or just right. Fixed costs are also crucial to track, in large part because they can be such a drain when business is slow.

Typical Expense Categories

As a general reference, here's a list of common expense categories:

- advertising
- automobile
- bank charges
- copying
- delivery, freight, and shipping
- dues and fees
- education (classes, workshops, and so on)
- employee wages
- equipment, furniture, and computers
- equipment rental
- insurance
- interest on business debt
- legal and professional fees
- meals (business related)
- membership
- office expenses and supplies
- office rent
- online services
- postage
- publications (books, magazines, and so on)
- software
- tax preparation fees
- taxes
- telephone
- travel, and
- utilities (gas and electric).

There's something of an art to defining the categories that are relevant for your business. You want them to be tightly defined—but not so narrow that you end up with dozens of tiny groups. For example, a handyman would likely use categories such as lumber, paint/sealants, hardware, and equipment rentals, but wouldn't go so far as to have a separate category for nails versus screws. A hair stylist might use categories like booth rental, cutting tools, and hair products; depending on her circumstances, she might want to further subcategorize the hair products into shampoos, conditioners and styling products. An experienced bookkeeper familiar with your field can be extremely helpful in setting up your categories and subcategories in a way that will help you generate the most meaningful reports for your business.

As for actually setting up the categories in your bookkeeping software, all programs make this really easy. Generally speaking, you'll create the categories when you set up the software; later, when you enter your transactions, you'll choose from the list of categories you've created. Undoubtedly over time you'll refine your bookkeeping system and your categories, and all bookkeeping software allows you to add, edit, and delete your categories whenever you want.

Entering Transactions

When it comes time to enter the information from your receipts (in other words, entering your transactions), you'll find that most bookkeeping software has an interface similar to a checkbook: Each transaction, whether an income or expense, is entered into a "register" where you'll include information including date, check number, payee, description, amount, category(ies), and any notes. With income transactions, remember to show any sales tax amounts separately from the total income. Bookkeeping software generally allows you to do this by "splitting" a transaction, showing a pretax subtotal separate from the sales tax amount.

TIP

Some states require nontaxable sales to be broken down into certain categories, such as wholesale sales, services, sales to out-of-state customers, or freight charges. Check with your state sales tax agency to find out which, if any, nontaxable subcategories you must use in your recordkeeping. As mentioned above, creating custom categories and subcategories in your bookkeeping software is incredibly easy.

When you have entered a receipt, mark the receipt as entered. Use whatever system works for you; you could handwrite an "E" on the receipt, use a stamp that says "Posted" or something similar. Then file the receipt away, ideally in a well-organized file system that will allow you easily to find a receipt should any questions arise later.

Finally, keep your bookkeeping records safe and regularly back them up. They will be essential to create financial reports revealing your business's financial health (explained in "Generating Financial Reports," below), and to complete your local, state, and federal tax returns. Losing your financial records can be an expensive disaster—dealing with an IRS audit without them is just one nightmare scenario—so be sure to treat them as the important business documents that they are.

TIP

Treat credit card purchases like cash. Even though the cash method of accounting records expenditures when they are paid, not when incurred, you should record purchases made with a credit card as if they were paid with cash. For whatever reason, the IRS considers credit card purchases paid on the date of purchase, not when payment is made on the credit card.

Step 3: Generating Financial Reports

Financial reports pull together various financial data to answer specific questions about your business's financial situation. For example, a profit and loss report compares monthly income to monthly expenses to show whether your business is making enough sales of products or services to cover costs each month. A cash flow projection shows similar information, but includes other sources of income, such as capital contributions from owners or loans (that is, not just revenues from sales), and organizes the information slightly differently to show you whether the timing of your income is adequate to pay your bills on time.

The financial reports discussed in this section are easily generated from your bookkeeping software—assuming that you've entered data consistently and correctly. When income and expenses have been entered and categorized accurately, you'll be ready to create the following reports showing you the financial health (or illness) of your business.

Profit and Loss Statement

If the typical owners of a small business start-up got a nickel for every time they asked themselves, "Will my business make a profit?" they'd probably be rich enough to retire before the doors were even open. A profit and loss statement (also called a P & L, or an income statement) is designed to answer this very question. Chapter 4 discussed creating a profit and loss statement with projected numbers. This section explains how to do it after you've opened your doors and have actual numbers to work with.

A P & L shows you pretty much what the name implies: how much profit or loss your business is making in a given period of time. You'll typically generate a profit and loss statement each month, as well as quarterly and annual summaries. We'll use a monthly period when describing the process of creating a P & L below.

In the most basic terms, a P & L is made by totaling your monthly revenues and then subtracting your monthly expenses from that total. If you use accounting software, it will generate a P & L at the click of a button based on the income and expense data you've already entered. For each month, you'll be able to see whether your revenues are higher or lower than your expenses and by how much. The monthly results are totaled to obtain your annual profit or loss.

An important detail involved in profit/loss calculations is that fixed costs need to be considered separately from variable costs. Fixed costs (also called overhead) are the costs associated with running your business in general, not with individual products or services themselves. Examples include rent, utilities, and insurance. Variable costs (also sometimes called costs of goods sold, or COGS) are the expenses that are directly tied to the product or service that you're selling. Examples include the costs of materials, packaging, and labor costs directly tied to producing the product or service (but note that labor costs can be tricky; see Tip below).

For example, say your business produces and sells greeting cards. Your variable costs would include the costs of the paper, printing costs, costs for packaging and labels, and the labor cost for the workers that package and distribute them. As the name implies, these costs will vary depending on the amount and type of product you make and sell or service you perform. For example, if you produce more or less of a particular greeting card or if you emboss or use a heavier grade of card stock, your variable expenses will be affected.

TIP

Labor costs: sometimes variable, sometimes fixed. If you ask a group of accountants whether the labor costs associated with making a product are fixed or variable, you're likely to get conflicting answers. Some argue that, as long as the workers will get paid regardless of whether they're working on that product, their salaries should be considered fixed, like rent or utilities. Others say that, to have accurate financial records, you need to reflect the cost of the labor that goes into a product. You or your accountant can decide how your business will categorize labor costs for making a product. Labor costs for providing services, on the other hand, are almost always treated as variable costs.

But other costs—your fixed costs—will not go up or down depending on the products you make or the services you perform. These costs, such as your rent, office utility bills, and insurance for your company vehicles, will be more or less the same, regardless of the amount or type of greeting cards you make. This is exactly why age-old business wisdom says to keep your overhead costs as low as you can. In times of slow sales, you want to be saddled with as few fixed costs as possible.

Now that you know the distinction between variable and fixed costs, you need to understand how they're each subtracted from your revenue on a typical profit and loss statement.

- A profit and loss statement starts with your total sales revenues, then subtracts your variable costs. The result is called your "gross profit"—how much money you've earned from sales of your products or services over and above their cost to you.
- Next, you subtract your fixed costs from your gross profit. Any money you're left with is usually called "net profit," but is sometimes called net income or pretax profit. Other than the various taxes you'll need to pay on this

income, this is your (and any other business owners') money.

To sum up, the formula used in a profit and loss statement is basically as follows:

Sales revenue
– Variable costs (costs of sale)
= Gross profit
– Fixed costs
= Net profit

A typical P & L is shown below.

A P & L not only will tell you whether you're making or losing money, but also will help you identify which aspects of your business need adjusting in order to boost profits. Often, a profitability problem can be found in your expenses. Being able to see the totals of each of your various expense categories over the course of several months, all on one report, can help you pinpoint areas in which you're spending too much money (and help give you the courage to do something about it). And, of course, accurately tracking income totals month by month will help you quickly spot a downturn in revenue and prompt you to take action to boost sales.

Cash Flow Projection

Chapter 4 discussed using cash flow projections as a way to determine whether your business will be able to pay its bills once it gets started. A cash flow projection is also a crucial tool to use in your ongoing business, as it tells you whether you'll have enough cash available at any given time to pay your operating costs. Having lots of customers and thriving sales isn't enough, especially if you sell on credit. If your customers pay you in 90 days, but you must pay your expenses in 30 days or even immediately, you may face a situation where, even though your financial statement says you are making a profit, you can't pay your staff, rent, utilities, insurance, delivery services, or other key bills. If you see the cash crunch well in advance, you'll usually be able to juggle expenses or take other measures, such as taking out a loan or a line of credit, to get through the squeeze. But if the cash crisis sneaks up on you without warning, you may not have enough time to react, possibly even forcing you to close up shop.

Helping you understand why you may not be able to pay your bills despite being profitable—and how to take steps to avoid this—is the role of a cash flow

20xx Profit/Loss Statement

	January	February	March	April	May		December	Year Total
Sales Revenues	$1,900	$1,950	$2,000	$1,850	$2,000		$2,100	$23,550
Variable Costs	300	310	350	300	325		350	3,840
Gross Profit	1,600	1,640	1,650	1,550	1,675		1,750	19,710
Fixed Expenses								
Rent	700	700	700	700	700		700	8,400
Supplies	150	100	75	90	125		100	1,220
Utilities	200	200	200	200	200		200	2,400
Advertising	150	150	150	150	150		150	1,800
Miscellaneous	75	80	65	70	75		85	830
Total Fixed Expenses	1,275	1,230	1,190	1,210	1,250		1,235	14,650
Net Income (Loss)	$325	$410	$460	$340	$425		$515	$5,060

projection. A cash flow projection focuses on the actual cash payments made to and by your business. These payments are called cash-ins and cash-outs (or inflows and outflows) to differentiate them from sales and expenses, which may not be paid right away. Estimating your cash-ins and cash-outs for upcoming months can help you predict when you might run short, allowing you to take action early, such as by tightening up on your credit terms, raising more capital, getting a loan or line of credit, or putting more effort into collecting accounts receivable.

Your cash flow projection will use most of the same numbers as your profit and loss statement, along with a few new ones. The big difference is that your cash flow projection will include all of your sources of income—not just sales income—and only income that's paid in cash (not credit). In other words, while your profit and loss statement is concerned with how much revenue your business is earning through sales of its products or services, your cash flow projection is designed to show you how much cash you will have on hand from all sources, including paid sales, loans, interest from investments, transfers from your personal accounts, lottery winnings, whatever. That's because when it comes to paying bills, the bottom line is whether you have enough money, period. Similarly, your cash flow projection will include all money you pay out of the business, whether for supplies, taxes (including any estimated taxes you owe; see Chapter 8), loan repayments, or any other expenditure.

The basic formula for cash flow analysis is:

Cash in bank at beginning of month
+ Cash receipts for the month
<u>– Cash disbursements for the month</u>
= Cash in bank at end of month

In a cash flow projection, each month starts with the amount of money you have in the bank. (This will generally be the same amount that's left over from the previous month.) Next, you'll add any cash that came in during the month in all relevant categories, such as sales income, loans, interest earned, and any personal money you put into the business—your total cash-ins for the month. Next, subtract the money you spent during the month: your cash-outs. The result is the cash left at the end of the month. Enter that figure into the beginning of the next month's column, and do the same process for the next month. If you use accounting software, a cash flow spreadsheet can be generated automatically once you've entered figures for income and expenses.

Now that you see the basic formula behind cash flow analysis, you need to understand that the real power of this tool is not in tracking actual cash-ins and cash-outs, but in predicting future cash flows. Periodically, say once a month or every couple of months, you should use your actual figures to help make estimates for upcoming months and complete a cash flow projection for the future, generally up to one year. Hopefully, you'll see that you will have enough cash to cover your expenses each month. If not, don't panic. First, pat yourself on the back for doing a cash flow analysis and figuring out ahead of time that you won't be able to cover all your expenses. Then come up with a plan—either put off some expenses that can wait; get more money (perhaps through collecting accounts receivable or getting a short-term loan or line of credit); or sell, sell, sell more product or services.

Especially when you're in the early stages of a business and don't have much of a business history, predicting cash-ins and cash-outs for future months isn't easy (though cash-outs are often easier to predict than cash-ins, because you have more control over them and many costs recur each month). You'll need to make estimates of how much income will come in and what expenses must be covered—a task that may seem only slightly easier than reading tea leaves.

The key is to do your best—with an emphasis on "do." Accept the fact that your estimates won't be 100% accurate, but make them anyway. As the months tick by and the flow of cash into and out from your business settles into daily, weekly, and monthly patterns, making estimates will inevitably become easier, and you'll find them increasingly more accurate.

An example of a cash flow projection you can do on a simple spreadsheet is shown below.

As you can see, arranging income and expense information into a cash flow projection reveals a lot about the financial workings of a business. For

Cash Flow Projection, Completed April, 20xx

	Jan	Feb	Mar	April	May	June	July	Aug	Sept	Oct	Nov	Dec
Cash at Beginning of Month	$2,000	$1,250	$600	$700	$350	$100	($300)	$150	$0	$0	($550)	$300
Cash-Ins												
Sales Paid	15,000	14,750	15,500	14,750	15,500	15,000	16,100	16,250	15,500	15,250	16,750	16,900
Loans and Transfers	0	0	0	0	0	0	0	0	0	0	0	0
Total Cash-Ins	15,000	14,750	15,500	14,750	15,500	15,000	16,100	16,250	15,500	15,250	16,750	16,900
Cash-Outs												
Variable Costs	3,000	3,100	3,500	3,000	3,250	3,150	3,450	3,500	3,250	3,300	3,400	3,550
Rent	7,000	7,000	7,000	7,000	7,000	7,000	7,000	7,000	7,000	7,000	7,000	7,000
Supplies	1,500	1,000	750	900	1,250	900	1,100	850	1,000	1,100	950	900
Utilities	2,000	2,000	2,000	2,000	2,000	2,000	2,000	2,000	2,000	2,000	2,000	2,000
Loan Payments	1,500	1,500	1,500	1,500	1,500	1,500	1,500	1,500	1,500	1,500	1,500	1,500
Miscellaneous	750	800	650	700	750	4,850	600	1,550	750	900	1,050	850
Total Cash-Outs	15,750	15,400	15,400	15,100	15,750	15,400	15,650	16,400	15,500	15,800	15,900	15,800
Cash at End of Month	$1,250	$600	$700	$350	$100	($300)	$150	$0	$0	($550)	$300	$1,400

example, the sample cash flow forecast shows that cash is tight each and every month (look at the "Cash at End of Month" row), so the business owner might consider ways to cut costs or to tighten credit terms.

Of more pressing importance is the projected cash shortfall starting in June. Knowing a few months in advance that a shortage is likely will help a business owner figure out what to do while there's still time to take action. The owner could contribute some personal money to the business (note that the cash flow didn't include any loans or personal transfers to the business) or could try to cut some nonessential expenses, at least until later in the year when there will be a bit (but only a small bit) more cash available.

 TIP

Credit lines provide cash flow flexibility. A very helpful resource for any small business is a revolving line of credit from the bank. A line of credit works on the same principle as a credit card, but generally offers better cash terms than credit card cash advance terms. The business can borrow funds up to the credit line limit on an as-needed basis and has to pay interest only on the outstanding balance (not the entire credit line). The business can choose to pay funds back and reborrow them as necessary during the time the credit line is open. Credit lines can be open for a specified period, such as five or ten years, or can be open-ended (like a credit card).

TIP

Compare your projection to reality. Each month, replace your projections with actual results from your accounting system. It's a great way to see how good a job of projecting you're doing.

Who Needs to Do a Cash Flow Analysis?

David Rothenberg, a CPA, gives the following advice: "If your business is wildly profitable, you have little or no debt, you are not planning on expanding your business anytime soon, and you don't grant your customers a long time to pay, you probably don't need to do a cash flow analysis—you already know you'll have plenty of cash to meet your needs. But if this doesn't sound like your business, then you probably will benefit from keeping a close eye on your cash flow. Remember, the cash flow statement isn't for the IRS, and it isn't for the bank; it's for you! That's right, YOU! You're the one who won't sleep at night if your bank account is empty. So what are you waiting for? Get out there and start projecting!"

Balance Sheet

A balance sheet is a financial report showing the net worth of your business at a particular point in time. Businesses typically generate balance sheets monthly, quarterly, and annually. In a nutshell, a balance sheet shows a complete picture of a business's financial situation by summarizing its assets, liabilities, and owner equity (sometimes called net worth) in the business. The general formula is:

$$\text{Assets} - \text{Liabilities} = \text{Equity}$$

Or, put another way:

$$\text{Assets} = \text{Liabilities} + \text{Equity}$$

As you'll see in the example below, the structure of a balance sheet reflects this second formulation. But they both mean the same thing, as described below.

The value of a balance sheet is that it provides a view into the business's financial position. It will reveal whether a business is, on one hand, overleveraged with too much debt, or perhaps on the other hand in a good position for expansion. In short, it offers a snapshot of the financial health of a company.

While balance sheets aren't quite as intuitive to read for the uninitiated, the elements that are included and how they related to each other aren't that complicated. As with the other financial reports described in this section, a balance sheet can easily be generated from your bookkeeping software, assuming all transactions have been entered and categorized correctly. But it's worth going through each element of a balance sheet so that you truly understand what it means and how to decipher one, rather than just relying on your software to spit one out for you without grasping the full meaning of the information it summarizes.

As mentioned above, a balance sheet reflects a business's assets, liabilities, and equity. In other words, when you subtract a business's liabilities from its assets, the result is the net equity the business owner(s) have in the business. This report is called a balance sheet because it reflects the balance between assets on one side of the equation and liabilities plus equity on the other side. When the data in your bookkeeping software are accurate, the assets will equal (or "balance") liabilities plus equity.

Let's look at each of these elements in a bit more detail.

Assets include anything of monetary value that your business owns. The standard balance sheet format lists assets in decreasing order of liquidity—in other words, how easy it is to convert the asset to cash. The following categories are typically used to reflect this breakdown:

- **Current assets** are those that can be converted to cash within one year. These include cash (of course), checking accounts, money market accounts, accounts receivable, and inventory.
- **Noncurrent assets** (sometimes called capital, long-term, or fixed assets) are defined as things with a useful business life of more than one year. These include land, buildings, vehicles, business equipment, and furniture. With the exception of land, tangible noncurrent assets depreciate, which means they lose value each year; this is reflected as a "depreciation

expense" in the balance sheet. If all assets are entered correctly into your bookkeeping software, including the type of asset and when it was purchased, the software should automatically calculate this overall depreciation figure for you. Other assets that would be considered noncurrent include intellectual property, such as patents, trade secrets, copyrights, trademarks, customer lists, or even company goodwill. Valuing these intangibles can be difficult, and they are typically heavily discounted on a balance sheet if included at all.

Liabilities are things that your business owes to others. Like assets, liabilities are typically divided into current and noncurrent:

- **Current liabilities** include debts your company owes within the next year. Examples include accounts payable, payroll owed to employees but not yet paid, accrued but unpaid taxes, loans that need to be repaid within the year, and credit card debt.

- **Noncurrent liabilities** include debts payable over a term longer than one year. This includes mortgages or other debts due more than one year from the date the balance sheet is prepared.

Equity is what's left over when you subtract liabilities from assets. This is the net worth of the business, which is essentially the amount that would be paid out to the owner(s) if the business liquidated. It includes:

- any **capital contributions** to the business, including money contributed by the owners and any stock sold to the public, and

- any **retained earnings**, which are the total of all annual profits since the beginning of the business (including the current year) that haven't been paid out to the owner(s) in draws or dividends.

Below is an example of how a balance sheet typically presents this information.

Balance Sheet

	Current 4/1/2010	Previous Year 4/1/2009	$ Change	% Change
Assets				
Current Assets				
Cash in bank	$15,700	$14,050	$1,650	11.74%
Accounts receivable	2,350	1,800	500	30.56%
Inventory	5,500	3,900	1,600	41.03%
Other current assets	0	0	0	0.00%
Total Current Assets	$23,500	$19,750	$3,800	19.24%
Fixed Assets				
Machinery and equipment	$13,500	$11,075	$2,425	21.90%
Furniture and fixtures	2,500	2,000	500	25.00%
Land and buildings	0	0	0	0.00%
Other fixed assets	0	0	0	0.00%
(Accumulated depreciation on all fixed assets)	−7,350	−7,155	−195	0.00%
Total Fixed Assets (net of depreciation)	$8,650	$5,920	$2,730	46.11%
Other Assets				
Intangibles	$0	$0	$0	0.00%
Goodwill	$0	$0	$0	0.00%
Other	$0	$0	$0	0.00%
Total Other Assets	$0	$0	$0	0.00%
TOTAL Assets	$32,200	$25,670	$6,530	25.44%
Liabilities and Equity				
Current Liabilities				
Accounts payable	$14,250	$2,985	$1,265	42.38%
Payroll unpaid	$0	$0	$0	0.00%
Taxes payable	1,700	985	715	72.59%
Short-term debt (due within 12 months)	$0	$0	$0	0.00%
Credit card debt	$0	$0	$0	0.00%
Other current liabilities	$0	$0	$0	0.00%
Total Current Liabilities	$5,950	$3,970	$1,980	49.87%
Long-Term Debt				
Bank loans payable	$0	$0	$0	0.00%
Other long-term debt	$0	$0	$0	0.00%
Total Long-Term Debt	$0	$0	$0	0.00%
TOTAL Liabilities	$5,950	$3,970	$1,980	49.87%
Owners' Equity				
Invested capital	$15,000	$15,000	$0	0.00%
Retained earnings	11,250	6,700	4,550	67.91%
Total Owners' Equity	$26,250	$21,700	$4,550	20.97%
TOTAL Liabilities and Equity	$32,200	$25,670	$6,530	25.44%

Chapter 11 Checklist:
Bookkeeping, Accounting, and Financial Management

☐ Decide whether to use the cash or accrual system of accounting.

☐ Keep records of all payments to and from your business. Create an organized system for keeping your receipts.

☐ Enter your income and expense information into bookkeeping software on a regular basis. Businesses with high volumes of sales or expenses should do this frequently—daily or weekly. If appropriate for your business, hire a part- or full-time bookkeeper to keep up with this task.

☐ On some regular basis—typically monthly, quarterly, and annually—generate financial reports such as a profit/loss statement and a cash flow analysis to show you the big picture of how your business is doing financially.

☐ Consult with an accountant or tax professional at least once a year to keep your system on track.

Small Business Marketing 101

So you've got a great product or service and have built a solid business infrastructure to support it. How will you get customers to buy it? The process of reaching out to potential customers and trying to attract them to your business is what's known as marketing. Some business owners look forward to the marketing process and enjoy the creative aspects of it; others find it intimidating and bewildering. The good news is that marketing your business does not have to be terribly time-consuming, complicated, or expensive. In fact, the best marketing methods are often the simplest and cheapest.

For example, encouraging good word of mouth and networking within a well-defined target audience will cost you little (if anything) and will greatly help your business develop name recognition and build a potential customer base. In fact, generating positive word of mouth is one of the most powerful ways for a business to develop its reputation and attract customers. Other inexpensive marketing methods, such as sending out press releases and fostering media coverage, can generate far better exposure than spending a fortune on advertising.

Before we dive into the nuts and bolts of marketing, keep in mind an important and often misunderstood distinction: Marketing is not synonymous with advertising. Paid advertising can be part of a marketing strategy, but it seldom makes sense for a small business to invest precious resources on ads. Paid advertising is much more expensive—and less effective—than many cheaper (or even free) methods of getting exposure. More efficient ways to promote your business include:

- networking with potential customers, other business owners, government officials, and community leaders
- creating incentives for your customers to pass good word of mouth about your business to others
- pitching stories about your business to local media
- organizing or participating in special events, such as a grand opening party, product demonstration, trade show, or informational seminar

- creating a website and promoting it
- distributing brochures, flyers, or other literature, and
- listing your business in local directories.

This chapter outlines a simple, affordable, and effective approach to marketing your business. The strategies and tips described here will help get your marketing machine up and running and can be expanded as your business grows.

 TIP

Valuable marketing lessons are all around you. We live in a world saturated by marketing appeals. As annoying as it is to be relentlessly courted by thousands of companies each day, constant exposure to marketing messages does have a bright side: Whether you've "studied" marketing or not, you've unwittingly absorbed some basic marketing know-how. As an experienced marketing target, you probably know more about marketing than you think you do. Use this knowledge to turn the tables—to think like a marketer, rather than a "marketee."

Defining Your Market

Your very first concern when marketing your business is making sure you understand who and what your market is. In fact, defining and learning about your market is a fundamental step in planning your business, period. You've probably heard this advice before, but what exactly does it mean to "know your market"? It's helpful to break the concept of "market" down into three components:

- your potential and actual customers
- your competition, and
- your industry.

Often, the term "market" is used as shorthand for your customer base. But it's crucial to understand that knowing your market also means knowing who your competition is and what the trends are in your industry. When you have a clear vision and understanding of all three—customers, competition, and industry—you'll be well positioned not only to tailor your business to a profitable customer base, but also to reach that customer base with effective marketing strategies.

Common Marketing Terms

So many terms are thrown around when referring to marketing efforts—it can be hard to understand the distinctions among specific types of marketing, such as publicity, public relations, and media relations. Truth be told, there's often only a fuzzy line among these categories. Here's a quick definition of some of the most common marketing terms as they are used in this chapter.

Marketing means just about any promotional activity: advertising, special events, direct mail, online discounts and promotions, and the like. Marketing includes all ways of promoting your business. This chapter uses more specific terms to refer to individual types of marketing activities.

Branding refers to the process of developing positive and specific associations in your target customers' minds regarding your business, above and beyond the basics of what products or services you provide. When a company has a well-developed brand, customers have an emotional tie to the company and a feeling of connection to the brand. For example, McDonald's is typically understood to be family friendly, cheerful, and fun. Volvo conveys the feeling of safety and quality. Levi Strauss & Co. projects a hip-yet-timeless vibe.

Advertising means buying space or airtime to deliver a promotional message designed to reach the general public, usually through print media, television, radio, or the Internet. Of course, just about anything can carry an advertising message, including the sides of buses, billboards, and park benches.

Listings or directories include phone books, business directories, and other specialized publications, both in print and online. Some, such as a directory of film production companies in a city, are highly targeted; others, like the yellow pages, are very broad. As you do with advertising, you must pay for a listing. But, unlike most ads, directories often serve as valuable resources that are used again and again, which means that they can be much more effective than typical display ads.

Public relations is another broad term that can refer to many different types of outreach efforts. In this chapter, public relations means a coordinated, multifaceted effort to get your business's message out to the public. Public relations might include sponsoring events, pitching stories to the media, inviting key people to participate in conferences, public speaking, and advertising—all coordinated to ensure clarity and consistency of message.

Media relations refers to contacting the media and pitching story ideas in hopes of obtaining editorial coverage—coverage in articles or feature stories not tied to advertising. Most commonly, media relations involves sending press releases to newspaper editors, reporters, and television producers to announce an event or provide information that could be the subject of a news story. Another media relations technique is to hold a press conference at which your business conveys a specific (and newsworthy) message to invited members of the press.

Publicity means exposure in the media and in public generated via a variety of methods, such as holding or participating in events, or making media appearances.

Let's look at each of the components of your market in a bit more detail.

Who Are Your Target Customers?

When you've come up with an idea for a business, one of the first questions you need to consider is whether there are enough potential customers to support the business. If there aren't enough people or other businesses willing to buy the product or service you plan to offer, you'll obviously have a hard time turning a profit.

To evaluate your potential customer base, start by putting careful thought into exactly whom you expect to be your most likely customers—in other words, your target customers. Part of the process of defining your target customers is learning as much as you can about them for a number of reasons: so you can make sure they are in fact a profitable customer base; so you can tailor your products or services to better suit their needs and desires; and so you can plan the most effective marketing outreach. We'll discuss methods of researching and learning about your target customers in "Learning About Your Market: Market Research," below. For now, we'll focus on why defining your target customers is so important, and how to develop a target customer profile.

TIP

Defining your target customers and learning about your market can be a circular process. Typically you'll start by identifying your best customer prospects based on your observations and intuition about your market (remember, your market includes not only customers, but also your competition and industry). Next, you'll want to do research to learn more about your market, such as what your target customers' buying habits are, what your competition is doing, and whether there are important industry trends. Based on this research, you may want to refine your target customer definition or refine your business idea to make the most of an unmet demand in the market. Also, remember that learning about your market and adjusting your business plan accordingly is an ongoing process, and lies at the heart of running a business. Successful business owners constantly monitor market conditions and make adjustments to their businesses in order to stay profitable.

Every business needs to have a clear idea of its most promising and likely customers. Without having a clear vision of your expected customer base, you will seriously diminish your business's chances of success for a number of reasons:

- You may fail to realize there are not enough potential customers for your business (in other words, there is not enough demand for your products or services).
- You may miss opportunities to tweak your business idea to better meet the needs of a potential customer base.
- You won't know how to reach your most promising prospects, which is another way of saying you won't know where to target your marketing efforts.
- You won't be able to craft your marketing messages appropriately—using the right tone, language, and attitude to appeal to your best prospects.

In a nutshell, defining your target customers means identifying specific characteristics of the people or businesses who you believe are most likely to actually buy your product or service. These characteristics are sometimes called a demographic profile. Common characteristics used to classify customers include:

- age
- gender
- income level
- buying habits
- occupation or industry
- marital status
- family status (children or no children)
- geographic location
- ethnic group
- political affiliations or leanings, and
- hobbies and interests.

Use these criteria to draw a profile of your most promising potential customers, those who have a real need or desire for your products or services. A maternity store specializing in professional wear, for example, may identify its target customer as 25- to 40-year-old pregnant, married women in the legal, financial, and real estate industries within a ten-mile radius of the store. A bike shop with a focus on single-track mountain biking gear might define its target customer as 18- to 25-year-old single males living within two miles of the local university.

Deciding how narrowly to define your target customer is more of an art than a science, but, in general, it helps to err on the side of being more specific. It's far more common for business owners to make the mistake of envisioning their customer base too broadly, making it very difficult to engage in effective marketing efforts. Remember: A solid definition of your target customer serves as a foundation for all your marketing activities. The more carefully you've defined your target market, the more likely your marketing efforts—even simple, low cost methods—will bear fruit.

 TIP

Defining a target market will not limit your business. New entrepreneurs sometimes resist defining a target customer base, thinking that it will somehow limit the business or reduce the number of potential customers. This is a misconception. For starters, identifying target customers in no way prevents a business from accepting customers that might not fit in the target. If a customer who completely does not fit your target profile walks through your door and wants to buy your product or service, great. But what's crucial to understand is this: Unless you have unlimited marketing resources, it's much more effective to focus your marketing efforts on potential customers who you have determined are *likely* to buy your

Defining a Niche

The term "niche" is somewhat of a buzzword in business. A niche is essentially a relatively narrow or specialized market; for example, a maternity clothing boutique specializing in corporate/professional wear or a law firm that specializes in immigration cases. In a crowded marketplace, a niche serves the critical function of distinguishing you from your competitors.

Focusing on a niche can be an effective and profitable strategy for small businesses because it is often too difficult and costly to try to cater to very broad audiences. Instead of trying to appeal to everyone, a small business usually will do better to develop a specialty in an area that is not being fully served by other businesses, and exploit that niche with cost-effective marketing strategies. Think of a niche as a hook that will help you reel in the potential customers that you have identified as the most profitable and likely prospects for your business.

There are two aspects of defining a niche: an operational aspect and a marketing aspect. Operationally, you'll have to decide to what degree your business will tailor its products or services for the target customer base. This is separate from the question of how you'll market your business to this target market. Targeting a niche usually involves both, to varying degrees— tailoring your products or services for a specific market segment, and actively reaching out to this segment with

your marketing efforts—and it's up to you how you balance the two aspects.

For example, a vegan catering business is an example of a business that is heavy on the operational component of defining its niche: Its services (providing vegan meals) are completely dictated by its aim to appeal to the vegan market. Of course, it will also focus its marketing efforts on outreach to vegans.

In contrast, consider a day spa that mostly caters to local residents, but that recognizes an opportunity to boost business from the sizable number of tourists who come to its city. Though the spa's massage and other services might not be highly specialized for tourists, it could focus its marketing efforts on this niche by reaching out to the city's hotels, tour group companies, and travel agents. While its operations might not be wholly dictated by its goal of attracting tourists, it might make small operational tweaks, such as offering a free shuttle service to local hotels or including maps of local tourist attractions in its lobby area.

The point to understand here is that marketing to a niche usually involves some combination of operational adjustments to appeal to a target audience, along with focusing your marketing outreach to this audience. When you do both well, you'll be on your way to carving out a niche for your business.

product or service—and not waste your time and money courting the vast world of prospects who merely *could* become customers.

Bear in mind that some businesses may focus on selling to other businesses rather than individuals. Selling products or services to other businesses (sometimes called B2B, for "business to business") can be lucrative because businesses usually buy in larger quantities than individuals. For example, a soap manufacturer might sell 50 bars of soap to individual customers via its website in a given month, but could sell 500 bars in just one sale to a hotel. If your business is targeting other businesses, you should still define your target customer, using characteristics such as:

- industry
- size, by number of employees or annual sales, and
- geographic location.

Evaluate Your Competition

Another crucial part of your market is your competition: the other businesses that are trying to sell similar products or services to roughly the same customers as you are. Knowing your competitors is just as essential as understanding your potential customers. Knowing who your competitors are and what they are doing will help you establish and maintain a competitive edge. The more that another business targets your customer base, the more important it is for you to develop compelling reasons for customers to choose your business instead of theirs.

When evaluating your competition, start with the businesses that are your closest, most direct competitors—the ones that target the same customers as you do. If you want to focus on a specific niche, you'll need to know whether other businesses are doing the same thing. If so, that niche may not have room for another business and you may want to find a different angle.

Niches that have little competition offer good opportunities for your business to be profitable. But keep in mind that a profitable niche that has little or no competition will likely not stay that way for long—you should expect competition to arise in any market that proves to be profitable. Sometimes, in fact, being the first business in a profitable niche isn't an advantage. Other businesses can observe and learn from the experiences of a "pioneer" business and improve upon the business model, sometimes beating out the original pioneer. The moral here is that profitable markets will either already have competition or will develop competition in the future. To keep your competitive edge, you'll need to stay current on what customers want and what the competition is offering. In addition, you'll want to know about industry trends, which we'll discuss next.

Know Your Industry

Anticipating change is essential for all businesses, and staying abreast of industry trends is an important way to stay ahead of the curve. Your industry is not the same as your competition; rather, it's the broad world of businesses that operate in your general field, some of which may be competitors. Learning about industry trends helps a business improve its competitive edge by incorporating trends that aren't being adopted by its competition. It also helps a business avoid trouble by knowing about trends that may pose a threat to it.

For example, any restaurant should know about trends in the restaurant industry, which may include learning about what is happening in New York and Los Angeles restaurants. For a restaurant in Austin, Texas, the New York and Los Angeles restaurants would not be actual competitors, but the Austin restaurant might want to read about their practices and experiences in order to learn valuable information about the restaurant industry. A trend, such as eliminating foie gras from menus because of inhumane farming practices, might be happening in New York and getting positive reactions from diners, but not happening at all in the Austin area. A smart Austin restaurant owner that is familiar with the trend could be the first to cut foie gras from the menu and reap valuable positive publicity.

Some trends can threaten entire industries, so being aware of them might be essential. The low-carb trend of the last several years was a serious blow for bakeries, pasta makers, and anyone serving or manufacturing carbohydrate products. The smart businesses learned about the trend and adapted their business strategies appropriately. Many restaurants began making rice or pasta optional in certain dishes, or offering burgers without a bun. For some businesses, like bakeries, the best way to respond was to offer other products, like expanded coffee and tea menus or deli items heavy on meat and cheese. Others responded not by changing their product offerings but with marketing messages trying to convince customers that not all carbs are bad. Whatever the strategy, the key was to recognize the trend in the first place and respond in time rather than be blindsided by it.

General economic conditions are also important to your business. General forecasts for your city or region can give you an idea of whether economic upturns or downturns are on the horizon. The health of other key industries may also have a big effect on your business, even if you're in a completely different industry. For example, if you run a restaurant in an area where a major hospital is facing huge layoffs, that will certainly impact your business. Keep a broad view when evaluating market conditions that can affect your bottom line.

TIP

A profitable niche may exist in bucking a trend. For example, a technology might become obsolete (technology businesses are particularly vulnerable to trends and market changes), which could open a possible niche of serving the few customers who continue to use the obsolete technology. If you're the only electronics shop in town that fixes or sells turntables, you may have a profitable niche with little competition, even though turntables and vinyl records are hardly a growing industry. As with any niche, the trick is to make sure it is big enough.

Learning About Your Market: Market Research

Effective marketing starts with knowing key information about your market—your potential customers, competition, and industry. Doing market research is an important and effective way of testing your assumptions and answering any questions

you may have about your market. For example, if you want to open a coffee shop, you may be confident that the university area would be a great location, but not be sure whether the students will be willing to pay a bit more for fair-trade coffee. Market research will help you test your assumption about the location and answer your question about pricing—and, in turn, give you valuable information upon which to base important business decisions.

The term "market research" tends to scare business owners who think it means hiring pricey firms and conducting complicated demographic studies. In fact, market research can be much simpler and just as effective. Most small businesses can do their own market research with a very limited budget. Large business ventures might hire a firm to do more extensive market research studies, but the simpler approach usually makes more sense for small to medium start-ups.

Market research can include primary and secondary research. Primary research involves doing studies with potential customers to find out how they feel about your product or service and your competitors' offerings and posing a myriad of other questions about their shopping habits and preferences. Secondary research involves studying what others have learned about your market; typically this involves reading trade journals, other business publications, or reports generated from studies that others have commissioned. Small businesses often focus on secondary research because they find primary research intimidating. But as described below, small businesses can easily and inexpensively tackle primary research—and there's no substitute for the information you get directly from your target prospects.

Clarifying Your Research Objectives

The first step in doing market research is figuring out exactly what questions you want to have answered: Specifically what do you want to learn about your market? A very helpful way to go about this is to approach each aspect of your market—potential customers, competition, and industry—separately.

The table below offers a breakdown of the types of questions and research methods that would be appropriate for each group. It's not an exhaustive list, but is meant to illustrate how your inquiry will shift depending on what you're researching and what you're trying to answer.

With a clear outline of what questions you want answered, you'll be in a good position to choose the best research methods. The best approach is to conduct both primary and secondary research—getting information from actual prospects (primary) and reading what others have to say about your market (secondary).

Primary Research Tools

Though primary research may not be quite as easy as reading a trade magazine, it's very doable and will generally yield much more valuable information because it comes directly from your prospects. The specific way that you'll ask questions to those prospects will depend on your type of business and the product or service you're offering, but, in general, there are three options: surveys and questionnaires, interviews, and focus groups. Let's look at each of these.

Using Surveys and Questionnaires

Presenting your target customers with surveys or questionnaires is a great way to answer specific questions you have about them. Start by identifying exactly what you want to learn; you can call these your research questions. Based on these research questions, you'll draft the actual survey questions themselves. It's a subtle but important distinction: Your research questions are not exactly the same as the survey questions. Instead, the survey questions should be crafted so they yield results that will help you answer your research questions. Your research questions will be more general than your survey questions, and you want your survey questions to be as specific as possible.

EXAMPLE: Solange plans to open a massage studio in San Francisco. She'd like to open it in the Nob Hill neighborhood because she thinks this neighborhood would appeal to her target customer base. To test her assumption,

Subject	Questions to Answer	Methods
Customers	• Who are your target customers? • What products or services do they need or want? • Where and how do they buy these products or services? • What do they typically pay for your type of products or service?	Primary research methods: • Surveys and questionnaires • Focus groups • One-on-one interviews or inquiries of trusted contacts Secondary research methods: • Magazine or trade journal articles • Reports from previously conducted studies
Competition	• What do they offer? • What do they charge? • How do they provide the products or services? • Who are their customers? • What is their competitive edge?	• Primary sources (marketing materials, websites, and so on) • Trade shows • Networking • Magazine or trade journal articles
Industry	• What are standard practices? • What are the latest trends? • What does the future hold?	• Magazine or trade journal articles • Trade shows • Books

she creates a survey and distributes it via email to her contacts who fit her target customer profile. Solange's research question is: "Is Nob Hill a good location for a massage studio?" To help her answer this fairly general and subjective question, Solange drafts more specific questions for the survey, such as:

- Do you consider parking in Nob Hill to be a problem?
- Do you currently get massage services in Nob Hill, and if so, where?
- What massage services are currently lacking in Nob Hill?
- What would be the ideal neighborhood for you to get massage services?

The survey responses indicate that there is a great desire for a massage studio in Nob Hill and only mild concern about parking. The primary complaint about the existing massage services is that they don't offer enough different massage styles such as hot stone therapy. The survey results solidify Solange's decision to open her studio in Nob Hill, and help her tailor the services to her target audience.

You can send surveys in hard copy via mail, in plain text format via email, or—even better—by using a Web-based service, many of which are free. At sites such as SurveyMonkey (www.surveymonkey.com) and Zoomerang (www.zoomerang.com), you can create professional-looking online surveys, invite your prospects by email, and tabulate the results in useful ways, all for free. More features are available if you upgrade to a paying account, but the excellent free versions are a great place to start.

Interviewing Prospects One on One

There are a few different ways of getting information directly from individuals. One way is simply to set up interviews with people whom you trust and who may have relevant opinions. For example, if you want to start a child care referral service, you could meet with people you know who have young children and ask them about their experiences. Or, if you're starting a software company that will focus on data management for construction companies,

set up lunch meetings with people you know in the construction business and pick their brains about their data management challenges.

Another way to interview people is to canvass them at locations where you are likely to encounter people within your target profile. A good example is going to a trade show related to your industry, standing in a high-traffic area, and asking people if they could answer a few short questions. The key here is to have just a few short questions that passers-by could answer quickly with concise answers ("yes" or "no" or a numerical answer, for example) that you can easily record on a clipboard or laptop computer. Other locations might include special events that appeal to your target audience.

Working With Focus Groups

A focus group is simply an event at which you provide a presentation or demonstration to potential customers and solicit their feedback. Often, feedback is gathered via a survey or questionnaire prepared in advance. Feedback is also obtained though oral question-and-answer sessions and discussions among the group, which are recorded by someone taking careful notes. Examples of possible focus groups include:

- a food manufacturer holding taste tests of a new salsa, asking participants to rate flavor and texture and to compare the new salsa to the competitors' versions
- a software company having users test its new time-management application, asking them to rate it on ease of use and timing them on how long it takes to complete certain tasks, and
- a nail salon demonstrating its signature pedicure on focus group participants, asking them for feedback on their experience during the pedicure and on the results.

While there's nothing inherently complex or expensive about conducting a focus group, it will require at least a nominal commitment of your time. If you don't have a retail or other space, you may need to rent an appropriate venue. Because of the preparation and possible expense involved, be sure to start the invitation process early enough to ensure that you get enough confirmed participants to justify the time and expense of doing the focus group.

Getting Started: A Basic Approach to Primary Research

Now that you have an overview of primary research tools, here's a simple approach to help get you started:

1. **Start by identifying the questions that you want answered—your research questions.** In other words, specify exactly what you want to learn.

2. **Decide the best way to get those questions answered.** As described above, the basic methods include surveys, interviews, and focus groups (usually in conjunction with a survey or questionnaire). The methods you choose will largely depend on the types of questions you want answered and the nature of your product or service.

3. **If you'll be using a survey or questionnaire, you'll need to draft the questions.** Your goal is to craft questions that will yield responses that will help you answer your research questions.

4. **Identify and invite your study's participants.** Start with your list of contacts and include people who fit your target customer profile. Build and expand your list by asking trusted contacts to suggest others that would be appropriate. Developing your list of contacts—particularly before you've started your business—is often a matter of networking, unless you want to pay for mailing lists. Networking is discussed under "Cost-Effective Marketing Tools," below.

5. **After conducting the study, compile the results.** Remember, doing market research is all about obtaining data, so don't neglect the essential task of assembling and analyzing your results. Once this is done, you'll be poised to make business decisions based on the information you've learned.

Secondary Research Tools

Doing secondary research is generally as simple as reading trade journals and other business publications. It's something that all businesses should

regularly do. Most businesses have at least one trade publication (many have several); identify the ones most relevant for you and read them as often as you can. Note that trade magazines do tend to be expensive, so read them at your local library if they're not in your budget. Also, particularly if your business will mostly have local customers, read your local newspapers and other media to keep an eye on your local economy.

Effective Marketing Starts With a Solid Organization

Lots of small businesses fail to understand the importance of having an efficient, organized operation in place *before* they start their marketing efforts. After all, you'll want to be ready to handle the heightened attention your marketing will bring to your business. For example, a restaurant should not start a big marketing campaign without already having a good chef and enough wait staff in place to handle a surge of diners. Otherwise, the unprepared restaurant's marketing efforts will likely result in unhappy diners and bad publicity.

Here's another way of saying this: Before you decide *how* to market, pay attention to *what* you're marketing. Make sure your house is in order before you worry about how to call attention to it. For more information on this and other common-sense tips for cost-effective marketing, read *Marketing Without Advertising,* by Michael Phillips and Salli Rasberry (Nolo).

 TIP

Read beyond the business pages. Valuable industry and other information is often found in other sections of your local newspaper. For instance, if you run a garden supply company, the home and garden section will have lots of information on trends and may feature other companies in your market. And an owner of a clothing store might find out about interesting fashion trends in the arts and culture section.

Cost-Effective Marketing Tools

There are endless ways to market your business—the key is to pick the methods that will give the most bang for the buck. Forget about the mega-budget strategies of the big businesses you see advertising on TV. The best bet for small to mid-sized businesses is to focus instead on building an excellent reputation and encouraging great word of mouth. Think about it: How did you choose a hair salon, plumber, or an auto mechanic? Chances are that you asked your friends and acquaintances for a recommendation. Likewise, you want your customers to recommend your business to their contacts. The more that you can motivate your customers and clients to rave about your business, the more likely your business will be a success.

This section provides an overview of the many ways you can market your business, focusing on some key, tried-and-true methods: networking, media relations, special events, and listing your business in directories.

Networking

Key contacts are essential to every business and the best way to develop these contacts is through networking. Networking involves actively cultivating relationships with people, businesses, community leaders, and others who present possible opportunities for your business—not just as potential customers, but also as vendors, partners, investors, or other roles. Networking is not the same thing as sales: Rather than the simple goal of making a sale, a huge goal of networking is to inform other businesspeople and influential people about what you do in hopes that they will recommend your business to their circle of contacts.

Lots of folks new to the world of business fear that successful networking requires unsavory schmoozing or pandering. These concerns are unfounded. In fact, if you adopt a sleazy wheeler-dealer approach, you risk alienating the very people whom you want to make your allies. Instead, successful networking is little more than sincere communication with others about what you do. You are "networking" every time you attend an event held by a local trade association, get to know other business owners and community leaders, write a letter to the editor, participate in an online discussion group, or have lunch with another local business owner.

TIP

Forge relationships with contacts before you need help from them. For example, if you need the support of a local politician on an upcoming city zoning decision, you'll have a better chance of getting the politician's vote if he or she already knows you and thinks favorably of your business than if you place a call to his or her office out of the blue.

While it may be easiest to meet someone at an event, introducing yourself to a potentially useful contact can be as simple as picking up the phone, writing a letter, or sending an email. In making your initial contact, you should be as formal or informal as is appropriate for the person with whom you are making contact. A letter of introduction on attractive letterhead might be best for an influential politician, for example, but a phone call might be fine to introduce yourself to a local business owner. In your letter, email, or phone call, explain who you are, what your business does, and why you thought that person might be interested in your products or services. Try to conclude by encouraging further communication in the future, such as inviting the contact to an event or asking if he or she would be interested in receiving email updates from your business. If you talk to someone on the phone, a follow-up email or letter thanking the contact for his or her time is always a smart idea.

TIP

Check out online networking. Social media, such as LinkedIn and Facebook, offer lots of opportunities for networking. See "Social Media: Facebook, Twitter, and More" in Chapter 13 for details.

Media Relations

Another excellent—and inexpensive—way to promote your business is to generate media coverage in newspapers or magazines or on radio, television, or the Internet. Your goal is to get "editorial" coverage, meaning some mention of your business or event in news or feature stories (as opposed to paid advertising). Because editorial coverage is far more credible than advertisements or paid publicity, it will have a greater impact. For example, a local newspaper article about your business being awarded a lucrative state contract will almost always generate a more favorable and lasting impression than any advertising.

The term "media relations" means the process of attempting to obtain editorial coverage. It is a fairly simple process: You contact the media on behalf of your business and encourage an editor, producer, or reporter to write or produce a story about your particular subject. As with most marketing efforts, the more specific and targeted your message, the more impact it will have. For example, you'll be much more likely to interest an editor in your business's recent expansion and opening of a new facility than the very general fact that your business exists.

The basic steps for conducting media relations are:

- **Write a press release.** A press release is a key tool to use when pitching a story idea. Typically, a press release is a one-page announcement outlining the information you want the media to cover. You have two main goals in writing a press release: (1) to capture the journalist's attention, and (2) to make it easy for the journalist to write the story you want published. Stylistically, press releases are usually written like news stories, offering journalists an example of the story you want them to produce. (See "Elements of a Strong Press Release," below, for more details on how to put together a winning pitch.)

- **Make the initial contact with a journalist by phone.** Make a preliminary phone call before sending a press release, so your release doesn't get lost in the shuffle. If you don't know which reporter would be likely to cover your story, call the news department, briefly describe the nature of your press release, and ask who might be the best person for you to contact. Once you have the name of a reporter, an editor, or a producer, give that person a call to introduce yourself and your business, briefly explain the nature of your news story, and tell the person you will be sending a press release. If you can't reach the journalist by phone (as is often the case), don't let it hold you up: Leave a message and send out your press release. While you could make this initial contact by email, a phone call makes a stronger impression. And creating lasting relationships with individual reporters is the best way to get positive coverage over the long term.

- **Send the press release by email, fax, or both.** Years ago, press releases were sent by mail. This practice has long since given way to delivery by fax. Today, it's a good strategy to send press releases via email as well, ideally as a both a PDF attachment and as plain text in the body of the email. Emailed press releases work because reporters like having an electronic copy from which to cut and paste when writing their stories; faxes work because they don't get lost or buried as easily as email. To cover your bases, send your press releases in both forms, or even better, ask the reporter which method he or she prefers.

- **Follow up after you send the press release.** Shortly after sending your press release—a few hours or a day later, depending on the timing of your announcement—follow up with another phone call or email to make sure your press contact received the release and to answer any questions he or she may have.

An example of a press release is shown below.

Some people feel timid about contacting the media and asking them to cover a specific story. While you shouldn't be a pest, you also shouldn't feel shy about pushing your story idea persistently. To do their jobs, journalists must come up with a constant stream of interesting new story ideas. Local business journalists are often particularly challenged in finding newsworthy business stories. Just as you need their help, they need yours. Because you will often know more than reporters do about a particular story, you can offer valuable information that they can use. If you are honest and reliable, you will usually be treated with respect.

Sample Press Release

FOR IMMEDIATE RELEASE
May 6, 2010

State of California Contracts With Data Solutions, Inc., for Data Communications Equipment and Services

OAKLAND, California—The state of California has entered into a purchasing contract with Data Solutions, Inc., for a wide array of data communications equipment, related software, and Data Solutions' award-winning network management services. Under this agreement, the equipment and services provided by Data Solutions will be available at special volume pricing to all California state agencies, municipalities, and educational institutions.

"We are thrilled that the state of California has chosen Data Solutions to fill its data communications needs," said Data Solutions CEO Steven Dutch. "As a growing California company, we are proud to play a role in keeping technology money in the California economy."

California's contract with Data Solutions will allow state procurement agencies to support and enhance their data communications networks with the highest quality products and support services. In addition to the data communications equipment included in the purchasing agreement, Data Solutions' engineers will be available under this contract to provide analysis, design, installation, training, and maintenance services for the equipment included in the contract.

The agreement will be effective until December 31, 2012.

About Data Solutions
Data Solutions is a privately held California-based company specializing in the design, implementation, support, and management of voice, video, and data communications infrastructures. Data Solutions offers unparalleled expertise in IP-based networking, including LAN, WAN, and IP multiservice technology. Data Solutions is headquartered in Oakland and has a second site in Portland, Oregon. More information about Data Solutions and its award-winning products and services is available at www.datasolutionswebsite.com.

Contact Information
Steven Dutch, CEO
Data Solutions, Inc.
510-555-1212 ext. 123
sdutch@datasolutionswebsite.com

Polly Harvey, Media Relations
Clarity Media
510-555-9876
polly@claritymedia.com

Elements of a Strong Press Release

The better your press release, the more likely a journalist will write about your business, giving you valuable exposure in the press. Reporters, editors, and producers are chronically busy and squeezed by deadlines; they need good story ideas and clear information to get their jobs done. The easier you can make it for them to cover your story, the more likely they are to oblige. If you write a strong, clear press release, they may even use parts of your release verbatim. But because most media people are flooded with press releases and story pitches, you'll need to keep your press release as succinct as possible.

Here are some tips on how to construct a compelling press release that is likely to generate media placements.

- **Start with a news hook.** Like a news story, your press release should have a strong first sentence, known in the news biz as the story's "lead" (sometimes spelled "lede" in publishing circles). What is the most important point you want to get across? Write it in a clear, straightforward style and you will have your lead. Compare the following examples:
  - **Weak lead:** "ClearVue Video Production Services provides professional videography and editing services."
  - **Strong lead:** "ClearVue Video Production Services recently launched a major new post-production facility, doubling the number of professional editing systems available for rental in the city."
- **Date, time, and location information should be easy to find.** If your press release is promoting an event, don't bury important information deep within long paragraphs. Include important event details such as date, location, and registration deadlines in the first sentence or two, the last sentence (perhaps in bold text), or summarized in bullet points at the end of the press release.
- **Include the most important information first.** Like stories in the newspaper, your press release

should include all important details up front, then work toward more general or background information in later paragraphs. You could even put background information at the end of the release, in a separate section.

- **Include quotes from yourself or other key people.** Reporters like to include quotes from real people in their stories, so include at least one or two catchy quotes in your press release. If you are writing the release and you are the best person to offer a quote, don't be shy about quoting yourself! It may feel strange but it's perfectly appropriate. Remember, you're offering the media a sample of the story you want them to write, so include a quote as if an outside reporter interviewed you.
- **Include a separate section with contact information.** The journalists who receive your release may have additional questions to ask you. Choose a point person who will be available to field any such questions and include his or her contact information clearly at the end of the release.
- **Create a news angle.** If it is appropriate and possible, tie your release into a topic that's currently in the news. For example, if your press release is announcing your furniture manufacturing company starting a new line featuring environmentally friendly materials, you'd certainly want to include a reference to the rapid growth of "green" businesses—a hot news topic.
- **Use statistics.** Reporters love statistics that show how prevalent a problem is or how many people are affected by an issue. Using the previous example, you could include recent statistics that 35% of people surveyed would be willing to pay a premium for environmentally friendly products.

If you don't get a response after an introductory phone call, a press release via email and fax, and a follow-up call, let the particular story idea rest; this will help you preserve your reputation as a pleasant, professional person to deal with the next time you want to pitch a story. A journalist may not cover your story because he or she does not think it is newsworthy or because there are other stories that take precedence. A few months later, when you try again, you may be pleasantly surprised to find that you've pitched the right story on the right day.

 TIP

Relationships with media people are gold. The most effective media relations come from relationships you build with reporters, editors, producers, and other media contacts. Because you are more likely to get news coverage from a reporter with whom you've worked before than from someone who's never heard of you, you should always treat your relationships with people in the media as the valuable resource they are.

Finally, keep in mind that having a story written about your business isn't the only way to get media coverage. Another great way to get exposure is to be interviewed and quoted for articles on subjects in which you have expertise. Ideally, you'll develop relationships with reporters who will understand you to be an expert in a certain area, so that they call you for a quote when covering that topic. Similarly you might be invited to participate in a local TV show on a topic within your expertise. Foster this type of coverage by making sure your reporter contacts understand your area of expertise and that you are willing to offer your opinions and information if they need them for a story.

Special Events

Holding events such as a grand opening party, a product demonstration, an informational workshop, or a holiday gala will help you forge a closer bond with your customers, while simultaneously generating valuable publicity for your business. Special events tend to grab the attention of the media, making them a particularly effective marketing method. The icing on the cake is that events can (and should!) be fun, both for you and your customers.

One reason that special events are such effective publicity tools is that the media is generally more responsive to specific, time-sensitive activities or events than to the business in the abstract. An event is an easy hook, particularly if there is any educational or public interest component to your event. For example, if your housewares store offers a half-day workshop on how to make your home more green, a reporter might well be able to craft a story around the event and discuss the timely topic of sustainable living.

Even if your event isn't newsworthy enough to merit a whole story, most events can be listed in local business calendars, usually for free. Most daily papers have a business section with events listings, and submitting your event is an easy way to get a dose of publicity.

Listings or Directories

Getting your business listed in appropriate directories is a great way to boost your visibility with your target customers. Listings work so well because consumers who consult a particular directory or directory category have already determined that they are looking for a specific type of business. In addition to every city's phone books, most communities have other types of directories—for example, the local chamber of commerce membership directory, a directory of women-owned businesses, or the African American business league's directory. Some directories are published in hard copy, though many directories are posted online.

Most business directories charge fees. You'll have to evaluate whether the fees fit into your budget and whether the directory exposes your business to the right audience. While most directory fees are modest, some are prohibitively expensive; these are not worth considering unless the audience you're trying to reach is extremely narrow and desirable and the directory is highly targeted to that audience.

Note also that some membership organizations include a directory listing as a benefit of membership. Chambers of commerce, for example, will typically list member businesses in their directories—

print, online, or both. As with regular directory fees, you'll have to judge whether the directory listing (plus any other benefits) are worth the membership fee.

With any kind of directory, the most important consideration is what audience the listing will reach. Ask about how and where the directory will be distributed, how many copies are printed, and how often a new edition is published.

To find all of the directories in which you should list your business, you'll have to do some homework. Looking online is a good start, but you should also check with local resources such as local government offices, chambers of commerce, economic development organizations, and trade associations.

Sponsorships

Sponsoring an event, sports team, nonprofit organization, or public television or radio station is a great way to develop your brand. Sponsorships are a lot like advertising in the sense that you pay money in exchange for having your business recognized in some way, usually with a display of your logo and sometimes a short marketing message. But unlike advertising in traditional media like newspapers or television, a sponsorship does more than just communicate your marketing message: it also conveys a sense of connection to whatever you are sponsoring and thus creates more positive associations in your potential customers' minds.

For example, if you sponsor a local golf tournament and have your logo prominently displayed on signs, event schedules, and other materials, the golf-oriented attendees will start to see your business as an ally and begin to develop an emotional connection to your business. Similarly, a business that sponsors a gay and lesbian film festival will develop a connection to the gay and lesbian community.

Sponsorship opportunities tend to fall in a few categories:

- **Events.** This includes events such as sport tournaments, film festivals, trade shows, street fairs, concerts, and just about any other event open to the public. Event organizers often want businesses to help fund an event in exchange for recognition, usually on signs, in printed materials, and in TV or radio ads.
- **Facilities.** New building projects such as sports arenas, courthouses, or university buildings sometimes ask for corporate and business sponsors, who are often recognized on a plaque, statue, or other sign in the building. Being recognized in this way helps show your business is a pillar in the community.
- **Nonprofit organizations.** Most nonprofits welcome sponsorship funds from businesses and will have specific benefits available for different levels of financial support. Sponsoring a nonprofit is an excellent way to build your reputation in the community served by and involved with the nonprofit.
- **Public television and radio.** While public TV and radio sponsorships are beginning to blur into the more traditional commercials, there still is a distinct difference in the perception of sponsors of public media. You'll also typically reach a more affluent, educated demographic via public media than with commercial stations.

Email Promotions

First off, we're not talking about spam here. While unsolicited junk mail is a huge problem, there is also a legitimate way to send out emails to your target customers to let them know about upcoming promotions, events, and other business information. This approach involves sending useful information to a list of people who have indicated a desire for your emails. See Chapter 13, "Email Marketing and E-Newsletters," for advice on email promotions.

Direct Mail

Besides sending out email promotions, you can send out hard-copy marketing materials by U.S. mail—a process that's called direct mail. People often perceive direct mail campaigns to be complex and expensive, and they can be both. However, direct mail campaigns can also be simple, targeted mailings that are effective without costing a fortune. If you keep the materials simple and develop your own mailing list instead of paying a firm for a list, you can engage in a direct mail campaign that's both thrifty and effective.

First, decide what the goal and subject of your direct mail campaign will be. As with most types of marketing outreach, the more specific your message, the better. Instead of sending out a general brochure about your printing business, for example, send out a postcard offering a 50% discount off the first order for new customers. Special promotions, discounts, or giveaways are the best way to capture people's attention amid all the junk mail.

You can take different approaches in developing your mailing lists, from simply compiling names of everyone you know and looking up their addresses, to hiring a mailing list firm and paying a fee for a list. You may be surprised at how many names you can come up with on your own. Start with the people within your target customer profile and work outward. Ask your friends for names of people they know who might be interested in your business. If you'll be targeting other businesses, scan other directories for their contact information.

Creating the printed materials for your mailing can be more affordable than you might expect. You don't need to produce a high-end direct mail package like the ones you get in your own mailbox, printed in full color on heavy paper with special die-cut shapes and other frills. Instead, focus on creating simple layouts of text and graphics on standard-sized pages or postcards. Ideally, you, a partner, or an employee can design your materials in-house, using relatively inexpensive software such as Adobe *InDesign*. Alternatively, a professional graphic designer can be immensely helpful, particularly if no one in your business has graphic design skills.

Samples

Everyone loves stuff for free. If you have a product that lends itself to being sampled, consider setting up a table at a trade show or other venue and offering freebies to the public. Sure, you'll always end up giving things away to people who have no intention of buying your product, but it's usually worth it to forge a connection with even a few potential buyers. Some examples of offering samples effectively include:

- a handmade soap maker offering small slices of beautiful soaps at a table in the health food store
- a coffee shop offering small, free cups of house-roasted coffee at a street fair, and
- a massage studio offering free, five-minute massages at a local trade show.

When offering samples, prepare in advance to ensure that you make a powerful and positive first impression. Have your business name and logo prominently displayed. And remember to have business cards or brochures available so that the people sampling your product or service can find you later.

Customer Loyalty Programs

The phrase "customer loyalty program" sounds much more involved than it really is. What we're talking about here is implementing ways to keep your current customers coming back for more. Here are a couple of ideas:

- **Offer punch cards for repeat customers.** Coffee shops often use these, but plenty of other businesses can use them too. After a number of purchases—measured either in units or dollar increments—the customer gets something free. For example, a coffee shop might offer customers a free cup of coffee after they have purchased ten cups, tracked on the punch card. Or a record shop might punch the card for every $10 spent, and after $100 is reached, customers get $10 off their next purchase.
- **Include freebies with each sale.** A shoe store, for example, could include a small tin of shoe polish with every order. A baby store could include a free rubber duckie with each sale. It's amazing how much customer goodwill you can generate by including something worth about 10¢ in each sale.

Print Materials

Brochures, business cards, flyers, letterhead, and other printed materials can help you spread the word about your business. It might be worth hiring a professional graphic designer to create these materials to ensure they convey a professional image. It's also important that your logo and other imagery remain consistent across all the media you produce, both in print and online.

Websites and Social Media

As described in detail in Chapter 13, every business should have at least a simple website with basic marketing information. These days, if a customer Googles your business and comes up empty-handed, they might think your business isn't very professional or stable and might keep looking, choosing one of your competitors that does have a useful site. In addition, there are endless ways to network online, including social media, such as Facebook, YouTube, and countless others. Read Chapter 13 for guidance on how to establish your business online and effectively network within online communities.

Publishing Articles or Newsletters

Publishing substantive information is a great way to establish your credibility and enhance your reputation, particularly for professional service businesses. Accountants and lawyers, for example, are perfect candidates for newsletters because the heart of their businesses is information. Newsletters—both print and email versions (discussed in Chapter 13)—are powerful marketing vehicles, helping to strengthen the relationship with existing clients and to broaden the customer base when existing customers pass on the newsletter to their friends and family.

On the flip side, newsletters do require a fairly sizable time commitment—and possible expenses if you need to hire someone to help. Writing and editing are time-consuming tasks (even for professional writers), and you might need to hire a designer for the layout work if you plan to distribute a hard-copy version.

Also bear in mind that by its nature, a newsletter is distributed periodically, so if you can't commit to whatever time frame—typically weekly, monthly, or quarterly—then don't do it at all. Starting to send a monthly newsletter and then having it disappear after six months will give a much poorer impression than never offering a newsletter in the first place.

If you really want to publish but can't commit to a newsletter, consider publishing occasional articles or white papers on certain topics, without any promise (explicit or implied) of when the next article will be issued. Or, consider sticking with marketing copy rather than substantive information. Putting out regular flyers or emails highlighting your products or services and any special events at your store is much easier than a substantive newsletter and might be all you need.

RESOURCE

Nolo's *Marketing Without Advertising* offers a whole book's worth of good marketing ideas. Written by Michael Phillips and Salli Rasberry, this excellent resource offers a wealth of information about how to build positive recognition without spending a dime on traditional advertising. Its insights into effective marketing techniques are valuable for any enterprise, particularly budget-minded ones.

Chapter 12 Checklist:
Small Business Marketing 101

☐ Define your target market—potential customers, competition, and industry—and learn everything you can about it. Based on what you learn, you might decide to tweak your target market or aspects of your business operations in order to better appeal to a profitable customer base.

☐ Engage in primary market research to get information directly from your potential customers. Web-based surveys are excellent tools to use.

☐ Have an efficient, organized operation in place before you start your marketing efforts.

☐ Focus on marketing strategies other than advertising—particularly on ways to encourage good word of mouth—that are usually less expensive and just as effective.

☐ Network by cultivating relationships with other businesses, community leaders, and others.

☐ Develop relationships with reporters and editors and pitch newsworthy stories about your business to them. Make your expertise clear to media people so that they contact you for quotes or interviews when writing stories on certain topics.

☐ Maintain at least a simple website and network online.

E-Business: Selling and Marketing Online

E-business these days encompasses much more than just creating a website. In many ways, today's possibilities for online business are incredibly exciting—new technologies are emerging every day that allow businesses to promote themselves and sell products and services online in novel and amazing ways. The downside is that the e-business landscape is constantly shifting and evolving, making it a real challenge to keep up with what's current and to separate the true opportunities from the hype.

Despite how bewildering the world of e-business can be, don't stick your head in the sand. Every business needs to consider to what degree it will operate online. At a minimum, a business should create a basic online presence to let the e-world know it exists; often this involves creating just a simple website as an "online business card" of sorts for a bricks-and-mortar business. At the other end of the spectrum, some businesses operate entirely online, with all revenues generated from online sales. In this situation, the website itself and its e-commerce functions will certainly need to be more complex, and it will be more important to implement a sophisticated online marketing strategy to drive traffic to the e-commerce operation.

In between having a basic marketing site and running a full e-commerce operation, there is a wide world of options for doing business—and in particular, promoting your business—online. Blogs and social media are transforming the way that businesses interact and develop relationships with potential customers online. And strategies for boosting your business's ranking with search engines, such as Google, (and thus driving more traffic to your site) have become a whole industry unto itself, known as search engine optimization or SEO.

What's true for all businesses is that taking your business online needs to be approached strategically. Most importantly, you need to establish how your e-business activities will fit into your overall business strategy, and do so *before* you start developing your site or other online ventures. For example, if you hire a Web developer to create a website and a blog without first giving careful thought to your e-business strategy, you might end up with a site

that is ineffective—or worse, one that unexpectedly drains your business's valuable resources.

Even when your strategy is clear, creating a website can be tricky. It's incredibly common for a business owner to think the site he or she envisions is simple or basic, when, in truth, it is anything but. Some business owners are tempted to build the site themselves to save money, but quickly discover they're out of their depth. Others decide to hire outside Web developers, but find they're at the mercy of programmers who push technologies the business doesn't need or who lack business savvy, resulting in sites that don't achieve business goals.

In this chapter, the term "e-business" refers to the broad range of ways your business can operate online, beyond simply maintaining a website. This chapter demystifies the process of taking your business online—starting by helping you clarify your strategy and understanding the range of opportunities online. We'll discuss a wide range of e-business issues, including:

- creating a website
- engaging in social media
- selling your products online
- driving traffic to your site through search engine optimization (SEO)
- how to find and work with Web developers
- how to evaluate alternatives such as template-based website builder services and open an affiliate store within e-commerce sites like Amazon, eBay, or Etsy
- the process of developing a website methodically, from strategy and concept to programming and testing, and
- domain name, copyright, and other intellectual property issues.

Defining Your Strategy and Goals

Way before you start thinking about the cool features or content you want to include at your website or how you'll promote your business on Facebook, put careful thought into your broad strategy for e-business and how it fits into your overall business strategy. In particular, you want to make sure that your online activities serve your business strategy and not the other way around. For example, don't let a Web developer talk you into an online store or a blog that doesn't directly serve your business needs or fit within your resources.

If your business was originally conceived as an online business—for example, an online-only athletic equipment retailer or an electronic publication—you probably already have a clear idea that your online activities will be the focus of your business. But if you are planning a website for a traditional offline business, such as a bakery or remodeling service, it's important to take the time to be clear about how your website or other online activities fit into your bigger business plan. Bricks-and-mortar businesses are vulnerable to stumbling into bigger e-business activities than they can handle. If you will be conducting business online, then you need to make sure that you have adequately accounted for these online operations in your business plan. If not, you'll need either to scale back your e-business plans or revise your business plan accordingly.

It's all too easy to be seduced by the latest inter-active features and other Web-based applications—online sales and publishing are common examples—and to lose focus of your core business operations. Online sales, in particular, tend to involve a whole new set of details you'll need to handle, such as managing online sales reports, shipping, and online customer service. If these activities weren't included in your original business plan, you might quickly find yourself overwhelmed and unable to keep customers happy—a bad situation for any business. With careful strategic thinking before launching a website or other e-business activities, you can plan for the resources you'll need and avoid this mistake.

> **EXAMPLE:** Michele is planning to open a store selling handmade jewelry. She wants to create a website and starts talking to Web developers to get an idea of what a site would cost. Many of the developers she talks with encourage her to create an online store to help increase sales. Without having put much thought into the website, Michele initially likes the idea. She figures that if the site generates even a few sales per month, it would be welcome additional income.
>
> When Michele takes the time to think more about an online jewelry store, though, she realizes she has several questions about how it would work. She calls back some of the developers she's talked to and asks about details such as how the site would be updated with photos of current pieces and how other tasks would be handled, such as shipping, billing, inventory control, and customer service. She learns that, indeed, while some tasks, such as billing, can be somewhat automated, other tasks would have to be handled either by her, an employee, or a subcontractor such as the Web developer.
>
> Michele realizes that her business plan did not account for the logistics involved in online sales and that she'd rather stick with her original plan and make sure to run her shop well, as she originally planned. In keeping with this, she decides to keep her website strategy simple, with a basic marketing website used to promote her business, not for online sales.

Beyond identifying an overall strategy for how your site and other online activities will fit within your business, you also need to define specific goals for your online efforts. All too often, business owners fail to do this with any specificity; many think the goal is simply to increase business. However, goals can and should be more specific so that your e-business efforts are well-tailored to them.

Typical goals for many small business owners would include:

- building recognition of the business and its brand
- attracting new clients and customers, either to come to a physical business or to call the business
- collecting email addresses or other contact information for marketing efforts
- showing work samples and portfolio items
- selling products—otherwise known as e-commerce
- answering common customer questions to decrease customer service phone calls

Web Jargon: Defined

In addition to the often bewildering technical jargon that's so often used by Web developers and consultants, even nontechnical terms can be confusing because the language of the Web is still evolving. To help stay clear about what's what, some of the most common terms are defined below. Because the e-world is relatively new, definitions are still fluid and other people might use these terms somewhat differently.

- **Blog** is short for "weblog," a website using a format of short posts, ordered in reverse chronological order (as in, the most recent post at the top of the page), which often include links to other sites. Blogs are regularly updated—often several times daily—with new information by one or more contributors, called bloggers. Blogs started out as largely personal communication vehicles, but an increasing number of reputable businesses and online publications are using the blog format.

- **E-business** is a very general term referring to the full range of ways a business can operate in the online world, from having a simple marketing website to sending out marketing emails to operating complex e-commerce sites, and everything in between. A website is generally—but not always—the focal point of e-business.

- **E-commerce** refers to an online sales operation, generally via a website that is set up to allow online orders and process credit card or other types of payments.

- **Email lists** are compilations of email addresses of people who have expressed interest in receiving promotional emails from a business. (If the content of the email is substantive in nature the email would usually be called an e-newsletter.) For example, your business could send emails about special promotions or events to an email list. It's critical that the recipients included in an email list have clearly expressed interest in receiving the emails. As you're probably aware, unsolicited marketing emails are known as spam and frowned upon by savvy businesspeople and their recipients alike.

- **Marketing websites** refer to basic websites that feature marketing-type information about a company, such as what its products or services are, pricing, and contact information. While an e-commerce site will usually include marketing information, a marketing website by definition does not include an e-commerce component. Very basic marketing websites are sometimes called brochure-ware, since they are analogous to a company brochure.

- **Listservs** are essentially email discussion groups about a specific topic that allow people who have signed up to them to share information with each other. Any subscriber can send an email to the listserv, and that email will automatically be sent to all other listserv subscribers. This differentiates a listserv from an email list, in which communications are typically only one-way from the administrator to the list.

- **Online presence** refers to the broad collection of ways a business is represented in the electronic world. For instance, in addition to having a website, you could maintain a blog; be listed in numerous online directories; be a regular commentor on other blogs and online forums; have a regular email newsletter; supply informative articles to other websites; or moderate a listserv. The sum of all these activities is often called your online presence.

- **Web developers** specialize in all aspects of creating websites, including organizing the information, graphic design, and programming. Avoid the term "Web designer" when referring to these individuals because graphic design is only one aspect of creating a website. Another acceptable term for Web developer is Web builder. Although some Web developers work alone as independent contractors, they typically involve teams to create a website: information architects, graphic designers, content developers, and programmers.

- attracting investors, and
- publishing late-breaking information, such as news about the latest bathroom fixtures available or recent technology releases.

By clearly defining goals, you'll be better able to decide what information is important to communicate to your audience. In addition, your specific goals will play a big part in determining how information is organized at your site. Content that is closely tied to high-priority goals should be featured prominently.

A Website: Your Online Base Camp

A few years ago, the concept of e-business was more or less synonymous with having a website. But as we start into the second decade of the 2000s, doing business online is much more expansive. A website is no longer one and the same as your e-business operations—rather, think of the website as the base camp for your e-business activities. Besides maintaining a site, you might maintain a Facebook page and actively network it among hundreds of "friends"; send out Twitter updates with business news or customer service tips; host a YouTube channel where you post informative or entertaining videos related to your business; and send out periodic promotional emails announcing special sales or other company news. Your website is still important as a central repository for business information and possibly a revenue center if you have an online store. But these days, a website typically does not work solo but in sync with a wider range of online activities that collectively serve to generate business.

As mentioned above, every business needs to evaluate its overall strategy to figure out to what degree it will engage in doing business online. If heavy social media networking doesn't make sense for your business, the conventional wisdom is that you still should have at least a simple website—for instance, one that includes basic information about what the business does and contact information. In some cases, this might be nothing more than a one-page site, similar to a listing in the yellow pages.

Whether to create a more extensive site or integrate it with other forms of online marketing (such as a social media outreach strategy) will depend on the specifics of your business.

Generally, even an ultrabasic site will offer several benefits to your business. Here are some of the main things it will help you do:

- **Project a professional image.** Some customers consider businesses that don't have websites to be less serious or less stable than businesses that have them.
- **Reach the ever-growing number of consumers who look for businesses online.** This is true for all kinds of businesses, not just Web-related ones. In our increasingly Web-reliant population, a growing number of people start their searches for a local plumber, a café, a clothing store, or any other type of business on the Web.
- **Communicate more information than you can typically fit on a business card or brochure.** When you include the Web address, called the URL for "uniform resource locator," on your business cards, brochures, or other printed materials, potential customers can go to your site for more in-depth information such as product details or portfolio pieces.
- **Create a permanent place where you can post information that potential customers can always refer to—unlike brochures or business cards that often get thrown away or lost.** This can be helpful to current customers or clients who may need to look up your phone number or payment mailing address.
- **Facilitate word-of-mouth marketing.** Your happy customers will easily be able to share information about your business with their friends and family simply by sharing your URL.
- **Market your business without paying print costs.** This can save you a lot of money if the information you want to communicate is lengthy or changes frequently, such as sales, specials, and new product arrivals. And of course, your website can use full color, which can be quite expensive to print.
- **Develop and refine your marketing messages before committing them to print.** For example, you could create a simple three-page site

with information about your services, your professional biography, and contact information—and refine these pieces of content for a month or two until you're satisfied with them; then create a print brochure with the information from the website.

- **Create a central place where all your marketing activities—both online and offline—can be referenced and linked.** For instance, your site can (and should) offer links to your Facebook, YouTube, and Twitter pages; a sign-up form for your email promotion list; and a calendar of special events or workshops your business is hosting.

Keep in mind that a website might offer even more opportunities for your particular business, such as the potential for profits from e-commerce and improved customer services. The bottom line is that even the simplest website will be an asset to your business. If more expansive online marketing efforts fit into your business strategy, then a website will serve as an important base of online operations.

The following sections discuss online marketing, blogging, social media, e-commerce, and other ways you can create an online presence for your business.

Online Outreach Methods

Though a website is generally the centerpiece of a business's online presence, there is an ever-expanding list of other online methods of communicating with potential customers. It's important to consider the big picture of how you plan to interact with potential customers beyond simply maintaining a website. The subsections below discuss the methods businesses commonly use these days to promote themselves online. Bear in mind that these methods are constantly evolving as new technologies are developed, so it's important to monitor trends and adapt your approach as circumstances warrant.

Email Marketing and E-Newsletters

Your business can email different kinds of information to customers who have signed up

for such communications. Broadly speaking, you can either send marketing information or more substantive information. Substantive information sent by email is usually called an e-newsletter. Marketing information sent by email is typically called an email announcement, email promotion, or marketing email. Of course, the line between marketing and substantive information can get awfully blurry, so here are some tips on how to communicate both types most effectively.

When emailing any type of information to your customers who have signed up for it, make sure that they receive the type of information they expected when they gave you their email address. In particular, don't send purely marketing information to customers who are expecting a more substantive newsletter with topic-based articles. Send marketing emails only to customers who have willingly signed up for that information.

Along these same lines, make sure anything that you call a "newsletter" actually lives up to its name. A newsletter—either in print or via email—does not have to be lengthy. In fact, short blurbs of useful information are generally more popular and reader friendly than lengthy articles. But a so-called newsletter that is little more than promotional copy for products and services will be sure to disappoint any customers expecting more substantive information. Considering how little tolerance people have for marketing emails, also known as "spam," be particularly careful not to send e-newsletters unless they contain truly useful information and are not just thinly disguised marketing copy. Some marketing information is fine in a newsletter, as long as substantive information is the focus. The best way to include marketing information in a newsletter is at the end of the more substantive information that offers some information of value to your readers.

 CAUTION
Publishing an e-newsletter or other substantive material requires an ongoing commitment. Publishing-oriented websites differ from marketing websites in that they focus on substantive information, such as articles or reports, not promotional copy. Be careful if you're considering an online newsletter or

other publishing activities; they will require a higher commitment and higher quality standards for the information you publish and more frequent updating.

What is appropriate content for a newsletter will vary significantly from one business to the next. It will largely depend on the expectations of your audience. Newsletters traditionally contain topic-based articles, but for some businesses it may be sufficient simply to announce upcoming events. For example, an e-newsletter for an independent cinema may send out a monthly newsletter with schedules and descriptions of upcoming screenings. Considering that the film screening schedules are the customers' primary interest, they would likely find that content valuable and happily accept that as an e-newsletter. But a monthly "e-newsletter" from a clothing store that has no content other than sales and specials would likely seem like just another marketing email and irritate its recipients. Instead, a short article or two each month about current fashion trends might be more appealing to interested readers. Or, the clothing store might reasonably conclude that an e-newsletter just isn't a good fit for its business and simply be clear with customers that its email announcements will consist of sales specials and other marketing information from the business.

True newsletters, particularly when they are done well, can take a fair amount of time to create. Though email newsletters may be simpler to create than print newsletters, don't underestimate the hours it will take you to write, edit, proofread, and send them. Similarly, don't underestimate the importance of well-written text that is free from errors and typos. In addition, when you commit to publishing a newsletter, it means that you commit to putting one out regularly, usually once a month or at least once a quarter. Make a realistic evaluation of whether you or a staffer has the writing skills and the time to be able to reliably create a quality newsletter. If not, then it's best to put off your newsletter plans until you have the resources in place.

When sending out any type of email to your customers, keep in mind the following tips:

- **Use the blind copy function to keep email addresses private.** By putting all the addresses in your email list in the blind copy, or Bcc

fields, the recipients will not be able to see all the other recipients' email addresses. Failing to do this risks irritating the members of your lists and making your business appear unprofessional.

- **Manage your email list scrupulously.** Managing hundreds or thousands of email addresses—including dealing with returned mail, address change requests, and unsubscribe requests—is no easy task. Using an email marketing service such as Constant Contact (www.constantcontact.com) or iContact (www.icontact.com) will help avoid mistakes that can cost you customer goodwill. Be careful, however, and don't use shady, unethical services that really are just spam companies. Stick with the well-known, trusted companies.

CAUTION

Avoid spam at all costs. To avoid being perceived as a spammer, send mass emails only to customers who have requested to be included on your list. Even better, use a "double–opt-in" system. In it, customers opt in the first time by indicating a willingness to receive your email communications—perhaps they signed up for your list at your website or signed a sheet at a tradeshow event. Then, you send an email to individual recipients asking them to confirm that they want to be included on your list. A doubl–opt-in system shows your commitment not to send spam—and ensures that the folks receiving your emails actually want them.

Blogging

Blogs have been around for several years but are just recently hitting their stride as an easy, effective way to communicate late-breaking information. Below we discuss big sites like Facebook that use blog formats; for now, let's consider a blog that you might start on your own.

A blog is basically just a website composed of chronologically ordered posts with the most recent entries at the top, much like an online journal. Photos or images are often included with individual posts. Posts tend to be short and almost always include one or more links to related information at other websites. In addition, many blogs allow readers to post comments. Inexpensive and free blog software (WordPress being the primary one these days) makes it easy to add new posts—much easier than it typically is to add content to traditional websites.

Early blogs tended to be more like personal journals, but now blogs have been embraced by businesses, media outlets, and issue-oriented websites seeking new ways to connect with audiences. A number of characteristics have made blogs attractive to the masses:

- They are easy to update.
- They allow an informal, friendly voice and more flexible coverage of topics.
- Perhaps most compelling, readers can easily comment on blogs, helping forge a connection between the blogger (that is, your business) and its readership (your potential customers).

The trick to a successful business blog is to offer information that's interesting to your potential customers and that favorably inclines them toward your business and products or services, without being too self-serving or marketing heavy. For example, if all your business blog posts are about how great your business is—and even worse, if it's all in marketing-speak—you'll quickly turn off readers. But if you present interesting topics to your readers in a sincerely helpful, information-sharing way, you'll be more likely to attract regular readers who develop a favorable impression of your business. This may even mean occasionally linking to competitors, if appropriate.

Blogs that allow users to post comments tend to develop a more loyal readership. Keep in mind, however, that allowing reader posts means you will have to monitor those comments for offensive, libelous, off-topic, or otherwise unacceptable material. It's up to you what line to draw, but inevitably you won't please everyone. If you leave offensive posts untouched, visitors will likely be turned off; while if you edit posts, people are sure to complain that you're censoring them. Still, allowing user posts is a great way to connect with your audience. Just strive to be fair in your policies in editing the posts.

A few examples of business blogging that could be done successfully include:

- a bakery's blog offering baking techniques and tips, allowing comments from readers and encouraging readers to submit photos of their results
- a yoga studio's blog about the health benefits of yoga and tips for doing various poses correctly, as well as links to external articles and studies about yoga's role in healthful living, and
- a landscaping company's blog sharing its experiences and projects, with photos of gardens as they grow, tips on gardening and landscaping, and links to sites with helpful information and/or quality products (such as seeds or landscaping materials).

Remember, the best blogs offer helpful, in-the-know tips and tidbits for readers—not straight-up marketing appeals. Rather than boosting sales directly, blogging is more likely to yield the indirect benefit of developing your brand as a reputable company that's in the know regarding industry developments. Keep this in mind when evaluating your expected results from a planned business blog.

Even more important are some fundamental realities to look at when considering a business blog. At a minimum, don't overlook the following:

- **The blog needs to be regularly updated, ideally a couple of times per week or more.** Don't start a blog unless you're sure that you or someone at your business has the time to keep it updated.
- **The blogger needs to be well informed on the topic and Web savvy.** Though the blogger doesn't have to be the world's top authority on your topic, he or she needs to know enough to create posts that are interesting and helpful to others seeking information on that topic. Part of this is being able to ferret out useful information online and provide links to that info.
- **The blogger needs to have some basic writing skills.** An informal, lively writing style is best on blogs. Avoid dry, academic writing or copy that sounds like a sales pitch.

Social Media: Facebook, Twitter, and More

If you spend any time online, you undoubtedly have at least heard of the terms "social media" or "Web 2.0," which refer to a major trend online towards websites with user-generated content, such as Facebook, MySpace, Yelp, YouTube, Flickr, or Twitter, to name just a few. In the broadest strokes, social media sites differ from traditional, old-school websites in that they consist almost entirely of content contributed by site users like you and me. After creating a user account, you can post all sorts of content including text, photos, videos and other multimedia. These sites are "social" in that users typically create networks of friends or followers, and in this way, build online communities within which they share information.

While some social media sites like LinkedIn are geared specifically towards professional and business networking, many others, such as Facebook and YouTube, began as vehicles for largely personal interaction among friends (Facebook started as an online network for Harvard students). But just about every sort of social media site has now been infiltrated (for better or worse) by businesses who have developed ways to use these sites to promote themselves and their brands. As you can imagine, some do it more effectively than others.

Very generally speaking, a business engages in social media by creating an account in the name of the business, then networking in whatever ways are appropriate within that community. There are endless ways to do this—so many, unfortunately, that the topic way exceeds the scope of this chapter. Without getting into details, here's a super-condensed list of some tips, ideas, and examples to get you on the right track.

- **Implement a comprehensive social media strategy.** As with any type of marketing, using social media to promote your business is best done with a well-thought-out plan and a clear idea of where you'll focus your efforts. Figure out which social media sites will work best for your business and what your communication goals are before jumping in. Keeping your strategy firmly in focus (and your audience;

see the next point) will also help you avoid being swayed by overhyped technologies that may not be a good fit.

- **Know your audience, and use social media sites that your audience uses.** Not surprisingly, many who use social media sites tend to be younger. Some sites, like Twitter, may have an even narrower base of particularly tech-happy users. If your target customers are 45- to 60-year-old executives, for example, you probably don't have to worry too much about Twittering. But for a target audience of young urban professionals, Twitter might offer some excellent opportunities for you to connect with them.
- **Understand the ins and outs of the online community(ies) you're thinking about joining.** Create a user account for yourself personally to learn how the community operates. Learning the conventions and customs that others use will help you avoid making any *faux pas*—more than just embarrassing, these kinds of missteps can damage your business's reputation and cost you customer goodwill.
- **Be creative!** From creating a hilarious or insanely clever YouTube video that goes viral to finding novel ways to use Twitter for customer service, there's no limit to the ways you can use social media for your business.

Bulletin Boards, Forums, and Listservs

Many businesses contribute their expertise and perspective by posting comments to online bulletin boards on topics related to their area of business. The key is to share information as an expert, not hustle for business. Including your business name and contact info in your signature is okay; actively soliciting business is generally a no-no.

Your business can also include an interactive forum at its website, where people can post messages and interact with each other on topics you choose. Your role is generally to moderate the discussion and remove posts that are off topic or offensive.

A listserv is similar to an email list, in that people who have signed up for the listserv receive emails.

However, with a listserv, the emails can be sent by anyone who is part of the listserv, not just by the manager of the listserv. For example, someone who reads a listserv email could respond to the whole group by sending an email to the listserv, which would be distributed to all recipients of the listserv. In contrast, email lists are one-directional, from the business to the list.

Listservs are most common in nonprofit organizations and schools, but some businesses also have customers who want to engage in an ongoing email discussion group. Business listservs tend to be appropriate only when a business's customer base has a compelling desire to interact, such as software companies whose customers like to share user tips with each other.

 RESOURCE

For more information on online publishing. Cheryl Woodard's *Starting & Running a Successful Newsletter or Magazine* (Nolo) includes a helpful, in-depth chapter on electronic publishing and establishing an online presence. It also offers the latest online communication methods and effective e-publishing strategies.

E-Commerce: What's Involved?

If you're planning to open a traditional brick-and-mortar store, you may see your website as a great way to expand sales. Or perhaps you have an idea for an online-only operation, such as selling vintage posters on your website. But keep in mind that selling products or services online adds complexity and cost to your website. (And don't forget the related logistical details your business will need to handle, such as shipping and customer service.) From a technical standpoint, your site will need to install "shopping cart" software that handles, at a minimum, the functions of the shopper selecting products and proceeding to checkout. Some shopping cart software does much more, such as allow you to provide discount codes, create custom categories of products, manage inventory, and more.

Besides shopping cart software, an e-commerce operation generally requires that your business have a "merchant account," which is essentially a business bank account specifically set up to accept credit and debit card payments. It's the same thing that a brick-and-mortar business needs to have in order to accept credit cards. In addition, an e-commerce site needs something called a "payment gateway," which is the service that securely processes the transfer of money from the buyer's payment instrument to the seller's merchant account. Think of the payment gateway as analogous to the credit card swipe machine that's used in brick-and-mortar businesses.

Each of these services charges its own set of fees. These can include an application fee, annual and/or monthly fees, and per-transaction fees, which may be a set amount or a percentage of the transaction total. With the hundreds of shopping carts, merchant accounts, and payment gateway services available and the complicated mix of fees they charge, picking the best suite of services for your e-commerce can be confusing, to say the least.

The good news is that there are a few standout e-commerce services have become well established. Services like PayPal, Google Checkout, and Yahoo! Merchant Solutions are particularly popular as they offer bundled services, including shopping carts, merchant accounts, and payment gateways. Each of these services offers a variety of options, but they simplify the process for customers by offering a streamlined, integrated suite of components rather than forcing you to research and choose them on your own.

If you don't use a bundled service, you'll need to choose shopping cart software (popular carts include FoxyCart, Zen Cart, and VirtueMart, but there are many, many others), set up a merchant account (it's not a bad idea to start by inquiring with your existing business bank), and choose a payment gateway (Authorize.net is a well-established and popular choice). Your shopping cart software, merchant account, and payment gateway need to be compatible with each other and with any other technology used at your website, such as a content management system (like Joomla or Drupal). The best bet is to ask your Web developer (discussed below in "Choosing and Working With a Web Developer") for recommendations, and ask other business owners you know for their experiences with various service providers. If you are interested in setting up an online store with Amazon, eBay, or Etsy, see "Website Builder Services and Affiliate Stores: Do or Don't?" below.

Website Builder Services and Affiliate Stores: Do or Don't?

A common question for small business owners embarking on their e-business plans is whether, instead of hiring a Web developer, they could use one of the many template-based website builder services currently available which cost significantly less than typical Web developer fees. Considering that many of these services can be quite inexpensive—say, as low as $50 or even $25 per month compared to a typical minimum $3,000 for a basic site built by a developer—it's certainly understandable that they are appealing to cash-strapped start-ups. Another attractive alternative is to create an affiliate store at an e-commerce site like Amazon, eBay, or Etsy.

There are a few different types of services here, so let's talk about them separately. First we'll look at template-driven sites created with "website builder" software, such as *WebSite Tonight*. Then, we'll consider options such as Amazon, eBay, and Etsy, which similarly allow you to do business online without having to hire a developer.

Using a Hosted Website Builder Service

Services such as GoDaddy's *WebSite Tonight* allow you to build a site using a simple browser-based interface that does not require any technical knowledge or skills. You will generally choose a prebuilt design template and customize it with menu headers, images, and text. For *WebSite Tonight*, GoDaddy charges a monthly fee that includes hosting and email and 24/7 customer support. Other similar services (often called website builder services) are often offered by website hosting companies. Fees, which typically include hosting, can be as low as $5 per month, but these lowest-end fees are generally only for personal websites.

Business sites can usually expect to pay in the range of $25 per month and up.

Generally speaking, these template-driven services might be appropriate only for the smallest of businesses that are truly pressed to get a minimal presence online. The biggest drawback is that these types of sites are seriously limited both in terms of design and functionality. While it's true that *WebSite Tonight* offers more than 1,500 design templates, customizing the template often results in shoddy looking sites, with poorly formatted text and clunky menus. Function-wise, it is often difficult or impossible to add features that you want, such as calendars, blogs, e-commerce, or interactive features. If it is possible to add these features at all, it will usually be only with whatever plug-in that the service provider has created for its template site, which may be primitive at best.

Another downside of using a do-it-yourself template site is that it usually takes more time, effort, and skill than these services claim. At the very least, inexperienced users will typically find they'll need to spend a fair amount of time learning the site building system, often through trial and error, before being able to get a site up and running. When considering a website builder service, be sure to look for user comments (often at websites separate from the builder service) to get a sense of how easy or difficult others found the service to use.

Even if you are able to figure out the builder software fairly easily, another issue to consider is that a lack of experience in designing a website will often result in a poorly organized site. Deciding what content to include and how to break up and organize that content at the site can be more complicated than you think. An experienced Web professional can make a huge difference in developing carefully considered content and organization—resulting in a site that's more tightly aligned with your strategic goals.

With all those downsides in mind, let's consider the positives: cost and convenience. Web builder services will significantly reduce the up-front cost of creating a site and minimize the complicated decisions and maintenance that are required when building your own site. These services generally include hosting and will usually handle software upgrades for free. Not having to deal with these issues can be a true relief for new business owners who are swarmed by the many other details of getting their businesses off the ground.

A final note: This field of template-driven, do-it-yourself sites is growing rapidly, and in coming years there may be solutions that offer better design and functionality than what is currently available. For example, a relatively new entrant into the field—Shopify, launched in 2006—is a good example of an e-commerce website builder service that appears to offer design and functionality of significantly higher quality than other similar services. Expect to see more develop in coming years.

Opening an Affiliate Store: Amazon, eBay, Etsy, and Others

Another alternative to hiring a Web developer to build your site is to open a store within an existing e-commerce site, such as Amazon, Etsy, or eBay. Creating a store within one of these e-commerce megaportals is definitely a quicker, easier, and less expensive way to get started selling your products online. Typically, the registration and set-up processes are easy to complete; as long as you have good photos of, and copy about, your products, you can be up and running in a day or two. (Again, remember this doesn't include the very important tasks of doing solid business planning to ensure your venture will be a success.)

There are downsides, however, to having just a store at Amazon or eBay and not your own website. The main drawback could perhaps best be described as getting lost within the shopping mall. Instead of developing name recognition for your business and its domain name, customers will have to find you amongst the thousands and thousands of other Amazon or eBay sellers. Anyone who has shopped at Amazon and other similar e-commerce sites can testify that finding a store or product can be like finding a needle in a haystack. Even if you give your store a specific name, shoppers within sites like Amazon are much less likely to remember your store name than if you had a custom-built store with its own domain name and that gave you the ability

to use the site design and content to develop your brand more strongly.

Another aspect to consider is that having a store within a big e-commerce operation restricts the content, design, and functions you can offer—and by extension, your ability to control and develop your brand image. With your own site built by a developer, you can use design elements to reinforce your brand and develop creative, strategic content to draw traffic—say, with a blog, an interactive customer service area, or other unique content. While stores within Amazon, Etsy, eBay, and others do allow you to offer some customized design and content, you'll be much more limited. Bear in mind that you can avoid this issue by having an affiliate store in addition to your own website that you use to develop your brand.

Planning a Website Project

After putting careful thought into your e-business strategy, including the methods that appear best suited for your specific goals, it's time to make some plans to implement your website and any related outreach activities. It's best to tackle some of the planning and preparation tasks before you contact a Web developer. If you take the time and effort to consider the issues discussed below before your first meeting, it will help create an efficient workflow and help you clearly convey to the developer what you want. Of course, it's normal to have some unresolved questions when you initially contact a Web developer and to work with him or her in refining your overall goals. The point is to do at least some planning and preparation in advance to get the most out of the working relationship.

If you want to take an alternative route by using a website builder service (like *WebSite Tonight*) or creating an affiliate store at a site like Amazon or eBay, read "Website Builder Services and Affiliate Stores: Do or Don't?" above. As we discuss in that section, there are several drawbacks to relying on these types of services to establish your online presence. In a nutshell, creating your own website will always give you more control over developing your brand online.

Identify Participants

Define early on which people in your company will be involved in the website project—in particular, who will have the authority to make decisions. With small start-ups, this is usually pretty straightforward: The business owners typically are involved, meaning they help to set goals, review the site in various stages of development, and have approval authority. However, if there are several business owners and one or more are not involved from the beginning, the possibility exists that they may raise objections down the line, after significant time and resources have already been spent on the site. To avoid this, make sure all business owners agree from the beginning who will have decision-making authority and what approval process will be followed.

> ⓘ **CAUTION**
>
> **If you outsource your site, retain control of strategic decisions.** Unless someone involved with your business has experience creating websites, it's generally best to outsource most aspects of the website creation process. (See "Creating A Website," below, for details.) Do not, however, give a consultant or Web development company complete discretion over your overall strategy for e-business. Even if you know and trust the developer you hire, you and any other business owners must be involved in these important strategic questions.

Research Other Sites

One of the best ways to educate yourself about the world of possibilities online and to generate specific ideas for features, designs, content, and other elements to include at your site is to browse the Web and look for examples of sites you like and don't like. Even if a site is very different from how you envision yours, there may be elements that could work for your site—for example, the color scheme, fonts, graphic images, or the organization of the information. Most Web developers will ask you for such examples, so it's a good idea to do this research before meeting with a developer.

Learn About Content Management Systems and Development Platforms

A short few years ago, website clients needed to decide whether to create a static site or a content-managed site (also called a "dynamic" site). In the most basic terms, static sites, which comprise individual HTML pages, require some technical knowledge to update, while content-managed sites, which use a browser-based content management system (CMS), can be updated much more easily by nontechnical folks. Static sites used to be considerably cheaper to build, but were more expensive to maintain because you'd typically have to hire a Web developer every time you wanted to make changes. If a small business needed a simple site and didn't anticipate making many changes over time, static sites were often advised. If they expected to make lots of updates to content or to an online store, a content-managed site would be a better option since the business would typically be able to make the changes on its own without having to pay a Web developer for help.

But as with all things technological, things have changed. These days, it's almost always best to create a content-managed site, even if you don't plan to update the site frequently. Why? A big reason is that content-managed sites have become considerably cheaper to build. With sites backed by robust CMSs now possible in the $3,000 dollar range (as opposed to, say, $5,000 and up a few years ago), there's little reason not to go the content-managed route which gives you several advantages, including the following:

- **Updatability:** A content-managed site uses a content management system, which simply means a browser-based interface allowing nontech folks to easily update site content, including text and images. Using whatever browser you normally use (*Firefox*, *Safari*, *Internet Explorer*, for example), you'll log in with a username and password, and then be able to access all the pages of content at your site. Details vary from one CMS to another, but, in general, you'll just go to whatever page you want to update, make changes to the text or photos, click "Save," and the changes will be live at the site. As you can see, having a CMS gives you lots of flexibility to make site updates without having to shell out more of your hard-earned money on technology consultants.

- **Scalability:** In addition to their updatability, content-managed sites are significantly more scalable than static sites, meaning that if you want to expand the site with new sections or add new features, it is much easier to do so if the site has a CMS. Even though you'll likely hire a developer to do this type of expansion or redesign, the developer will have much less work to do—meaning you'll spend much less money—if the site is content managed. In fact, major revisions to a static site often require the developer to start from scratch.

- **Solid technology:** Most content-managed sites these days are built using a development platform, which are continually updated to take advantage of the latest security technologies and other Web standards. In addition, most professional Web developers now no longer work with static sites, for many of the same reasons listed here. This leaves static sites largely in the realm of Web newbies, students, and that cousin of yours who keeps offering to do your site for a few cases of beer. It's perhaps for this reason that most static sites these days look awfully unprofessional.

Assuming you choose to create a content-managed site, there's also the question of what development platform will be used to build the site. Typically your developer will suggest a development platform, so you'll need to understand a little about this topic in order to make an informed decision. Here's the scoop.

In recent years a number of development platforms have emerged that are, in a sense, "prefab" websites with essential modules preprogrammed. Instead of writing code from scratch, a developer configures the modules to meet the website client's specific needs and design specifications. Development platforms can be either proprietary or open source; the former require licensing fees to be paid (usually annually) to the platform owner; open-source platforms are free to use. The clear trend

these days is to use open-source platforms which not only are free to use, but, in the case of popular platforms, are supported by an extensive community of developers who constantly test and make enhancements to the platform. The most popular open-source platforms include Drupal, Joomla, WordPress, and Plone; in the world of proprietary platforms, ExpressionEngine is fairly popular.

The question of which development platform to use (or whether to use one at all; more on this question in a moment) depends on the content and features you plan for your site. In very general terms, Drupal and Joomla are appropriate for a wide range of small business sites; WordPress works well for blogs but can also be customized to look like a regular, nonblog site; Plone works well for large enterprise websites, especially ones that will have visitors sign in and manage account information.

Finally, keep in mind that while using a development platform is the best, most cost-efficient option for most businesses, some businesses with high budgets and very specific design or other requirements may opt not to use a platform at all, instead opting for a totally custom site built from scratch. In reality, while development platforms offer excellent flexibility in terms of technology and design, they do sometimes run into limitations. Say for instance that you have a $25,000 budget for your website, some of which is being paid to a top design firm to develop color mock-ups of site pages and simulations of interactive features. When it comes time to program these mock-ups, a development platform might not allow enough flexibility to achieve them exactly as specified. In this case, you might need to hire a developer to build a custom website from scratch.

TIP

Some Web developers specialize in certain development platforms. As you interview potential Web developers, ask them what platform they recommend and why. Beware, however, that some developers may not have experience with some platforms and may therefore express a bias against them. Make sure that whatever developer you choose uses a development platform that is relatively common; otherwise you may end up with a site built with technology that hardly anyone else knows how to work with—not a good situation if you ever want to hire a different developer down the road. We discuss more tips in "Choosing and Working With a Web Developer," below.

Set a Realistic Budget

You don't need to spend a fortune creating a website, but you certainly can—and you can do so either by choice, or by letting costs spiral out of control. An essential step in preventing costs from smothering your best intentions is to set a budget for what your business can realistically afford for website creation and maintenance. It's best to do this before you start talking to Web developers to get a clear answer from those you contact about whether they can do what you want within your budget. You'll likely get quite a wide range of fees and rates from different developers, often determined by how many years they've been in business and what technologies they use. As long as your budget is realistic to begin with, you'll likely be able to find someone who can create something close to the site you want within your budget.

When attempting to set a realistic budget, keep a few parameters in mind. Very generally speaking, a basic content-managed site built upon an open-source development platform will typically cost somewhere between $3,000 and $5,000. To build any additional features—e-commerce functions, a photo gallery, a graphical calendar, an online registration system, a blog, and so on—the price will go up. Remember also that there are often third-party fees beyond what the Web developer charges, such as payment processing and security certificate fees for e-commerce sites and domain name and hosting fees. The bottom line is that the more features and functionality a site has, the more it will cost. Major, complex websites can cost in the tens or hundreds of thousands of dollars to create.

TIP

You get what you pay for. Even simple websites require several components: information architecture, graphic design, content creation, and programming. To have all these done well, you'll generally need a bare minimum budget of $3,000. You are not likely to get a quality, professional site—even a simple one—for $1,000. Sites in this low price range are often based on website templates which tend not to look professional or to meet specific business needs. It's better to pay a bit more for a site that is customized for you and that has a professional look and feel.

In addition, it's essential to consider the cost of maintaining your site after it has been created. Assuming you create a site with a content management system, you should be able to handle a significant portion of updating on your own. But don't underestimate the time commitment required; you'll need to define an updating schedule, establish who will be doing the updating work, and make realistic estimates for the time it will take to get the updates done.

Even with a CMS you may want to hire a Web developer to make deeper technical changes, say to add a calendar function or change the layout of an HTML template. With Web developer fees ranging from $50 to $150 an hour, outsourcing maintenance can get expensive.

Finally, remember that every site should have a periodic software and security update. Development platforms, such as Drupal, Joomla, and others, continually release new versions to address bugs or security issues and to add functionality. You should plan on hiring a developer at least once a year— twice a year or quarterly is even safer—to review the available updates for the technology being used at your site and upgrade the software when warranted.

Besides software and security updates, the following maintenance and updating tasks are typical:

- writing new content
- adding, removing, or editing products and descriptions in an online store
- taking new photographs—particularly for e-commerce operations when new products are added
- responding to emails from site visitors
- generating and analyzing traffic or sales reports, and
- promoting and marketing the website.

Establish a Schedule

For some business owners, the timing of the launch of their website is crucial—say, it absolutely needs to go live before an important trade show or before a grand opening. For others, it may not matter very much at all. The point is to consider whether the timing of your website project is an important issue, and if so, schedule accordingly.

It typically takes *at least* one month from the start of the website project until the site's launch, and usually longer—for complex sites, considerably longer. If holiday online sales are a big part of your business strategy, get the ball rolling in time to get your site up and running by mid-October; this means at a bare minimum getting a contract signed with a developer by September, which means starting your search for a developer and other preparations in early summer. Of course, even this is cutting it close, considering the time it takes to market a site and gain exposure for it. The essential thing is to start the process well before you need your site to be launched.

Also, consider your own busy schedule when planning a Web project. Web developers typically need a fair amount of input from you during the development process, which may require several meetings. For example, you'll likely need to review and approve diagrams or design mockups and provide guidance on site content. Definitely do not assume that once you start the project, the Web developer will just run with it and finish it off; you'll absolutely need to account for the time necessary to participate, review, and provide information to the developer.

Finally, your cash flow can be an issue in timing your Web project. Make sure you'll have the necessary cash or credit for any advance deposits and other payments.

Draft an Outline of Site Content

Drafting at least a rough outline of the content you want to feature at your site is a good idea for a few reasons. The most compelling reason is that your site content should be closely related to your site strategy and goals—and because you know these best, it's wise not to turn this task over entirely to

a developer. In addition, drafting the initial content outline may help to reduce costs by reducing the work that a Web developer will have to do. Finally, it generally makes sense for you to take the first stab at outlining content because you know best what kind of content exists or can easily be created for your business. Your Web developer can—and likely will—help you refine a content outline, but you are in the best position to make the first draft.

What to Include

A content outline is pretty much what it sounds like. It's not the content itself, but an organized list of topics and subsections that you envision for the site.

When deciding on what to include, focus on the content that will directly help you achieve your goals for the website. For example, if you are creating a simple marketing site with a goal of motivating clients to call you, effective content might include a well-presented portfolio and testimonials from customers, which will impress site visitors about the quality of your work. If you want to create a successful online store, you will want to make it easy for customers to choose among your products: Make sure to include important information like dimensions, specifications, installation instructions, or other informative text that will make customers feel confident in choosing a product. If your goal is to attract investors, a downloadable PDF of your business plan would be an obvious piece of valuable content, as would your business history and resumes of the owners.

In addition to your substantive content, always include easy-to-find contact information—your phone number, email address, and location. Or, if a site goal is to reduce customer service calls, then only include an email address. Again, think strategically and include content that fits with your strategy.

Tips on Drafting

In drafting your content outline, just use the same approach you learned in school: List sections and subsections and possibly third-level or fourth-level subsections. For example, a website for a photography studio might look something like this:

1. Home page
2. Services
3. About the studio
   a. History
   b. Photographer bio
4. Location and map
5. Portfolio
   a. Weddings
   b. Graduation photos
   c. Professional head shots
6. Tips for great photos
7. Links

Keep in mind that each section may or may not correspond to its own separate Web page. At this stage of the game, don't worry too much about the specifics of each section or the details of whether certain information will be grouped on one page or on separate pages. Instead, focus on the overall scope of the site and which sections will be offered. Later, as you work with your Web developer, you'll refine your outline into a more detailed blueprint for the website.

Choosing and Working With a Web Developer

Ironically, lots of Web developers are poor communicators and tend to drown potential clients in tech-speak, making it hard to discern whether they understand what you want or what they're offering. Obviously, you want a developer who is easy to communicate with, clearly understands your vision, and does quality, professional work.

This section offers advice on how to find a Web developer—and gives tips on what to consider when choosing one.

Starting Your Search

Just as when you are looking for any professional, the best way to find a Web developer is to ask other business owners for recommendations. In addition, look for examples of good local websites and find out who built them. Sometimes a website will include a credit saying who built it; other times you may have to ask the business owner.

Keep in mind that in the last few years, Web developers have multiplied like little tech-savvy rabbits. Lots of talented developers—and plenty not so talented—operate under the radar, often with no yellow pages listing or other advertising presence. Because of this, traditional approaches such as searching the phone book or other listings are likely to miss a significant number of prospects. It's much better to talk with plenty of other business owners to get the word on the street about who does great work, at a reasonable price.

What to Look for in a Web Developer

Before you consider hiring any Web developer, visit other sites that he or she has created. Web developers' own websites will usually have online portfolios showing websites they've done. Visit those sites and poke around to make sure they work well. Ideally, the developer will have experience with sites and features that are similar to what you want. Even better, the developer has experience working with businesses similar to yours. As discussed earlier in this chapter, strategic considerations are critical in website projects, so the more your developer understands your business and the strategies driving it, the better.

Clare Zurawski, Albuquerque Regional Manager for WESST Corp., a New Mexico nonprofit dedicated to helping people start or grow their own businesses:

WesstArtisans.com is an e-commerce site showcasing handcrafted gifts and housewares made by New Mexican artisans. The steepest learning curve related to developing and maintaining WesstArtisans.com was my role as project manager. In the Web development industry, it seems there are few generalists and many specialists. So I had to become the generalist and negotiate contracts with several consultants at once, including a professional product photographer, a graphic designer, an HTML programmer, and a search engine specialist.

To make sure the site reflects our regional flavor, we include a black-and-white photo of each artisan at the top of their product pages. We also provide a link to their biographies and artists' statements. This way a personal connection can be made, and there is no mistaking their work as being mass-produced in a factory somewhere.

At the time we launched WesstArtisans.com in late 2000, we weren't sure how large the site would eventually be. To reduce our expenses, we opted for a static website with 200 items programmed for sale. At its height a few years later, the site had more than 1,000 items for sale, and it is now clear that we should have spent the extra money up front to make it dynamic (database driven) from the start. We are now spending more than we'd like to on HTML programming to add or update product content to the shopping cart. Converting the site to a database is always possible, but costly.

Professional Skills

Web development involves several different components and skills. Ideally, you'll find a Web development firm that can offer a team with skills in the following areas:

- designing the organization of the information at your site, also called information architecture
- designing the graphical elements of your site, including choosing a color palette, fonts, and images
- programming the site, and
- creating and finalizing necessary content, including text and images.

Some individual Web developers may say they can handle all these tasks on their own—but this is usually a risky way to go. You'll almost always get a better result from a firm that employs or contracts with specialists, such as information architects, graphic designers, programmers, and content developers. This isn't to say that each task absolutely needs to be handled by a separate person, just that it's important that the folks handling the variety of tasks have the right specific skills. For example, many graphic designers sell themselves as Web developers, often calling themselves "Web designers," even if they have minimal skills in information architecture or programming.

Ask directly about whether professional information architects, graphic designers, programmers, and writers will be used. If the person or firm pitching services to you has loads of expertise in one element, such as graphic design or programming, but not in other important aspects of Web development, such as information architecture or content development, it may be wise to keep looking.

If you plan to handle certain aspects of Web development in-house, another consideration is to find a Web developer who can work collaboratively with you. For example, if you want your in-house graphic designer to create the design templates for the site, make this fact clear to the prospective developer and evaluate whether that type of working relationship will be successful.

Use of Technologies and Standards

Some Web developers use specialized development platforms and other technologies that are proprietary or difficult for others to use. So if you end up parting ways with your developer, you might get stuck with a website that is difficult or nearly impossible for others to maintain and update.

When considering Web developers, ask them what technologies they use, whether they are widely supported, and what difficulties might arise for other developers in maintaining the site. You may feel uncomfortable asking this, but it's a perfectly legitimate question that the developer should answer clearly.

In addition, ask whether the developer conforms to Web standards—specifically, the standards established by the World Wide Web Consortium, otherwise known as W3C. Generally, think of Web standards as guidelines that help ensure the best accessibility and compatibility for websites that conform to them. The benefits of conforming to W3C standards are multifold: The website will be compatible with more browsers; it will be easier and cheaper to modify; it will be accessible on other devices such as cell phones and handheld devices; and people with disabilities such as vision limitations will be able to access your content.

Project Management Approach

An important but often overlooked issue is how well a Web developer manages and coordinates all the various aspects of the project—such as defining the information organization, doing the graphic design, creating the content, and programming the site—to ensure a smooth process.

Web developers should have a clear process in which you, the business owner, are asked to approve the Web developer's progress at various stages. For example, if a Web developer does not follow a methodical process and does not obtain your approval of early stages of site development, you may find yourself presented with a nearly finished site that has no resemblance to what you envisioned. If this happens, the developer may virtually have to start all over again—a situation that could have been averted if approvals had been requested along the way.

Don't find out the hard way how time-consuming —and sometimes, costly—a poorly managed website project can be. Make sure your developer uses a systematic, methodical approach with a clear review and approval process. If you get the sense that a developer's approach is to wing it, it's not a good sign.

"Creating a Website," below, offers a broad-strokes outline of a sensible process for Web development. While it's not intended to be a definitive, end-all approach, it should give you a general idea of how the process should go. Use it as a general model when asking Web developers about their processes and approaches.

Proposals, Quotes, and Contracts

After you have met with a few potential developers and have narrowed your list down to a few prospects, ask each of them to give you a proposal and quote in writing. Generally speaking, it's best to get at least two or three proposals or quotes to compare. Some developers might give bare-bones quotes focused on numbers; others will give proposals that outline their planned approaches. Though an exhaustive, novel-length proposal isn't necessary, a proposal is better than a strictly numbers-oriented quote, because it will demonstrate whether the developer understands your specific needs and has come up with the right solution for you.

Also, watch out for developers who balk at putting a quote or proposal in writing or who merely want to give you a total quote without a breakdown of services and fees. At the very least, a quote should show what specific services will be offered; ideally the cost will be broken down into an itemized list.

Once you choose a developer, it's essential that you write and sign a contract clearly outlining the project. At a minimum, that contract should include:

- **An overview of the scope of services:** Make sure that you and the Web developer are on the same page regarding who will be responsible for what tasks. Don't assume he or she will create or edit content for you. Web developers typically will work with your text and photographs, but will not write text from scratch or take photographs without charging extra.
- **A list of deliverables:** In other words, anything the developer will deliver to you, such as a site map, a color mock-up, an HTML template, or anything else that he or she promises to deliver as the project progresses and at the end of the project.

- **A clear schedule:** Giving deadlines for various aspects of the project, often tied to deliverables.
- **Intellectual property provisions:** Detailing who will own the materials developed in the project—including graphic designs, templates, written content, photographs, software programming, and any other material subject to intellectual property protection.
- **Compensation and payment terms:** Including specifics on how fees will be calculated if work goes beyond the scope originally anticipated.
- **Termination provisions:** Detailing what will happen if the working relationship falls apart or either party wants to end the project.

> **CAUTION**
>
> **Get it in writing.** This advice cannot be over-stated: Do not work with a Web developer without a contract. If the developer is reluctant to create or sign a written contract, it's a clear sign that he or she lacks the professional standards that you want. Even worse, without a contract the Web developer may own copyright to the code, content, or other aspects of your site that he or she has created. Avoid this at all costs by insisting on a contract that addresses intellectual property ownership. For more on this crucial issue, see "Intellectual Property: Who Owns Your Website?" later in this chapter.

> **RESOURCE**
>
> **For more help with Web issues.** This chapter focuses on helping you understand the most important considerations when starting a website for your business. For in-depth information on the process itself, you should consult other resources. Here is a short list of some particularly helpful sources:
>
> - *How to Build a Website and Stay Sane*, by Jonathan Oxer (Oft Press), focuses on how to find a Web developer who's a good match and how to build an effective working relationship in which you retain control of the end result. The Australia-specific information does not detract from its helpful focus on the process of website creation. You can download it free from www.stay-sane.com.

- *HTML for the World Wide Web With XHTML and CSS: Visual QuickStart Guide*, by Elizabeth Castro (Peachpit Press), demystifies HTML code with lots of illustrations and screen shots. Beginners and experienced Web developers alike will find it a useful reference.
- *The Non-Designer's Web Book: An Easy Guide to Creating, Designing, and Posting Your Own Web Site*, by Robin Williams and John Tollett (Peachpit Press), is especially helpful for beginners. It offers a solid introduction to technical concepts and principles of effective design.
- *Legal Guide to Web & Software Development*, by Stephen Fishman (Nolo), discusses the specific intellectual property issues that relate to Web and technology projects.

Creating a Website

As has been mentioned previously, an efficient, methodical process will go a long way toward making your website a success. This is true whether you create a website in-house or hire a Web developer to help you. This section outlines a simple, generalized approach that will help ensure an efficient workflow between the Web developer and your business—all the participants you've included. Keep in mind these steps aren't written in stone; there's always a certain amount of fluidity in Web development projects.

In particular, be aware that it's common for Web projects to get a bit circular at times and that you may need to revisit earlier steps to make modifications. For example, you may need to refine your site's information architecture after you create content if some of that content does not fit into your original design. This is normal, as long as it's not chronic and extensive. The reality is that following a methodical process will improve efficiency. Even if you're planning a small, simple site, following a process similar to the one described here will help increase your chances of success.

The planning process will generally involve the following steps, many of which have been discussed earlier in this chapter—and each of which are outlined below. Those steps include:

1. Clarify strategy and goals.
2. Define content and organization, or information architecture.
3. Define design elements or the look and feel of the site.
4. Create content, including text and graphics.
5. Build the website, including any necessary HTML coding, database creation, or programming.
6. Test the site to ensure it functions smoothly before being unleashed on the public.

Clarify Your Strategy and Goals

All website projects should start by clearly identifying a strategy and goals. (See "Defining Your Strategy and Goals," above.) It's crucial in this early stage that you and your Web developer have open and clear communication about these issues.

Workshop-type meetings in which your business's Web project participants—and possibly other staffers or associates—contribute ideas are usually helpful. And it's often a good idea to solicit comments from a wide range of people in the early stage, even if those people won't be involved in the project as it progresses. Soliciting feedback from people who will be affected by the website—such as your customer service team or some trusted potential customers—helps ensure that you will include a wide range of perspectives and avoid tunnel vision.

Define Information Architecture

The term "information architecture" may sound like tech-speak, but it's actually an accurate description of an important, fundamental aspect of all websites: how the information is organized. This is also sometimes called information design or content mapping. In all websites, defining the information architecture is the first step in actually starting to build the site.

A basic tool in defining information architecture is called a site map. Closely related to a simple content outline, a site map is a visual representation of content modules and how they are related to one other.

Another fundamental tool is called a user interface diagram, or UI diagram, which is a mock layout of how content and other elements, such as links and images, will be organized on the site pages, which is another way of saying how the pages will look to users. A UI diagram is nearly analogous to an architectural blueprint for a building. Because it deals with information rather than building materials, however, a UI will be based in logic rather than mechanical physics.

To help understand the difference between a site map and a UI diagram, bear in mind that a site map shows what content will be at a site, and a UI diagram shows how it will be displayed to site users.

Web developers will generally ask you to approve the site map before creating UI diagrams—and to approve the UI diagrams before moving to the next steps.

On the following pages, you'll find examples of both a site map and a UI diagram for a fictional site (Juno Designs).

Define the Website's Look and Feel

Once a site map and UI diagrams are approved, the developer will usually start working on the graphic design and other visual elements of the website, which as a whole are generally called the site's look and feel. Color palettes and typefaces are major elements to consider, as well as images and composition. Web developers will typically ask you for some initial direction, such as whether you want your site to appear traditional, modern, funky, high tech, or whimsical. You'll also usually be asked about what colors you envision at the site. Your input at this stage is important so that the site conveys the right message and strikes the right tone for your business. Then, based on your guidance, the developer will usually make mock Web pages, sometimes called color comprehensives, for you to review and approve.

Create Content

With information architecture and visual elements approved, you can get started on creating the content that will populate the website's pages. You may have already spent some time developing brochures, flyers, or other written information about your business. Don't reinvent the wheel: Use what

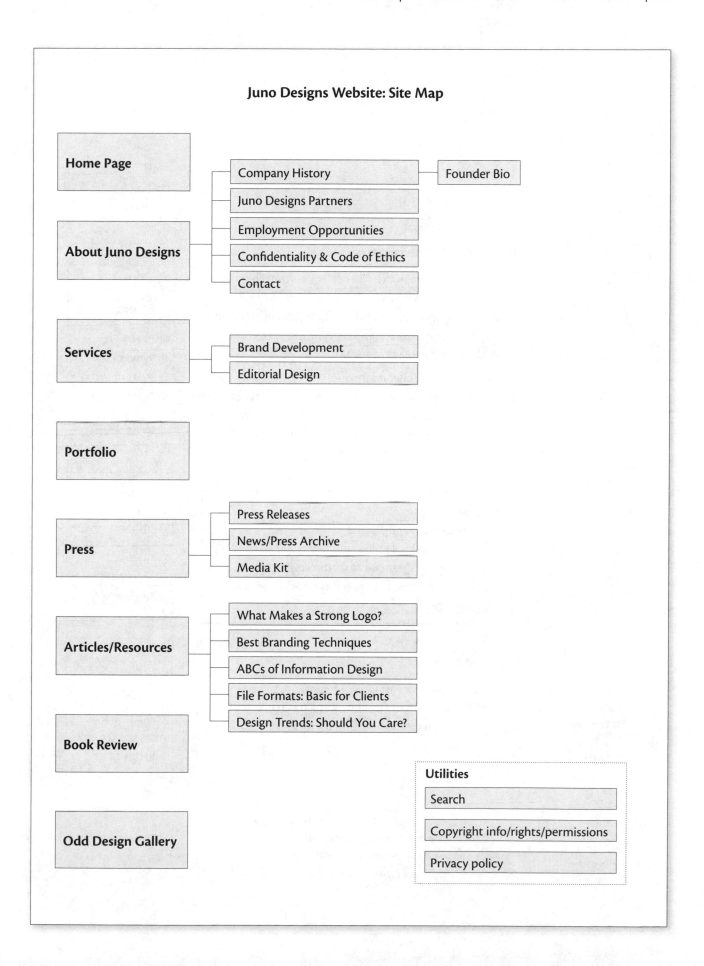

Juno Designs Website: Site Map

Home Page

About Juno Designs
- Company History — Founder Bio
- Juno Designs Partners
- Employment Opportunities
- Confidentiality & Code of Ethics
- Contact

Services
- Brand Development
- Editorial Design

Portfolio

Press
- Press Releases
- News/Press Archive
- Media Kit

Articles/Resources
- What Makes a Strong Logo?
- Best Branding Techniques
- ABCs of Information Design
- File Formats: Basic for Clients
- Design Trends: Should You Care?

Book Review

Odd Design Gallery

Utilities
- Search
- Copyright info/rights/permissions
- Privacy policy

Juno Designs Website: UI Diagram

Juno Designs logo

image

Search site

Company Information

Home

About

Services

Portfolio

Press

Juno Designs
555 Main St.
Palm Springs, CA 12345
555-987-6543
info@junodesigns.com

Partner Sites

Spitz Software

Smart Dog Printing

Main Street Independent Business Alliance

Welcome to Juno Designs

Juno Designs is a graphic design firm specializing in brand development and editorial design. We have helped businesses, nonprofits, trade associations, and others define their brands, develop a compelling company image, and produce award-winning collateral.

The links at the left offer information about our company and services. The links at the right offer a wide range of informational resources on graphic design issues. Please feel free to contact us directly at 555-987-6543 or drop an email to info@junodesigns.com.

Featured Article:
What Makes a Strong Logo?
A strong logo helps develop your brand and ingrains your business in the minds of customers. This short article outlines some principles driving effective logo design. More ...

Featured Projects

image

Annual Report Design. Client: AAA Corp. Juno Designs recently completed a project designing a 150-page report for AAA Corp. More ...

Books

Image

Reviews of the best art and design titles

Articles

Information articles on design strategies

Odd Design Gallery

Image

Old ads, trademarks, and other odd designs of today and yesteryear

Home | About | Services | Portfolio | Press
Books | Articles | Odd Design Gallery
Search | Site Map

you have as a basis for your website's content. You may need to rework the existing content to make it shorter and more concise for the Web, but it's still much easier to adapt something that's already written than to start from scratch.

If you don't have any written materials, someone will need to start writing. Generally speaking, less is more when it comes to online content. Due to the space constraints of computer screens and the ever-shortening attention spans of some computer users, nothing will turn visitors away from your website faster than dense, lengthy paragraphs. The best Web content is concise and easy to digest, so don't be afraid to get right to the point and condense information into lists, bullet points, and short blurbs.

If you decide to publish longer material—for example, a user manual or an industry report—either break it up into sections or provide the document in a downloadable format, such as a PDF, or Portable Document Format, file. Better yet, offer both an HTML version searchable and navigable by section and a downloadable version, so that your visitors can read the document in whatever manner they prefer.

Finally, make sure that at least two people are involved in creating the website's content to make sure that it is clear, concise, and free from errors. At a minimum, one person should write the material and another person should review and edit it. Even if the writer is experienced, a second set of eyes can really make a difference. A little bit of care in these areas will go a long way toward giving a professional tone to your site and enhancing the credibility of your business.

When you're done creating and formatting your content, you'll provide it to the Web developer to be incorporated into the site pages. Make sure the content is formatted so that the developer can easily see which information belongs in a header, where paragraphs should break, which information belongs in bullet points, and so on. You'll need to review the content again once it's on the site to be sure it formats and flows well and logically.

 CAUTION

Banish bad clip art from your site. In addition to lack of planning, another major fault of too many websites is an unprofessional appearance. Though a discussion of design aesthetics is beyond the scope of this chapter, one thing to watch out for is bad clip art. If you're new to this term, "clip art" refers to small illustrations and graphics—sometimes animated—that are widely available online, often for free. Some clip art is of high quality, but the vast majority tends to be very amateurish looking and will make your site look amateurish as well. Don't pepper your site with angels, teddy bears, or animated dragons because you think they look cute. An unprofessional-looking website is simply bad business.

Build the Website

Often, while the content is being written and photographed, the programmer is busy building the site based on the approved site architecture diagrams and design mock-ups. When the build is complete, it will be ready for the content (both text and images) to be entered into the CMS. Depending on your contract, either the Web developer or you will do the content entry. If you do it, you'll likely need some guidance as to how to use the CMS first, which may be a minitraining in addition to the full training done at the conclusion of the project (see "Train the Site Administrators," below).

Though your Web developer may build the site on a test server, he or she may prefer to build the site on the Web server where it will ultimately have its home. If so, you'll need to tackle domain name registration and Web hosting before the build is started. (See "Domain Names and Hosting," below.)

Test the Website

When your site is complete, it should be thoroughly and methodically tested, and all glitches—or bugs—fixed. It's normal and not a bad reflection on the Web developer if the site contains some bugs. What's important is to find them and fix them before launching your site to the public. Professional Web developers should include a testing phase. Once it is completed and all bugs reported and corrected, the site is ready to be launched.

How Content Can Help Drive Traffic and Boost Search Engine Rankings

When developing your content, there are a couple of things to keep in mind regarding how well your site ranks in search engine results. The practice of trying to improve your site's search engine results ranking is called search engine optimization, or SEO. While SEO is a complex and constantly evolving topic, there are a few basic strategies you can use to boost your site's rankings in search engine results. In a nutshell, your content affords you two simple SEO opportunities:

- **Developing inbound links:** Quality content that results in other sites linking to your site does more than just boost site traffic. Having many inbound links will have a strong effect on how well your site ranks with search engines.
- **Relevant keywords:** Content that contains appropriate words and phrases will also improve your search engine results.

Let's discuss each of these in a bit more detail.

Inbound Links

One of the most powerful ways to rank highly with search engines, such as Google and Yahoo!, is to have lots of other sites link to yours—in other words, to have a lot of inbound links. This concept is sometimes called "link popularity." Search engines have developed complex formulas to determine how many inbound links a site has, and, all things being equal, sites that have more inbound links will rank higher than other sites. The thinking goes, if other reputable sites find the content at a website useful, then that is a powerful indicator that the site is a quality one that deserves to rank highly for relevant searches.

How this relates to site content is pretty simple: Sites with quality content tend to have more inbound links than sites with meager or inferior content. For example, consider two websites that both sell tennis equipment. One is a straightforward e-commerce site that sells tennis rackets, shoes, tennis balls, and other equipment. The second site sells similar equipment, but also has informative how-to articles and a few streaming videos showing techniques, such as a primer on serving and a demonstration of different backhand techniques. Hundreds of other tennis- and sport-related websites

link to the second, content-rich site for its informative content, while far fewer link to the first e-commerce site. So, when people search for "tennis," "rackets," or make other tennis-related searches, the second site ranks way above the first site in Google's search engine results.

As you can see, quality content has a doubly powerful affect on bringing traffic to your site: Besides merely attracting more visitors by virtue of being useful or compelling, content that many other sites have linked to will also raise a site's visibility by helping to improve its search engine rankings.

To attract links (and plain old traffic) to your site, include content that is useful, entertaining, or otherwise interesting to your target audience. Blogs that allow user comments can be very effective at drawing traffic. How-to articles are always popular, as are lists such as "Top 10 Ways to Make Your Home Greener" or "Five Tips to Improve Your Forehand."

Keywords

When creating content, you'll also want to use certain words and phrases—called keywords—that potential customers are likely to use when searching for your site with search engines such as Google and Yahoo! Including appropriate keywords in your site content should help improve its search engine rankings.

When choosing keywords, put yourself in the mind of potential customers: What words and phrases would they use when searching the Web for a business such as yours? For example, if you own an electronics store selling audio and video equipment, typical keywords (which should include single words and multiple-word phrases) might include: audio, video, home audio, home video, home entertainment, stereo, surround sound, CD player, mp3 player, speakers, DVD player, DVR, television, TV, plasma TV, LCD TV, flat-screen TV.

The trick is to identify appropriate keywords, then use them in your site content so that they read naturally. Don't create awkward text that is crammed with keywords; site visitors can usually see through this tactic or at the very least will be turned off by your poorly written copy.

How Content Can Help Drive Traffic and Boost Search Engine Rankings (cont'd)

Besides looking for keywords in your site's content, search engines also look at the page titles for relevant keywords. The title is what appears in the top bar of the browser window. Title text is set in the HTML code for a web page; assuming you're hiring a Web developer to create your site, he or she will know how to set the page title text. If your Web developer has expertise in search engine optimization, he or she can be a big help in choosing keywords and drafting title text; otherwise it's fairly simple for you as the business owner to do it.

Page titles should generally not be much longer than 80 characters, so you should include your most important, strategic keywords here. Ideally, you'll have custom keywords for each individual page. For example, instead of having the same title for every page of your plumbing supply e-commerce website, each page's title should accurately describe what's on the page. The home page title could be "McGee's Plumbing Supply—Clawfoot Faucets, Restoration Hardware, Vintage Accessories," while the title on the Faucets category page could be, "Clawfoot Faucets: Wall Mount, Tub Mount, Gooseneck; Hand Showers; Bronze, Chrome, Brass." Again, put yourself in the mind of your potential customers and think of words or phrases they would use when looking for your products or services.

Train the Site Administrators

When the site is finished, the Web developer will generally offer a one- to three-hour training to whomever at your company will be in charge of maintaining the site (the site administrators). If you'll be outsourcing maintenance to the Web developer or an experienced outside contractor, the training may not be necessary.

Drive Traffic to Your Site

There are a number of ways to market your site and drive traffic to it. The extent of your website marketing activities will depend on how your website fits into your overall marketing strategy for your business. If you're planning an e-commerce site that will be the sole source of sales and income for your business, then marketing your site will be critical. If, on the other hand, your website is a basic marketing site that isn't a significant source of referrals and doesn't play a major role in marketing your business, don't worry too much about actively promoting it. That said, all businesses should do simple things such as including their website URL on their business cards, flyers, any ads they run, and other materials they produce.

If driving traffic to your site is a priority, one of the best approaches is to develop inbound links to your site as discussed above. Besides the obvious traffic-boosting effect of having many other sites link to yours, another benefit is that sites with many inbound links will rank more highly in search engine results. Here are some simple methods for getting other sites to link to yours.

Create content at your site that other sites will want to link to. Sometimes called "link baiting," this strategy is discussed above under "How Content Can Help Drive Traffic and Boost Search Engine Rankings." Taking this a step further, you can share your site's content by licensing it to other sites with a requirement that the other site provide a link back to your site.

TIP

Search engines include the quality of the inbound links in their algorithms. To favorably influence your search engine rankings, the inbound links must come from other reputable sites—not from shady sites such as "link farms," which are meaningless Web pages with hundreds or thousands of links created by unethical Web marketing firms trying to trick search engines. Quality inbound links are from legitimate sites, such as online publications, trade associations, or other businesses in related industries.

Include sharing and syndication buttons at your site. As discussed earlier in this chapter, the Web has evolved towards sites that allow users to interact with others who share the same interests and sites that customize the information users receive. For example, users of sites such as Facebook can easily share their favorite articles with other Facebook members. Other sites, like Digg or Del.icio.us, sometimes called "social bookmarking" sites, allow users to rate articles in a public forum. Google and other sites allow users to "subscribe" to blogs and other information sources, aggregating headlines from selected sites onto one page. The list goes on and on. One way to take advantage of this trend is to include buttons at your site that allow users to share your content or receive it in a feed. For example, if your site features a how-to article on home repair, you could include a Facebook button, allowing a user to click on it and quickly share the article with their Facebook contacts. Or if you write a blog on the latest digital audio technology, you could include an "Add to Google" button allowing users to receive updated headlines from your blog on their personalized page where they track dozens of blogs.

Write for other sites. If you have expertise in a certain area, find online publications that are looking for writers; you'd be surprised how many there are. You may not get paid for your writing but can usually get a link to your site. Remember that it's best to be brief when writing for websites, so you usually won't need to write much more than 500 words, often less.

Submit press releases to online newswires. As discussed in Chapter 12, sending press releases to local reporters and editors is a great way to get exposure for your business. On the Web, you can submit press releases to distribution services such as PRWeb (www.prweb.com) or SourceWire (www.sourcewire.com) which, for a fee, can get your release picked up by Google News and Yahoo! News as well as hundreds of other news outlets. When your press release includes one or more links back to your website, this can result in quality inbound links.

List your business in online directories. There are loads of directories online, grouped by industry type, location, or other criteria. As long as the directories are fairly reputable and not "link farms" (see "Tip," above), this can be a great way to develop inbound links. Some directories charge fees, so do some research before deciding where to list. Pick the ones that look like they get the most traffic and that fit into your budget.

Join membership organizations that provide an online directory listing. Related to the above, keep in mind that some organizations, such as your local chamber of commerce or other trade organizations, will list your business in their online and print directories as a benefit of membership. Again, evaluate the membership fees and estimated distribution of the directories before deciding on which ones to join.

Clare Zurawski, Albuquerque Regional Manager of WESST Corp, a New Mexico nonprofit dedicated to helping people start or grow their own businesses:
Although there are aspects of search marketing that do involve meticulous technical details, in general SEO strategy is coming full circle to align with good old-fashioned target marketing and public relations. There are no shortcuts anymore. Essentially, an optimized website must contain relevant content that's well presented in the eyes of your customers.

 RESOURCE

For more on search engine optimization, see these books and websites:

- *Search Engine Optimization: An Hour a Day*, by Jennifer Grappone and Gradiva Couzin (Sybex), is a detailed and practical book that's aimed at busy business owners who are short on time but who need to take search engine optimization seriously. The authors maintain a blog at www.yourseoplan.com to offer the latest breaking information.
- Search Engine Watch (www.searchenginewatch.com) is a website devoted to tracking the latest developments, trends, and tips for search engine optimization.
- SEO Book (www.seobook.com) is another excellent resource online, with information and tools to help you optimize your site.

Domain Names and Hosting

Before you can post your Web pages for the world to see, you must register a domain name and sign up with a Web hosting company. Your domain name is part of the address visitors will use to access your site, such as nolo.com or amazon.com. Your Web host is the company that keeps your site pages on computer servers that are connected to the Internet 24 hours a day, so the pages are always available for visitors to view.

Choosing and Registering a Domain Name

Your first task is to choose an available domain name—that is, a name that is not currently registered to, or being used by, another group. (See "Choosing a Domain Name," in Chapter 2.)

Your domain name has tremendous potential marketing value, so you should take the time to choose it carefully. Remember that it may not be just your business name that attracts customers; names of your popular products and services are also good candidates for domain names. Considering how inexpensive domain name registration is—roughly $10 per year—it makes little sense not to register multiple names if they are appropriate for your business.

In addition, it often makes sense to register your domain name in multiple domains in addition to the .com domain in order to establish the widest presence possible for your domain name. Beyond the most common .com domain, the .biz and .net domains are appropriate for for-profit businesses. However, don't make the mistake of registering a .org address for a for-profit business. The .org domain is intended for nonprofit organizations only. Even though this rule is not enforced by the .org registry, it's misleading and inappropriate to use a .org address for your for-profit business. At the very least, using a .org address will make your business look ignorant of domain name rules; at worst, customers will think you are trying to mislead them into believing you are a nonprofit.

Once you select an available name, register it online at a domain name registrar. There are hundreds of options out there. If you'd like to do some comparison shopping, you can find a list of approved registrars at www.internic.org.

RESOURCE

How one domain name registrar works. One popular registrar is GoDaddy at www.godaddy.com (as discussed above, GoDaddy also offers website builder services). Here's how the process works: At the GoDaddy website, you will first be prompted to enter your proposed domain name to see if it has already been registered. If not, you will be allowed to proceed and register the name yourself.

Fees vary depending on the options you choose; all are generally affordable. Registering one name for one year through GoDaddy costs under $10. Once you've chosen your options, simply enter information about your business and provide credit card information. Or, if you prefer, call GoDaddy at 480-505-8877 and do it by phone.

Although registering a domain name is pretty simple, there are a few potential pitfalls. In particular, if you allow your Web host to take care of domain name registration or renewal—a common practice—you must make sure it lists your business or an authorized representative as the domain name registrant and administrative contact. If anyone but an authorized representative of your business is listed as the domain name registrant, you might find that your control over your domain name is seriously compromised. Web host companies have developed a nasty habit of registering their clients' domain names under the host company's name, rather than the name of the client. This creates serious domain name ownership and control issues.

For example, if your Web host handles the domain name registration process for your business and lists itself as the registrant of the domain name you've chosen, you might not be able to make any changes to your host account or even your domain name account, because you are not listed as the registrant. In this way, the Web host company can hold your domain name hostage, preventing you from switching hosts or otherwise managing this crucial part of your business's identity.

Your domain name is an asset, and the people or organizations listed in the domain name registration have varying degrees of authority over the asset. Be particularly careful about whom you list as:

- **Registrant.** The registrant is the legal owner of the domain name. Use your business's legal name, not your Web host company's name.
- **Administrative contact.** The administrative contact should be someone in your business who has authority to make policy decisions, particularly with regard to the domain name. Again, you should not list your Web host company here.
- **Technical contact.** This is the person the registrar may contact with technical issues. You may list your Web host company here.

If your Web host handles domain name registration or renewal, make sure it uses the names you want. Otherwise, it may cost you many times the original registration fee to get the registration back in your rightful name. Register.com, for instance, charges a $200 fee to transfer the registrant from one name to another, even if you never intended to list your Web host or someone else as the registrant in the first place. One way to avoid this fee is to transfer the domain name from the registrar where it is currently registered under the wrong name to another registrar, making sure to use the correct names when you transfer the registration.

Clare Zurawski, Albuquerque Regional Manager for WESST Corp., a New Mexico nonprofit dedicated to helping people start or grow their own businesses:

Because WESST Corp. is the parent nonprofit to our e-commerce site WesstArtisans.com, it was important we used the same spelling of the nonprofit name in our domain name. But if somebody heard "WesstArtisans.com" without seeing it, they would probably not be aware of the unusual spelling. So we also bought the domain "WestArtisans.com" which, sure enough, attracts some customers. Visitors to the misspelled domain name are automatically sent to the correct address.

Choosing a Web Host

A Web host is a company that maintains servers, which are simply high-performance computers that are connected to the Internet continuously, serving the Web pages stored on it to the world. When your website files have been uploaded to the host's server and your Web host has configured your domain name correctly, your website will be live and all the information it offers will be available to visitors around the globe, 24 hours a day, 365 days a year.

To choose from the many Web hosts out there, get recommendations from other business owners to find one that offers reliable servers and good customer service. Make sure there are reasonable customer service hours during which you can talk to an actual human. More than a few host companies offer no live-person customer service which can be infuriating if you're experiencing any problems.

Web hosts may charge by the month or by the year. Fees are based on how much data you need the server to store—that is, the size of your website in disk space—or how much data you transfer to and from your website each month.

Intellectual Property: Who Owns Your Website?

Intellectual property laws establish ownership rights and other rules for various types of works, such as text and artwork protected by copyright, marks used in business protected by trademark, and inventions protected by patents. Copyright is of particular importance in Web development projects, as many of the components of websites are protected by copyright. As mentioned earlier, it's crucial that your contract with a Web developer includes clear, detailed terms on ownership and permissions for any materials developed for the website protected by copyright. Other intellectual property laws such as trademark or patent also may come into play, though not as often.

Copyrightable materials include text, photos, artwork, and designs, as well as technology developed for your site, such as databases and programming. As you can imagine, serious troubles can arise if ownership of any aspect of your website is in dispute. The way to avoid this is by including clear copyright terms in your contract with the Web developer. This section gives a quick overview of copyright basics and the specific issues that arise in Web development projects, to help you head off any copyright conflict.

 RESOURCE

In-depth resources on copyright and intellectual property issues. For the full treatment on copyright and the permissions process, see *Getting Permission: How to License & Clear Copyrighted Materials Online & Off*, by Richard Stim (Nolo). In addition, Nolo's *Legal Guide to Web & Software Development*, by Stephen Fishman, discusses the specific intellectual property issues that relate to Web and technology projects.

Copyright Basics

When someone owns copyright to certain works, it means that others may not reproduce, modify, distribute, or sell the works without the copyright owner's permission. In legal terms, permission to use someone else's copyrighted content is known as a license. When you license content, you do not own it; you simply obtain the right to use it in specific circumstances. In contrast, buying the copyrights to a creative work, known in legal terms as an assignment, gives you all the rights to the work as if you were the original copyright owner.

The general rule is that the person who creates content owns the copyright. However, if the work qualifies as a "work for hire," then the hiring party, not the creator, legally owns the copyright to it. The rules regarding what constitutes a work for hire vary depending on whether the work is created by an employee or an independent contractor.

Rules for Employees

When an employee creates any work in the course of employment, the work is considered a work for hire, so that the employer—not the employee—owns the copyright to that work. Having your website created by employees, not contractors, is the simplest and most straightforward way for your business to make sure that it owns copyright in all aspects of the site.

Unfortunately, this isn't an option for many start-up businesses. But fortunately, there are other ways to make the work a work for hire, even if it is created by an independent contractor, not an employee.

Rules for Independent Contractors

When an independent contractor creates certain types of content, the hiring party owns the copyright in the work if the contractor and hiring party have made a written agreement stating that the work is a work for hire. The written agreement is essential: Work-for-hire agreements are necessary whenever a nonemployee creates the work. Without a written work-for-hire agreement, the nonemployee Web developer owns copyright to the materials he or she develops for the website.

But there's an important wrinkle: You cannot turn every kind of creative work into a work for hire using a written agreement. According to copyright law, a work-for-hire agreement will give copyright to the hiring party only if the content is:

- part of a larger literary work, such as an article in a magazine or a poem or story in an anthology
- part of a motion picture or other audiovisual work, such as a screenplay
- a translation
- a supplementary work, such as an afterword, introduction, chart, editorial note, bibliography, appendix, or index
- a compilation
- an instructional text
- a test or answer material for a test, or
- an atlas.

Without trying to puzzle through how on earth lawyers came up with these categories, it's important to understand that depending on whom you ask, the categories may not include the components of websites. This naturally raises the question: If website materials cannot be the subject of work-for-hire agreements, how can you obtain ownership from a Web development contractor? The answer is that you'll need to have a written and signed copyright assignment—an outright sale of all copyright from the contractor to your business. Though it's possible that website materials might legally fall into one of the work-for-hire categories, the safest route is to assume they do not, and to handle ownership transfer with a copyright assignment.

To sum up, to obtain ownership of materials created by a Web developer for your website, you'll need to:

- hire the creator as an employee—which usually is not a practical option, unless you already planned to hire a Web developer on staff, or
- have a written copyright assignment, signed by both you and the developer, usually within your website development contract.

Employee or Independent Contractor?

A number of laws govern whether a worker is an independent contractor (IC) or an employee, and each of these laws has a different way of looking at the issue. For example, the IRS has one method of determining whether a person is an independent contractor, but your state workers' compensation board may use a different test. Because of all these different laws, often referred to as "worker classification" rules, the issue of whether a worker is an IC is not always straightforward.

The IRS is probably the most important agency to satisfy when it comes to classifying a worker as an IC. Under the IRS's test, workers are considered employees if the company they work for has the right to direct and control the way they work—including the details of when, where, and how the job is accomplished. In contrast, the IRS will consider workers independent contractors if the company they work for does not manage how they work except to accept or reject their final result. (See "Employees Versus Independent Contractors," in Chapter 15, for a more complete discussion of distinguishing between these types of workers.)

RESOURCE

For more on intellectual property contracts for Web development projects. *Legal Guide to Web & Software Development,* by Stephen Fishman (Nolo), includes a standard Web Development Agreement and information on intellectual property issues related to Web and technology projects.

Protecting Your Interests

It's obviously in your interest to own all aspects of your website so that you have the legal right to do anything you want with the site. For example, if you fail to obtain a copyright to the site's text content from the Web developer, the developer could potentially prevent you from making any changes to the text on the site. The same is true for images, graphic designs, and technologies created by the Web developer for the website. This may sound far-fetched to you now, but consider what might happen if you and the developer ever got into a conflict and decided to part ways. A developer with a bone to pick who owns any rights to your site could deal a serious blow to your online business.

Be aware that sometimes, a Web developer will not want to assign copyright ownership to your company for certain aspects of the site. As discussed below, this may be perfectly legitimate. What's crucial in this situation is for you to get permission— legally, a license—from the Web developer to use his or her copyrighted work as necessary for you to get the full benefits of your website. Without such permission, you'll be at the mercy of your Web developer when you want to edit content or make changes to technology owned by the developer —a situation you definitely want to avoid.

There are a number of situations in which it might make sense for a Web developer to retain ownership. Developers sometimes will not transfer ownership of technology that they have developed, such as content management systems, shopping carts, or other functions. Developing Web applications and using them for multiple clients is the lifeblood of some Web firms, so they naturally are not willing to transfer ownership of that programming code to your company. Instead, they'll give your business permission, or a license, to use the technology in specified ways. This is perfectly legitimate, but you'll need to be careful about a couple of things:

- **You need to protect your company's ability to make changes to the site down the road.** You should always think about—and ask prospective developers about—what will happen if you end your relationship with the developer in the future. If the developer creates the site with proprietary technology, you may find it difficult or impossible to make changes without using the original developer. More than a few businesses have learned this lesson the hard way and have had to create a new website from scratch after ending their relationship with a previous developer who refused to grant permission to the business to make changes to the code the developer owned.

- **If you are hiring the developer to create functions or other programming code that will give your business a competitive edge online, then you'll want to obtain full ownership of that code so that it can't be used for other businesses.** This isn't usually the case with small, basic websites that simply want to establish an online presence. But if you are paying a developer to create an innovative shopping cart or search function that will help distinguish you from your online competition, it's essential that you own that code when it's complete so that it can't be used by anyone else without your permission (and possible licensing fees paid to you). Don't be surprised to be charged a premium for this type of full transfer of rights.

At the end of the day, the important thing is that you and the developer are on the same page about who owns what. Consider another possible scenario: Say your business has only a tiny budget for photographs for the site, and cannot afford the rates a developer would charge to take photos and transfer all rights to your company. As an alternative, your website development contract could specify that the developer will retain all rights to any photos it takes for the site, and that the developer grants your company a license (permission) to post the photos at the site indefinitely. In this case, your contract should state specifically *how* you are allowed to use the photos—and you must abide by the license agreement. With an agreement like this, you typically will not be allowed to use the photos in advertisements, on T-shirts, or in any other ways. As long as having broad use of the photos isn't important to you, letting the developer retain copyright is a good way to keep your website project costs down.

EXAMPLE: Marina is negotiating contract terms with the Web developer she chose to create her pottery store's website. To keep costs down, Marina and the developer agree that Marina will be responsible for taking photos. However, they also agree that the developer may take photos for the site, and that he will retain the copyright to those photographs. To make sure she retains control over the website, Marina gets a provision in the contract granting her business a license to display any of the developer's photos at her website indefinitely. In addition, Marina asks the developer if he would be willing to include a license allowing her to modify the size and the brightness of the photos in case they ever need such adjustments. The developer agrees to a license to modify that is limited to size and brightness, but no other modifications.

In deciding what ownership or licensing arrangements will work for your business, keep in mind the following rule: The more important content or technology is to your site, the more crucial it is that you either get ownership or a broad license to use and possibly modify those materials. This is true whether or not the Web developer has a valid reason to retain ownership. If it's essential that you own copyright ownership in a database or other technology, don't enter into an agreement that won't confer the rights you need.

Chapter 13 Checklist:
E-Business: Selling and
Marketing Online

☐ Assess your strategy and goals for your site and any other e-business activities and how they fit into your overall business plan.

☐ Consider the wide range of ways your business can reach out to customers online, such as with a blog, email lists, e-newsletters, listservs, e-commerce, and others when crafting an e-business plan.

☐ Research other sites to get examples of organization, design, content, and features that might work well for your site.

☐ Choose a Web developer who has strong project management skills.

☐ Develop compelling content that will attract traffic to your site, and actively encourage inbound links to that content.

☐ Insist upon a written contract with your Web developer, and make sure your business will obtain copyright ownership of most, if not all, content and technology developed for the site.

Planning for Changes in Ownership

As discussed in Chapter 1, choosing a legal structure is a fundamental task for every new business owner. Whether you operate as a sole proprietorship, partnership, an LLC, or a corporation has important implications for liability issues and taxes—two areas definitely worthy of your close attention.

For businesses with more than one owner, there's another important and related concern: how to handle any future changes in business ownership. It probably won't be top-of-mind in your early, exciting start-up days, but the fact is that businesses commonly face situations that raise serious—and often unexpected—ownership questions. An incapacitating illness or untimely death are just two of the more extreme situations that call the business's ownership into question. What if an incapacitated owner wants to sell to someone the other owners don't like? Will a deceased owner's child inherit the ownership interest and become an active owner of the business? Plenty of other situations can also have an impact on the ownership of the business; they're discussed later in this chapter.

The best way to handle all these situations is to make an agreement about how the business will deal with them. This type of agreement is known as a buy-sell agreement; the phrase "buy-sell" refers to the rules it outlines for how a company's ownership shares may be bought or sold. By anticipating certain events and defining what will happen if they arise, a buy-sell agreement can lessen the chaos that ownership changes can inflict on a business.

Busy as you may be with the details and concerns of starting up your business, it makes the best sense to address these issues even before you get up and running. Because buy-sell provisions generally limit what owners can and cannot do with their ownership interests, it's crucial to create fair, impartial rules while everyone is on an equal footing. If you wait until something happens that puts ownership on the brink of change—for example, one owner becomes incapacitated and desperate to sell out—you'll have a much harder time imposing rules that are comfortable for everyone involved. And addressing buy-sell provisions early on is one of the best ways to build and maintain harmonious relationships among business co-owners.

This chapter starts by explaining who should consider drafting a buy-sell agreement and why. Then it defines buy-sell agreements, explaining the essential provisions you'll typically find. Finally, it offers sample buy-sell provisions to help you get started in drafting your own agreement.

RESOURCE

For more in-depth information. While you'll learn the basic, essential elements of buy-sell agreements in this chapter, *Business Buyout Agreements: A Step-by-Step Guide for Co-Owners*, by Anthony Mancuso and Bethany K. Laurence (Nolo), covers much more ground. It walks you through the process of drafting a comprehensive buy-sell agreement that addresses a wide range of issues, such as structuring and funding buyouts and tax and estate planning concerns.

When You Need a Written Agreement

If your business—whether a partnership, an LLC, or a corporation—has more than one owner, you would be wise to have a written buy-sell agreement in place. Although hopeful co-owners of a new business usually want to think their alliance will last forever, this attitude is unrealistic. Even the most compatible, fair-minded business owners commonly face all sorts of life events that can bring ownership into question: death, divorce, illness, bankruptcy, or simply a decision to change life's direction. Rather than let ownership changes sneak up on you and wreak havoc on your company, it's much smarter to accept that the ownership will likely change at some point, and plan for that day.

If you still need convincing, consider some common situations and how they can impact a business.

An Owner Leaves or Retires

It's often said that being a co-owner of a business is like being in a marriage—and the pressures of running the business can lead to bitter break-ups. But even when co-owners get along famously, one of them may simply want to retire or do something different. Perhaps the business didn't provide an owner with the satisfaction anticipated, prompting a decision to change course and leave the business.

Whatever the circumstances, the potential departure of an owner raises serious questions. What if an owner decides to stop working for the company but refuses to sell the share in the business, hoping to earn income without contributing to it? Assuming an owner does plan to sell the interest in the business, can the sale be to anyone at all? Clearly, the remaining co-owners would not be happy to learn the departing owner sold out to someone they all detest. How will the price of the departing owner's interest be determined if offered for sale? Valuing the company and determining share price can be quite contentious, particularly when continuing owners want to purchase the share.

On the flip side, consider what would happen if you wanted to retire. What if you couldn't find someone to buy your interest, and your co-owners didn't want or couldn't afford to buy your share? Would you be stuck, unable to cash out? Failing to address these issues early in the life of your company can result in a real quagmire if they arise in real life.

An Owner Becomes Disabled

If one owner has a debilitating stroke, is paralyzed in a car accident, or suffers some other incapacitating illness, the remaining owners face some big questions: Can they force the disabled owner to sell out? Can the departing owner sell to whomever he or she pleases? If the sale is to the continuing owners, what price must they pay for that share?

Again, the issues shift a bit for the person who becomes disabled and wants—or, more likely, needs—to sell. If you find yourself in this situation, you'd likely be concerned about being able to sell your ownership interest for cash to help pay medical bills and get through the tough time. Truth is, it's often difficult for small business owners to find outside buyers, especially for a minority ownership interest. If your co-owners are uninterested or unable to buy you out and you have no buy-sell agreement in place, you could find yourself in a really tight spot.

An Owner Dies

The death of a co-owner is sure to be a traumatic situation for everyone in the business. In the midst of it, the co-owners will be faced with the burden of figuring out who will own the deceased owner's share. For example, will they be forced to accept anyone who inherits the ownership interest as a new, active owner? What if the person who inherits the share wants to sell it for cash to the current owners or to an outside buyer?

Similarly, if you die, these questions will be dropped into the laps of your grieving family members or the people who may take over your ownership share. They may need money for funeral expenses, not to mention living expenses once you aren't earning any income.

A buy-sell agreement can anticipate and provide a clear plan for these emotionally laden situations. Without an agreement, the trauma of losing an owner can go from bad to worse if the current owners and the deceased owner's successors can't agree.

An Owner Divorces

You don't need to be reminded that divorce is a possibility, even when marital harmony and bliss seem certain. Roughly half of all marriages end in divorce, so you absolutely must deal with the question of how a marital split might affect your business.

The most glaring possibility is that when a co-owner gets divorced, the ex can become a new owner of the business. Except when a premarital agreement or "prenup" prevents it—and, in reality, many prenups are hard to enforce—spouses of business partners often have a legal interest in the business. This legal right is most clear in community property states—which includes California—in which each spouse owns half of the couple's community property, usually most of the property gained during the marriage. But even in noncommunity property states, laws often require that a couple's property be divided fairly during divorce.

Having an ex suddenly on board can, of course, can be a true disaster, especially if former spouses each have an ownership share and must run the business together. Even if the original co-owner sells out of the business and the ex remains an owner, there's a huge potential for drama and trouble—particularly if the divorce was a nasty one. If the divorce was friendly, an ex who has no business experience or is just plain incompetent may still be unwelcome as an owner. In short, there are ample and compelling reasons to preemptively avoid these situations by implementing a sound buy-sell agreement.

Specific contract language is discussed in "Sample Buy-Sell Provisions," below. For now, keep in mind that to avoid the situations outlined above, all the spouses of current business owners should read and sign the buy-sell agreement.

An Owner Becomes a Liability

Sometimes conflict with a business owner goes beyond the occasional squabbling and sniping typical of many business relationships. In extreme cases, the conflict crosses the line and some of the owners agree that it's time to push out one of the other owners. This situation can arise for all kinds of reasons: The owner may be inherently unreasonable and difficult, suffering from alcoholism or substance abuse, mentally ill, or engaged in criminal behavior.

Whatever the root cause, once things have deteriorated to an intolerable level, it's important to have a mechanism in place to expel an owner. Having rules—for instance, outlining the situations that call for expulsion—will help make this nasty situation a little less nasty.

To sum up, when any of these often-painful situations occurs, you can depend on a buy-sell agreement to dictate an orderly transfer of ownership interests according to rules all have consented to beforehand. As discussed in more detail below, a buy-sell agreement can outline straightforward rules about when ownership shares can or must be sold, to whom they may be sold, and how to determine the share's selling price.

Buy-Sell Agreement Basics

A buy-sell agreement is a contract among a business's owners that spells out, in varying degrees of detail, some or all of the following issues:

- who can buy a departing owner's interest
- when the owners can force another owner to sell a share of the business
- when one owner can force the other owners to buy a share
- what price will be paid for a departing owner's share, and
- how a buyout will actually happen, including specific payment terms.

In practice, a buy-sell agreement typically has a few standard provisions to handle these issues. Buy-sell provisions can either be assembled into their own stand-alone agreement or inserted into other business documents such as your partnership agreement, LLC operating agreement, or corporate bylaws. The term buy-sell agreement in this chapter includes any buy-sell provisions your company has adopted, whether they're in a separate agreement or included in another business document.

The three provisions at the heart of buy-sell agreements establish:

- transfer of ownership interests with the right of first refusal
- the right to force buyouts, and
- a set price or a formula to determine share price.

Limiting Ownership Transfers

When an owner wants to leave a business and sell an ownership interest, it can create real and lasting chaos if the share is sold to someone the other owners don't want as a co-owner. But if there is a buy-sell agreement that establishes limits on the transfers of ownership shares, this possibility can be avoided.

The best way to avoid unwanted outsiders gaining ownership of your business is with a provision known as a "right of first refusal." This provision gives the company or the remaining co-owners the right to buy a departing owner's interest before it's transferred—that is, sold or given—to an outsider.

It works like this: A departing owner who receives an offer to purchase his or her interest from an outsider may not accept it outright. Instead, the right of first refusal requires the departing owner to give written notice to the company stating the intention to sell the shares and describing the terms of the proposed sale. At that point, the company and the continuing owners have the option to buy the departing owner's interest. Depending on how you structure your right of first refusal, the company and continuing owners will be entitled to purchase the shares either at the same price as the outsider offered or at a price previously agreed upon and included in the agreement. If the co-owners don't want to buy the ownership interest at those terms, then the departing owner has 60 days to sell it to the outsider according to the terms outlined in the notice.

The right of first refusal focuses on preventing unwanted outsiders from gaining ownership interest in your company. Since this is a fundamental issue, it is important for all business owners to put this provision in place.

But you can also include solutions such as the following for dealing with related issues in the right of first refusal.

- **Extend the right to potential sales to current owners.** If the right of first refusal is structured this way, when a departing owner offers a share to another current owner, all the co-owners must be given the option to buy it. The main reason to use this arrangement is to prevent one or more co-owners from seizing control of the business by buying a departing owner's share.
- **Create different rules for gifts or transfers to trusts.** It's possible to have the right of first refusal apply to sales of ownership shares, as described above, but not to other types of transfers, such as gifts or transfers to trusts. Generally, giving ownership shares to family members or putting them in a trust is done for estate planning purposes—to save estate taxes and avoid probate. If you and your co-owners want more freedom to engage in estate planning techniques with your ownership shares, you may not want the right of first refusal provisions to apply to gifts and transfers to trusts.
- **Prohibit all transfers.** Current owners may keep the tightest grip on control of company ownership by banning all ownership transfers outright. However, since this approach is so rigid and unhelpful to owners who may really need to sell out of a business, it is generally not a good idea.

FORM ON CD-ROM

You can find suggested language for a right of first refusal in "Sample Buy-Sell Agreement Provisions," below, and on the CD-ROM in the back of this book.

Forcing Buyouts

In addition to controlling who owns a business, an important function of a buy-sell agreement is to provide answers to the questions that can arise when the ownership setup is thrown into question. What if one of your co-owners dies? Will the heirs become co-owners in your business? What if a co-owner slides into crippling alcoholism or substance abuse? Will you be stuck with an inebriated business partner? What if your co-owner gets divorced and the dreaded ex-spouse gets an ownership share as part of the divorce settlement? Is there anything you can do?

You can remove the uncertainty from all of these situations by taking preventive action. By adopting forced buyout provisions in a buy-sell agreement, you'll establish rules for different scenarios, such as death, divorce, bankruptcy, retirement, and other business-disrupting events. When the rules are triggered by specific events, an owner can be forced to sell shares, or continuing owners can be forced to buy out a departing owner's share. Forced buyout rules help keep the business stable during difficult times and make ownership transitions as smooth as possible.

As you can imagine, a crucial fact about forced buyout provisions is that they must be agreed to well in advance of any situation that will trigger them. It goes without saying that the situations that trigger these provisions—such as death, disease, and divorce—often cause emotions to run high. You and your co-owners should discuss the possible scenarios and come to a consensus on what rules will apply in those situations before any owner is personally affected.

In a nutshell, there are two different kinds of forced buyouts: Either an owner can be forced to sell out, or a departing owner can force the other owners to buy the departing owner's share.

Forcing Owners to Sell

Business owners can force an owner or other person who has obtained an interest in the business to sell out of it—and sell the shares back to the company or to the continuing owners at a specified price. They do it by including an option-to-purchase provision in the buy-sell agreement.

This provision can force any of the following people to sell back to the continuing owners:

- any one of the owners—for specified reasons, such as retirement, disability, bankruptcy, loss of professional license, or misconduct
- the executor or administrator of a deceased owner's estate, and
- an owner's ex-spouse who gains an interest in the business through a divorce settlement.

The rules vary depending on which situation triggers the forced buyout, but the overall goal is the same: to keep control over the company's ownership and keep out anyone unacceptable to the continuing owners. This includes people who stand to gain ownership through inheritance, divorce, or bankruptcy—as well as current owners whom other owners want to push out.

All options to purchase should also address the price at which the shares will be sold. Usually this is accomplished by referring to the agreement price outlined in a separate buy-sell provision. (Price provisions are discussed in "Establishing the Price for Sales," below.)

Forcing Owners to Buy

The flip side of an option-to-purchase provision is the right to force a sale. Without a right-to-force-a-sale provision, an owner who wants to sell out might be stuck if a current owner doesn't want—or doesn't have the funds—to purchase his or her share. But with a forced buyout provision, anyone with an ownership interest in the business can force the other owners to buy that interest at a specified price. Common scenarios include an owner who's retiring or becomes disabled who wants to sell out of the business or a deceased owner's survivors who want to cash out the ownership interest they got in a will.

Beware that while a forced buyout provision protects owners from being stuck in a business, it also has the potential to seriously damage a company that doesn't have the means to pay out departing owners, particularly when business isn't so hot.

But there is a way to both protect business owners who don't want to be chained to the business forever and to protect the business from bleeding money from cashing out owners. Your right-to-force-a-sale clause can allow owners to cash out of the business only after a certain time, by which you expect your business to be stable and profitable enough to pay out a departing owner. Anyone who chooses to cash out before that time—for example, three or five years—will only receive a fraction of the value of ownership share—say, 50%. This creates a disincentive for any owner to leave early in the life of the business, when cash reserves may be crucial.

FORM ON CD-ROM

You can find suggested language for a right of forced buyout in "Sample Buy-Sell Agreement Provisions," below, and on the CD-ROM in the back of this book.

Negotiations can easily get tangled up on price issues, so it's important that the right-to-force-a-sale provision addresses the price at which the shares will be sold. Generally it will refer to a separate pricing provision, which is discussed next.

CAUTION

Wrinkles for co-owners with unequal shares. If your company has one controlling owner and one or more owners with small minority shares, the controlling owner may not want to be subject to the same rules as the minority owners. For example, say a company has a majority owner who is very identified with the company and who has played the primary role in building it over many years. The majority owner may balk at the idea that the minority owners could force his or her children to sell their shares, elevating the minority owners to control the company. Majority owners should consider consulting an experienced business lawyer before signing a buy-sell agreement. Before doing that, it's a good idea to read *Business Buyout Agreements: A Step-by-Step Guide for Co-Owners*, by Anthony Mancuso and Bethany K. Laurence (Nolo), which explains the subtleties of buy-sell agreements in much greater detail than this chapter.

Establishing the Price for Sales

In addition to spelling out ownership transfer rules for specific situations, a buy-sell agreement should outline how to set the price for shares being sold. In essence, this determines how to value the company. It's all too common for departing and continuing owners to have significantly different ideas about a company's value. Without a consensus as to how to determine the company's value and the price of its shares, negotiations can be stymied or sunk.

In addition, a buy-sell agreement can define details of the ownership transfer, such as how it will be funded, payment terms, and other specifics.

Equipment, property, and accounts receivable are simple enough to total, but it's much harder to put a price tag on intangibles, such as business reputation or customer lists. When owners don't agree on how to establish a company's value, the haggling involved in an ownership transfer can get gnarly. If the ownership transfer is due to death, divorce, or some other wrenching event, you can count on the negotiations being even tougher.

To avoid these conflicts, a buy-sell agreement establishes in advance a value for the company or a formula that will be used to determine it. Any owner's share can then be calculated by multiplying the ownership percentage by the overall company value.

There are several different ways to value a business, and you can include any of them in your buy-sell agreement.

One approach is to establish a preset value for the company. Though the simplicity of this approach may be attractive, the obvious weakness is that the fixed price is likely to become outdated and may not accurately reflect the current value of the business— particularly if the business is growing or shrinking

rapidly. One way to remedy this is to update the fixed price periodically, say, every year.

A better approach is to use a valuation formula in your agreement. With a formula, you and your co-owners will have a clearly defined way to figure out the value of the business and, by extension, the ownership shares up for sale. Even better, the value generated by a formula will be more meaningful than a fixed value, since the formula will be based on up-to-date data such as current assets or income.

There are a few different valuation formulas and methods possible. Here is a look at the most common ones.

Book Value

A company's book value is simply its assets minus its liabilities, the same as the information on a balance sheet. Because the figures used to calculate book value are readily available from various financial statements, this is an easy formula to use and to understand. Though book value does not include intangibles such as reputation, earnings potential, or customer goodwill, this may not be a big issue for new businesses that haven't had the time or luck to develop much of a reputation or goodwill. Another issue is that this method uses the depreciated value of assets, which typically results in a low value overall. As your business grows, you may be wise to switch to a valuation method that reflects more and provides a higher buyout price.

Multiple of Book Value

This method is based on the book value approach, but goes further and includes intangible assets such as customer goodwill, a solid client base, a desirable location, a recently implemented marketing campaign, and intellectual property owned by the business. The overall value is reached by taking the business's book value and multiplying it by a predetermined number, aptly called a multiplier. The co-owners will need to choose a multiplier to include in the buy-sell agreement—and choosing is more of an art than a science. You'll find a wide range of multipliers used, from just over one to six or more. Do some research into your particular industry before choosing a multiplier.

Capitalization of Earnings

Also called "multiple of earnings," the capitalization of earnings method bases a company's value on its record of profits. Because brand-new businesses won't have a profit record, do not use this method until you develop an earnings history. The valuation begins with the company's annual profit (gross revenues minus costs) multiplied by a predetermined number—a multiplier, sometimes called a capitalization rate. Co-owners will choose a multiplier based on several factors, including general economic conditions, type of business, business age, risk involved in business, or multipliers of similar businesses. Multipliers for the capitalization of earnings method can go as high as ten in some cases.

Appraisal Value

Rather than doing it yourselves, you can hire a professional business appraiser to determine a business's value once an ownership transfer is imminent. That certainly makes things easier for the co-owners, but it's not without drawbacks. One is cost: Appraisers don't come cheap. Expect to pay at least $1,000 for an appraisal of a small company, and up to $10,000 for large businesses with annual sales into the millions. Appraisals can also take valuable time, which may be an issue when an owner is eager to sell.

At the end of the day, you'll need to choose the valuation method that works best for your company. As a general rule, methods based on book value tend not to be good choices for service businesses that may have few assets. For such businesses, basing valuation on earnings history makes more sense.

TIP

Address other issues, such as payment terms and the funding source. Because ownership shares can involve big sums of money, buyouts cannot always be paid for all at once. It's a good idea to outline specific payment terms in your agreement—for instance, monthly payments of principal and interest or some other arrangement. It's also wise to address where the money will come from in the case of a buyout. Businesses commonly need to take out a loan to pay departing owners or to use proceeds from life or disability insurance. If you don't plan in advance how you'll fund buyouts, you might find there's not enough time to scramble the money together once something triggers a buyout.

FORM ON CD-ROM

You can find suggested language for agreement prices in "Sample Buy-Sell Agreement Provisions," below, and on the CD-ROM in the back of this book.

Implementing Buy-Sell Provisions

In general, buy-sell provisions either can be assembled into their own document or can be added to your existing business-governing document. For corporations, this is the bylaws; for LLCs, it's the operating agreement; for partnerships, it's the partnership agreement. If you want to use the sample provisions provided below, it is best to insert them into your existing business-governing document, because only the basic clauses are provided in the template here.

To insert clauses into the existing document that governs your business, either type or cut and paste the clauses into your document file, preferably near the end. Be sure to renumber the sections as needed to conform with the existing numbering of your document.

Note that many of the standard clauses in the sample agreement have multiple options with checkboxes. Feel free either to copy and paste all the possible options and use the checkboxes to indicate your choices or to copy and paste only the clauses you choose to use. However, it is not a good idea to select partial language; instead, choose among the clearly defined alternative options.

Before finalizing your agreement, you must tackle an important legal task: a consistency check. This requires scrutinizing whether any of the buy-sell provisions conflicts with any existing business documents. Essentially, you need to make sure that your existing documents don't contain any language contradicting any of the buy-sell provisions. Generally, if there are no clauses in your existing document that explicitly contradict the buy-sell provisions, then you will be in the clear. Still, analyzing the provisions for conflict can be confusing, and you may want simply to pay a lawyer to review the existing document and the buy-sell provisions.

CAUTION

Consistency checks are important business. Often, inconsistencies in documents will be obvious, even to a nonlawyer. For example, say your existing LLC operating agreement states that any person who is at the receiving end of an ownership transfer will have economic rights only—as in, no voting rights or management authority. Your buy-sell provisions, on the other hand, are based on the assumption that full ownership rights are being transferred, including voting and management rights. This should trigger alarm bells. One option is to delete the limited-ownership-rights provision from your existing operating agreement. Or, if you'd prefer, see a lawyer who can make the necessary changes for you.

Sample Buy-Sell Provisions

Sample buy-sell clauses are provided below for you to use as a starting point when drafting your own agreement. The sample clauses are also included on the CD-ROM in the back of this book.

The samples are of the three most important clauses:

- a limitation on the transfer of ownership interests or right of first refusal
- a right to force buyouts, and
- a method to determine share price.

You'll also find a fourth provision, payment terms, which outlines a few alternatives for how a buyout will be paid.

Keep in mind that these sample provisions stick to the basics and should be seen as a skeletal version of a full buy-sell agreement. There are many other details and issues you should consider once you're serious about putting your agreement together. All businesses owners would be wise to take these issues seriously from the get-go, but it's especially important for businesses that have accumulated significant assets, and for business owners who are concerned about estate planning.

RESOURCE

Getting help with the details. For a more detailed agreement that anticipates a comprehensive range of issues and potential situations, consult *Business Buyout Agreements: A Step-by-Step Guide for Co-Owners*, by Anthony Mancuso and Bethany K. Laurence (Nolo).

CAUTION

Running your buy-sell agreement by an expert. Although buy-sell basics aren't hard to understand, it may be a good idea to have an attorney or business consultant review yours once you've drafted it. The expert may be able to point out potential additional issues that are not covered in depth in this chapter, such as tax and estate planning considerations.

Sample Buy-Sell Agreement Provisions

Section 1: Limiting the Transfer of Ownership Interests

Right of First Refusal

(a) No owner ("transferring owner") shall have the right to sell, transfer, or dispose of any or all of an ownership interest, for consideration or otherwise, unless he or she delivers to the company written Notice of Intent to Transfer the interest stating the name and the address of the proposed transferee and the terms and conditions of the proposed transfer. Delivery of this notice shall be deemed an offer by the transferring owner to sell to the company and the continuing owners the interest proposed to be transferred.

   If the proposed transfer is a sale of the owner's interest, these terms shall include the price to be paid for the interest by the proposed transferee, and a copy of the offer to purchase the interest on these terms, dated and signed by the proposed transferee, shall be attached to the notice.

(b) The company and the nontransferring owners then have an option, but not an obligation (unless otherwise stated in this agreement), to purchase the interest proposed for transfer, and may do so within 60 days after the date on which the company receives notice or becomes aware of the event triggering the Option to Purchase.

   If the company and the nontransferring owners do not elect to purchase all of the interest stated in the notice, the transferring owner may then transfer his or her interest to the proposed transferee stated in the notice within 60 days after the nontransferring owners' purchase option ends.

(c) Price and terms:
   [Check either Option 1a or Option 1b below.]

   ☐ **Option 1a: Price and terms in offer**
   The company and the nontransferring owners shall have the right to purchase the interest of the transferring owner only at the purchase price and payment terms stated in the Notice of Intent to Transfer submitted to the company by the transferring owner. The price and terms in this notice override the general Agreement Price selected in the "Agreement Price" and "Payment Terms" sections of this agreement.

   ☐ **Option 1b: Price and terms in agreement**
   The company and the nontransferring owners shall have the right to purchase the interest of the transferring owner at the Agreement Price and payment terms selected in the "Agreement Price" and "Payment Terms" sections of this agreement.

Section 2: Providing the Right to Force Buyouts

Scenario 1. When an Active Owner Retires or Quits the Company's Employ
[You may check Option 1, Option 2, both, or neither below. Check Option 1 if you want the company and continuing owners to have the option to buy a retiring owner's interest.]

☐ **Option 1: Option of Company and Continuing Owners
to Purchase a Retiring Owner's Interest**

An owner who voluntarily retires or quits the company's employ is deemed to have offered his or her ownership interest to the company and the continuing owners for sale. The company and the continuing owners shall then have an option, but not an obligation (unless otherwise stated in this agreement), to purchase all or part of the ownership interest within 60 days after the date on which the company receives notice or becomes aware of the event triggering the Option to Purchase. The price to be paid, the manner of payments, and other terms of the purchase shall be according to the "Agreement Price" and "Payment Terms" sections of this agreement. An owner who stops working for the company is referred to as a "retiring owner" below.

[Check Option 2 if you want a retiring owner to be able to force the company to buy his or her interest. This right can be in addition to Option 1 (company and continuing owners' option to purchase) above.]

☐ **Option 2: Right of Retiring Owner to Force a Sale**

An owner who voluntarily retires or quits the company's employ can require the company and the continuing owners to buy all, but not less than all, of his or her ownership interest by delivering to the company at least 60 days before departing a notice of intention to force a sale ("Notice of Intent to Force a Sale"). The notice shall include the date of departure, the name and address of the owner, a description and amount of the owner's interest in the company, and a statement that the owner wishes to force a sale due to the owner's retirement as provided in this provision. The price to be paid, the manner of payments, and other terms of the purchase shall be according to this section and the "Agreement Price" and "Payment Terms" sections of this agreement. An owner who requests that an interest be purchased is referred to as a "retiring owner" below.

Scenario 2. When an Owner Becomes Disabled

[You may check Option 1, Option 2, both, or neither below. Check Option 1 if you want the company and continuing owners to have the option to buy a disabled owner's interest. If you check Option 1, insert the amount of time an owner must be disabled before the company or the continuing owners can purchase the available interest.]

☐ **Option 1: Option of Company and Continuing Owners
to Purchase a Disabled Owner's Interest**

An owner who becomes permanently and totally disabled, and such disability lasts at least ____ months (the "waiting period"), either consecutively or cumulatively, is deemed to have offered his or her ownership interest to the company and the continuing owners for sale. The company and the continuing owners shall then have an option, but not an obligation (unless otherwise stated in this agreement), to purchase all or part of the ownership interest within 60 days after the date on which the company receives notice or becomes aware of the event triggering the Option to Purchase. The price to be paid, the manner of payments, and other terms of the purchase shall be according to this section and the "Agreement Price" and "Payment Terms" sections of this agreement.

An owner who is unable to perform his or her regular duties is considered disabled. If disability insurance is used to fund a buyout under this provision, the insurance company shall establish whether an owner is disabled; without disability insurance, the owner's doctor will establish whether an owner is disabled. An owner who becomes disabled according to this section is referred to as a "disabled owner" below.

[Check Option 2 if you want a disabled owner to be able to force the company to buy his or her interest. This right can be in addition to Option 1 (company and continuing owners' option to purchase) above. If you check Option 2, insert the amount of time an owner must be disabled before forcing the company to purchase an interest.]

☐ **Option 2: Right of Disabled Owner to Force a Sale**

An owner who becomes permanently and totally disabled, and such disability lasts at least _____months (the "waiting period"), either consecutively or cumulatively, can require the company and the continuing owners to buy all, but not less than all, of his or her ownership interest by delivering to the company, within 30 days of the expiration of the waiting period, a notice of intention to force a sale ("Notice of Intent to Force a Sale") in writing. The notice shall include the name and address of the owner, a description and amount of the owner's interest in the company, and a statement that the owner wishes to force a sale due to disability as provided in this provision. The price to be paid, the manner of payments, and other terms of the purchase shall be according to this section and the "Agreement Price" and "Payment Terms" sections of this agreement.

An owner is who is unable to perform his or her regular duties is considered disabled. If disability insurance is used to fund a buyout under this provision, the insurance company shall establish whether an owner is disabled; without disability insurance, the owner's doctor will establish whether an owner is disabled. An owner who becomes disabled according to this section is referred to as a "disabled owner" below.

Scenario 3. When an Owner Dies

[You may check Option 1, Option 2, both, or neither below. Check Option 1 if you want the company and continuing owners to have the right to buy a deceased owner's interest.]

☐ **Option 1: Option of Company and Continuing Owners to Purchase a Deceased Owner's Interest**

An owner who dies and the executor or administrator of the estate or the trustee of a trust holding the ownership interest are deemed to have offered the deceased owner's interest to the company and the continuing owners for sale as of the date of the notice of death received orally or in writing by the company. The company and the continuing owners shall then have an option, but not an obligation (unless otherwise stated in this agreement), to purchase all or part of the ownership interest within 60 days after the date on which the company receives notice or becomes aware of the death. The price to be paid, the manner of payments, and other terms of the purchase shall be according to the "Agreement Price" and "Payment Terms" sections of this agreement. An owner who has died is referred to as a "deceased owner" below.

[Check Option 2 below if you want the estate, trust, or inheritors of a deceased owner to be able to force the company to buy his or her interest. This right can be in addition to Option 1 (company and continuing owners' right to purchase) above.]

☐ **Option 2: Right of Estate, Trust, or Inheritors to Force a Sale**

When an owner dies, the executor or administrator of the deceased owner's estate, the trustee of a trust holding the deceased owner's ownership interest, or the deceased owner's inheritors can require the company and the continuing owners to buy all, but not less than all, of the deceased owner's interest by delivering to the company within 60 days a notice of intention to force a sale ("Notice of Intent to Force a Sale") in writing. The notice shall include the name and address of the deceased owner, the date of death, a description and amount of the owner's interest in the company, the name and address of the person exercising the right to force the sale, and a statement that this person wishes to force a sale of the interest due to the owner's death as provided in this provision. The price to be paid, the manner of payments, and other terms of the purchase shall be according to the "Agreement Price" and "Payment Terms" sections of this agreement. An owner who has died is referred to as a "deceased owner" below.

Scenario 4. When an Owner's Interest Is Transferred to His or Her Former Spouse

[Check Option 1 if you want the company and owners to have the right to buy a divorced owner's interest from his or her former spouse.]

☐ **Option 1: Option of Company and Continuing Owners to Purchase Former Spouse's Interest**

(a) If, in connection with the divorce or dissolution of the marriage of an owner, a court issues a decree or order that transfers, confirms, or awards part or all of an ownership interest to a divorced owner's former spouse, the former spouse is deemed to have offered the newly acquired ownership interest to the divorced owner for purchase on the date of the court award or settlement, according to the terms of this agreement. If the divorced owner does not elect to make such purchase within 30 days of the date of the court award or settlement, the former spouse of the divorced owner is deemed to have offered the newly acquired ownership interest to the company and the co-owners (including the divorced owner) for purchase, according to the terms of this agreement. The divorced owner must send notice to the company, in writing, that his or her former spouse now owns an ownership interest in the company. The notice shall state the name and address of the owner, the name and address of the divorced owner's former spouse, a description and amount of the interest awarded to the former spouse, and the date of the court award. If the company does not receive notice from the divorced owner, an offer to the company and the co-owners is deemed to have occurred when the company actually receives notice orally or in writing of the court award or settlement transferring the divorced owner's interest to the owner's former spouse. The company and the co-owners (including the divorced owner) shall then have an option, but not an obligation (unless otherwise stated in this agreement), to purchase all or part of the ownership interest within 60 days after the date on which the company receives notice or becomes aware of the event triggering the Option to Purchase. The price to be paid, the manner of payments, and other terms of the purchase shall be according to the "Agreement Price" and "Payment Terms" sections of this agreement.

(b)　A former spouse who sells an ownership interest back to the company or continuing owners agrees to be responsible for any taxes owed on those sales proceeds.

Scenario 5. Expulsion of Owner

[Check Option 1 below if you want to give the company and the continuing owners the option to purchase an expelled owner's interest. If you check Option 1, also check and fill in Options 1a through 1f.]

☐ **Option 1: Option of Company and Continuing Owners to Purchase an Expelled Owner's Interest**

(a)　When the company has three or more owners, situations may arise in which a group of owners wishes to expel another owner. An owner may be expelled upon a unanimous vote of all other owners for adequate cause. Upon such expulsion, the expelled owner is deemed to have offered to sell all of his or her interest to the company and the continuing owners. The company and the continuing owners shall then have an option, but not an obligation (unless otherwise stated in this agreement), to purchase all or part of the ownership interest within 30 days after the vote to expel the owner. The price to be paid shall be as specified in this section; if not so specified, then according to the "Agreement Price" section of this agreement. The manner of payments and other terms of the purchase shall be according to the "Payment Terms" section of this agreement. An owner who has been expelled is referred to as an "expelled owner" below.

(b)　Adequate cause includes, but is not limited to:

☐ **Option 1a: Any criminal conduct against the company (such as embezzlement)**

☐ **Option 1b: A serious breach of the owner's duties or of any written policy of the company**

☐ **Option 1c:** _____

(c)　If an owner is expelled for a reason listed in Subsection (b), the price that the company or the continuing owners will pay for the expelled owner's ownership interest will be:

☐ **Option 1d: The full Agreement Price according to the "Agreement Price" section of this agreement**

☐ **Option 1e: Decided by an independent appraisal, according to the Appraised Value Method in the "Agreement Price" section of this agreement**

☐ **Option 1f: The Agreement Price as established in the "Agreement Price" section of this agreement, decreased by _____%.**

Section 3: Agreement Price

Unless otherwise provided in this agreement, the undersigned agree that the method checked below for valuing the company shall be used to determine a price for ownership interests under this agreement.

[You must check one and only one of the valuation methods below:]

☐ **Valuation Method 1: Agreed Value**

The agreed value of the company shall be $_____, or such other amount as fixed by all owners of the company after the date this agreement is adopted as specified in a written statement signed by each owner of the company. If more than one such statement is signed by the owners after this agreement is adopted, the statement with the latest date shall control for purposes of fixing a price for the purchase of ownership interests under this agreement. The value of an individual owner's interest shall be the entire value for the company as determined under this paragraph, multiplied by his or her ownership percentage.

☐ **Valuation Method 2: Book Value**

The value of the company shall be its book value (its assets minus its liabilities as shown on the balance sheet of the company) as of the end of the most recent fiscal year prior to the purchase of an ownership interest under this agreement. The value of an individual owner's interest shall be the entire value for the company as determined under this paragraph, multiplied by his or her ownership percentage.

☐ **Valuation Method 3: Multiple of Book Value**

The value of the company shall be _____times its book value (its assets minus its liabilities as shown on the balance sheet of the company) as of the end of the most recent fiscal year prior to the purchase of an ownership interest under this agreement. The value of an individual owner's interest shall be the entire value for the company as determined under this paragraph, multiplied by his or her ownership percentage.

☐ **Valuation Method 4: Capitalization of Earnings (Adjusted for Income Taxes)**

The value of the company shall be determined on the basis of _____times the average net earnings (annual gross revenues of the company minus annual expenses and minus any annual federal, state, and local income taxes payable by the company) for the _____ fiscal years of the company (or the number of fiscal years the company has been in existence, if fewer) that have occurred prior to the purchase of an ownership interest under this agreement. The value of an individual owner's interest shall be the entire value for the company as determined under this paragraph, multiplied by his or her ownership percentage.

☐ **Valuation Method 5: Appraised Value**

The value of the company shall be its fair market value as determined by an independent appraiser mutually selected by the Buyer(s) and Seller of the ownership interest subject to purchase under this agreement. If the Buyer(s) and Seller are unable to agree upon an independent appraiser within 30 days, within the next 10 days, each shall select an independent appraiser. If the selected appraisers are unable, within 60 days, to agree on the fair market value of the company, then the appraisers shall select an additional independent appraiser within the next 10 days, who shall, within 30 days, determine the fair market value of the company. The Buyer(s) and Seller shall equally share all costs of an appraiser mutually selected by the Buyer(s) and Seller or of an additional appraiser. All costs of an individually selected appraiser shall be paid by the party selecting the appraiser. The value of an individual owner's interest shall be the entire value for the company as determined under this paragraph, multiplied by his or her ownership percentage.

Section 4: Payment Terms

Unless otherwise provided in this agreement, the undersigned agree that the payment terms checked below shall be used for the purchase of ownership interests.

[You must check one and only one of the payment terms alternatives below.]

☐ **Payment Terms Alternative 1: Full Cash Payment**

Cash payment for the Seller's ownership interest shall be made by the Buyer(s) to the Seller within _____ days of the date the company provides a Notice of Intent to Purchase to the Seller under this agreement.

☐ **Payment Terms Alternative 2: Monthly Installments of Principal and Interest**

The Buyer(s) shall pay the Seller the purchase price for an ownership interest in equal install-ments over a term of _____ months, with interest added to the amount of each installment computed at an annual rate of _____ and compounded annually on the unpaid continuing balance of the purchase price of the ownership interest. The Buyer shall make the first installment payment to the Seller by _____ , and the continuing payments shall be made on the _____ of every month, until the full purchase price, together with any interest owed, is paid in full.

☐ **Payment Terms Alternative 3: Customized Schedule for Payment for Ownership Interest**

The Buyer(s) shall pay the Seller the purchase price for the ownership interest according to the schedule and other terms included below:

_____

_____

_____

_____

_____

_____

_____

Chapter 14 Checklist:
Planning for Changes in Ownership

☐ If your business will have more than one owner, consider the various situations that may raise ownership questions: retirement, illness, disability, death, divorce, or conflict among business owners.

☐ To control the transfer of ownership shares in your business, include buy-sell provisions in your business formation document, such as your partnership agreement or LLC operating agreement, or in a separate agreement. (The sample clauses in this chapter are to be used in your existing business formation document.)

☐ To limit the ability of a business owner to sell a business interest to an outsider, use a right of first refusal clause.

☐ To force an owner or someone who has acquired an interest in the business to sell the interest to the current owners, use an option to purchase clause.

☐ To force the other owners of the business to purchase a departing owner's share, include a forced buyout clause.

☐ Remember to include provisions for how the price will be set for ownership shares being sold and payment terms.

Building Your Business and Hiring Workers

I f all your careful planning, hard work, and good karma pay off, you may soon find yourself needing help to handle your thriving business. While part of you will surely be happy that your business is taking off, another, more practical side of you may worry about what's involved in hiring help. This chapter offers a broad overview of the many legal requirements that apply to businesses that have one or more employees. If you're thinking about hiring an employee but aren't sure about how or whether to do it, the information we give here should help you understand what you might be getting into—and help you figure out if there's a better way to go.

In addition to the practical and financial concerns involved in hiring one or more people to work for your business, you need to be aware of several legal rules that apply to businesses with outside workers. First of all, you'll need to understand the difference between two types of workers: employees and independent contractors. This distinction is crucial, because different rules will apply to your business depending on what kind of workers you hire. If the government considers your workers to be employees, you'll have to follow a number of state and federal laws and pay employment-related taxes. If, on the other hand, your workers can be characterized as independent contractors, you'll be spared many—but not all—of these financial and legal requirements.

Employees Versus Independent Contractors

Anyone who works for your business—other than a business owner—is either an employee or an independent contractor (IC). In a nutshell, an employee is someone who works for you, on your site, with your tools and equipment, and according to your rules and procedures. Independent contractors, on the other hand, are in business for themselves; they work on their own time and with their own tools, and perform services for a number of different clients.

This is not a distinction to be taken lightly. Businesses that hire employees owe a number of employment taxes, such as payroll tax and unemployment tax, while those that hire only independent contractors do not owe these taxes. If you treat an employee as an independent contractor and fail to pay employment taxes, you risk subjecting yourself to a huge back-tax bill, plus interest and other state and federal penalties. More than a few businesses have been torpedoed and sunk into bankruptcy after making this mistake.

With that warning in mind, here's the lowdown on classifying your workers.

Controlling Government Agencies

Because paying taxes is the main drawback to classifying workers as employees, it shouldn't surprise you to learn that the IRS takes a great interest in whether your workers are classified properly. At the federal level, the IRS will take swift and severe action if it finds out that you're treating a worker as an independent contractor, when in fact the worker meets the criteria of an employee.

At the state level, the California Employment Development Department (EDD) (the agency that collects employment taxes) will also punish a business that avoids paying taxes by misclassifying workers. Don't make the mistake of ignoring state rules and requirements—state penalties can be at least as harsh as those imposed by the IRS.

Determining a Worker's Classification

IRS Publication 15-A, *Employer's Supplemental Tax Guide*, offers information and examples to help you determine whether a worker is, in fact, an independent contractor or an employee. It's available online at www.irs.gov. The EDD also has a brochure that gives some guidance on the issue, though for the most part the EDD uses the same standards as the IRS. (See Appendix A for contact information for the EDD.)

A worker should normally be considered an employee, not an independent contractor, when he or she:

- works only for you and not for any other business
- works on your premises
- uses your tools and equipment
- follows work hours you set

- follows your instructions on how to complete a job
- receives reimbursement for expenses incurred in doing a job
- supervises any of your other workers, or
- receives any employee benefits, such as holiday pay, paid vacation, or health insurance.

On the flip side, a worker should probably be considered an independent contractor if he or she:

- works for a number of different businesses or clients
- has a personal office, studio, garage, or other permanent place to work
- owns the equipment and tools used for the work
- sets his or her own hours
- uses independent judgment as to how best to complete a job
- doesn't get reimbursed for expenses incurred in doing a job, or
- advertises services to the public.

Of course, a worker you hire might display some characteristics of both categories, which makes it harder to say for sure how that worker should be classified. Ultimately, you'll need to consider all these factors and weigh them against each other to decide whether a worker should be classified as an employee or as an independent contractor.

EXAMPLE 1: Bob does a lot of freelance proofreading for a publisher of books on alternative health, Wholeness Press. He often works for Wholeness Press (about ten projects per year), but he also does four or five jobs per year for other publishers. He always works at home, receives minimal instructions as to how to do his work, and does his proofreading whenever he feels like it. Bob can probably be categorized as an independent contractor.

EXAMPLE 2: Susan programs almost exclusively for one software developer, Fizz Games, but she also does approximately one outside project per year. She sometimes works from home, but often uses a computer at Fizz Games' office. She works closely with the software development team at Fizz Games, following instructions from some of the developers while training some of the newer

workers in programming techniques. The government is likely to see Susan as an employee. It would be risky to try to treat her as an independent contractor.

In borderline situations, it's safer to treat a worker as an employee than risk the penalties that may result if the IRS or the EDD decides you've misclassified an employee as an independent contractor. Keep in mind that the IRS and the EDD tend to disfavor independent contractor status. They'd much rather see borderline workers classified as employees, so that they can collect taxes on them.

If you can't decide how one of your workers should be classified, there are a few ways you can proceed. One is to consult a lawyer or an accountant who understands business tax laws. Another option is to go straight to the horse's mouth and ask the IRS or the EDD to tell you how they would classify a certain worker. You can file Form SS-8, *Determination of Worker Status,* to request a formal ruling from the IRS on a worker's status. You can get this form from an IRS office or from the agency's website at www.irs.gov, and a copy is in Appendix C and on the CD-ROM that goes with this book.

As mentioned, however, don't be surprised if the IRS classifies your worker as an employee. For an EDD determination, file Form DE 1870, *Determination of Employment Taxes and Personal Income Tax Withholding,* which is also available online or from an EDD office (see www.edd.ca.gov for contact information for the EDD). Like the IRS, the EDD commonly classifies workers as employees rather than independent contractors. You'll have to decide for yourself whether it makes sense to leave the determination up to these agencies, or whether you feel confident enough to classify your workers on your own.

SKIP AHEAD

For businesses with ICs only. If you decide that all of your workers will be independent contractors, the rest of the rules in this chapter won't apply to you. You may still want to read on, however, if you'd like to get an overview of the regulations that apply to businesses with employees.

Classifying Workers: Don't Make the Same Mistake Microsoft Did

Who would think that lowly temporary workers would be able to beat Microsoft, one of the world's mightiest economic juggernauts? But that's just what they did, which should be a lesson to all businesses that hire independent contractors. Like many software companies, Microsoft supplemented its regular core of employees with a pool of workers it classified as "freelancers," paying them cash compensation (sometimes more than its employees) but providing them with none of the fringe benefits available to regular employees. Microsoft had the workers sign agreements specifying that they were ICs, which meant Microsoft wouldn't give them fringe benefits or withhold or pay any taxes for them.

The problem with Microsoft's designation of these workers as ICs was that it failed to treat them like ICs—that is, people running their own independent businesses. Instead, Microsoft integrated the workers into its workforce: They often worked on teams along with regular employees, sharing the same supervisors, performing identical functions, and working the same core hours. And because Microsoft required that they work onsite, they received admittance card keys, office equipment, and supplies from the company. Microsoft's treatment of the workers clearly spelled out "employee," not IC.

When the IRS audited the company's payroll tax accounts in 1989 and 1990, it determined that Microsoft treated the workers as employees—not ICs who control the manner and means of how their services are performed—and therefore, owed employment taxes for them. Microsoft agreed with the IRS and admitted that the workers should have been classified as employees for tax purposes. The company paid back-payroll taxes and overtime for the workers and moved some of them to permanent employee status.

Upon learning of the IRS's decision, eight of the formerly misclassified workers sued Microsoft for full employee benefits for the time they worked as independent contractors. The workers finally won their lawsuit, and Microsoft had to pay a small fortune to its misclassified workers. (*Vizcaino v. Microsoft Corp.*, 120 F.3d 1006 (9th Cir. 1997).)

This case demonstrates that merely having a worker sign an agreement that he or she is an IC will not change the worker's status in the eyes of the law. Rather, the worker must be treated like an IC on the job. Because the penalties for misclassification can be severe, make sure that everyone who deals with ICs in your company understands that they can't be supervised or otherwise controlled in the same way as employees.

CAUTION

Hiring ICs triggers some requirements. If you pay any independent contractor over $600 in a year, you need to report those payments on IRS Form 1099-MISC, then send it to the worker and to the IRS. In addition, if you are required to file a federal 1099-MISC (*Miscellaneous Income*), you must also report certain information about that contractor to the EDD. More information about this requirement is available from the EDD; see www.edd.ca. gov. For in-depth information about hiring independent contractors, see *Working With Independent Contractors*, by Stephen Fishman (Nolo).

Special Hurdles for Employers

As soon as you hire your first employee, you unleash a swarm of legal requirements that apply specifically to employers. Not only will you have to pay a number of employment taxes, but you'll also need to register with certain government agencies, pay for certain types of insurance, and comply with various laws, such as those requiring you to keep a smoke-free workplace and to post certain notices at your business premises.

Though the many laws that apply to employers are beyond the scope of this book, here's an overview of the major requirements that apply to businesses with employees. If you can't meet your needs by hiring an independent contractor and you must hire an employee, you'll need to consult additional resources to make sure you comply with the many state and federal laws governing employers. (Some additional resources are included at the end of this chapter.)

In general, owners of businesses with one or more employees are required to take a number of steps.

- Report all new hires to the EDD within 20 days of the employee's first day of work, as part of the New-Employee Registration Program—a government system designed to help states track down parents who owe child support. (See www.edd.cahwnet.gov; click on the "Payroll Taxes" tab, then the "Reporting Requirements" link.)

- Obtain workers' compensation insurance and follow rules on notifying employees of their rights to workers' compensation benefits. You may purchase this insurance from the State Compensation Insurance Fund (visit online at www.scif.com) or from a private insurance company.

- Comply with state and federal job safety laws, administered by the federal Occupational Safety and Health Administration (OSHA) and California's Department of Industrial Relations, Division of Occupational Safety and Health (DOSH). This includes filing an illness and injury prevention plan, reporting work-related injuries and illnesses that result in lost work time, and keeping a log of all work-related injuries and illnesses. For more information about OSHA regulations, visit the OSHA website at www.osha.gov, or the California OSHA Consultation Services's website at www.dir.ca.gov/DOSH/consultation.html. Or, call the Cal/OSHA assistance line at 800-963-9424.

- Withhold federal income taxes and FICA taxes (which basically consist of Social Security and Medicare taxes) from employees' paychecks and periodically report and send these withheld taxes to the IRS. See IRS Publication 15 (Circular E), *Employer's Tax Guide*, for details.

- Report wages and withholding to each employee and to the IRS with Form W-2.

- Pay the employer's portion of Social Security and Medicare tax for each employee, based on the employee's wages. The employer's portion is the same amount as the employee's share: 7.65% of the employee's wages up to $106,800 in 2009, and 1.45% of wages in excess of that amount.

- Withhold state income taxes from employees' paychecks and periodically deposit them with the Franchise Tax Board.

- Withhold employees' contributions to the State Disability Insurance (SDI) program from their paychecks and periodically deposit them with the state. (See www.edd.ca.gov for current rates; click on the "Payroll Taxes" tab, then the "Rates & Withholding" section.)

- Register and pay the California Unemployment Insurance (UI) tax. The range in 2009 is between 1.5% and 6.2% of the first $7,000 of wages per employee. Unlike disability insurance, the employer is solely responsible for paying unemployment insurance tax and may not deduct it from employees' paychecks. (See www.edd.ca.gov for more information.)

- Pay federal unemployment taxes. It's the sole responsibility of the employer to pay the Federal Unemployment Tax (FUTA) directly to the IRS; you may not deduct it from employees' paychecks. The general rule is that you must pay FUTA taxes if you paid a total of $1,500 or more in wages in any calendar quarter or if you had one or more employees for at least some part of a day in each of 20 or more calendar weeks (not necessarily consecutive) during the year. If you have to pay FUTA taxes, you must pay a 6.2% tax on the first $7,000 of wages that you pay each employee during the year. However, if you paid the state unemployment tax on the same wages on time, you are allowed a state credit of up to 5.4%. The federal tax rate becomes a mere 0.8% after this credit. The FUTA tax is reported annually on IRS Form 940, *Employer's Annual Federal Unemployment Tax Return.*

- Confirm employee eligibility to work in the United States by completing U.S. Citizenship and Immigration Services (USCIS) Form I-9 (available at www.uscis.gov).

Thinking twice about becoming an employer? There's no way around it: Adding employees to your business will greatly complicate your life. (And we haven't even discussed providing optional benefits, such as health insurance and 401(k) plans.)

If there's a way to meet your needs with independent contractors rather than employees, it may be a much more practical road to take. At the very least, you shouldn't jump into hiring employees without having a clear reason to do so.

Hiring and Managing Staff

If you've decided you're ready to take the leap and hire one or more employees, it's essential to hire and manage them with care. Obviously, it's important to hire only those people who can achieve the goals set for them. (This presumes that goals have been set for workers before you start the hiring process—as discussed in more detail below.) These workers will also need ongoing management to make sure they're doing a good job and dealing with any obstacles along the way.

This section outlines a simple, systematic approach to recruiting people to work for your business. The focus of this approach is on creating clearly defined positions and organizing them into an efficient structure.

Determine What Tasks Need to Be Done

The first step in hiring staff is to clearly define what needs to be done. Do you need help answering phones? Managing a retail store? Making donuts? The clearer you are about what needs to be done, the easier it will be for workers to meet these expectations.

Defining tasks can be somewhat overwhelming for business owners in the start-up stage. When considering what you need help with, your initial reaction will probably be, "Everything!" The best way to clear this hurdle is to evaluate your business plan and make sure to develop solid systems for all aspects of your business. For example, you'll want a well-established system or procedure for how the business will provide its products or services, how it will track inventory, what records it will keep and how it will keep them, how it will track employees' time, and so on. When you have sketched out a system for each of the essential tasks of your business, it will be much easier to see specifically what tasks need to be handled. This is where your needs for one or more employees will come into sharper focus.

Create Positions and Job Descriptions

With a solid and realistic task list in hand, the next step is to group tasks together for each position. Certain activities will fall together naturally. For instance, the tasks of answering phones, updating databases, managing office supplies, and doing very basic bookkeeping might combine well into one position. Ordering inventory and managing retail sales might similarly fall into a distinct task set.

Once tasks are grouped together, you can create job positions to handle those areas. The office tasks mentioned above, for instance, could go to an office manager. Tasks such as ordering inventory and managing sales might well be headed by a sales manager. Obviously, how you define specific positions for your business will depend on many different factors.

It's also important to write out a formal job description for each permanent position. Creating a job description for each position not only will help in the hiring process but will also be valuable when it's time to review the employee's performance. Fortunately, writing job descriptions should be easy if you have created the position from a task-based to-do list; the job description can simply restate the list in a slightly more polished form.

Develop Staff Hierarchies

Progressive-minded folks sometimes look at staff hierarchies as undemocratic or somehow oppressive. Without getting into a treatise on the virtues or evils of various types of power structures, suffice it to say that a little structure goes a long way toward ensuring the efficient operation of any organization. That's not to say that it's necessary to create a multilayered, command-and-control reporting system. If your business will have five or more regular employees, however, it's important to take the time to designate clear lines of authority and accountability. In small businesses, this often means that everyone reports to one of the business owners. As the business grows, you'll probably want to add a second layer of managerial accountability—for example, to require marketing associates to report to the sales and marketing manager, not directly to the business owner.

Create Review Procedures

Every business should implement an evaluation procedure before hiring anyone. That way, new employees know what to expect from the very first day. The review procedure needn't be complex; it might simply identify who will participate in reviews, when they will occur, and the criteria by which staff will be measured.

Create an Employee Handbook

A handbook for employees serves a vital role, giving everyone ready access to important information about their jobs. Even more important, creating an employee handbook is a powerful way to minimize the risks posed by anyone that works for your business. As discussed in more detail in Chapter 7, a business's potential risk of a liability or contract lawsuit go way up as soon as you hire even one employee. Not only can that worker potentially harm someone and expose the business to a lawsuit, but he or she also could sue the business for a host of discrimination, wrongful termination, or other claims.

Creating a guidebook that outlines clear policies for employees will go a long way toward minimizing these risks. To create a handbook, the business owner or high-level manager will have to spend some time coming up with a set of rules for employees to follow and procedures the business

will use in dealing with workers. Facing and answering these questions will help ensure that your employment practices are sound. And compiling these policies in a guidebook promotes positive staff relations by demonstrating your business's commitment to fair treatment for all workers according to the same set of rules. By offering clearly stated expectations and procedures for treating employees consistently, a handbook provides a powerful deterrent to future workplace trouble.

Employee handbooks typically include information on:

- hiring
- hours and flex time
- sick and vacation leave
- parental leave
- employee benefits
- performance review procedures
- workplace behavior
- health and safety
- employee privacy
- conflicts of interest
- discrimination and harassment
- grievance procedures, and
- termination.

Lots of new business owners find the prospect of creating a staff handbook too overwhelming in their harried early days. While this is understandable, it's a good idea to tackle the task earlier rather than later—it will be easier to create a handbook before the staff grows large and complex. It's simply unwise to have more than a few employees without a written policy manual.

 RESOURCE

Resources for creating your employee handbook. All businesses with employees would be wise to take this task seriously. An excellent guide is Nolo's *Create Your Own Employee Handbook,* by Lisa Guerin and Amy DelPo. This book walks you step-by-step through creating an employee handbook, explaining the issues and offering sample language you can modify to fit your workplace.

Orient New Employees

When employees come on board, it's important to take some time to introduce them to your world. For efficiency's sake, it's a great idea to create a standard orientation process—it could be a short meeting and video shown in a conference room, a walk-through of the office, or a get-together at your house—to explain the ins and outs of working for the business. If and when you have several employees coming on board at once, you can save time by orienting them as a group.

All new hires should receive basic information about the business, but you'll want to provide a more extensive orientation for higher-level positions. For example, you may want to spend a significant amount of time with a general manager—say, a series of meetings over a few days—to make sure he or she really understands what the business is about and how you want it to be run. This might include discussing the business's history and any past problems that you do not want to see repeated. For regular employees, on the other hand, this much information would be overkill. The point here is to keep those whom you are orienting in mind when deciding what information to include in your orientation sessions.

A good starting point is to provide each new employee with a copy of your employee handbook. Beyond that, the type of orientation may well depend on how many staffers are involved. If you're starting out with just a handful of employees, perhaps a couple of hours of orientation followed by lunch might work. As your staff grows, you may want to have new hires attend presentations by a manager or supervisor. Pairing new employees with experienced ones for a mentorship period is also a good way to bring newcomers on board.

RESOURCE

For more information on being an employer. *The Employer's Legal Handbook*, by Fred S. Steingold, is an indispensable, comprehensive reference for employers that covers the legal rules on hiring, firing, taxes, workplace safety, and much more. First-time employers, see *Hiring Your First Employee*, also by Fred S. Steingold. For practical information and guidance on handling workplace issues—including performance evaluations, investigations, discipline, and firing—see *Dealing With Problem Employees*, by Amy Delpo and Lisa Guerin. Or, if you're strapped for time, but want a quick guide to steering clear of legal problems with your employees, check out *The Manager's Legal Handbook*, by Lisa Guerin and Amy DelPo. For information on hiring independent contractors, be sure to read *Working With Independent Contractors*, by Stephen Fishman. (All are published by Nolo.)

Chapter 15 Checklist: Building Your Business and Hiring Workers

☐ Become familiar with the legal differences between employees and independent contractors.

☐ Before hiring help, determine whether you need to hire employees or whether you could hire independent contractors instead.

☐ Don't avoid your obligations by misclassifying your workers as independent contractors. If the IRS or the EDD decides that your workers are really employees, you can face serious penalties, including payment of back payroll taxes.

☐ Make sure you're ready to take care of all the legal, bureaucratic, and tax requirements that apply to businesses with employees before hiring your first one.

Getting Professional Help

Most business owners, especially sole proprietors and partners in general partnerships, won't need to rely on professional help for the vast majority of their day-to-day business affairs. As the chapters in this book have shown, the legal tasks required to start a business, as well as many of those relating to its ongoing operation, involve nothing more than complying with simple bureaucratic requirements, filling out standard forms, and paying fees.

But life's not always so simple, of course. From time to time, you may find yourself feeling like you're in over your head. Maybe you're struggling to decide whether it's a good time, financially speaking, to expand your business. Or perhaps there's a dispute brewing between you and a business partner. These are just a couple of examples of the types of situations in which an expert can come in handy.

Even when things are running smoothly, virtually every business should at least occasionally consult an accountant or other tax expert for help in preparing tax returns. A tax professional can also help you manage your business's finances to keep down your business taxes. Contacting both a lawyer and a tax professional early in your business life is often a sensible step. As your business grows, you'll be able to consult these experts for help with ongoing questions.

Once you decide you want to hire a professional, your next question very likely will be, "How do I find someone I can trust?" This chapter will offer strategies that will help you find and hire a professional, such as a lawyer or an accountant, who's competent and aboveboard.

Working With Lawyers

Despite the fact that the attorney section of the yellow pages is often the biggest section of the phone book, a good lawyer can be hard to find. This section explains how to find a lawyer who meets your needs and how to make sure you're getting the most for your hard-earned money.

What to Look for in a Lawyer

Make sure to find an attorney who has some experience with small business issues, preferably for your specific type of small business. Plus, you want someone who's intelligent and competent—two qualities that don't necessarily go hand in hand with having a law degree. And, of course, you want a lawyer whom you can trust.

In today's world of ever-increasing specialization, lawyers often focus their areas of expertise rather narrowly. For example, an expert negotiator may not be an effective courtroom lawyer, and vice versa. Make sure that your lawyer can handle the particular type of problem you're facing, in terms of both its subject matter and the type of work involved.

In addition to finding a lawyer with the skills and experience relevant to your situation, it's important that you and the lawyer get along on a personal level. If an otherwise perfect lawyer—smart, experienced, and trustworthy—is condescending or rude, you should keep looking for someone with better personal skills. This general rule is especially true for a small business owner, who will ideally develop a long-term relationship with a lawyer. An attorney who knows you and your business will be better equipped to provide the best advice and assistance for your specific situation.

Finally, you may want to make a special effort to find a lawyer who is willing to work with you collaboratively on certain matters that you can handle at least partially on your own. Handling some routine legal issues, such as amending your partnership agreement or executing a contract for services, may be well within your abilities, though you may be more comfortable having a lawyer review your work or give you limited advice. While lawyers traditionally offered their services on an all-or-nothing basis (and charged fees accordingly), a trend has recently emerged where lawyers act as coaches for their clients, giving only as much service as the clients want. (See "Using a Lawyer as a Coach," below.)

How to Find a Lawyer

Unfortunately, the easiest and quickest ways to find a lawyer are usually the least effective. Sure, you'll find hundreds of lawyers' names in the yellow pages, but how will you choose among them? You'll have the same problem if you look in legal newspapers for attorney ads or check out lawyer referral services operated by bar associations because you don't always know what you're getting in terms of the lawyers' expertise and skills. By the way, flashy, aggressive advertising is not necessarily a good indicator of quality legal services.

RESOURCE

Check out Nolo's Lawyer Directory. Nolo offers a lawyer directory at http://lawyers.nolo.com. The Nolo directory offers comprehensive profiles of the lawyers who advertise there, including each attorney's education, background, areas of expertise, fees, and practice philosophy—including whether the lawyer is willing to review documents or coach clients who are doing their own legal work. Nolo has confirmed that every attorney advertiser has a valid license and is in good standing with the state bar association where the attorney practices.

The best way to find a good lawyer is to get a personal referral, such as from your accountant or banker, but preferably from another person who runs a small business. Even better is a referral from someone who owns a business that's similar to yours. Book publishers, for instance, face different types of legal issues than do auto repair shops, and would be best served by a lawyer familiar with legal areas such as copyright and freedom of speech.

If you just can't find anyone who can give you a personal referral, try investigating lawyers who work in your industry. One good way to do this is to keep your eyes and ears open for names of attorneys who have worked on cases in your field. For example, a trade magazine might have an article about a current lawsuit involving a business similar to yours and mention the names of the attorneys working on it. You can also contact organizations and visit websites that focus on your type of business. They can often direct you to lawyers who have worked in your

industry. Once you get some names, try calling those lawyers and asking if they're available. If not, there's a good chance they will know someone else who might be able to help you.

TIP

Speak with the lawyer personally. You can probably get a good idea of how the attorney operates by paying close attention to the way your initial call is handled. Is the lawyer available right away, and, if not, is your call promptly returned? Is the lawyer willing to spend at least a few minutes talking with you to determine whether the two of you are a good fit? Do you get a good feeling from your conversation? The way you're treated during your initial call can be a good indicator of how the lawyer treats clients in general.

Using a Lawyer as a Coach

In a traditional attorney/client relationship, a client hires an attorney to take care of a legal problem and then hands over all responsibility for—and control over—the matter to the lawyer. Though some clients like it this way, many would rather be more involved in their cases, both to maintain some control and to save money on legal fees. But until recently, limited legal help from a lawyer wasn't much of an option. Most lawyers wouldn't take cases unless they could handle them fully on their own.

A new model of legal services has finally emerged. In this approach, sometimes called "legal coaching" or "unbundled legal services," a lawyer provides only the services that a client wants, and nothing more. For example, a client who wants legal help in drafting a contract can arrange a short consultation with a lawyer to get answers to general questions, go home and draft the contract, then fax it to the lawyer, who will review it and suggest changes. Or a client who wants to represent himself or herself in small claims court can use a lawyer to help draft motions and prepare for hearings, but otherwise pursue the case alone.

For the owner of a small business, using a lawyer as a coach can be especially useful. More often than not, the legal issues that arise in the course of business are relatively simple, and—with a bit of good legal advice—most businesspeople can handle them fairly easily. Many times, a business owner needs nothing more than some guidance through the bureaucratic maze that small businesses need to navigate. For instance, a businessperson facing a zoning conflict may be perfectly served by a five-minute explanation from a legal coach on the process of appealing a planning commission's decision. Rather than hiring an attorney for upwards of $1,000 to deal with the problem, using a coach might cost $50 and enable the business owner to proceed alone.

Despite the good sense of this approach, it still can take some effort to find a lawyer who is willing to be just a coach. To find a legal coach, use the same strategies discussed above (personal referrals, for example) but take the extra step of asking the lawyer directly whether he or she is willing to help you in your efforts to solve your own legal problems. If you don't find one right away, be persistent.

Dealing With Bills and Payments

Before you hire any lawyer, be sure you fully understand how your fees will be calculated. All too often, clients are unpleasantly surprised by their bills because they didn't pay enough attention to the billing terms when they hired the lawyer. For instance, make sure you understand who's responsible for paying for things such as court fees, copy fees, transcription costs, and phone bills. These costs aren't trivial and can quickly send your otherwise affordable bill into the keep-you-awake-at-night range.

Lawyers generally use one of the following methods of calculating fees for their services:

- **Hourly fees.** This arrangement works just like it sounds: You pay an hourly rate for the number of hours the attorney spends working on your case. Simple as this system is, there are some details to consider. First, find out what hourly increments the lawyer uses for billing. For instance, if an attorney bills in half-hour increments, you'll be charged for a full half-hour even if you talk for just five minutes. That can easily total $100 or more for a five-minute phone call—a rate that would make even AT&T blush. You'd be better off if your lawyer

uses ten- or 15-minute periods, though not all attorneys break down their time into such small increments.

Another issue to ask about is whether all time spent on the case—even if the attorney isn't doing the work—is billed at the attorney's regular rate. For example, it's reasonable to expect a discounted rate for time spent by the attorney's administrative staff on making copies or organizing paperwork. Make sure that the hourly fee for the attorney applies only to the work of the actual attorney.

Hourly fees for attorneys range from $100 or so to over $400 per hour. High rates may reflect a lawyer's extensive experience—or they might simply reflect a need to pay for a swank office. Don't pay the highest rates unless you feel the lawyer's expertise—not that Armani suit—is worth it.

- **Flat fees.** For some types of cases, attorneys will charge a flat fee for a specific task, such as negotiating a contract or filing Articles of Incorporation. As long as the job goes as expected, you'll pay only the agreed-upon price, regardless of how many hours the lawyer spent on the job. If the lawyer hits a snag, however, or if the case becomes convoluted for some reason, the price can go up. Be sure you and the lawyer are on the same page regarding the situations that may result in a higher fee. Also, find out if any expenses, such as court costs or copy fees, are charged in addition to the flat fee.

- **Contingency fees.** In a contingency fee arrangement, you pay an attorney's fee only if the lawyer wins money for you through a court judgment or negotiated settlement. In that case, the fee you'd pay would be a percentage of the monetary award, usually one-third to one-half. In contingency fee arrangements, you need to be especially careful of costs such as travel expenses, transcription fees, and phone bills. If you lose your case, you won't owe attorneys' fees (because your lawyer didn't recover any money), but you will often be responsible for the lawyer's out-of-pocket expenses accrued while working on your case.

Small business matters don't typically require contingency fee arrangements. This payment method is usually used in personal injury cases and others in which a plaintiff sues someone in hopes of winning a large money award.

- **Retainers.** Sometimes you can hire a lawyer to be more or less "on call" by paying a regular fee (usually monthly) called a retainer. This type of arrangement is useful when you have regular, ongoing legal needs, such as contract review or negotiation. Based upon your expected needs, you and the lawyer settle on a mutually acceptable monthly fee. Then, you simply have the lawyer take care of any routine legal matters that arise. If you run into a sudden, complex legal dispute or if your problems escalate greatly, you'll likely have to make additional payments. For this type of arrangement to work, it's important that you and the lawyer have a clear understanding of the routine services that you expect. Unless your legal needs are regular and predictable, a retainer arrangement is probably not your best option.

By California law, your fee agreement must be in writing if your lawyer estimates the total cost of legal services to be more than $1,000, or if you have a contingency fee arrangement. Even if it's not legally required, it's always a good idea to get your fee agreement in writing. A written agreement will help prevent disputes over billing and is the best way to avoid getting gouged.

Working With Accountants and Other Financial Professionals

Many of the issues that small businesses face can be solved by professionals other than lawyers. In particular, tax professionals are often indispensable in helping you deal with tax laws, which have a huge impact on your business both financially and legally. In fact, tax advice is so essential to a successful small business that we recommend that every small business owner consult with a tax expert at least occasionally—say, once a year.

Obviously, you want to manage your business and the money flowing through it so as to minimize your tax bill. But you also need to be extremely careful not to violate any tax laws—which are insanely complex—and to avoid making simple mistakes that can result in costly penalties. Complicated tax troubles may indeed call for a tax attorney, but many other more common questions can be answered by an accountant.

Matching People to Your Needs

For routine maintenance of your books, you probably don't need the experience—or expense—of an accountant (certified or otherwise). An experienced bookkeeper will be able to implement an effective system of tracking your income and expenses and staying on top of your important bills, including the various taxes your business will owe. Depending on the complexity of your business, you may even decide to do your own bookkeeping—a job that's undoubtedly easier these days with the availability of accounting software. As your business grows, however, an experienced bookkeeper will likely become an invaluable investment.

If you find yourself seeking specific tax advice or encountering a tricky financial problem, you may need to go up a step on the professional ladder and hire an accountant who's intimate with tax laws. The top dogs of accountants are called certified public accountants (CPAs) and are licensed and regulated by the state. California also licenses uncertified accountants called public accountants. Because the licensing requirements for CPAs are more stringent, these accountants are considered to be the most experienced and knowledgeable, and accordingly will be the most expensive.

In addition to bookkeepers and accountants, there are other professionals out there who specialize in tax preparation. The main thing to keep in mind is that some are licensed and some are not. An enrolled agent (EA) is a tax professional, licensed by the IRS, who can answer tax questions and help you prepare your returns. Others who simply use the title "tax preparer" or "tax return preparer" may not be licensed at all. If a tax professional doesn't have a license as an enrolled agent or as a public or certified public accountant, it may mean that the "professional" has no official qualifications whatsoever.

The bottom line is that you should hire the person who is best equipped to meet your particular needs. Obviously, you shouldn't pay a CPA to do simple bookkeeping, nor should you use a bookkeeper for preparing complex tax returns.

Finding Good Professional Help

Finding a tax professional is a lot like finding a lawyer: Your goal is to find someone both competent and trustworthy. The strategies discussed above for finding a lawyer are equally useful in finding other professionals. Getting a personal referral is the best way to find someone you can trust. Referrals from businesspeople in your field are particularly valuable. Since virtually every business has consulted a tax pro at one point or another, it shouldn't be too hard to get a decent list of names.

As with attorneys, choose your tax professional carefully, with an eye to developing a long-term relationship. Don't be shy about asking questions. Find out about the person's experience with small businesses similar to yours, and about his or her knowledge of bookkeeping methods, the tax code, the IRS, or anything else that's relevant to the work you want the professional to do for you.

Also be sure you understand the professional's fee structure up front, before he or she does any work. Most charge hourly fees, which vary a great deal depending on what kind of qualifications the professional has. Like your attorney fee agreement, your fee agreement with a tax professional should be in writing; written fee agreements reduce the possibility of disputes over the bill.

Internet Legal Research

Some of the legal questions you may run into won't warrant an expensive consultation with an attorney, but may be beyond the scope of a self-help book. For instance, you may need to look up specific consumer protection regulations on warranties and advertising or find out what California's rules are on hiring and firing practices. If you don't want to call your lawyer every time you have a question, you might consider doing a little legal research yourself.

Finding basic small business law is usually not difficult—much of the information you'll need can be found on the Internet. Start by visiting Nolo's website at www.nolo.com and checking under the "Business, LLCs & Corporations" tab to see if your question has already been answered or to get some background information in the area of the law in which you're interested.

Here are some other websites that offer helpful information on small business and tax law:

- National Federation of Independent Business at www.nfib.com. Here you can find small business news and practical information.
- Internal Revenue Service at www.irs.gov. You can download forms and instructions as well as a wide range of publications that do a fairly good job of explaining the tax laws.
- U.S. Small Business Administration at www.sba .gov. This site has a lot of good information on starting and financing your own business. The SBA also offers links to state websites related to business issues.
- SCORE (Service Corps of Retired Executives) at www.score.org. SCORE's association of retired executives and business owners offers email counseling and mentoring and an excellent directory of small business resources on the Web.
- A great resource for information on California law is the Official California Legislative Information website at www.leginfo.ca.gov. It offers searchable databases of existing California law, as well as pending legislation.
- The Thomas Legislative Information site at http://thomas.loc.gov. Here you can read small business bills pending in Congress as well as laws that have recently been adopted.

RESOURCE

Help with legalese. If, during your legal meandering, you come across strange phrases like "blue sky," "naked option," or "commercial frustration," and you just know there's got to be a legal meaning behind them, try looking them up in Nolo's Plain-English Law Dictionary at www.nolo.com under the "Legal Encyclopedia" tab.

RESOURCE

More help with legal research. This chapter has given you a few helpful hints on getting answers to your small business questions, but there may be times when you'll need more guidance. For basic advice on doing legal research and checking out federal, state, and local laws, see the Legal Research section (under the "Legal Encyclopedia" tab) at www.nolo.com. An excellent resource that teaches you how to find answers to your legal questions is Nolo's book *Legal Research: How to Find & Understand the Law*, by Stephen R. Elias and the Editors of Nolo. Learning how to use legal resources online or at the law library will empower you to take care of a wide range of simple, everyday matters yourself rather than paying someone else to handle them.

Chapter 16 Checklist: Getting Professional Help

☐ Ask business associates and friends for recommendations for lawyers, as well as accountants or other tax professionals. Also check trade magazines and other industry sources.

☐ Try to find a lawyer who will work as a legal coach, if that approach appeals to you.

☐ Get your fee agreements in writing.

☐ Become familiar with online sources of legal information, such as nolo.com, the IRS website (www.irs.gov), and the legislative information site of the State of California (www.leginfo.ca.gov).

California Small Business Resources and Contact Information

This appendix offers names and website addresses for various government agencies (federal, state of California, and county clerk/recorders' offices in California) plus associations that deal with businesses and taxes for California. If a resource can be located on the Web, its website address, along with information about what's available online, is included here. There's also a separate section for interactive websites—those that offer more than merely another way to contact a particular office. For instance, the searchable federal trademark database gets its own listing under "Websites," even though it's also listed in the "Government Agencies" section under the U.S. Patent and Trademark Office.

Government Agencies

Government agencies are a lot like Russian dolls: One office often contains another office, which often contains yet another office, in a long, confusing chain of government subbranches. Getting the right phone number and the right government clerk can be incredibly frustrating. Be patient, and be persistent. Don't be afraid to ask questions. Do your best to explain what or who you need as clearly as you can; the clerk on the other end of the line is often your best source of accurate contact information.

Internal Revenue Service (IRS)

Find the IRS before it finds you. In addition to collecting income taxes, the IRS is also in charge of issuing federal employer identification numbers (FEINs, sometimes called EINs) to new businesses. For general questions on taxes, forms, or FEINs, call 800-829-4933. You can also visit the IRS on the Web at www.irs.gov. If you have a computer, a printer, and Internet access, getting forms and instructions online is convenient—and much more pleasant than spending an eternity on hold.

Small Business Administration (SBA)

The SBA specializes in assisting small businesses with financing, often by guaranteeing loans. If your small business is having trouble securing a loan through a bank, the SBA may guarantee all or part of it, which will make the bank much more likely to approve the loan. There are many different SBA loan programs that you can learn about at a local SBA office; contact information for district offices appears below. Or visit the SBA online at www.sba.gov.

San Francisco SBA District Office
455 Market Street, 6th Floor
San Francisco, CA 94105-2420
415-744-6820

Sacramento SBA District Office
6501 Sylvan Road, Suite 100
Citrus Heights, CA 95610
916-735-1700

San Diego SBA District Office
550 West C Street, Suite 550
San Diego, CA 92101
619-557-7250

Santa Ana SBA District Office
200 W. Santa Ana Boulevard, #700
Santa Ana, CA 92701
714-550-7420

Fresno SBA District Office
2719 N. Air Fresno Drive, Suite 200
Fresno, CA 93727
559-487-5791

Los Angeles SBA District Office
330 N. Brand Boulevard, Suite 1200
Glendale, CA 91203
818-552-3215

U.S. Patent and Trademark Office (PTO)

The PTO offers federal trademark information and forms. You can call the general information line at 800-PTO-9199 or 571-272-1000. Better yet is to visit the trademark area of the PTO's website, at www .uspto.gov. In addition to the extensive information on trademark law and procedure available online, you can search the PTO's trademark database free and fill out and submit your trademark application electronically.

California Employment Development Department (EDD)

For information on payroll taxes and other rules for employers, contact the EDD at 888-745-3886. Or visit the EDD's website, which offers contact details for the EDD offices in your area and substantive information on the laws that apply to employers. The Web address is www.edd.ca.gov.

California Board of Equalization (BOE)

For sales tax and seller's permit information and forms, contact the California Board of Equalization (BOE) at 800-400-7115. Or visit the BOE's website at www.boe.ca.gov. Many forms and informational pamphlets are available for downloading. You'll also find useful information about property taxes, which are assessed and collected by counties but regulated by the BOE. You can download the free publication, *California Property Tax: An Overview*, which contains lots of valuable information, including calendars of important tax deadlines and contact details for each county assessor.

California Secretary of State

The California Secretary of State handles a number of different business-related issues, including corporate and LLC filings and trademark and service mark registrations. The phone number for general information is 916-653-6814. Or visit the Secretary of State online at www.sos.ca.gov, where you'll find a wide range of information and downloadable forms.

Contact information for local offices follows.

Sacramento Headquarters
1500 11th Street
Sacramento, CA 95814
916-657-5448

Los Angeles Branch
300 S. Spring Street, Room 12513
Los Angeles, CA 90013-1233
213-897-3062

San Diego Branch
1350 Front Street, Suite 2060
San Diego, CA 92101-3690
619-525-4113

The California Franchise Tax Board (FTB)

The FTB is California's version of the IRS. This is the agency that collects state income taxes from individuals, corporations, and LLCs. For general information, call 800-852-5711. Most California tax forms and instructions are also available online. The FTB's Web address is www.ftb.ca.gov.

Associations

The California Small Business Association (CSBA)

As every new entrepreneur quickly learns, city and state laws and regulations—from zoning issues to sales tax laws—have a significant impact on small businesses each and every day. The CSBA is a nonprofit grassroots organization dedicated to advocating the interests of small businesses to government officials. In addition to political activism, this group offers member benefits, such as discounted health insurance and Internet access. Contact CSBA at 800-350-CSBA. Or visit its website at www.csba.com.

California Chamber of Commerce

The California Chamber of Commerce tracks business-related legislation in California and lobbies for business interests. The Chamber also publishes a number of business guides. To find your local chamber, contact the central office at 916-444-6670. Or visit its website at www.calchamber.com.

Graphic Artists Guild (GAG)

The GAG is an excellent resource for anyone in the business of visual art. In advocating for the rights and interests of working artists, GAG has been a leader in the effort to reform California sales tax laws as well as laws regulating home businesses. The Guild is also a good source of information about copyright and contract issues for professional artists. The Northern California chapter of GAG has a website at http://norcal.gag.org.

Websites

CalGOLD

CalGOLD is a website sponsored by the California Environmental Protection Agency, but the help it offers isn't limited to environmental matters. After prompting you to enter a bit of information about the business you're starting, this interactive site directs you to the government agencies whose registration requirements may apply to you. CalGOLD is located at www.calgold.ca.gov.

California Demographic Research Unit

The California Department of Finance sponsors a website by the California Demographic Research Unit, which offers a range of state demographic data. At this site you can obtain a number of different free reports and research papers on California's population, such as the annual percentage growth in each city and county. For small business owners, this information can be really useful—not to mention fascinating. The Web address is www.dof.ca.gov/research.

Franchise Tax Board (FTB)

Download the latest California tax forms at www.ftb.ca.gov.

Board of Equalization (BOE)

Download a seller's permit application and other BOE publications from www.boe.ca.gov.

The Internal Revenue Service (IRS)

Download the latest federal tax forms at www.irs.gov.

U.S. Patent and Trademark Office (PTO)

You can now search the online database of federal trademarks and apply for a trademark online at the website run by the U.S. Patent and Trademark Office. Go to www.uspto.gov.

InterNic

For a list of approved domain name registrars, go to www.internic.net. This site allows you to look up who owns a particular domain name (known as a "whois" search) and offers general information about domain names and the registration process.

County Clerk/Recorders' Offices

Alameda County Clerk
www.acgov.org/auditor/clerk

Alpine County Clerk
www.alpinecountyca.gov

Amador County Recorder
www.co.amador.ca.us

Butte County Clerk-Recorder
http://clerk-recorder.buttecounty.net

Calaveras County Clerk
www.co.calaveras.ca.us/cc

Colusa County Clerk-Recorder
www.colusacountyclerk.com

Contra Costa County Clerk-Recorder
www.co.contra-costa.ca.us

Del Norte County Clerk-Recorder
www.dnco.org

El Dorado County Recorder-Clerk
www.co.el-dorado.ca.us/countyclerk

Fresno County Clerk
www.co.fresno.ca.us

Glenn County Clerk-Recorder
www.countyofglenn.net

Humboldt County Clerk-Recorder
http://co.humboldt.ca.us/portal/business

Imperial County Clerk-Recorder
www.co.imperial.ca.us/recorder

Inyo County Clerk
www.inyocounty.us

Kern County Clerk
www.co.kern.ca.us

Kings County Clerk
www.countyofkings.com

Lake County Clerk-Auditor
www.co.lake.ca.us

Lassen County Clerk
http://lassencounty.org

Los Angeles Register-Recorder/County Clerk
www.lavote.net

Madera County Clerk
www.madera-county.com/countyclerk/clerk

Marin County Clerk-Recorder
www.co.marin.ca.us/depts/CC/main

Mariposa County Clerk
www.mariposacounty.org

Mendocino County Clerk
www.co.mendocino.ca.us/acr/clerk.htm

Merced County Clerk
www.co.merced.ca/us

Modoc County Clerk
www.modoccounty.us

Mono County Clerk
www.monocounty.ca.gov

Monterey County Clerk
www.co.monterey.ca.us/Recorder

Napa County Clerk-Recorder
www.co.napa.ca.us

Nevada County Recorder
www.mynevadacounty.com/recorder

Orange County Clerk-Recorder
http://egov.ocgov.com/ocgov

Placer County Recorder
www.placer.ca.gov/departments/recorder.aspx

Plumas County Clerk
http://countyofplumas.com/clerkrecorder

Riverside County Clerk and Recorder
http://riverside.asrclkrec.com

Sacramento County Business License Section
www.ccr.saccounty.net

San Benito County Clerk
www.san-benito.ca.us

San Bernardino Fictitious Businesses
www.co.san-bernardino.ca.us/ACR

San Diego Recorder-County Clerk
http://arcc.co.san-diego.ca.us

San Francisco County Clerk
www.sfgov.org/site/countyclerk_index.asp

San Joaquin County Recorder
www.sjgov.org/recorder

San Luis Obispo County Clerk-Recorder
www.slocounty.ca.gov/clerk.htm

San Mateo Special Services
www.smcare.org

Santa Barbara County Clerk-Office South
http://sbcassessor.com

Santa Clara County Clerk-Recorder
www.clerkrecorder.org/portal/site/rec

Santa Cruz County Clerk
www.sccoclerk.com

Shasta County Clerk
www.co.shasta.ca.us

Sierra County Clerk-Recorder
www.sierracounty.ws

Siskiyou County Clerk
www.co.siskiyou.ca.us/clerk/index.htm

Solano Tax Collector-County Clerk
www.co.solano.ca.us

Sonoma County Clerk
www.sonoma-county.org/clerk/index.htm

Stanislaus County Clerk
www.co.stanislaus.ca.us

Sutter County Recorder
www.co.sutter.ca.us

Tehama County Clerk-Recorder
www.co.tehama.ca.us

Trinity Recorder
www.trinitycounty.org

Tulare County Clerk-Recorder

www.co.tulare.ca.us

Tuolumne County Clerk

www.tuolumnecounty.ca.gov

Ventura County Clerk

http://recorder.countyofventura.org/venclrk.htm

Yolo County Clerk-Recorder

www.yolorecorder.org

Yuba County Clerk-Recorder

www.co.yuba.ca.us

How to Use the Forms CD-ROM

The CD-ROM included with this book can be used with Windows computers. It installs files that use software programs that need to be on your computer already. It is not a stand-alone software program.

In accordance with U.S. copyright laws, the CD-ROM and its files are for your personal use only.

Please read this appendix and the "Readme.htm" file included on the CD-ROM for instructions on using it. For a list of files and their file names, see the end of this appendix.

Note to Macintosh users: This CD-ROM and its files should also work on Macintosh computers. Please note, however, that Nolo cannot provide technical support for non-Windows users.

Note to eBook users: You can access the CD-ROM files mentioned here from the bookmarked section of the eBook, located on the left-hand side.

How to View the README File

To view the "Readme.htm" file, insert the CD-ROM into your computer's CD-ROM drive and follow these instructions.

Windows XP, Vista, and 7
1. On your PC's desktop, double-click the **My Computer** icon.
2. Double-click the icon for the CD-ROM drive into which the CD-ROM was inserted.
3. Double-click the file "Readme.htm."

Macintosh
1. On your Mac desktop, double-click the icon for the CD-ROM that you inserted.
2. Double-click the file "Readme.htm."

Installing the Files Onto Your Computer

To work with the files on the CD-ROM, you first need to install them onto your hard disk. Here's how.

Windows XP, Vista, and 7

Follow the CD-ROM's instructions that appear on the screen.

If nothing happens when you insert the CD-ROM, then:
1. Double-click the **My Computer** icon.
2. Double-click the icon for the CD-ROM drive into which the CD-ROM was inserted.
3. Double-click the file "Setup.exe."

Macintosh

If the **CA Business Start-Up CD** window is not open, double-click the **CA Business Start-Up CD** icon. Then:
1. Select the **CA Business Start-Up Forms** folder icon.
2. Drag and drop the folder icon onto your computer.

Where Are the Files Installed?
Windows

By default, all the files are installed to the **CA Business Start-Up Forms** folder in the **Program Files** folder of your computer. A folder called **CA Business Start-Up Forms** is added to the **Programs** folder of the **Start** menu.

Macintosh

All the files are located in the **CA Business Start-Up Forms** folder.

Using the Word Processing Files to Create Documents

The CD-ROM includes word processing files that you can open, complete, print, and save with your word processing program. All word processing files come in Rich Text Format and have the extension ".rtf." For example, the form for the partnership agreement discussed in Chapter 1 is on the file "Partnership. rtf." RTF files can be read by most recent word processing programs, including MS *Word*, Windows *WordPad*, and recent versions of *WordPerfect*.

The following are general instructions. Because each word processor uses different commands to open, format, save, and print documents, refer to your word processor's help file for specific instructions.

Do not call Nolo's technical support if you have questions on how to use your word processor or your computer.

Opening a File

You can open word processing files in any of the three following ways:

1. Windows users can open a file by selecting its shortcut.
    i. Click the Windows **Start** button.
    ii. Open the **Programs** folder.
    iii. Open the **CA Business Start-Up Forms** folder.
    iv. Click the shortcut to the file you want to work with.
2. Both Windows and Macintosh users can open a file by double-clicking it.
    i. Use **My Computer** or **Windows Explorer** (Windows XP, Vista, or 7) or the Finder (Macintosh) to go to the **CA Business Start-Up Forms** folder.
    ii. Double-click the file you want to open.
3. Windows and Macintosh users can open a file from within their word processors.
    i. Open your word processor.
    ii. Go to the **File** menu and choose the **Open** command. This opens a dialog box.
    iii. Select the location and name of the file. (Navigate to the version of the **CA Business Start-Up Forms** folder that you've installed on your computer.)

Editing Your Document

Here are tips for working on your document.

- Refer to the book's instructions and sample agreements for help.
- Underlines indicate where to enter information, frequently including bracketed instructions. Delete the underlines and instructions before finishing your document.
- Signature lines should appear on a page with at least some text from the document itself.

Editing Files That Have Optional or Alternative Text

Some files have checkboxes that appear before text. Checkboxes indicate:

- optional text that you can choose to include or exclude, or
- alternative text that you select to include, excluding the other alternatives.

If you are using the tear-out forms in Appendix C, mark the appropriate box to make your choice.

When you are using the CD-ROM, we recommend doing the following:

Optional text

Delete optional text you do not want to include and keep that which you do. In either case, delete the checkbox and the italicized instructions. If you choose to delete an optional numbered clause, renumber the subsequent clauses after deleting it.

Alternative text

Delete the alternatives that you do not want to include first. Then, delete the remaining checkboxes, as well as the italicized instructions to select one of the alternatives provided.

Printing Out the Document

Use your word processor's or text editor's **Print** command to print out your document.

Saving Your Document

Use the **Save As** command to save and rename your document. You will be unable to use the **Save** command because the files are read-only. If you save the file without renaming it, the underlines that indicate where you need to enter your information will be lost, and you will be unable to create a new document with this file without recopying the original file from the CD-ROM.

Using Government Forms

The CD-ROM includes government forms in Adobe Acrobat PDF format. These form files were created by government agencies, not by Nolo.

To use them, you need Adobe *Reader* installed on your computer. If you don't already have this software, you can download it for free at www.adobe.com.

Some of these forms have fill-in text fields. To use such a form:

1. Open a file.
2. Fill in the text fields using either your mouse or the TAB key to navigate from field to field.
3. Print out the form.

Opening a Form

PDF files, like the word processing files, can be opened in any of the three following ways:

1. Windows users can open a file by selecting its shortcut.
    i.   Click the Windows **Start** button.
    ii. Open the **Programs** folder.
    iii. Open the **CA Business Start-Up Forms** subfolder.
    iv. Click the shortcut to the form you want to work with.
2. Both Windows and Macintosh users can open a file directly by double-clicking it.
    i.   Use **My Computer** or **Windows Explorer** (Windows XP, Vista, or 7) or the Finder (Macintosh) to go to the folder you created and copied the CD-ROM's files to.
    ii. Double-click the specific file you want to open.
3. Both Windows and Macintosh users can open a PDF file from within Adobe *Reader*.
    iii. Open Adobe *Reader*.
    iv. Go to the **File** menu and choose the **Open** command. This opens a dialog box.
    v.   Tell the program the location and name of the file. (Navigate through the directory tree to get to the folder on your hard disk where the CD's files have been installed.)

For further assistance, check Adobe *Reader*'s help. Nolo's technical support department is unable to help with the use of Adobe *Reader*.

Filling in a Form

Newer government forms enable you to fill in your form on your computer using Adobe *Reader* 5.1 or higher. If this feature is available, when you open the form you will see a message box about document rights. If you are using an earlier version of Adobe *Reader*, you will be prompted to download a newer version.

Use your mouse or the TAB key to navigate from field to field within these forms. To complete forms without fill-in fields, print them and fill them in either by hand or with a typewriter.

Saving a Filled-In Form

If document rights are enabled, after completing your form onscreen you can save it using *Reader* 5.1 or higher.

If document rights are not enabled, although you cannot save the form, you can print it out.

Using the Spreadsheets

This section concerns the spreadsheet files, which are in Microsoft's *Excel* format and have the extension ".xls." For example, the cash flow projection worksheet discussed in Chapter 4 is on the file "CashFlow.xls." Such files can be opened and edited with Microsoft's *Excel* and other spreadsheet programs that read XLS files.

The following are general instructions. Because each spreadsheet program uses different commands to open, format, save, and print documents, read your spreadsheet program's help files for specific instructions. Nolo's technical support department is unable to assist with your spreadsheet software.

To complete a spreadsheet:

1. Open the file in a spreadsheet program that is compatible with XLS files.
2. Fill in the needed fields.
3. Print out the form.
4. Rename and save your revised file.

Opening a File

There are three ways to open the spreadsheets.

1. Windows users can open a file by selecting its shortcut.
   i. Click the Windows **Start** button.
   ii. Open the **Programs** folder.
   iii. Open the **CA Business Start-Up Forms** subfolder.
   iv. Open the **Business Planning Spreadsheets** subfolder.
   v. Click on the shortcut to the spreadsheet you want to work with.
2. Both Windows and Macintosh users can open a file by double clicking it.
   i. Use **My Computer** or **Windows Explorer** (Windows XP, Vista, or 7) or the **Finder** (Macintosh) to go to the **CA Business Start-Up Forms** folder you installed on your computer.
   ii. Double-click the file you want to open.
3. Windows and Macintosh users can open a file from within their spreadsheet programs. To do this:
   i. Start your spreadsheet program.
   ii. Go to the **File** menu and choose the **Open** command. This opens a dialog box.
   iii. Select the location and name of the file. (Navigate to the **CA Business Start-Up Forms** folder that you installed on your computer.)

Entering Information Into the Spreadsheet

Here are a couple of tips:

- While you are filling in information, you can consult the instructions and sample spreadsheets in the book for help.
- Some spreadsheets are created to perform automatic calculations as you fill the cells.

Printing Out the Spreadsheet

Use your spreadsheet program's **Print** command to print out your document.

Saving Your Spreadsheet

After filling in the form, use **Save As** and rename the file. You will be unable to use the **Save** command because the files are read-only. Saving a file without renaming it overwrites the original spreadsheet. In this case, recopy the original file from the CD-ROM to create a new document.

Files on the CD-ROM

The following word processing files are in Rich Text Format (RTF):

Form Name	File Name
Partnership Agreement	Partnership.rtf
Sample Buy-Sell Agreement Provisions	BuySellSample.rtf

The following government forms are in Portable Document Format (PDF):

Form Name	File Name
IRS Instructions for Form SS-4	iss4.pdf
IRS Form SS-4	fss4.pdf
IRS Form 8716	f8716.pdf
IRS Form SS-8	fss8.pdf
IRS Form 8832	f8832.pdf
California Limited Liability Company Tax Voucher	05_3522.pdf
California Resale Certificate	boe230.pdf
California Application for Seller's Permit and Instructions	boe400spa.pdf
California Swap Meets, Flea Markets, or Special Events Certification	boe410d.pdf
California Board of Equalization Publications Order Form	boe663.pdf
California Sample Articles of Incorporation	corp_artsclose.pdf
California Fictitious Business Name Statement	fictbus.pdf
California LLC Articles of Organization	llc-1.pdf
California Registered Limited Liability Partnership Registration	llp-1.pdf
California Certificate of Limited Partnership	lp-1.pdf

The following business planning spreadsheets are in Microsoft's *Excel* format (XLS):

Form Name	File Name
Cash Flow Projection Worksheet	CashFlow.xls
Profit/Loss Forecast Worksheet	ProfitLoss.xls
Break-Even Analysis Worksheet	BreakEven .xls
Billable Rate Worksheet	BillableRate.xls
Warranty Track Worksheet	Warranty.xls

Tear-Out Forms for California Businesses*

Partnership Agreement

California Registered Limited Liability Partnership Registration

California LLC Articles of Organization

California Sample Articles of Incorporation

California Certificate of Limited Partnership

Application for Employer Identification Number (IRS Form SS-4)

Instructions for IRS Form SS-4

California Fictitious Business Name Statement

California Application for Seller's Permit and Instructions (Individuals, Partnerships, Corporations, and Organizations)

California Resale Certificate

California Swap Meets, Flea Markets, or Special Events Certification (BOE-410-D)

California Board of Equalization Publications Order Form

California Limited Liability Company Tax Voucher (FTB Form 3522)

Entity Classification Election (IRS Form 8832)

Election To Have a Tax Year Other Than a Required Tax Year (IRS Form 8716)

Determination of Worker Status for Purposes of Federal Employment Taxes and Income Tax Withholding (IRS Form SS-8)

* All forms are also included on the CD-ROM included in this book.

Partnership Agreement

1. Partners

_____ (Partners) make the following

Partnership Agreement.

2. Creation of Partnership

As of _____, the Partners agree to enter into a Partnership for the purpose of operating a

business known as: _____

(Partnership Business).

The name of the Partnership (if different from name of Partnership Business) shall be: _____

_____ (Partnership Name).

3. Nature of Partnership Business

The Partnership Business will consist of the following business activities: _____

_____

4. Contributions to the Partnership

The Partners will make the following contributions to the Partnership:

Partner Name	Cash Contribution	Other Contribution (describe property and/or work; give cash value)	Total Contribution Value
	$	Total cash value:	$
	$	Total cash value:	$
	$	Total cash value:	$
	$	Total cash value:	$

5. Profit and Loss Allocation

The Partners will share business profits and losses as follows:

☐ in the same proportions as their contributions to the business

☐ as follows: _____

6. Management of Partnership Business

The Partners will have the following management powers and responsibilities:

☐ The Partners will have equal management powers and responsibilities.

☐ The Partners will share management powers and responsibilities as follows: _____

_____

7. Addition of a Partner

A new Partner may be added to the Partnership under the following conditions:

☐ unanimous vote of all Partners

☐ majority vote of Partners

☐ other conditions: _____

8. Departure of a Partner

A Partner can be expelled by:

☐ unanimous vote of the other Partners

☐ majority vote of the other Partners

Any Partner who leaves voluntarily will give at least 30 days' written notice.

If any Partner leaves the Partnership for any reason, including voluntary withdrawal, expulsion, or death, the Partnership will ☐ survive ☐ dissolve.

If the Partnership survives, the remaining Partner(s) will pay, within a reasonable time, the departing Partner, or the deceased Partner's estate, the fair market value of the departing Partner's share of the business as of the date of his or her departure. The Partnership's accountant will determine the fair market value of the departing Partner's share of the business according to the following method: _____

_____ .

9. Dispute Resolution

If a dispute arises under this Agreement, the Partners agree to first try to resolve the dispute with the help of a mutually agreed-on mediator. Any costs and fees other than attorney fees will be shared equally by the Partners. If it is impossible to arrive at a mutually satisfactory solution, the Partners agree to submit the dispute to binding arbitration in the same city or region, conducted on a confidential basis pursuant to the Commercial Arbitration Rules of the American Arbitration Association.

10. Amendment of Agreement

This agreement cannot be amended without the written consent of all Partners.

11. Partner Signatures

Date: _____   Date: _____

Name: _____   Name: _____

Address: _____   Address: _____

_____   _____

SSN: _____   SSN: _____

Signature: _____   Signature: _____

File #_____

State of California
Secretary of State

REGISTERED LIMITED LIABILITY PARTNERSHIP REGISTRATION

A $70.00 filing fee must accompany this form.
IMPORTANT – Read instructions before completing this form.

This Space For Filing Use Only

1. Name of the registered limited liability partnership or foreign limited liability partnership:
   (End the name with the word "Registered Limited Liability Partnership" or "Limited Liability Partnership" or one of the abbreviations "L.L.P.", "LLP", "R.L.L.P.", or "RLLP.")

2. ☐ Domestic (California) **OR** ☐ Foreign (Not in California) | 3. Jurisdiction

4. Address of the principal office: City   State   Zip Code

5. Name the agent for service of process in this state and check the appropriate provision below:
   _____ which is

   [ ] an individual residing in California. Proceed to item 6.
   [ ] a corporation which has filed a certificate pursuant to California Corporations Code Section 1505. Proceed to item 7.

6. If an individual, California address of the agent for service of process:
   Address
   City   State **CA**   Zip Code

7. Indicate the business in which the limited liability partnership shall engage: (check one)
   ☐ Practice of Architecture   ☐ Practice of Public Accountancy
   ☐ Practice of Law   ☐ Related:_____

8. Indicate whether the limited liability partnership is complying with the alternative security provisions (California Corporations Code 16956[c]): ☐ Yes. Attach Alternative Security Provision (LLP-3) ☐ No

9. Future Effective Date, if any   Month   Day   Year

10. Other matters to be included in this registration may be set forth on separate attached pages and are made a part of this registration. Total number of pages attached, if any:

11. **Declaration:** By filing this Registered Limited Liability Partnership (LLP-1) with the Secretary of State, the partnership named above is registering as a domestic registered limited liability partnership or foreign limited liability partnership. **(DO NOT ALTER THIS STATEMENT)** Further, I declare that I am the person who executed this instrument, which execution is my act and deed.

_____   _____
Signature of Authorized Partner/Person   Type or Print Name of Authorized Partner/Person   Date

12. **RETURN TO:**

    NAME

    FIRM

    ADDRESS

    CITY/STATE

    ZIP CODE

INSTRUCTIONS FOR COMPLETING THE REGISTERED LIMITED LIABILITY PARTNERSHIP REGISTRATION (LLP-1)

DO NOT ALTER THIS FORM
Type or legibly print in black ink.

Statutory filing provisions are found in California Corporations Code Sections 16953 and 16959, unless otherwise indicated.

FILING FEE: The fee for filing the Registered Limited Liability Partnership Registration (LLP-1) is $70 (Government Code Section12189).

For further information contact the Business Filings Section at (916) 657-5448.

- **Make check(s) payable to the Secretary of State.** Send the executed document and filing fee to: California Secretary of State, Document Filing Support Unit, P.O. Box 944228, Sacramento, CA 94244-2280

- The original and at least two copies of the document should be included with your submittal. The Secretary of State will certify two copies of the filed document without charge, **provided that the copies are submitted to this office along with the original to be filed.** Any additional copies submitted with the original will be certified upon request and the payment of the $8.00 (per copy) certification fee.

Fill in the items as follows:

Item 1. Enter the name of the registered limited liability partnership or foreign limited liability partnership. The name of the limited liability partnership shall contain the words "Limited Liability Partnership," "Registered Limited Liability Partnership," or one of the abbreviations "L.L.P.," "LLP," "R.L.L.P.," or "RLLP" (California Corporations Code Section 16952).

Item 2. Check if the registering limited liability partnership is Domestic (California) or Foreign (not in California). If it is a foreign limited liability partnership, attach an original certificate of good standing from an authorized public official of the jurisdiction under which the foreign limited liability partnership was formed. If issuance of such a certificate is not permissible in that jurisdiction, then attach a statement by the foreign limited liability partnership indicating such.

Item 3. Enter the jurisdiction of formation of the foreign limited liability partnership.

Item 4. Enter the complete address, including the zip code, of the principal office. Do not abbreviate the name of the city.

Item 5. Enter the name and address of agent for service of process in this state. The agent for service of process must be an individual residing in California or a corporation which has filed a certificate pursuant to California Corporations Code Section 1505. Check the appropriate provision.

Item 6. If an individual is designated as the agent for service of process, enter an address in California. Do not enter "in care of" (c/o) or abbreviate the name of the city. DO NOT enter an address if a corporation is designated as the agent for service of process.

Item 7. Check the appropriate provision indicating whether the limited liability partnership shall engage in the practice of architecture, the practice of public accountancy, the practice of law, or a related activity as provided in Section 16101(6)(A).

The inclusion of the practice of architecture as a professional limited liability partnership service permitted by Section 16101 commenced January 1, 1999 and shall extend only until January 1, 2012.

Item 8. Upon registering as a registered limited liability partnership or foreign limited liability partnership, and while transacting intrastate business, the limited liability partnership shall provide security for claims against it. Check the appropriate provision indicating whether the limited liability partnership is complying with the alternative security provisions. If the limited liability partnership is complying with such alternative security provisions, attach the Alternative Security Provision using form LLP-3 (California Corporations Code Section 16956[c]).

If the limited liability partnership is not utilizing the Alternative Security Provisions, information regarding the security for claims against the limited liability partnership or foreign limited liability partnership is not required to be filed with the Secretary of State.

Item 9. Enter the future effective date of the Registered Limited Liability Partnership Registration (LLP-1), if any. If none is indicated, the Registration shall be effective upon filing with the California Secretary of State.

Item 10. The Registered Limited Liability Partnership Registration (LLP-1) may include other matters that the person filing the Registration determines to include. If other matters are to be included, attach one or more pages setting forth the other matters. Enter the number of pages attached, if any. All attachments should be 8½" x 11", one-sided and legible.

Item 11. The Registered Limited Liability Partnership Registration (LLP-1) must be executed with the original signatures of one or more partners authorized to execute a registration, if a domestic limited liability partnership, or by an authorized person if a foreign limited liability partnership.

Execution of this document confirms the following statement, which has been preprinted on this form and may not be altered. "BY FILING THIS REGISTERED LIMITED LIABILITY PARTNERSHIP REGISTRATION (LLP-1) WITH THE SECRETARY OF STATE, THE PARTNERSHIP NAMED ABOVE IS REGISTERING AS A DOMESTIC REGISTERED LIMITED LIABILITY PARTNERSHIP OR FOREIGN LIMITED LIABILITY PARTNERSHIP."

Item 12. Enter the name and address of the individual or firm to whom a copy of the filing is to be returned.

LLC-1   File # _____

State of California
Secretary of State

LIMITED LIABILITY COMPANY
ARTICLES OF ORGANIZATION

A $70.00 filing fee must accompany this form.

IMPORTANT – Read instructions before completing this form.

This Space For Filing Use Only

ENTITY NAME (End the name with the words "Limited Liability Company," or the abbreviations "LLC" or "L.L.C." The words "Limited" and "Company" may be abbreviated to "Ltd." and "Co.," respectively.)

1. NAME OF LIMITED LIABILITY COMPANY

PURPOSE (The following statement is required by statute and should not be altered.)

2. THE PURPOSE OF THE LIMITED LIABILITY COMPANY IS TO ENGAGE IN ANY LAWFUL ACT OR ACTIVITY FOR WHICH A LIMITED LIABILITY COMPANY MAY BE ORGANIZED UNDER THE BEVERLY-KILLEA LIMITED LIABILITY COMPANY ACT.

INITIAL AGENT FOR SERVICE OF PROCESS (If the agent is an individual, the agent must reside in California and both Items 3 and 4 must be completed. If the agent is a corporation, the agent must have on file with the California Secretary of State a certificate pursuant to Corporations Code section 1505 and Item 3 must be completed (leave Item 4 blank).

3. NAME OF INITIAL AGENT FOR SERVICE OF PROCESS

4. IF AN INDIVIDUAL, ADDRESS OF INITIAL AGENT FOR SERVICE OF PROCESS IN CALIFORNIA   CITY   STATE   ZIP CODE

CA

MANAGEMENT (Check only one)

5. THE LIMITED LIABILITY COMPANY WILL BE MANAGED BY:

☐ ONE MANAGER

☐ MORE THAN ONE MANAGER

☐ ALL LIMITED LIABILITY COMPANY MEMBER(S)

ADDITIONAL INFORMATION

6. ADDITIONAL INFORMATION SET FORTH ON THE ATTACHED PAGES, IF ANY, IS INCORPORATED HEREIN BY THIS REFERENCE AND MADE A PART OF THIS CERTIFICATE.

EXECUTION

7. I DECLARE I AM THE PERSON WHO EXECUTED THIS INSTRUMENT, WHICH EXECUTION IS MY ACT AND DEED.

_____
DATE

_____
SIGNATURE OF ORGANIZER

_____
TYPE OR PRINT NAME OF ORGANIZER

LLC-1 (REV 04/2007)   APPROVED BY SECRETARY OF STATE

INSTRUCTIONS FOR COMPLETING THE ARTICLES OF ORGANIZATION (FORM LLC-1)

For easier completion, this form is available on the Secretary of State's website at http://www.sos.ca.gov/business/ and can be viewed, filled in and printed from your computer. The completed form along with the applicable fees can be mailed to Secretary of State, Document Filing Support Unit, P.O. Box 944228, Sacramento, CA 94244-2280 or delivered in person to the Sacramento office, 1500 11th Street, 3rd Floor, Sacramento, CA 95814. If you are not completing this form online, please type or legibly print in black or blue ink. This form is filed only in the Sacramento office.

Statutory filing requirements are found in California Corporations Code sections 17051 and 17052. All statutory references are to the California Corporations Code, unless otherwise stated.

FEES: The fee for filing Form LLC-1 is $70.00. There is an additional $15.00 special handling fee for processing a document delivered in person to the Sacramento office. The special handling fee must be remitted by separate check for each submittal and will be retained whether the document is filed or rejected. The preclearance and/or expedited filing of a document within a guaranteed time frame can be requested for an additional fee (in lieu of the special handling fee). Please refer to the Secretary of State's website at http://www.sos.ca.gov/business/precexp.htm for detailed information regarding preclearance and expedited filing services. The special handling fee or preclearance and expedited filing services are not applicable to documents submitted by mail. Check(s) should be made payable to the Secretary of State.

COPIES: The Secretary of State will certify two copies of the filed document(s) without charge, provided that the copies are submitted to the Secretary of State with the document(s) to be filed. Any additional copies submitted will be certified upon request and payment of the $8.00 per copy certification fee.

Pursuant to Section 17375, a domestic limited liability company may not render professional services, as defined in Sections 13401(a) and 13401.3. Professional services are defined as any type of professional services that may be lawfully rendered only pursuant to a license, certification, or registration authorized by the Business and Professions Code, the Chiropractic Act, the Osteopathic Act or the Yacht and Ship Brokers Act. If your business is required to be licensed, certified or registered, it is recommended that you contact the appropriate licensing authority before filing with the Secretary of State's office in order to determine whether your services are considered professional.

Filing this document shall obligate most limited liability companies to pay an annual minimum tax of $800.00 to the Franchise Tax Board pursuant to Revenue and Taxation Code section 17941.

Complete the Articles of Organization (Form LLC-1) as follows:

Item 1. Enter the name of the limited liability company. The name must end with the words "Limited Liability Company," or the abbreviations "LLC" or "L.L.C." The words "Limited" and "Company" may be abbreviated to "Ltd." and "Co.," respectively. The name of the limited liability company may not contain the words "bank," "trust," "trustee," "incorporated," "inc.," "corporation," or "corp.," and must not contain the words "insurer" or "insurance company" or any other words suggesting that it is in the business of issuing policies of insurance and assuming insurance risks.

Item 2. This statement is required by statute and should not be altered. Provisions limiting or restricting the business of the limited liability company may be included as an attachment.

Items 3 & 4 Enter the name of the agent for service of process in California. An agent is an individual, whether or not affiliated with the limited liability company, who resides in California or a corporation designated to accept service of process if the company is sued. The agent should agree to accept service of process on behalf of the limited liability company prior to designation.

If a corporation is designated as agent, that corporation must have previously filed with the Secretary of State, a certificate pursuant to Corporations Code section 1505. Note, **a limited liability company cannot act as its own agent** and no domestic or foreign corporation may file pursuant to Section 1505 unless the corporation is currently authorized to engage in business in California and is in good standing on the records of the Secretary of State.

If an individual is designated as agent, complete Items 3 and 4. If a corporation is designated as agent, complete Item 3 and proceed to Item 5 (do not complete Item 4).

Item 5. Check the appropriate provision indicating whether the limited liability company is to be managed by one manager, more than one manager or all limited liability company members. Only one box may be checked.

Item 6. Attach any other information to be included in Form LLC-1, provided that the information is not inconsistent with law.

Item 7. Form LLC-1 must be signed by the organizer. The person signing Form LLC-1 need not be a member or manager of the limited liability company.

- If Form LLC-1 is signed by an attorney-in-fact, the signature should be followed by the words "Attorney-in-fact for (name of person)."

- If Form LLC-1 is signed by an entity, the person who signs on behalf of the entity should note their name and position/title and the entity name. Example: If a limited liability company ("Smith LLC") is the organizer, the signature of the person signing on behalf of the Smith LLC should be reflected as Joe Smith, Manager of Smith LLC, Organizer.

- If Form LLC-1 is signed by a trust, the trustee should sign as follows:_____, trustee for _____ trust (including the date of the trust, if applicable). Example: Mary Todd, trustee of the Lincoln Family Trust (U/T 5-1-94).

Any attachments to Form LLC-1 are incorporated by reference. All attachments should be 8 ½" x 11", one-sided and legible.

Secretary of State
Business Programs Division

1500 11th Street, 3rd Floor
Sacramento, CA 95814

Business Entities
(916) 657-5448

Organization of California Close Corporations

Business corporations authorized to issue stock, excluding such special organizations as cooperatives, credit unions, etc., are organized pursuant to the General Corporation Law, California Corporations Code, Title 1, Division 1, Chapter 2.

California Corporations Code sections 200-202 outline the minimum content requirements of Articles of Incorporation for stock corporations. California Corporations Code section 158 specifically contains additional provisions for statutory close corporations. The attached sample has been drafted to meet minimum statutory requirements. The sample may be used as a guide in preparing documents to be filed with the Secretary of State. It is suggested that you seek private counsel for advice regarding the proposed corporation's specific business needs, which may require the inclusion of special article provisions, or require the formation of the corporation as a general stock corporation rather than formation as a close corporation. The Secretary of State does not provide a standardized form due to the many possible drafting variations.

Where to File

Documents can be delivered in person (drop off) to any office location between the hours of 8:00 a.m. and 4:30 p.m., Monday through Friday (excluding holidays) or mailed to the Sacramento office. The mailing address and office locations are as follows:

Sacramento Office
Business Entities Section
1500 11th Street, 3rd Floor
Sacramento, CA 95814
(916) 657-5448

Mailing Address
Document Filing Support Unit
P.O. Box 944260
Sacramento, CA 94244-2600

Los Angeles Regional Office
300 South Spring Street, Room 12513
Los Angeles, CA 90013
(213) 897-3062

San Diego Regional Office
1350 Front Street, Suite 2060
San Diego, CA 92101
(619) 525-4113

To facilitate the processing of documents mailed to our Sacramento office, a self-addressed envelope and a letter referencing the corporate name as well as your own name, return address and telephone number should also be submitted. Please refer to our Mail Processing Times webpage at www.sos.ca.gov/business/be/mail-processing-times.htm for current mail processing times.

Note: The regional offices are only able to process organizational documents delivered in person (drop off). Please refer to our Regional Offices webpage at www.sos.ca.gov/business/regional.htm for detailed information regarding the submission of documents to the regional offices.

Fees

The fee for filing Articles of Incorporation for a close corporation is $100.00. A $15.00 special handling fee is applicable for processing documents delivered in person (drop off) to the Sacramento office or to any of the regional offices. The special handling fee is in addition to the filing fee, should be included in a separate check, and will be retained whether the document is filed or rejected.

Fees (continued)

The preclearance and/or expedited filing of a document *within a guaranteed time frame* can be requested in the Sacramento office for an additional fee in lieu of the special handling fee. Please refer to the Secretary of State's website at www.sos.ca.gov/business/be/preclearance-expedited-services.htm for detailed information regarding preclearance and expedited filing services. The special handling fee or preclearance and expedited filings services are not applicable to documents submitted by mail.

Payments for documents submitted:

- by mail to Sacramento can be made by check or money order.
- in person (drop off) at the Sacramento office can be made by check, money order, cash, or credit card (Visa or MasterCard).
- in person (drop off) at a regional office can be made by check, money order, or credit card (Visa or MasterCard). Regional offices are not able to accept cash.

Checks or money orders should be made payable to the Secretary of State.

Copies

The Secretary of State will certify up to two copies of the filed document without charge, **provided that the copies are submitted to the Secretary of State with the document to be filed**. Any additional copies submitted will be certified with payment of $8.00 per copy.

Franchise Tax Requirements

A close corporation is a taxable entity and subject each year to an **$800** minimum franchise tax. Therefore, the corporation must file a return and pay the associated tax every year until the corporation is formally dissolved. For further information regarding franchise tax requirements, refer to the Franchise Tax Board's website at www.ftb.ca.gov or call the Franchise Tax Board at:

From within the United States (toll free) .... (800) 852-5711
From outside the United States (not toll free) .... (916) 845-6500
Automated Telephone Service - From within the United States (toll free) .... (800) 338-0505
Automated Telephone Service - From outside the United States (not toll free)...................... (916) 845-6600

Additional Resources

All corporations are subject to state and federal tax laws and may be subject to additional requirements depending on the type of corporation and/or the type of business conducted. Please refer to our Business Resources webpage at www.sos.ca.gov/business/be/resources.htm for a list of other agencies you may need to contact to ensure proper compliance. Note: The Secretary of State does not license corporations. For licensing requirements, please contact the city and/or county where the principal place of business is located and/or the state agency with jurisdiction over the activities of the corporation.

Organization of California Close Corporations

Close Corporations

The statutory concept of a "close" corporation is often confused with two other concepts having some elements in common. The three differing concepts are as follows:

a) Statutory close corporation, as defined in California Corporations Code section 158.

b) Issuance of shares under a notice filing procedure with the Commissioner of Corporations pursuant to California Corporations Code section 25102(f) or 25102(h).

c) "S" corporation election pursuant to Internal Revenue Code section 1372.

Adding to the confusion, the terms "close" corporation, "closed" corporation or "closely held" corporation are often used in a nontechnical sense simply to describe a corporation having a relatively small number of shareholders.

Each of the three concepts: statutory close corporation, notice filing procedure, and "S" election, is independent of the other two. It is not a condition to the use of the notice filing procedure or to the making of an "S" corporation election that the Articles of Incorporation state that the corporation is a close corporation or limit the number of shareholders of record. Experienced corporate counsel advise that the appropriate use of the statutory close corporation, even among corporations having 35 or fewer shareholders, is infrequent.

There are three differences in the mandatory provisions of Articles of Incorporation forming a statutory close corporation and the Articles of Incorporation forming a general stock corporation; the name style requirement; the inclusion of wording denoting close corporation status; and the reference to the number of persons entitled to hold issued shares.

Organization of California Close Corporations

INSTRUCTIONS:

Articles of Incorporation must be drafted to include all the provisions required by the California Corporations Code. Articles of Incorporation may include other provisions as permitted under California law (e.g., the name and address of each initial director). The attached sample meets the minimum statutory requirements and should only be used as a guide in preparing Articles of Incorporation. The document should be typed with letters in dark contrast to the paper. Documents not suitable for reproduction will be returned unfiled. Note: The file date of Articles of Incorporation is generally the date the document complying with applicable law is received in the Secretary of State's office.

Article I: The articles must include a statement of the name of the corporation.

Note: The name must be exactly as you want it to appear on the records of the California Secretary of State. The name of a close corporation must include the word "corporation", "incorporated" or "limited" or an abbreviation of one of these three words.

Article II: This exact statement is required by the California Corporations Code and should not be altered.

Article III: The articles must include the name of the initial agent for service of process.[1]

- If an individual is designated as agent, include the agent's business or residential **street** address in California (a P.O. Box address is not acceptable). Please do not use "in care of" (c/o) or abbreviate the name of the city.

- If another corporation is designated as agent, do not include the address of the designated corporation.

Note: Before another corporation may be designated as agent, that corporation must have previously filed with the Secretary of State a certificate pursuant to California Corporations Code section 1505. **A corporation cannot act as its own agent** and no domestic or foreign corporation may file pursuant to Section 1505 unless the corporation is currently authorized to engage in business in California and is in good standing on the records of the California Secretary of State.

Article IV: The articles must include a statement of the total number of shares the corporation will be authorized to issue.

Note: Before shares of stock are sold or issued the corporation must comply with the Corporate Securities Law administered by the Department of Corporations. Information regarding permits to issue shares can be obtained from the Department of Corporation's website at www.corp.ca.gov or by calling the Department of Corporations at (213) 573-7500.

Article V: The articles must include a statement that the corporation is a close corporation and must include the number of persons entitled to hold issued shares. Note: The number of persons cannot exceed 35.

Execution: The articles must be signed by each incorporator, or by each initial director named in the articles. If initial directors are named, each director must both sign and acknowledge the articles. Note: If initial directors are not named in the articles, the individual(s) executing the document is the incorporator(s) of the corporation. The name of each incorporator or initial director should be typed beneath their signatures.

---

[1] An "agent for service of process" is an individual (director, officer or any other person, whether or not affiliated with the corporation) who resides in California or another corporation designated to accept service of process if the corporation is sued. Note: The agent must agree to accept service of process on behalf of the corporation prior to designation.

ARTICLES OF INCORPORATION

I

The name of this corporation is _____ *(NAME OF CORPORATION)* _____ .

II

The purpose of the corporation is to engage in any lawful act or activity for which a corporation may be organized under the **General Corporation Law** of California other than the banking business, the trust company business or the practice of a profession permitted to be incorporated by the California Corporations Code.

III

The name and address in the State of California of this corporation's initial agent for service of process is:

Name _____

Address _____

City _____ State **CALIFORNIA** Zip _____

IV

This corporation is authorized to issue only one class of shares of stock; and the total number of shares which this corporation is authorized to issue is _____ .

V

This corporation is a **Close Corporation**. All of the corporation's issued shares of stock, of all classes, shall be held of record by not more than _____ persons.

_____ *(Signature of Incorporator)* _____
(Typed Name of Incorporator), Incorporator

If an individual is designated as the initial agent for service of process, include the agent's business or residential street address in California (a P.O. Box address is not acceptable). If another corporation is designated as the initial agent for service of process, do not include the address of the designated corporation.

This sample is provided to be used as a guideline ONLY in the preparation of the original document for filing with the Secretary of State.

State of California
Secretary of State

LP-1

File # _____

CERTIFICATE OF LIMITED PARTNERSHIP

A $70.00 filing fee must accompany this form.

IMPORTANT – Read instructions before completing this form.

This Space For Filing Use Only

ENTITY NAME (End the name with the words "Limited Partnership" or the abbreviation "LP" or "L.P.")

1. NAME OF LIMITED PARTNERSHIP

INITIAL DESIGNATED OFFICE ADDRESS (Do not abbreviate the name of the city.)

2. ADDRESS OF INITIAL DESIGNATED OFFICE IN CALIFORNIA   CITY   STATE   ZIP CODE

CA

INITIAL AGENT FOR SERVICE OF PROCESS (If the initial agent is an individual, the agent must reside in California and both Items 3 and 4 must be completed. If the initial agent is a corporation, the agent must have on file with the California Secretary of State a certificate pursuant to Corporations Code section 1505 and Item 3 must be completed (leave Item 4 blank).

3. NAME OF INITIAL AGENT FOR SERVICE OF PROCESS

4. IF AN INDIVIDUAL, ADDRESS OF INITIAL AGENT FOR SERVICE OF PROCESS IN CA   CITY   STATE   ZIP CODE

CA

GENERAL PARTNERS (Enter the names and addresses of all the general partners. Attach additional pages, if necessary.)

5a. NAME   ADDRESS   CITY   STATE   ZIP CODE

5b. NAME   ADDRESS   CITY   STATE   ZIP CODE

ADDITIONAL INFORMATION

6. ADDITIONAL INFORMATION SET FORTH ON THE ATTACHED PAGES, IF ANY, IS INCORPORATED HEREIN BY THIS REFERENCE AND MADE A PART OF THIS CERTIFICATE.

EXECUTION (This certificate must be signed by all of the general partners. If additional signature space is necessary, the signatures may be made on an attachment to this certificate.)

7. I DECLARE I AM THE PERSON WHO EXECUTED THIS INSTRUMENT, WHICH EXECUTION IS MY ACT AND DEED.

_____
DATE

_____
SIGNATURE OF GENERAL PARTNER

_____
TYPE OR PRINT NAME OF GENERAL PARTNER

_____
SIGNATURE OF GENERAL PARTNER

_____
TYPE OR PRINT NAME OF GENERAL PARTNER

LP-1 (REV 01/2008)   APPROVED BY SECRETARY OF STATE

INSTRUCTIONS FOR COMPLETING THE
CERTIFICATE OF LIMITED PARTNERSHIP (FORM LP-1)

For easier completion, this form is available on the Secretary of State's website at http://www.sos.ca.gov/business/ and can be viewed, filled in and printed from your computer. The completed form along with the applicable fees can be mailed to Secretary of State, Document Filing Support Unit, P.O. Box 944225, Sacramento, CA 94244-2250 or delivered in person to the Sacramento office, 1500 11th Street, 3rd Floor, Sacramento, CA 95814. If you are not completing this form online, please type or legibly print in black or blue ink. This form is filed only in the Sacramento office.

LEGAL AUTHORITY: Statutory filing requirements are found in California Corporations Code section 15902.01. All statutory references are to the California Corporations Code, unless otherwise stated. **Note:** Signing Form LP-1 constitutes an affirmation under penalty of perjury that the facts stated in the certificate are true. (Section 15902.08(b).)

FEES: The fee for filing Form LP-1 is $70.00. There is an additional $15.00 special handling fee for processing a document delivered in person to the Sacramento office. The special handling fee must be remitted separately for each submittal and will be retained whether the document is filed or rejected. The preclearance and/or expedited filing of a document *within a guaranteed time frame* can be requested for an additional fee (in lieu of the special handling fee). Please refer to the Secretary of State's website at http://www.sos.ca.gov/business/precexp.htm for detailed information regarding preclearance and expedited filing services. The special handling fee or preclearance and expedited filing services are not applicable to documents submitted by mail. Check(s) should be made payable to the Secretary of State.

COPIES: The Secretary of State will certify two copies of the filed document(s) without charge, provided that the copies are submitted to the Secretary of State with the document(s) to be filed. Any additional copies submitted will be certified upon request and payment of the $8.00 per copy certification fee.

MINIMUM TAX REQUIREMENT: Filing this document shall obligate most limited partnerships to pay an annual minimum tax of $800.00 to the Franchise Tax Board pursuant to California Revenue and Taxation Code section 17935.

Complete the Certificate of Limited Partnership (Form LP-1) as follows:

Item 1. Enter the name of the limited partnership. The name must end with the words "Limited Partnership," or the abbreviation "LP" or "L.P." and may not contain the words "bank," "insurance," "trust," "trustee," "incorporated," "inc.," "corporation," or "corp." (Section 15901.08.)

Item 2. Enter the address, including the zip code, of the initial designated office in California. Please do not abbreviate the name of the city. The "designated office" address may, but need not, be the place of the limited partnership's activity in California. (Sections 15901.02(e) and 15901.14.)

Items 3 & 4. Enter the name of the initial agent for service of process in California. An agent is an individual, whether or not affiliated with the limited partnership, who resides in California or a corporation designated to accept service of process if the limited partnership is sued. The agent should agree to accept service of process on behalf of the limited partnership prior to designation. If a corporation is designated as agent, that corporation must have previously filed with the Secretary of State, a certificate pursuant to Corporations Code section 1505. Note: **A limited partnership cannot act as its own agent** and no domestic or foreign corporation may file pursuant to Section 1505 unless the corporation is currently authorized to engage in business in California and is in good standing on the records of the Secretary of State.

If an individual is designated as the initial agent, complete Items 3 and 4. If a corporation is designated as the initial agent, complete only Item 3 and proceed to Item 5 (do not complete Item 4).

Items 5a - 5b. Enter the name and address of each general partner. Please do not abbreviate the name of the city. The limited partnership must have one or more general partners. (Section 15901.02(q).) If there are more than two general partners, please attach additional pages. Note: If a general partner is a trust, both the name of the trust (including the date of the trust, if applicable) and the trustee should be listed. Example: Mary Todd, trustee of the Lincoln Family Trust U/T/A 5-1-94.

Item 6. Attach any other information to be included in Form LP-1 (e.g., the number of general partners' signatures required for filing merger or conversion documents with the California Secretary of State, if less than all) provided that the information is not inconsistent with law.

Item 7. Form LP-1 must be signed by all of the general partners. (Section 15902.04.) If additional signature space is necessary, the signatures may be made on an attachment to Form LP-1.

- If Form LP-1 is signed by any person other than the general partner(s), the signature must be followed by the words "signature pursuant to Section _____" identifying the appropriate statutory authority. (Section 15902.05.)

- If Form LP-1 is signed by an attorney-in-fact, the signature should be followed by the words "Attorney-in-fact for (name of the partner)." (Section 15902.04.)

- If a trust is designated as a general partner, Form LP-1 should be signed by a trustee as follows: _____ trustee for _____ trust (including the date of the trust, if applicable). Example: Mary Todd, trustee of the Lincoln Family Trust (U/T/A 5-1-94).

Any attachments to Form LP-1 are incorporated by reference and made part of Form LP-1. All attachments should be 8 ½" x 11", one-sided and legible.

Secretary of State
Business Programs Division

1500 11th Street, 3rd Floor
Sacramento, CA 95814

Business Entities
(916) 657-5448

LIMITED PARTNERSHIPS

California Tax Information

Registration of a limited partnership with the California Secretary of State will obligate a limited partnership to pay to the Franchise Tax Board an annual minimum tax of $800.00. The tax is required to be paid for the taxable year of registration and each taxable year, or part thereof, until a Certificate of Cancellation is filed with the California Secretary of State. (California Revenue and Taxation Code section 17935.)

A limited partnership is not subject to the taxes imposed by Revenue and Taxation Code section 17935 if the limited partnership did no business in California during the taxable year and the taxable year was 15 days or less. (California Revenue and Taxation Code section 17936.)

For further information regarding franchise tax requirements, refer to the Franchise Tax Board's website at www.ftb.ca.gov or call the Franchise Tax Board at:

From within the United States (toll free) .... (800) 852-5711
From outside the United States (not toll free) .... (916) 845-6500
Automated Service - From within the United States (toll free) .... (800) 338-0505
Automated Service - From outside the United States (not toll free) .... (916) 845-6600

Form **SS-4** (Rev. January 2009) Department of the Treasury Internal Revenue Service	**Application for Employer Identification Number** (For use by employers, corporations, partnerships, trusts, estates, churches, government agencies, Indian tribal entities, certain individuals, and others.) ▶ See separate instructions for each line.　▶ Keep a copy for your records.	OMB No. 1545-0003 **EIN**

Type or print clearly.

1	Legal name of entity (or individual) for whom the EIN is being requested	

2	Trade name of business (if different from name on line 1)	3	Executor, administrator, trustee, "care of" name

4a	Mailing address (room, apt., suite no. and street, or P.O. box)	5a	Street address (if different) (Do not enter a P.O. box.)
4b	City, state, and ZIP code (if foreign, see instructions)	5b	City, state, and ZIP code (if foreign, see instructions)

6	County and state where principal business is located

7a	Name of principal officer, general partner, grantor, owner, or trustor	7b	SSN, ITIN, or EIN

8a	Is this application for a limited liability company (LLC) (or a foreign equivalent)? . . . . ☐ Yes ☐ No	8b	If 8a is "Yes," enter the number of LLC members . . . . ▶

8c　If 8a is "Yes," was the LLC organized in the United States? . . . . ☐ Yes ☐ No

9a Type of entity (check only one box). **Caution.** If 8a is "Yes," see the instructions for the correct box to check.

☐ Sole proprietor (SSN) _____
☐ Partnership
☐ Corporation (enter form number to be filed) ▶ _____
☐ Personal service corporation
☐ Church or church-controlled organization
☐ Other nonprofit organization (specify) ▶ _____
☐ Other (specify) ▶

☐ Estate (SSN of decedent) _____
☐ Plan administrator (TIN) _____
☐ Trust (TIN of grantor) _____
☐ National Guard　☐ State/local government
☐ Farmers' cooperative　☐ Federal government/military
☐ REMIC　☐ Indian tribal governments/enterprises
Group Exemption Number (GEN) if any ▶

9b	If a corporation, name the state or foreign country (if applicable) where incorporated	State	Foreign country

10 Reason for applying (check only one box)

☐ Started new business (specify type) ▶ _____
_____
☐ Hired employees (Check the box and see line 13.)
☐ Compliance with IRS withholding regulations
☐ Other (specify) ▶

☐ Banking purpose (specify purpose) ▶ _____
☐ Changed type of organization (specify new type) ▶ _____
☐ Purchased going business
☐ Created a trust (specify type) ▶ _____
☐ Created a pension plan (specify type) ▶ _____

11	Date business started or acquired (month, day, year). See instructions.	12	Closing month of accounting year

13	Highest number of employees expected in the next 12 months (enter -0- if none).	14	Do you expect your employment tax liability to be $1,000 or less in a full calendar year? ☐ Yes ☐ No (If you expect to pay $4,000 or less in total wages in a full calendar year, you can mark "Yes.")

Agricultural	Household	Other

15 First date wages or annuities were paid (month, day, year). **Note.** If applicant is a withholding agent, enter date income will first be paid to nonresident alien (month, day, year) . . . . ▶

16 Check **one** box that best describes the principal activity of your business.

☐ Construction　☐ Rental & leasing　☐ Transportation & warehousing
☐ Real estate　☐ Manufacturing　☐ Finance & insurance

☐ Health care & social assistance　☐ Wholesale-agent/broker
☐ Accommodation & food service　☐ Wholesale-other　☐ Retail
☐ Other (specify)

17 Indicate principal line of merchandise sold, specific construction work done, products produced, or services provided.

18 Has the applicant entity shown on line 1 ever applied for and received an EIN? ☐ Yes ☐ No
If "Yes," write previous EIN here ▶

Third Party Designee	Complete this section **only** if you want to authorize the named individual to receive the entity's EIN and answer questions about the completion of this form.	
	Designee's name	Designee's telephone number (include area code) ( )
	Address and ZIP code	Designee's fax number (include area code) ( )

Under penalties of perjury, I declare that I have examined this application, and to the best of my knowledge and belief, it is true, correct, and complete.

Name and title (type or print clearly) ▶	Applicant's telephone number (include area code) ( )
Signature ▶　　　　　　　　Date ▶	Applicant's fax number (include area code) ( )

For Privacy Act and Paperwork Reduction Act Notice, see separate instructions.　　Cat. No. 16055N　　Form **SS-4** (Rev. 1-2009)

Do I Need an EIN?

File Form SS-4 if the applicant entity does not already have an EIN but is required to show an EIN on any return, statement, or other document.[1] See also the separate instructions for each line on Form SS-4.

IF the applicant...	AND...	THEN...
Started a new business	Does not currently have (nor expect to have) employees	Complete lines 1, 2, 4a–8a, 8b–c (if applicable), 9a, 9b (if applicable), and 10–14 and 16–18.
Hired (or will hire) employees, including household employees	Does not already have an EIN	Complete lines 1, 2, 4a–6, 7a–b (if applicable), 8a, 8b–c (if applicable), 9a, 9b (if applicable), 10–18.
Opened a bank account	Needs an EIN for banking purposes only	Complete lines 1–5b, 7a–b (if applicable), 8a, 8b–c (if applicable), 9a, 9b (if applicable), 10, and 18.
Changed type of organization	Either the legal character of the organization or its ownership changed (for example, you incorporate a sole proprietorship or form a partnership)[2]	Complete lines 1–18 (as applicable).
Purchased a going business[3]	Does not already have an EIN	Complete lines 1–18 (as applicable).
Created a trust	The trust is other than a grantor trust or an IRA trust[4]	Complete lines 1–18 (as applicable).
Created a pension plan as a plan administrator[5]	Needs an EIN for reporting purposes	Complete lines 1, 3, 4a–5b, 9a, 10, and 18.
Is a foreign person needing an EIN to comply with IRS withholding regulations	Needs an EIN to complete a Form W-8 (other than Form W-8ECI), avoid withholding on portfolio assets, or claim tax treaty benefits[6]	Complete lines 1–5b, 7a–b (SSN or ITIN optional), 8a, 8b–c (if applicable), 9a, 9b (if applicable), 10, and 18.
Is administering an estate	Needs an EIN to report estate income on Form 1041	Complete lines 1–6, 9a, 10–12, 13–17 (if applicable), and 18.
Is a withholding agent for taxes on non-wage income paid to an alien (i.e., individual, corporation, or partnership, etc.)	Is an agent, broker, fiduciary, manager, tenant, or spouse who is required to file Form 1042, Annual Withholding Tax Return for U.S. Source Income of Foreign Persons	Complete lines 1, 2, 3 (if applicable), 4a–5b, 7a–b (if applicable), 8a, 8b–c (if applicable), 9a, 9b (if applicable), 10, and 18.
Is a state or local agency	Serves as a tax reporting agent for public assistance recipients under Rev. Proc. 80-4, 1980-1 C.B. 581[7]	Complete lines 1, 2, 4a–5b, 9a, 10, and 18.
Is a single-member LLC	Needs an EIN to file Form 8832, Classification Election, for filing employment tax returns and excise tax returns, or for state reporting purposes[8]	Complete lines 1–18 (as applicable).
Is an S corporation	Needs an EIN to file Form 2553, Election by a Small Business Corporation[9]	Complete lines 1–18 (as applicable).

[1] For example, a sole proprietorship or self-employed farmer who establishes a qualified retirement plan, or is required to file excise, employment, alcohol, tobacco, or firearms returns, must have an EIN. A partnership, corporation, REMIC (real estate mortgage investment conduit), nonprofit organization (church, club, etc.), or farmers' cooperative must use an EIN for any tax-related purpose even if the entity does not have employees.

[2] However, do not apply for a new EIN if the existing entity only (a) changed its business name, (b) elected on Form 8832 to change the way it is taxed (or is covered by the default rules), or (c) terminated its partnership status because at least 50% of the total interests in partnership capital and profits were sold or exchanged within a 12-month period. The EIN of the terminated partnership should continue to be used. See Regulations section 301.6109-1(d)(2)(iii).

[3] Do not use the EIN of the prior business unless you became the "owner" of a corporation by acquiring its stock.

[4] However, grantor trusts that do not file using Optional Method 1 and IRA trusts that are required to file Form 990-T, Exempt Organization Business Income Tax Return, must have an EIN. For more information on grantor trusts, see the Instructions for Form 1041.

[5] A plan administrator is the person or group of persons specified as the administrator by the instrument under which the plan is operated.

[6] Entities applying to be a Qualified Intermediary (QI) need a QI-EIN even if they already have an EIN. See Rev. Proc. 2000-12.

[7] See also *Household employer* on page 4 of the instructions. **Note.** State or local agencies may need an EIN for other reasons, for example, hired employees.

[8] See *Disregarded entities* on page 4 of the instructions for details on completing Form SS-4 for an LLC.

[9] An existing corporation that is electing or revoking S corporation status should use its previously-assigned EIN.

Instructions for Form SS-4

(Rev. January 2009)

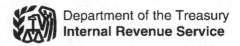

Department of the Treasury
Internal Revenue Service

Application for Employer Identification Number

Section references are to the Internal Revenue Code unless otherwise noted.

What's New

Disregarded entities. Beginning in 2008, disregarded entities, including single-member limited liability companies (LLCs) that are disregarded as separate from their owner and qualified subchapter S subsidiaries, are required to file certain excise tax returns using the disregarded entity's name and EIN rather than its owner's name and EIN. This new filing requirement for disregarded entities also applies to employment tax returns, effective for wages paid on or after January 1, 2009. Disregarded entities not previously needing an EIN may now need to obtain an EIN for the payment and reporting of these taxes. See *Disregarded entities* on page 4 for details.

General Instructions

Use these instructions to complete Form SS-4, Application for Employer Identification Number. Also see *Do I Need an EIN?* on page 2 of Form SS-4.

Purpose of Form

Use Form SS-4 to apply for an employer identification number (EIN). An EIN is a nine-digit number (for example, 12-3456789) assigned to sole proprietors, corporations, partnerships, estates, trusts, and other entities for tax filing and reporting purposes. The information you provide on this form will establish your business tax account.

 An EIN is for use in connection with your business activities only. Do not use your EIN in place of your social security number (SSN).

Reminders

Apply online. Generally, you can apply for and receive an EIN online using the Internet. See *How To Apply* later.

 This is a free service offered by the Internal Revenue Service at www.irs.gov. Beware of websites on the Internet that charge for this free service.

File only one Form SS-4. Generally, a sole proprietor should file only one Form SS-4 and needs only one EIN, regardless of the number of businesses operated as a sole proprietorship or trade names under which a business operates. However, if the proprietorship incorporates or enters into a partnership, a new EIN is required. Also, each corporation in an affiliated group must have its own EIN.

EIN applied for, but not received. If you do not have an EIN by the time a return is due, write "Applied For" and the date you applied in the space shown for the number. Do not show your SSN as an EIN on returns.

If you do not have an EIN by the time a tax deposit is due, send your payment to the Internal Revenue Service Center for your filing area as shown in the instructions for the form that you are filing. Make your check or money order payable to the "United States Treasury" and show your name (as shown on Form SS-4), address, type of tax, period covered, and date you applied for an EIN.

Electronic filing and payment. Now, more than ever before, businesses can enjoy the benefits of filing and paying their federal taxes electronically. Whether you rely on a tax professional or handle your own taxes, IRS offers you convenient programs to make filing and paying easier. Spend less time and worry on taxes and more time running your business. Use e-file and the Electronic Federal Tax Payment System (EFTPS) to your benefit.
- For e-file, visit *www.irs.gov* for additional information.
- For EFTPS, visit *www.eftps.gov* or call EFTPS Customer Service at 1-800-555-4477, 1-800-733-4829 (TDD), or 1-800-244-4829 (Spanish).

Federal tax deposits. New employers that have a federal tax obligation will be pre-enrolled in the Electronic Federal Tax Payment System (EFTPS). EFTPS allows you to make all of your federal tax payments online at *www.eftps.gov* or by telephone. Shortly after we have assigned you your EIN, you will receive instructions by mail for activating your EFTPS enrollment. You will also receive an EFTPS Personal Identification Number (PIN) that you will use to make your payments, as well as instructions for obtaining an Internet password you will need to make payments online.

If you are not required to make deposits by EFTPS, you can use Form 8109, Federal Tax Deposit (FTD) Coupon, to make deposits at an authorized depositary. If you would like to receive Form 8109, call 1-800-829-4933. Allow 5 to 6 weeks for delivery. For more information on federal tax deposits, see Pub. 15 (Circular E), Employer's Tax Guide.

How To Apply

You can apply for an EIN online, by telephone, by fax, or by mail depending on how soon you need to use the EIN. Use only one method for each entity so you do not receive more than one EIN for an entity.

Online. Taxpayers and authorized third party designees located within the United States and U.S. possessions can receive an EIN online and use it immediately to file a return or make a payment. Go to the IRS website at *www.irs.gov/businesses* and click on *Employer ID Numbers*.

 Taxpayers who apply online have an option to view, print, and save their EIN assignment notice at the end of the session. (Authorized third party designees will receive the EIN but the notice will be mailed to the applicant.)

 Applicants who are not located within the United States or U.S. possessions cannot use the online application to obtain an EIN. Please use one of the other methods to apply.

Telephone. You can receive your EIN by telephone and use it immediately to file a return or make a payment. Call the IRS at 1-800-829-4933. The hours of operation are 7:00 a.m. to 10:00 p.m. local time (Pacific time for Alaska and Hawaii). The person making the call must be authorized to sign the form or be an authorized designee. See *Third Party Designee* and *Signature* on page 6. Also see the *TIP* on page 2.

Note. International applicants must call 215-516-6999.

If you are applying by telephone, it will be helpful to complete Form SS-4 before contacting the IRS. An IRS representative will use the information from the Form SS-4 to establish your account and assign an EIN. Write the number you are given on the upper right corner of the form and sign and date it. Keep this copy for your records.

If requested by an IRS representative, mail or fax (facsimile) the signed Form SS-4 (including any Third Party Designee authorization) within 24 hours to the IRS address provided by the IRS representative.

 *Taxpayer representatives can apply for an EIN on behalf of their client and request that the EIN be faxed to their client on the same day. **Note.** By using this procedure, you are authorizing the IRS to fax the EIN without a cover sheet.*

Fax. Under the Fax-TIN program, you can receive your EIN by fax within 4 business days. Complete and fax Form SS-4 to the IRS using the appropriate Fax-TIN number listed below. A long-distance charge to callers outside of the local calling area will apply. Fax-TIN numbers can only be used to apply for an EIN. The numbers may change without notice. Fax-TIN is available 24 hours a day, 7 days a week.

Be sure to provide your fax number so the IRS can fax the EIN back to you.

Note. By using this procedure, you are authorizing the IRS to fax the EIN without a cover sheet.

Mail. Complete Form SS-4 at least 4 to 5 weeks before you will need an EIN. Sign and date the application and mail it to the service center address for your state. You will receive your EIN in the mail in approximately 4 weeks. See also *Third Party Designee* on page 6.

Call 1-800-829-4933 to verify a number or to ask about the status of an application by mail.

Where to File or Fax

If your principal business, office or agency, or legal residence in the case of an individual, is located in:	File or fax with the "Internal Revenue Service Center" at:
One of the 50 states or the District of Columbia	Attn: EIN Operation Cincinnati, OH 45999 Fax-TIN: 859-669-5760
If you have no legal residence, principal place of business, or principal office or agency in any state:	Attn: EIN Operation Philadelphia, PA 19255 Fax-TIN: 215-516-1040

How To Get Forms and Publications

Internet. You can access the IRS website 24 hours a day, 7 days a week at *www.irs.gov* to download forms, instructions, and publications.

Phone. Call 1-800-TAX-FORM (1-800-829-3676) to order forms, instructions, and publications. You should receive your order or notification of its status within 10 workdays.

DVD for Tax Products. For small businesses, return preparers, or others who may frequently need tax forms or publications, a DVD containing over 2,000 tax products (including many prior year forms) can be purchased from the National Technical Information Service (NTIS).

To order Pub.1796, IRS Tax Products CD, call 1-877-233-6767 or connect to *www.irs.gov/cdorders*.

Tax Help for Your Business

IRS-sponsored Small Business Workshops provide information about your federal and state tax obligations. For information about workshops in your area, call 1-800-829-4933.

Related Forms and Publications

The following forms and instructions may be useful to filers of Form SS-4.
- Form 990-T, Exempt Organization Business Income Tax Return.
- Instructions for Form 990-T.
- Schedule C (Form 1040), Profit or Loss From Business.
- Schedule F (Form 1040), Profit or Loss From Farming.
- Instructions for Form 1041 and Schedules A, B, D, G, I, J, and K-1, U.S. Income Tax Return for Estates and Trusts.
- Form 1042, Annual Withholding Tax Return for U.S. Source Income of Foreign Persons.
- Instructions for Form 1065, U.S. Return of Partnership Income.
- Instructions for Form 1066, U.S. Real Estate Mortgage Investment Conduit (REMIC) Income Tax Return.
- Instructions for Forms 1120 and 1120-A.
- Form 2553, Election by a Small Business Corporation.
- Form 2848, Power of Attorney and Declaration of Representative.
- Form 8821, Tax Information Authorization.
- Form 8832, Entity Classification Election.

For more information about filing Form SS-4 and related issues, see:
- Pub. 51 (Circular A), Agricultural Employer's Tax Guide;
- Pub. 15 (Circular E), Employer's Tax Guide;
- Pub. 538, Accounting Periods and Methods;
- Pub. 542, Corporations;
- Pub. 557, Tax-Exempt Status for Your Organization;
- Pub. 583, Starting a Business and Keeping Records;
- Pub. 966, The Secure Way to Pay Your Federal Taxes for Business and Individual Taxpayers;
- Pub. 1635, Understanding Your EIN;
- Package 1023, Application for Recognition of Exemption Under Section 501(c)(3) of the Internal Revenue Code; and
- Package 1024, Application for Recognition of Exemption Under Section 501(a).

Specific Instructions

Print or type all entries on Form SS-4. Follow the instructions for each line to expedite processing and to avoid unnecessary IRS requests for additional information. Enter "N/A" (nonapplicable) on the lines that do not apply.

Line 1. Legal name of entity (or individual) for whom the EIN is being requested. Enter the legal name of the entity (or individual) applying for the EIN exactly as it appears on the social security card, charter, or other applicable legal document. An entry is required.

Individuals. Enter your first name, middle initial, and last name. If you are a sole proprietor, enter your individual name, not your business name. Enter your business name on line 2. Do not use abbreviations or nicknames on line 1.

Trusts. Enter the name of the trust as it appears on the trust instrument.

Estate of a decedent. Enter the name of the estate. For an estate that has no legal name, enter the name of the decedent followed by "Estate."

Partnerships. Enter the legal name of the partnership as it appears in the partnership agreement.

Corporations. Enter the corporate name as it appears in the corporate charter or other legal document creating it.

Plan administrators. Enter the name of the plan administrator. A plan administrator who already has an EIN should use that number.

Line 2. Trade name of business. Enter the trade name of the business if different from the legal name. The trade name is the "doing business as" (DBA) name.

 Use the full legal name shown on line 1 on all tax returns filed for the entity. (However, if you enter a trade name on line 2 and choose to use the trade name instead of the legal name, enter the trade name on all returns you file.) To prevent processing delays and errors, always use the legal name only (or the trade name only) on all tax returns.

Line 3. Executor, administrator, trustee, "care of" name. Trusts enter the name of the trustee. Estates enter the name of the executor, administrator, or other fiduciary. If the entity applying has a designated person to receive tax information, enter that person's name as the "care of" person. Enter the individual's first name, middle initial, and last name.

Lines 4a–b. Mailing address. Enter the mailing address for the entity's correspondence. If the entity's address is outside the United States or its possessions, you must enter the city, province or state, postal code, and the name of the country. Do not abbreviate the country name. If line 3 is completed, enter the address for the executor, trustee or "care of" person. Generally, this address will be used on all tax returns.

If the entity is filing the Form SS-4 only to obtain an EIN for the Form 8832, use the same address where you would like to have the acceptance or nonacceptance letter sent.

 File Form 8822, Change of Address, to report any subsequent changes to the entity's mailing address.

Lines 5a–b. Street address. Provide the entity's physical address only if different from its mailing address shown in lines 4a–b. Do not enter a P.O. box number here. If the entity's address is outside the United States or its possessions, you must enter the city, province or state, postal code, and the name of the country. Do not abbreviate the country name.

Line 6. County and state where principal business is located. Enter the entity's primary physical location.

Lines 7a–b. Name of principal officer, general partner, grantor, owner, or trustor. Enter the first name, middle initial, last name, and SSN of (a) the principal officer if the business is a corporation, (b) a general partner if a partnership, (c) the owner of an entity that is disregarded as separate from its owner (disregarded entities owned by a corporation enter the corporation's name and EIN), or (d) a grantor, owner, or trustor if a trust.

If the person in question is an alien individual with a previously assigned individual taxpayer identification number (ITIN), enter the ITIN in the space provided and submit a copy of an official identifying document. If necessary, complete Form W-7, Application for IRS Individual Taxpayer Identification Number, to obtain an ITIN.

You must enter an SSN, ITIN, or EIN unless the only reason you are applying for an EIN is to make an entity classification election (see Regulations sections 301.7701-1 through 301.7701-3) and you are a nonresident alien or other foreign entity with no effectively connected income from sources within the United States.

Lines 8a–c. Limited liability company (LLC) information. An LLC is an entity organized under the laws of a state or foreign country as a limited liability company. For federal tax purposes, an LLC may be treated as a partnership or corporation or be disregarded as an entity separate from its owner.

By default, a domestic LLC with only one member is disregarded as an entity separate from its owner and must include all of its income and expenses on the owner's tax return (for example, Schedule C (Form 1040)). Also by default, a domestic LLC with two or more members is treated as a partnership. A domestic LLC may file Form 8832 to avoid either default classification and elect to be classified as an association taxable as a corporation. For more information on entity classifications (including the rules for foreign entities), see the instructions for Form 8832.

If the answer to line 8a is "Yes," enter the number of LLC members. If the LLC is owned solely by a husband and wife in a community property state and the husband and wife choose to treat the entity as a disregarded entity, enter "1" on line 8b.

 Do not file Form 8832 if the LLC accepts the default classifications above. If the LLC is eligible to be treated as a corporation that meets certain tests and it will be electing S corporation status, it must timely file Form 2553. The LLC will be treated as a corporation as of the effective date of the S corporation election and does not need to file Form 8832. See the Instructions for Form 2553.

Line 9a. Type of entity. Check the box that best describes the type of entity applying for the EIN. If you are an alien individual with an ITIN previously assigned to you, enter the ITIN in place of a requested SSN.

 This is not an election for a tax classification of an entity. See Disregarded entities on page 4.

Sole proprietor. Check this box if you file Schedule C, C-EZ, or F (Form 1040) and have a qualified plan, or are required to file excise, employment, alcohol, tobacco, or firearms returns, or are a payer of gambling winnings. Enter your SSN (or ITIN) in the space provided. If you are a nonresident alien with no effectively connected income from sources within the United States, you do not need to enter an SSN or ITIN.

Corporation. This box is for any corporation other than a personal service corporation. If you check this box, enter the income tax form number to be filed by the entity in the space provided.

 If you entered "1120S" after the "Corporation" checkbox, the corporation must file Form 2553 no later than the 15th day of the 3rd month of the tax year the election is to take effect. Until Form 2553 has been received and approved, you will be considered a Form 1120 filer. See the Instructions for Form 2553.

Personal service corporation. Check this box if the entity is a personal service corporation. An entity is a personal service corporation for a tax year only if:
● The principal activity of the entity during the testing period (prior tax year) for the tax year is the performance of personal services substantially by employee-owners, and
● The employee-owners own at least 10% of the fair market value of the outstanding stock in the entity on the last day of the testing period.

Personal services include performance of services in such fields as health, law, accounting, or consulting. For more information about personal service corporations, see the Instructions for Forms 1120 and 1120-A and Pub. 542.

 If the corporation is recently formed, the testing period begins on the first day of its tax year and ends on the earlier of the last day of its tax year, or the last day of the calendar year in which its tax year begins.

Other nonprofit organization. Check this box if the nonprofit organization is other than a church or church-controlled organization and specify the type of nonprofit organization (for example, an educational organization).

 If the organization also seeks tax-exempt status, you must file either Package 1023 or Package 1024. See Pub. 557 for more information.

If the organization is covered by a group exemption letter, enter the four-digit group exemption number (GEN) in the last entry. (Do not confuse the GEN with the nine-digit EIN.) If you do not know the GEN, contact the parent organization. Get Pub. 557 for more information about group exemption numbers.

If the organization is a section 527 political organization, check the box for *Other nonprofit organization* and specify "section 527 organization" in the space to the right. To be recognized as exempt from tax, a section 527 political organization must electronically file Form 8871, Political Organization Notice of Section 527 Status, within 24 hours of the date on which the organization was established. The organization may also have to file Form 8872, Political Organization Report of Contributions and Expenditures. See *www.irs.gov/polorgs* for more information.

Plan administrator. If the plan administrator is an individual, enter the plan administrator's taxpayer identification number (TIN) in the space provided.

REMIC. Check this box if the entity has elected to be treated as a real estate mortgage investment conduit (REMIC). See the Instructions for Form 1066 for more information.

State/local government. If you are a government employer and you are not sure of your social security and Medicare coverage options, go to *www.ncsssa.org/ssaframes.html* to obtain the contact information for your state's Social Security Administrator.

Other. If not specifically listed, check the "Other" box, enter the type of entity and the type of return, if any, that will be filed (for example, "Common Trust Fund, Form 1065" or "Created a Pension Plan"). Do not enter "N/A." If you are an alien individual applying for an EIN, see the *Lines 7a–b* instructions on page 3.
- **Household employer.** If you are an individual that will employ someone to provide services in your household, check the "Other" box and enter "Household Employer" and your SSN. If you are a trust that qualifies as a household employer, you do not need a separate EIN for reporting tax information relating to household employees; use the EIN of the trust.
- **Household employer agent.** If you are an agent of a household employer that is a disabled individual or other welfare recipient receiving home care services through a state or local program, check the "Other" box and enter "Household Employer Agent." (See Rev. Proc. 80-4, 1980-1 C.B. 581 and Notice 2003-70, 2003-43 I.R.B. 916.) If you are a state or local government also check the box for state/local government.
- **QSub.** For a qualified subchapter S subsidiary (QSub) check the "Other" box and specify "QSub."
- **Withholding agent.** If you are a withholding agent required to file Form 1042, check the "Other" box and enter "Withholding Agent."

Disregarded entities. A disregarded entity is an eligible entity that is disregarded as separate from its owner for federal income tax purposes. Disregarded entities include single-member limited liability companies (LLCs) that are disregarded as separate from their owners, qualified subchapter S subsidiaries (qualified subsidiaries of an S corporation), and certain qualified foreign entities. See the instructions for Form 8832 and Regulations section 301.7701-3 for more information on domestic and foreign disregarded entities.

A disregarded entity must have an EIN if it is subject to employment taxes or certain excise taxes. For wages paid during 2008 and in prior years, the reporting and payment of employment taxes for employees could be made using the name and EIN of either the owner or the disregarded entity (as explained in Notice 99-6, 1999-3 I.R.B. 12). For wages paid on or after January 1, 2009, the disregarded entity is required to use its name and EIN for reporting and payment of employment taxes. A disregarded entity is also required to use its name and EIN to register for excise tax activities on Form 637, pay and report excise taxes reported on Forms 720, 730, 2290, and 11-C, and claim any refunds, credits, and payments on Form 8849. This requirement for reporting and paying excise taxes became effective after December 31, 2007. See the instructions for the employment and excise tax returns for more information.

Complete Form SS-4 for disregarded entities as follows.
- If a disregarded entity is filing Form SS-4 to obtain an EIN because it is required to report and pay employment and excise taxes (see above) or for non-federal purposes such as a state requirement, check the "Other" box for line 9a and write "disregarded entity" (or "disregarded entity-sole proprietorship" if the owner of the disregarded entity is an individual).
- If the disregarded entity is requesting an EIN for purposes of filing Form 8832 to elect classification as an association taxable as a corporation, or Form 2553 to elect classification as an association and S corporation status, check the "Corporation" box for line 9a and write "single-member" and the form number of the return that will be filed (Form 1120 or 1120S).
- If the disregarded entity is requesting an EIN because it has acquired one or more additional owners and its classification has changed to partnership under the default rules of Regulations section 301.7701-3(f), check the "Partnership" box for line 9a.

For more reporting information, see Treasury Decision (T.D.) 9356, available at *www.irs.gov/irb/2007-39_IRB/ar11.html*.

Line 10. Reason for applying. Check only one box. Do not enter "N/A." A selection is required.

Started new business. Check this box if you are starting a new business that requires an EIN. If you check this box, enter the type of business being started. Do not apply if you already have an EIN and are only adding another place of business.

Hired employees. Check this box if the existing business is requesting an EIN because it has hired or is hiring employees and is therefore required to file employment tax returns. Do not apply if you already have an EIN and are only hiring employees. For information on employment taxes (for example, for family members), see Pub. 15 (Circular E).

 You may have to make electronic deposits of all depository taxes (such as employment tax, excise tax, and corporate income tax) using the Electronic Federal Tax Payment System (EFTPS). See Federal tax deposits on page 1; section 11, Depositing Taxes, of Pub. 15 (Circular E); and Pub. 966.

Banking purpose. Check this box if you are requesting an EIN for banking purposes only, and enter the banking purpose (for example, a bowling league for depositing dues or an investment club for dividend and interest reporting).

Changed type of organization. Check this box if the business is changing its type of organization. For example, the business was a sole proprietorship and has been incorporated or has become a partnership. If you check this box, specify in the space provided (including available space

-4-

immediately below) the type of change made. For example, "From Sole Proprietorship to Partnership."

Purchased going business. Check this box if you purchased an existing business. Do not use the former owner's EIN unless you became the "owner" of a corporation by acquiring its stock.

Created a trust. Check this box if you created a trust, and enter the type of trust created. For example, indicate if the trust is a nonexempt charitable trust or a split-interest trust.

Exception. Do not file this form for certain grantor-type trusts. The trustee does not need an EIN for the trust if the trustee furnishes the name and TIN of the grantor/owner and the address of the trust to all payers. However, grantor trusts that do not file using Optional Method 1 and IRA trusts that are required to file Form 990-T, Exempt Organization Business Income Tax Return, must have an EIN. For more information on grantor trusts, see the Instructions for Form 1041.

 Do not check this box if you are applying for a trust EIN when a new pension plan is established. Check "Created a pension plan."

Created a pension plan. Check this box if you have created a pension plan and need an EIN for reporting purposes. Also, enter the type of plan in the space provided.

 Check this box if you are applying for a trust EIN when a new pension plan is established. In addition, check the "Other" box on line 9a and write "Created a Pension Plan" in the space provided.

Other. Check this box if you are requesting an EIN for any other reason; and enter the reason. For example, a newly-formed state government entity should enter "Newly-Formed State Government Entity" in the space provided.

Line 11. Date business started or acquired. If you are starting a new business, enter the starting date of the business. If the business you acquired is already operating, enter the date you acquired the business. If you are changing the form of ownership of your business, enter the date the new ownership entity began. Trusts should enter the date the trust was funded. Estates should enter the date of death of the decedent whose name appears on line 1 or the date when the estate was legally funded.

Line 12. Closing month of accounting year. Enter the last month of your accounting year or tax year. An accounting or tax year is usually 12 consecutive months, either a calendar year or a fiscal year (including a period of 52 or 53 weeks). A calendar year is 12 consecutive months ending on December 31. A fiscal year is either 12 consecutive months ending on the last day of any month other than December or a 52-53 week year. For more information on accounting periods, see Pub. 538.

Individuals. Your tax year generally will be a calendar year.

Partnerships. Partnerships must adopt one of the following tax years.
• The tax year of the majority of its partners.
• The tax year common to all of its principal partners.
• The tax year that results in the least aggregate deferral of income.
• In certain cases, some other tax year.

See the Instructions for Form 1065 for more information.

REMICs. REMICs must have a calendar year as their tax year.

Personal service corporations. A personal service corporation generally must adopt a calendar year unless it meets one of the following requirements.

• It can establish a business purpose for having a different tax year.
• It elects under section 444 to have a tax year other than a calendar year.

Trusts. Generally, a trust must adopt a calendar year except for the following trusts.
• Tax-exempt trusts.
• Charitable trusts.
• Grantor-owned trusts.

Line 13. Highest number of employees expected in the next 12 months. Complete each box by entering the number (including zero ("-0-")) of "Agricultural," "Household," or "Other" employees expected by the applicant in the next 12 months.

Line 14. Do you expect your employment tax liability to be $1,000 or less in a full calendar year? Check the appropriate box to indicate if you expect your annual tax liability to be $1,000 or less in a full calendar year. Generally, if you pay $4,000 or less in wages subject to social security and Medicare taxes and federal income tax withholding, you are likely to pay $1,000 or less in employment taxes.

 For employers in the U.S. possessions, generally, if you pay $6,536 or less in wages subject to social security and Medicare taxes, you are likely to pay $1,000 or less in employment taxes.

For more information on employment taxes, see Pub. 15 (Circular E); or Pub. 51 (Circular A) if you have agricultural employees (farmworkers).

Line 15. First date wages or annuities were paid. If the business has employees, enter the date on which the business began to pay wages. If the business does not plan to have employees, enter "N/A."

Withholding agent. Enter the date you began or will begin to pay income (including annuities) to a nonresident alien. This also applies to individuals who are required to file Form 1042 to report alimony paid to a nonresident alien.

Line 16. Check the one box on line 16 that best describes the principal activity of the applicant's business. Check the "Other" box (and specify the applicant's principal activity) if none of the listed boxes applies. You must check a box.

Construction. Check this box if the applicant is engaged in erecting buildings or engineering projects (for example, streets, highways, bridges, tunnels). The term "Construction" also includes special trade contractors (for example, plumbing, HVAC, electrical, carpentry, concrete, excavation, etc. contractors).

Real estate. Check this box if the applicant is engaged in renting or leasing real estate to others; managing, selling, buying, or renting real estate for others; or providing related real estate services (for example, appraisal services). Also check this box for mortgage real estate investment trusts (REITS). Mortgage REITS are engaged in issuing shares of funds consisting primarily of portfolios of real estate mortgage assets with gross income of the trust solely derived from interest earned.

Rental and leasing. Check this box if the applicant is engaged in providing tangible goods such as autos, computers, consumer goods, or industrial machinery and equipment to customers in return for a periodic rental or lease payment. Also check this box for equity real estate investment trusts (REITS). Equity REITS are engaged in issuing shares of funds consisting primarily of portfolios of real estate assets with gross income of the trust derived from renting real property.

Manufacturing. Check this box if the applicant is engaged in the mechanical, physical, or chemical transformation of materials, substances, or components into new products. The assembling of component parts of manufactured products is also considered to be manufacturing.

Transportation & warehousing. Check this box if the applicant provides transportation of passengers or cargo; warehousing or storage of goods; scenic or sight-seeing transportation; or support activities related to transportation.

Finance & insurance. Check this box if the applicant is engaged in transactions involving the creation, liquidation, or change of ownership of financial assets and/or facilitating such financial transactions; underwriting annuities/insurance policies; facilitating such underwriting by selling insurance policies; or by providing other insurance or employee-benefit related services.

Health care & social assistance. Check this box if the applicant is engaged in providing physical, medical, or psychiatric care or providing social assistance activities such as youth centers, adoption agencies, individual/family services, temporary shelters, daycare, etc.

Accommodation & food services. Check this box if the applicant is engaged in providing customers with lodging, meal preparation, snacks, or beverages for immediate consumption.

Wholesale–agent/broker. Check this box if the applicant is engaged in arranging for the purchase or sale of goods owned by others or purchasing goods on a commission basis for goods traded in the wholesale market, usually between businesses.

Wholesale–other. Check this box if the applicant is engaged in selling goods in the wholesale market generally to other businesses for resale on their own account, goods used in production, or capital or durable nonconsumer goods.

Retail. Check this box if the applicant is engaged in selling merchandise to the general public from a fixed store; by direct, mail-order, or electronic sales; or by using vending machines.

Other. Check this box if the applicant is engaged in an activity not described above. Describe the applicant's principal business activity in the space provided.

Line 17. Use line 17 to describe the applicant's principal line of business in more detail. For example, if you checked the "Construction" box on line 16, enter additional detail such as "General contractor for residential buildings" on line 17. An entry is required. For mortgage REITS indicate mortgage REIT and for equity REITS indicate what type of real property is the principal type (residential REIT, nonresidential REIT, miniwarehouse REIT).

Line 18. Check the applicable box to indicate whether or not the applicant entity applying for an EIN was issued one previously.

Third Party Designee. Complete this section only if you want to authorize the named individual to receive the entity's EIN and answer questions about the completion of Form SS-4. The designee's authority terminates at the time the EIN is assigned and released to the designee. You must complete the signature area for the authorization to be valid.

Signature. When required, the application must be signed by (a) the individual, if the applicant is an individual, (b) the president, vice president, or other principal officer, if the applicant is a corporation, (c) a responsible and duly

authorized member or officer having knowledge of its affairs, if the applicant is a partnership, government entity, or other unincorporated organization, or (d) the fiduciary, if the applicant is a trust or an estate. Foreign applicants may have any duly-authorized person (for example, division manager) sign Form SS-4.

Privacy Act and Paperwork Reduction Act Notice. We ask for the information on this form to carry out the Internal Revenue laws of the United States. We need it to comply with section 6109 and the regulations thereunder, which generally require the inclusion of an employer identification number (EIN) on certain returns, statements, or other documents filed with the Internal Revenue Service. If your entity is required to obtain an EIN, you are required to provide all of the information requested on this form. Information on this form may be used to determine which federal tax returns you are required to file and to provide you with related forms and publications.

We disclose this form to the Social Security Administration (SSA) for their use in determining compliance with applicable laws. We may give this information to the Department of Justice for use in civil and/or criminal litigation, and to cities, states, the District of Columbia, and U.S. commonwealths and possessions for use in administering their tax laws. We may also disclose this information to other countries under a tax treaty, to federal and state agencies to enforce federal nontax criminal laws, and to federal law enforcement and intelligence agencies to combat terrorism.

We will be unable to issue an EIN to you unless you provide all of the requested information that applies to your entity. Providing false information could subject you to penalties.

You are not required to provide the information requested on a form that is subject to the Paperwork Reduction Act unless the form displays a valid OMB control number. Books or records relating to a form or its instructions must be retained as long as their contents may become material in the administration of any Internal Revenue law. Generally, tax returns and return information are confidential, as required by section 6103. Section 6109 requires paid preparers to provide their identifying number.

The time needed to complete and file this form will vary depending on individual circumstances. The estimated average time is:

Recordkeeping	8 hrs., 36 min.
Learning about the law or the form	42 min.
Preparing the form	52 min.
Copying, assembling, and sending the form to the IRS	- - - - -

If you have comments concerning the accuracy of these time estimates or suggestions for making this form simpler, we would be happy to hear from you. You can write to Internal Revenue Service, Tax Products Coordinating Committee, SE:W:CAR:MP:T:T:SP, IR-6526, 1111 Constitution Avenue, NW, Washington, DC 20224. Do not send the form to this address. Instead, see *Where to File or Fax* on page 2.

Office of the County Clerk	Fees	FILING STAMP ONLY
Address _____ City _____ ☐ First Filing ☐ Renewal Filing	$ _____ for 1 FBN and registrant $ _____ for each additional FBN filed on same statement and doing business at same location $ _____ for each additional registrant	 **File Number:** _____

FICTITIOUS BUSINESS NAME STATEMENT

THE FOLLOWING PERSON(S) IS (ARE)

1
Fictitious Business Name(s)
1

2

3.

Articles of Incorporation Number (if applicable)
AL#

2 Street Address & City of Principal Place of Business in California (P.O. Box alone not acceptable) — Zip Code

3 Full Name of Registrant — if corporation—incorporated in what state

Residence Street Address — City — State — Zip Code

3a Full Name of Registrant — if corporation—incorporated in what state

Residence Street Address — City — State — Zip Code

3b Full Name of Registrant — if corporation—incorporated in what state

Residence Street Address — City — State — Zip Code

4 This Business is conducted by:
( ) an individual   ( ) a general partnership   ( ) joint venture   ( ) a business trust
( ) co-partners   ( ) husband and wife   ( ) a corporation   ( ) a limited partnership
( ) an unincorporated association other than a partnership   ( ) other—please specify _____

5
( ) The registrant commenced to transact business under name or names listed on (date): _____
( ) Registrant has not yet begun to transact business under the fictitious business name or names listed herein.

6 If registrant is not a corporation or a limited liability company sign below:

_____   _____
SIGNATURE   TYPE OR PRINT NAME

_____   _____
SIGNATURE   TYPE OR PRINT NAME

_____   _____
SIGNATURE   TYPE OR PRINT NAME

6a If registrant is a corporation or a limited liability company sign below:

_____
COMPANY NAME

_____
SIGNATURE & TITLE

_____
TYPE OR PRINT NAME AND TITLE

This statement was filed with the County Clerk of _____ County on date indicated by file stamp above.

NOTICE—THIS FICTITIOUS NAME STATEMENT EXPIRES FIVE YEARS FROM DATE IT WAS FILED IN THE OFFICE OF THE COUNTY CLERK.

A NEW FICTITIOUS BUSINESS NAME STATEMENT MUST BE FILED PRIOR TO THAT DATE. The filing of this statement does not of itself authorize the use in this state of a fictitious business name in violation of the rights of another under federal, state, or common law (SEE SECTION 14400 et seq., Business and Professional Code).

This form should be __typed__ or __printed__ legibly in __black ink__.

California Seller's Permit Application

for Individuals/Partnerships/Corporations/Organizations
(Regular or Temporary)

≈ State Board of Equalization

Frequently Asked Questions

Who must have a permit?

You are generally required to obtain a California seller's permit if you sell or lease merchandise, vehicles, or other tangible personal property in California. A seller's permit allows you to sell items at the wholesale or retail level. If your sales are ongoing, you should apply for a "Regular" permit. If your sales are of a temporary nature (90 days or less), apply for a "Temporary" permit. You cannot legally sell taxable items in California until you have been issued a seller's permit.

Do I need more than one permit?

Each location where sales of taxable items are made requires, and must display, a seller's permit. If you have more than one selling location, attach a list that includes the address for each location, and we will issue the permits needed. If your application is for a temporary permit, one permit will be enough, but you need to display a copy of that permit at each temporary location.

Is there a charge for a permit?

No. However, we may require a security deposit. Deposits are used to cover any unpaid taxes that may be owed at the time a business closes.

Is information about my account subject to public disclosure?

State laws that protect your privacy generally cover your records. Some records are subject to public disclosure, such as the information on your seller's permit, names of owners or partners, your business address, and your permit status. See the disclosure information on the back page.

Why do you need a copy of my driver license?

When it is required, it is used to ensure the accuracy of the information provided and to protect against fraudulent use of your identification.

Why am I being asked if I sell tires, covered electronic devices, or tobacco products at retail?

Effective January 1, 2001, California retailers of new tires began collecting a tire fee (currently $1.75) for each new tire sold to consumers. Beginning January 1, 2005, retailers must collect a recycling fee on the retail sale or lease of certain new or refurbished video display devices that have a screen size of more than four inches measured diagonally. Video display devices subject to the fee are called "covered electronic devices" (CEDs). They include televisions, computer monitors, or any other product that contains a cathode ray tube, including "bare" cathode ray tubes, computer monitors, and laptop computers that use a liquid crystal display. For more information on the Electronic Recycling Fee Program or CEDs, visit: *www.boe.ca.gov/ sptaxprog/ewaste.htm.* Effective June 30, 2004, if you sell cigarettes and/or tobacco products, you must obtain a license (separate from a seller's permit) for each location you intend to sell these products. Depending on your response to each question and the type of business, the BOE will send you information about these license and fee programs.

What are my rights and responsibilities as a seller?

When you obtain a seller's permit, you acquire certain rights and responsibilities.

- **You may buy property for resale without paying tax to your supplier**. By providing the vendor a completed resale certificate, you are not required to pay sales tax on property you are buying for resale. You cannot use a resale certificate to buy property for your own use (even if you plan to sell it after its use).

- **You must keep records** to substantiate your sales, purchases, and return deductions and keep them for four years.

- **You must file returns** according to the BOE's instructions for the filing basis that we determine from your application. You must file a return even if you have no tax to report.

- **You must pay the sales tax due** on your retail sales in California. You may be reimbursed by collecting the amount of tax from your customers.

- **You must notify the BOE of any business changes.** A permit is issued only to the owner and address listed on the permit. If you change ownership, address, add another location, sell or close your business, add or drop a partner, you must notify the BOE by calling or in writing. Your notification will help us close your account and return any security on deposit. If you do not, you could be held liable for continuing business taxes. Note: Notify us immediately if you drop or add a partner in order to protect former partners from tax liabilities incurred by the business after the partnership changes.

TAXPAYER INFORMATION SECTION

800-400-7115

TDD/TTY 800-735-2929

FIELD OFFICES

CALL FOR ADDRESSES

City	Area Code	Number
Bakersfield	661	395-2880
Chula Vista	619	409-7440
Culver City	310	342-1000
El Centro	760	352-3431
Eureka*	707	576-2100
Fresno	559	248-4219
Irvine	949	440-3473
Norwalk	562	466-1694
Oakland	510	622-4100
Rancho Mirage	760	770-4828
Redding	530	224-4729
Riverside	951	680-6400
Sacramento	916	227-6700
Salinas	831	443-3003
San Diego	619	525-4526
San Francisco	415	356-6600
San Jose	408	277-1231
San Marcos	760	510-5850
Santa Rosa	707	576-2100
Suisun City	707	428-2041
Van Nuys	818	904-2300
Ventura	805	677-2700
West Covina	626	480-7200

Business Located Out-of-State

916-227-6600

*Office closed June 30, 2005. For dates and times of services in the Eureka area, please visit our website at *www.boe.ca.gov* or call the Taxpayer Information Section at 800-400-7115.

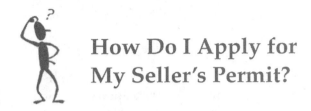

How Do I Apply for My Seller's Permit?

Step 1: Complete Your Application

Complete the application on page 5. If your business is an ongoing operation, check permit type "Regular." If your business will operate at the location(s) for 90 days or less, check "Temporary." Please provide **all** the information requested on the application. If you do not, this will delay the issuance of your permit. Refer to the "Tips" on page 4. If you need assistance, please call your local BOE office or the Taxpayer Information Section at 800-400-7115.

Note: If your business is located outside California, you also need to complete form BOE-403-B, *Registration Information for Out-of-State Account.* Visit our website at *www.boe.ca.gov,* call the Out-of-State Office at 916-227-6600, or the Taxpayer Information Section at 800-400-7115, to request a copy by mail or by fax (select the automated fax-back option).

For information regarding whether or not your out-of-state corporation qualifies to transact business in the State of California, you may visit the Secretary of State's website at *www.ss.ca.gov.* For information regarding the minimum franchise tax for corporations, please visit the California Taxes Information Center's website at *www.taxes.ca.gov.*

Step 2: Send Your Application for Processing

Send or take your application to the district office nearest your place of business. If you plan to apply in person, contact the local office to find out when they are open. Note: A permit is required before you begin making sales. Advise the BOE if you have an urgent need for a permit.

Step 3: After Your Application Is Approved

If your application is complete, you should receive your permit in about two weeks. Based on the information in your application, the BOE will provide you with regulations, forms, and other publications that may help you with your business. Or, you may choose to view and download information from our website at *www.boe.ca.gov.* You will also be informed as to when to file tax returns: monthly, quarterly, fiscal or calendar yearly. Electronic filing is the BOE's method for filing your sales and use tax return and making payment. Visit our website for details.

Post your permit at your place of business in a location easily seen by your customers.

Tips for Filling Out Your Application

Item 1: Permit Type

Check whether you are applying for a **regular** or **temporary** permit. You may apply for a temporary permit if you intend to make sales for a period of 90 days or less. Otherwise, you must apply for a regular permit.

Items 2–8: Business Identification Information

Check your type of ownership and provide all of the information requested. Partnerships should provide a copy of their written partnership agreement, if one exists. If it is filed with us at the time you apply for a permit and it specifies that all business assets are held in the name of the partnership, we will attempt to collect any delinquent tax liability from the partnership's assets before we attempt to collect from the partners' personal assets. The "Registered Domestic Partnership" ownership box should only be checked if both persons are registered as domestic partners with the Office of the Secretary of State.

Items 9–35: Ownership Information

Indicate whether those listed are owners, partners, etc., and enter their driver license or California Identification Card number and, except in the case of corporate officers, their social security number. Also, provide a reference for each person, who does not live with that person. This information will be kept in strict confidence. If mailing your application, you must provide a photocopy of your driver license or California Identification Card.

Items 36–49, 66: Type of Business, Selling Locations, and Landlord Information

Check whether the business is a retailer, wholesaler, etc., and whether the business is full time or part time. Describe the types of items you will sell. Avoid using broad descriptions, such as "general merchandise." Instead, list specific examples such as sports equipment or garden supplies. Indicate the number of selling locations, the address, telephone number, email address, and website of the business, as well as the landlord's name, address, and telephone number. If there are multiple selling locations, additional addresses can be listed on the reverse side (Item 66). Correspondence will be sent to the business address unless a different mailing address is specified (Item 42).

Items 50–51: Projected Monthly Sales

Indicate your projected monthly gross and taxable sales. If unsure, provide an estimate. Your projection helps to determine how often you will need to file a return. If your actual sales vary, we may adjust your filing frequency.

Items 52–55: Related Program Information

Provide your Alcoholic Beverage Control license number, if applicable. Indicate if you will be selling new tires, covered electronic devices, or tobacco products. We will contact you to determine if you need to register for any of these other programs.

Items 56–65: Related Party Information

Identify the person maintaining your records, your bank, and if you accept credit cards, your merchant card account. Also, identify major California-based suppliers and the products that you purchase from them.

Items 67–74: Ownership and Organizational Changes

If you are purchasing a business, or changing from one type of business organization to another, provide the previous owner's name and seller's permit number. If you are purchasing a business, you should request a tax clearance in advance to assure that you won't have to pay any taxes owed by the previous owner.

Items 75–82: Temporary Permit Event Information

Applicants for a temporary permit must complete each item in this section.

Certification

Each owner, co-owner, partner, or corporate officer must sign the application.

APPLICATION FOR SELLER'S PERMIT

STATE OF CALIFORNIA
BOARD OF EQUALIZATION

---

1. PERMIT TYPE: *(check one)* ☐ **Regular** ☐ **Temporary**

FOR BOE USE ONLY			

2. TYPE OF OWNERSHIP *(check one)*   * Must provide partnership agreement

☐ Sole Owner
☐ Corporation
☐ General Partnership
☐ Limited Partnership (LP)*
☐ Registered Domestic Partnership
☐ Other *(describe)* _____

☐ Married Co-ownership
☐ Limited Liability Company (LLC)
☐ Unincorporated Business Trust
☐ Limited Liability Partnership (LLP)*
(Registered to practice law, accounting or architecture)

FOR BOE USE ONLY

TAX	IND	OFFICE	PERMIT NUMBER
S			

NAICS CODE | BUS CODE | A.C.C. | REPORTING BASIS | TAX AREA CODE

PROCESSED BY | PERMIT ISSUE DATE ___/___/___

RETURN TYPE ☐ (1) 401-A ☐ (2) 401-EZ
VERIFICATION ☐ DL ☐ PA ☐ Other

3. NAME OF SOLE OWNER, CORPORATION, LLC, PARTNERSHIP, OR TRUST

4. STATE OF INCORPORATION OR ORGANIZATION

5. BUSINESS TRADE NAME/"DOING BUSINESS AS" [DBA] *(if any)*

6. DATE YOU WILL BEGIN BUSINESS ACTIVITIES *(month, day, and year)*

7. CORPORATE, LLC, LLP OR LP NUMBER FROM CALIFORNIA SECRETARY OF STATE

8. FEDERAL EMPLOYER IDENTIFICATION NUMBER (FEIN)

CHECK ONE ☐ Owner/Co-Owners ☐ Partners ☐ Registered Domestic Partners ☐ Corp. Officers ☐ LLC Officers/Managers/Members ☐ Trustees/Beneficiaries

Use additional sheets to include information for more than three individuals.

9. FULL NAME *(first, middle, last)*

10. TITLE

11. SOCIAL SECURITY NUMBER *(corporate officers excluded)*

12. DRIVER LICENSE NUMBER *(attach copy)*

13. HOME ADDRESS *(street, city, state, zip code)*

14. HOME TELEPHONE NUMBER ( )

15. NAME OF A PERSONAL REFERENCE NOT LIVING WITH YOU

16. ADDRESS *(street, city, state, zip code)*

17. REFERENCE TELEPHONE NUMBER ( )

18. FULL NAME OF ADDITIONAL PARTNER, OFFICER, OR MEMBER *(first, middle, last)*

19. TITLE

20. SOCIAL SECURITY NUMBER *(corporate officers excluded)*

21. DRIVER LICENSE NUMBER *(attach copy)*

22. HOME ADDRESS *(street, city, state, zip code)*

23. HOME TELEPHONE NUMBER ( )

24. NAME OF A PERSONAL REFERENCE NOT LIVING WITH YOU

25. ADDRESS *(street, city, state, zip code)*

26. REFERENCE TELEPHONE NUMBER ( )

27. FULL NAME OF ADDITIONAL PARTNER, OFFICER, OR MEMBER *(first, middle, last)*

28. TITLE

29. SOCIAL SECURITY NUMBER *(corporate officers excluded)*

30. DRIVER LICENSE NUMBER *(attach copy)*

31. HOME ADDRESS *(street, city, state, zip code)*

32. HOME TELEPHONE NUMBER ( )

33. NAME OF A PERSONAL REFERENCE NOT LIVING WITH YOU

34. ADDRESS *(street, city, state, zip code)*

35. REFERENCE TELEPHONE NUMBER ( )

---

36. TYPE OF BUSINESS (check one that best describes your business)

☐ Retail ☐ Wholesale ☐ Mfg. ☐ Repair ☐ Service ☐ Construction Contractor ☐ Leasing

37. NUMBER OF SELLING LOCATIONS *(if 2 or more, see Item No. 66)*

38. WHAT ITEMS WILL YOU SELL?

39. CHECK ONE ☐ Full Time ☐ Part Time

40. BUSINESS ADDRESS *(street, city, state, zip code) [do not list P.O. Box or mailing service]*

41. BUSINESS TELEPHONE NUMBER ( )

42. MAILING ADDRESS *(street, city, state, zip code) [if different from business address]*

43. BUSINESS FAX NUMBER ( )

44. BUSINESS EMAIL ADDRESS

45. BUSINESS WEBSITE ADDRESS WWW.

46. DO YOU MAKE INTERNET SALES? ☐ Yes ☐ No

47. NAME OF BUSINESS LANDLORD

48. LANDLORD ADDRESS *(street, city, state, zip code)*

49. LANDLORD TELEPHONE NUMBER ( )

50. PROJECTED MONTHLY GROSS SALES $

51. PROJECTED MONTHLY TAXABLE SALES $

52. ALCOHOLIC BEVERAGE CONTROL LICENSE NUMBER *(if applicable)* ___ ___ - ___ ___ ___ ___

53. SELLING NEW TIRES AT RETAIL? ☐ Yes ☐ No

54. SELLING COVERED ELECTRONIC DEVICES? ☐ Yes ☐ No

55. SELLING TOBACCO AT RETAIL? ☐ Yes ☐ No

(continued on reverse)

56. NAME OF PERSON MAINTAINING YOUR RECORDS	57. ADDRESS *(street, city, state, zip code)*	58. TELEPHONE NUMBER ( )
59. NAME OF BANK OR OTHER FINANCIAL INSTITUTION *(note whether business or personal)*		60. BANK BRANCH LOCATION
61. NAME OF MERCHANT CREDIT CARD PROCESSOR *(if you accept credit cards)*		62. MERCHANT CARD ACCOUNT NUMBER

63. NAMES OF MAJOR CALIFORNIA-BASED SUPPLIERS	64. ADDRESSES *(street, city, state, zip code)*	65. PRODUCTS PURCHASED

ADDITIONAL SELLING LOCATIONS (List All Other Selling Locations)

66. PHYSICAL LOCATION OR STREET ADDRESS *(attach separate list, if required)*

OWNERSHIP AND ORGANIZATIONAL CHANGES (Do Not Complete for Temporary Permits)

67. ARE YOU BUYING AN EXISTING BUSINESS?

☐ Yes ☐ No If yes, complete items 70 through 74.

68. ARE YOU CHANGING FROM ONE TYPE OF BUSINESS ORGANIZATION TO ANOTHER (FOR EXAMPLE, FROM A SOLE OWNER TO A CORPORATION OR FROM A PARTNERSHIP TO A LIMITED LIABILITY COMPANY, ETC.)?

☐ Yes ☐ No If yes, complete items 70 and 71.

69. OTHER OWNERSHIP CHANGES *(please describe)*:

70. FORMER OWNER'S NAME	71. SELLER'S PERMIT NUMBER
72. PURCHASE PRICE $	73. VALUE OF FIXTURES & EQUIPMENT $

74. IF AN ESCROW COMPANY IS REQUESTING A TAX CLEARANCE ON YOUR BEHALF, PLEASE LIST THEIR NAME, ADDRESS, TELEPHONE NUMBER, AND THE ESCROW NUMBER

TEMPORARY PERMIT EVENT INFORMATION

75. PERIOD OF SALES FROM: ___ / ___ / ___ THROUGH: ___ / ___ / ___	76. ESTIMATED EVENT SALES $	77. SPACE RENTAL COST *(if any)* $	78. ADMISSION CHARGED? ☐ Yes ☐ No
79. ORGANIZER OR PROMOTER OF EVENT *(if any)*	80. ADDRESS *(street, city, state, zip code)*	81. TELEPHONE NUMBER ( )	

82. ADDRESS OF EVENT *(If more than one, use line 66, above. Attach separate list, if required.)*

CERTIFICATION

All Corporate Officers, LLC Managing Members, Partners, or Owners must sign below.

I am duly authorized to sign the application and certify that the statements made are correct to the best of my knowledge and belief.
I also represent and acknowledge that the applicant will be engaged in or conduct business as a seller of tangible personal property.

NAME *(typed or printed)*	SIGNATURE	DATE
NAME *(typed or printed)*	SIGNATURE	DATE
NAME *(typed or printed)*	SIGNATURE	DATE

FOR BOE USE ONLY

SECURITY REVIEW

☐ BOE-598 ($ _____) *or* ☐ BOE-1009

REQUIRED BY   APPROVED BY

FORMS

☐ BOE-8 ☐ BOE-400-Y
☐ BOE-162 ☐ BOE-519
☐ BOE-467 ☐ BOE-1241-D

REGULATIONS

☐ REG. 1668 ☐ REG. 1698
☐ REG. 1700 ☐ _____

PUBLICATIONS

☐ PUB 73 ☐ PUB DE 44

_____

_____

RETURNS

_____

_____

Where Can I Get Help?

No doubt you will have questions about how the Sales and Use Tax Law applies to your business operations. For assistance, you may take advantage of the resources listed below.

INTERNET

www.boe.ca.gov

You can log onto our website for additional information. For example, you can find out what the tax rate is in a particular county, or you can download numerous publications — such as laws, regulations, pamphlets, and policy manuals — that will help you understand how the law applies to your business. You can also verify sellers' permit numbers online, read about upcoming Taxpayers' Bill of Rights hearings, and obtain information on BOE field office addresses and telephone numbers.

Another good resource — especially for starting businesses — is the California Tax Information Center at *www.taxes.ca.gov.*

CLASSES

You may enroll in a basic sales and use tax class offered by some local BOE offices. You should call ahead to find out when your local office conducts classes for beginning sellers.

WRITTEN TAX ADVICE

It is best to get tax advice from the BOE in writing. You may be relieved of tax, penalty, or interest charges if we determine you did not correctly report tax because you reasonably relied on our written advice regarding a transaction.

For this relief to apply, your request for advice must be in writing, identify the taxpayer to whom the advice applies, and fully describe the facts and circumstances of the transaction.

Send your request for written advice to: State Board of Equalization; Audit and Information Section, MIC:44; PO Box 942879, Sacramento, CA 94279-0044.

TAXPAYER INFORMATION SECTION
800-400-7115

TDD/TTY 800-735-2929

Customer service representatives are available from 8 a.m. through 5 p.m., Monday-Friday, excluding state holidays.

Faxback Service. To order fax copies of selected forms and notices, call 800-400-7115 and choose the faxback option. You can call at any time for this service.

Translator Services. We can provide bilingual services for persons who need assistance in a language other than English.

TAXPAYERS' RIGHTS ADVOCATE OFFICE

If you would like to know more about your rights as a taxpayer or if you are unable to resolve an issue with the BOE, please contact the Taxpayers' Rights Advocate office for help at 916-324-2798 (or toll-free, 888-324-2798). Their fax number is 916-323-3319.

If you prefer, you can write to: State Board of Equalization; Taxpayers' Rights Advocate, MIC:70; PO Box 942879; Sacramento, CA 94279-0070.

To obtain a copy of publication 70, *The California Taxpayers' Bill of Rights,* you may visit our website or call our Taxpayer Information Section.

FIELD OFFICES

See page 3.

Sales and Use Tax Privacy Notice

Information Provided to the Board of Equalization

We ask you for information so that we can administer the state's sales and use tax laws (Revenue and Taxation Code sections 6001-7176, 7200-7226, 7251-7279.6, 7285-7288.6). We will use the information to determine whether you are paying the correct amount of tax and to collect any amounts you owe. You must provide all of the information we request, including your social security number (used for identification purposes [see Title 42 U.S. Code sec.405(c)(2)(C)(i)]).

What happens if I don't provide the information?

If your application is incomplete, we may not issue your seller's permit or use tax certificate. If you do not file complete returns, you may have to pay penalties and interest. Penalties may also apply if you don't provide other information we request or that is required by law, or if you give us fraudulent information. In some cases, you may be subject to criminal prosecution.

In addition, if you don't provide information we request to support your exemptions, credits, exclusions, or adjustments, we may not allow them. You may end up owing more tax or receiving a smaller refund.

Can anyone else see my information?

Your records are covered by state laws that protect your privacy. However, we may share information regarding your account with certain government agencies. We may also share certain information with companies authorized to represent local governments.

Under some circumstances we may release to the public the information printed on your permit, account start and closeout dates, and names of business owners or partners. When you sell a business, we can give the buyer or other involved parties information regarding your outstanding tax liability.

With your written permission, we can release information regarding your account to anyone you designate.

We may disclose information to the proper officials of the following agencies, among others:

- United States government agencies: U.S. Attorney's Office; Bureau of Alcohol, Tobacco and Firearms; Depts. of Agriculture, Defense, and Justice; Federal Bureau of Investigation; General Accounting Office; Internal Revenue Service; Interstate Commerce Commission

- State of California government agencies and officials: Air Resources Board; Dept. of Alcoholic Beverage Control; Auctioneer Commission; Dept. of Motor Vehicles; Employment Development Department; Energy Commission; Exposition and Fairs; Dept. of Food and Agriculture; Board of Forestry; Forest Products Commission; Franchise Tax Board; Dept. of Health Services; Highway Patrol; Dept. of Housing and Community Development; California Parent Locator Service

- State agencies outside of California for tax enforcement purposes

- City attorneys and city prosecutors; county district attorneys, police and sheriff departments.

Can I review my records?

Yes. Please contact your closest Board office (see the white pages of your phone book). If you need more information, you may contact our Disclosure Officer in Sacramento by calling 916-445-2918. You may also want to obtain publication 58-A, *How to Inspect and Correct Your Records.* For a copy, go to *www.boe.ca.gov* or call our Information Center at 800-400-7115.

Who is responsible for maintaining my records?

The deputy director of the Sales and Use Tax Department, whom you may contact by calling 916-445-6464 or writing to the address shown.

Deputy Director
Sales and Use Tax Department, MIC:43
450 N Street
Sacramento, CA 95814

California Resale Certificate

I HEREBY CERTIFY:

1. I hold valid seller's permit number:

2. I am engaged in the business of selling the following type of tangible personal property:

_____

3. This certificate is for the purchase from _____ of the item(s) I have
   listed in paragraph 5 below.   [Vendor's name]

4. I will resell the item(s) listed in paragraph 5, which I am purchasing under this resale certificate in the form of tangible personal property in the regular course of my business operations, and I will do so prior to making any use of the item(s) other than demonstration and display while holding the item(s) for sale in the regular course of my business. I understand that if I use the item(s) purchased under this certificate in any manner other than as just described, I will owe use tax based on each item's purchase price or as otherwise provided by law.

5. Description of property to be purchased for resale:

6. I have read and understand the following:

   For Your Information: A person may be guilty of a misdemeanor under Revenue and Taxation Code section 6094.5 if the purchaser knows at the time of purchase that he or she will not resell the purchased item prior to any use (other than retention, demonstration, or display while holding it for resale) and he or she furnishes a resale certificate to avoid payment to the seller of an amount as tax. Additionally, a person misusing a resale certificate for personal gain or to evade the payment of tax is liable, for each purchase, for the tax that would have been due, plus a penalty of 10 percent of the tax or $500, whichever is more.

_____
NAME OF PURCHASER

_____
SIGNATURE OF PURCHASER, PURCHASER'S EMPLOYEE OR AUTHORIZED REPRESENTATIVE

PRINTED NAME OF PERSON SIGNING	TITLE

_____
ADDRESS OF PURCHASER

TELEPHONE NUMBER ( )	DATE

SWAP MEETS, FLEA MARKETS, OR
SPECIAL EVENTS CERTIFICATION

People who sell merchandise in California are generally required to hold a seller's permit.

You **may not** sell at this event unless you have a seller's permit or are not required to hold a permit. You are required to have a permit if you are selling, even temporarily, new or handcrafted items or used items you purchased for the purpose of reselling to others. You are not required to hold a permit if you are only making "occasional" sales, selling products that are not taxable when sold at retail, or selling on behalf of a section 6015 retailer.

Seller's permits can be obtained at any local Board of Equalization office at no cost to you. To find a Board office near you, call our Information Center at 800-400-7115 or check our website at *www.boe.ca.gov*. Permit applications can also be found online at *www.boe.ca.gov/sutax/sutprograms.htm*. If you obtain a temporary seller's permit, the business address on your temporary permit should be the address of the temporary selling location and the mailing address should be your permanent place of business or residence.

Occasional and Nontaxable Sales - Occasional sellers are usually people who are not required to hold a seller's permit because they will not be making a series of qualifying sales. A person who has cleared their garage of used items *accumulated for their own use* and who sells *only* those items would usually qualify as an occasional seller, provided they make sales no more than twice in a 12-month period. Some sellers who make only nontaxable sales are also not required to hold seller's permits. Examples include sellers of fresh produce or other cold food products sold "to go." Please note, however, some food sales are taxable, including sales of food for consumption in places where admission is charged.

Section 6015 Retailers - Revenue and Taxation Code section 6015 relieves certain individuals of the requirement to obtain a seller's permit when: (1) the product supplier is a Board approved section 6015 retailer, (2) the product supplier reports and pays tax on the actual "retail selling price," (3) the individual is selling only those items purchased from the section 6015 retailer, and (4) the individual provides the name of the product supplier. Typical section 6015 retailers include multi-level marketing retailers that solicit sales through a network of individual salespeople/representatives (e.g., Avon, Tupperware).

Verification of a seller's status is required by law. Please complete all four sections of this form. Please print.

1. EVENT INFORMATION

EVENT NAME AND PLACE

EVENT DATE(S)

TABLE/BOOTH/LOCATION ID#

2. VENDOR/EXHIBITOR INFORMATION

OWNER'S NAME

MAILING ADDRESS *(street number or P.O. box)*

(city, state and zip code)

TELEPHONE NUMBER
(   )

DRIVER LICENSE NUMBER OR STATE ID NUMBER AND STATE

TYPE OF BUSINESS, DESCRIPTION OF ITEMS TO BE SOLD/DISPLAYED

3. STATUS — *Check appropriate boxes, and provide requested information*

☐ I hold a valid seller's permit. My number is: **S**

☐ No sales of tangible personal property are being made or solicited at this event.

☐ I am not required to hold a seller's permit because:
  ☐ My retail product sales are not subject to tax   ☐ My sales are exempt occasional sales
  ☐ I sell on behalf of a section 6015 retailer

4. CERTIFICATION — *Partners/additional sellers, complete a separate copy of this form*

The above statements are certified to be correct to the best knowledge and belief of the undersigned.

NAME *(typed or printed)*

TITLE

SIGNATURE

DATE

See reverse for disclosure information.

Sales and Use Tax Privacy Notice

Information Provided
to the Board of Equalization

We ask you for information so that we can administer the state's sales and use tax laws (Revenue and Taxation Code sections 6001-7176, 7200-7226, 7251-7279.6, 7285-7288.6). We will use the information to determine whether you are paying the correct amount of tax and to collect any amounts you owe. You must provide all of the information we request, including your social security number (used for identification purposes [see Title 42 U.S. Code sec.405(c)(2)(C)(i)]).

What happens if I don't provide the information?

If your application is incomplete, we may not issue your seller's permit or use tax certificate. If you do not file complete returns, you may have to pay penalties and interest. Penalties may also apply if you don't provide other information we request or that is required by law, or if you give us fraudulent information. In some cases, you may be subject to criminal prosecution.

In addition, if you don't provide information we request to support your exemptions, credits, exclusions, or adjustments, we may not allow them. You may end up owing more tax or receiving a smaller refund.

Can anyone else see my information?

Your records are covered by state laws that protect your privacy. However, we may share information regarding your account with certain government agencies. We may also share certain information with companies authorized to represent local governments.

Under some circumstances we may release to the public the information printed on your permit, account start and closeout dates, and names of business owners or partners. When you sell a business, we can give the buyer or other involved parties information regarding your outstanding tax liability.

With your written permission, we can release information regarding your account to anyone you designate.

We may disclose information to the proper officials of the following agencies, among others:

- United States government agencies: U.S. Attorney's Office; Bureau of Alcohol, Tobacco and Firearms; Depts. of Agriculture, Defense, and Justice; Federal Bureau of Investigation; General Accounting Office; Internal Revenue Service; Interstate Commerce Commission

- State of California government agencies and officials: Air Resources Board; Dept. of Alcoholic Beverage Control; Auctioneer Commission; Dept. of Motor Vehicles, Employment Development Department; Energy Commission; Exposition and Fairs; Dept. of Food and Agriculture; Board of Forestry; Forest Products Commission; Franchise Tax Board; Dept. of Health Services; Highway Patrol; Dept. of Housing and Community Development; California Parent Locator Service

- State agencies outside of California for tax enforcement purposes

- City attorneys and city prosecutors; county district attorneys, police and sheriff departments.

Can I review my records?

Yes. Please contact your closest Board office (see the white pages of your phone book). If you need more information, you may contact our Disclosure Officer in Sacramento by calling 916- 445-2918. You may also want to obtain publication 58-A, *Inspecting and Correcting Your Records.* You may order a copy from our Information Center: 800-400-7115 or download it from the Internet: *www.boe.ca.gov* (look under "Forms and Publications").

Who is responsible for maintaining my records?

The deputy director of the Sales and Use Tax Department, whom you may contact by calling 916-445-6464 or writing at the address shown.

Deputy Director, Sales and Use Tax Department MIC:43
450 N Street
Sacramento, CA 95814

PUBLICATIONS ORDER

Please enter the quantity of each publication you wish to order and send your completed order form to the State Board of Equalization, Supply Unit, 3920 West Capitol Avenue, West Sacramento, CA 95691 or FAX your order to (916) 372-6078.

NAME OF BUSINESS	FOR OFFICE USE ONLY	REQUEST ☐ New ☐ One Time ☐ Replacement
ATTENTION	RECEIVED BY	IS FOR ☐ Distribution Change
MAILING ADDRESS	DATE REQUEST RECEIVED	
CITY STATE ZIP	SHIPPED BY	
TELEPHONE NUMBER ( )	DATE MATERIAL SHIPPED	

PAMPHLETS *(No Charge)*

QTY.	NO.	TITLE	QTY.	NO.	TITLE
_____	1	Sales and Use Tax Law	_____	31K	Tax Tips for Grocery Stores (Korean)
_____	2	Uniform Local Sales & Use Tax Law and Transactions & Use Tax Law	_____	31S	Tax Tips for Grocery Stores (Spanish)
			_____	31V	Tax Tips for Grocery Stores (Vietnamese)
_____	3	Use Fuel Tax Law	_____	32	Tax Tips for Sales to Purchasers from Mexico
_____	4	California Cigarette and Tobacco Products Tax Law	_____	32S	Tax Tips for Sales to Purchasers from Mexico (Spanish)
_____	5	Alcoholic Beverage Tax Law	_____	33AC	Making Sales in California (Arabic)
_____	6	Motor Vehicle Fuel License Tax Law	_____	33AN	Making Sales in California (Armenian)
_____	6A	Motor Vehicle Tax Law	_____	33CN	Making Sales in California (Cambodian)
_____	7	Tax on Insurers Law	_____	33GN	Making Sales in California (German)
_____	8	Private Railroad Car Tax Law	_____	33HG	Making Sales in California (Hmong)
_____	9	Tax Tips for Construction and Building Contractors	_____	33HI	Making Sales in California (Hindi)
_____	10	Energy Resources Surcharge Law	_____	33JE	Making Sales in California (Japanese)
_____	11	Energy Resources Surcharge Regulations	_____	33PE	Making Sales in California (Portuguese)
_____	12	California Use Fuel Tax: A Guide for Vendors and Users	_____	33PI	Making Sales in California (Pilipino)
_____	14	Motor Vehicle Fuel License Tax Regulations	_____	33PO	Making Sales in California (Punjabi)
_____	15	Cigarette Tax Regulations	_____	34	Tax Tips for Motor Vehicle Dealers (New & Used)
_____	16	Alcoholic Beverage Tax Regulations and Instructions	_____	35	Tax Tips for Interior Designers and Decorators
_____	17	Appeals Procedures: Sales & Use Taxes and Special Taxes	_____	36	Tax Tips for Veterinarians
_____	18	Tax Tips for Nonprofit Organizations	_____	39	Emergency Telephone Users Surcharge Regulations
_____	19	Diesel Fuel Tax Law	_____	40	Tax Tips for the Watercraft Industry
_____	20	California Emergency Telephone Users Surcharge Law	_____	41	Taxes and Fees Administered by the Board of Equalization
_____	21	State Board of Equalization	_____	42	Resale Certificate Tips
_____	22	Tax Tips for the Dining and Beverage Industry	_____	42S	Resale Certificate Tips (Spanish)
_____	22K	Tax Tips for the Dining and Beverage Industry (Korean)	_____	43	Timber Yield Tax Law
			_____	44	Tax Tips for District Taxes
_____	22S	Tax Tips for the Dining and Beverage Industry (Spanish)	_____	45	Tax Tips for Hospitals
			_____	46	Tax Tips for Leasing of Tangible Personal Property in California
_____	24	Tax Tips for Liquor Stores	_____	47	Tax Tips for Mobilehomes and Factory-Built Housing
_____	25	Tax Tips for Auto Repair Garages and Service Stations			
_____	25S	Tax Tips for Auto Repair Garages and Service Stations (Spanish)	_____	48	Property Tax Exemptions for Religious Organizations
_____	26	Tax Information Bulletin Index	_____	49	California Underground Storage Tank Maintenance Fee Law
_____	27	Tax Tips for Drug Stores			
_____	28	Tax Information for City and County Officials Sales and Use Tax	_____	50	Guide to the International Fuel Tax Agreement
			_____	50S	Guide to the International Fuel Tax Agreement (Spanish)
_____	29	California Property Tax: An Overview			
_____	30	Residential Property Assessment Appeals	_____	50-A	Introduction to the International Fuel Tax Agreement
_____	31	Tax Tips for Grocery Stores	_____	50-A-S	Introduction to the International Fuel Tax Agreement (Spanish)
_____	31C	Tax Tips for Grocery Stores (Chinese)			

QTY.	NO.	TITLE	QTY.	NO.	TITLE
_____	51	Guide to Board of Equalization Services	_____	86	Timber Yield Tax (brochure)
_____	51C	Guide to Board of Equalization Services (Chinese)	_____	87	Guide to the Timber Yield Tax
_____	51K	Guide to Board of Equalization Services (Korean)	_____	88	Underground Storage Tank Fee
_____	51S	Guide to Board of Equalization Services (Spanish)	_____	90	Environmental Fee
_____	51V	Guide to Board of Equalization Services (Vietnamese)	_____	91	Tire Recycling Fee
_____	52	Vehicles and Vessels: How to Request a Use Tax Clearance for DMV Registration	_____	92	Alcoholic Beverage Tax
_____	54	Tax Collection Procedures	_____	93	Cigarette & Tobacco Products Tax
_____	55	Homeowners & Renters Assistance Appeals	_____	94	Occupational Lead Poisoning Prevention Fee
_____	56	Offers In Compromise	_____	100	Shipping and Delivery Charges
_____	58-A	How to Inspect & Correct Your Records	_____	100S	Shipping and Delivery Charges (Spanish)
_____	59	Local Motor Vehicle Fuel Taxation Law	_____	101	Sales Delivered Outside California
_____	60	Hazardous Substances Tax Law	_____	101S	Sales Delivered Outside California (Spanish)
_____	61	Sales and Use Taxes: Exemptions and Exclusions	_____	102	Sales to the U.S. Government
_____	62	Tax Tips for Locksmiths	_____	102S	Sales to the U.S. Government (Spanish)
_____	64	Tax Tips for Jewelry Stores	_____	103	Sales for Resale
_____	66	Tax Tips for Retail Feed and Farm Supply Stores	_____	103S	Sales for Resale (Spanish)
_____	68	Tax Tips for Photographers, Photo Finishers and Film Processing Laboratories	_____	104	Sales to Residents of Other Countries
_____	69	California Integrated Waste Management Fee Law	_____	104S	Sales to Residents of Other Countries (Spanish)
_____	70	The California Taxpayers' Bill of Rights	_____	105	District Taxes and Delivered Sales
_____	70C	The California Taxpayers' Bill of Rights (Chinese)	_____	105S	District Taxes and Delivered Sales (Spanish)
_____	70K	The California Taxpayers' Bill of Rights (Korean)	_____	106	Gift Wrapping Charges
_____	70S	The California Taxpayers' Bill of Rights (Spanish)	_____	107	Do You Need a California Sellers Permit?
_____	70V	The California Taxpayers' Bill of Rights (Vietnamese)	_____	107S	Do You Need a California Sellers Permit? (Spanish)
_____	71	California City and County Sales and Use Tax Rates	_____	108	When Is Labor Taxable?
_____	71C	California City and County Sales and Use Tax Rates (Chinese)	_____	108S	When Is Labor Taxable? (Spanish)
_____	71S	California City and County Sales and Use Tax Rates (Spanish)	_____	109	Are Your Internet Sales Taxable?
_____	72	Summary of Constitutional & Statutory Authorities	_____	109S	Are Your Internet Sales Taxable? (Spanish)
_____	73	Your California Seller's Permit	_____	110	California Use Tax Basics
_____	73C	Your California Seller's Permit (Chinese)	_____	110S	California Use Tax Basics (Spanish)
_____	73F	Your California Seller's Permit (Farsi)	_____	111	Operators of Swap Meets, Flea Markets and Special Events
_____	73K	Your California Seller's Permit (Korean)	_____	111S	Operators of Swap Meets, Flea Markets and Special Events (Spanish)
_____	73S	Your California Seller's Permit (Spanish)	_____	112	Purchases From Out-of-State Vendors
_____	73V	Your California Seller's Permit (Vietnamese)	_____	112S	Purchases From Out-of-State Vendors (Spanish)
_____	74	Closing Out Your Seller's Permit	_____	113	Coupons and Sales Tax
_____	74C	Closing Out Your Seller's Permit (Chinese)	_____	113S	Coupons and Sales Tax (Spanish)
_____	74S	Closing Out Your Seller's Permit (Spanish)	_____	114	Consignment Sales
_____	75	Interest and Penalty Payments	_____	115	Applying Sales Tax to Tips
_____	76	Audits	_____	115S	Applying Sales Tax to Tips (Spanish)
_____	76F	Audits (Farsi)	_____	116	Sales and Use Tax Records
_____	76K	Audits (Korean)	_____	Other	_____
_____	76S	Audits (Spanish)			_____
_____	77	Out-of-State Sellers: Do You Need to Register with California			_____
_____	79	Documented Vessels & California Tax			_____
_____	79A	Aircraft and California Tax			_____
_____	79B	California Individual Use Tax			_____
_____	80	Electronic Funds Transfer Program			
_____	81	Franchise and Personal Income Tax Appeals			
_____	82	Prepaid Sales Tax on Sales of Fuel			
_____	83	Tire Recycling Fee Law			
_____	84	Use Fuel Permit Requirements			

MISCELLANEOUS *(No Charge)*

_____ Annual Calendar of Board Meetings

_____ Annual Report of the State Board of Equalization

_____ State of California Sales Tax Reimbursement Schedules

_____ Tax Information Bulletin (published quarterly)

Issue (mo./year) _____

_____ Other _____

Instructions for Form FTB 3522
LLC Tax Voucher

General Information

Use form FTB 3522, LLC Tax Voucher, to pay the annual limited liability company (LLC) tax of $800 for taxable year 2009. An LLC should use this form if any of the following apply:

- The LLC has articles of organization accepted by the California Secretary of State (SOS).
- The LLC has a certificate of registration issued by the SOS.
- The LLC is doing business in California.

You can download, view, and print California tax forms and publications from our website at **ftb.ca.gov**.

Access other state agencies' websites through the State Agencies Directory on California's website at **ca.gov**.

Round Cents to Dollars – Round cents to the nearest whole dollar. For example, round $50.50 up to $51 or round $25.49 down to $25.

Who Must Pay the Annual LLC Tax

Every LLC that is doing business in California or that has articles of organization accepted or a certificate of registration issued by the SOS **is subject to the $800.00 annual tax.** The tax must be paid for each taxable year until a certificate of cancellation of registration or of articles of organization is filed with the SOS.

For taxable years beginning on or after January 1, 2003, an LLC as described in Internal Revenue Code Section 501(c)(2) and 501(c)(25) and California Revenue and Taxation Code Sections 23701h and 23701x is exempt from the annual LLC tax.

How to Complete Form FTB 3522

Enter all the information requested using blue or black ink. To ensure the timely and proper application of the payment to the LLC's account, enter the SOS file number (assigned upon registration with the SOS), and the federal employer identification number (FEIN).

Series LLC – After the name for each series, write "Series LLC # ___." In addition, write "Series LLC" in red on the top right margin of the form. Only the first series to pay tax or file a return may use a California SOS number. For all other series, enter zeroes in the Secretary of State (SOS) file number field. We will assign a number and notify each series. See FTB Pub. 3556, Limited Liability Companies, for more information.

Private Mail Box

Include the Private Mail Box (PMB) in the address field. Write "PMB" first, then the box number. Example: 111 Main Street PMB 123.

Where to File

Make a check or money order payable to the "Franchise Tax Board." Write the SOS file number, FEIN, and "2009 FTB 3522" on the check or money order. Detach the payment form from the bottom of the page. Enclose, but do **not** staple, your payment to the form and mail to:

FRANCHISE TAX BOARD
PO BOX 942857
SACRAMENTO CA 94257-0631

Make all checks or money orders payable in U.S. dollars and drawn against a U.S. financial institution. **If no payment is due, do not mail this form.**

When to Pay the Annual LLC Tax

The annual LLC tax is due and payable **by the 15th day of the 4th month** after the **beginning** of the LLC's taxable year (fiscal year) or April 15, 2009 (calendar year).

The first taxable year of an LLC that was not previously in existence begins when the LLC is organized or registered with the California SOS.

If the 15th day of the 4th month of an existing foreign LLC's taxable year has passed before the foreign LLC commences business in California or registers with the SOS, the annual LLC tax should be paid immediately after commencing business or registering with the SOS.

Example: LLC1, a newly-formed calendar year taxpayer, organizes as an LLC in Delaware on June 1, 2009. LLC1 registers with the SOS on August 13, 2009, and begins doing business in California on August 14, 2009. Because LLC1's initial taxable year began on June 1, 2009 the annual LLC tax is due by September 15, 2009 (the 15th day of the 4th month of the short period taxable year). LLC1's short period (June 1, 2009-December 31, 2009) tax return is due by April 15, 2010. The annual tax payment for taxable year 2010, with form FTB 3522 also is due by April 15, 2010.

Penalties and Interest

If the LLC fails to pay its annual tax by the 15th day of the 4th month after the beginning of the taxable year, a late payment penalty plus interest will be assessed for failure to pay the annual LLC tax by the due date. The FTB may waive the late penalty, based on reasonable cause, where the greater of the annual tax or 90% of the tax shown on the return is paid by the original due date of the return. The penalty and interest will be computed from the due date of the tax to the date of payment.

Late Payment of Prior Year Annual LLC Tax

If a prior year LLC tax of $800 was not paid by the 15th day of the 4th month after the beginning of the taxable year, the tax should be paid as soon as possible, using the **appropriate taxable year** form FTB 3522. **Do not** use any other form for payment of the tax. This will assure proper application of the payment to the LLC's account.

✂- - DETACH HERE _ _ _ _ _ _ _ **IF NO PAYMENT IS DUE, DO NOT MAIL THIS FORM** _ _ _ _ _ _ DETACH HERE - ✂

Fiscal year: File and Pay by the 15th day of the 4th month after the beginning of the taxable year.
Calendar year: File and Pay by APRIL 15, 2009.

TAXABLE YEAR   CALIFORNIA FORM

2009   LLC Tax Voucher   3522

For calendar year 2009 or fiscal year beginning month_____ day_____ year _____, and ending month_____ day_____ year_____.

Limited liability company name	Secretary of State (SOS) file number
DBA	FEIN

Address (including suite, room, PO Box, or PMB no.).

City		State	ZIP Code

Contact Telephone no.	Amount of payment
( )	_ _ _ _ _ _.00

6111093   FTB 3522 2008

Form **8832**
(Rev. March 2007)
Department of the Treasury
Internal Revenue Service

Entity Classification Election

OMB No. 1545-1516

Type or Print

Name of eligible entity making election	Employer identification number

Number, street, and room or suite no. If a P.O. box, see instructions.

City or town, state, and ZIP code. If a foreign address, enter city, province or state, postal code and country. Follow the country's practice for entering the postal code.

▶ Check if: ☐ Address change

---

1 **Type of election** (see instructions):

a ☐ Initial classification by a newly-formed entity. Skip lines 2a and 2b and go to line 3.

b ☐ Change in current classification. Go to line 2a.

2a Has the eligible entity previously filed an entity election that had an effective date within the last 60 months?

☐ **Yes.** Go to line 2b.
☐ **No.** Skip line 2b and go to line 3.

2b Was the eligible entity's prior election for initial classification by a newly formed entity effective on the date of formation?

☐ **Yes.** Go to line 3.
☐ **No.** Stop here. You generally are not currently eligible to make the election (see instructions).

3 Does the eligible entity have more than one owner?

☐ **Yes.** You can elect to be classified as a partnership or an association taxable as a corporation. Skip line 4 and go to line 5.
☐ **No.** You can elect to be classified as an association taxable as a corporation or disregarded as a separate entity. Go to line 4.

4 If the eligible entity has only one owner, provide the following information:

a Name of owner ▶ ....

b Identifying number of owner ▶ ....

5 If the eligible entity is owned by one or more affiliated corporations that file a consolidated return, provide the name and employer identification number of the parent corporation:

a Name of parent corporation ▶ ....

b Employer identification number ▶ ....

For Paperwork Reduction Act Notice, see instructions.   Cat. No. 22598R   Form **8832** (Rev. 3-2007)

6   Type of entity (see instructions):

a ☐   A domestic eligible entity electing to be classified as an association taxable as a corporation.

b ☐   A domestic eligible entity electing to be classified as a partnership.

c ☐   A domestic eligible entity with a single owner electing to be disregarded as a separate entity.

d ☐   A foreign eligible entity electing to be classified as an association taxable as a corporation.

e ☐   A foreign eligible entity electing to be classified as a partnership.

f ☐   A foreign eligible entity with a single owner electing to be disregarded as a separate entity.

7   If the eligible entity is created or organized in a foreign jurisdiction, provide the foreign country of organization ▶ ....

8   Election is to be effective beginning (month, day, year) (see instructions) . . . . ▶ ___ / ___ / ___

9 Name and title of contact person whom the IRS may call for more information	**10** Contact person's telephone number
	( )

Consent Statement and Signature(s) (see instructions)

Under penalties of perjury, I (we) declare that I (we) consent to the election of the above-named entity to be classified as indicated above, and that I (we) have examined this consent statement, and to the best of my (our) knowledge and belief, it is true, correct, and complete. If I am an officer, manager, or member signing for all members of the entity, I further declare that I am authorized to execute this consent statement on their behalf.

Signature(s)	Date	Title

General Instructions

Section references are to the Internal Revenue Code unless otherwise noted.

What's New

This revision of the Form 8832 instructions reflects an update to the filing locations. Our previous revision (December 2006) stated that all entity classification elections were sent to the service center in Ogden, UT. *This is no longer the case.* Now the form is filed either in Cincinnati or Ogden depending upon your principal business location. See *Where To File* on page 4 for your filing location.

• You are not required to sign the copy of Form 8832 filed with your tax return. See *Consent statement and signature(s)* on page 6.

• New questions on lines 2a and 2b highlight the general rule which limits an eligible entity's ability to change its classification by election again during the 60 months after the effective date of making an earlier entity classification election.

• All single-owner eligible entities electing either corporate or disregarded entity status must provide the name and identifying number of their owner on lines 4a and 4b. Previously this requirement applied only to single-owner eligible entities electing disregarded entity status.

• All eligible entities owned by one or more affiliated corporations that file a consolidated return must provide the name and employer identification number (EIN) of their parent corporation on lines 5a and 5b. Previously this requirement applied only to single-owner eligible entities electing disregarded entity status.

• All foreign eligible entities making an entity classification election, including those also organized under domestic law, must provide the name of the foreign country in which they are organized on line 7. Previously this requirement applied only to single-owner foreign eligible entities electing disregarded entity status.

Purpose of Form

An eligible entity uses Form 8832 to elect how it will be classified for federal tax purposes, as a corporation, a partnership, or an entity disregarded as separate from its owner. An eligible entity is classified for federal tax purposes under the default rules described below unless it files Form 8832 or Form 2553, Election by a Small Business Corporation, to elect a classification or change its current classification. See *Who Must File* on page 4.

 A new eligible entity should not file Form 8832 if it will be using its default classification (see Default Rules below).

Eligible entity. An eligible entity is a business entity that is not included in items 1, or 3 through 9, under the definition of **corporation** provided under *Definitions.*

Eligible entities include limited liability companies (LLCs), partnerships, and any foreign entity that is not identified as a corporation under Regulations section 301.7701-2(b)(8) (see item 3 below).

Generally, corporations are not eligible entities. However, the following types of corporations are treated as eligible entities:

1. An eligible entity that previously elected to be an association taxable as a corporation by filing Form 8832. An entity that elects to be classified as a corporation by filing Form 8832 can make another election to change its classification (see the *60-month limitation rule* discussed below in the instructions for lines 2a and 2b).

2. A foreign eligible entity that became an association taxable as a corporation under the foreign default rule described below.

3. A foreign corporation that is not identified as a corporation under Regulations section 301.7701-2(b)(8). If a foreign corporation is not identified on the list included in these regulations, it qualifies as an eligible entity. See the list of *Foreign Entities Classified as Corporations for Federal Tax Purposes* under this regulation on page 6. Refer to the regulations for any changes to the list made after these instructions were printed.

The IRS will use the information entered on this form to establish the entity's filing and reporting requirements for federal tax purposes.

Default Rules

Existing entity default rule. Certain domestic and foreign entities that were in existence before January 1, 1997, and have an established federal tax classification generally do not need to make an election to continue that classification. If an existing entity decides to change its classification, it may do so subject to the 60-month limitation rule. See the instructions for lines 2a and 2b. See Regulations sections 301.7701-3(b)(3) and 301.7701-3(h)(2) for more details.

Domestic default rule. Unless an election is made on Form 8832, a domestic eligible entity is:

1. A partnership if it has two or more members.

2. Disregarded as an entity separate from its owner if it has a single owner.

A change in the number of members of an eligible entity classified as an **association** (defined below) does not affect the entity's classification. However, an eligible entity classified as a partnership

will become a disregarded entity when the entity's membership is reduced to one member and a disregarded entity will be classified as a partnership when the entity has more than one member.

Foreign default rule. Unless an election is made on Form 8832, a foreign eligible entity is:

1. A partnership if it has two or more members and at least one member does not have limited liability.

2. An association taxable as a corporation if all members have limited liability.

3. Disregarded as an entity separate from its owner if it has a single owner that does not have limited liability.

Definitions

Association. For purposes of this form, an association is an eligible entity taxable as a corporation by election or, for foreign eligible entities, under the default rules (see Regulations section 301.7701-3).

Business entity. A business entity is any entity recognized for federal tax purposes that is not properly classified as a trust under Regulations section 301.7701-4 or otherwise subject to special treatment under the Code regarding the entity's classification. See Regulations section 301.7701-2(a).

Corporation. For federal tax purposes, a corporation is any of the following:

1. A business entity organized under a federal or state statute, or under a statute of a federally recognized Indian tribe, if the statute describes or refers to the entity as incorporated or as a corporation, body corporate, or body politic.

2. An association (as determined under Regulations section 301.7701-3).

3. A business entity organized under a state statute, if the statute describes or refers to the entity as a joint-stock company or joint-stock association.

4. An insurance company.

5. A state-chartered business entity conducting banking activities, if any of its deposits are insured under the Federal Deposit Insurance Act, as amended, 12 U.S.C. 1811 et seq., or a similar federal statute.

6. A business entity wholly owned by a state or any political subdivision thereof, or a business entity wholly owned by a foreign government or any other entity described in Regulations section 1.892-2T.

7. A business entity that is taxable as a corporation under a provision of the Code other than section 7701(a)(3).

8. A foreign business entity listed on page 6. See Regulations section 301.7701-2(b)(8) for any exceptions and inclusions to items on this list and for any revisions made to this list since these instructions were printed.

9. An entity created or organized under the laws of more than one jurisdiction (business entities with multiple charters) if the entity is treated as a corporation with respect to any one of the jurisdictions. See Regulations section 301.7701-2(b)(9) for examples.

Disregarded entity. A disregarded entity is an eligible entity that is treated as an entity not separate from its single owner. Its separate existence will be ignored for federal tax purposes unless it elects corporate tax treatment.

Limited liability. A member of a foreign eligible entity has limited liability if the member has no personal liability for any debts of or claims against the entity by reason of being a member. This determination is based solely on the statute or law under which the entity is organized (and, if relevant, the entity's organizational documents). A member has personal liability if the creditors of the entity may seek satisfaction of all or any part of the debts or claims against the entity from the member as such. A member has personal liability even if the member makes an agreement under which another person (whether or not a member of the entity) assumes that liability or agrees to indemnify that member for that liability.

Partnership. A partnership is a business entity that has at least two members and is not a corporation as defined on page 3 under *Corporation.*

Who Must File

File this form for an eligible entity that is one of the following:

● A domestic entity electing to be classified as an association taxable as a corporation.

● A domestic entity electing to change its current classification (even if it is currently classified under the default rule).

● A foreign entity that has more than one owner, all owners having limited liability, electing to be classified as a partnership.

● A foreign entity that has at least one owner that does not have limited liability, electing to be classified as an association taxable as a corporation.

● A foreign entity with a single owner having limited liability, electing to be an entity disregarded as an entity separate from its owner.

● A foreign entity electing to change its current classification (even if it is currently classified under the default rule).

Do not file this form for an eligible entity that is:

● Tax-exempt under section 501(a);

● A real estate investment trust (REIT), as defined in section 856; or

● Electing to be classified as an S corporation. An eligible entity that timely files Form 2553 to elect classification as an S corporation and meets all other requirements to qualify as an S corporation is deemed to have made an election under Regulations section 301.7701-3(c)(v) to be classified as an association taxable as a corporation.

All three of these entities are deemed to have made an election to be classified as an association.

Effect of Election

The federal tax treatment of elective changes in classification as described in Regulations section 301.7701-3(g)(1) is summarized as follows:

● If an eligible entity classified as a partnership elects to be classified as an association, it is deemed that the partnership contributes all of its assets and liabilities to the association in exchange for stock in the association, and immediately thereafter, the partnership liquidates by distributing the stock of the association to its partners.

● If an eligible entity classified as an association elects to be classified as a partnership, it is deemed that the association distributes all of its assets and liabilities to its shareholders in liquidation of the association, and immediately thereafter, the shareholders contribute all of the distributed assets and liabilities to a newly formed partnership.

● If an eligible entity classified as an association elects to be disregarded as an entity separate from its owner, it is deemed that the association distributes all of its assets and liabilities to its single owner in liquidation of the association.

● If an eligible entity that is disregarded as an entity separate from its owner elects to be classified as an association, the owner of the eligible entity is deemed to have contributed all of the assets and liabilities of the entity to the association in exchange for the stock of the association.

Note. For information on the federal tax consequences of elective changes in classification, see Regulations section 301.7701-3(g).

When To File

An election specifying an eligible entity's classification cannot take effect more than 75 days prior to the date the election is filed, nor can it take effect later than 12 months after the date the election is filed.

Late election relief. A newly formed entity may be eligible for late election relief under Rev. Proc. 2002-59, 2002-39 I.R.B. 615 if:

● The entity failed to obtain its desired classification solely because Form 8832 was not timely filed,

● The due date for the entity's desired classification tax return (excluding extensions) for the tax year beginning with the entity's formation date has not passed, and

● The entity has reasonable cause for its failure to make a timely election.

To obtain relief, a newly formed entity must file Form 8832 on or before the due date of the first federal tax return (excluding extensions) of the entity's desired classification. The entity must also write "FILED PURSUANT TO REV. PROC. 2002-59" at the top of the form. The entity must attach a statement to the form explaining why it failed to file a timely election. If Rev. Proc. 2002-59 does not apply, an entity may seek relief for a late entity election by requesting a private letter ruling and paying a user fee in accordance with Rev. Proc. 2006-1, 2006-1 I.R.B. 1 (or its successor).

Where To File

File Form 8832 with the Internal Revenue Service Center for your state listed below.

Attach a copy of Form 8832 to the entity's federal tax return for the tax year of the election. If the entity is not required to file a return for that year, a copy of its Form 8832 must be attached to the federal tax returns of all direct or indirect owners of the entity for the tax year of the owner that includes the date on which the election took effect. Failure to attach a copy of Form 8832 will not invalidate an otherwise valid election, but penalties may be assessed against persons who are required to, but do not, attach Form 8832.

Each member of the entity is required to file their return consistent with the entity election. Penalties apply to returns filed inconsistent with the entity's election.

If the entity's principal business, office, or agency is located in:	Use the following Internal Revenue Service Center address:
Connecticut, Delaware, District of Columbia, Illinois, Indiana, Kentucky, Maine, Maryland, Massachusetts, Michigan, New Hampshire, New Jersey, New York, North Carolina, Ohio, Pennsylvania, Rhode Island, South Carolina, Vermont, Virginia, West Virginia, Wisconsin	Cincinnati, OH 45999

If the entity's principal business, office, or agency is located in:	Use the following Internal Revenue Service Center address:
Alabama, Alaska, Arizona, Arkansas, California, Colorado, Florida, Georgia, Hawaii, Idaho, Iowa, Kansas, Louisiana, Minnesota, Mississippi, Missouri, Montana, Nebraska, Nevada, New Mexico, North Dakota, Oklahoma, Oregon, South Dakota, Tennessee, Texas, Utah, Washington, Wyoming	Ogden, UT 84201
A foreign country or U.S. possession	Ogden, UT 84201-0023

Note. Also attach a copy to the entity's federal income tax return for the tax year of the election.

Acceptance or Nonacceptance of Election

The service center will notify the eligible entity at the address listed on Form 8832 if its election is accepted or not accepted. The entity should generally receive a determination on its election within 60 days after it has filed Form 8832.

Care should be exercised to ensure that the IRS receives the election. If the entity is not notified of acceptance or nonacceptance of its election within 60 days of the date of filing, take follow-up action by calling 1-800-829-0115, or by sending a letter to the service center to inquire about its status. Send any such letter by certified or registered mail via the U.S. Postal Service, or equivalent type of delivery by a designated private delivery service (see Notice 2004-83, 2004-52 I.R.B. 1030 (or its successor)).

If the IRS questions whether Form 8832 was filed, an acceptable proof of filing is:

• A certified or registered mail receipt (timely postmarked) from the U.S. Postal Service, or its equivalent from a designated private delivery service;

• Form 8832 with an accepted stamp;

• Form 8832 with a stamped IRS received date; or

• An IRS letter stating that Form 8832 has been accepted.

Specific Instructions

Name. Enter the name of the eligible entity electing to be classified.

Employer identification number (EIN). Show the EIN of the eligible entity electing to be classified.

Caution. Do not put "Applied For" on this line.

Note. Any entity that has an EIN will retain that EIN even if its federal tax classification changes under Regulations section 301.7701-3.

If a disregarded entity's classification changes so that it becomes recognized as a partnership or association for federal tax purposes, and that entity had an EIN, then the entity must continue to use that EIN. If the entity did not already have its own EIN, then the entity must apply for an EIN and not use the identifying number of the single owner.

A foreign person that makes an election under Regulations section 301.7701-3(c) and (d) must also use its own taxpayer identifying number. See sections 6721 through 6724 for penalties that may apply for failure to supply taxpayer identifying numbers.

If the entity electing to be classified using Form 8832 does not have an EIN, it must apply for one on Form SS-4, Application for Employer Identification Number. If the filing of Form 8832 is the only reason the entity is applying for an EIN, check the "Other" box on line 9 of Form SS-4 and enter "Form 8832" to the right of that box. The entity must have received an EIN by the time Form 8832 is filed in order for the form to be processed. An election will not be accepted if the eligible entity does not provide an EIN. **Caution.** Do not apply for a new EIN for an existing entity that is changing its classification if the entity already has an EIN.

Address. Enter the address of the entity electing a classification. All correspondence regarding the acceptance or nonacceptance of the election will be sent to this address. Include the suite, room, or other unit number after the street address. If the Post Office does not deliver mail to the street address and the entity has a P.O. box, show the box number instead of the street address. If the electing entity receives its mail in care of a third party (such as an accountant or an attorney), enter on the street address line "C/O" followed by the third party's name and street address or P.O. box.

Address change. If the eligible entity has changed its address since filing Form SS-4 or the entity's most recently-filed return (including a change to an "in care of" address), check the box for an address change.

Note. If a change of address occurs after the later of the filing of Form SS-4 or the most recently-filed return, use Form 8822, Change of Address, to notify the IRS of the new address. A new address shown on Form 8832 will not update the entity's address of record with the IRS.

Line 1. Check box 1a if the entity is choosing a classification for the first time (i.e., the entity does not want to be classified under the applicable default classification). Do not file this form if the

entity wants to be classified under the default rules.

Check box 1b if the entity is changing its current classification.

Lines 2a and 2b. 60-month limitation rule. Once an eligible entity makes an election to *change* its classification, the entity generally cannot change its classification by election again during the 60 months after the effective date of the election. However, the IRS may (by private letter ruling) permit the entity to change its classification by election within the 60-month period if more than 50% of the ownership interests in the entity, as of the effective date of the election, are owned by persons that did not own any interests in the entity on the effective date or the filing date of the entity's prior election.

Note. The 60-month limitation does not apply if the previous election was made by a *newly formed* eligible entity and was effective on the date of formation.

Line 4. If an eligible entity has only one owner, provide the name of its owner on line 4a and the owner's identifying number (social security number, or Individual taxpayer identification number, or EIN) on line 4b. Enter "DE" if the owner is a disregarded entity that does not have an identifying number. If the owner is a foreign person or entity and does not have a U.S. identifying number, enter "none" on line 4b.

Line 5. If the eligible entity is owned by one or more members of an affiliated group of corporations that file a consolidated return, provide the name and EIN of the parent corporation.

Line 6. Check the appropriate box if you are changing a current classification (no matter how achieved), or are electing out of a default classification. Do not file this form if you fall within a default classification that is the desired classification for the new entity.

Line 7. If the entity making the election is created or organized in a foreign jurisdiction, enter the name of the foreign country in which it is organized. This information must be provided even if the entity is also organized under domestic law.

Line 8. Generally, the election will take effect on the date you enter on line 8 of this form, or on the date filed if no date is entered on line 8. An election specifying an entity's classification for federal tax purposes can take effect no more than 75 days prior to the date the election is filed, nor can it take effect later than 12 months after the date on which the election is filed. If line 8 shows a date more than 75 days prior to the date on which the election is filed, the election will default to 75 days before the date it is filed. If line 8 shows an effective date more than 12 months from the filing date, the election will take effect 12 months after the date the election is filed.

Consent statement and signature(s).
Form 8832 must be signed by:

1. Each member of the electing entity who is an owner at the time the election is filed; or

2. Any officer, manager, or member of the electing entity who is authorized (under local law or the organizational documents) to make the election. The elector represents to having such authorization under penalties of perjury.

If an election is to be effective for any period prior to the time it is filed, each person who was an owner between the date the election is to be effective and the date the election is filed, must sign.

If you need a continuation sheet or use a separate consent statement, attach it to Form 8832. The separate consent statement must contain the same information as shown on Form 8832.

Note. Do not sign the copy that is attached to your tax return.

Paperwork Reduction Act Notice

We ask for the information on this form to carry out the Internal Revenue laws of the United States. You are required to give us the information. We need it to ensure that you are complying with these laws and to allow us to figure and collect the right amount of tax.

You are not required to provide the information requested on a form that is subject to the Paperwork Reduction Act unless the form displays a valid OMB control number. Books or records relating to a form or its instructions must be retained as long as their contents may become material in the administration of any Internal Revenue law. Generally, tax returns and return information are confidential, as required by section 6103.

The time needed to complete and file this form will vary depending on individual circumstances. The estimated average time is:

Recordkeeping . . . . 1 hr., 49 min.

Learning about the law or the form . . . . 2 hr., 7 min.

Preparing and sending the form to the IRS . . . . . 23 min.

If you have comments concerning the accuracy of these time estimates or suggestions for making this form simpler, we would be happy to hear from you. You can write to the Internal Revenue Service, Tax Products Coordinating Committee, SE:W:CAR:MP:T:T:SP, 1111 Constitution Ave. NW, IR-6406, Washington, DC 20224. Do not send the form to this address. Instead, see *Where To File* on page 4.

Foreign Entities Classified as Corporations for Federal Tax Purposes:

American Samoa—Corporation
Argentina—Sociedad Anonima
Australia—Public Limited Company
Austria—Aktiengesellschaft
Barbados—Limited Company
Belgium—Societe Anonyme
Belize—Public Limited Company
Bolivia—Sociedad Anonima
Brazil—Sociedade Anonima
Canada—Corporation and Company
Chile—Sociedad Anonima
People's Republic of China—Gufen Youxian Gongsi
Republic of China (Taiwan)—Ku-fen Yu-hsien Kung-szu
Colombia—Sociedad Anonima
Costa Rica—Sociedad Anonima
Cyprus—Public Limited Company
Czech Republic—Akciova Spolecnost
Denmark—Aktieselskab
Ecuador—Sociedad Anonima or Compania Anonima
Egypt—Sharikat Al-Mossahamah
El Salvador—Sociedad Anonima
Estonia—Aktsiaselts
European Economic Area/European Union—Societas Europaea
Finland—Julkinen Osakeyhtio/ Publikt Aktiebolag
France—Societe Anonyme
Germany—Aktiengesellschaft
Greece—Anonymos Etairia
Guam—Corporation
Guatemala—Sociedad Anonima
Guyana—Public Limited Company
Honduras—Sociedad Anonima
Hong Kong—Public Limited Company
Hungary—Reszvenytarsasag
Iceland—Hlutafelag
India—Public Limited Company
Indonesia—Perseroan Terbuka
Ireland—Public Limited Company
Israel—Public Limited Company
Italy—Societa per Azioni
Jamaica—Public Limited Company
Japan—Kabushiki Kaisha
Kazakstan—Ashyk Aktsionerlik Kogham
Republic of Korea—Chusik Hoesa
Latvia—Akciju Sabiedriba
Liberia—Corporation
Liechtenstein—Aktiengesellschaft
Lithuania—Akcine Bendroves
Luxembourg—Societe Anonyme

Malaysia—Berhad
Malta—Public Limited Company
Mexico—Sociedad Anonima
Morocco—Societe Anonyme
Netherlands—Naamloze Vennootschap
New Zealand—Limited Company
Nicaragua—Compania Anonima
Nigeria—Public Limited Company
Northern Mariana Islands—Corporation
Norway—Allment Aksjeselskap
Pakistan—Public Limited Company
Panama—Sociedad Anonima
Paraguay—Sociedad Anonima
Peru—Sociedad Anonima
Philippines—Stock Corporation
Poland—Spolka Akcyjna
Portugal—Sociedade Anonima
Puerto Rico—Corporation
Romania—Societe pe Actiuni
Russia—Otkrytoye Aktsionernoy Obshchestvo
Saudi Arabia—Sharikat Al-Mossahamah
Singapore—Public Limited Company
Slovak Republic—Akciova Spolocnost
Slovenia—Delniska Druzba
South Africa—Public Limited Company
Spain—Sociedad Anonima
Surinam—Naamloze Vennootschap
Sweden—Publika Aktiebolag
Switzerland—Aktiengesellschaft
Thailand—Borisat Chamkad (Mahachon)
Trinidad and Tobago—Limited Company
Tunisia—Societe Anonyme
Turkey—Anonim Sirket
Ukraine—Aktsionerne Tovaristvo Vidkritogo Tipu
United Kingdom—Public Limited Company
United States Virgin Islands—Corporation
Uruguay—Sociedad Anonima
Venezuela—Sociedad Anonima or Compania Anonima

See Regulations section 301.7701-2(b)(8) for any exceptions and inclusions to items on this list and for any revisions made to this list since these instructions were printed.

Form **8716**
(Rev. December 2008)

Department of the Treasury
Internal Revenue Service

Election To Have a Tax Year Other Than a Required Tax Year

OMB No. 1545-1036

Type or Print

Name

Employer identification number

Number, street, and room or suite no. (or P.O. box number if mail is not delivered to street address)

City or town, state, and ZIP code

1 Check applicable box to indicate type of entity:
☐ Partnership
☐ S corporation (or C corporation electing to be an S corporation)
☐ Personal service corporation (PSC)

2 Name and telephone number (including area code) of person who may be called for information:

3 Enter ending date of the tax year for the entity's last filed return. A new entity should enter the ending date of the tax year it is adopting . . . .

Month	Day	Year

4 Enter ending date of required tax year determined under section 441(i), 706(b), or 1378 . .

Month	Day

5 **Section 444(a) Election.** Check the applicable box and enter the ending date of the first tax year for which the election will be effective that the entity is (see instructions):
☐ Adopting ☐ Retaining ☐ Changing to

Month	Day	Year

Under penalties of perjury, I declare that the entity named above has authorized me to make this election under section 444(a), and that the statements made are, to the best of my knowledge and belief, true, correct, and complete.

▶ _____
Signature and title (see instructions)

▶ _____
Date

General Instructions

Section references are to the Internal Revenue Code unless otherwise noted.

Purpose of Form

Form 8716 is filed by partnerships, S corporations, and personal service corporations (as defined in section 441(i)(2)) to elect under section 444 to have a tax year other than a required tax year.

When To File

Form 8716 must be signed and filed by the earlier of:

1. The 15th day of the 5th month following the month that includes the 1st day of the tax year the election will be effective or

2. The due date (not including extensions) of the income tax return for the tax year resulting from the section 444 election.

Items **1** and **2** relate to the tax year, or the return for the tax year, for which the ending date is entered on line 5 above.

Under Regulations section 301.9100-2, the entity is automatically granted a 12-month extension to make an election on Form 8716. To obtain an extension, type or legibly print "Filed Pursuant To Section 301.9100-2" at the top of Form 8716, and file the form within 12 months of the original due date.

Where To File

File Form 8716 at the applicable IRS address shown below.

If the entity's principal place of business or principal office or agency is located in ▼	Use the following address ▼
Connecticut, Delaware, District of Columbia, Georgia, Illinois, Indiana, Kentucky, Maine, Maryland, Massachusetts, Michigan, New Hampshire, New Jersey, New York, North Carolina, Ohio, Pennsylvania, Rhode Island, South Carolina, Tennessee, Vermont, Virginia, West Virginia, Wisconsin	Department of the Treasury Internal Revenue Service Center Cincinnati, OH 45999
Alabama, Alaska, Arizona, Arkansas, California, Colorado, Florida, Hawaii, Idaho, Iowa, Kansas, Louisiana, Minnesota, Mississippi, Missouri, Montana, Nebraska, Nevada, New Mexico, North Dakota, Oklahoma, Oregon, South Dakota, Texas, Utah, Washington, Wyoming	Department of the Treasury Internal Revenue Service Center Ogden, UT 84201

An entity without a principal office or agency or principal place of business in the United States must file Form 8716 with the Internal Revenue Service Center, P.O. Box 409101, Ogden, UT 84409.

Also file a copy of Form 8716 with your income tax return for the first tax year for which the election is made. To enable electronic filing, you may file an unsigned Form 8716 containing the same information as on the signed Form 8716 you filed separately.

Effect of Section 444 Election

Partnerships and S corporations. An electing partnership or S corporation must file Form 8752, Required Payment or Refund Under Section 7519, for each year the election is in effect. Form 8752 is used to figure and make the payment required under section 7519 or to obtain a refund of net prior year payments. File Form 8752 by May 15 following the calendar year in which each applicable election year begins.

The section 444 election will end if the partnership or S corporation is penalized for willfully failing to make the required payments.

Personal service corporations (PSC). An electing PSC should not file Form 8752. Instead, it must comply with the minimum distribution requirements (see next paragraph) of section 280H for each year the election is in effect. If the PSC does not meet these requirements, the applicable amounts it may deduct for payments made to its employee-owners may be limited.

For Paperwork Reduction Act Notice, see instructions.

Cat. No. 64725S

Form **8716** (Rev. 12-2008)

Use Schedule H (Form 1120), Section 280H Limitations for a Personal Service Corporation (PSC), to figure the required minimum distribution and the maximum deductible amount. Attach Schedule H to the income tax return of the PSC for each tax year the PSC does not meet the minimum distribution requirements.

The section 444 election will end if the PSC is penalized for willfully failing to comply with the requirements of section 280H.

Members of Certain Tiered Structures May Not Make Election

No election may be made under section 444(a) by an entity that is part of a tiered structure other than a tiered structure that consists entirely of partnerships and/or S corporations all of which have the same tax year. An election previously made will be terminated if an entity later becomes part of a tiered structure that is not allowed to make the election. See Temporary Regulations section 1.444-2T for other details.

Acceptance of Election

After your election is received and accepted by the service center, the center will stamp it "Accepted" and return a copy to you. Be sure to keep a copy of the form marked "Accepted" for your records.

End of Election

The election is made only once. It remains in effect until the entity changes its accounting period to its required tax year or some other permitted year or it is penalized for willfully failing to comply with the requirements of section 280H or 7519. If the election is terminated, the entity may not make another section 444 election.

Signature

Form 8716 is not a valid election unless it is signed. For partnerships, a general partner or a member-manager of a limited liability company must sign and date the election.

For corporations, the election must be signed and dated by the president, vice president, treasurer, assistant treasurer, chief accounting officer, or any other corporate officer (such as tax officer) authorized to sign its tax return.

If a receiver, trustee in bankruptcy, or assignee controls the entity's property or business, that person must sign the election.

Specific Instructions

Line 1

Check the applicable box to indicate whether the entity is classified for federal income tax purposes as a partnership, an S corporation (or a C corporation electing to be an S corporation), or a PSC.

A corporation electing to be an S corporation that wants to make a section 444 election is not required to attach a copy of Form 8716 to its Form 2553, Election by a Small Business Corporation. However, the corporation is required to state on Form 2553 its intention to make a section 444 election (or a backup section 444 election). If a corporation is making a backup section 444 election (provided for in Part II, item Q, of Form 2553), it must type or print the words "Backup Election" at the top of the Form 8716 it files. See Temporary Regulations section 1.444-3T for more details.

Line 2

Enter the name and telephone number (including the area code) of a person that the IRS may call for information needed to complete the processing of the election.

Line 4

Required tax year. The required tax year for an S corporation or PSC is a calendar year. Generally, the required tax year for a partnership is the tax year of a majority of its partners (see Regulations section 1.706-1(b) for details).

Line 5

The following limitations and special rules apply in determining the tax year an entity may elect.

New entity adopting a tax year. An entity adopting a tax year may elect a tax year under section 444 only if the deferral period of the tax year is not more than 3 months. See *Deferral period* below.

Existing entity retaining a tax year. In certain cases, an entity may elect to retain its tax year if the deferral period is not more than 3 months. If the entity does not want to elect to retain its tax year, it may elect to change its tax year as explained below.

Existing entity changing a tax year. An existing entity may elect to change its tax year if the deferral period of the elected tax year is not more than the shorter of 3 months or the deferral period of the tax year being changed. If the tax year being changed is the entity's required tax year, the deferral period for that year is zero and the entity is not permitted to make a section 444 election.

Example. ABC, a C corporation that historically used a tax year ending October 31, elects S status and wants to make a section 444 election for its tax year

beginning November 1. ABC's required tax year under section 1378 is a calendar tax year. In this case, the deferral period of the tax year being changed is 2 months. Thus, ABC may elect to retain its tax year beginning November 1 and ending October 31 or elect a tax year beginning on December 1 (with a deferral period of one month). However, it may not elect a tax year beginning October 1 because the 3-month deferral period would be longer than the 2-month deferral period of the tax year being changed. If ABC elects a tax year beginning on December 1, it must file a short tax year return beginning November 1 and ending November 30.

Deferral period. The term "deferral period" means the number of months between the last day of the elected tax year and the last day of the required tax year. For example, if you elected a tax year that ends on September 30 and your required tax year is the calendar year, the deferral period would be 3 months (the number of months between September 30 and December 31).

Paperwork Reduction Act Notice. We ask for the information on this form to carry out the Internal Revenue laws of the United States. You are required to give us the information. We need it to ensure that you are complying with these laws and to allow us to figure and collect the right amount of tax.

You are not required to provide the information requested on a form that is subject to the Paperwork Reduction Act unless the form displays a valid OMB control number. Books or records relating to a form or its instructions must be retained as long as their contents may become material in the administration of any Internal Revenue law. Generally, tax returns and return information are confidential, as required by section 6103.

The time needed to complete and file this form will vary depending on individual circumstances. The estimated average time is:

Recordkeeping . . . . 2 hr., 37 min.

Learning about the law or the form . . . . 1 hr., 12 min.

Preparing and sending the form to the IRS . . . 1 hr., 16 min.

If you have comments concerning the accuracy of these time estimates or suggestions for making this form simpler, we would be happy to hear from you. You can write to the Internal Revenue Service, Tax Products Coordinating Committee, SE:W:CAR:MP:T:T:SP, 1111 Constitution Ave. NW, IR-6526, Washington, DC 20224. Do not send the form to this address. Instead, see *Where To File* on page 1.

Form SS-8
(Rev. November 2006)
Department of the Treasury
Internal Revenue Service

Determination of Worker Status
for Purposes of Federal Employment Taxes
and Income Tax Withholding

OMB No. 1545-0004

Name of firm (or person) for whom the worker performed services	Worker's name

Firm's address (include street address, apt. or suite no., city, state, and ZIP code)	Worker's address (include street address, apt. or suite no., city, state, and ZIP code)

Trade name	Daytime telephone number ( )	Worker's social security number

Telephone number (include area code) ( )	Firm's employer identification number	Worker's employer identification number (if any)

Note. If the worker is paid by a firm other than the one listed on this form for these services, enter the name, address, and employer identification number of the payer. ▶

Disclosure of Information

The information provided on Form SS-8 may be disclosed to the firm, worker, or payer named above to assist the IRS in the determination process. For example, if you are a worker, we may disclose the information you provide on Form SS-8 to the firm or payer named above. The information can only be disclosed to assist with the determination process. If you provide incomplete information, we may not be able to process your request. See *Privacy Act and Paperwork Reduction Act Notice* on page 5 for more information. **If you do not want this information disclosed to other parties, do not file Form SS-8.**

Parts I–V. All filers of Form SS-8 must complete all questions in Parts I–IV. Part V must be completed if the worker provides a service directly to customers or is a salesperson. If you cannot answer a question, enter "Unknown" or "Does not apply." If you need more space for a question, attach another sheet with the part and question number clearly identified.

Part I   General Information

1 This form is being completed by: ☐ Firm ☐ Worker; for services performed _____ (beginning date) to _____ (ending date) .

2 Explain your reason(s) for filing this form (for example, you received a bill from the IRS, you believe you erroneously received a Form 1099 or Form W-2, you are unable to get worker's compensation benefits, or you were audited or are being audited by the IRS). _____

----

3 Total number of workers who performed or are performing the same or similar services _____ .

4 How did the worker obtain the job? ☐ Application ☐ Bid ☐ Employment Agency ☐ Other (specify) _____

5 Attach copies of all supporting documentation (contracts, invoices, memos, Forms W-2 or Forms 1099-MISC issued or received, IRS closing agreements, IRS rulings, etc.). In addition, please inform us of any current or past litigation concerning the worker's status. If no income reporting forms (Form 1099-MISC or W-2) were furnished to the worker, enter the amount of income earned for the year(s) at issue $ _____ .

If both Form W-2 and Form 1099-MISC were issued or received, explain why. ------------------------------------
----

6 Describe the firm's business. --
----

7 Describe the work done by the worker and provide the worker's job title. -----------------------------------
----

8 Explain why you believe the worker is an employee or an independent contractor. ---------------------------
----
----

9 Did the worker perform services for the firm in any capacity before providing the services that are the subject of this determination request?
☐ Yes ☐ No ☐ N/A
If "Yes," what were the dates of the prior service? --
If "Yes," explain the differences, if any, between the current and prior service. ------------------------------
----
----

10 If the work is done under a written agreement between the firm and the worker, attach a copy (preferably signed by both parties). Describe the terms and conditions of the work arrangement. --
----

Part II   Behavioral Control

1   What specific training and/or instruction is the worker given by the firm? ....

....

2   How does the worker receive work assignments? ....

....

3   Who determines the methods by which the assignments are performed? ....

4   Who is the worker required to contact if problems or complaints arise and who is responsible for their resolution? ....

....

5   What types of reports are required from the worker? Attach examples. ....

....

6   Describe the worker's daily routine such as, schedule, hours, etc. ....

....

....

7   At what location(s) does the worker perform services (e.g., firm's premises, own shop or office, home, customer's location, etc.)? Indicate the appropriate percentage of time the worker spends in each location, if more than one. ....

....

8   Describe any meetings the worker is required to attend and any penalties for not attending (e.g., sales meetings, monthly meetings, staff meetings, etc.). ....

9   Is the worker required to provide the services personally? . . . .   ☐ **Yes**   ☐ **No**

10 If substitutes or helpers are needed, who hires them? ....

11 If the worker hires the substitutes or helpers, is approval required? . . . .   ☐ **Yes**   ☐ **No**

    If "Yes," by whom? ....

12 Who pays the substitutes or helpers? ....

13 Is the worker reimbursed if the worker pays the substitutes or helpers? . . . .   ☐ **Yes**   ☐ **No**

    If "Yes," by whom?

Part III   Financial Control

1   List the supplies, equipment, materials, and property provided by each party:

    The firm ....

    The worker ....

    Other party ....

2   Does the worker lease equipment? . . . .   ☐ **Yes**   ☐ **No**

    If "Yes," what are the terms of the lease? (Attach a copy or explanatory statement.) ....

....

3   What expenses are incurred by the worker in the performance of services for the firm? ....

....

4   Specify which, if any, expenses are reimbursed by:

    The firm ....

    Other party ....

5   Type of pay the worker receives: ☐ Salary   ☐ Commission   ☐ Hourly Wage   ☐ Piece Work

    ☐ Lump Sum   ☐ Other (specify) ....

    If type of pay is commission, and the firm guarantees a minimum amount of pay, specify amount $ _____ .

6   Is the worker allowed a drawing account for advances? . . . .   ☐ **Yes**   ☐ **No**

    If "Yes," how often? ....

    Specify any restrictions. ....

....

7   Whom does the customer pay? . . . .   ☐ Firm   ☐ Worker

    If worker, does the worker pay the total amount to the firm?   ☐ **Yes**   ☐ **No**   If "No," explain. ....

....

8   Does the firm carry worker's compensation insurance on the worker? . . . .   ☐ **Yes**   ☐ **No**

9   What economic loss or financial risk, if any, can the worker incur beyond the normal loss of salary (e.g., loss or damage of equipment, material, etc.)? ....

....

Part IV   Relationship of the Worker and Firm

1   List the benefits available to the worker (e.g., paid vacations, sick pay, pensions, bonuses, paid holidays, personal days, insurance benefits). ....

2   Can the relationship be terminated by either party without incurring liability or penalty? . . . . ☐ **Yes**   ☐ **No**
    If "No," explain your answer. ....
    ....

3   Did the worker perform similar services for others during the same time period? . . . . ☐ **Yes**   ☐ **No**
    If "Yes," is the worker required to get approval from the firm? . . . . ☐ **Yes**   ☐ **No**

4   Describe any agreements prohibiting competition between the worker and the firm while the worker is performing services or during any later period. Attach any available documentation. ....
    ....

5   Is the worker a member of a union? . . . . ☐ **Yes**   ☐ **No**

6   What type of advertising, if any, does the worker do (e.g., a business listing in a directory, business cards, etc.)? Provide copies, if applicable. ....

7   If the worker assembles or processes a product at home, who provides the materials and instructions or pattern? ....
    ....

8   What does the worker do with the finished product (e.g., return it to the firm, provide it to another party, or sell it)? ....
    ....

9   How does the firm represent the worker to its customers (e.g., employee, partner, representative, or contractor)? ....
    ....

10 If the worker no longer performs services for the firm, how did the relationship end (e.g., worker quit or was fired, job completed, contract ended, firm or worker went out of business)? ....

Part V   For Service Providers or Salespersons. Complete this part if the worker provided a service directly to customers or is a salesperson.

1   What are the worker's responsibilities in soliciting new customers? ....
    ....

2   Who provides the worker with leads to prospective customers? ....

3   Describe any reporting requirements pertaining to the leads. ....
    ....

4   What terms and conditions of sale, if any, are required by the firm? ....

5   Are orders submitted to and subject to approval by the firm? . . . . ☐ **Yes**   ☐ **No**

6   Who determines the worker's territory? ....

7   Did the worker pay for the privilege of serving customers on the route or in the territory? . . . . ☐ **Yes**   ☐ **No**
    If "Yes," whom did the worker pay? ....
    If "Yes," how much did the worker pay? . . . . $ _____

8   Where does the worker sell the product (e.g., in a home, retail establishment, etc.)? ....
    ....

9   List the product and/or services distributed by the worker (e.g., meat, vegetables, fruit, bakery products, beverages, or laundry or dry cleaning services). If more than one type of product and/or service is distributed, specify the principal one. ....

10 Does the worker sell life insurance full time? . . . . ☐ **Yes**   ☐ **No**

11 Does the worker sell other types of insurance for the firm? . . . . ☐ **Yes**   ☐ **No**
    If "Yes," enter the percentage of the worker's total working time spent in selling other types of insurance . . . . _____ %

12 If the worker solicits orders from wholesalers, retailers, contractors, or operators of hotels, restaurants, or other similar establishments, enter the percentage of the worker's time spent in the solicitation . . . . _____ %

13 Is the merchandise purchased by the customers for resale or use in their business operations? . . . . ☐ **Yes**   ☐ **No**
    Describe the merchandise and state whether it is equipment installed on the customers' premises. ....
    ....

Sign Here ▶

Under penalties of perjury, I declare that I have examined this request, including accompanying documents, and to the best of my knowledge and belief, the facts presented are true, correct, and complete.

_____   Title ▶ _____   Date ▶ _____
Type or print name below signature.

General Instructions

Section references are to the Internal Revenue Code unless otherwise noted.

Purpose

Firms and workers file Form SS-8 to request a determination of the status of a worker for purposes of federal employment taxes and income tax withholding.

A Form SS-8 determination may be requested only in order to resolve federal tax matters. If Form SS-8 is submitted for a tax year for which the statute of limitations on the tax return has expired, a determination letter will not be issued. The statute of limitations expires 3 years from the due date of the tax return or the date filed, whichever is later.

The IRS does not issue a determination letter for proposed transactions or on hypothetical situations. We may, however, issue an information letter when it is considered appropriate.

Definition

Firm. For the purposes of this form, the term "firm" means any individual, business enterprise, organization, state, or other entity for which a worker has performed services. The firm may or may not have paid the worker directly for these services.

If the firm was not responsible for payment for services, be sure to enter the name, address, and employer identification number of the payer on the first page of Form SS-8, below the identifying information for the firm and the worker.

The SS-8 Determination Process

The IRS will acknowledge the receipt of your Form SS-8. Because there are usually two (or more) parties who could be affected by a determination of employment status, the IRS attempts to get information from all parties involved by sending those parties blank Forms SS-8 for completion. Some or all of the information provided on this Form SS-8 may be shared with the other parties listed on page 1. The case will be assigned to a technician who will review the facts, apply the law, and render a decision. The technician may ask for additional information from the requestor, from other involved parties, or from third parties that could help clarify the work relationship before rendering a decision. The IRS will generally issue a formal determination to the firm or payer (if that is a different entity), and will send a copy to the worker. A determination letter applies only to a worker (or a class of workers) requesting it, and the decision is binding on the IRS. In certain cases, a formal determination will not be issued. Instead, an information letter may be issued. Although an information letter is advisory only and is not binding on the IRS, it may be used to assist the worker to fulfill his or her federal tax obligations.

Neither the SS-8 determination process nor the review of any records in connection with the determination constitutes an examination (audit) of any federal tax return. If the periods under consideration have previously been examined, the SS-8 determination process will not constitute a reexamination under IRS reopening procedures. Because this is not an examination of any federal tax return, the appeal rights available in connection with an examination do not apply to an SS-8 determination. However, if you disagree with a determination and you have additional information concerning the work relationship that you believe was not previously considered, you may request that the determining office reconsider the determination.

Completing Form SS-8

Answer all questions as completely as possible. Attach additional sheets if you need more space. Provide information for all years the worker provided services for the firm. Determinations are based on the entire relationship between the firm and the worker. Also indicate if there were any significant changes in the work relationship over the service term.

Additional copies of this form may be obtained by calling 1-800-829-4933 or from the IRS website at *www.irs.gov.*

Fee

There is no fee for requesting an SS-8 determination letter.

Signature

Form SS-8 must be signed and dated by the taxpayer. A stamped signature will not be accepted.

The person who signs for a corporation must be an officer of the corporation who has personal knowledge of the facts. If the corporation is a member of an affiliated group filing a consolidated return, it must be signed by an officer of the common parent of the group.

The person signing for a trust, partnership, or limited liability company must be, respectively, a trustee, general partner, or member-manager who has personal knowledge of the facts.

Where To File

Send the completed Form SS-8 to the address listed below for the firm's location. However, only for cases involving federal agencies, send Form SS-8 to the Internal Revenue Service, Attn: CC:CORP:T:C, Ben Franklin Station, P.O. Box 7604, Washington, DC 20044.

Firm's location:	Send to:
Alaska, Arizona, Arkansas, California, Colorado, Hawaii, Idaho, Illinois, Iowa, Kansas, Minnesota, Missouri, Montana, Nebraska, Nevada, New Mexico, North Dakota, Oklahoma, Oregon, South Dakota, Texas, Utah, Washington, Wisconsin, Wyoming, American Samoa, Guam, Puerto Rico, U.S. Virgin Islands	Internal Revenue Service SS-8 Determinations P.O. Box 630 Stop 631 Holtsville, NY 11742-0630
Alabama, Connecticut, Delaware, District of Columbia, Florida, Georgia, Indiana, Kentucky, Louisiana, Maine, Maryland, Massachusetts, Michigan, Mississippi, New Hampshire, New Jersey, New York, North Carolina, Ohio, Pennsylvania, Rhode Island, South Carolina, Tennessee, Vermont, Virginia, West Virginia, all other locations not listed	Internal Revenue Service SS-8 Determinations 40 Lakemont Road Newport, VT 05855-1555

Instructions for Workers

If you are requesting a determination for more than one firm, complete a separate Form SS-8 for each firm.

Form SS-8 is not a claim for refund of social security and Medicare taxes or federal income tax withholding.

If the IRS determines that you are an employee, you are responsible for filing an amended return for any corrections related to this decision. A determination that a worker is an employee does not necessarily reduce any current or prior tax liability. For more information, call 1-800-829-1040.

Time for filing a claim for refund. Generally, you must file your claim for a credit or refund within 3 years from the date your original return was filed or within 2 years from the date the tax was paid, whichever is later.

Filing Form SS-8 does not prevent the expiration of the time in which a claim for a refund must be filed. If you are concerned about a refund, and the statute of limitations for filing a claim for refund for the year(s) at issue has not yet expired, you should file Form 1040X, Amended U.S. Individual Income Tax Return, to protect your statute of limitations. File a separate Form 1040X for each year.

On the Form 1040X you file, do not complete lines 1 through 24 on the form. Write "Protective Claim" at the top of the form, sign and date it. In addition, you should enter the following statement in Part II, Explanation of Changes: "Filed Form SS-8 with the Internal Revenue Service Office in (Holtsville, NY; Newport, VT; or Washington, DC; as appropriate). By filing this protective claim, I reserve the right to file a claim for any refund that may be due after a determination of my employment tax status has been completed."

Filing Form SS-8 does not alter the requirement to timely file an income tax return. Do not delay filing your tax return in anticipation of an answer to your SS-8 request. In addition, if applicable, do not delay in responding to a request for payment while waiting for a determination of your worker status.

Instructions for Firms

If a **worker** has requested a determination of his or her status while working for you, you will receive a request from the IRS to complete a Form SS-8. In cases of this type, the IRS usually gives each party an opportunity to present a statement of the facts because any decision will affect the employment tax status of the parties. Failure to respond to this request will not prevent the IRS from issuing a determination letter based on the information he or she has made available so that the worker may fulfill his or her federal tax obligations. However, the information that you provide is extremely valuable in determining the status of the worker.

If you are requesting a determination for a particular class of worker, complete the form for one individual who is representative of the class of workers whose status is in question. If you want a written determination for more than one class of workers, complete a separate Form SS-8 for one worker from each class whose status is typical of that class. A written determination for any worker will apply to other workers of the same class if the facts are not materially different for these workers. Please provide a list of names and addresses of all workers potentially affected by this determination.

If you have a reasonable basis for not treating a worker as an employee, you may be relieved from having to pay employment taxes for that worker under section 530 of the 1978 Revenue Act. However, this relief provision cannot be considered in conjunction with a Form SS-8 determination because the determination does not constitute an examination of any tax return. For more information regarding section 530 of the 1978 Revenue Act and to determine if you qualify for relief under this section, you may visit the IRS website at *www.irs.gov*.

Privacy Act and Paperwork Reduction Act Notice. We ask for the information on this form to carry out the Internal Revenue laws of the United States. This information will be used to determine the employment status of the worker(s) described on the form. Subtitle C, Employment Taxes, of the Internal Revenue Code imposes employment taxes on wages. Sections 3121(d), 3306(a), and 3401(c) and (d) and the related regulations define employee and employer for purposes of employment taxes imposed under Subtitle C. Section 6001 authorizes the IRS to request information needed to determine if a worker(s) or firm is subject to these taxes. Section 6109 requires you to provide your taxpayer identification number. Neither workers nor firms are required to request a status determination, but if you choose to do so, you must provide the information requested on this form. Failure to provide the requested information may prevent us from making a status determination. If any worker or the firm has requested a status determination and you are being asked to provide information for use in that determination, you are not required to provide the requested information. However, failure to provide such information will prevent the IRS from considering it in making the status determination. Providing false or fraudulent information may subject you to penalties. Routine uses of this information include providing it to the Department of Justice for use in civil and criminal litigation, to the Social Security Administration for the administration of social security programs, and to cities, states, and the District of Columbia for the administration of their tax laws. We may also disclose this information to other countries under a tax treaty, to federal and state agencies to enforce federal nontax criminal laws, or to federal law enforcement and intelligence agencies to combat terrorism. We may provide this information to the affected worker(s), the firm, or payer as part of the status determination process.

You are not required to provide the information requested on a form that is subject to the Paperwork Reduction Act unless the form displays a valid OMB control number. Books or records relating to a form or its instructions must be retained as long as their contents may become material in the administration of any Internal Revenue law. Generally, tax returns and return information are confidential, as required by section 6103.

The time needed to complete and file this form will vary depending on individual circumstances. The estimated average time is: Recordkeeping, 22 hrs.; Learning about the law or the form, 47 min.; and Preparing and sending the form to the IRS, 1 hr., 11 min. If you have comments concerning the accuracy of these time estimates or suggestions for making this form simpler, we would be happy to hear from you. You can write to the Internal Revenue Service, Tax Products Coordinating Committee, SE:W:CAR:MP:T:T:SP, 1111 Constitution Ave. NW, IR-6406, Washington, DC 20224. Do not send the tax form to this address. Instead, see *Where To File* on page 4.

Index

Keep Up to Date

 Go to **Nolo.com/newsletters/index.html** to sign up for free newsletters and discounts on Nolo products.

- **Nolo Briefs.** Our monthly email newsletter with great deals and free information.

- **BizBriefs.** Tips and discounts on Nolo products for business owners and managers.

- **Landlord's Quarterly.** Deals and free tips just for landlords and property managers, too.

- **Nolo's Special Offer.** A monthly newsletter with the biggest Nolo discounts around.

 Don't forget to check for updates at **Nolo.com.** Under "Products," find this book and click "Legal Updates."

Let Us Hear From You

 Comments on this book? We want to hear 'em. Email us at feedback@nolo.com.

OPEN8